THE WESTMINSTER
COLLECTION OF

CHRISTIAN
QUOTATIONS

THE WESTMINSTER
COLLECTION OF

CHRISTIAN QUOTATIONS

Compiled by
Martin H. Manser

Westminster John Knox Press
LOUISVILLE
LONDON • LEIDEN

Book design by Sharon Adams
Cover design by Pam Poll Graphic Design

First edition
Published by Westminster John Knox Press
Louisville, Kentucky

Library of Congress Cataloging-in-Publication Data

The Westminster collection of Christian quotations / compiled by Martin Manser.—1st ed.
    p. cm.
Includes indexes.
ISBN 0-664-22258-7 (hardcover)
    1. Spiritual life—Christianity—Quotations, maxims, etc. 2. Bible—Quotations. I. Manser, Martin H.

PN6084.R3 W47 2001
230—dc21   00-054081

CONTENTS

*All-Knowing, Anger of, Creator,
Faithfulness of, Goodness of, Grace and
Mercy of, Greatness of, Hiddenness of,
Holiness of, Infiniteness of, Judgment of,
Justice of, Love of, Mystery of, Name of,
Personal Descriptions of, Presence of,
Self-Existence of, Sovereignty of,
Transcendence of, Trinity, Voice of,
Will of, Wisdom of*

LIST OF ABBREVIATIONS

CEV	Contemporary English Version
GNB	Good News Bible
KJV	King James Version
NIV	New International Version
NJB	The New Jerusalem Bible
NRSV	New Revised Standard Version
REB	The Revised English Bible
RSV	Revised Standard Version

INTRODUCTION

The Westminster Collection of Christian Quotations is an anthology of over 6,000 quotations arranged under nearly 500 topics and subtopics. The topics cover not only the different aspects of the Christian life and faith, e.g. *Christ-likeness, Cross, Discipleship, Kingdom of God*, and *Prayer*, but also practical aspects such as *Families, Fellowship, Guidance*, and *Speech*. Quotations are drawn from an extensive range of Christians of different traditions through the ages and throughout the world, as well as from the Bible itself.

Here you will read the relatively well-known "My grace is sufficient for thee: for my strength is made perfect in weakness" (*2 Corinthians 12:9*), "Thou hast made us for Thyself, and the heart of man is restless until it finds rest in Thee" (*St. Augustine*), "Expect great things from God. Attempt great things for God" (*William Carey*). You will also find the lesser known "This is eternal life: to know you the only true God, and Jesus Christ whom you have sent" (*John 17:3*), "I sometimes think that the whole secret of the Christian life is to know how to use the word 'Therefore'" (*D.M. Lloyd-Jones*), and "A good marriage is the union of two forgivers" (*Ruth Bell Graham*).

The quotations are arranged under topics in alphabetical order and, for some major subjects such as *Church, God, Jesus Christ, Prayer*, and *Spirit*, are divided into subtopics. Within each topic, quotations are given in the following order: quotations from the Bible (in Bible-book order), and then quotations arranged by alphabetical order of surname. An extensive range of cross references is also included to related topics.

As well as the alphabetical arrangement of topics within the main text, we have also included the following indexes: list of authors and topics, brief notes on authors, Bible references (in alphabetical order of Bible book).

This anthology has been designed as a resource for preachers to help encapsulate a thought in a perceptive saying, for use in personal devotions as an inspiration and encouragement, and simply as a source of insight and challenge on our spiritual journey.

The editor would like to express his gratitude to the following who made significant contributions to the compilation and production of the text: Lynn Elias, Greta Chang, and Margarett Oakley.

Martin H. Manser
Aylesbury, Buckinghamshire, England
September 2000

Ability

See also Gifts

To one he gave five talents, to another two, to another one, to each according to his ability.

Matthew 25:15 NRSV

[On the day of Pentecost] All of them were filled with the Holy Spirit and began to speak in other languages, as the Spirit gave them ability.

Acts 2:4 NRSV

The disciples determined that according to their ability, each would send relief to the believers living in Judea.

Acts 11:29 NRSV

God does not ask about our ability or our inability, but our availability.

Anon.

It is not my ability, but my response to God's ability, that counts.

Corrie ten Boom

Anybody can do their best, but we are helped by the Spirit of God to do better than our best.

Catherine Bramwell Booth

There is a great deal of unmapped country within us.

George Eliot

Alas for those who never sing, but die with all their music in them.

Oliver Wendell Holmes

Do what you can, with what you have, where you are.

Theodore Roosevelt

When love and skill work together, expect a masterpiece.

John Ruskin

No talent can survive the blight of neglect.

Edgar A. Whitney

The real tragedy of life is not in being limited to one talent, but in the failure to use the one talent.

Edgar W. Work

Acceptance

See also Peace, of Mind

If you do well, will you not be accepted? And if you do not do well, sin is lurking at the door; its desire is for you, but you must master it.

Genesis 4:7 NRSV

To do what is right and just is more acceptable to the Lord than sacrifice.

Proverbs 21:3 NIV

Accept one another, then, for the glory of God, as Christ has accepted you.

Romans 15:7 GNB

To the praise of the glory of his grace, wherein he hath made us accepted in the beloved.

Ephesians 1:6 KJV

Accept surprises that upset your plans, shatter your dreams, give a completely different turn to your day and who knows?— to your life. Leave the Father free himself to weave the pattern of your days.

Dom Helder Câmara

We can do nothing if we hate ourselves, or feel that all our actions are doomed to failure because of our own worthlessness. We have to take ourselves, good and bad alike, on trust before we can do anything.

Martin Israel

Acceptance says, True, this is my situation at the moment. I'll look unblinkingly at the reality of it. But I'll also open my hands to accept willingly whatever a loving Father sends.

Catherine Wood Marshall

Christianity is about acceptance, and if God accepts me as I am, then I had better do the same.

Hugh Montefiore

God, give us grace to accept with serenity the things that cannot be changed, courage to change the things that should be changed, and the wisdom to distinguish the one from the other.

(Karl Paul) Reinhold Niebuhr

Accept the fact that you are accepted.

Paul Tillich

Peace comes not by establishing a calm outward setting so much as by inwardly surrendering to whatever the setting.

Hubert van Zeller

Action

I will give them singleness of heart and action, so that they will always fear me for their own good and the good of their children after them.

Jeremiah 32:39 NIV

It is by action and not by faith alone that a man is justified.

James 2:24 REB

Prepare your minds for action; discipline yourselves; set all your hope on the grace that Jesus Christ will bring you when he is revealed.

1 Peter 1:13 NRSV

A man can be so busy making a living that he forgets to make a life.

William Barclay

Action springs not from thought, but from a readiness for responsibility.

Dietrich Bonhoeffer

Conviction, were it never so excellent, is worthless till it convert itself into conduct.

Thomas Carlyle

Well done is better than well said.

Benjamin Franklin

Action is the proper fruit of knowledge.

Thomas Fuller

Our problem is not that we take refuge from action in spiritual things, but that we take refuge from spiritual things in action.

Monica Furlong

We ascend to the heights of contemplation by the steps of the active life.

St. Gregory I

The road to holiness necessarily passes through the world of action.

Dag Hammarskjöld

Never be entirely idle, but either be reading, or writing, or praying, or meditating, or endeavoring something for the public good.

Thomas à Kempis

I sometimes think that the whole secret of the Christian life is to know how to use the word "Therefore."

David Martyn Lloyd-Jones

I find the doing of the will of God leaves me no time for disputing about His plans.

George MacDonald

Tomorrow God isn't going to ask, "What did you dream? What did you think? What did you plan? What did you preach?" He's going to ask, "What did you do?"

Michel Quoist

Ere the sun goes down think of some one action which may tend to the conversion of some one person, and do it with all your might.

Charles Haddon Spurgeon

Between the great things we cannot do and the little things we will not do, the danger is that we will do nothing.

H.G. Weaver

Adam and Eve

The Lord God formed a human being from the dust of the ground and breathed into his nostrils the breath of life, so that he became a living creature.

Genesis 2:7 REB

The Lord God then put the man into a deep sleep and, while he slept, he took one of the man's ribs and closed up the flesh over the place. The rib he had taken out of the man the Lord God built up into a woman, and he brought her to the man. The man said: "This one at last is bone from my bones, flesh from my flesh! She shall be called woman, for from man was she taken." That is why a man leaves his father and mother and attaches himself to his wife, and the two become one.

Genesis 2:21–24 REB

Adam called his wife's name Eve; because she was the mother of all living.

Genesis 3:20 KJV

Just as sin entered the world through one

man, and death through sin . . . in this way death came to all men, because all sinned.

Romans 5:12 NIV

I am afraid that as the serpent deceived Eve by its cunning, your thoughts will be led astray from a sincere and pure devotion to Christ.

2 Corinthians 11:3 NJB

The man without a navel still lives in me.

Sir Thomas Browne

Adam was created to be the friend and companion of God; he was to have dominion over all the life in the air and earth and sea, but one thing he was not to have dominion over, and that was himself.

Oswald Chambers

The way the serpent beguiled Eve through his subtlety was by enticing her away from personal faith in God to depend on her reason alone.

Oswald Chambers

Adam switched off from God's design. Instead of maintaining his dependence on God, he took his rule over himself and thereby introduced sin into the world.

Oswald Chambers

The woman was made of a rib out of the side of Adam; not made out of his head to rule over him, not out of his feet to be trampled on by him; but out of his side to be equal to him, under his arm to be protected, and near his heart to be loved.

Matthew Henry

Adam while he spake not, had paradise at will.

William Langland

When Eve was brought unto Adam, he became filled with the Holy Spirit, and gave her the most sanctified, the most glorious of appelations. He called her Eva, that is to say, the Mother of All. He did not style her wife, but simply mother—mother of all living creatures. In this consists the glory and the most precious ornament of woman.

Martin Luther

Adam was but human—this explains it all. He did not want the apple for the apple's sake, he wanted it only because it was forbidden.

Mark Twain

Adoption

See also Children

To all who received him, who believed in his name, he gave power to become children of God.

John 1:12 NRSV

We also, to whom the Spirit is given as the firstfruits of the harvest to come, are groaning inwardly whilst we look forward eagerly to our adoption, our liberation from mortality.

Romans 8:23 REB

God was kind and decided that Christ would choose us to be God's adopted children.

Ephesians 1:5 CEV

How great is the love the Father has lavished on us, that we should be called children of God! And that is what we are!

1 John 3:1 NIV

Adoption gives us the privilege of sons, regeneration, the nature of sons.

Stephen Charnock

The least degree of sincere sanctification, being an effect of regeneration, is a certain

sign of adoption, and may minister a sure argument to him that has it, that he is the adopted child of God.

Thomas Gataker

Affliction is the badge of adoption.

Thomas Watson

A man adopts one for his son and heir that does not at all resemble him; but whosoever God adopts for His child is like Him; he not only bears His heavenly Father's name, but His image.

Thomas Watson

Adoration

See also Love, for God; Prayer, Adoration; Worship

And now, Israel, what doth the Lord thy God require of thee, but to fear the Lord thy God, to walk in all his ways, and to love him, and to serve the Lord thy God with all thy heart and with all thy soul.

Deuteronomy 10:12 KJV

I will praise you my God and King, and always honor your name. I will praise you each day and always honor your name. You are wonderful, Lord, and you deserve all praise, because you are so much greater than anyone can understand. Each generation will announce to the next your wonderful and powerful deeds.

Psalm 145:1–3 CEV

How great are God's riches! How deep are his wisdom and knowledge! Who can explain his decisions? Who can understand his ways? As the scripture says, "Who knows the mind of the Lord? Who is able to give him advice? Who has ever given him anything, so that he had to pay it back?" For all things were created by him, and all things exist through him and for him. To God be the glory for ever!

Romans 11:33–36 GNB

If we would understand divine things, we must cultivate an attitude of humble adoration. Who does not begin by kneeling down, runs every possible risk.

Ernest Hello

It is magnificent to be clothed like the lilies of the field . . . but the supreme glory is to be nothingness in adoration.

Søren Kierkegaard

Praise to the Lord, the Almighty, the King of creation; / O my soul, praise Him, for he is thy health and salvation; / All ye who hear, / Brothers and sisters, draw near, / Praise Him in glad adoration.

Joachim Neander

Man is most truly himself . . . not when he toils but when he adores. And we are learning more and more that all innocent joy in life may be a form of adoration.

Vida Scudder

This is adoration; not a difficult religious exercise, but an attitude of the soul.

Evelyn Underhill

Advent

See also Jesus Christ, Incarnation; Light

The Lord says, "Bethlehem Ephrathah, you are one of the smallest towns in Judah, but out of you I will bring a ruler for Israel, whose family line goes back to ancient times." . . . When he comes, he will rule his people with the strength that comes from the Lord and with the majesty of the Lord

God himself. His people will live in safety because people all over the earth will acknowledge his greatness, and he will bring peace.

Micah 5:2, 4–5 GNB

See, I am sending my messenger to prepare the way before me, and the Lord whom you seek will suddenly come to his temple. The messenger of the covenant in whom you delight— indeed, he is coming, says the LORD of hosts.

Malachi 3:1 NRSV

He [John the Baptist] said, I am the voice of one crying in the wilderness, Make straight the way of the Lord. . . . I baptize with water: but there standeth one among you, whom ye know not; He it is, who coming after me is preferred before me, whose shoe's latchet I am not worthy to unloose.

John 1:23, 26–27 KJV

Advent. The coming of quiet joy. Arrival of radiant light in our darkness.

Anon.

The best way to prepare for the coming of Christ is never to forget the presence of Christ.

William Barclay

I'm ever and always a stranger to grace. I need this annual angel visitation . . . to know the virgin conceives and God is with us.

Eugene H. Peterson

Adversity, *see* Suffering; Trials; Trouble

Advice

See also Guidance

I will instruct you and teach you the way you should go; I will counsel you with my eye upon you.

Psalm 32:8 NRSV

A fool's conduct is right in his own eyes; to listen to advice shows wisdom.

Proverbs 12:15 REB

Plans are established by taking advice.

Proverbs 20:18 NRSV

Whenever my advice is followed I confess that I always feel oppressed with a greater burden of responsibility, and I can never be confident, and always await the outcome with anxiety.

St. Bernard of Clairvaux

Advice is seldom welcome: and those who want it the most always like it the least.

Philip Dormer Stanhope, Lord Chesterfield

To profit from good advice requires more wisdom than to give it.

John Churton Collins

No gift is more precious than good advice.

Desiderius Erasmus

We are better persuaded by the reasons we discover ourselves than by those given to us by others.

Blaise Pascal

Affection, *see* Love

Age, *see* Old Age; Youth

Agnosticism and Atheism

See also Doubt; Unbelief

The wicked in his arrogance does not look very far; "There is no God," is his only thought.

Psalm 10:4 NJB

Fools say in their hearts, "There is no God." They are corrupt, they do abominable deeds; there is no one who does good.

Psalm 14:1 NRSV

They [sinful people] know everything that can be known about God, because God has shown it all to them. God's eternal power and character cannot be seen. But from the beginning of creation, God has shown what these are like by all he has made. That's why those people don't have any excuse.

Romans 1:19–20 CEV

People who tell me there is no God are like a six-year-old boy saying there is no such thing as passionate love—they just haven't experienced it.

William Alfred

A little philosophy inclineth a man's mind to atheism, but depth in philosophy bringeth a man's mind about to religion.

Francis Bacon

Atheism is rather in the lip than in the heart of man.

Francis Bacon

Where there is no God, there is no man.

Nikolai Aleksandrovich Berdyaev

Nobody talks so constantly about God as those who insist there is no God.

Heywood Campbell Broun

An atheist is a man with no invisible means of support.

Henry Emerson Fosdick

The basic atheism is unwillingness to commit our lives to God's keeping.

Georgia Harkness

He who proselytizes in the cause of unbelief is basically a man in need of belief.

Eric Hoffer

I can see how it might be possible to look down upon the earth and be an atheist, but I cannot conceive how one could look into the heavens and say there is no God.

Abraham Lincoln

Every effort to prove there is no God is in itself an effort to reach for God.

Charles Edward Locke

Agnosticism solves not, but merely shelves the mysteries of life. When agnosticism has done its withering work in the mind of man, the mysteries remain as before: all that has been added to them is a settled despair.

Vincent McNabb

Agnosticism leads inevitably to moral indifference. It denies us all power to esteem or to understand moral values, because it severs our spiritual contact with God who alone is the source of all morality.

Thomas Merton

I do not see much difference between avowing that there is no God, and implying that nothing definite can for certain be known about him.

John Henry Newman

Atheists put on a false courage and alacrity in the midst of their darkness and apprehensions, like children who, when they fear to go in to the dark, will sing with fear.

Alexander Pope

The agnostic's prayer: "O God, if there is a god, save my soul, if I have a soul."

Joseph Ernst Renan

We are not to be guilty of that practical atheism, which, seeing no guidance for human affairs but its own limited foresight, endeavors itself to play the God, and decide what will be good for mankind and what bad.

Herbert Spencer

The worst moment for an atheist is when he feels grateful and doesn't know who to thank.

Wendy Ward

The religion of the atheist has a God-shaped blank at its heart.

Herbert George (H.G.) Wells

Ambition

Do you seek great things for yourself? Do not seek them.

Jeremiah 45:5 NRSV

It has always been my ambition to preach the gospel where Christ was not known, so that I would not be building on someone else's foundation.

Romans 15:20 NIV

Do nothing from selfish ambition or conceit, but in humility regard others as better than yourselves.

Philippians 2:3 NRSV

In our natural life our ambitions are our own. In the Christian life we have no aim of our own, and God's aim looks like missing the mark because we are too short-sighted to see what he is aiming at.

Oswald Chambers

Most of the trouble in the world is caused by people wanting to be important.

T.S. Eliot

Nothing can make a man truly great but being truly good and partaking of God's holiness.

Matthew Henry

Hew not too high lest the chip fall in thine eye.

John Heywood

Most people would succeed in small things if they were not troubled by great ambition.

Henry Wadsworth Longfellow

And he that strives to touch the stars, Oft stumbles at a straw.

Edmund Spenser

Personal ambition and empire building are hindering the spread of the gospel.

John R.W. Stott

Angels

He has given his angels orders about you to guard you wherever you go.

Psalm 91:11 NJB

When the Son of Man comes in his glory with all of his angels, he will sit on his royal throne.

Matthew 25:31 CEV

Are not all angels spirits in the divine service, sent to serve for the sake of those who are to inherit salvation?

Hebrews 1:14 NRSV

The servants of Christ are protected by invisible, rather than visible, beings. But if these guard you, they do so because they have been summoned by your prayers.

St. Ambrose

Everlasting God, you have ordained and constituted in a wonderful order the ministries of angels and mortals: Mercifully grant that, as your holy angels always serve and worship you in heaven, so by your appointment they may help and defend us here on earth; through Jesus Christ our Lord, who lives and reigns with you and the Holy Spirit, one God, for ever and ever. Amen.

Book of Common Prayer

The angels are the dispensers and administrators of the divine beneficence toward us; they regard our safety, undertake our defense, direct our ways, and exercise a constant solicitude that no evil befalls us.

John Calvin

If you pray truly, you will feel within yourself a great assurance: and the angels will be your companions.

Evagrius of Pontus

They take different forms at the bidding of their master, God, and thus reveal themselves to men and unveil the divine mysteries to them.

St. John of Damascus

An angel is a spiritual being created by God without a body, for the service of Christendom and the Church.

Martin Luther

Angels, help us to adore Him; / Ye behold Him face to face; / Sun and moon, bow down before Him, / Dwellers all in time and space. / Praise Him! Praise Him! / Praise with us the God of grace.

Henry Francis Lyte

Millions of spiritual creatures walk the earth unseen, both when we sleep and when we awake.

John Milton

Angels, from the realms of glory, / wing your flight o'er all the earth / Ye who sang creation's story, / now proclaim Messiah's birth:

/ Come and worship, come and worship, / worship Christ the newborn King.

James Montgomery

Angels mean messengers and ministers. Their function is to execute the plan of divine providence, even in earthly things.

St. Thomas Aquinas

Anger

See also God, Anger of

It's smart to be patient, but it's stupid to lose your temper.

Proverbs 14:29 CEV

A soft answer turns away wrath, but a harsh word stirs up anger.

Proverbs 15:1 NRSV

You have heard that it was said to those of ancient times, "You shall not murder"; and "whoever murders shall be liable to judgment." But I say to you that if you are angry with a brother or sister, you will be liable to judgment.

Matthew 5:21–22 NRSV

Even if you are angry, do not sin: never let the sun set on your anger.

Ephesians 4:26 NJB

The wrath of man worketh not the righteousness of God.

James 1:20 KJV

Speak when you are angry and you will make the best speech you will ever regret.

Ambrose Bierce

I was angry with my friend; / I told my wrath, my wrath did end. / I was angry with my foe; / I told it not, my wrath did grow.

William Blake

Anger is quieted by a gentle word just as fire is quenched by water.

Bishop Jean Pierre Camus

There is no sin nor wrong that gives a man such a foretaste of hell in this life as anger and impatience.

St. Catherine of Siena

There is a holy anger, excited by zeal, which moves us to reprove with warmth those whom our mildness failed to correct.

St. Jean Baptist de la Salle

The sun must not set upon anger, much less will I let the sun set upon the anger of God toward me.

John Donne

To build one's activity on love and non-violence demands the greatest inner purification; one must constantly rid one's heart of inordinate desires, fears, and anxieties, but above all, one must cleanse oneself of anger.

William Johnston

He that would be angry and sin not must not be angry with anything but sin.

Thomas Secker

Animals

See also Creation

So out of the ground the LORD God formed every animal of the field and every bird of the air, and brought them to the man to see what he would call them; and whatever the man called every living creature, that was its name. The man gave names to all cattle, and to the birds of the air, and to every animal of the field.

Genesis 2:19–20 NRSV

But ask the animals, and they will teach you; the birds of the air, and they will tell you; ask the plants of the earth, and they will teach you; and the fish of the sea will declare to you. Who among all these does not know that the hand of the LORD has done this? In his hand is the life of every living thing and the breath of every human being.

Job 12:7–10 NRSV

You make him [a human being] master over all that you have made, putting everything in subjection under his feet: all sheep and oxen, all the wild beasts, the birds in the air, the fish in the sea, and everything that moves along ocean paths.

Psalm 8:6–8 REB

You make darkness, and it is night, when all the animals of the forest come creeping out. O LORD, how manifold are your works! In wisdom have you made them all; the earth is full of your creatures. Yonder is the sea, great and wide, creeping things innumerable are there, living things both small and great.

Psalm 104:20, 24–25 NRSV

Are not five sparrows sold for two pennies? Yet not one of them is forgotten in God's sight.

Luke 12:6 NRSV

Our thoughts ought instinctively to fly upwards from animals, men, and natural objects to their Creator. If things created are so full of loveliness, how resplendent with beauty must be he who made them! The wisdom of the Worker is apparent in His handiwork.

St. Antony of Padua

Animals are such agreeable friends—they ask no questions, they pass no criticisms.

George Eliot

Though I am far from denying that the counsels of Divine Goodness regarding dumb creatures are, for us, involved in deep obscurity, yet Scripture foretells for them a "glorious liberty." And we are assured that the compassion of Heaven will not be wanting to them.

John Keble

Antichrist

He shall speak words against the Most High, shall wear out the holy ones of the Most High, and shall attempt to change the sacred seasons and the law; and they shall be given into his power for a time, two times, and half a time.

Daniel 7:25 NRSV

Do not let anyone deceive you in any way. For the Day will not come until the final Rebellion takes place and the Wicked One appears, who is destined to hell. He will oppose every so-called god or object of worship and will put himself above them all. He will even go in and sit down in God's Temple and claim to be God. . . . The Mysterious Wickedness is already at work, but what is going to happen will not happen until the one who holds it back is taken out of the way. Then the Wicked One will be revealed, but when the Lord Jesus comes, he will kill him with the breath from his mouth and destroy him with his dazzling presence. The Wicked One will come with the power of Satan and perform all kinds of false miracles and wonders, and use every kind of wicked deceit on those who will perish. They will perish because they did not welcome and love the truth so as to be saved.

2 Thessalonians 2:3–4, 7–10 GNB

Every spirit that confesseth not that Jesus Christ is come in the flesh is not of God: and this is that spirit of antichrist, whereof ye have heard that it should come; and even now already is it in the world.

1 John 4:3 KJV

And I stood upon the sand of the sea and saw a beast rise up out of the sea.

Revelation 13:1 KJV

And he opened his mouth in blasphemy against God, to blaspheme his name, and his tabernacle, and them that dwell in Heaven.

Revelation 13:6 KJV

When Scripture speaks of Antichrist it includes the whole duration of his reign.

John Calvin

The name Antichrist does not designate a single individual, but a single kingdom, which extends throughout many generations.

John Calvin

What will finally destroy us is not communism or fascism, but man acting like God.

Malcolm Muggeridge

Anxiety

See also Fear; Stress

Cast your burden on the LORD, and he will sustain you; he will never permit the righteous to be moved.

Psalm 55:22 NRSV

When I was burdened with worries, you comforted me and made me feel secure.

Psalm 94:19 CEV

Do not worry about tomorrow, for tomorrow will worry about itself. Each day has enough trouble of its own.

Matthew 6:34 NIV

Martha, Martha, thou art careful and troubled about many things: But one thing is needful: and Mary hath chosen that good part, which shall not be taken away from her.

Luke 10:41–42 KJV

Do not be anxious about anything, but in everything, by prayer and petition, with thanksgiving, present your requests to God.

Philippians 4:6 NIV

Cast all your anxiety on him, because he cares for you.

1 Peter 5:7 NRSV

Anxiety has its use, stimulating us to seek with keener longing for that security where peace is complete and unassailable.

St. Augustine of Hippo

Do not worry at being worried; but accept worry peacefully. Difficult but not impossible.

John Chapman

Anxiety is the natural result when our hopes are centered in anything short of God and his will for us.

William Franklin (Billy) Graham

Worry is an intrusion into God's providence.

John Edmund Haggai

Anxiety is the interest paid on trouble before it's due.

William Ralph Inge

Anxiety is not only a pain which we must ask God to assuage but also a weakness we must ask him to pardon—for he's told us to take no care for the morrow.

Clive Staples (C.S.) Lewis

Anxiety comes from strain, and strain is

caused by too complete a dependence on ourselves, on our own devices, our own plans, our own idea of what we are able to do.

Thomas Merton

The beginning of anxiety is the end of faith and the beginning of true faith is the end of anxiety.

George Müller

Anxiety does not empty tomorrow of its sorrow—only today of its strength.

Charles Haddon Spurgeon

Beware of anxiety. Next to sin, there is nothing that so troubles the mind, strains the heart, distresses the soul and confuses the judgment.

William Bernard Ullathorne

Apostasy, *see* Falling Away

Arrogance, *see* Conceit; Pride

Art and Architecture

Make the tabernacle with ten curtains of fine twisted linen, and blue, purple, and crimson yarns; you shall make them with cherubim skilfully worked into them.

Exodus 26:1 NRSV

There was cedar wood round the inside of the Temple, ornamentally carved with gourds and rosettes.

1 Kings 6:18 NJB

Solomon had the inside walls of the temple's main room paneled first with pine and then with a layer of gold, and he had them decorated with carvings of palm trees and designs that looked like chains. He used precious stones to decorate the temple, and he used gold imported from Parvaim to decorate the ceiling beams, the doors, the door frames, and the walls. Solomon also had the workers carve designs of winged creatures into the walls.

2 Chronicles 3:5–7 CEV

Nature is the art of God Eternal.

Dante Alighieri

It has been said that Gothic architecture represents the soul aspiring to God, and the Renaissance or Romanesque architecture represents God tabernacling with men.

Robert Hugh Benson

Just as good literature and good art raise and ennoble character, so bad literature and bad art degrade it.

(Frederick) Donald Coggan

Art is a collaboration between God and the artist, and the less the artist does the better.

André Gide

All great art is the expression of man's delight in God's work, not his own.

John Ruskin

Art is not a handicraft, it is the transmission of feeling the artist has experienced.

Count Leo Tolstoy

Where the spirit does not work with the hand there is no art.

Leonardo da Vinci

Varieties of uniformities make complete beauty.

Christopher Wren

Ascension, *see* Jesus Christ, Ascension of

Assurance, *see* Confidence

Atheism, *see* Agnosticism and Atheism

Atonement

See also Jesus Christ, Death of; Jesus Christ, Savior; Redemption

You shall lay your hand on the head of the burnt offering, and it shall be acceptable in your behalf as atonement for you.

Leviticus 1:4 NRSV

Being justified freely by his grace through the redemption that is in Christ Jesus: Whom God hath set forth to be a propitiation through faith in his blood, to declare his righteousness for the remission of sins that are past, through the forbearance of God.

Romans 3:24–25 KJV

He is the atoning sacrifice for our sins, and not only for ours but also for the sins of the whole world.

1 John 2:2 NIV

Guilty, vile, and helpless, we; / Spotless Lamb of God was He: / Full atonement!—can it be? / Hallelujah! What a Savior!

Philipp Paul Bliss

When we are filled with the Holy Spirit, he unites us body, soul, and spirit with God until we are one with God even as Jesus was. This is the meaning of the Atonement—at-onement with God.

Oswald Chambers

Jesus alone can make atonement because he is the atonement—the at-onement of God and man.

Gonville ffrench-Beytagh

In the cross, God descends to bear in his own heart the sins of the world. In Jesus, he atones at unimaginable cost to himself.

Woodrow A. Grier

A great many people are trying to make peace, but that has already been done. God has not left it for us to do; all we have to do is to enter into it.

Dwight Lyman (D.L.) Moody

God requires satisfaction because he is holiness, but he makes satisfaction because he is love.

Augustus Hopkins Strong

Authority

See also Government and Politics; Jesus Christ, Authority of; Power

He called his twelve disciples to him and gave them authority to drive out evil spirits and to heal every disease and sickness.

Matthew 10:1 NIV

Jesus came and said to them [the eleven disciples], "All authority in heaven and on earth has been given to me."

Matthew 28:18 NRSV

But Peter and the apostles answered, "We must obey God rather than any human authority."

Acts 5:29 NRSV

Everyone is to obey the governing authorities, because there is no authority except from God and so whatever authorities exist have been appointed by God.

Romans 13:1 NJB

No authority has power to impose error, and if it resists the truth, the truth must be upheld until it is admitted.

Lord John Acton

It is right to submit to higher authority whenever a command of God would not be violated.

St. Basil the Great

Cast away authority, and authority shall forsake you.

Robert Hugh Benson

Self-chosen authority is an impertinence. Jesus said that the great ones in this world exercise authority but that in his kingdom it is not so; no one exercises authority over another because in his kingdom the king is servant of all. If a saint tries to exercise authority, it is a proof he is not rightly related to Jesus Christ.

Oswald Chambers

Authority is not a short way to the truth; it is the only way to many truths; and for men on earth, it is the only way to divine truths.

Vincent McNabb

Men desire authority for its own sake that they may rule, command, and control other men, and live uncommanded and uncontrolled themselves.

Sir Thomas More

Authority is like a bar of soap—the more you use it the less you have.

John Richard Wimber

Babies, *see* Birth; Children

Backsliding, *see* Falling Away

Baptism

See also Church

I [John the Baptist] baptize you with water for repentance, but one who is more powerful than I is coming after me . . . He will baptize you with the Holy Spirit and fire.

Matthew 3:11 NRSV

Go, therefore, make disciples of all nations; baptize them in the name of the Father and of the Son and of the Holy Spirit.

Matthew 28:19 NJB

Repent and be baptized, every one of you, in the name of Jesus Christ for the forgiveness of your sins. And you will receive the gift of the Holy Spirit.

Acts 2:38 NIV

Don't you know that all who share in Christ Jesus by being baptized also share in his death? When we were baptized, we died and were buried with Christ. We were baptized, so that we would live a new life, as Christ was raised to life by the glory of God the Father. If we shared in Jesus' death by being baptized, we will be raised to life with him.

Romans 6:3–5 CEV

For we were all baptized by one Spirit into one body—whether Jews or Greeks, slave or free—and we were all given the one Spirit to drink.

1 Corinthians 12:13 NIV

No athlete is admitted to the contest of virtue, unless he has first been washed of all stains of sins and consecrated with the gift of heavenly grace.

St. Ambrose

An outward and visible sign of an inward and spiritual grace given unto us.

Book of Common Prayer

You have been baptized, but think not that you are straightaway a Christian. . . . The flesh is touched with salt: what then if the mind remains unsalted? The body is anointed, yet the mind remains unanointed. But if you are buried with Christ within, and already practise walking with Him in newness of life, I acknowledge you as a Christian.

Desiderius Erasmus

Baptism signifies that the old Adam in us is to be drowned by daily sorrow and repentance, and perish with all sins and evil lusts;

and that the new man should daily come forth again and rise, who shall live before God in righteousness and purity forever.

Martin Luther

Baptism points back to the work of God, and forward to the life of faith.

J. Alec Motyer

To be baptized is to be born according to Christ; it is to receive existence, to come into being out of nothing.

St. Nicholas Cabasilas

In baptism, the Christian is born. His old self is buried and the new self emerges. Whether in the case of infants or adults, baptism signifies this more as a promise than as an actually fulfilled fact. The direction is indicated rather than the arrival.

Friedrich Rest

Beatitudes

See also Blessings

Blessed are the poor in spirit, for theirs is the kingdom of heaven. Blessed are those who mourn, for they will be comforted. Blessed are the meek, for they will inherit the earth. Blessed are those who hunger and thirst for righteousness, for they will be filled. Blessed are the merciful, for they will receive mercy. Blessed are the pure in heart, for they will see God. Blessed are the peacemakers, for they will be called children of God. Blessed are those who are persecuted for righteousness' sake, for theirs is the kingdom of heaven. Blessed are you when people revile you and persecute you and utter all kinds of evil against you falsely on my account.

Matthew 5:3–11 NRSV

The man who is poor in spirit is the man who has realized that things mean nothing, and that God means everything.

William Barclay

If the Sermon on the Mount is the précis of all Christian doctrine, the eight beatitudes are the précis of the whole of the Sermon on the Mount.

Jacques Bénigne Bossuet

We have too many men of science, too few men of God. We have grasped the mystery of the atom, and rejected the Sermon on the Mount. The world has achieved brilliance without wisdom, power without conscience.

Omar Nelson Bradley

The character which we find in the Beatitudes is, beyond all question, nothing less than our Lord's own character, put into words. It is the description set side by side with an example.

William Franklin (Billy) Graham

"Poor in spirit" refers, not precisely to humility, but to an attitude of dependence on God and detachment from earthly supports.

Ronald Arbuthnott Knox

The more we live and try to practice the Sermon on the Mount, the more shall we experience blessing.

David Martyn Lloyd-Jones

Meek endurance and meek obedience, the accepting of His dealings, of whatever complexion they are and however they may tear and desolate our hearts, without murmuring, without sulking, without rebellion or resistance, is the deepest conception of the meekness which Christ pronounced blessed.

Alexander Maclaren

Beatitudes, just by virtue of having been spoken by him, have enriched our mortal existence beyond imagination, putting a yeast of love into the unlovely dough of human greed and human spite and human willfulness, so that it can rise marvelously.

Malcolm Muggeridge

The beatitudes are a call to us to see ourselves, to live with ourselves, in a way that probably does not come easily to most of us.

Simon Tugwell

Beauty

See also Creation

Worship the Lord in the beauty of holiness.

1 Chronicles 16:29 KJV

As it is written, "How beautiful are the feet of those who bring good news!"

Romans 10:15 NRSV

Your beauty should not come from outward adornment, such as braided hair and the wearing of gold jewelry and fine clothes. Instead, it should be that of your inner self, the unfading beauty of a gentle and quiet spirit, which is of great worth in God's sight. For this is the way the holy women of the past who put their hope in God used to make themselves beautiful.

1 Peter 3:3–5 NJB

Good in the heart works its way up into the face and prints its own beauty there.

Anon.

Beauty is indeed a good gift of God; but that the good may not think it a great good, God dispenses it even to the wicked.

St. Augustine of Hippo

Beauty may be said to be God's trademark in creation.

Henry Ward Beecher

O world, as God has made it! All is beauty.

Robert Browning

Wherever ugliness is kept at bay, there the Spirit of God, who is the God of Beauty, is doing His creative and re-creative labor.

(Frederick) Donald Coggan

Cheerfulness and content are great beautifiers, and are famous preservers of good looks.

Charles Dickens

Love built on beauty, soon as beauty, dies.

John Donne

Though we travel the world over to find the beautiful, we must carry it with us or we find it not.

Ralph Waldo Emerson

Beauty is the mark God sets upon virtue.

Ralph Waldo Emerson

God is beauty.

St. Francis of Assisi

God passes through the thicket to the world, and wherever his glance falls he turns all things to beauty.

St. John of the Cross

Beauty is God's handwriting. Welcome it in every fair face, every fair day, every fair flower.

Charles Kingsley

God's fingers can touch nothing but to mold it into loveliness.

George MacDonald

A rose is but a rose, it blooms because it blooms; / It thinks not on itself, nor asks if it is seen.

Angelus Silesius

In all ranks of life the human heart yearns for the beautiful; and the beautiful things that God makes are his gifts to all alike.

Harriet Beecher Stowe

Belief

See also Creeds; Faith; Trust

Everything is possible to one who believes.

Mark 9:23 REB

Those who believe in me, even though they die, will live, and everyone who lives and believes in me will never die.

John 11:25–26 NRSV

Believe on the Lord Jesus, and you will be saved, you and your household.

Acts 16:31 NRSV

Without faith it is impossible to please him: for he that cometh to God must believe that he is, and that he is a rewarder of them that diligently seek him.

Hebrews 11:6 KJV

A belief is not true because it is useful.

Henri-Frédéric Amiel

If you believe in the Gospel what you like, and reject what you don't like, it is not the Gospel you believe, but yourself.

St. Augustine of Hippo

I believe in God the Father Almighty, Maker of heaven and earth: And in Jesus Christ his only Son our Lord, Who was conceived by the Holy Ghost, Born of the Virgin Mary, Suffered under Pontius Pilate, Was crucified, dead, and buried: He descended into hell; The third day he rose again from the dead; He ascended into heaven, And sitteth on the right hand of God the Father Almighty; From thence he shall come to judge the quick and the dead. I believe in the Holy Ghost; The holy Catholick Church; The Communion of Saints; The Forgiveness of sins; The Resurrection of the body, And the life everlasting. Amen.

Book of Common Prayer

There is nothing that can help you to understand your beliefs more than trying to explain them to an inquisitor.

Frank A. Clark

Belief consists in accepting the affirmations of the soul; unbelief in denying them.

Ralph Waldo Emerson

He does not believe that does not live according to his belief.

Thomas Fuller

You never know how much you really believe anything until its truth or falsehood becomes a matter of life and death to you.

Clive Staples (C.S.) Lewis

We can believe what we choose. We are answerable for what we choose to believe.

John Henry Newman

Belief is truth held in the mind; faith is fire in the heart.

Joseph Fort Newton

For the most part we live upon successes, not promises. Unless we see and feel the print of victories we will not believe.

John Owen

There are three roads to belief: reason, habit, revelation.

Blaise Pascal

What I believe about God is the most important thing about me.

Aiden Wilson (A.W.) Tozer

Bereavement

See also Grief; Loss; Sadness

Yea, though I walk through the valley of the shadow of death, I will fear no evil: for thou art with me; thy rod and thy staff they comfort me.

Psalm 23:4 KJV

You have turned my mourning into dancing; you have taken off my sackcloth and clothed me with joy.

Psalm 30:11 NRSV

The spirit of the Lord God is upon me because the Lord has anointed me . . . to comfort all who mourn, to give them garlands instead of ashes, oil of gladness instead of mourners' tears, a garment of splendour for the heavy heart.

Isaiah 61:1–3 REB

Jesus wept.

John 11:35 KJV

When I buried my husband, I buried all my earthly love with him, for though I loved him as my own soul, I would not for a penny buy back his life against the will of God . . . Now my soul will love God only.

St. Bridget of Sweden

If they are with Christ and Christ is with us, then they cannot be very far away.

Pierre Teilhard de Chardin

I have lost all! Oh, my beloved brother—oh, the friend of my heart—oh, my good and

pious husband, thou art dead, and hast left me in misery! How shall I live without thee? Ah, poor lonely widow and miserable woman that I am; may he who forsakes not widows and orphans console me. Oh! my God, console me! Oh, my Jesus, strengthen me in my weakness.

Elizabeth of Hungary

When we lose one we love our bitterest tears are called forth by the memory of hours when we loved not enough.

Maurice Maeterlinck

They that love beyond the world cannot be separated by it. Death cannot kill what never dies, nor can spirits ever be divided that love and live in the same divine principle.

William Penn

Death has sealed off those married years like a capped bottle of perfume. Our marriage cannot be lost or shattered. Nothing can touch it now. It's safe—one of my treasures laid up in heaven where not mothy resentment or rusty dissolution can erode it. In a sense our marriage was like a flower that matured into a fruit, sweet and wholesome, and I am like a seed dropped from that mature fruit, now withered and dead. I am the result of a long relationship and I want to fall in good ground and produce more fruit—of what kind God and I will have to determine.

Luci Shaw

The grave is but the threshold of eternity.

Robert Southey

Death hides, but it does not divide, they are but on Christ's other side. Thou art with Christ and Christ with me. In Him I am close to thee.

Elizabeth Urch

Bible

See also Reading; Study; Word of God

Authority of

Heaven and earth will pass away, but my words will never pass away.

Matthew 24:35 GNB

When you received the word of God that you heard from us, you accepted it not as a human word but as what it really is, God's word.

1 Thessalonians 2:13 NRSV

The faith will totter if the authority of the Holy Scriptures loses its hold on men. We must surrender ourselves to the authority of Holy Scripture, for it can neither mislead nor be misled.

St. Augustine of Hippo

You cannot criticize the New Testament. It criticizes you.

John Jay Chapman

There is only one real inevitability: it is necessary that the Scripture be fulfilled.

Carl F.H. Henry

Men do not reject the Bible because it contradicts itself but because it contradicts them.

E. Paul Hovey

All experience must be subservient to the discipline of Scripture.

Erroll Hulse

God the Father is the giver of Holy Scripture; God the Son is the theme of Holy Scripture; and God the Spirit is the author, authenticator, and interpreter of Holy Scripture.

James Innell (J.I.) Packer

Back to the Bible, or back to the jungle.

Luis Palau

If we come to Scripture with our minds made up, expecting to hear from it only an echo of our own thoughts and never the thunderclap of God's, then indeed he will not speak to us and we shall only be confirmed in our own prejudices. We must allow the Word of God to confront us, to disturb our security, to undermine our complacency and to overthrow our patterns of thought and behavior.

John R.W. Stott

All the knowledge you want is comprised in one book, the Bible.

John Wesley

Inspiration of

All scripture is inspired by God.

2 Timothy 3:16 NRSV

No prophecy of the scripture is of any private interpretation. For the prophecy came not in old time by the will of man: but holy men of God spake as they were moved by the Holy Ghost.

2 Peter 1:20–21 KJV

Be astounded that God should have written to us.

St. Antony of Egypt

How firm a foundation, ye saints of the Lord; / Is laid for your faith in His excellent word; / What more can He say than to you He hath said; / You who unto Jesus for refuge have fled?

K in Rippon's Selection

The Lord has more truth yet to break forth out of His holy Word.

John Robinson

The Bible is especially dangerous if we call it "the Word of God" and think that divine inspiration means that everything in it we read is right . . . The Bible is accepted as the Word of God when communities of faith understand God to be speaking to them in and through its message.

Letty M. Russell

If I did not believe the infallibility of this book I would rather be without it. If I am to judge the book, it is no judge of me.

Charles Haddon Spurgeon

It is one thing to be told that the Bible has authority because it is divinely inspired, and another thing to feel one's heart leap out and grasp its truth.

Leslie Weatherhead

Interpretation of

You pore over the scriptures, believing that in them you can find eternal life; it is these scriptures that testify to me, and yet you refuse to come to me to receive life!

John 5:39–40 NJB

In the Old Testament the New lies hidden, in the New Testament the Old is laid open.

St. Augustine of Hippo

All the Word of God is given by the Spirit of God, so each word must be interpreted to us by that same Spirit.

Book of Common Prayer

Explain the Scriptures by the Scriptures.

Clement of Alexandria

Compare Scripture with Scripture. False doctrines, like false witnesses, agree not among themselves.

William Gurnall

What you bring away from the Bible depends to some extent on what you carry to it.

Oliver Wendell Holmes

When you read God's word, you must constantly be saying to yourself, "It is talking to me, and about me."

Søren Kierkegaard

The Bible without the Holy Spirit is a sun-dial by moonlight.

Dwight Lyman (D.L.) Moody

God's truth always agrees with itself.

John Robinson

The devil can cite Scripture for his purpose.

William Shakespeare

Read the Scripture, not only as a history, but as a love-letter sent to you from God.

Thomas Watson

The Scripture is to be its own interpreter, or rather the Spirit speaking in it; nothing can cut the diamond but the diamond; nothing can interpret the Scripture but Scripture.

Thomas Watson

Power and Influence of

Thy word is a lamp unto my feet, and a light unto my path.

Psalm 119:105 KJV

Is not my word like as a fire? saith the Lord; and like a hammer that breaketh the rock in pieces?

Jeremiah 23:29 KJV

Jesus answered and said unto them, Ye do err, not knowing the scriptures, nor the power of God.

Matthew 22:29 KJV

For the word of God is quick, and powerful, and sharper than any two-edged sword, piercing even to the dividing asunder of soul and spirit, and of the joints and marrow, and is a discerner of the thoughts and intents of the heart.

Hebrews 4:12 KJV

As in Paradise, God walks in the Holy Scriptures, seeking man.

St. Ambrose

I have sometimes seen more in a line of the Bible that I could well tell how to stand under, yet at another time the whole Bible hath been to me as dry as a stick.

John Bunyan

It is a great thing, this reading of the Scriptures! For it is not possible ever to exhaust the mind of the Scriptures. It is a well that has no bottom.

St. John Chrysostom

I have found in the Bible words for my inmost thoughts, songs for my joy, utterances for my hidden griefs and pleadings for my shame and feebleness.

Samuel Taylor Coleridge

The Bible—banned, burned, beloved. More widely read, more frequently attacked than any other book in history. Generations of intellectuals have attempted to discredit it; dictators of every age have outlawed it and executed those who read it. Yet soldiers carry it into battle believing it more powerful than their weapons. Fragments of it smuggled into solitary prison cells have transformed ruthless killers into gentle saints.

Charles W. Colson

The Bible is a window in this prison-world, through which we may look into eternity.

Timothy Dwight

These writings bring back to you the living image of that most holy mind, the very Christ himself speaking, healing, dying, rising, in fact so entirely present, that you would see less of him if you beheld him with your eyes.

Desiderius Erasmus

Shallows where a lamb could wade and depths where an elephant could drown.

Matthew Henry

Lay hold on the Bible until the Bible lays hold on you.

William H. Houghton

If a man's Bible is coming apart, it is an indication that he himself is fairly well put together.

James Jennings

I believe that the Bible is the best gift that God has ever given to man. All the good from the Savior of the world is communicated to us through this book. I have been driven many times to my knees by the overwhelming conviction that I had nowhere else to go.

Abraham Lincoln

The Bible is alive, it speaks to me; it has feet, it runs after me; it has hands, it lays hold on me.

Martin Luther

By reading of Scripture I am so renewed that all nature seems renewed around me and with me. The sky seems to be a purer, a cooler blue, the trees a deeper green, light is sharper on the outlines of the forest and the hills and the whole world is charged with the glory of God.

Thomas Merton

One of the many divine qualities of the Bible is this, that it does not yield its secrets to the irreverent and censorious.

James Innell (J.I.) Packer

The Bible is the greatest traveler in the world. It penetrates to every country, civilized and uncivilized. It is seen in the royal palace and in the humble cottage. It is the friend of emperors and beggars. It is read by the light of the dim candle amid Arctic snows. It is read under the glare of the equatorial sun. It is read in city and country, amid the crowds and in solitude. Wherever the message is received, it frees the mind from bondage and fills the heart with gladness.

Arthur Tappan (A.T.) Pierson

We cannot segregate God's word from the historical reality in which it is proclaimed. It would not then be God's word. It would be history, it would be a pious book, a Bible that is just a book in our Library. It becomes God's word because it verifies, enlightens, contrasts, repudiates, praises what is going on today in this society.

Oscar Romero

If a man is not familiar with the Bible, he has suffered a loss which he had better make all possible haste to correct.

Theodore Roosevelt

Arm yourself with a thorough knowledge of the written Word of God. Read your Bible. . . . Neglect your Bible and nothing that I know of can prevent you from error if a plausible advocate of false teaching shall happen to meet you.

John Charles Ryle

Many books in my library are now behind and beneath me. They were good in their way once, and so were the clothes I wore when I was ten years old; but I have outgrown them. Nobody ever outgrows Scripture; the book widens and deepens with our years.

Charles Haddon Spurgeon

Most people are bothered by those passages in Scripture which they cannot understand; but as for me, I always noticed that the passages in Scripture which trouble me most are those that I do understand.

Mark Twain

Leave not off reading the Bible till you find your hearts warmed. . . . Let it not only inform you, but inflame you.

Thomas Watson

The Bible is a rock of diamonds, a chain of pearls, the sword of the Spirit; a chart by which the Christian sails to eternity; the map by which he daily walks; the sundial by which he sets his life; the balance in which he weighs his actions.

Thomas Watson

Give the Bible to the people, unadulterated, pure, unaltered, unexplained, uncheapened, and then see it work through the whole nature. It is very difficult indeed for a man or for a boy who knows the Scriptures to get away from it. It follows him like the memory of his mother. It haunts him like an old song. It reminds him like the word of an old and revered teacher. It forms a part of the warp and woof of his life.

(Thomas) Woodrow Wilson

Purpose of

The unfolding of your words gives light; it imparts understanding to the simple.

Psalm 119:130 NRSV

From infancy you have known the holy Scriptures, which are able to make you wise for salvation through faith in Jesus Christ. All Scripture is God-breathed and is useful for teaching, rebuking, correcting and training in righteousness, so that the man of God may be thoroughly equipped for every good work.

2 Timothy 3:15–17 NIV

Divine Scripture is the feast of wisdom, and the single books are the various dishes.

St. Ambrose

The Bible is God's chart for you to steer by, to keep you from the bottom of the sea, and to show you where the harbor is, and how to reach it without running on rocks and bars.

Henry Ward Beecher

[Of all the holy Scriptures] hear them, read, mark, learn, and inwardly digest them.

Book of Common Prayer

The Bible is like a telescope. If a man looks through his telescope, then he sees worlds beyond; but if he looks at his telescope, then he does not see anything but that. The Bible is a thing to looked through, to see that which is beyond.

Phillips Brooks

The Scriptures teach us the best way of living, the noblest way of suffering, and the most comfortable way of dying.

John Flavel

The storehouse of God's word was never meant for mere scrutiny, nor even primarily for study but for sustenance.

Vance Havner

The Bible is a letter God has sent to us; prayer is a letter we send to him.

Matthew Henry

God has favored us with his autobiography so that we might know and think his thoughts in every department of our lives.

Robert Horn

If the Bible is to get into us we must get into the Bible.

Robert Horn

The Bible calls itself food. The value of food is not in the discussion it arouses but in the nourishment it imparts.

William H. Houghton

Ignorance of the Scripture is ignorance of Christ.

St. Jerome

There is a book, who runs may read, / Which heavenly truth imparts; / And all the love its scholars need, / Pure eyes and Christian hearts.

John Keble

As we go to the cradle only in order to find the baby, so we go to the Scriptures only to find Christ.

Martin Luther

We ought to open the Holy Book as we would go into a sanctuary where we were sure of meeting our heavenly Father face to face, of hearing His voice.

Dwight Lyman (D.L.) Moody

The Scriptures were not given to increase our knowledge but to change our lives.

Dwight Lyman (D.L.) Moody

The Holy Scriptures tell us what we could never learn any other way: they tell us what we are, who we are, how we got here, why we are here, and what we are required to do while we remain here.

Aiden Wilson (A.W.) Tozer

Doers of the Word are the best hearers.

Thomas Watson

Birth

See also Jesus Christ, Birth of; New Birth

To the woman he said: I shall give you intense pain in childbearing, you will give birth to your children in pain. Your yearning will be for your husband, and he will dominate you.

Genesis 3:16 NJB

On you I have leaned from birth; you brought me from my mother's womb; to you I offer praise at all times.

Psalm 71:6 REB

The time came for the baby to be born, and she gave birth to her firstborn, a son. She wrapped him in cloths and placed him in a manger, because there was no room for them in the inn.

Luke 2:6–7 NIV

When a woman is in labor, she has pain, because her hour has come. But when her child is born, she no longer remembers the anguish because of the joy of having brought a human being into the world.

John 16:21 NRSV

No human birth can compare to the supernatural birth of a child of God.

James Montgomery Boice

The birth of every new baby is God's vote of confidence in the future of man.

Imogene Fey

Birth is the beginning of death.

Thomas Fuller

Baby: Unwritten history! Unfathomed mystery!

Josiah Gilbert Holland

Birthdays and Anniversaries

The third day was Pharaoh's birthday and he gave a banquet for all his officials.

Genesis 40:20 NJB

The Lord has helped us and taken care of us during the past forty years that we have been in this huge desert. We've had everything we needed, and the Lord has blessed us and made us successful in whatever we have done.

Deuteronomy 2:7 CEV

The people started crying when God's Law was read to them. Then Nehemiah the governor, Ezra the priest and teacher, and the Levites who had been teaching the people all said, "This is a special day for the Lord your God. So don't be sad and don't cry!" Nehemiah told the people, "Enjoy your good food and wine and share some with those who didn't have anything to bring. Don't be sad. This is a special day for the Lord, and he will make you happy and strong."

Nehemiah 8:9–10 CEV

For all our days pass away under your wrath; our years come to an end like a sigh. The days of our life are seventy years, or perhaps eighty, if we are strong; even then their span is only toil and trouble; they are soon gone, and we fly away.

Psalm 90:9–10 NRSV

I see not a step before me as I tread on another year; but I've left the past in God's keeping— the future in his mercy shall clear; and what looks dark in the distance may brighten as I draw near.

Mary Gardiner Brainard

The year is closed, the record made, / The last deed done, the last word said, / The memory alone remains / Of all its joys, its grief, its gains, / And now with purpose full and clear, / We turn to meet another year.

Robert Browning

Be at war with your vices, at peace with your neighbors, and let every new year find you a better man.

Benjamin Franklin

The holiest of all holidays are those kept by ourselves in silence and apart; the secret anniversaries of the heart.

Henry Wadsworth Longfellow

Bishops, *see* Church, Leaders of

Bitterness

See also Hatred

I loathe my life; I will give free utterance to my complaint; I will speak in the bitterness of my soul.

Job 10:1 NRSV

Foolish children are a grief to their father and bitterness to her who bore them.

Proverbs 17:25 NRSV

And Peter remembered the word of the Lord, how he had said unto him, Before the cock crow, thou shalt deny me thrice. And Peter went out, and wept bitterly.

Luke 22:61–62 KJV

Let all bitterness and wrath, and anger, and clamor, and evil speaking, be put away from you, with all malice.

Ephesians 4:31 KJV

He who cannot forgive others, breaks the bridge over which he himself must pass.

Corrie ten Boom

If there is the tiniest grudge in your mind against anyone . . . your spiritual penetration into the knowledge of God stops.

Oswald Chambers

Malice and envy are but two branches growing out of the same bitter root. Self-love

and evil-speakings are the fruit they bear. Malice is properly the procuring or wishing another's evil; envy, the repining at his good. And these vent themselves by evil-speaking.

Robert Leighton

If you hug to yourself any resentment against anybody else, you destroy the bridge by which God would come to you.

Peter Marshall

Animosity cloaked in piety is a demon even if it sits in church praising the Creator.

Calvin Miller

Those who say they will forgive but can't forget, simply bury the hatchet, but leave the handle out for immediate use.

Dwight Lyman (D.L.) Moody

There is no torment like the inner torment of an unforgiving spirit. It refuses to be soothed, it refuses to be healed, it refuses to forget.

Charles R. Swindoll

Blasphemy

See also Holy Spirit, Sin Against

You shall not make wrongful use of the name of the LORD your God, for the LORD will not acquit anyone who misuses his name.

Exodus 20:7 NRSV

Every human sin and blasphemy will be forgiven, but blasphemy against the Spirit will not be forgiven.

Matthew 12:31 NJB

[In the last days] Men shall be lovers of their own selves, covetous, boasters, proud, blasphemers.

2 Timothy 3:2 KJV

Watch over yourselves that you may never swear. I invoked God my helper and he afforded me his succor not to swear, now nothing is more easy to me than not to swear.

St. Augustine of Hippo

Beware of worshiping Jesus as the Son of God and professing your faith in him as the Savior of the world, while you blaspheme him by the complete evidence in your daily life that he is powerless to do anything in and through you.

Oswald Chambers

For eighty and six years have I been his [Christ's] servant, and he has done me no wrong, and how can I blaspheme my King who saved me?

St. Polycarp

Profanity fixes the other person's attention on my words rather than my thoughts.

Hugh Prather

Profanity is the use of strong words by weak people.

William Arthur Ward

Blessings

See also Beatitudes

The LORD bless you and keep you; the LORD make his face to shine upon you, and be gracious to you; the LORD lift up his countenance upon you, and give you peace.

Numbers 6:24–26 NRSV

[Jesus and little children] Then he embraced them, laid his hands on them and gave them his blessing.

Mark 10:16 NJB

Do not repay wrong with wrong, or abuse with abuse; on the contrary, respond with blessing, for a blessing is what God intends you to receive.

1 Peter 3:9 REB

God is more anxious to bestow His blessings on us than we are to receive them.

St. Augustine of Hippo

Prosperity is the blessing of the Old Testament; adversity is the blessing of the New.

Francis Bacon

The greatest blessing we ever get from God is to know that we are destitute spiritually.

Oswald Chambers

Reflect upon your present blessings, of which every man has many; not on your past misfortunes, of which all men have some.

Charles Dickens

To bless God for mercies is the way to increase them; to bless Him for miseries is the way to remove them.

William Dyer

Blessed is the influence of one true, loving soul on another.

George Eliot

Blessed is he who does good to others and desires not that others should do good to him.

Br. Giles (of Assisi)

Those blessings are sweetest that are won with prayers and worn with thanks.

Thomas Goodwin

The best things are nearest: breath in your nostrils, light in your eyes, flowers at your feet, duties at your hand, the path of God just before you.

Robert Louis Stevenson

Blessed are those who saw Christ in the flesh. But still more blessed are we who see his image portrayed in the Gospels, and hear his voice speaking from them.

Tikhon of Zadonsk

The more we count the blessings we have, the less we crave the luxuries we haven't.

William Arthur Ward

Among my list of blessings infinite stands this the foremost—that my heart has bled.

Edward Young

Blindness, *see* Spiritual Blindness

Blood, *see* Jesus Christ, Death of

Boasting, *see* Conceit

Body

See also Church

Nothing about me is hidden from you! I was secretly woven together deep in the earth below, but with your own eyes you saw my body being formed. Even before I was born, you had written in your book everything I would do.

Psalm 139:15–16 CEV

You must not allow sin to reign over your mortal bodies and make you obey their desires; or give any parts of your bodies over to sin to be used as instruments of evil. Instead, give . . . every part of your bodies to God to be instruments of uprightness.

Romans 6:12–13 NJB

Know ye not that your body is the temple of the Holy Ghost which is in you, which ye have of God, and ye are not your own? For ye are bought with a price; therefore glorify

God in your body, and in your spirit, which are God's.

1 Corinthians 6:19–20 KJV

For I received from the Lord what I also passed on to you: The Lord Jesus, on the night he was betrayed, took bread, and when he had given thanks, he broke it and said, "This is my body, which is for you; do this in remembrance of me."

1 Corinthians 11:23 NIV

Now you are the body of Christ and individually members of it.

1 Corinthians 12:27 NRSV

Put to death in the body, he [Christ] was brought to life in the spirit.

1 Peter 3:18 REB

Whether in this life, or in death, or in resurrection, the body is of great service to the soul that loves the Lord. First, it produces the fruits of penitence, second, it brings the gift of rest, and third, the final state of beatitude.

St. Bernard of Clairvaux

My body was made for the love of God. Every cell in my body is a hymn to my creator and a declaration of love.

Ernesto Cardenal

Thank God we are not going to be angels, we are going to be something tenfold better. By the redemption of Jesus Christ there is a time coming when our bodies will be in the image of God.

Oswald Chambers

Our body is the most gracious gift God has given us, and if we hand over the mainspring of our life to God we can work out in our bodily life all that he works in. It is through our bodily lives that Satan works and, thank

God, it is through our bodily lives that God's Spirit works. God gives us his grace and his Spirit; he puts right all that was wrong, he does not suppress it nor counteract it, but readjusts the whole thing; then begins our work.

Oswald Chambers

How can I hate this body of mine when it is my nature to love it? How can I break away from it when I am bound to it for ever? How can I escape from it when it is going to rise with me?

St. John Climacus

The body is deified along with the soul.

Gregory Palamas

The body is matter, but it is God's creation. . . . When it is neglected or scoffed at, God himself is insulted.

Michel Quoist

The human body is probably the most amazing example of teamwork anywhere. Every part needs the other. When the stomach is hungry, the eyes spot the hamburger. The nose smells the onions, the feet run to the snack stand, the hands douse the burger with mustard and shove it back into the mouth, where it goes down to the stomach. Now that's cooperation!

Joni Eareckson Tada

Boldness, *see* Confidence; Courage

Bondage

See also Freedom

Moses reported this to the Israelites, but they did not listen to him because of their discouragement and cruel bondage.

Exodus 6:9 NIV

The creation itself will be set free from its bondage to decay and will obtain the freedom of the glory of the children of God.

Romans 8:21 NRSV

Stand fast therefore in the liberty wherewith Christ hath made us free, and be not entangled again with the yoke of bondage.

Galatians 5:1 KJV

The peculiar characteristic of slavery is to be always in fear.

St. Ambrose

Worldly people imagine that the saints must find it difficult to live with so many restrictions, but the bondage is with the world, not with the saints. There is no such thing as freedom in the world, and the higher we go in the social life the more bondage there is.

Oswald Chambers

Himself is his dungeon.

George MacDonald

Jesus Christ is the key which unlocks the door of the prison cell of our own making and sets us free to live in the wide world of God's love and purpose.

Kenneth Pillar

There is no real bondage, but what is either from, or for sin.

Vavasor Powell

Boredom, *see* Monotony

Borrowing, *see* Debt

Bribes, *see* Corruption

Brothers and Sisters, *see* Families

Calling, *see* Vocation

Calm, *see* Quiet and Stillness; Rest

Caring

See also Pastoral Care

The Lord is a sure protection in time of trouble, and cares for all who make him their refuge.

Nahum 1:7 REB

My illness must have caused you some trouble, but you didn't hate me or turn me away because of it. You welcomed me as though I were one of God's angels or even Christ Jesus himself.

Galatians 4:14 CEV

Be shepherds of God's flock that is under your care, serving as overseers—not because you must, but because you are willing, as God wants you to be; not greedy for money, but eager to serve; not lording it over those entrusted to you, but being examples to the flock.

1 Peter 5:2–3 NIV

People will not care what you know until they know that you care.

Anon.

Have a heart that never hardens, and a temper that never tires, and a touch that never hurts.

Charles Dickens

The Christian with social concern must champion all those who need champions, not just those whose championing is currently popular.

Os Guinness

Christianity has taught us to care. Caring is the greatest thing, caring matters most.

Baron Friedrich von Hügel

Keep Jesus Christ in your hearts and you will recognize his face in every human being. You will want to help him out in all his needs; the needs of your brothers and sisters.

John Paul II

The gospel of a broken heart begins with the ministry of bleeding hearts. As soon as we cease to bleed we cease to bless.

John Henry Jowett

Christianity demands a level of caring that transcends human inclinations.

Erwin W. Lutzer

We tend to look at caring as an attitude of the strong toward the weak, of the powerful toward the powerless, of the haves toward the have-nots. . . . Still, when we honestly ask ourselves which persons in our lives mean the most to us, we often find that it is those who, instead of giving much advice, solutions, or cures, have chosen rather to share our pain and touch our wounds with a gentle and tender hand. The friend who can be silent with us in a moment of despair or confusion, who can stay with us in an hour of grief and bereavement, who can tolerate not-knowing, not-curing, not-healing and face with us the reality of our powerlessness, that is the friend who cares.

Henri J.M. Nouwen

God cares, God is concerned. And since God is concerned his people have an obligation to be concerned too.

Foy Valentine

Painful wounds call for love, understanding, and healing.

David Watson

Celebration

See also Praise; Worship

The people of Israel, the priests and the Levites, and the rest of the returned exiles, celebrated the dedication of this house of God with joy.

Ezra 6:16 NRSV

Each generation will announce to the next your wonderful and powerful deeds. I will keep thinking about your marvelous glory and your mighty miracles. Everyone will talk about your fearsome deeds, and I will tell all nations how great you are. They will celebrate and sing about your matchless mercy and your power to save.

Psalm 145:4–7 CEV

"Bring the calf we have been fattening, and kill it; we will celebrate by having a feast, because this son of mine was dead and has come back to life; he was lost and is found." And they began to celebrate.

Luke 15:23–24 NJB

All our life is a celebration for us; we are convinced, in fact, that God is always everywhere. We sing while we work, we sing hymns while we sail, we pray while we carry out all life's other occupations.

Clement of Alexandria

In celebration the high and the mighty regain their balance, and the weak and lowly receive new stature. Who can be high or low at the festival of God?

Richard J. Foster

Lord, turn the routines of work into celebrations of love.

John Oxenham

Yet if we celebrate, let it be that he has invaded our lives with purpose.

Luci Shaw

The camera follows a young woman as she makes her way through the stands to an area set aside for repentance and conversion. But Jesus' stories imply that far more may be going on out there: beyond that stadium scene, in a place concealed from all camera lenses, a great party has erupted, a gigantic celebration in the unseen world.

Philip Yancey

Celibacy, *see* Singleness

Change

See also Spiritual Growth

I am the Lord, I change not.

Malachi 3:6 KJV

And be not conformed to this world: but be ye transformed by the renewing of your mind, that ye may prove what is that good, and acceptable, and perfect, will of God.

Romans 12:2 KJV

But we all, with open face beholding as in a glass the glory of the Lord, are changed into the same image from glory to glory, even as by the Spirit of the Lord.

2 Corinthians 3:18 KJV

Every generous act of giving, with every perfect gift, is from above, coming down from the Father of lights, with whom there is no variation or shadow due to change.

James 1:17 NRSV

Change is here to stay.

Anon.

Keep changing. When you're through changing, you're through.

Bruce Fairchild Barton

We can change, slowly and steadily, if we set our will to it.

Robert Hugh Benson

Today is not yesterday. We ourselves change. How then, can our works and thoughts, if they are always to be the fittest, continue always the same. Change, indeed, is painful, yet ever needful; and if memory have its force and worth, so also has hope.

Thomas Carlyle

Change is the nursery of music, joy, life and eternity.

John Donne

The nature of human beings is to be inactive unless influenced by some affection: love or hatred, desire, hope, fear, etc. These affections are the "spring of action", the things that set us moving in our lives, that move us to engage in activities. . . . It is the affection we call covetousness that moves a person to seek worldly profits; it is the affection we call ambition that moves a person to pursue worldly glory; it is the affection we call lust that moves a person to pursue sensual delights. Just as worldly affections are the spring of worldly actions, so the religious affections are the spring of religious actions. . . . No-one is ever changed, either by doctrine, by hearing the Word, or by the preaching or teaching of another, unless the affections are moved by these things.

Jonathan Edwards

He that never changes his opinions, never corrects his mistakes, will never be wiser tomorrow than he is today.

Tryon Edwards

Christians are supposed not merely to endure change, nor even to profit by it, but to cause it.

Harry Emerson Fosdick

He who shall introduce into public affairs the principles of primitive Christianity will change the face of the world.

Benjamin Franklin

The world does need changing, society needs changing, the nation needs changing, but we never will change it until we ourselves are changed.

William Franklin (Billy) Graham

Change is not made without inconvenience, even from worse to better.

Richard Hooker

In a higher world it is otherwise; but here below to live is to change, and to be perfect is to have changed often.

John Henry Newman

God, give us grace to accept with serenity the things that cannot be changed, courage to change the things that should be changed, and the wisdom to distinguish the one from the other.

(Karl Paul) Reinhold Niebuhr

Everyone thinks of changing the world, but no one thinks of changing himself.

Count Leo Tolstoy

Character

See also Christ-likeness; Maturity; Spiritual Growth

The LORD said to Samuel, "Do not look on his appearance or on the height of his stature, because I have rejected him; for the LORD does not see as mortals see; they look on the outward appearance, but the LORD looks on the heart."

1 Samuel 16:7 NRSV

We also boast in our sufferings, knowing that suffering produces endurance, and endurance produces character, and character produces hope, and hope does not disappoint us, because God's love has been poured into our hearts through the Holy Spirit.

Romans 5:3–5 NRSV

Do not be misled: "Bad company corrupts good character."

1 Corinthians 15:33 NIV

The Christian character is the flower of which sacrifice is the seed.

Fr. Andrew

Resolved, to live with all my might while I do live. Resolved, never to lose one moment of time, to improve it in the most profitable way I can. Resolved, never to do anything which I should despise or think meanly in another. Resolved, never to do anything out of revenge. Resolved, never to do anything which I should be afraid to do if it were the last hour of my life.

Lord Arthur James Balfour

Character is better than ancestry, and personal conduct is of more importance than the highest parentage.

Dr. Thomas John Barnardo

A good name is better than great riches.

Miguel de Cervantes

God alters our disposition, but he does not make our character. When God alters my disposition, the first thing the new disposition will do is to stir up my brain to think along God's line. As I begin to think, begin to work out what God has worked in, it will become character. Character is consolidated thought. God makes me pure in heart; I must make myself pure in conduct.

Oswald Chambers

Just as good literature and good art raise and ennoble character, so bad literature and bad art degrade it.

(Frederick) Donald Coggan

We first make our habits, then our habits make us.

John Dryden

The fruit of the Spirit is not excitement or orthodoxy, it is character.

G.B. Duncan

Talent develops in quiet places, character in the full current of human life.

Johann Wolfgang von Goethe

I am sure that most of us, looking back, would admit that whatever we have achieved in character we have achieved through conflict.

J. Wallace Hamilton

Character cannot be developed in ease and quiet. Only through experience of trial and suffering can the soul be strengthened, vision cleared, ambition inspired, and success achieved.

Helen Adams Keller

The discipline of desire is the background of character.

John Locke

More is at stake than your personal victory. Conflict is the main ingredient in God's character development program.

Erwin W. Lutzer

Character is what you are in the dark.

Dwight Lyman (D.L.) Moody

If I take care of my character, my reputation will take care of itself.

Dwight Lyman (D.L.) Moody

Strive to be like a well-regulated watch, of pure gold, with open face, busy hands and full of good works.

David Newquist

Reputation is what men and women think of us. Character is what God and the angels know of us.

Thomas Paine

The Sermon on the Mount cuts across differences of temperament and variations in capacity. It outlines the kind of character which is possible for any man, gifted or relatively ungifted, strong or weak, clever or slow. Once more we find Christ placing his finger, not upon the externals, but upon the vital internal attitude.

John Bertram (J.B.) Phillips

God is more concerned about our character than our comfort. His goal is not to pamper us physically but to perfect us spiritually.

Paul W. Powell

A man never shows his own character so plainly as by the way he describes another's.

Jean Paul Richter

Character is not in the mind. It is in the will.

Fulton John Sheen

Charity, *see* Love

Chastity, *see* Purity; Singleness

Childbirth, *see* Birth

Children

See also Adoption; Families; Parents; Sons and Daughters

Children are a blessing and a gift from the Lord. Having a lot of children to take care of you in your old age is like a warrior with a lot of arrows. The more you have, the better off you will be, because they will protect you when your enemies attack with arguments.

Psalm 127:3–5 CEV

Train children in the right way, and when old, they will not stray.

Proverbs 22:6 NRSV

Suffer the little children to come unto me, and forbid them not: for of such is the kingdom of God. Verily I say unto you, Whosoever shall not receive the kingdom of God as a little child, he shall not enter therein. And he took them up in his arms, put his hands upon them, and blessed them.

Mark 10:14–16 KJV

Children, be obedient to your parents in the Lord—that is what uprightness demands. The first commandment that has a promise attached to it is: Honor your father and mother, and the promise is: so that you may have long life and prosper in the land.

Ephesians 6:1–3 NJB

Children have never been very good at listening to their elders, but they have never failed to imitate them.

James Arthur Baldwin

Children are innocent and love justice, while most adults are wicked and prefer mercy.

Gilbert Keith (G.K.) Chesterton

Children must be valued as our most priceless possession.

James Dobson

Children are not casual guests in our home. They have been loaned to us temporarily for the purpose of loving them and instilling a foundation of values on which their future lives will be built.

James Dobson

A world without children is a world without newness, regeneration, color and vigor.

James Dobson

Give me a child for the first seven years, and you may do what you like with him afterwards.

St. Francis Xavier

Give me the children until they are seven and anyone may have them afterwards.

St. Francis Xavier

Virtue and a trade are the best portion for children.

George Herbert

Every child should be taught that useful work is worship and that intelligent labor is the highest form of prayer.

Robert Green Ingersoll

One laugh of a child will make the holiest day more sacred still.

Robert Green Ingersoll

It is common sense to put the seal to the wax while it is soft.

Arthur Jackson

Children have more need of models than of critics.

Joseph Joubert

Children learn what they observe. If children live with criticism, they learn to condemn and be judgmental. If children live with hostility, they learn to be angry and fight. If children live with ridicule, they learn to be shy and withdrawn. If children live with shame, they learn to feel guilt. If children live with tolerance, they learn to be patient. If children live with encouragement, they learn confidence. If children live with praise, they learn to appreciate. If children live with families, they learn justice. If children live with security, they learn to have faith. If children live with approval, they learn to like themselves. If children live with acceptance and friendship, they learn to find love in the world.

Dorothy Knolte

There is just one way to bring up a child in the way he should go and that is to travel that way yourself.

Abraham Lincoln

But with much trouble I was corrupted and made to learn the dirty devices of the world which I am now unlearning and becoming as it were a little child again, so that I may enter into the Kingdom of God.

Thomas Traherne

Choices

See also Decisions

I call heaven and earth to record this day against you, that I have set before you life and death, blessing and cursing: therefore choose life, that both thou and thy seed may live.

Deuteronomy 30:19 KJV

But if serving the Lord seems undesirable to you, then choose for yourselves this day whom you will serve, whether the gods your forefathers served beyond the River, or the gods of the Amorites, in whose land you are living. But as for me and my household, we will serve the Lord.

Joshua 24:15 NIV

Be ready to protect me because I have chosen to obey your laws.

Psalm 119:173 CEV

Do you not realize that love for the world is hatred for God? Anyone who chooses the world for a friend is constituted an enemy of God.

James 4:4 NJB

Choose to love—rather than hate. Choose to smile—rather than frown. Choose to build— rather than destroy. Choose to persevere—

rather than quit. Choose to praise—rather than gossip. Choose to heal—rather than wound. Choose to give—rather than grasp. Choose to act—rather than delay. Choose to forgive—rather than curse. Choose to pray—rather than despair.

Anon.

Every act is an act of self-sacrifice. When you choose anything you reject everything else—just as when you marry one woman you give up all the others.

Gilbert Keith (G.K.) Chesterton

This world and that to come are two enemies. We cannot therefore be friends to both; but we must resolve which we would forsake and which we would enjoy.

Clement of Alexandria

O Lord, may I be directed what to do and what to leave undone.

Elizabeth Fry

When you have to make a choice and don't make it, that is in itself a choice.

William James

The power of choosing good or evil is within the reach of all.

Origen of Alexandria

There is a time when we must firmly choose the course we will follow, or the relentless drift of events will make the decision.

Herbert V. Prochnow

Every day the choice between good and evil is presented to us in simple ways.

William Edwyn Robert Sangster

God always gives his very best to those who leave the choice with him.

James Hudson Taylor

Men are free to decide their own moral choices, but they are also under the necessity to account to God for those choices.

Aiden Wilson (A.W.) Tozer

Christ, *see* Jesus Christ

Christianity

See also Christ-likeness; Jesus Christ; Religions and Religion

It was at Antioch that the believers were first called Christians.

Acts 11:26 GNB

Agrippa said to Paul, "Are you so quickly persuading me to become a Christian?" Paul replied, "Whether quickly or not, I pray to God that not only you but also all who are listening to me today might become such as I am—except for these chains."

Acts 26:28–29 NRSV

Your attitude should be the same as that of Christ Jesus: Who, being in very nature God, did not consider equality with God something to be grasped, but made himself nothing, taking the very nature of a servant, being made in human likeness. And being found in appearance as a man, he humbled himself and became obedient to death—even death on a cross! Therefore God exalted him to the highest place and gave him the name that is above every name, that at the name of Jesus every knee should bow, in heaven and on earth and under the earth, and every tongue confess that Jesus Christ is Lord, to the glory of God the Father.

Philippians 2:5–11 NIV

If a man cannot be a Christian where he is, he cannot be a Christian anywhere.

Henry Ward Beecher

Christians showed themselves at that time to all the heathen in the most brilliant light; for the Christians were the only people who, in the midst of so much and so great tribulation, proved by deeds their sympathy and love of their kind.

Eusebius of Caesarea

It is unnatural for Christianity to be popular.

William Franklin (Billy) Graham

There is no more profound or more dangerous enemy to Christianity than anything which shrinks it and makes it narrow.

Abbé Henri Huvelin

To be a Christian is a great thing, not merely to seem one. And somehow or other those please the world most who please Christ least.

St. Jerome

It would scarcely be necessary to expound doctrine if our lives were radiant enough. If we behaved like true Christians, there would be no pagans.

John XXIII

Christianity is the highest perfection of humanity.

Samuel Johnson

Christianity, if false, is of no importance, and if true, of infinite importance. The one thing it cannot be is moderately important.

Clive Staples (C.S.) Lewis

To hold on to the plow while wiping our tears—this is Christianity.

Watchman Nee

Christianity is not a collection of truths to be believed, of laws to be obeyed. . . . Christianity is a person, one who loved us so much,

one who calls for our love. Christianity is Christ.

Oscar Romero

Christ cannot live his life today in the world without our mouth, without our eyes, without our going and coming, without our heart. When we love, it is Christ loving through us. This is Christianity.

Leon Joseph Suenens

The primary declaration of Christianity is not, "This do!" but "This happened!"

Evelyn Underhill

The Christian believes that he was created to know, love, and serve God in this world and to be happy with him in the next. That is the sole reason for his existence.

Evelyn Waugh

Christianity can be condensed into four words: admit, submit, commit and transmit.

Samuel Wilberforce

Christ-likeness

See also Discipleship; Humility

A disciple is not above the teacher, nor a slave above the master; it is enough for the disciple to be like the teacher, and the slave like the master.

Matthew 10:24–25 NRSV

Those whom God had already chosen he also set apart to become like his Son, so that the Son would be the first among many brothers.

Romans 8:29 GNB

All of us, with unveiled faces, seeing the glory of the Lord as though reflected in a mirror, are being transformed into the same image from one degree of glory to another.

2 Corinthians 3:18 NRSV

Beloved, now are we the sons of God, and it doth not yet appear what we shall be: but we know that when he shall appear, we shall be like him; for we shall see him as he is.

1 John 3:2 KJV

The most deeply felt obligation on earth is that which the Christian feels to imitate the Redeemer.

Albert Barnes

The expression of Christian character is not good doing, but God-likeness. If the Spirit of God has transformed you within, you will exhibit divine characteristics in your life, not good human characteristics. God's life in us expresses itself as God's life, not as human life trying to be godly. The secret of a Christian is that the supernatural is made natural in him by the grace of God, and the experience of this works out in the practical details of life, not in times of communion with God.

Oswald Chambers

To become like Christ is the only thing in the world worth caring for, the thing before which every ambition of man is folly and all lower achievement vain. Those only who make this quest the supreme desire and passion of their lives can even begin to hope to reach it.

John Drummond

If you were arrested for being a Christian, would there be enough evidence to convict you?

David Otis Fuller

Being a Christian is more than just an instantaneous conversion—it is a daily process whereby you grow to be more and more like Christ.

William Franklin (Billy) Graham

God creates out of nothing. Therefore until a man is nothing God can make nothing out of him.

Martin Luther

It is time that Christians were judged more by their likeness to Christ than their notions of Christ.

Lucretia Mott

On account of Him there have come to be many Christs in the world, even all who, like Him, loved righteousness and hated iniquity.

Origen of Alexandria

To be like Christ is to be a Christian.

William Penn

If Christ lives in us, controlling our personalities, we will leave glorious marks on the lives we touch. Not because of our lovely characters, but because of his.

Eugenia Price

We cannot help conforming ourselves to what we love.

St. Francis de Sales

To be like Christ. That is our goal, plain and simple. It sounds like a peaceful, relaxing, easy objective. But stop and think. He learned obedience by the things he suffered. So must we. It is neither easy nor quick nor natural. It is impossible in the flesh, slow in coming, and supernatural in scope. Only Christ can accomplish it within us.

Charles R. Swindoll

You and I were created to tell the truth about God by reflecting his likeness. That is normality. How many lies have you told about God today?

Ian Thomas

Christmas

See also Jesus Christ, Birth of

For unto us a child is born, unto us a son is given: and the government shall be upon his shoulder: and his name shall be called Wonderful, Counselor, The mighty God, The everlasting Father, the Prince of Peace.

Isaiah 9:6 KJV

In the countryside close by there were shepherds out in the fields keeping guard over their sheep during the watches of the night. An angel of the Lord stood over them and the glory of the Lord shone round them. They were terrified, but the angel said, "Do not be afraid. Look, I bring you news of great joy, a joy to be shared by the whole people. Today in the town of David a Savior has been born to you; he is Christ the Lord. And here is a sign for you: you will find a baby wrapped in swaddling clothes and lying in a manger." And all at once with the angel there was a great throng of the hosts of heaven, praising God with the words: Glory to God in the highest heaven, and on earth peace for those he favors.

Luke 2:8–16 NJB

And the Word was made flesh, and dwelt among us, (and we beheld his glory, the glory as of the only begotten of the Father,) full of grace and truth.

John 1:14 KJV

But when the fullness of time had come, God sent his Son, born of a woman, born under the law, in order to redeem those who were under the law, so that we might receive adoption as children.

Galatians 4:4–5 NRSV

Christmas began in the heart of God. It is complete only when it reaches the heart of man.

Anon.

The character of the Creator cannot be less than the highest. He has created and the highest is that babe born to Mary on that first Christmas morning.

A. Ian Burnett

Christmas is the gift from heaven of God's Son given for free; If Christmas isn't found in your heart, you won't find it under the tree.

Charlotte Carpenter

It is good to be children sometimes, and never better than at Christmas, when its mighty Founder was a child Himself.

Charles Dickens

Christmas is based on an exchange of gifts: the gift of God to man—his Son; and the gift of man to God—when we first give ourselves to God.

Vance Havner

To travel the road to Bethlehem is to keep a rendezvous with wonder, to answer the call of wisdom, and to bow the knee in worship.

John A. Knight

O come, all ye faithful, / Joyful and triumphant, / O come ye, O come ye to Bethlehem; / Come and behold Him, / Born the King of angels: / O come, let us adore Him, / O come, let us adore Him, / O come, let us adore Him, Christ the Lord!

Latin, tr. Frederick Oakeley

There were only a few shepherds at the first Bethlehem. The ox and the ass understood more of the first Christmas than the high priests in Jerusalem. And it is the same today.

Thomas Merton

You can never truly enjoy Christmas until

you can look up into the Father's face and tell him you have received his Christmas gift.

John R. Rice

The simple shepherds heard the voice of an angel and found their Lamb; the wise men saw the light of a star and found their Wisdom.

Fulton John Sheen

Christmas is the day that holds all time together.

Alexander Smith

The Christian should resemble a fruit tree, not a Christmas tree! For the gaudy decorations of a Christmas tree are only tied on, whereas fruit grows on a fruit tree.

John R.W. Stott

At Christmas play and make good cheer, / For Christmas comes but once a year.

Thomas Tusser

To perceive Christmas through its wrapping becomes more difficult every year.

E.B. White

Church

Leaders of

See also Leadership

Whoever wishes to become great among you must be your servant, and whoever wishes to be first among you must be slave of all.

Mark 10:43–44 NRSV

Now you are the body of Christ, and each one of you is a part of it. And in the church God has appointed first of all apostles, second prophets, third teachers, then workers of miracles, also those having gifts of healing, those able to help others, those with gifts of administration, and those speaking in different kinds of tongues.

1 Corinthians 12:27–28 NIV

It is he who has given some to be apostles, some prophets, some evangelists, some pastors and teachers, to equip God's people for work in his service, for the building up of the body of Christ.

Ephesians 4:11–12 REB

My friends, we ask you to be thoughtful of your leaders who work hard and tell you how to live for the Lord. Show them great respect and love because of their work.

1 Thessalonians 5:12–13 CEV

Knox once remarked that the Church gets on by hook or crook, by the hook of the fisherman and the crook of the shepherd.

Sir Arnold Lunn

A good leader is not the person who does things right, but the one who finds the right things to do.

Anthony T. Padovano

The spiritual leader influences others not by the power of his own personality alone but by that personality irradiated and interpenetrated and empowered in the Holy Spirit. Because he permits the Holy Spirit undisputed control of his life, the Spirit's power can flow through him to others unhindered.

J. Oswald Sanders

A true and safe leader is likely to be one who has no desire to lead but is forced into a position of leadership by the inward pressure of the Holy Spirit and the press of the external situation.

Aiden Wilson (A.W.) Tozer

I believe it might be accepted as a fairly reliable rule of thumb that the man who is ambitious to lead is disqualified as a leader.

Aiden Wilson (A.W.) Tozer

Mission and Ministry of

See also Evangelism

Go therefore and make disciples of all nations, baptizing them in the name of the Father and of the Son and of the Holy Spirit, and teaching them to obey everything that I have commanded you.

Matthew 28:19–20 NRSV

He called the Twelve together and gave them power and authority over all devils and to cure diseases, and he sent them out to proclaim the kingdom of God and to heal.

Luke 9:1–2 NJB

The gifts that we have differ according to the grace that was given to each of us. . . . If it is a gift of practical service, let us devote ourselves to serving.

Romans 12:6–7 NJB

You are God's chosen and special people. You are a group of royal priests and a holy nation. God has brought you out of darkness into his marvelous light. Now you must tell all the wonderful things that he has done.

1 Peter 2:9 CEV

Whoever serves must do so with the strength that God supplies, so that God may be glorified in all things through Jesus Christ.

1 Peter 4:11 NRSV

There is little good in filling churches with people who go out exactly the same as they came in; the call of the Church is not to fill churches but to fill heaven.

Fr. Andrew

We do the works, but God works in us the doing of the works.

St. Augustine of Hippo

The church exists by mission as a fire exists by burning.

Heinrich Emil Brunner

The special person called to do missionary work is every person who is a member of the church of Christ. The call does not come to a chosen few, it is to every one of us.

Oswald Chambers

The purpose of the Church in the world is to be the worshiping and witnessing spearhead of all that is in accordance with the will of God as it has been revealed in Jesus Christ.

(Frederick) Donald Coggan

There is nothing small in the service of God.

St. Francis de Sales

The Church as a whole must be concerned with both evangelism and social action. It is not a case of either–or; it is both–and. Anything less is only a partial Gospel, not the whole counsel of God.

Robert D. De Haan

The service we render for others is really the rent we pay for our room on this earth.

Sir Wilfred Thomason Grenfell

Educating people to die meaningful deaths is one way to describe the teaching mission of the church.

John A. Harms

The service that counts is the service that costs.

Howard G. Hendricks

The living Church, though never neat, keeps God's world from complete disaster.

Lord George Fielden MacLeod

The Spirit of Christ is the spirit of missions, and the nearer we get to him the more intensely missionary we must become.

Henry Martyn

Christian mission is the only reason for our being on earth.

Andrew Murray

The Church has many tasks but only one mission.

Arthur Preston

The Christian Church is the one organization in the world that exists purely for the benefit of non-members.

William Temple

We must reach the point of preferring to die rather than to have a ministry without fruit and without power.

Fernando Vangioni

The church's service and mission in the world is absolutely dependent on its being different from the world, being in the world but not of the world.

Jim Wallis

The church has nothing to do but to save souls; therefore spend and be spent in this work. It is not your business to speak so many times, but to save souls as you can; to bring as many sinners as you possibly can to repentance.

John Wesley

To go to people and say "Jesus loves you!" and yet do nothing to help change their circumstances is not a complete message.

John Richard Wimber

Nature of

For as in one body we have many members, and not all the members have the same function, so we, who are many, are one body in Christ, and individually we are members one of another.

Romans 12:4–5 NRSV

Know ye not that ye are the temple of God, and that the Spirit of God dwelleth in you?

1 Corinthians 3:16 KJV

The church . . . which is his [Christ's] body, the fullness of him who fills everything in every way.

Ephesians 1:22 NIV

So then, you Gentiles are not foreigners or strangers any longer; you are now fellow-citizens with God's people and members of the family of God. You, too, are built upon the foundation laid by the apostles and prophets, the cornerstone being Christ Jesus himself. He is the one who holds the whole building together and makes it grow into a sacred temple dedicated to the Lord. In union with him you too are being built together with all the others into a place where God lives through his Spirit.

Ephesians 2:19–22 GNB

But you are a chosen race, a royal priesthood, a holy nation, God's own people, in order that you may proclaim the mighty acts of him who called you out of darkness into his marvelous light.

1 Peter 2:9 NRSV

He cannot have God for his father who refuses to have the Church for his mother.

St. Augustine of Hippo

What matters in the Church is not religion but the form of Christ, and its taking form amidst a band of men.

Dietrich Bonhoeffer

The Church of Christ is not an institution, it is a new life with Christ and in Christ, guided by the Holy Spirit.

Sergei Nikolaevich Bulgakov

Biblically the church is an organism not an organization—a movement, not a monument. It is not a part of the community; it is a whole new community. It is not an orderly gathering; it is a new order with new values, often in sharp conflict with the values of the surrounding society.

Charles W. Colson

A person who says he believes in God but never goes to church is like one who says he believes in education but never goes to school.

Franklin Clark Fry

The Church is in Christ as Eve was in Adam.

Richard Hooker

The Church cannot exercise democracy. The Church does not belong to its members nor is it dependent on its members for its life or existence. It belongs to Christ.

Rev. David J. Howson

This gift of God was entrusted to the Church that all the members might receive of him and be made alive; and none are partakers of him who do not assemble with the Church but defraud themselves of life. For where the Church is there is the Spirit of God, and where the Spirit of God is, there is the Church and all grace.

St. Irenaeus

God never intended his Church to be a refrigerator in which to preserve perishable piety. He intended it to be an incubator in which to hatch converts.

F. Linicome

In one form or another the Church is the only society which points people to God through Jesus Christ. By baptism and the response of faith individuals exercise their membership and in so doing commit themselves to God.

Bishop Peter Mumford

It may take a crucified Church to bring a crucified Christ before the eyes of the world.

William Edwin Orchard

The Church is not a finished, solidly built and furnished house, in which all that changes is the successive generations who live in it. The Church is a living reality which has had a history of its own and still has one.

Karl Rahner

Locality, nationality, particularity are essential marks of the universal Church; the local congregation is the embodiment at a given place and time of the Church of all the world.

Alan Richardson

The Church as historical institution tends to sacralize the established social order—its political as well as familial hierarchies. . . . By contrast, the concept of the church as spirit-filled community tends to break down these social hierarchies.

Rosemary Radford Ruether

The church's one foundation / Is Jesus Christ her Lord; / She is His new creation / By water and the Word; / From heaven He came and sought her / To be His holy bride; / With His own blood He bought her, / And for her life He died.

Samuel John Stone

The church exists for those outside it.

William Temple

We are members of that body which was

nailed to the cross, laid in a tomb and raised to life on the third day. There is only one organism of the new creation, and we are members of that organism which is Christ.

Lional Thornton

The meeting-place is the training-place for the market-place.

John Richard Wimber

Unity of

How good and how pleasant it is to live together as brothers in unity!

Psalm 133:1 REB

Can two walk together, except they be agreed?

Amos 3:3 KJV

[Jesus' prayer] That they may all be one. As you, Father, are in me and I am in you, may they also be in us, so that the world may believe that you have sent me.

John 17:21 NRSV

Now the whole group of those who believed were of one heart and soul, and no one claimed private ownership of any possessions, but everything they owned was held in common.

Acts 4:32 NRSV

Make every effort to keep the unity of the Spirit through the bond of peace. There is one body and one Spirit—just as you were called to one hope when you were called— one Lord, one faith, one baptism; one God and Father of all, who is over all and through all and in all.

Ephesians 4:3–6 NIV

The whole Christian life is that we are totally one with each other in his Church, that Christ has given himself totally to us in this oneness.

Fr. Peter Ball

For one sect then to say, Ours is the true Church, and another say, Nay, but ours is the true Church, is as mad as to dispute whether your hall or kitchen, or parlor, or coal-house is your house, and for one to say, This is the house, and another, Nay, but it is that; when a child can tell them, that the best is but a part, and the house containeth them all.

Richard Baxter

And I believe in one Catholick and Apostolick Church.

Book of Common Prayer

In God and in his Church there is no difference between living and dead, and all are one in the love of the Father. Even the generations yet to be born are part of this one divine humanity.

Sergei Nikolaevich Bulgakov

The real ecumenical crisis today is not between Catholic and Protestant but between traditional and experimental forms of Church life.

Harvey Cox

I do not want the walls of separation between different orders of Christians to be destroyed, but only lowered, that we may shake hands a little easier over them.

Rowland Hill

Form all together one choir, so that, with the symphony of your feelings and having all taken the tone of God, you may sing with one voice to the Father through Jesus Christ, that He may listen to you and know you from your chant as the canticle of His only Son.

St. Ignatius of Antioch

For the whole Church which is throughout the whole world possesses one and the same God.

St. Irenaeus

Division has done more to hide Christ from the view of men than all the infidelity that has ever been spoken.

George MacDonald

If we would but observe unity in essentials, liberty in non-essentials, charity in all things, our affairs would certainly be in the best possible situation.

Robert Maldenius

None understand better the nature of real distinction than those who have entered into unity.

Johann Tauler

Church unity is like peace, we are all for it, but we are not willing to pay the price.

Willem Adolf Visser't Hooft

It's hard enough resisting the real enemy. That's a full-time job. If we start fighting other Christians we're fighting two wars—and one of them is suicidal.

John Richard Wimber

Citizenship, *see* Society

Civilization, *see* Society

Comfort

Comfort, O comfort my people, says your God. Speak tenderly to Jerusalem, and cry to her that she has served her term, that her penalty is paid, that she has received from the LORD's hand double for all her sins.

Isaiah 40:1–2 NRSV

Don't be afraid, I am with you. Don't tremble with fear. I am your God. I will make you strong, as I protect you with my arm and give you victories.

Isaiah 41:10 CEV

Take courage, my daughter; the Lord of heaven grant you joy in place of your sorrow. Take courage my daughter.

Tobit 7:16 NRSV

Blessed are they that mourn: for they shall be comforted.

Matthew 5:4 KJV

Come unto me, all ye that labor and are heavy laden, and I will give you rest.

Matthew 11:28 KJV

Praise be to the God and Father of our Lord Jesus Christ, the Father of compassion and the God of all comfort, who comforts us in all our troubles, so that we can comfort those in any trouble with the comfort we ourselves have received from God.

2 Corinthians 1:3–4 NIV

Our High Priest is not one who cannot feel sympathy for our weaknesses. On the contrary, we have a High Priest who was tempted in every way that we are, but did not sin. Let us have confidence, then, and approach God's throne, where there is grace. There we will receive mercy and find grace to help us just when we need it.

Hebrews 4:15–16 GNB

He cares for you, so cast all your anxiety on him.

1 Peter 5:7 REB

God sometimes snuffs out our brightest candle that we may look up to his eternal stars.

Vance Havner

God does not comfort us to make us comfortable, but to make us comforters.

John Henry Jowett

All human comfort is vain and short.

Thomas à Kempis

How sweet the Name of Jesus sounds in a believer's ear! It soothes his sorrows, heals his wounds, and drives away his fear!

John Newton

Although today He prunes my twigs with pain, / Yet doth His blood nourish and warm my root; / Tomorrow I shall put forth buds again / And clothe myself with fruit.

Christina Georgina Rossetti

To need consolation and to console are human, just as human as Christ was.

Dorothy Soelle

The refiner is never very far from the mouth of the furnace when his gold is in the fire.

Charles Haddon Spurgeon

Let nothing disturb thee, nothing afright thee; All things are passing; God never changeth; Patient endurance attaineth to all things; Who God possesseth in nothing is wanting; Alone God sufficeth.

St. Teresa of Avila

Commitment

See also Covenant; Discipleship; Obedience

Asa's heart was fully committed to the Lord all his life.

1 Kings 15:14 NIV

Whoever loves father or mother more than me is not worthy of me; and whoever loves son or daughter more than me is not worthy of me; and whoever does not take up the cross and follow me is not worthy of me.

Matthew 10:37–38 NRSV

As slaves of Christ do the will of God wholeheartedly.

Ephesians 6:6 REB

Lord, take my lips and speak through them, take my mind and think through it; take my heart and set it on fire.

W.H.H. Aitken

One can always measure a man's devotion to the cause of Christ by his readiness to be called to responsibility, by his diligence in it, by the personal risks he runs through his involvement in it, or by the ease with which he lays it down.

Anon.

All to Thee is yielded, / I am not my own; / Blissful, glad surrender—/ I am Thine alone.

E. May Crawford

Don't touch Christianity unless you mean business. I promise you a miserable existence if you do.

Henry Drummond

He is no fool who gives what he cannot keep to gain what he cannot lose.

Jim Elliot

Take my life, and let it be / Consecrated, Lord, to Thee; / Take my moments and my days, / Let them flow in ceaseless praise.

Frances Ridley Havergal

Teach us, good Lord, to serve Thee as Thou deservest. To give and not to count the cost; to fight and not to heed the wounds; to toil and not seek for rest; to labor and not to ask for any reward save that of knowing that we do Thy will.

St. Ignatius of Loyola

Give me a person who says, "This one thing I do, and not these fifty things I dabble in."

Dwight Lyman (D.L.) Moody

To take up the cross of Christ is no great action done once for all; it consists in the continual practice of small duties which are distasteful to us.

John Henry Newman

Being aware of the absolute importance and arduous nature of the service in which he is engaged, the true Christian sets about his task with vigor and diligence. He is prepared to meet difficulties and is not discouraged when they occur.

William Wilberforce

Commitment is spelled M–O–N–E–Y.

John Richard Wimber

Communion, *see* Eucharist; Fellowship

Community, *see* Society

Compassion

See also Jesus Christ, Compassion of; Love, for Others; Kindness; Pity

It is of the Lord's mercies that we are not consumed, because his compassions fail not. They are new every morning: great is thy faithfulness.

Lamentations 3:22–23 KJV

When he saw the crowds, he had compassion for them, because they were harassed and helpless, like sheep without a shepherd.

Matthew 9:36 NRSV

As the chosen of God, then, the holy people whom he loves, you are to be clothed in heartfelt compassion.

Colossians 3:12 NJB

Jesus teaches that human need must always be helped; that there is no greater task than to relieve someone's pain and distress and

that the Christian's compassion must be like God's—unceasing. Other work may be laid aside but the work of compassion never.

William Barclay

Compassion will cure more sins than condemnation.

Henry Ward Beecher

Let everything be done in moderation. Let the weakness of the old and the very young be always taken into account. Let the weaker be helped so that they may not do their work in sadness.

St. Benedict

By compassion we make others' misery our own, and so, by relieving them, we relieve ourselves also.

Sir Thomas Browne

God tempers the wind to the shorn lamb.

Henri Estienne

Man is never nearer the Divine than in his compassionate moments.

Joseph H. Hertz

Every act of kindness and compassion done by any man for his fellow Christian is done by Christ working within him.

Julian of Norwich

There is no wilderness so terrible, so beautiful, so arid, so fruitful, as the wilderness of compassion. It is the only desert that shall truly flourish like a lily.

Thomas Merton

I would rather make mistakes in kindness and compassion than work miracles in unkindness and hardness.

Mother Teresa

Conceit

See also Pride

Woe unto them that are wise in their own eyes, and prudent in their own sight!

Isaiah 5:21 KJV

For by the grace given to me I say to everyone among you not to think of yourself more highly than you ought to think, but to think with sober judgment, each according to the measure of faith that God has assigned.

Romans 12:3 NRSV

Let us not be conceited or provocative and envious of one another.

Galatians 5:26 NJB

God hates those who praise themselves.

St. Clement I of Rome

It's ludicrous for any Christian to believe that he or she is the worthy object of public worship; it would be like the donkey carrying Jesus into Jerusalem believing the crowds were cheering and laying down their garments for him.

Charles W. Colson

Talent is God-given; be thankful. Conceit is self-given; be careful.

Thomas La Mance

God sends no one away empty except those who are full of themselves.

Dwight Lyman (D.L.) Moody

The Christ we manifest is too small because in ourselves we have grown too big.

Watchman Nee

Beware of no man more than yourself; we carry our worst enemies within us.

Charles Haddon Spurgeon

If we think we can do anything of ourselves, all we shall get from God is the opportunity to try.

Charles Haddon Spurgeon

God will not go forth with that man who marches in his own strength.

Charles Haddon Spurgeon

He is two fools that is wise in his own eyes.

John Trapp

Confession

See also Prayer, Confession; Repentance

I have sinned, O Lord, I have sinned, and I acknowledge my transgressions.

Prayer of Manasseh 12 REB

If you confess with your lips that Jesus is Lord and believe in your heart that God raised him from the dead, you will be saved. For one believes with the heart and so is justified, and one confesses with the mouth and so is saved.

Romans 10:9–10 NRSV

Confess your sins to one another, and pray for one another, that you may be healed.

James 5:16 REB

Before God can deliver us we must undeceive ourselves.

St. Augustine of Hippo

We have erred and strayed from thy ways like lost sheep. We have followed too much the devices and desires of our own hearts. We have offended against thy holy laws. We have left undone those things which we ought to have done. And we have done those things which we ought not to have done. And there is no health in us.

Book of Common Prayer

Confessing sin is not informing God, it is agreeing with him.

Derek Cleave

It is better for a man to confess his sins than to harden his heart.

St. Clement I of Rome

Confession is the first step to repentance.

Edmund Gayton

For him who confesses, shams are over and realities have begun.

William James

Confession, which means to agree with God regarding our sin, restores our fellowship. It is a form of discipline which God requires.

Erwin W. Lutzer

Never be ashamed to own you have been in the wrong; 'tis but saying you are wiser today than you were yesterday.

Jonathan Swift

Confession may be considered as a sort of exorcism in which Christ does battle against the powers of evil.

Max Thurian

Confidence

See also Courage

In returning and rest shall ye be saved; in quietness and confidence shall be your strength.

Isaiah 30:15 KJV

For we are the circumcision, which worship God in the spirit, and rejoice in Christ Jesus, and have no confidence in the flesh.

Philippians 3:3 KJV

We have then, brothers, complete confidence through the blood of Jesus in entering the sanctuary.

Hebrews 10:19 NJB

The greater and more persistent your confidence in God, the more abundantly you will receive all that you ask.

Albert the Great

Confidence in the natural world is self-reliance, in the spiritual world it is God-reliance.

Oswald Chambers

I sometimes think that the very essence of the whole Christian position and the secret of a successful spiritual life is just to realize two things. . . . I must have complete, absolute confidence in God and no confidence in myself.

David Martyn Lloyd-Jones

Faith is a living and unshakeable confidence, a belief in the grace of God so assured that a man would die a thousand deaths for its sake.

Martin Luther

Only he who can say, "The Lord is the strength of my life," can say, "Of whom shall I be afraid?"

Alexander Maclaren

Seeing is not believing. Seeing is seeing. Believing is being confident without seeing.

George Campbell Morgan

No condemnation now I dread; / Jesus, and all in Him, is mine! / Alive in Him, my living Head, / And clothed in righteousness divine, / Bold I approach the eternal throne, / And claim the crown, through Christ my own.

Charles Wesley

I felt my heart strangely warmed, I feel I did trust in Christ, Christ alone, for salvation; an assurance was given me that he had taken away my sins, even mine, and saved me from the law of sin and death.

John Wesley

Our confidence in Christ does not make us lazy, negligent, or careless, but on the contrary it awakens us, urges us on, and makes us active in living righteous lives and doing good. There is no self-confidence to compare with this.

Ulrich Zwingli

Conflict

See also Spiritual Warfare; War and Warfare

We know that the Law is spiritual; but I am a mortal man, sold as a slave to sin. I do not understand what I do; for I don't do what I would like to do, but instead I do what I hate. Since what I do is what I don't want to do, this shows that I agree that the Law is right. So I am not really the one who does this thing; rather it is the sin that lives in me. I know that good does not live in me—that is, in my human nature. For even though the desire to do good is in me, I am not able to do it. I don't do the good I want to do; instead, I do the evil that I do not want to do. If I do what I don't want to do, this means that I am no longer the one who does it; instead, it is the sin that lives in me. So I find that this law is at work: when I want to do what is good, what is evil is the only choice I have. My inner being delights in the law of God. But I see a different law at work in my body—a law that fights against the law which my mind approves of. It makes me a prisoner to the law of sin which is at work in my body. What an unhappy man I am! Who will rescue me from this body that is taking me to death? Thanks be to God, who does this through our Lord Jesus Christ!

Romans 7:14–25 GNB

If you are guided by the Spirit, you won't obey your selfish desires. The Spirit and your desires are enemies of each other. They are always fighting each other and keeping you from doing what you feel you should.

Galatians 5:16–17 CEV

Put on the whole armor of God, so that you may be able to stand against the wiles of the devil. For our struggle is not against enemies of blood and flesh, but against the rulers, against the authorities, against the cosmic powers of this present darkness, against the spiritual forces of evil in the heavenly places.

Ephesians 6:11–12 NRSV

Without Contraries is no progression. Attraction and Repulsion, Reason and Energy, Love and Hate, are necessary to Human existence.

William Blake

The devil wrestles with God, and the field of battle is the human heart.

Fyodor Dostoevsky

Stand up, stand up for Jesus! / Stand in His strength alone: / The arm of flesh will fail you: / Ye dare not trust your own. / Put on the gospel armor, / Each piece put on with prayer; / Where duty calls, or danger, / Be never wanting there.

George Duffield

Life is a hard fight, a struggle, a wrestling with the principle of evil, hand to hand, foot to foot. Every inch of the way is disputed. The night is given to us to take breath and to pray, to drink deep at the fountain of power. The day, to use the strength which has been given to us, to go forth to work with it till the evening.

Florence Nightingale

Conscience

I try my best to have a clear conscience in whatever I do for God or for people.

Acts 24:16 CEV

To the pure all things are pure, but to the corrupt and unbelieving nothing is pure. Their very minds and consciences are corrupted.

Titus 1:15 NRSV

We cannot make our consciences clear by offering gifts and sacrifices. These rules are merely about such things as eating and drinking and ceremonies for washing ourselves. And rules about physical things will last only until the time comes to change them for something better.

Hebrews 9:9–10 CEV

Let us draw near to God with a sincere heart in full assurance of faith, having our hearts sprinkled to cleanse us from a guilty conscience and having our bodies washed with pure water.

Hebrews 10:22 NIV

My dear friends, if our conscience does not condemn us, then we can approach God with confidence.

1 John 3:21 REB

Conscience and reputation are two things. Conscience is due to yourself, reputation to your neighbor.

St. Augustine of Hippo

Conscience is a check to beginners in sin, reclaiming them from it and rating them for it; but this in longstanders becometh useless; either failing to discharge its office, or assaying it to no purpose: having often been slighted, it will be weary of chiding; or if it be not wholly dumb, we shall be deaf to its reproof: as those who continue to live by cataracts or downfalls of water, are, by continual noise, so deafened as not to hear or mind it.

Isaac Barrow

A good conscience is a mine of wealth. And in truth, what greater riches can there be, what thing more sweet than a good conscience?

St. Bernard of Clairvaux

When a man is content with the testimony of his own conscience, he does not care to shine with the light of another's praise.

St. Bernard of Clairvaux

Most of us follow our conscience as we follow a wheelbarrow. We push it in front of us in the direction we want to go.

William Franklin (Billy) Graham

If we take care to keep a good conscience, we may leave it to God to take care of our good name.

Matthew Henry

There is a conscience in man; therefore there is a God in heaven.

Ezekiel Hopkins

Have a good conscience and you will always have gladness; for a good conscience is able to endure a great deal, and be glad even in adversity, whereas a bad conscience is always fearful and restless.

Thomas à Kempis

My conscience is captive to the Word of God.

Martin Luther

It is neither safe nor prudent to do anything against conscience.

Martin Luther

Conscience implies a relation between the soul and a something exterior . . . a relation to an excellence which it does not possess, and to a tribunal over which it has no power.

John Henry Newman

Labor to keep alive in your breast that little spark of celestial fire called conscience.

George Washington

Contemplation, *see* Meditation and Contemplation; Prayer

Contentment

See also Happiness; Peace

I have learned to manage with whatever I have. I know how to live modestly, and I know how to live luxuriously too: in every way now I have mastered the secret of all conditions: full stomach and empty stomach, plenty and poverty.

Philippians 4:11–12 NJB

There is great gain in godliness combined with contentment; for we brought nothing into the world, so that we can take nothing out of it; but if we have food and clothing, we will be content with these.

1 Timothy 6:6–8 NRSV

Be content with such things as ye have: for he hath said, I will never leave thee, nor forsake thee.

Hebrews 13:5 KJV

Contentment is a pearl of great price, and whoever procures it at the expense of ten thousand desires makes a wise and a happy purchase.

John Balguy

The rarest feeling that ever lights the human face is the contentment of a loving soul.

Henry Ward Beecher

He who is not contented with little will never be satisfied with much.

Thomas Benton Brooks

Those who face that which is actually before them, unburdened by the past, undistracted by the future, these are they who live, who make the best use of their lives; these are those who have found the secret of contentment.

Alban Goodier

The children of Israel did not find in the manna all the sweetness and strength they might have found in it; not because the manna did not contain them, but because they longed for meat.

St. John of the Cross

When we cannot find contentment in ourselves it is useless to seek it elsewhere.

François de La Rochefoucauld

It is right to be contented with what we have, but never with what we are.

Sir James Mackintosh

Conversion

See also New Birth

The law of the Lord is perfect, converting the soul: the testimony of the Lord is sure, making wise the simple.

Psalm 19:7 KJV

Can the Ethiopian change his skin, or the leopard his spots?

Jeremiah 13:23 KJV

In truth I tell you, unless you change and become like little children you will never enter the kingdom of Heaven.

Matthew 18:3 NJB

You [Paul] are to open their eyes and turn them from the darkness to the light and from the power of Satan to God, so that through their faith in me they will have their sins forgiven and receive their place among God's chosen people.

Acts 26:18 GNB

Conversion may occur in an instant, but the process of coming from sinfulness into a new life can be a long and arduous journey.

Charles W. Colson

It is not culture but conversion that we need first. Not education, but transformation. Not new knowledge, but a new nature. We must become new creations by the regenerating power of the Holy Spirit before we are ready to live Christ's life and bear His image.

Robert C. Cunningham

The almighty power of God in the conversion of a sinner is the most mysterious of all the works of God.

Thomas Hooker

In the Trinity Term of 1929 I gave in, and admitted that God was God . . . perhaps the most dejected and reluctant convert in all England.

Clive Staples (C.S.) Lewis

A man can accept what Christ has done without knowing how it works; indeed he certainly won't know how it works until he's accepted it.

Clive Staples (C.S.) Lewis

Do not let any conversion astonish you; be astonished rather, that anyone should possibly remain unconverted.

David Martyn Lloyd-Jones

People who think that once they are converted all will be happy, have forgotten Satan.

David Martyn Lloyd-Jones

Repentance is the golden key that opens the palace of eternity.

John Milton

A faithful ministry will usually be sealed by the conversion of sinners.

Thomas V. Moore

I think I am the only person who was actually converted at his own confirmation service.

Robert Runcie

If any minister can be satisfied without conversions, he shall have no conversions.

Charles Haddon Spurgeon

Conviction

See also Confession; Sin

For I acknowledge my transgressions; and my sin is ever before me. Against thee, thee only, have I sinned, and done this evil in thy sight: that thou mightest be justified when thou speakest, and be clear when thou judgest.

Psalm 51:3–4 KJV

When he [the Holy Spirit] comes, he will convict the world of guilt in regard to sin and righteousness and judgment.

John 16:8 NIV

When they heard this, they were cut to the heart and said to Peter and to the other apostles, "Brothers, what should we do?"

Acts 2:37 NRSV

Never, for the sake of peace and quiet, deny your own experience or convictions.

Dag Hammarskjöld

The great thing in this world is not so much where we stand, as in what direction we are moving.

Oliver Wendell Holmes

God will never plant the seed of his life upon the soil of a hard, unbroken spirit. He will only plant that seed where conviction of his Spirit has brought brokenness, where the soil has been watered with the tears of repentance as well as the tears of joy.

Alan Redpath

Many people confuse the conviction of sin with such feelings as inferiority, lack of self–confidence and so on. Yet whoever observes people closely can see that these feelings and the conviction of sin are not only different from each other but in certain regards are mutually exclusive. A diffuse and vague guilt feeling kills the personality, whereas the conviction of sin gives life to the personality. The former depends on people, on public opinion, while the latter depends on God.

Paul Tournier

He that is not open to conviction is not qualified for discussion.

Richard Whately

Corruption

See also Sin; Sinful Nature

The earth also was corrupt before God, and the earth was filled with violence. And God looked upon the earth, and, behold, it was corrupt; for all flesh had corrupted his way upon the earth.

Genesis 6:11–12 KJV

The Lord looks out from heaven on all the human race to see if any act wisely, if any seek God. But all are unfaithful, altogether corrupt; no one does good, no, not even one.

Psalm 14:2–3 REB

Being greedy causes trouble for your family, but you protect yourself by refusing bribes.

Proverbs 15:27 CEV

He has given us . . . his precious and very great promises, so that through them you may escape from the corruption that is in the world because of lust, and may become participants of the divine nature.

2 Peter 1:4 NRSV

Every sin should convince us of the general truth of the corruption of our nature.

John Calvin

As we get to know ourselves better we always find ourselves to be more depraved than we thought.

François de la Mothe Fénelon

Man is not evolving upward toward a knowledge of God. He was created with a knowledge of God and has been going the other way ever since.

Vance Havner

Grace does not run in the blood, but corruption does. A sinner begets a sinner, but a saint does not beget a saint.

Matthew Henry

The history of man is his attempt to escape his own corruption.

Daniel Mullis

Man is a double-dyed villain. He is corrupted by nature and afterwards by practice.

Augustus Hopkins Strong

Counsel, *see* Advice

Courage

See also Confidence; Fear; Risk

Have I not commanded thee? Be strong and of a good courage; be not afraid, neither be thou dismayed: for the Lord thy God is with thee whithersoever thou goest.

Joshua 1:9 KJV

But Jesus immediately said to them [his disciples]: "Take courage! It is I. Don't be afraid."

Matthew 14:27 NIV

And now, Lord, take note of their threats and help your servants to proclaim your message with all fearlessness.

Acts 4:29 NJB

God's Spirit doesn't make cowards out of us. The Spirit gives us power, love, and self-control.

2 Timothy 1:7 CEV

Courage is fear that has said its prayers.

Dorothy Bernard

Have plenty of courage. God is stronger than the Devil. We are on the winning side.

John Wilbur Chapman

Courage is almost a contradiction in terms. It means a strong desire to live taking the form of a readiness to die.

Gilbert Keith (G.K.) Chesterton

Behold the turtle, he makes progress only when he sticks his neck out.

James Bryant Conant

Facing the darkness, admitting the pain, allowing the pain to be pain, is never easy.

That is why courage—big-heartedness—is the most essential virtue on the spiritual journey.

Matthew Fox

Fear can keep a man out of danger, but courage can support him in it.

Thomas Fuller

Have courage for the great sorrows of life, and patience for the small ones. And when you have laboriously accomplished your daily task, go to sleep in peace. God is awake.

Victor Hugo

Courage is not simply one of the virtues, but the form of every virtue at the testing point, which means at the point of highest reality.

Clive Staples (C.S.) Lewis

Courage is not the absence of fear; it is the making of action in spite of fear, the moving against the resistance engendered by fear into the unknown and into the future. On some level spiritual growth, and therefore love, always requires courage and involves risk.

M. Scott Peck

The courage to be is rooted in the God who appears when God has disappeared in the anxiety of doubt.

Paul Tillich

Father, hear the prayer we offer; / Not for ease that Prayer shall be, / But for strength that we may ever / Live our lives courageously.

Love Maria Willis

Covenant

See also Commitment

Moses took the blood from the bowls and sprinkled it on the people. Next, he told them, "With this blood the Lord makes his agreement with you."

Exodus 24:8 CEV

You are standing here in order to enter into a covenant with the Lord your God, a covenant the Lord is making with you this day and sealing with an oath, to confirm you this day as his people, that he may be your God as he promised you and as he swore to your fathers, Abraham, Isaac and Jacob.

Deuteronomy 29:12–13 NIV

This is my blood of the covenant, which is poured out for many for the forgiveness of sins.

Matthew 26:28 NRSV

For this is the covenant that I will make with the house of Israel after those days, saith the Lord; I will put my laws into their mind, and write them in their hearts: and I will be to them a God, and they shall be to me a people.

Hebrews 8:10 KJV

His oath, His covenant, and blood / Support me in the 'whelming flood: / When all around my soul gives way, / He then is all my hope and stay.

Edward Mote

The bond of the covenant is able to bear the weight of the believer's heaviest burden.

William S. Plummer

The first covenant made with man was a covenant of works, wherein life was promised to Adam, and in him to his posterity, upon condition of perfect and personal obedience. Man by his fall having made himself incapable of life by that covenant, the Lord was pleased to make a second commonly called the Covenant of Grace: whereby he freely offereth unto sinners life and salvation by Jesus Christ, requiring of them faith in him, that they may be saved; and promising to give unto all those that are ordained unto life his Holy Spirit to make them willing and able to believe.

Westminster Confession of Faith

Covetousness

See also Greed

Thou shalt not covet thy neighbor's house, thou shalt not covet thy neighbor's wife, nor his manservant, nor his maidservant, nor his ox, nor his ass, nor any thing that is thy neighbor's.

Exodus 20:17 KJV

All day long the wicked covet, but the righteous give and do not hold back.

Proverbs 21:26 NRSV

What causes fights and quarrels among you? Don't they come from your desires that battle within you? You want something but don't get it. You kill and covet, but you cannot have what you want. You quarrel and fight. You do not have, because you do not ask God. When you ask, you do not receive, because you ask with wrong motives, that you may spend what you get on your pleasures.

James 4:1–3 NIV

The more of heaven we cherish, the less of earth we covet.

Anon.

The man who covets is always poor.

Claudian

Riches have made more covetous men than covetousness hath made rich men.

Thomas Fuller

He is much happier that is always content, though he has ever so little than he that is always coveting, though he has ever so much.

Matthew Henry

One can be covetous when he has little, much, or anything between, for covetousness comes from the heart, not from the circumstances of life.

Charles Caldwell Ryrie

He is not a covetous man, who lays up something providentially, but he is a covetous man, who gives out nothing willingly.

William Secker

They are fools that fear to lose their wealth by giving, but fear not to lose themselves by keeping it.

John Trapp

All the danger is when the world gets into the heart. The water is useful for the sailing of the ship; all the danger is when the water gets into the ship; so the fear is when the world gets into the heart. "Thou shalt not covet."

Thomas Watson

Cowardice

The fear of others lays a snare, but one who trusts in the LORD is secure.

Proverbs 29:25 NRSV

You did not receive a spirit that makes you a slave again to fear, but you received the Spirit of sonship. And by him we cry, "Abba, Father."

Romans 8:15 NIV

The legacy for cowards . . . is the second death in the burning lake of sulphur.

Revelation 21:8 NJB

Not seldom we refrain from rebuke because of mistaken kindness, or because of the desire to avoid trouble. But there is a time when to avoid trouble is to store up trouble and then to seek for a lazy and a cowardly peace is to court a still greater danger.

William Barclay

A dog barks when his master is attacked. I would be a coward if I saw that God's truth is attacked and yet would remain silent, without giving any sound.

John Calvin

A man without courage is a knife without an edge.

Benjamin Franklin

Spiritual cowardice is not only weakness but wickedness.

J.B. Gambrell

To sin by silence when they should protest makes cowards out of men.

Abraham Lincoln

No one is afraid to climb the heights, at least not if they have brave hearts and high courage. But the heart that is little from lack of love does not dare to undertake any great task, and does not venture to climb the heights.

Margaret Porette

The coward seeks release from pressure. The courageous pray for strength.

Frances J. Roberts

He that would not die when he must, and he that would die when he must not, are both of them cowards alike.

George Swinnock

Creation

See also God, Creator

In the beginning God created heaven and earth.

Genesis 1:1 NJB

The heavens declare the glory of God: and the firmament sheweth his handywork. One day telleth another: and one night certifieth another. There is neither speech nor language: but their voices are heard among them. Their sound is gone out into all lands: and their words into the ends of the world.

Psalm 19:1–4 BCP

Lift your eyes and look to the heavens: Who created all these? He who brings out the starry host one by one; and calls them each by name. Because of his great power and mighty strength, not one of them is missing. . . . Do you not know? Have you not heard? The Lord is the everlasting God, the Creator of the ends of the earth.

Isaiah 40:26, 28 NIV

For the creation waits with eager longing for the revealing of the children of God; for the creation was subjected to futility, not of its own will but by the will of the one who subjected it, in hope that the creation itself will be set free from its bondage to decay and will obtain the freedom of the glory of the children of God. We know that the whole creation has been groaning in labor pains until now; and not only the creation, but we ourselves, who have the first fruits of the Spirit, groan inwardly while we wait for adoption, the redemption of our bodies.

Romans 8:19–23 NRSV

He is the image of the invisible God, the first-born of all creation; for in him all things in heaven and on earth were created, things visible and invisible, whether thrones or dominions or rulers or powers—all things have been created through him and for him.

Colossians 1:15–16 NRSV

Thus does the world forget You, its Creator, and falls in love with what You have created instead of with You.

St. Augustine of Hippo

Every flower of the field, every fiber of a plant, every particle of an insect, carries with it the impress of its Maker, and can—if duly considered—read us lectures on ethics or divinity.

Sir Thomas Pope Blount

The more we learn about the wonders of our universe, the more clearly we are going to perceive the hand of God.

Frank Borman

Earth's crammed with heaven. Any every common bush afire with God.

Elizabeth Barrett Browning

The universe is but one vast symbol of God.

Thomas Carlyle

Think of the number of trees and blades of grass and flowers, the extravagant wealth of beauty no one ever sees! Think of the sunrises and sunsets we never look at! God is lavish in every degree.

Oswald Chambers

The world is the first Bible that God made for the instruction of man.

Clement of Alexandria

The probability of life originating from accident is comparable to the probability of the unabridged dictionary resulting from an explosion in a printing shop.

Edwin G. Conklin

Love all God's creation, the whole of it, love every grain of sand. Love every leaf, every ray of God's light! Love the animals, love the plants, love everything. If you love everything, you will perceive the divine mystery in things. And once you have perceived it, you will be able to comprehend it ceaselessly more and more every day.

Fyodor Dostoevsky

Nature is a first volume, in itself incomplete, and demanding a second volume, which is Christ.

Charles Gore

God writes the gospel not in the Bible alone, but on trees, and flowers, and clouds, and stars.

Martin Luther

Laws of nature are God's thoughts thinking themselves out in the orbits and the tides.

Charles Henry Parkhurst

Posterity will some day laugh at the foolishness of modern materialistic philosophy. The more I study nature, the more I am amazed at the Creator.

Louis Pasteur

Creation not only exists, it also discharges truth. . . . Wisdom requires a surrender, verging on the mystical, of a person to the glory of existence.

Gerard von Rad

That the universe was formed by a fortuitous concourse of atoms, I will no more believe than that the accidental jumbling of the alphabet would fall into a most ingenious treatise of philosophy.

Jonathan Swift

Creeds

See also Teachers and Teaching

Hear, O Israel: The Lord our God is one Lord: And thou shalt love the Lord thy God with all thine heart, and with all thy soul, and with all thy might.

Deuteronomy 6:4–5 KJV

Simon Peter answered and said, Thou art the Christ, the Son of the living God.

Matthew 16:16 KJV

No one can deny how great is the secret of our religion: He appeared in human form, was shown to be right by the Spirit, and was seen by angels. He was preached among the nations, was believed in throughout the world, and was taken up to heaven.

1 Timothy 3:16 GNB

I believe in God the Father Almighty; Maker of heaven and earth. And in Jesus Christ his only Son our Lord; who was conceived by the Holy Spirit, born of the virgin Mary; suffered under Pontius Pilate, was crucified, dead and buried; the third day he rose from the dead; he ascended into heaven; and sitteth at the right hand of God the Father Almighty; from thence he shall come to judge the quick and the dead. I believe in the Holy Spirit; the holy catholic Church; the communion of saints; the forgiveness of sins; the resurrection of the body; and the life everlasting. Amen.

The Apostles' Creed

We believe in God, Creator of the earth, Creator of life and freedom, hope of the poor. We believe in Jesus Christ, friend in suffering, companion in the resurrection, way of peace. We believe in the Spirit, that holy force impelling the poor to build a church of the beatitudes.

Guillermo Chavez

The Church retains these ancient Creeds, not because they are wholly satisfying, but because they express with great dignity, and the large prestige of their antiquity and

Catholick authority, truths which it holds to be vital. When we can gain a more satisfactory formulation of what we believe, we may replace the Creeds.

Herbert Hensley Henson

The church, though scattered throughout the whole world to the ends of the earth, has received from the apostles and their disciples this faith; in one God, the Father almighty, maker of heaven and earth and the sea and all things in them; and in one Christ Jesus, the Son of God, who was made flesh for our salvation; and in the Holy Spirit, who through the prophets proclaimed God's saving dealings with man and the coming, virgin birth, passion, resurrection from the dead, and bodily ascension into heaven of our beloved Lord Jesus Christ and his second coming from heaven in the glory of the Father to sum up all things and to raise up all human flesh so that . . . he should execute just judgment upon all men.

St. Irenaeus

A man's liberty to travel is not cramped by signposts; on the contrary, they save his time by showing what roads he must avoid if he wishes to reach his destination. The creeds perform the same function.

C.B. Moss

We believe in one God, the Father almighty, maker of heaven and earth and of all things visible and invisible; And in one Lord Jesus Christ, the only-begotten Son of God, begotten from the Father before all ages, light from light, true God from true God, begotten not made, of one substance *homoousios* with the Father. By him all things were made. For us men and for our salvation he came down from heaven, was made flesh from the Holy Spirit and Mary the virgin and became man. He was crucified for us under Pontius Pilate, suffered and was buried. He rose again on the third day, according to the Scriptures, and ascended into the heavens. He sits on the right hand of the Father and will come again with glory to judge the living and the dead. His kingdom will not end; And in the Holy Spirit, the Lord and life-giver, who proceeds from the Father. Together with the Father and the Son he is worshiped and glorified. He spoke through the prophets; And in one holy catholic and apostolic church. We confess one baptism for the remission of sins. We look forward to the resurrection of the dead and the life of the age to come. Amen.

Nicene Creed

A dead creed is of no use; we must have our creed baptized with the Holy Ghost.

Charles Haddon Spurgeon

Criticism, *see* Judging Others

Cross

See also Good Friday; Jesus Christ, Death of; Seven Last Words

And whosoever doth not bear his cross, and come after me, cannot be my disciple.

Luke 14:27 KJV

This man was handed over to you by God's set purpose and foreknowledge; and you, with the help of wicked men, put him to death by nailing him to the cross.

Acts 2:23 NIV

The message about the cross is foolishness to those who are perishing, but to us who are being saved it is the power of God.

1 Corinthians 1:18 NRSV

God forbid that I should glory, save in the cross of our Lord Jesus Christ, by whom the world is crucified unto me, and I unto the world.

Galatians 6:14 KJV

He was humble and walked the path of obedience all the way to death—his death on the cross.

Philippians 2:8 GNB

Through him God was pleased to reconcile to himself all things, whether on earth or in heaven, by making peace through the blood of his cross.

Colossians 1:20 NRSV

The cross is the ladder to heaven.

Thomas Drake

The greatest of all crosses is self—if we die in part every day, we shall have but little to do on the last. These little daily deaths will destroy the power of the final dying.

François de la Mothe Fénelon

God gives the cross, and the cross gives us God.

Madame Jeanne Marie Guyon

One who does not seek the Cross of Jesus isn't seeking the glory of Christ.

St. John of the Cross

The cross preceded the resurrection; but the resurrection has not abolished the cross. Suffering, sin, betrayal, cruelty of every kind, continued to exist after the crucifixion and they continue still. This is the failure of the cross. God made failure an instrument of victory.

Una Kroll

Nobody who has truly seen the cross of Christ can ever again speak of hopeless cases.

George Campbell Morgan

The cross is a way of life; the way of love meeting all hate with love, all evil with good, all negatives with positives.

Rufus Moseley

The cross has revealed to good men that their goodness has not been good enough.

Johann H. Schroeder

There are no crown-wearers in Heaven who were not cross-bearers here below.

Charles Haddon Spurgeon

The way of winning a knowledge of the Cross is by feeling the whole weight of the Cross.

Edith Stein

This one event of the cross of Christ is a final revelation both of the character and consequence of human sin and of the wonder and sacrifice of divine love.

Alan M. Stibbs

The cross possesses such power and strength that, whether they like it or not, it attracts and draws and carries away those who bear it.

Heinrich Suso

Nothing in my hand I bring, / Simply to Thy cross I cling; / Naked, come to Thee for dress; / Helpless, look to Thee for grace; / Foul, I to the fountain fly; / Wash me, Savior, or I die.

Augustus Montague Toplady

The cross of Christ is the most revolutionary thing ever to appear among men.

Aiden Wilson (A.W.) Tozer

There are three marks of one who is crucified. One, he is facing in only one direction. Two, he can never turn back. And three, he no longer has any plans of his own.

Aiden Wilson (A.W.) Tozer

The cross is a picture of violence, yet the key to peace, a picture of suffering, yet the key to healing, a picture of death, yet the key to life.

David Watson

When I survey the wondrous cross / On which the Prince of glory died, / My richest gain I count but loss, / And pour contempt on all my pride.

Isaac Watts

Were the whole realm of nature mine, / That were an offering far too small; / Love so amazing, so Divine, / Demands my soul, my life, my all.

Isaac Watts

Cruelty

See also Oppression

A righteous man regardeth the life of his beast: but the tender mercies of the wicked are cruel.

Proverbs 12:10 KJV

Some had to bear being pilloried and flogged, or even chained up in prison. They were stoned, or sawn in half, or killed by the sword; they were homeless, and wore only the skins of sheep and goats; they were in want and hardship, and maltreated.

Hebrews 11:36–37 NJB

Cruelty is a detested sport that owes its pleasures to another's pain.

William Cowper

Your cruelty does not profit you, however exquisite. Instead, it tempts people to our sect. As often as you mow us down, the more we grow in number. The blood of the Christians is the seed of the church.

Quintus Tertullian

In order to obtain and hold power a man must love it. Thus the effort to get it is not likely to be coupled with goodness, but with the opposite qualities of pride, craft, and cruelty.

Count Leo Tolstoy

Darkness

See also Light

In the beginning God created the heaven and the earth. And the earth was without form, and void; and darkness was upon the face of the deep. And the Spirit of God moved upon the face of the waters. And God said, Let there be light: and there was light. And God saw the light, that it was good: and God divided the light from the darkness. And God called the light Day, and the darkness he called Night.

Genesis 1:1–5 KJV

If I say, "Surely the darkness shall cover me, and the light around me become night," even the darkness is not dark to you; the night is as bright as the day, for darkness is as light to you.

Psalm 139:11–12 NRSV

God is light, and in him is no darkness at all.

1 John 1:5 KJV

There is not enough darkness in all the world to put out the light of even one small candle.

Robert Atkin

Lighten our darkness, we beseech thee, O Lord; and by thy great mercy defend us from all perils and dangers of this night.

Book of Common Prayer

Almighty God, give us grace that we may cast away the works of darkness, and put upon us the armor of light, now in the time of this mortal life.

Book of Common Prayer

No matter how deep our darkness, he is deeper still.

Corrie ten Boom

I would rather work with God in the dark than go alone in the light.

Mary Gardiner Brainard

Darkness is my point of view, my right to myself; light is God's point of view.

Oswald Chambers

Facing the darkness, admitting the pain, allowing the pain to be pain, is never easy. That is why courage—big-heartedness— is the most essential virtue on the spiritual journey.

Matthew Fox

In such times of darkness there is one crucial point—to form no conclusions, to take no decisions, to change nothing during such crises.

Baron Friedrich von Hügel

Live in faith and hope, though it be in darkness, for in this darkness God protects the soul. Cast your care upon God, for you are His and He will not forget you.

St. John of the Cross

Afflictions are but the shadow of God's wings.

George MacDonald

We must welcome the night. It's the only time that the stars shine.

Michel Quoist

Faith grows only in the dark. You've got to trust him when you can't trace him. That's faith.

Lyell Rader

The stars are constantly shining, but often we do not see them until the dark hours.

Earl Riney

Whate'er my darkness be, / 'Tis not, O Lord, of Thee: / The light is Thine alone; / The shadows, all my own.

John Bannister Tabb

Daughters, *see* Children; Sons and Daughters

Deacons, *see* Church, Leaders of

Death

See also Jesus Christ, Death of; Self-Denial

A mortal, born of woman, few of days, and few of trouble

Job 14:1 NRSV

Their soul abhorred all manner of meat: and they were even hard at death's door.

Psalm 107:18 BCP

Precious in the sight of the Lord is the death of his saints.

Psalm 116:15 KJV

And when he was at the last gasp, he said, Thou like a fury takest us out of the present life, but the King of the world shall raise us up, who have died for his laws, unto everlasting life.

2 Maccabees 7:9 KJV

For the wages of sin is death, but the free gift of God is eternal life in Christ Jesus our Lord.

Romans 6:23 NRSV

O death, where is thy sting? O grave, where is thy victory?

1 Corinthians 15:55 KJV

[H]is grace . . . has now been revealed through the appearing of our Savior Christ Jesus, who abolished death and brought life and immortality to light through the gospel.

2 Timothy 1:9–10 NRSV

We know that we have passed from death to life because we love one another. Whoever does not love abides in death.

1 John 3:14 NRSV

The foolish fear death as the greatest of evils, the wise desire it as a rest after labors and the end of ills.

St. Ambrose

For man is by nature afraid of death and of the dissolution of the body; but there is this most startling fact, that he who has put on the faith of the cross despises even what is naturally fearful, and for Christ's sake is not afraid of death.

St. Athanasius of Alexandria

When I die, I should like to slip out of the room without fuss—for what matters is not what I am leaving, but where I am going.

William Barclay

Death is the supreme festival on the road to freedom.

Dietrich Bonhoeffer

Death is but a passage out of a prison into a palace.

John Bunyan

Our Lord makes little of physical death, but he makes more of moral and spiritual death.

Oswald Chambers

The final heartbeat for the Christian is not the mysterious conclusion to a meaningless existence. It is, rather, the grand beginning to a life that will never end.

James Dobson

Were it not for sin, death had never had a beginning, and were it not for death sin would never have had an ending.

William Dyer

Death has nothing terrible which life has not made so. A faithful Christian life in this world is the best preparation for the next.

Tryon Edwards

The greatest of all crosses is self—if we die in part every day, we shall have but little to do on the last. These little daily deaths will destroy the power of the final dying.

François de la Mothe Fénelon

And thou, most kind and gentle death / Waiting to hush our latest breath / O Praise Him—Alleluia / Thou leadest home the child of God / And Christ our Lord the way hath trod.

St. Francis of Assisi

It is in dying that we are born to eternal life.

St. Francis of Assisi

Death, that final curb on freedom, has itself suffered a death blow through the resurrection of Jesus.

Michael Green

Do not seek death. Death will find you, but seek the road which makes death a fulfilment.

Dag Hammarskjöld

In the last analysis it is our conception of death which decides the answers to all the questions that life puts to us.

Dag Hammarskjöld

This is my coronation day, I have been looking forward to it for years.

Dwight Lyman (D.L.) Moody

Death is not extinction in any use of the word. It is always separation.

Charles Caldwell Ryrie

To be, or not to be—that is the question; / Whether 'tis nobler in the mind to suffer / The slings and arrows of outrageous fortune, / Or to take arms against a sea of troubles, / And by opposing end them?

To die, to sleep— / No more: and by a sleep to say we end / The heart-ache and the thousand natural shocks / That flesh is heir to, 'tis a consummation / Devoutly to be wish'd. To die, to sleep; / To sleep, perchance to dream. Ay, there's the rub; / For in that sleep of death what dreams may come, / When we have shuffled off this mortal coil, / Must give us pause.

William Shakespeare

It is an easy matter for one to die that hath died in heart and affection before.

Richard Sibbes

If I may die as I have seen some die, I court the grand occasion. I would not wish to escape death by some by-road if I may sing as they sang.

Charles Haddon Spurgeon

A beautiful death is for people who have lived like animals to die like angels.

Mother Teresa

Death is the flowering of life, the consummation of union with God.

Abbé Henri de Tourville

Death helps us to see what is worth trusting and loving and what is a waste of time.

J. Neville Ward

He may look on death with joy, who can look on forgiveness with faith.

Thomas Watson

Take care of your life and the Lord will take care of your death.

George Whitefield

My happiest moment will be when God puts his hand on my heart and stops it beating.

Arthur Skevington Wood

Debt

See also Money

The wicked borrow, and do not pay back, but the righteous are generous and keep giving.

Psalm 37:21 NRSV

And forgive us our sins; for we also forgive every one that is indebted to us.

Luke 11:4 KJV

Leave no debt outstanding, but remember the debt of love you owe one another.

Romans 13:8 REB

People come to poverty in two ways; accumulating debts and paying them off.

Anon.

He that cannot pay; let him pray.

Thomas Fuller

Are we as willing to go into debt for the work of God as we are for a vacation to Hawaii?

Erwin W. Lutzer

Neither a borrower nor a lender be; / For loan oft loses both itself and friend, / And borrowing dulls the edge of husbandry. / This above all: to thine own self be true, / And it must follow, as the night the day, / Thou canst not then be false to any man.

William Shakespeare

Deceit

See also Dishonesty

The thoughts of the righteous are right: but the counsels of the wicked are deceit.

Proverbs 12:5 KJV

Bread gained by deceit is sweet, but afterward the mouth will be full of gravel.

Proverbs 20:17 NRSV

The heart is deceitful above all things, and desperately wicked: who can know it?

Jeremiah 17:9 KJV

The pride of thine heart hath deceived thee.

Obadiah 1:3 KJV

If we say that we have no sin, we deceive ourselves, and the truth is not in us.

1 John 1:8 NRSV

I have met with many that would deceive; who would be deceived, no one.

St. Augustine of Hippo

Nothing is more offensive to God than deceit in commerce.

Matthew Henry

You can fool some of the people all of the time, and all of the people some of the time, but you cannot fool all of the people all of the time.

Abraham Lincoln

Indeed, it is not in human nature to deceive others for any long time, without in a measure deceiving ourselves too.

John Henry Newman

Decisions

See also Choices

Elijah went up to the people and said, "How much longer will it take you to make up your minds? If the Lord is God, worship him; but if Baal is God, worship him!"

1 Kings 18:21 GNB

The lot is cast into the lap, but the decision is the LORD's alone.

Proverbs 16:33 NRSV

Multitudes, multitudes, in the valley of decision! For the day of the LORD is near in the valley of decision.

Joel 3:14 NRSV

You cannot be the slave of two masters! You will like one more than the other or be more loyal to one than the other. You cannot serve both God and money.

Matthew 7:24 CEV

We make our decisions, and then our decisions turn around and make us.

Francis William (F.W.) Boreham

In any moment of decision the best thing you can do is the right thing, the next best thing is the wrong thing, and the worst thing you can do is nothing.

Theodore Roosevelt

All heaven's glory is within and so is hell's fierce burning. You must yourself decide in which direction you are turning.

Angelus Silesius

The roads we take are more important than the goals we announce. Decisions determine destiny.

Frederick Speakman

One person we cannot avoid—the inevitable Christ; one dilemma we must face—"What shall I do with Jesus, which is called Christ?"

John Watson

Dedication, *see* Commitment

Deliverance, *see* Demons

Demons

See also Devil; Occult

That evening they brought to him many who were possessed with demons; and he cast out the spirits with a word, and cured all who were sick.

Matthew 8:16 NRSV

Calling the Twelve together he gave them power and authority to overcome all demons and to cure diseases.

Luke 9:1 REB

For it is not against human enemies that we have to struggle, but against the principalities and the ruling forces who are masters of the darkness in this world, the Spirits of evil in the heavens.

Ephesians 6:12 NJB

Envious of us Christians, the demons meddle in everything in their efforts to stop us getting to heaven: they do not want us to make it to the place from which they fell.

St. Antony of Egypt

If hereafter you wish to come to the Blessed City, avoid the company of demons. They can be satisfied with the worship of rogues, to whom immorality is pleasing. Therefore let your gods be erased from your worship by a Christian cleansing, just as the stage-players have been removed from honorable society by the action of the censors.

St. Augustine of Hippo

And them all the Lord transformed to devils, because they his deeds and word would not revere.

Caedmon

The demons say one thing to get us into sin, and another to overwhelm us in despair.

St. John Climacus

Let us arm ourselves against our spiritual enemies with courage. They think twice about engaging with one who fights boldly.

St. John Climacus

In days of old, evil spirits appeared in various guises and defiled women and corrupted boys, and made a show of horrors. Men were seized with dread and failed to understand that they were wicked spirits; instead they called them gods and addressed them by all the titles that the demon bestowed on himself.

St. Justin Martyr

There are two equal and opposite errors into which our race can fall about the devils. One is to disbelieve in their existence. The other is to believe, and to feel an excessive and unhealthy interest in them.

Clive Staples (C.S.) Lewis

They who worship images are slaves to demons. Do you address as lords and greet with bowed head men whom you see enslaved to wood and stone? They worship gold and silver under the name of gods, and their religion is one that corrupt greed also loves.

St. Paulinus

It is no more difficult to believe in demons than to believe in God, Christ, the Holy Spirit, angels or the devil.

J.W. Roberts

Depression

See also Comfort

After this Job opened his mouth and cursed the day of his birth. Job said: "Let the day perish in which I was born, and the night that said, 'A man-child is conceived.' Let that day be darkness! May God above not seek it, or light shine upon it."

Job 3:1–4 NRSV

I am weary with my moaning; every night I flood my bed with tears; I drench my couch with my weeping. My eyes waste away because of grief; they grow weak because of all my foes.

Psalm 6:6–7 NRSV

How much longer, Lord, will you forget about me? Will it be forever? How long will you hide? How long must I be confused and miserable all day? How long will my enemies keep beating me down?

Psalm 13:1–2 CEV

The spirit of a man will sustain his infirmity; but a wounded spirit who can bear?

Proverbs 18:14 KJV

Give no place to despondency. God's designs regarding you, and his methods of bringing about these designs, are infinitely wise.

Madame Jeanne Marie Guyon

Vicissitude of day and night in the spiritual life is neither new nor unexpected to those that are acquainted with the ways of God; for the ancient prophets and most eminent saints have all experienced an alternation of visitation and desertion. . . . If this interchange of light and darkness, joy and sorrow, was the common state of the greater saints surely such poor and infirm creatures as we ought not to despair, when we are sometimes elevated by fervor and sometimes depressed by coldness.

Thomas à Kempis

A vague feeling of anguish is prowling around in me like a caged beast, immobilizing my energies and concentration. The feeling has no shape and I don't know what to call it. I am its prisoner. I've got to shake it off. I need all my energy at the moment, at every moment, if I'm to live my life in its fullness. But I won't be free of it until I've let the bad feeling wash over me, then faced it without fear, grabbed it with both hands and offered it to God who can bring new life out of sin.

Michel Quoist

The Christian's chief occupational hazards are depression and discouragement.

John R.W. Stott

Sometimes I battle with depression. I never know all the reasons for this "dark pit," as it seems to me. Some of it may be hurt pride. Sometimes it is obviously exhaustion, physical, mental, emotional and spiritual. At times, when I am tired and strained, I can get angry over an incident that may be quite trivial in itself; and then I get angry with myself for getting angry. As I suppress both forms of anger, depression is the result. I am then even more difficult to live with than usual. I do not want people to get too near to me, but I hope very much that they will not go too far away either.

David Watson

Desert

The wilderness and the solitary place shall be glad for them; and the desert shall rejoice, and blossom as the rose.

Isaiah 35:1 KJV

The voice of him that crieth in the wilderness, Prepare ye the way of the Lord, make straight in the desert a highway for our God. Every valley shall be exalted, and every mountain and hill shall be made low: and the crooked shall be made straight, and the rough places plain.

Isaiah 40:3–4 KJV

Filled with the Holy Spirit, Jesus left the Jordan and was led by the Spirit into the desert, for forty days being put to the test by the devil.

Luke 4:1–2 NJB

The desert does not mean the absence of men, it means the presence of God.

Carlo Carretto

The lives that are getting stronger are lives in the desert, deep-rooted in God.

Oswald Chambers

But has not the moment passed when God speaks in the desert, and must we now not understand that "He who is" is not to be heard in this place or that, for the heights where He dwells are not inaccessible mountains but a more profound sphere of things? The secret of the world lies wherever we can discern the transparency of the universe.

Pierre Teilhard de Chardin

It's tough in the desert. It's bewildering. It's destructive. It's hellish. Yet the testimony of the Old Testament, and ever more strongly, of the New, is that out of it comes new growth, new insight, new certainty that a God of love is at home among us.

Charles Elliott

The Promised Land always lies on the other side of a wilderness.

Henry Havelock Ellis

The desert is the place where human powers must be renounced. In the desert there can be no more trickery, no illusions as to getting out by one's own means, no possibility of placing hope in natural sources of help.

Jacques Ellul

The desert . . . is a place of revelation and revolution. In the desert we wait, we weep, we learn to live.

Alan Jones

This, then is our desert; to live facing despair, but not to consent. To trample it down under hope in the Cross. To wage war against despair unceasingly. That war is our wilderness. If we wage it courageously, we will find Christ at our side. If we cannot face it, we will never find him.

Thomas Merton

The desert is the place where God's people learn hard lessons of life and faith. It is a place to learn the real priorities and there are no margins for error. In the desert there is no room for luxuries and no respect of human status or strength. To contemplate the desert, then, is to understand the call to walk by faith in God alone. It is a place that simplifies us, down to our true selves, until we are ready to meet the God of life and death.

David Runcorn

The desert bears the sign of man's complete helplessness as he can do nothing to subsist alone and by himself, and thus discovers his weakness and the necessity of seeking help and strength in God.

René Voillaume

The desert has bred fanaticism and frenzy and fear; but it has also bred heroic gentleness.

Helen Waddell

Desertion, *see* Rejection

Desire

See also Hope; Love

Delight thyself also in the Lord; and he shall give thee the desires of thine heart.

Psalm 37:4 KJV

He brought me to the banqueting house, and his banner over me was love.

Song of Solomon 2:4 KJV

Set me as a seal upon thine heart, as a seal upon thine arm: for love is strong as death; jealousy is cruel as the grave: the coals thereof are coals of fire, which hath a most vehement flame. Many waters cannot quench love, neither can the floods drown it: if a man would give all the substance of his house for love, it would utterly be condemned.

Song of Solomon 8:6–7 KJV

Follow the way of love and eagerly desire spiritual gifts, especially the gift of prophecy.

1 Corinthians 14:1 NIV

Beloved, I urge you as aliens and exiles to abstain from the desires of the flesh that wage war against the soul.

1 Peter 2:11 NRSV

For desire never ceases to pray even though the tongue be silent. If ever desiring, then ever praying.

St. Augustine of Hippo

To desire to love God is to love to desire Him, and hence to love Him, for love is the root of all desire.

Bishop Jean Pierre Camus

It became so clear to me that it must be either obedience to the Divine challenge or failure to grow in the spiritual life, that all desire for smoking suddenly left me, and from that day to this I have never even wanted to take it up again; some greater desire had mastered the old habit, it was desire to know God.

J. Rowntree Gillett

For those who love, nothing is hard; and no task is difficult if your desire is great.

St. Jerome

Let temporal things serve thy use, but the eternal be the object of thy desire.

Thomas à Kempis

Thirst must be quenched! If our desires are not met by God, we will quickly find something else to alleviate our thirst.

Erwin W. Lutzer

Man finds it hard to get what he wants because he does not want the best; God finds it hard to give because he would give the best and man will not take it.

George MacDonald

The desire of Love, Joy; / The desire of life, Peace; / The desire of the soul, Heaven; / The desire of God—a flame-white secret for ever.

William Sharp

None of us ever desired anything more ardently than God desires to bring men to a knowledge of himself.

Johann Tauler

If we do go down into ourselves we find that we possess exactly what we desire.

Simone Weil

Any unmortified desire which a man allows in will effectually drive and keep Christ out of the heart.

Charles Wesley

Despair

See also Hope

A despairing man should have the devotion of his friends, even though he forsakes the fear of the Almighty.

Job 6:14 NIV

We are subjected to every kind of hardship, but never distressed; we see no way out but we never despair; we are pursued but never cut off; knocked down but still have some life in us, always we carry with us in our body the death of Jesus so that the life of Jesus, too, may be visible in our body.

2 Corinthians 4:8–10 NJB

I would say to my soul, O my soul this is not the place of despair; this is not the time to despair in. As long as mine eyes can find a promise in the Bible, as long as there is a moment left me of breath or life in this world, so long will I wait or look for mercy, so long will I fight against unbelief and despair.

John Bunyan

God does not despair of you, therefore you ought not to despair of yourself.

C.C. Grafton

Give no place to despondency. This is a dangerous temptation to the adversary. Melancholy contracts and withers the heart.

Madame Jeanne Marie Guyon

There are no hopeless situations. There are only people who have grown hopeless about them.

Clare Boothe Luce

It is impossible for that man to despair who remembers that his Helper is omnipotent.

Jeremy Taylor

Hope thinks nothing is difficult; despair tells us that difficulty is unsurmountable.

Isaac Watts

Let us never despair while we have Christ as our leader!

George Whitefield

Destiny

See also Future; Goals

It is better to go to a house of mourning than to go to a house of feasting, for death is the destiny of every man; the living should take this to heart.

Ecclesiastes 7:2 NIV

In Christ we have also obtained an inheritance, having been destined according to the purpose of him who accomplishes all things according to his counsel and will.

Ephesians 1:11 NRSV

They [the enemies of Christ's cross] are destined to be lost; their god is the stomach; they glory in what they should think shameful, since their minds are set on earthly things.

Philippians 3:19 NJB

Destiny is not a matter of chance; it is a matter of choice.

Anon.

The destiny of every human being depends on his relationship to Jesus Christ. It is not on his relationship to life, or on his service or his usefulness, but simply and solely on his relationship to Jesus Christ.

Oswald Chambers

Destiny waits in the hand of God, not in the hands of statesmen.

Thomas Stearns (T.S.) Eliot

We are not permitted to choose the frame of our destiny. But what we put into it is ours.

Dag Hammarskjöld

We are called to be a great living cloth of gold with not only the woof going from God to man and from man to God, but also the warp going from man to man.

Baron Friedrich von Hügel

Devil

See also Demons

Then Satan answered the LORD, "Does Job fear God for nothing? Have you not put a fence around him and his house and all that he has, on every side? You have blessed the work of his hands, and his possessions have increased in the land. But stretch out your hand now, and touch all that he has, and he will curse you to your face."

Job 1:9–11 NRSV

If it is Satan who drives out Satan, he is divided against himself; how then can his kingdom stand?

Matthew 12:26 REB

He rebuked Peter and said to him, "Get behind me, Satan! You are thinking not as God thinks, but as human beings do."

Mark 8:33 NJB

You are the children of your father, the Devil, and you want to follow your father's desires. From the very beginning he was a murderer and he has never been on the side of truth, because there is no truth in him. When he tells a lie, he is only doing what is natural to him, because he is a liar and the father of all lies.

John 8:44 GNB

The god of this world hath blinded the minds of them which believe not, lest the light of the glorious gospel of Christ, who is the image of God, should shine unto them.

2 Corinthians 4:4 KJV

Even Satan tries to make himself look like an angel of light.

2 Corinthians 11:14 CEV

Everyone who commits sin is a child of the devil; for the devil has been sinning from the beginning. The Son of God was revealed for this purpose, to destroy the works of the devil.

1 John 3:8 NRSV

Then the devil, who led them astray, was hurled into the lake of fire and sulphur, where the beast and the false prophet are, and their torture will not come to an end, day or night, for ever and ever.

Revelation 20:10 NJB

The devil's snare does not catch you, unless you are first caught by the devil's bait.

St. Ambrose

When the devil is called the god of this world, it is not because he made it, but because we serve him with our worldliness.

St. Thomas Aquinas

Satan wastes no ammunition on those who are dead in trespasses and sins.

Corrie ten Boom

The devil has one good quality, that he will flee if we resist him. Though cowardly, it is safety for us.

Tryon Edwards

If you don't believe in the devil's existence, just try resisting him for a while.

Charles Grandison Finney

Satan is quite content for us to make any number of beginnings as long as we never complete anything.

St. Francis de Sales

Satan is not fighting churches; he is joining them. He does more harm by sowing tares than by pulling up wheat. He accomplishes more by imitation than by outright opposition.

Vance Havner

It is so stupid of modern civilization to have given up belief in the devil when he is the only explanation of it.

Ronald Arbuthnott Knox

For where God built a church, there the devil would also build a chapel. Thus is the devil ever God's ape.

Martin Luther

No matter how many pleasures Satan offers you, his ultimate intention is to ruin you. Your destruction is his highest priority.

Erwin W. Lutzer

That there is a devil is a thing doubted by none but such as are under the influence of the devil. For any to deny the being of a devil must be from an ignorance or profaneness worse than diabolical.

Cotton Mather

Satan deals with confusion and lies. Put the truth in front of him and he is gone.

Paul Mattock

I believe Satan to exist for two reasons; first,

the Bible says so; and second, I've done business with him.

Dwight Lyman (D.L.) Moody

The devil can cite Scripture for his purpose.

William Shakespeare

The use of a counterfeit is Satan's most natural method of resisting the purposes of God.

Stephen Slocum

The devil is a better theologian than any of us and is a devil still.

Aiden Wilson (A.W.) Tozer

Satan finds some mischief still / For idle hands to do.

Isaac Watts

Devotion, *see* Faithfulness; Love

Dignity

See also Respect

For your brother Aaron make sacred vestments, to give him dignity and grandeur.

Exodus 28:2 REB

[A capable wife] Strength and dignity are her clothing, and she laughs at the time to come.

Proverbs 31:25 NRSV

Deacons, likewise, must be dignified, not indulging in double talk, given neither to excessive drinking nor to money-grubbing.

1 Timothy 3:8 REB

If the value of an article is dependent upon the price paid for it, Christ's death made our value skyrocket.

Let no one say we are worthless. God is

not a foolish speculator; he would never invest in worthless property.

Erwin W. Lutzer

There is nothing small in the service of God.

St. Francis de Sales

Man's dignity is derived and dependent, not intrinsic.

Robert Charles (R.C.) Sproul

The meanest work for Jesus is a grander thing than the dignity of an emperor.

Charles Haddon Spurgeon

Our greatest claim to nobility is our created capacity to know God, to be in personal relationship with him, to love him and to worship him. Indeed, we are most truly human when we are on our knees before our Creator.

John R.W. Stott

No race can prosper until it learns that there is as much dignity in tilling a field as in writing a poem.

Booker T. Washington

Diligence

See also Work

A slack hand brings poverty, but the hand of the diligent brings forth wealth.

Proverbs 10:4 NJB

Those who are far off shall come and help to build the temple of the LORD . . . if you diligently obey the voice of the LORD your God.

Zechariah 6:15 NRSV

Brethren, give diligence to make your calling and election sure: for if ye do these things, ye shall never fall.

2 Peter 1:10 KJV

In doing what we ought we deserve no praise.

St. Augustine of Hippo

"Take your needle, my child, and work at your pattern; it will come out a rose by and by." Life is like that; one stitch at a time taken patiently, and the pattern will come out all right like embroidery.

Oliver Wendell Holmes

Few things are impossible to diligence and skill.

Samuel Johnson

The leading rule for a man of every calling is diligence; never put off until tomorrow what you can do today.

Abraham Lincoln

Patience and diligence, like faith, remove mountains.

William Penn

The first principle God's honor, the second man's happiness, the means prayer and unremitting diligence.

Anthony Ashley Cooper,
Seventh Earl of Shaftesbury

Disability

Do not treat the deaf with contempt, or put an obstacle in the way of the blind; you are to fear your God. I am the Lord.

Leviticus 19:14 REB

Here [the pool of Bethesda] a great number of disabled people used to be—the blind, the lame, the paralyzed.

John 5:3 NIV

Lift your drooping hands and strengthen your weak knees, and make straight paths for your feet, so that what is lame may not be put out of joint, but rather be healed.

Hebrews 12:12–13 NRSV

Whosoever believeth in him should not perish. . . . With these words my sense of inferiority, my fear of handicaps, dropped away. It meant that I, a humble Negro girl, had just as much chance as anybody in the sight and love of God.

Mary McLeod Bethune

Cripple him, and you have a Sir Walter Scott. Lock him in a prison cell, and you have a John Bunyan. Bury him in the snows of Valley Forge, and you have a George Washington. Raise him in abject poverty, and you have an Abraham Lincoln. Strike him down in infantile paralysis, and he becomes Franklin Roosevelt. Deafen him, and you have a Ludwig van Beethoven. Have him or her born black in a society filled with racial discrimination, and you have a Booker T. Washington, a Marian Anderson, a George Washington Carver. . . . Call him a slow learner, "retarded," and write him off as uneducable, and you have an Albert Einstein.

Ted W. Engstrom

To be blind is bad, but worse is it to have eyes and not to see.

Helen Adams Keller

I thank God for my handicaps; for, through them, I have found myself, my work, and my God.

Helen Adams Keller

Beethoven composed his deepest music after becoming totally deaf. Pascal set down his most searching observations about God, man, life, and death in brief intervals of release from a prostrating illness.

Robert J. McCracken

Here I sit in the middle of eternity . . . This wheelchair has helped me sit still. I've observed with curiosity the way we Christians grasp for the future, as if the present didn't quite satisfy. How we, in spiritual fits and starts, scrape and scratch our way along, often missing the best of life while looking the other way, preoccupied with shaping our future. In my least consistent moments I too try to wrest the future out of his hands. Or worse, I sink back into the past and rest on long-ago laurels. But God is most concerned with the choices I make now. . . . God, standing silently and invisibly and presently with us in the middle of eternity, is interested in a certain kind of change. . . . He brings us choices through which we never-endingly change, fresh and new, into his likeness.

Joni Eareckson Tada

Discipleship

See also Christ-likeness; Commitment; Jesus Christ, Example of

Follow me, and I will make you fishers of men.

Matthew 4:19 KJV

Go to the people of all nations and make them my disciples. Baptize them in the name of the Father, the Son, and the Holy Spirit, and teach them to do everything I have told you. I will be with you always, even until the end of the world.

Matthew 28:19–20 CEV

If any man come to me, and hate not his father, and mother, and wife, and children, and brethren, and sisters, yea, and his own life also, he cannot be my disciple. And whosoever doth not bear his cross, and come after me, cannot be my disciple.

Luke 14:26–27 KJV

If any man serve me, let him follow me; and where I am, there shall also my servant be: if any man serve me, him will my Father honor.

John 12:26 KJV

By this everyone will know that you are my disciples, if you have love for one another.

John 13:35 NRSV

Jesus calls us! O'er the tumult / Of our life's wild restless sea, / Day by day His sweet voice soundeth, / Saying, "Christian, follow Me."

Cecil Frances Alexander

When Christ calls a man he bids him come and die.

Dietrich Bonhoeffer

Jesus invited us, not to a picnic, but to a pilgrimage; not to a frolic, but to a fight. He offered us, not an excursion, but an execution. Our Savior said that we would have to be ready to die to self, sin, and the world.

William Franklin (Billy) Graham

Salvation is free, but discipleship costs everything we have.

William Franklin (Billy) Graham

What our Lord said about cross-bearing and obedience is not in fine type. It is in bold print on the face of the contract.

Vance Havner

To follow the Savior is to participate in salvation; to follow the light is to perceive the light.

St. Irenaeus

On account of him there have come to be many Christs in the world, even all who, like him, loved righteousness and hated iniquity.

Origen of Alexandria

Discipleship is more than getting to know what the teacher knows. It is getting to be what he is.

Juan Carlos Ortiz

The making of a disciple means the creating of a duplicate.

Juan Carlos Ortiz

What other people think of me is becoming less and less important; what they think of Jesus because of me is critical.

Sir Cliff Richard

Christ cannot live his life today in this world without our mouth, without our eyes, without our going and coming, without our hearts. When we love, it is Christ loving through us.

Leon Joseph Suenens

If we were willing to learn the meaning of real discipleship and actually to become disciples, the Church in the West would be transformed, and the resultant impact on society would be staggering.

David Watson

The disciple is one who, intent upon becoming Christ-like and so dwelling in his "faith and practice," systematically and progressively rearranges his affairs to that end.

Dallas Willard

When no mark of the cross appears in our discipleship, we may doubt the ownership. We should be branded for Christ.

Mary S. Wood

Discipline

See also Children; Self-Control

My child, do not despise the LORD's discipline or be weary of his reproof, for the LORD reproves the one he loves, as a father the son in whom he delights.

Proverbs 3:11–12 NRSV

Endure hardship as discipline; God is treating you as sons. For what son is not disciplined by his father? If you are not disciplined (and everyone undergoes discipline), then you are illegitimate children and not true sons. Moreover, we have all had human fathers who disciplined us and we respected them for it. How much more should we submit to the Father of our spirits and live! Our fathers disciplined us for a little while as they thought best; but God disciplines us for our good, that we may share in his holiness. No discipline seems pleasant at the time, but painful. Later on, however, it produces a harvest of righteousness and peace for those who have been trained by it.

Hebrews 12:7–11 NIV

All whom I love I reprove and discipline. Be wholehearted therefore in your repentance.

Revelation 3:19 REB

Discipline puts back in its place that something in us which should serve but wants to rule.

Anon.

God can never make us wine if we object to the fingers he uses to crush us with. If God would only use his own fingers, and make us broken bread and poured out wine in a special way! But when he uses someone whom we dislike, or some set of circumstances to which we said we would never submit, and makes those the crushers, we object.

Oswald Chambers

Discipline and love are not antithetical; one is a function of the other.

James Dobson

God never strikes except for motives of love, and never takes away but in order to give.

François de la Mothe Fénelon

No horse gets anywhere until he is harnessed. No steam or gas ever drives anything until it is confined. No Niagara is ever turned into light and power until it is tunneled. No life ever grows great until it is focused, dedicated, disciplined.

Harry Emerson Fosdick

Pruning creates strength, richness, depth, though temporarily pruning hurts and conjures up doubt and fear. It takes a wise gardener to know when and how and how much to cut back a beautiful rose. . . . It takes a wise individual to prune himself or herself according to one's unique needs and timing.

Matthew Fox

God does not discipline us to subdue us, but to condition us for a life of usefulness and blessedness.

William Franklin (Billy) Graham

We must be anchored in self-discipline if we are to venture successfully in freedom.

Harold E. Kohn

It is one thing to show a man that he is in error, and another to put him in possession of truth.

John Locke

Discipline is a proof of our sonship.

Erwin W. Lutzer

Discipline is the basic set of tools we require to solve life's problems.

M. Scott Peck

It is in mercy and in measure that God chastiseth His children.

John Trapp

Better be pruned to grow than cut up to burn.

John Trapp

Discouragement

Have I not commanded thee? Be strong and of a good courage: be not afraid, neither be thou dismayed: for the Lord thy God is with thee whithersoever thou goest.

Joshua 1:9 KJV

The Lord says that you don't need to be afraid or let this powerful army discourage you. God will fight on your side!

2 Chronicles 20:15 CEV

Fathers, do not embitter your children, or they will become discouraged.

Colossians 3:21 NIV

Never think you could do something if you only had a different lot and sphere assigned you. What you call hindrances, obstacles, discouragements, are probably God's opportunities.

Horace Bushnell

Discouragement comes when we insist on having our own way.

Oswald Chambers

Every step toward Christ kills a doubt. Every thought, word and deed for him carries you away from discouragement.

Theodore Ledyard Cuyler

No one has a right to sit down and feel hopeless. There's too much work to do.

Dorothy Day

There is no disappointment to those whose wills are buried in the will of God.

Frederick William Faber

Should we feel at times disheartened and discouraged, a confiding thought, a simple movement of heart toward God will renew our powers. Whatever he may demand of us, he will give us at the moment the strength and the courage that we need.

François de la Mothe Fénelon

The occupational hazard of the Christian ministry and evangelism is discouragement.

John R.W. Stott

When we yield to discouragement, it is usually because we give too much thought to the past or to the future.

St. Thérèse of Lisieux

Dishonesty

See also Deceit; Falsehood

All who act dishonestly, are abhorrent to the LORD your God.

Deuteronomy 25:16 NRSV

You cheated others, but everything you gained will fly away, like birds hatched from stolen eggs. Then you will discover what fools you are.

Jeremiah 17:11 CEV

Anyone who is trustworthy in little things is trustworthy in great; anyone who is dishonest in little things is dishonest in great.

Luke 16:10 NJB

Man can certainly keep on lying (and does so) but he cannot make truth falsehood.

Karl Barth

Better to bear than to swear, and to die than to lie.

Thomas Benton Brooks

It is easy to tell one lie, hard to tell but one lie.

Thomas Fuller

Sin has many tools, but a lie is the handle that fits them all.

Oliver Wendell Holmes

Disobedience

See also Obedience; Rebellion

With the spirit and power of Elijah he [John the Baptist] will go before him, to turn the hearts of parents to their children, and the disobedient to the wisdom of the righteous, to make ready a people prepared for the Lord.

Luke 1:17 NRSV

For as by one man's disobedience many were made sinners, so by the obedience of one shall many be made righteous.

Romans 5:19 KJV

[In the last days] people will be self-centered and avaricious, boastful, arrogant and rude; disobedient to their parents, ungrateful, irreligious; heartless and intractable.

2 Timothy 3:2 NJB

Judas heard all Christ's sermons.

Thomas Goodwin

The Fall is simply and solely disobedience— doing what you have been told not to do; and it results from pride—from being too big for your boots, forgetting your place, thinking that you are God.

Clive Staples (C.S.) Lewis

God has established Government but he has not made it autonomous. Thus if the office bearer commands that which is contrary to God's Law his authority is abrogated. At this point it is the Christian's duty to disobey.

Francis August Schaeffer

Distress, *see* Suffering

Divorce

See also Marriage

I hate divorce, says the LORD, the God of Israel.

Malachi 2:16 NRSV

It was also said, "Whoever divorces his wife, let him give her a certificate of divorce." But I say to you that anyone who divorces his wife, except on the ground of unchastity, causes her to commit adultery; and whoever marries a divorced woman commits adultery.

Matthew 5:31–32 NRSV

They [some Pharisees] said to him [Jesus], "Why then did Moses command us to give a certificate of dismissal and to divorce her?" He said to them, "It was because you were so hard-hearted that Moses allowed you to divorce your wives, but from the beginning it was not so. And I say to you, whoever divorces his wife, except for unchastity, and marries another commits adultery."

Matthew 19:7–9 NRSV

The Law says that a man's wife must remain his wife as long as he lives. But once her husband is dead, she is free to marry someone else. However, if she goes off with another man while her husband is still alive, she is said to be unfaithful.

Romans 7:2–3 CEV

Divorce courts are packed with people who tried to base their marriages on "If you do this, I'll do that."

Mary Garson

Divorce is an easy escape, many think. But . . . the guilt and loneliness they experience can be even more tragic than living with their problems.

William Franklin (Billy) Graham

I have such a hatred of divorce that I prefer bigamy to divorce.

Martin Luther

When Christians break the marriage vow it is primarily because they fail to accept God's plan for their marriage.

Walter Schoedel

Most divorces are not bad marriages, just poorly prepared marriages.

Jim Talley

Failure and the evil inherent in divorce would destroy us were it not for the fact that God keeps his promises and continues to love even when we break our promises and our love fails.

William H. Willimon

Doctrine, *see* Education; Orthodoxy; Teachers and Teaching; Theology

Doubt

See also Faith; Unbelief

Jesus answered them, "Truly I tell you, if you have faith and do not doubt, not only will you do what has been done to the fig tree, but even if you say to this mountain, 'Be lifted up and thrown into the sea,' it will be done."

Matthew 21:21 NRSV

Thomas said, "First, I must see the nail scars in his hands and touch them with my finger. I must put my hand where the spear went into his side. I won't believe unless I do this!"

John 20:25 CEV

Prayer must be made with faith, and no trace of doubt, because a person who has doubts is like the waves thrown up in the sea by the buffeting of the wind.

James 1:6 NJB

If a man begins with certainties, he shall end in doubts; but if he begins with doubts, he shall end in certainties.

Francis Bacon

When we say: "Yes, I doubt, but I do believe in God's love more than I trust my own doubts," it becomes possible for God to act.

Anthony Bloom

Doubt is not always a sign that a man is wrong; it may be a sign that he is thinking.

Oswald Chambers

Every step towards Christ kills a doubt.

Theodore Ledyard Cuyler

Believe your beliefs and doubt your doubts; do not make the mistake of doubting your beliefs and believing your doubts.

Charles F. Deems

Christ never failed to distinguish between doubt and unbelief. Doubt is can't believe; unbelief is won't believe. Doubt is honesty; unbelief is obstinacy. Doubt is looking for light; unbelief is content with darkness.

John Drummond

Never doubt in the dark what God told you in the light.

Victor Raymond Edman

It need not discourage us if we are full of doubts. Healthy questions keep faith dynamic. Unless we start with doubts we cannot have a deep-rooted faith. One who believes lightly and unthinkingly has not much of a belief. He who has a faith which is not to be shaken has won it through blood and tears—has worked his way from doubt to truth as one who reaches a clearing through a thicket of brambles and thorns.

Helen Adams Keller

The man that feareth, Lord, to doubt, In that fear doubteth thee.

George MacDonald

Ten thousand difficulties do not make one doubt, as I understand the subject; difficulty and doubt are incommensurate.

John Henry Newman

If we are sensible we will not doubt God, we will doubt our world and we will doubt ourselves.

Agnes Sanford

Our doubts are traitors. And make us lose the good we oft might win by fearing to attempt.

William Shakespeare

Doubt is not the opposite of faith; it is one element of faith.

Paul Tillich

Doxologies

See also Praise

David said, "Blessed are you, O LORD, the God of our ancestor Israel, forever and ever. Yours, O LORD, are the greatness, the power, the glory, the victory, and the majesty; for all that is in the heavens and on the earth is yours; yours is the kingdom, O LORD, and you are exalted as head above all. Riches and honor come from you, and you rule over all. In your hand are power and might; and it is in your hand to make great and to give strength to all. And now, our God, we give thanks to you and praise your glorious name."

1 Chronicles 29:10–13 NRSV

Oh, the depth of the riches of the wisdom and knowledge of God! How unsearchable his judgments, and his paths beyond tracing out! "Who has known the mind of the Lord? Or who has been his counselor?" "Who has ever given to God, that God should repay him?" For from him and through him and to him are all things. To him be the glory for ever!

Romans 11:33–36 NIV

Jesus Christ . . . who is the blessed and only Potentate, the King of kings, and Lord of lords; Who only hath immortality, dwelling in the light which no man can approach unto; whom no man hath seen, nor can see: to whom be honor and power everlasting. Amen.

1 Timothy 6:14–16 KJV

Now unto him that is able to keep you from falling, and to present you faultless before the presence of his glory with exceeding joy. To the only wise God our Savior, be glory and majesty, dominion and power, both now and ever. Amen.

Jude 24–25 KJV

"Holy, holy, holy the Lord God Almighty, who was and is and is to come."

Revelation 4:8 NRSV

"Worthy is the Lamb who was slain, to receive power and wealth, wisdom and might, honor and glory and praise!" Then I heard all created things, in heaven, on earth, under the earth, and in the sea, crying: "Praise and honor, glory and might, to him who sits on the throne and to the Lamb for ever!"

Revelation 5:12–13 REB

Glory to God, Source of all being, Eternal Word and Holy Spirit: as it was in the beginning, is now, and shall be for ever.

Book of Common Prayer

Glory be to the Father and to the Son and to the Holy Spirit. As it was in the beginning is now and ever shall be, world without end.

Book of Common Prayer

God hath in Himself all power to defend you, all wisdom to direct you, all mercy to pardon you, all grace to enrich you, all righteousness to clothe you, all goodness to supply you, and all happiness to crown you.

Thomas Benton Brooks

The God and Father of our Lord Jesus Christ open all our eyes, that we may see that blessed hope to which we are called; that we may altogether glorify the only true God and Jesus Christ, whom he hath sent down to us from heaven; to whom with the Father and the Holy Spirit be rendered all honor and glory to all eternity.

John Jewel

Glory be to thee, O Lord, glory to thee, O holy One, glory to thee, O King!

St. John Chrysostom

To God the Father, who first loved us, and made us accepted in the beloved: To God the Son, who loved us, and washed us from our sins in his own blood: To God the Holy Ghost, who sheds the love of God abroad in our hearts: Be all love and all glory, for all time and for eternity.

Thomas Ken

Blessing and honor and thanksgiving and praise, more than we can utter, more than we can conceive, be unto thee, O holy and glorious Trinity, Father, Son, and Holy Ghost, by all angels, by all men, all creatures, for ever and ever.

Thomas Ken

Glory be to thee, O God, the Father, the Maker of the world: Glory be to thee, O God, the Son, the Redeemer of mankind: Glory be to thee, O God, the Holy Ghost, the Sanctifier of thy people.

Brooke Foss Westcott

Dreams

See also Visions

One time Joseph had a dream, and when he told his brothers about it, they hated him even more.

Genesis 37:5 GNB

Listen to my words! If there is a prophet among you, I reveal myself to him in a vision, I speak to him in a dream.

Numbers 12:6 NJB

For dreams come with many cares, and a fool's voice with many words.

Ecclesiastes 5:3 NRSV

The king asked Daniel (also called Belteshazzar), "Are you able to tell me what I saw in my dream and interpret it?" Daniel replied, "No wise man, enchanter, magician or diviner can explain to the king the mystery he has asked about, but there is a God in heaven who reveals mysteries. He has shown King Nebuchadnezzar what will happen in days to come."

Daniel 2:26–28 NIV

I will pour out my spirit on all flesh; your sons and your daughters shall prophesy, your old men shall dream dreams, and your young men shall see visions.

Joel 2:28 NRSV

The angel of the Lord appeared unto him in a dream, saying, Joseph, thou son of David, fear not to take unto thee Mary thy wife: for that which is conceived in her is of the Holy Ghost.

Matthew 1:20 KJV

God's gifts put man's best dreams to shame.

Elizabeth Barrett Browning

Our heart oft times wakes when we sleep, and God can speak to that, either by words, by proverbs, by signs and similitudes, as well as if one was awake.

John Bunyan

I have a dream that my four little children will one day live in a nation where they will not be judged by the color of their skin but by the content of their character.

Martin Luther King Jr.

I have a dream that one day this nation will rise up, live out the true meaning of its creed.

Martin Luther King Jr.

When the dream in our heart is one that God has planted there, a strange happiness flows into us. At that moment all of the spiritual resources of the universe are released to help us. Our praying is then at one with the will of God and becomes a channel for the Creator's always joyous, triumphant purposes for us and our world.

Catherine Wood Marshall

God is the great reality. His resources are available and endless. His promises are real and glorious, beyond our wildest dreams.

John Bertram (J.B.) Phillips

Dreams are the touchstones of our characters. For in dreams we but act a part which must have been learned and rehearsed in our waking hours. . . . Our truest life is when we are in dreams awake.

Henry David Thoreau

Drink, *see* Drunkenness; Food and Drink

Drunkenness

See also Temperance

Who is always in trouble? Who argues and fights? Who has cuts and bruises? Whose eyes are red? Everyone who stays up late, having just one more drink. Don't even look at that colorful stuff bubbling up in the glass! It goes down so easily, but later it bites like a poisonous snake. You will see weird things, and your mind will play tricks on you. You will feel tossed about like someone trying to sleep on a ship in a storm. You will be bruised all over, without even remembering how it all happened. And you will lie awake asking, "When will morning come, so I can drink some more?"

Proverbs 23:29–35 CEV

Let us behave decently, as in the daytime, not in orgies and drunkenness.

Romans 13:13 NIV

Don't destroy yourself by getting drunk, but let the Spirit fill your life.

Ephesians 5:18 CEV

While the wine is in thy hand, thou art a man; when it is in thine head, thou art become a beast.

Thomas Adams

Drunkenness is the ruin of a person. It is premature old age. It is temporary death.

St. Basil the Great

Overdoing is the ordinary way of undoing.

Richard Baxter

Drink has drained more blood, hung more crepes, sold more homes, plunged more people into bankruptcy, armed more villains, slain more children, snapped more wedding rings, defiled more innocence, blinded more eyes, twisted more limbs, dethroned more reason, wrecked more manhood, dishonored more womanhood, broken more hearts, driven more to suicide and dug more graves than any other poisonous scourge that ever swept its death-dealing waves across the world.

Evangeline Cory Booth

Drink moderately, for drunkenness neither keeps a secret, nor observes a promise.

Miguel de Cervantes

No man ever drank lard into his tub, or flour into his sack, nor meal into his barrel, nor happiness into his home, nor God into his heart.

Benjamin Franklin

Alcohol does not drown care, but waters it and makes it grow faster.

Benjamin Franklin

He that will never drink less than he may, sometimes will drink more than he should.

Thomas Fuller

The drunken man is a living corpse.

St. John Chrysostom

Duty

See also Responsibility

Fear God, and keep his commandments; for that is the whole duty of everyone.

Ecclesiastes 12:13 NRSV

He hath shewed thee, O man, what is good; and what doth the Lord require of thee, but to do justly, and to love mercy, and to walk humbly with thy God?

Micah 6:8 KJV

So likewise ye, when ye shall have done all those things which are commanded you, say, We are unprofitable servants: we have done that which was our duty to do.

Luke 17:10 KJV

But you [Timothy], keep your head in all situations, endure hardship, do the work of an evangelist, discharge all the duties of your ministry.

2 Timothy 4:5 NIV

No duty is more urgent than that of returning thanks.

St. Ambrose

In doing what we ought we deserve no praise, it is our duty.

St. Augustine of Hippo

Our main business is not to see what lies dimly at a distance, but to do what lies clearly at hand.

Thomas Carlyle

When the law of God is written in our hearts, our duty will be our delight.

Matthew Henry

No better citizen is there, whether in time of peace or war, than the Christian who is mindful of his duty; but such a one should be ready to suffer all things, even death itself, rather than abandon the cause of God or of the Church.

Leo XIII

Let us have faith that right makes might, and in that faith let us to the end dare to do our duty as we understand it.

Abraham Lincoln

You would not think any duty small if you yourself were great.

George MacDonald

Duty does not have to be dull. Love can make it beautiful and fill it with life.

Thomas Merton

Never think yourself safe because you do your duty in ninety-nine points; it is the hundredth which is to be the ground of your self-denial.

John Henry Newman

God never imposes a duty without giving time to do it.

John Ruskin

Every duty which we omit, obscures some truth which we should have known.

John Ruskin

There is no duty we so much underrate as the duty of being happy.

Robert Louis Stevenson

There are only two duties required of us—the love of God and the love of our neighbor, and the surest sign of discovering whether we observe these duties is the love of our neighbor.

St. Teresa of Avila

The whole duty of man is summed up in obedience to God's will.

George Washington

Earth, *see* Creation; Environment

Easter

See also Jesus Christ, Resurrection of; Resurrection

For just as Jonah was three days and three nights in the belly of the sea monster, so for three days and three nights the Son of Man will be in the heart of the earth.

Matthew 12:40 NRSV

He is not here: for he is risen, as he said.

Matthew 28:6 KJV

[The angel to the women at the tomb] "Do not be alarmed; you are looking for Jesus of Nazareth, who was crucified. He has been raised; he is not here."

Mark 16:6 NRSV

Jesus said, "I am the resurrection and the life. Whoever has faith in me shall live, even though he dies; and no one who lives and has faith in me shall ever die."

John 11:25–26 REB

The best news the world ever had came from a graveyard.

Anon.

The stone at the tomb of Jesus was a pebble to the Rock of Ages inside.

Frederick Beck

The great Easter truth is not that we are to live newly after death, but that we are to be new here and now by the power of the resurrection.

Phillips Brooks

Lo! Jesus meets us, risen from the tomb; / Lovingly He greets us, scatters fear and gloom; / Let the Church with gladness hymns of triumph sing, / For her Lord now liveth, death hath lost its sting. / Thine be the glory, risen, conquering Son, / Endless is the victory Thou o'er death hast won.

Edmund Louis Budry

Christ has turned all our sunsets into dawns.

Clement of Alexandria

Easter says you can put truth in a grave, but it won't stay there.

Clarence W. Hull

Our Lord has written the promise of the resurrection, not in books alone, but in every leaf in springtime.

Martin Luther

Easter means hope prevails over despair. Jesus reigns as Lord of Lords and King of Kings. . . . Easter says to us that despite everything to the contrary, his will for us will prevail, love will prevail over hate, justice over injustice and oppression, peace over exploitation and bitterness.

Desmond Tutu

Lift your voices in triumph on high, / For Jesus is risen and man cannot die.

Henry Ware

Christ, the Lord, is risen today, / Hallelujah! / Sons of men and angels say: / Raise your joys and triumphs high; / Sing, ye heavens, and earth reply. / Vain the stone, the watch, the seal; / Christ hath burst the gates of hell; / Death in vain forbids Him rise; / Christ hath opened paradise.

Charles Wesley

Ecumenism, *see* Church, Unity

Eden, *see* Creation; Paradise

Education

See also Knowledge; Study; Teachers and Teaching

No other nation, no matter how great, has laws so just as those that I have taught you today. Be on your guard! Make certain that you do not forget, as long as you live, what you have seen with your own eyes. Tell your children and your grandchildren about the day you stood in the presence of the Lord your God at Mount Sinai. . . . I want them to hear what I have to say, so that they will learn to obey me as long as they live and so that they will teach their children to do the same.

Deuteronomy 4:7–10 GNB

We will tell to the coming generation the glorious deeds of the LORD, and his might, and the wonders that he has done. He established a decree in Jacob, and appointed a law in Israel, which he commanded our ancestors to teach to their children; that the next generation might know them.

Psalm 78:4–6 NRSV

If you have good sense instruction, will help you to have even better sense. And if you live right, education will help you to know even more.

Proverbs 9:9 CEV

Train up a child in the way he should go: and when he is old, he will not depart from it.

Proverbs 22:6 KJV

Moses was educated in all the wisdom of the Egyptians and was powerful in speech and action.

Acts 7:22 NIV

Of the same kind, too, are those men who insinuate themselves into families in order to get influence over silly women who are obsessed with their sins and follow one craze after another, always seeking learning, but unable ever to come to knowledge of the truth.

2 Timothy 3:6–7 NJB

God often works more by the illiterate seeking the things that are God's than by the learned seeking the things that are their own.

St. Anselm of Canterbury

See how the unlearned start up and take heaven by storm whilst we with all our learning grovel upon the earth.

St. Augustine of Hippo

There is no such thing on earth as an uninteresting subject: the only thing that can exist is an uninterested person.

Gilbert Keith (G.K.) Chesterton

To train a citizen is to train a critic. The whole point of education is that it should give a man abstract and eternal standards, by which he can judge material and fugitive conditions.

Gilbert Keith (G.K.) Chesterton

Anyone who stops learning is old, whether at twenty or eighty. Anyone who keeps learning stays young. The greatest thing in life is to keep your mind young.

Henry Ford

One of the reasons mature people stop learning is that they become less and less willing to risk failure.

John (William) Gardner

We must learn to get on in the world—not in the commercial and materialistic sense—but as a means to getting Heavenwards. Any education which neglects this fact, and to the extent to which it neglects it, is false education because it is false to man.

Arthur Eric Rowton Gill

I think it's important to teach our children—as the Bible says—line upon line, precept upon precept, here a little, there a little. If you try to teach a child too rapidly, much will be lost. But the time for teaching and training is preteen. When they reach the teenage years, it's time to shut up and start listening.

Ruth Bell Graham

The supreme end of education is expert discernment in all things—the power to tell the good from the bad, the genuine from the counterfeit, and to prefer the good and the genuine to the bad and the counterfeit.

Samuel Johnson

Learning is not to be blamed, nor the mere knowledge of anything which is good in itself and ordained by God; but a good conscience and a virtuous life are always to be preferred before it.

Thomas à Kempis

Education without religion, as useful as it is, seems rather to make man a more clever devil.

Clive Staples (C.S.) Lewis

The end of all learning is to know God, and out of that knowledge to love and imitate Him.

John Milton

Every method of education founded wholly or in part, on the denial or forgetfulness of original sin and grace, and relying solely on the power of human nature, is unsound.

Pius XI

When you educate a man in mind and not in morals you educate a menace to society.

Franklin D. Roosevelt

An education which is not religious is atheistic, there is no middle way. If you give to children an account of the world from which God is left out, you are teaching them to understand the world without reference to God.

William Temple

Elders, *see* Church, Leaders of

Election

See also Grace; Predestination

It was not because you were more numerous than any other people that the LORD set his heart on you and chose you—for you were the fewest of all peoples. It was because the LORD loved you and kept the oath that he swore to your ancestors, that the LORD has brought you out with a mighty hand, and redeemed you from the house of slavery, from the hand of Pharaoh king of Egypt.

Deuteronomy 7:7–8 NRSV

Those whom God had already chosen he also set apart to become like his Son, so that the Son would be the first among many brothers. And so those whom God set apart, he called; and those he called, he put right with himself, and he shared his glory with them. . . . Who will accuse God's chosen people?

Romans 8:29–30, 33 GNB

He hath chosen us in him before the foundation of the world, that we should be holy and without blame before him in love: Having predestined us unto the adoption of children by Jesus Christ to himself, according to the good pleasure of his will.

Ephesians 1:4–5 KJV

To God's elect, strangers in the world . . . who have been chosen according to the foreknowledge of God the Father, through the sanctifying work of the Spirit, for obedience to Jesus Christ and sprinkling by his blood.

1 Peter 1:1–2 NIV

Man is not converted because he wills to be, but he wills to be because he is ordained to election.

St. Augustine of Hippo

The elect are whosoever will; the non-elect are whosoever won't.

Henry Ward Beecher

If we are searching for God's fatherly love and grace, we must look to Christ, in whom alone the Father is well pleased. If we are searching for salvation, life, and immortality, we must turn to him again, since he alone is the fountain of life, the anchor of salvation, and the heir of the kingdom. The purpose of election is no more than that, when we are adopted as sons by the heavenly Father, we will inherit salvation and eternal life through his favor.

John Calvin

Every departure from the doctrine of election in any degree has been a departure from the gospel, for such departure always involves the introduction of some obligation on man's part to make a contribution toward his own salvation, a contribution he simply cannot make.

Arthur C. Custance

The calling of God never leaves men where it finds them.

Joseph Hall

The saved are singled out not by their own merits but by the grace of the Mediator.

Martin Luther

This doctrine affords comfort: thy unworthiness may dismay thee, but remember that thy election depends not upon thy worthiness but upon the will of God.

Elnathan Parr

I believe the doctrine of election, because I am quite sure that if God had not chosen me I would never have chosen him; and I am sure he chose me before I was born, or else he never would have chosen me afterward.

Charles Haddon Spurgeon

The marvel of marvels is not that God, in his infinite love, has not elected all of this guilty race to be saved, but that he has elected any.

Benjamin Breckinridge Warfield

God never repents of his electing love.

Thomas Watson

Let us then ascribe the whole work of grace to the pleasure of God's will. God did not choose us because we were worthy, but by choosing us He makes us worthy.

Thomas Watson

Encouragement

See also Prayer, Encouragements to

We have different gifts, according to the grace given us. If a man's gift is . . . encouraging, let him encourage.

Romans 12:6, 8 NIV

Let us consider how to provoke one another to love and good deeds, not neglecting to meet together, as is the habit of some, but encouraging one another, and all the more as you see the Day approaching.

Hebrews 10:24–25 NRSV

More people fail for lack of encouragement than for any other reason.

Anon.

Encouragement is oxygen to the soul.

George M. Adams

One of the highest of human duties is the duty of encouragement. There is a regulation of the Royal Navy which says: "No officer shall speak discouragingly to another officer in the discharge of his duties."

William Barclay

Correction does much, but encouragement does more. Encouragement after censure is as the sun after a shower.

Johann Wolfgang von Goethe

There is a point with me in matters of any size when I must absolutely have encouragement as much as crops rain: afterwards I am independent.

Gerard Manley Hopkins

Take courage. We walk in the wilderness today and in the Promised Land tomorrow.

Dwight Lyman (D.L.) Moody

If you wish to be disappointed, look to others. If you wish to be downhearted, look to yourself. If you wish to be encouraged, look upon Jesus Christ.

Erich Sauer

I have yet to find the man, however exalted his station, who did not do better work and put forth greater effort under a spirit of approval than under a spirit of criticism.

Charles M. Schwab

Endurance

See also Patience; Perseverance

You will be hated by all because of my name. But the one who endures to the end will be saved.

Matthew 10:22 NRSV

We know that suffering is a source of endurance, endurance of approval, and approval of hope.

Romans 5:3–4 REB

Let us keep our eyes fixed on Jesus, who leads us in our faith and brings it to perfection: for the sake of the joy which lay ahead of him, he endured the cross.

Hebrews 12:2 NJB

What we obtain too easy, we value too lightly; it is the cost that gives value.

Anon.

Patient endurance is the perfection of charity.

St. Ambrose

Endurance is not just the ability to bear a hard thing, but to turn it into glory.

William Barclay

There remain times when one can only endure. One lives on, one doesn't die, and the only thing that one can do, is to fill one's mind and time as far as possible with the concerns of other people. It doesn't bring immediate peace, but it brings the dawn nearer.

Arthur Christopher Benson

Nothing great was ever done without much enduring.

St. Catherine of Siena

The root of all steadfastness is in consecration to God.

Alexander Maclaren

We conquer—not in any brilliant fashion—we conquer by continuing.

George Matheson

Bear in mind, if you are going to amount to anything, that your success does not depend on the brilliancy and the impetuosity with which you take hold, but upon the everlasting and sanctified bull-doggedness with which you hang on after you have taken hold.

A.B. Meldrum

Enemies

See also Hatred; Oppression

When we please the Lord, even our enemies make friends with us.

Proverbs 16:7 CEV

You have heard that it was said, "You shall love your neighbor and hate your enemy." But I say to you, Love your enemies and pray for those who persecute you.

Matthew 5:43–44 NRSV

For if, when we were enemies, we were reconciled to God by the death of his Son, much more, being reconciled, we shall be saved by his life.

Romans 5:10 KJV

There is only one true way of conquering enemies in this warring world, and that is to make your enemy your friend.

Fr. Andrew

You never so touch the ocean of God's love as when you forgive and love your enemies.

Corrie ten Boom

If is infinitely better to have the whole world for our enemies and God for our friend, than to have the whole world for our friends and God for our enemy.

John Brown

The Bible tells us to love our neighbors, and also to love our enemies; probably because they are generally the same people.

Gilbert Keith (G.K.) Chesterton

Love your enemies, for they tell you your faults.

Benjamin Franklin

Do good to your friend to keep him, to your enemy to gain him.

Benjamin Franklin

Nature teaches us to love our friends, but religion our enemies.

Thomas Fuller

I owe much to my friends, but all things considered, it strikes me that I owe even more to my enemies. The real person springs to life under a sting, even better than under a caress.

André Gide

Could we read the secret history of our enemies, we should find in each man's life, sorrow and suffering enough to disarm all hostility.

Henry Wadsworth Longfellow

We should conduct ourselves toward our enemy as if he were one day to be our friend.

John Henry Newman

Enemies are not those who hate us, but rather those whom we hate.

Dagobert Runes

Environment

See also Creation; Stewardship

And God said, Let us make man in our image, after our likeness: and let them have dominion over the fish of the sea, and over the fowl of the air, and over the cattle, and over all the earth, and over every creeping thing that creepeth upon the earth.

Genesis 1:26 KJV

For six years you shall sow your land and gather in its yield; but the seventh year you shall let it rest and lie fallow, so that the poor of your people may eat; and what they leave the wild animals may eat.

Exodus 23:10–11 NRSV

When you are attacking a town, don't chop down its fruit trees, not even if you have had the town surrounded for a long time. Fruit trees aren't your enemies, and they produce fruit that you can eat, so don't cut them down.

Deuteronomy 20:19 CEV

The world and all that is in it belong to the Lord; the earth and all who live on it are his.

Psalm 24:1 GNB

Do not dishonor to the earth lest you dishonor the spirit of man.

Henry Benson

Earth with her thousand voices praises God.

Samuel Taylor Coleridge

All of creation God gives to human–kind to use. If this privilege is misused, God's justice permits creation to punish humanity.

St. Hildegard of Bingen

Man thinks of himself as a creator instead of a user, and this delusion is robbing him, not only of his natural heritage, but perhaps of his future.

Helen Hoover

We abuse land because we regard it as a commodity belonging to us. When we see land as a community to which we belong we may begin to use it with love and respect.

Aldo Leopold

The ground is holy, being even as it came from the Creator. Keep it, guard it, care for it, for it keeps men, guards men, cares for men. Destroy it and man is destroyed.

Alan Stewart Paton

Envy

See also Jealousy

Fret not thyself because of the ungodly; neither be thou envious against the evildoers.

Psalm 37:1 BCP

A sound heart is the life of the flesh: but envy the rottenness of the bones.

Proverbs 14:30 KJV

For he [Pilate] knew it was out of envy that they had handed Jesus over to him.

Matthew 27:18 NIV

Now the works of the flesh are manifest . . . envyings, murders, drunkenness.

Galatians 5:19, 21 KJV

Envy and hatred try to pierce our neighbor with a sword. But the blade cannot reach him unless it first pass through our own body.

St. Augustine of Hippo

Envy is a denial of providence.

Stephen Charnock

If envy was not such a tearing thing to feel it would be the most comic of sins. It is usually, if not always, based on a complete mis-understanding of another person's situation.

Monica Furlong

Envy takes the joy, happiness, and content-ment out of living.

William Franklin (Billy) Graham

Too many Christians envy the sinners their pleasure and the saints their joy, because they don't have either one.

Martin Luther

Envy of another man's calling can work havoc in our own.

Watchman Nee

Envy is sin, and it punisheth itself like gluttony; for it fretteth the heart, shorteneth the life, and eateth the flesh.

Henry Smith

A little grit in the eye destroyeth the sight of the very Heavens; and a little Malice or Envy, a World of Joy.

Thomas Traherne

Envy comes from people's ignorance of, or lack of belief in, their own gifts.

Jean Vanier

Equality, *see* Justice

Eternity

You have always been God—long before the birth of the mountains, even before you created the earth and the world. At your command we die and turn back to dust, but a thousand years mean nothing to you! They are merely a day gone by or a few hours in the night.

Psalm 90:2–4 CEV

Your throne is set firm from of old, from all eternity you exist.

Psalm 93:2 NJB

He has made everything beautiful in its time. He has also set eternity in the hearts of men, yet they cannot fathom what God has done from beginning to end.

Ecclesiastes 3:11 NIV

For God so loved the world, that he gave his only begotten Son, that whosoever believeth in him should not perish, but have everlasting life.

John 3:16 KJV

Then said Jesus unto the twelve, Will ye also go away? Then Simon Peter answered him, Lord, to whom shall we go? Thou hast the words of eternal life.

John 6:67–68 KJV

This is eternal life: to know you the only true God, and Jesus Christ whom you have sent.

John 17:3 REB

For the wages of sin is death, but the free gift of God is eternal life in Christ Jesus our Lord.

Romans 6:23 NRSV

Jesus Christ the same yesterday, and to day, and for ever.

Hebrews 13:8 KJV

Those who are born drive out those who preceded them. But there, in the hereafter, we shall all live on together. There will be no successors there, for neither will there be departures.

St. Augustine of Hippo

The sole purpose of life in time is to gain merit for life in eternity.

St. Augustine of Hippo

I thank thee, O Lord, that thou hast so set eternity within my heart that no earthly thing can ever satisfy me wholly.

John Baillie

The only way to get out values right is to see, not the beginning, but the end of the way, to see things, not in the light of time, but in the light of eternity.

William Barclay

To see a World in a grain of sand, / And a Heaven in a wild flower, / Hold Infinity in the palm of your hand, / And Eternity in an hour.

William Blake

As it was in the beginning, is now and ever shall be: world without end. Amen.

Book of Common Prayer

The created world is but a small parenthesis in eternity.

Sir Thomas Browne

He who has no vision of eternity will never get a true hold of time.

Thomas Carlyle

Eternity is not something that begins after you are dead. It is going on all the time. We are in it now.

Charlotte Gilman

Those who hope for no other life are dead even for this.

Johann Wolfgang von Goethe

In the presence of eternity the mountains are as transient as the clouds.

Robert Green Ingersoll

It is eternity now. I am in the midst of it. It is about me in the sunshine; I am in it, as the butterfly in the light-laden air. Nothing has to come, it is now. Now is eternity, now is immortal life.

Richard Jeffries

For a small living, men run a great way; for eternal life, many will scarce move a single foot from the ground.

Thomas à Kempis

The seed dies into a new life, and so does man.

George MacDonald

Some day you will read in the papers that D.L. Moody, of East Northfield, is dead. Don't you believe a word of it! At that moment I shall be more alive than I am now.

Dwight Lyman (D.L.) Moody

Learn to hold loosely all that is not eternal.

Agnes Maud Royden

God has given to man a short time here upon earth, and yet upon this short time eternity depends.

Jeremy Taylor

The life of faith does not earn eternal life; it is eternal life. And Christ is its vehicle.

William Temple

He who provides for this life, but takes no care for eternity, is wise for a moment, but a fool forever.

John Tillotson

Eternity to the godly is a day that has no sunset; eternity to the wicked is a night that has no sunrise.

Thomas Watson

Eucharist

See also Church; Jesus Christ, Death of

As they were eating, Jesus took bread, and blessed it, and broke it, and gave it to the disciples, and said, Take, eat; this is my body. And he took the cup, and gave thanks, and gave it to them, saying, Drink ye all of it; For this is my blood of the new testament, which is shed for many for the remission of sins.

Matthew 26:26–28 KJV

When we drink from the cup that we ask God to bless, isn't that sharing in the blood of Christ? When we eat the bread that we break, isn't that sharing in the body of Christ? By sharing in the same loaf of bread, we become one body, even though there are many of us.

1 Corinthians 10:16–17 CEV

For I received from the Lord what I also handed on to you, that the Lord Jesus on the night when he was betrayed took a loaf of bread, and when he had given thanks, he broke it and said, "This is my body that is for you. Do this in remembrance of me." In the same way he took the cup also, after supper, saying, "This cup is the new covenant in my blood. Do this, as often as you drink it, in remembrance of me." For as often as you eat this bread and drink the cup, you proclaim the Lord's death until he comes.

1 Corinthians 11:23–26 NRSV

We eat the Body of Christ that we may be able to be partakers of eternal life.

St. Ambrose

Therefore you hear that as often as sacrifice is offered, the Lord's death, the Lord's resurrection, the Lord's ascension and the remission of sins is signified, and will you not take the Bread of Life daily? He who has a wound needs medicine. The wound is that we are under sin; the medicine is the heavenly and venerable Sacrament.

St. Ambrose

When it comes to the consecration of this venerable sacrament, the priest no longer uses his own language, but he uses the language of Christ. Therefore, the word of Christ consecrates this sacrament.

St. Ambrose

Christ bore himself in his hands when he said, "This is my Body."

St. Augustine of Hippo

Here, O my Lord, I see thee face to face; / Here would I touch and handle things unseen, / Here grasp with firmer hand th' eternal grace, / And all my weariness upon thee lean.

Horatius Bonar

An outward and visible sign of an inward and spiritual grace given unto us.

Book of Common Prayer

The Blood of our Lord Jesus Christ, which was shed for thee, preserve thy body and soul unto everlasting life: Drink this in remembrance that Christ's Blood was shed for thee, and be thankful.

Book of Common Prayer

The Body of our Lord Jesus Christ, which was given for thee, preserve thy body and soul unto everlasting life: Take and eat this in remembrance that Christ died for thee, and feed on him in thy heart by faith with thanksgiving.

Book of Common Prayer

Draw near with faith.

Book of Common Prayer

The Eucharist must invade my life. My life must become, as a result of the sacrament, an unlimited and endless contact with you— that life which seemed, a few moments ago, like a baptism with you in the waters of the world, now reveals itself to me as a communion with you through the world. It is the sacrament of life.

Pierre Teilhard de Chardin

The appropriateness of the name "Eucharist" rests upon the giving of thanks by Jesus at the Last Supper and upon the character of the rite itself which is the supreme act of Christian thanksgiving.

J.G. Davies

Always seek communion. It is the most precious thing men possess. In this respect, the symbol of the religious is indeed full of majesty. Where there is communion there is something that is more than human, there is surely something divine.

Georges Duhamel

The body you receive in the sacrament accomplished its purpose by nailing to a tree. You are to become this body, you are to be nailed . . . the nails that hold you are God's commandments.

Austin Farrer

Love is that liquor sweet and most divine, / Which my God feels as blood; but I as wine.

George Herbert

I am—we are all—the Body of Christ. Nourished by God, we must bear God into the world and give God away with ourselves.

Nancy Mairs

The heart preparing for communion should be as a crystal vial filled with clear water in which the least mote of uncleanliness will be seen.

Elizabeth Ann Bayley Seton

The great eucharistic prayer is a proclamation of the fundamental fact: Christ is dead, Christ is risen.

Jean-François Six

Evangelism

See also Church, Mission and Ministry of; Witness

When the Holy Spirit comes upon you, you will be filled with power, and you will be witnesses for me in Jerusalem, in all Judea and Samaria, and to the ends of the earth.

Acts 1:8 GNB

Then Philip began to speak, and starting with this scripture, he proclaimed to him the good news about Jesus.

Acts 8:35 NRSV

To the weak became I as weak, that I might gain the weak: I am made all things to all men, that I might by all means save some.

1 Corinthians 9:22 KJV

And he gave some, apostles; and some, prophets; and some, evangelists . . . For the perfecting of the saints, for the work of the ministry, for the edifying of the body of Christ.

Ephesians 4:11–12 KJV

You must stay calm and be willing to suffer. You must work hard to tell the good news and to do your job well.

2 Timothy 4:5 CEV

The Christian is called upon to be the partner of God in the work of the conversion of men.

William Barclay

Some like to live within the sound of church or chapel bell; / I'd rather run a rescue shop within a yard of hell.

William Booth

Go for souls, and go for the worst.

William Booth

God is not saving the world; it is done. Our business is to get men and women to realize it.

Oswald Chambers

Evangelism is truth demanding a verdict.

Lionel Fletcher

The way from God to a human heart is through a human heart.

Samuel Dickey (S.D.) Gordon

God will hold us responsible as to how well we fulfil our responsibilities to this age and take advantage of our opportunities.

William Franklin (Billy) Graham

Evangelism never seemed to be an "issue" in the New Testament. That is to say, one does not find the apostles urging, exhorting, scolding, planning and organizing for evangelistic programmes . . . evangelism happened! Issuing effortlessly from the community of believers as light from the sun, it was automatic, spontaneous, continuous, contagious.

Richard Christian Halverson

People matter so much to God that every one warrants an all-out search.

Bill Hybels

The truth is that we do not truly understand the Gospel if we spend all our time preaching it to Christians. . . . The Gospel is communication of news to those who do not know it, and we only really understand it as we are involved in so communicating it.

James Edward Lesslie Newbigin

It is as absurd to argue men, as to torture them, into believing.

John Henry Newman

Evangelism is one beggar telling another beggar where to get bread.

Daniel Thambirajah (D.T.) Niles

To earn the right to speak words of love, we must first willingly demonstrate deeds of love with the hurting people of our cities.

Steve Sjogren

In the last resort, we engage in evangelism today not because we want to, or because we choose to, or because we like to, but because we have been told to.

John R.W. Stott

Ultimately, evangelism is not a technique. It is the Lord of the Church who reserves to Himself His sovereign right to add to His Church.

John R.W. Stott

There is a net of love by which you can catch souls.

Mother Teresa

My gracious Master and my God, / Assist me to proclaim, / To spread through all the earth abroad, / The honors of Thy name.

Charles Wesley

I look upon all the world as my parish, this far I mean, that, in whatever part of it I am, I judge it meet, right and my bounden duty to declare unto all that are willing to hear, the glad tidings of salvation.

John Wesley

When social action is mistaken for evangelism the Church has ceased to manufacture its own blood cells and is dying of leukemia.

Sherwood Eliot Wirt

Evangelism is not primarily a matter of method. It is a channel of the Word.

Arthur Skevington Wood

Evangelism is not a human enterprise; it is a divine operation.

Arthur Skevington Wood

It is impossible to save a life from burning and avoid the heat of the fire.

Mary S. Wood

Eve, *see* Adam and Eve

Evil

See also Good; Virtues and Vices

There is no peace, saith the Lord, unto the wicked.

Isaiah 48:22 KJV

Your eyes are too pure to behold evil, and you cannot look on wrongdoing.

Habakkuk 1:13 NRSV

Out of your heart come evil thoughts, vulgar deeds, stealing, murder.

Mark 7:21 CEV

See that none render evil for evil unto any man; but ever follow that which is good, both among yourselves, and to all men.

1 Thessalonians 5:15 KJV

The love of money is a source of all kinds of evil. Some have been so eager to have it that they have wandered away from the faith and have broken their hearts with many sorrows.

1 Timothy 6:10 GNB

God judged it better to bring good out of evil than to suffer no evil to exist.

St. Augustine of Hippo

A truth that's told with bad intent / Beats all the lies you can invent.

William Blake

The deceits of the world, the flesh, and the devil.

Book of Common Prayer

For evil to triumph, it is only necessary for good men to do nothing.

Edmund Burke

It is tempting to deny the existence of evil since denying it obviates the need to fight it.

Alexis Carrel

Evil is a fact, not to be explained away, but to be accepted; and accepted, not to be endured, but to be conquered. It is a challenge neither to our reason nor to our patience, but to our courage.

John Haynes Holmes

Science may have found a cure for most evils: but it has found no remedy for the worst of them all—the apathy of human beings.

Helen Adams Keller

He who passively accepts evil is as much involved in it as he who helps to perpetuate it. He who accepts evil without protesting against it is really co-operating with it.

Martin Luther King Jr.

Nothing can withstand evil except the power of love.

Una Kroll

People do not need Satan to recruit them to evil. They are quite capable of recruiting themselves.

M. Scott Peck

We have to carry on the struggle against the evil that is in mankind, not by judging others, but by judging ourselves. Struggle with oneself and veracity toward oneself are the means by which we influence others.

Albert Schweitzer

God is so powerful that he can direct any evil to a good end.

St. Thomas Aquinas

Exile

The Lord will let you and your king be taken captive to a country that you and your ancestors have never even heard of, and there you will have to worship idols of wood and stone.

Deuteronomy 28:36 CEV

If you return to me and observe my commandments and fulfill them, I shall gather those of you who have been scattered to the far corners of the world and bring you to the place I have chosen as a dwelling for my name.

Nehemiah 1:9 REB

For God listens to the poor, he has never scorned his captive people.

Psalm 69:33 NJB

By the rivers of Babylon, there we sat down, yea, we wept, when we remembered Zion.

Psalm 137:1 KJV

The House of Israel were exiled for their guilt; because they were unfaithful to me, I hid my face from them and put them into the clutches of their enemies.

Ezekiel 39:23 NJB

Others have their families, but to a solitary and an exile his friends are everything.

Willa Sibert Cather

Shall I tell you what supported me through all these years of exile, among a people whose language I could not understand and whose attitude toward me was always uncertain and often hostile? It was this: "Lo, I am with you always even unto the end of the world."

David Livingstone

I had heard of the underground prisons of Beirut: "the Lebanese Gulag" as Terry Anderson described them. There were stories of prisoners being incarcerated for years in such places. I sat down again and began to prepare myself for an ordeal. First, I would strengthen my will by fasting; I would refuse all food for at least a week. Secondly, I would make three resolutions to support me through whatever was to come: no regrets, no false sentimentality, no self-pity. Then I did what generations of prisoners have done before me. I stood up and, bending my head, I began to walk round and round and round and round. . . .

Terry Waite

Experience

See also Longing for God

With the ancient is wisdom; and in length of days understanding.

Job 12:12 KJV

The Lord says, "Wise men should not boast of their wisdom, nor strong men of their strength, nor rich men of their wealth. If anyone wants to boast, he should boast that he knows and understands me, because my love is constant, and I do what is just and right. These are the things that please me."

Jeremiah 9:23–24 GNB

The sheep know their shepherd's voice. He calls each of them by name and leads them out. When he has led out all of his sheep, he walks in front of them, and they follow, because they know his voice.

John 10:3–4 CEV

By faith Enoch was taken so that he did not experience death.

Hebrews 11:5 NRSV

All experience is an arch to build upon.

Henry Brooks Adams

Experience is the best of schoolmasters, only the school fees are heavy.

Thomas Carlyle

Emotion may vary in religious experience. Some people are stoical and others are demonstrative, but the feeling will be there. There is going to be a tug at the heart.

William Franklin (Billy) Graham

Never, for the sake of peace and quiet, deny your own experience or convictions.

Dag Hammarskjöld

All experience must be subservient to the discipline of Scripture.

Erroll Hulse

Truth divorced from experience will always dwell in doubt.

Henry Krause

It is the heart which experiences God and not the reason.

Blaise Pascal

Hold sacred every experience.

Frances J. Roberts

The long experience of the Church is more likely to lead to correct answers than is the experience of the lone individual.

(David) Elton Trueblood

Present we know Thou art, / But O Thyself reveal! / Now, Lord, let every pounding heart / Thy mighty comfort feel.

Charles Wesley

Exploitation, *see* Bondage; Oppression

Failure

See also Success; Weakness

My flesh and my heart may fail, but God is the strength of my heart and my portion forever.

Psalm 73:26 NRSV

I do not understand my own behavior; I do not act as I mean to, but I do things that I hate. While I am acting as I do not want to, I still acknowledge the Law as good, so it is not myself acting, but the sin which lives in me. And really, I know of nothing good living in me—in my natural self, that is—for though the will to do what is good is in me, the power to do it is not; the good thing I want to do, I never do; the evil thing which I do not want—that is what I do.

Romans 7:15–19 NJB

Examine yourselves: are you living the life of faith? Put yourselves to the test. Surely you recognize that Jesus Christ is among you? If not, you have failed the test. I hope you will come to see that we have not failed. Our prayer to God is that you may do no wrong, not that we should win approval; we want you to do what is right, even if we should seem failures.

2 Corinthians 13:5–7 REB

The Christian message is for those who have done their best and failed!

Anon.

Beware of succumbing to failure as inevitable; make it the stepping-stone to success.

Oswald Chambers

With the right attitude, all the problems in the world will not make you a failure. With the wrong mental attitude, all the help in the world will not make you a success.

Warren Deaton

He who is fretted by his own failings will not correct them; all profitable correction comes from a calm, peaceful mind.

St. Francis de Sales

One of the reasons mature people stop learning is that they become less and less willing to risk failure.

John (William) Gardner

A failure is not someone who has tried and failed; it is someone who has given up trying and resigned himself to failure; it is not a condition, but an attitude.

Sydney J. Harris

The perfect Christian is the one who, having a sense of his own failure, is minded to press toward the mark.

Ernest F. Kevan

It's the nature of God to make something out of nothing; therefore, when anyone is nothing, God may yet make something of him.

Martin Luther

Often we assume that God is unable to work in spite of our weakness, mistakes, and sins. We forget that God is a specialist; he is well able to work our failures into his plans.

Erwin W. Lutzer

Far better it is to dare mighty things, to win glorious triumphs, even though checkered by failure, than to take rank with those poor spirits who neither enjoy much nor suffer much because they live in the gray twilight that knows not victory nor defeat.

Theodore Roosevelt

I'd rather attempt to do something great and fail than attempt to do nothing and succeed.

Robert Harold Schuller

More people would learn from their mistakes if they weren't so busy denying them.

Harold J. Smith

Great accomplishments are often attempted but only occasionally reached. Those who reach them are usually those who missed many times before. Failures are only temporary tests to prepare us for permanent triumphs.

Charles R. Swindoll

Failure is as much a part of life as success is and by no means something in front of which one sits down and howls as though it is a scandal and a shame.

J. Neville Ward

The greatest failure is the failure to try.

William Arthur Ward

God is not defeated by human failure.

William J.C. White

Faith

See also Belief; Doubt; Trust

The just shall live by his faith.

Habakkuk 2:4 KJV

Those [signs] written here have been recorded in order that you may believe that Jesus is the Christ, the Son of God, and that through this faith you may have life by his name.

John 20:31 REB

Now that we have been put right with God through faith, we have peace with God through our Lord Jesus Christ.

Romans 5:1 GNB

For we walk by faith, not by sight.

2 Corinthians 5:7 KJV

Now faith is the assurance of things hoped for, the conviction of things not seen.

Hebrews 11:1 NRSV

The first mark of the gift of faith is the love of truth.

Fr. Andrew

Great faith is not the faith that walks always in the light and knows no darkness, but the faith that perseveres in spite of God's seeming silences, and that faith will most certainly and surely get its reward.

Fr. Andrew

To choose what is difficult all one's days as if it were easy, that is faith.

W.H. Auden

Do not rejoice in earthly reality, rejoice in Christ, rejoice in his word, rejoice in his law. . . . There will be peace and tranquillity in the Christian heart; but only as long as our faith is watchful; if, however, our faith sleeps, we are in danger.

St. Augustine of Hippo

Faith is to believe what you do not yet see: the reward for this faith is to see what you believe.

St. Augustine of Hippo

I am one of those who would rather sink with faith than swim without it.

Stanley Baldwin

Faith is a gift which can be given or withdrawn; it is something infused into us, not produced by us.

Robert Hugh Benson

You do right when you offer faith to God: you do right when you offer works. But if you separate the two, then you do wrong. For faith without works is dead; and lack of charity in action murders faith, just as Cain murdered Abel, so that God cannot respect your offering.

St. Bernard of Clairvaux

The act of faith is more than a bare statement of belief, it is a turning to the face of the living God.

Christopher Bryant

You can do very little with faith but you can do nothing without it.

Nicholas Murray Butler

Fear imprisons, faith liberates; fear paralyzes, faith empowers, fear disheartens, faith encourages; fear sickens, faith heals; fear makes useless, faith makes serviceable—and, most of all, fear puts hopelessness at the heart of life, while faith rejoices in its God.

Harry Emerson Fosdick

It is cynicism and fear that freeze life; it is faith that thaws it out, releases it, sets it free.

Harry Emerson Fosdick

One of the mysteries of faith is that, although it constitutes our deepest response to God for what he has done for us in Jesus Christ, yet it is, at the same time, a gift from him when we lift our eyes beyond ourselves. He meets us with faith when we want to have faith.

John Gunstone

Faith tells us of things we have never seen, and cannot come to know by our natural senses.

St. John of the Cross

Faith is required of thee, and a sincere life, not loftiness of intellect, nor deepness in the mysteries of God.

Thomas à Kempis

I do not want merely to possess faith; I want a faith that possesses me.

Charles Kingsley

Faith, like light, should always be simple, and unbending; whilst love, like warmth, should beam forth on every side and bend to every necessity of our brethren.

Martin Luther

Believing in God means getting down on your knees.

Martin Luther

Faith is the sight of the inward eye.

Alexander Maclaren

A man cannot have faith without asking, neither can he ask it without faith.

Edward Marbury

Ultimately, faith is the only key to the universe. The final meaning of human existence, and the answers to the questions on which all our happiness depends cannot be found in any other way.

Thomas Merton

Faith is illuminative, not operative; it does not force obedience, though it increases responsibility; it heightens guilt, it does not prevent sin; the will is the source of action.

John Henry Newman

Belief is a truth held in the mind. Faith is a fire in the heart.

Joseph Fort Newton

Faith is what you have in the absence of knowledge.

Mary Flannery O'Connor

Very often, when people first turn toward God and realize that God loves them and that everything about them matters to Him, a wave of joyful emotion overwhelms them. But actual faith is mostly the realization that, even though we don't in the least deserve it, God believes in us and finds us loveable. This is astonishing.

Philip Pare

For me the greatest danger for faith continues to be the divorce between faith and life with its commitments.

Juan Luis Segundo

Faith is nothing at all tangible. It is simply believing God; and, like sight, it is nothing apart from its object. You might as well shut your eyes and look inside to see whether you have sight, as to look inside and discover if you have faith.

Hannah Whitall Smith

Onward is faith—and leave the rest to Heaven.

Robert Southey

Your faith is what you believe, not what you know.

John Lancaster Spalding

Faith is reason at rest in God.

Charles Haddon Spurgeon

As the flower is before the fruit, so is faith before good works.

Richard Whately

Faith is the root of works. A root that produces nothing is dead.

Thomas Wilson

Faithfulness

See also God, Faithfulness of; Loyalty

Know therefore that the Lord thy God, he is God, the faithful God, which keepeth covenant and mercy with them that love him and keep his commandments.

Deuteronomy 7:9 KJV

"Well done, you good and faithful servant!" said his master. "You have been faithful in managing small amounts, so I will put you in charge of large amounts. Come on in and share my happiness!"

Matthew 25:21 GNB

He that is faithful in that which is least is faithful also in much.

Luke 16:10 KJV

The fruit of the Spirit is . . . faithfulness.

Galatians 5:22 NIV

If we are faithless, he remains faithful—for he cannot deny himself.

2 Timothy 2:13 NRSV

Our prayers will be most like the prayer of Christ if we do not ask God to show us what is going to be, or to make any particular thing happen, but only pray that we may be faithful in whatever happens.

Fr. Andrew

Watch where Jesus went. The one dominant note in his life was to do his Father's will. His is not the way of wisdom or of success, but the way of faithfulness.

Oswald Chambers

It is, however, only by fidelity in little things that a true and constant love of God can be distinguished from a passing fervor of spirit.

François de la Mothe Fénelon

God requires a faithful fulfilment of the merest trifle given us to do, rather than the most ardent aspiration to things to which we are not called.

St. Francis de Sales

He does most in God's great world who does his best in his own little world.

Thomas Jefferson

Faithfulness in little things is a big thing.

St. John Chrysostom

In God's house we must try to accept any job: cook or kitchen boy, waiter, stable boy, baker. If it pleases the king to call us into his private council, then we must go there, but without being too excited, for we know that our rewards depend not on the job itself but on the faithfulness with which we serve him.

John Paul I

He who is faithful over a few things is a lord of cities. It does not matter whether you preach in Westminster Abbey, or teach a ragged class, so you be faithful. The faithfulness is all.

George MacDonald

It is better to be faithful than famous.

Theodore Roosevelt

Fall

See also Disobedience; Falling Away; Sin; Sinful Nature

Now the serpent was more subtle than any beast of the field which the Lord God had made. And he said unto the woman, Yea, hath God said, Ye shall not eat of every tree of the garden? . . . And the serpent said unto the woman, Ye shall not surely die. . . . And when the woman saw that the tree was good for food, and that it was pleasant to the eyes, and a tree to be desired to make one wise, she took of the fruit thereof, and did eat, and gave also unto her husband with her; and he did eat. And the eyes of them both were opened, and they knew that they were naked; and they sewed fig leaves together and made themselves aprons . . . and Adam and his wife hid themselves from the presence of the Lord God amongst the trees of the garden.

Genesis 3:1, 4, 6–8 KJV

Adam sinned, and that sin brought death into the world. Now everyone has sinned, and so everyone must die.

Romans 5:12 CEV

For since death came through a human being, the resurrection of the dead has also come through a human being; for as all die in Adam, so all will be made alive in Christ.

1 Corinthians 15:21–22 NRSV

At the Fall, man's natural gifts were corrupted through sin, while his supernatural gifts were entirely lost.

St. Augustine of Hippo

The desire of power in excess caused the angels to fall; the desire of knowledge in excess caused man to fall.

Francis Bacon

The fruit of the tree of knowledge always drives man from some paradise or other.

William Ralph Inge

Of man's first disobedience, and the fruit, / Of that forbidden tree, whose mortal taste / Brought death into the world, and all our woe.

John Milton

We are not part of a nice neat creation, set in motion by a loving God; we are part of a mutinous world where rebellion against God is the order of the day.

Samuel Moor Shoemaker

Falling Away

The one who received the seed that fell on rocky places is the man who hears the word and at once receives it with joy. But since he has no root, he lasts only a short time. When trouble or persecution comes because of the word, he quickly falls away.

Matthew 13:20–21 NIV

For it is impossible for those who were once enlightened, and have tasted of the heavenly gift, and were made partakers of the Holy Ghost, And have tasted the good word of God, and the powers of the world to come, If they shall fall away, to renew them again unto repentance; seeing they crucify to themselves the Son of God afresh, and put him to an open shame.

Hebrews 6:4–6 KJV

For if we willfully persist in sin after having received the knowledge of the truth, there no longer remains a sacrifice for sins.

Hebrews 10:26 NRSV

The Spirit says clearly that some people will abandon the faith in later times; they will obey lying spirits and follow the teachings of demons.

1 Timothy 4:1 GNB

If thou wilt fly from God, the devil will lend thee both spurs and a horse.

Thomas Adams

Apostasy is a perversion to evil after a seeming conversion from it.

Timothy Cruso

None sink so far into hell as those that come nearest heaven, because they fall from the greatest height.

William Gurnall

The best way never to fall is ever to fear.

William Jenkyn

To forsake Christ for the world, is to leave a treasure for a trifle . . . eternity for a moment, reality for a shadow.

William Jenkyn

The backslider is a man who, because of his relationship to God, can never really enjoy anything else.

David Martyn Lloyd-Jones

Apostasy must be called what it is—spiritual adultery.

Francis August Schaeffer

If I were called upon to identify the principal trait of the entire twentieth century, I would be unable to find anything more precise than to repeat once again, "Men have forgotten God."

Alexander Solzhenitsyn

Falsehood

See also Hypocrisy; Truth

Neither shalt thou bear false witness against thy neighbor.

Deuteronomy 5:20 KJV

I hate and abhor falsehood, but I love your law.

Psalm 119:163 NRSV

So then, putting away falsehood, let all of us speak the truth to our neighbors, for we are members of one another.

Ephesians 4:25 NRSV

To profess to love God while leading an unholy life is the worst of falsehoods.

St. Augustine of Hippo

It is a sovereign remedy against lying to unsay the lie on the spot.

St. Francis de Sales

If I speak what is false, I must answer for it; if truth, it will answer for me.

Thomas Fuller

He who permits himself to tell a lie once finds it much easier to do it a second and a third time till at length it becomes habitual.

Thomas Jefferson

The cruelest lies are often told in silence.

Robert Louis Stevenson

That a lie which is all a lie may be met and fought with outright. / But a lie which is part a truth is a harder matter to fight.

Alfred, Lord Tennyson

As for conforming outwardly, and living your own life inwardly, I do not think much of that.

Henry David Thoreau

Stand against that which is wrong, show why it is wrong, overcome it and plant truth in its place.

Aiden Wilson (A.W.) Tozer

Falsehoods not only disagree with truths, but usually quarrel among themselves.

Daniel Webster

Peace is the first casualty of untruthfulness.

Rowan Williams

Families

See also Children; Parents

Grandchildren are the crown of old age, and parents are the pride of their children.

Proverbs 17:6 REB

So then, whenever we have an opportunity, let us work for the good of all, and especially for those of the family of faith.

Galatians 6:10 NRSV

People who don't take care of their relatives, and especially their own families, have given up their faith.

1 Timothy 5:8 CEV

The religion of a child depends on what its mother and father are, and not on what they say.

Henri-Frédéric Amiel

The union of the family lies in love; and love is the only reconciliation of authority and liberty.

Robert Hugh Benson

Fathers and mothers, if you have children, they must come first. Your success as a family, our success as a society, depends not on what happens at the White House, but on what happens inside your house.

Barbara Bush

The family is the most basic unit of government. As the first community to which a person is attached and the first authority under which a person learns to live, the family establishes society's most basic values.

Charles W. Colson

Each of us will have our own different ways of expressing love and care for the family. But unless that is a high priority, we will find that we may gain the whole world and lose our own children.

Michael Green

Every effort to make society sensitive to the importance of the family is a great service to humanity.

John Paul II

I believe the family was established long before the church, and my duty is to my family first. I am not to neglect my family.

Dwight Lyman (D.L.) Moody

If Christ is in your house your neighbors will soon know it.

Dwight Lyman (D.L.) Moody

The best test of a sanctified man is to ask his family about him.

Charles Thomas (C.T.) Studd

A family is a place where principles are hammered and honed on the anvil of everyday living.

Charles R. Swindoll

A family that prays together stays together.

Mother Teresa

Loving relationships are a family's best protection against the challenges of the world.

Bernie Wiebe

Fanaticism

See also Zeal

It is not good to have zeal without knowledge, nor to be in too great a hurry and so miss the way.

Proverbs 19:2 REB

Jews from Asia, who had seen him in the temple, stirred up the whole crowd. . . . Then all the city was aroused, and the people rushed together. They seized Paul and dragged him out of the temple. . . . When Paul came to the steps, the violence of the mob was so great that he had to be carried by the soldiers. The crowd that followed kept shouting, "Away with him!"

Acts 21:27, 30, 35–36 NRSV

In the matter of the Law, I was a Pharisee; as for religious fervor, I was a persecutor of the Church.

Philippians 3:5–6 NJB

It is part of the nature of fanaticism that it loses sight of the totality of evil and rushes like a bull at the red cloth instead of at the man who holds it.

Dietrich Bonhoeffer

A fanatic is one who can't change his mind and won't change the subject.

Sir Winston Churchill

History teaches us that no one feels so disgustingly certain of victory, or is so unteachably sure, and immune to reason, as the fanatic, and that no one is so absolutely certain of ultimate defeat.

Theodor Heacker

We often excuse our own want of [involvement] by giving the name of fanaticism to the more ardent zeal of others.

Henry Wadsworth Longfellow

By the time the average Christian gets his temperature up to normal, everybody thinks he's got a fever.

Watchman Nee

Even fanaticism is to be preferred to indiffer-

ence. I had sooner risk the dangers of a tornado of religious excitement than see the air grow stagnant with a dead formality.

Charles Haddon Spurgeon

A fanatic is a person who loves Jesus more than you do.

George Verwer

All fanaticism is a strategy to prevent doubt from becoming conscious.

H.A. Williams

Fasting

See also Self-Denial

Is not this the fast that I choose: to loose the bonds of injustice, to undo the thongs of the yoke, to let the oppressed go free, and to break every yoke? Is it not to share your bread with the hungry, and bring the homeless poor into your house; when you see the naked, to cover them, and not to hide yourself from your own kin?

Isaiah 58:6–7 NRSV

He fasted forty days and forty nights, and afterwards he was famished.

Matthew 4:2 NRSV

Moreover when ye fast, be not, as the hypocrites, of a sad countenance: for they disfigure their faces, that they may appear unto men to fast. Verily I say unto you, They have their reward. But thou, when thou fastest, anoint thine head, and wash thy face; That thou appear not unto men to fast, but unto thy Father which is in secret: and thy Father, which seeth in secret, shall reward thee openly.

Matthew 6:16–18 KJV

Your hunger will serve as a call to prayer. It

will remind you of your physical life, but your abstinence in the name of God will declare your avowed belief in the supremacy of the spiritual over the physical.

Anon.

He who fasteth and doeth no good, saveth his bread but loseth his soul.

Henry George Bohn

Since [fasting] is a holy exercise both for the humbling of men and for their confession of humility, why should we use it less than the ancients did?

John Calvin

What we gain from fasting does not compensate for what we lose in anger.

John Cassian

Lenten fasts make me feel better, stronger, and more active than ever.

Catherine of Genoa

Fasting alone accomplishes little except perhaps to cause us to eat more at the next meal. Prayer by itself is often limited or blocked in some way. But prayer and fasting together provide miracles.

Marjorie Cooney

Fasting is the voluntary denial of a normal function for the sake of intense spiritual activity.

Richard J. Foster

The best of all medicines are resting and fasting.

Benjamin Franklin

When the stomach is full it is easy to talk of fasting.

St. Jerome

By fasting, the body learns to obey the soul; by praying, the soul learns to command the body.

William Secker

Fasting is calculated to bring a note of urgency and importance into our praying, and to give force to our pleading in the court of heaven. The man who prays with fasting is giving heaven notice that he is truly in earnest.

Arthur Wallis

Fate, *see* Destiny

Fathers and Fatherhood

See also God, Personal Description of; Husbands and Wives; Mothers and Motherhood; Parents

A fool despiseth his father's instruction: but he that regardeth reproof is prudent.

Proverbs 15:5 KJV

Fathers, provoke not your children to wrath: but bring them up in the nurture and admonition of the Lord.

Ephesians 6:4 KJV

We can never afford to forget that we teach our children to call God Father, and the only conception of fatherhood that they can have is the conception which we give them. Human fatherhood should be molded and modeled on the pattern of the fatherhood of God.

William Barclay

Every parent is at some time the father of the unreturned prodigal with nothing to do but keep his house open to hope.

John Ciardi

There is something ultimate in a father's love, something that cannot fail, something to be believed against the whole world. We almost attribute practical omnipotence to our father in the days of our childhood.

Frederick William Faber

The most important thing a father can do for his children is to love their mother.

Theodore Martin Hesburgh

It is easier for a father to have children than for children to have a real father.

John XXIII

The best gift a father can give to his son is the gift of himself—his time. For material things mean little, if there is not someone to share them with.

Neil C. Strait

Fear

See also Courage; Reverence

The man answered, "I was naked, and when I heard you walking through the garden, I was frightened and hid!"

Genesis 3:10 CEV

Do not fear those who kill the body but cannot kill the soul; rather fear those who can destroy both soul and body in hell.

Matthew 10:28 NRSV

Do not be afraid, little flock, for your Father is pleased to give you the Kingdom.

Luke 12:32 GNB

For ye have not received the spirit of bondage again to fear; but ye have received the Spirit of adoption, whereby we cry, Abba, Father.

Romans 8:15 KJV

It is a fearful thing to fall into the hands of the living God.

Hebrews 10:31 KJV

In love there is no room for fear, but perfect loves drive out fear, because fear implies punishment and no one who is afraid has come to perfection in love.

1 John 4:18 NJB

All fear is bondage.

Anon.

Fear is never a good counselor and victory over fear is the first spiritual duty of man.

Nikolai Aleksandrovich Berdyaev

There is never a fear that has not a corresponding "Fear not."

Amy Wilson Carmichael

Fear imprisons, faith liberates; fear paralyzes, faith empowers, fear disheartens, faith encourages; fear sickens, faith heals; fear makes useless, faith makes serviceable—and, most of all, fear puts hopelessness at the heart of life, while faith rejoices in its God.

Harry Emerson Fosdick

The best answer to fear is to have a firm grasp of what it means to be accepted by God.

John Gunstone

The chains of love are stronger than the chains of fear.

William Gurnall

We fear men so much, because we fear God so little. One fear cures another. When man's terror scares you, turn your thoughts to the wrath of God.

William Gurnall

Men who fear God face life fearlessly. Men who do not fear God end up fearing everything.

Richard Christian Halverson

Courage faces fear and thereby masters it. Cowardice represses fear and is thereby mastered by it.

Martin Luther King Jr.

God incarnate is the end of fear; and the heart that realizes that he is in the midst . . . will be quiet in the midst of alarm.

Frederick Brotherton (F.B.) Meyer

Fear not that your life shall come to an end, but rather fear that it shall never have a beginning.

John Henry Newman

The cure for fear is faith.

Norman Vincent Peale

The fear of death is ingrafted in the common nature of all men, but faith works it out of Christians.

Vavasor Powell

Of all the passions, fear weakens judgment most.

Cardinal de Retz

Jesus! the Name that charms our fears, / That bids our sorrows cease; / 'Tis music in the sinner's ears, / 'Tis life, and health, and peace.

Charles Wesley

It is only the fear of God that can deliver us from the fear of man.

John Witherspoon

Fellowship

See also Church; Eucharist; Prayer; Union with God

They devoted themselves to the apostles' teaching and fellowship, to the breaking of bread and the prayers.

Acts 2:42 NRSV

All the Lord's followers often met together, and they shared everything they had.

Acts 2:44 CEV

May the grace of the Lord Jesus Christ, and the love of God, and the fellowship of the Holy Spirit be with you all.

2 Corinthians 13:14 NIV

We declare to you the eternal life which was with the Father and was made visible to us. It is this which we have seen and heard that we declare to you also, in order that you may share with us in a common life, that life which we share with the Father and his Son Jesus Christ.

1 John 1:2–3 REB

Individuals cannot cohere closely unless they sacrifice something of their individuality.

Robert Hugh Benson

We do weep with those who weep; we do not know enough of rejoicing with those who rejoice.

A. Neave Brayshaw

There is no brotherhood of man without the fatherhood of God.

Henry Martyn Field

Try as hard as you like, but in the end only the language of the heart can ever reach another heart, while mere words, as they slip from your tongue, don't get past your listener's ear.

St. Francis de Sales

If you really believe in the brotherhood of

man, and you want to come into its fold, you've got to let everyone else in too.

Oscar Hammerstein

To live in prayer together is to walk in love together.

Margaret Moore Jacobs

In that Mystical Body, thanks to the communion of saints, no good can be done, no virtue practiced by individual members, without its contributing something also to the salvation of all.

Pius XII

God calls us not to solitary sainthood but to fellowship in a company of committed men.

David Schuller

Satan watches for those vessels that sail without a convoy.

George Swinnock

The reality of our communion with Christ and in him with one another is the increase of love in our hearts.

William Temple

The union of men with God is the union of men with one another.

St. Thomas Aquinas

If thy heart be as my heart, give me thy hand.

John Wesley

Femininity, *see* God, Personal Description of; Women and Womanhood

Fidelity, *see* Faithfulness; Loyalty

Following Jesus, *see* Discipleship

Food and Drink

Every moving thing that lives shall be food for you; and just as I gave you the green plants, I give you everything.

Genesis 9:3 NRSV

You let the earth produce grass for cattle, plants for our food, wine to cheer us up, olive oil for our skin, and grain for our health.

Psalm 104:14–15 CEV

Look not thou upon the wine when it is red, when it giveth his color in the cup, when it moveth itself aright.

Proverbs 23:31 KJV

All of us should eat and drink and enjoy what we have worked for. It is God's gift.

Ecclesiastes 3:13 GNB

Give us this day our daily bread.

Matthew 6:11 NRSV

"My food," Jesus said to them, "is to obey the will of the one who sent me and to finish the work he gave me to do."

John 4:34 GNB

Drink no longer water, but use a little wine for thy stomach's sake and thine often infirmities.

1 Timothy 5:23 KJV

Brown bread and the gospel is good fare.

Anon.

The question of bread for myself is a material question: but the question of bread for my neighbor, for everybody, is a spiritual and a religious question.

Nikolai Aleksandrovich Berdyaev

We must not anticipate food before the time for it and we must not overdo it; on the other hand, when the due hour comes, we must have our food and our sleep, regardless of our reluctance.

John Cassian

The history of man from the beginning has been the history of the struggle for daily bread.

Jesús de Castro

One ought to arise from a meal able to apply oneself to prayer and study.

St. Jerome

Hunger and thirst are healthy drives unless you eat and drink solely for your own pleasure and in excess of what is reasonable. We must eat to live, and not live to eat.

Michel Quoist

Irrational feeding darkens the soul and makes it unfit for spiritual experiences.

St. Thomas Aquinas

Foolishness

See also Wisdom

Fools say in their hearts, "There is no God."

Psalm 14:1 NRSV

Do not answer fools according to their folly, or you will be a fool yourself. Answer fools according to their folly, or they will be wise in their own eyes.

Proverbs 26:4–5 NRSV

Like a dog that returns to its vomit is a fool who reverts to his folly.

Proverbs 26:11 NRSV

For fools speak folly, and their minds plot iniquity: to practice ungodliness, to utter error concerning the LORD, to leave the craving of the hungry unsatisfied, and to deprive the thirsty of drink.

Isaiah 32:6 NRSV

Anyone who hears my teachings and doesn't obey them is like a foolish person who built a house on sand. The rain poured down, the rivers flooded, and the winds blew and beat against that house. Finally, it fell with a crash.

Matthew 7:26–27 CEV

The natural man receiveth not the things of the Spirit of God: for they are foolishness unto him: neither can he know them, because they are spiritually discerned.

1 Corinthians 2:14 KJV

Nothing looks so like a man of sense as a fool who holds his tongue.

Anon.

We were deceived by the wisdom of the serpent, but we are freed by the foolishness of God.

St. Augustine of Hippo

A man that extols himself is a fool and an idiot.

John Calvin

If fifty million people say a foolish thing, it is still a foolish thing.

Anatole France

Hate and despise all human glory, for it is nothing else but human folly. It is the greatest snare and the greatest betrayer that you can possibly admit into your heart.

William Law

Fools rush in where angels fear to tread.

Alexander Pope

He who provides for this life, but takes no care for eternity, is wise for a moment, but a fool forever.

John Tillotson

Forgiveness

See also Sin

As far as the east is from the west, so far he removes our transgressions from us.

Psalm 103:12 NRSV

Who is a god like you? You take away guilt, you forgive the sins of the remnant of your people.

Micah 7:18 REB

And forgive us our trespasses, as we forgive them that trespass against us.

Matthew 6:12 BCP

For by the blood of Christ we are set free, that is, our sins are forgiven. How great is the grace of God, which he gave to us in such large measure!

Ephesians 1:7–8 GNB

And be kind to one another, tenderhearted, forgiving one another, as God in Christ has forgiven you.

Ephesians 4:32 NRSV

Without the shedding of blood there is no forgiveness of sins.

Hebrews 9:22 NRSV

If we confess our sins, he who is faithful and just will forgive us our sins and cleanse us from all unrighteousness.

1 John 1:9 NRSV

Christ's Passion is the true and proper cause of forgiveness of sins.

St. Thomas Aquinas

"I can forgive, but I cannot forget," is only another way of saying, "I cannot forgive."

Henry Ward Beecher

The glory of Christianity is to conquer by forgiveness.

William Blake

Forgiveness is the key that unlocks the door of resentment and the handcuffs of hate. It is a power that breaks the chains of bitterness and the shackles of selfishness.

Corrie ten Boom

Forgiveness is man's deepest need and highest achievement.

Horace Bushnell

Nothing is this world bears the impress of the Son of God so surely as forgiveness.

Alice Cary

The most marvelous ingredient in the forgiveness of God is that he also forgets, the one thing a human being can never do. Forgetting with God is a divine attribute; God's forgiveness forgets.

Oswald Chambers

Pardon one another so that later on you will not remember the injury. The remembering of an injury is itself a wrong: it adds to our anger, feeds our sin and hates what is good. It is a rusty arrow and poison for the soul.

Francis of Paola

He that cannot forgive others breaks the bridge over which he must pass himself; for every man has need to be forgiven.

Thomas Fuller

In these days of guilt complexes, perhaps the most glorious word in the English language is "forgiveness."

William Franklin (Billy) Graham

There's no point in burying a hatchet if you're going to put a marker on the site.

Sydney J. Harris

The sin which is not too great to be forsaken, is not too great to be forgiven.

Thomas Horton

The only true forgiveness is that which is offered and extended even before the offender has apologized and sought it.

Søren Kierkegaard

We pardon as long as we love.

François, Duc de La Rochefoucauld

Everyone says forgiveness is a lovely idea, until they have something to forgive.

Clive Staples (C.S.) Lewis

The man who is truly forgiven and knows it, is a man who forgives.

David Martyn Lloyd-Jones

Forgiveness is not an occasional art, it is a permanent attitude.

Martin Luther

To err is human, to forgive divine.

Alexander Pope

Humanity is never so beautiful as when praying for forgiveness or else forgiving another.

Jean Paul Richter

When God pardons, he consigns the offense to everlasting forgetfulness.

Merv Rosell

Only one petition in the Lord's Prayer has any condition attached to it: it is the petition for forgiveness.

William Temple

It is by forgiving that one is forgiven.

Mother Teresa

God does not want to punish you; He has provided for your forgiveness.

Colin Urquhart

There is so much for us all to forgive that we shall never get it done without putting in a lot of practice.

J. Neville Ward

A man may as well go to hell for not forgiving as for not believing.

Thomas Watson

We need not climb up into heaven to see whether our sins are forgiven; let us look into our hearts, and see if we can forgive others. If we can, we need not doubt but God has forgiven us.

Thomas Watson

Plenteous grace with Thee is found, / Grace to cover all my sins; / Let the healing streams abound, / Make and keep me pure within.

Charles Wesley

The Bible knows nothing of mere pardon. There can be no pardon except on the ground of satisfaction of justice.

Geoffrey B. Wilson

Free Will

See also Choices; Decisions

See, I am setting before you today a blessing and a curse: the blessing, if you obey the commandments of the LORD your God that I am commanding you today; and the curse, if you do not obey the commandments of the LORD your God.

Deuteronomy 11:26–27 NRSV

Seek ye the Lord while he may be found, call ye upon him while he is near.

Isaiah 55:6 KJV

"For me everything is permissible"; maybe, but not everything does good. True, for me everything is permissible, but I am determined not to be dominated by anything.

1 Corinthians 6:12 NJB

We are not constrained by servile necessity, but act with free will, whether we are disposed to virtue or inclined to vice.

St. Ambrose

While the Savior does not reject the willing, He does not constrain the unwilling; while He does not deny Himself to whose who seek Him, He does not strive with those who cast Him out.

St. Ambrose

He who created us without our help will not save us without our consent.

St. Augustine of Hippo

There are no galley slaves in the royal vessel of divine love—every man works his oar voluntarily.

Bishop Jean Pierre Camus

Our destiny is not determined for us, but it is determined by us. Man's free will is part of God's sovereign will. We have freedom to take which course we choose, but not freedom to determine the end of that choice. God makes clear what he desires, we must choose, and the result of the choice is not the inevitableness of law, but the inevitableness of God.

Oswald Chambers

God has so constituted us that there must be a free willingness on our part. This power is at once the most fearful and the most glorious power.

Oswald Chambers

God gave us a free choice because there is no significance to love that knows no alternative.

James Dobson

We have freedom to do good or evil; yet to make choice of evil, is not to use, but to abuse our freedom.

St. Francis de Sales

God, having placed good and evil in our power, has given us full freedom of choice; he does not keep back the unwilling, but embraces the willing.

St. John Chrysostom

The power of choosing good and evil is within the reach of all.

Origen of Alexandria

No one learns to make right decisions without being free to make wrong ones.

Kenneth Sollitt

Freedom

See also Bondage

The spirit of the Lord GOD is upon me, because the LORD has anointed me; he has sent me to bring good news to the oppressed, to bind up the brokenhearted, to proclaim liberty to the captives, and release to the prisoners.

Isaiah 61:1 NRSV

Jesus said to those who believed in him, "If you obey my teachings, you are really my disciples; you will know the truth, and the truth will set you free." . . . Jesus said to them, "I am telling you the truth: everyone who sins is a slave of sin. A slave does not belong to a family permanently, but a son belongs there forever. If the Son sets you free, then you will be really free."

John 8:31–32, 34–36 GNB

Now this Lord is the Spirit and where the Spirit of the Lord is, there is freedom.

2 Corinthians 3:17 NJB

Christ has set us free! This means we are really free. Now hold on to your freedom and don't ever become slaves of the Law again.

Galatians 5:1 CEV

Freedom is not the right to do as you please; it is the liberty to do as you ought.

Anon.

There is no true liberty except the liberty of the happy who cleave to the eternal law.

St. Augustine of Hippo

The author of peace and lover of concord, in knowledge of whom standeth our eternal life, whose service is perfect freedom.

Book of Common Prayer

No man in this world attains to freedom from any slavery except by entrance into some higher servitude. There is no such thing as an entirely free man conceivable.

Phillips Brooks

God forces no one, for love cannot compel, and God's service, therefore, is a thing of perfect freedom.

Hans Denck

True freedom is only to be found when one escapes from oneself and enters into the liberty of the children of God.

François de la Mothe Fénelon

Christianity promises to make men free; it does not promise to make them independent.

William Ralph Inge

There are two freedoms—the false, where a man is free to do what he likes; the true, where a man is free to do what he ought.

Charles Kingsley

The Spirit of God first imparts love; he next inspires hope, and then gives liberty; and that is about the last thing we have in many of our churches.

Dwight Lyman (D.L.) Moody

The only lasting treasure is spiritual; the only perfect freedom is serving God.

Malcolm Muggeridge

Liberty has brought us the freedom to be the slaves of righteousness.

Charles Caldwell Ryrie

Freedom does not mean I am able to do whatever I want to do. That's the worst kind of bondage. Freedom means I have been set free to become all that God wants me to be, to achieve all that God wants me to achieve, to enjoy all that God wants me to enjoy.

Warren W. Wiersbe

Friends

There are friends who point the way to ruin, others are closer than a brother.

Proverbs 18:24 NJB

Faithful are the wounds of a friend; but the kisses of an enemy are deceitful.

Proverbs 27:6 KJV

You are better off to have a friend than to be all alone, because then you will get more enjoyment out of what you earn. If you fall, your friend can help you up. But if you fall without having a friend nearby, you are really in trouble. If you sleep alone, you won't have anyone to keep you warm on a cold night. Someone might be able to beat up one of you, but not both of you. As the saying goes, "A rope made from three strands of cord is hard to break."

Ecclesiastes 4:9–12 CEV

Faithful friends are a sturdy shelter: whoever finds one has found a treasure. Faithful friends are beyond price; no amount can balance their worth. Faithful friends are life-saving medicine; and those who fear the Lord find them.

Ecclesiasticus 6:14–16 NRSV

Do not abandon old friends, for new ones cannot equal them. A new friend is like new wine; when it has aged, you can drink it with pleasure.

Ecclesiasticus 9:10 NRSV

Greater love hath no man than this, that a man lay down his life for his friends. Ye are my friends, if ye do whatsoever I command you. Henceforth I call you not servants; for the servant knoweth not what his lord doeth: but I have called you friends; for all things that I have heard of my Father I have made known unto you.

John KJV

Abraham had faith in God, and God was pleased with him. That's how Abraham became God's friend.

James 2:23 CEV

Friendship improves happiness, and abates misery, by doubling our joy, and dividing our grief.

Joseph Addison

No medicine is more valuable, none more efficacious, none better suited to the cure of all our temporal ills than a friend to whom we may turn for consolation in time of trouble—and with whom we may share our happiness in time of joy.

St. Aelred

What brings joy to the heart is not so much the friend's gift as the friend's love.

St. Aelred

The highest privilege there is, is the privilege of being allowed to share another's pain. You talk about your pleasures to your acquaintances; you talk about your troubles to your friends.

Fr. Andrew

No man can be a friend of Jesus Christ who is not a friend to his neighbor.

Robert Hugh Benson

The essence of a perfect friendship is that each friend reveals himself utterly to the other, flings aside his reserves and shows himself for what he truly is.

Robert Hugh Benson

Friendship is like money, easier made than kept.

Samuel Butler

True friendship is like sound health, the value of it is seldom known until it be lost.

Charles Caleb Colton

A Friend may well be reckoned the master-piece of Nature.

Ralph Waldo Emerson

The only way to have a friend is to be one.

Ralph Waldo Emerson

Friendships begun in this world will be taken up again, never to be broken off.

St. Francis de Sales

The better friends you are, the straighter you can talk, but while you are only on nodding terms, be slow to scold.

St. Francis Xavier

To know someone here or there with whom you feel there is understanding in spite of distances or thoughts unexpressed—that can make of this earth a garden.

Johann Wolfgang von Goethe

A true friend can never have a hidden motive for being a friend. He can have no hidden agenda. A friend is simply a friend, for the sake of friendship.

James Houston

From acquaintances, we conceal our real selves. To our friends we reveal our weaknesses.

George Basil Hume

If a man does not make new acquaintance as he advances through life, he will soon find himself left alone. A man, Sir, should keep his friendship in constant repair.

Samuel Johnson

Job endured everything—until his friends came to comfort him, then he grew impatient.

Søren Kierkegaard

The typical expression of opening Friendship would be something like, "What? You too? I thought I was the only one."

Clive Staples (C.S.) Lewis

Friendship must be about something even if it were only an enthusiasm for dominoes or white mice.

Clive Staples (C.S.) Lewis

It is mutual respect which makes friendship lasting.

John Henry Newman

The impulse of love that leads us to the doorway of a friend is the voice of God within and we need not be afraid to follow it.

Agnes Sanford

Friendship is one of the sweetest joys of life. Many might have failed beneath the bitterness of their trial had they not found a friend.

Charles Haddon Spurgeon

True friendship is a plant of slow growth, and must undergo and withstand the shocks of adversity before it is entitled to the appellation.

George Washington

Fruitfulness

See also Maturity; Spiritual Growth

God blessed them, and God said to them, "Be fruitful and multiply, and fill the earth and subdue it."

Genesis 1:28 NRSV

I am the real vine, and my Father is the gardener. He breaks off every branch in me that does not bear fruit, and he prunes every branch that does bear fruit, so that it will be clean and bear more fruit. . . . A branch cannot bear fruit by itself; it can do so only if it remains in the vine. In the same way you cannot bear fruit unless you remain in me. I am the vine, and you are the branches. Those who remain in me, and I in them, will bear much fruit; for you can do nothing without me. . . . My Father's glory is shown by your bearing much fruit; and in this way you become my disciples.

John 15:1–2, 4–5, 8 GNB

The fruit of the Spirit is love, joy, peace, long-suffering, gentleness, goodness, faith, meekness, temperance: against such there is no law.

Galatians 5:22–23 KJV

The fruit of the Spirit is not excitement or orthodoxy, it is character.

G.B. Duncan

Joy is love exalted; peace is love in repose; long-suffering is love enduring; gentleness is love in society; goodness is love in action; faith is love on the battlefield; meekness is love in school; and temperance is love in training.

Dwight Lyman (D.L.) Moody

Religious work can be done by natural men without the gifts of the Spirit, and it can be done well and skillfully. But work designed for eternity can only be done by the eternal Spirit.

Aiden Wilson (A.W.) Tozer

Futility

The LORD knows our thoughts, that they are but an empty breath.

Psalm 94:11 NRSV

I have seen everything that is done under the sun: how futile it all is, mere chasing after the wind!

Ecclesiastes 1:14 NJB

Beware of the barrenness of a busy life.

Anon.

Much of our activity these days is nothing more than a cheap anesthetic to deaden the pain of an empty life.

Richard J. Foster

Our Adversary majors in three things: noise, hurry, and crowds. If he can keep us engaged in "muchness" and "manyness" he will rest satisfied.

Richard J. Foster

Seeking to perpetuate one's name on earth is like writing on the sand by the seashore.

Dwight Lyman (D.L.) Moody

And so, from hour to hour, we ripe and ripe, / And then, from hour to hour, we rot and rot; / And thereby hangs a tale.

William Shakespeare

Like as the waves make towards the pebbled shore, / So do our minutes hasten to their end.

William Shakespeare

No matter what a man does, no matter how successful he seems to be in any field, if the Holy Spirit is not the chief energizer of his activity, it will all fall apart when he dies.

Aiden Wilson (A.W.) Tozer

Future

See also Destiny; Goals

Life is hard, but there is a time and a place for everything, though no one can tell the future.

Ecclesiastes 8:6–7 CEV

The Day of the Lord will come like a thief. On that Day the heavens will disappear with a shrill noise, the heavenly bodies will burn up and be destroyed, and the earth with everything in it will vanish. Since all these things will be destroyed in this way, what kind of people should you be? Your lives should be holy and dedicated to God.

2 Peter 3:10–11 GNB

Most men prefer and strive for the present, we for the future.

St. Ambrose

Men must pursue things which are just in the present, and leave the future to divine Providence.

Francis Bacon

Never be afraid to trust an unknown future to a known God.

Corrie ten Boom

I've read the last page of the Bible. It's all going to turn out all right.

William Franklin (Billy) Graham

There is only one real inevitability: it is necessary that the Scripture be fulfilled.

Carl F.H. Henry

The only light upon the future is faith.

Theodor Hoecker

We should all be concerned about the future because we will have to spend the rest of our lives there.

Charles Kettering

His divinity is understood as the power of the future making our present appear in a new light. The future is God's: which means that,

wherever the individual being goes, in life or death, God is there.

Hans Küng

The most effective way to ensure the value of the future is to confront the present courageously and constructively.

Rollo May

We know not what the future holds, but we do know who holds the future.

Willis J. Ray

God's plans, like lilies, pure and white, unfold; / We must not tear the close-shut leaves apart; / Time will reveal the chalices of gold.

May Louise Riley Smith

One God, one law, one element, / And one far-off divine event, / To which the whole creation moves.

Alfred, Lord Tennyson

Generosity

See also Unselfishness

It is well with those who deal generously and lend, who conduct their affairs with justice.

Psalm 112:5 NRSV

Give, and there will be gifts for you: a full measure, pressed down, shaken together, and overflowing, will be poured into your lap; because the standard you use will be the standard used for you.

Luke 6:38 NJB

We want you to know, brothers and sisters, about the grace of God that has been granted to the churches of Macedonia; for during a severe ordeal of affliction, their abundant joy and their extreme poverty have overflowed in a wealth of generosity on their part.

2 Corinthians 8:1–2 NRSV

Remind the rich to be generous and share what they have.

1 Timothy 6:18 CEV

The test of generosity is not how much you give, but how much you have left.

Anon.

A man there was, though some did count him mad, the more he cast away, the more he had.

John Bunyan

A cheerful giver does not count the cost of what he gives. His heart is set on pleasing and cheering him to whom the gift is given.

Julian of Norwich

If you are not generous with a meager income, you will never be generous with abundance.

Harold Nye

He who is not liberal with what he has, does but deceive himself when he thinks he would be liberal if he had more.

William S. Plummer

He who gives what he would as readily throw away, gives without generosity; for the essence of generosity is in self-sacrifice.

Sir Henry Talor

You do not have to be rich to be generous. If he has the spirit of true generosity, a pauper can give like a prince.

Corrine U. Wells

Gentleness

See also Meekness

Take the yoke I give you. Put it on your shoulders and learn from me. I am gentle and humble, and you will find rest.

Matthew 11:29 CEV

The fruit of the Spirit is . . . gentleness.

Galatians 5:22 KJV

Let your gentleness be known to everyone. The Lord is near.

Philippians 4:5 NRSV

A servant of the Lord must not be quarrelsome; he must be kindly towards all. He should be a good teacher, tolerant, and gentle when he must discipline those who oppose him.

2 Timothy 2:24–25 REB

Nothing is so strong as gentleness, nothing so gentle as real strength.

St. Francis de Sales

If you would reap praise, sow the seeds; gentle words and useful deeds.

Benjamin Franklin

Soft words are hard arguments.

Thomas Fuller

Only the truly strong and great can be truly tender. Tenderness is a mark of nobility, not of weakness.

James Philip

Gifts

See also Generosity; Spiritual Gifts

A gift opens doors; it gives access to the great.

Proverbs 18:16 NRSV

Like clouds and wind without rain is one who boasts of a gift never given.

Proverbs 25:14 NRSV

There came a certain poor widow, and she threw in two mites, which make a farthing. And he called unto him his disciples and saith unto them, Verily I say unto you, that this poor widow hath cast more in, than all they which have cast into the treasury: For all they did cast in of their abundance; but she of her want did cast in all that she had, even all her living.

Mark 12:42–44 KJV

In all this I have given you an example that by such work we must support the weak, remembering the words of the Lord Jesus, for he himself said, "It is more blessed to give than to receive."

Acts 20:35 NRSV

You should each give, then, as you have decided, not with regret or out of a sense of duty; for God loves the one who gives gladly.

2 Corinthians 9:7 GNB

Every good and perfect gift comes down from the Father who created all the lights in the heavens.

James 2:17 CEV

The man who gives little with a smile gives more than the man who gives much with a frown.

Anon.

The hand that gives, gathers.

Anon.

The highest love of all finds its fulfillment not in what it keeps but in what it gives.

Fr. Andrew

It is easy to want things from the Lord and yet not want the Lord Himself; as though the gift could ever be preferable to the Giver.

St. Augustine of Hippo

The desire for power caused the angels to fall; the desire for knowledge in excess caused man to fall, but in charity there is no excess, neither can angel nor man come in danger by it.

Francis Bacon

Have you ever stopped to think that Christ never gave anyone money? The riches of the world were his for the taking and his to give away, yet when the poor and the hungry came to him, he didn't give them money, and he rarely gave them food; he gave them love and service and the greatest gift of all—himself.

Henry Ward Beecher

It is possible to give without loving, but it is impossible to love without giving.

Richard Braunstein

God's gifts put man's best dreams to shame.

Elizabeth Barrett Browning

He that bestows his goods upon the poor, shall have as much again, and ten times more.

John Bunyan

You can give without loving, but you cannot love without giving.

Amy Carmichael

Not how much we give, but what we do not give, is the test of our Christianity.

Oswald Chambers

We make a living by what we get, but we make a life by what we give.

Sir Winston Churchill

Our prayers and fastings are of less avail, unless they are aided by almsgiving.

St. Cyprian

God does not need our money. But you and I need the experience of giving.

James Dobson

For it is in giving that we receive, it is in loving that we are loved and it is in dying that we are born to eternal life.

St. Francis of Assisi

Complete possession is proved only by giving. All you are unable to give possesses you.

André Gide

God has given us two hands—one for receiving and the other for giving.

William Franklin (Billy) Graham

Giving much to the poor / Doth enrich a man's store: / It takes much from the account / To which his sin doth amount.

George Herbert

Give unto all, lest he whom thou deny'st may chance to be no other man but Christ.

Robert Herrick

He is truly great who hath great charity.

Thomas à Kempis

It could be argued that in the Old Testament tithes were paid, and therefore do not, strictly speaking, come under the heading of giving at all. Christian giving only begins when we give more than a tenth.

Kenneth F.W. Prior

Lots of people think they are charitable if they give away their old clothes and things they don't want.

Myrtle Reed

There are three kinds of giving: grudge giving, duty giving, and thanksgiving. Grudge giving says, "I hate to"; duty giving says, "I ought to"; thanksgiving says, "I want to." The first comes from constraint, the second from a sense of obligation, the third from a full heart. Nothing much is conveyed in grudge giving since "the gift without the giver is bare." Something more happens in duty giving, but there is no song in it. Thanksgiving is an open gate into the love of God.

Robert N. Rodenmayer

Whatever we hold to ourselves is loss. Whatever we give to God is gain.

Gilbert Shaw

Feel for others—in your pocket.

Charles Haddon Spurgeon

True charity is the desire to be useful to others without thought of recompense.

Emanuel Swedenborg

We are never more like God than when we give.

Charles R. Swindoll

Giving, *see* Generosity; Gifts

Glory

See also God, Greatness of; Salvation

All the earth shall be filled with the glory of the LORD.

Numbers 14:21 NRSV

Glorious things are spoken of thee, O city of God.

Psalm 87:3 KJV

And yet I say unto you, That even Solomon in all his glory was not arrayed like one of these.

Matthew 6:29 KJV

He that speaketh of himself seeketh his own glory: but he that seeketh his glory that sent him, the same is true, and no unrighteousness is in him.

John 7:18 KJV

I reckon that the sufferings of this present time are not worthy to be compared with the glory which shall be revealed in us.

Romans 8:18 KJV

There is the glory of the sun, and another glory of the moon, and another glory of the stars: for one star differeth from another star in glory.

1 Corinthians 15:41 KJV

But we all, with open face beholding as in a glass the glory of the Lord, are changed into the same image from glory to glory, even as by the Spirit of the Lord.

2 Corinthians 3:18 KJV

Provided that God be glorified, we must not care by whom.

St. Francis de Sales

The paths of glory lead but to the grave.

Thomas Gray

The glory of God is a living man; and the life of man consists in beholding God.

St. Irenaeus

Short is the glory that is given and taken by men; and sorrow followeth ever the glory of this world. . . . But true glory and holy joy is to glory in Thee and not in one's self; to rejoice in Thy name, and not to be delighted in one's own virtue, nor in any creature, save only for Thy sake.

Thomas à Kempis

By faith we know his existence; in glory we shall know his nature.

Blaise Pascal

The cross of Christ is Christ's glory. Man seeks to win his glory by the sacrifice of others—Christ by the sacrifice of himself. Men seek to get crowns of gold—he sought a crown of thorns. Men think that glory lies in being exalted over others—Christ thought that his glory did lie in becoming "a worm and no man," a scoff and reproach among all that beheld him. He stooped when he conquered; and he counted that the glory lay as much in the stooping as in the conquest.

Charles Haddon Spurgeon

We must not reject man in favor of God, nor reject God in favor of man, for the glory of God is man alive, supremely in Christ.

Leon Joseph Suenens

Our great honor lies in being just what Jesus was and is. To be accepted by those who accept him, rejected by all who reject him, loved by those who love him and hated by everyone who hates him. What greater glory could come to any man?

Aiden Wilson (A.W.) Tozer

Goals

See also Destiny; Future

So we make it our goal to please him.

2 Corinthians 5:9 NIV

I press on toward the goal for the prize of the heavenly call of God in Christ Jesus.

Philippians 3:14 NRSV

You have not seen him, yet you love him; and still without seeing him you believe in him and so are already filled with a joy so glorious that it cannot be described; and you are sure of the goal of your faith, that is, the salvation of your souls.

1 Peter 1:8–9 NJB

God is the only goal worthy of man's efforts; the fitting end of human existence is a loving union with God.

St. Augustine of Hippo

My goal is God himself, not joy nor peace, / Nor even blessing, but himself, my God, / 'Tis his to lead me there, not mine but his / At any cost, dear Lord, by any road!

E. Brook

A good archer is not known by his arrows but his aim.

Thomas Fuller

If you would hit the mark, you must aim a little above it; / Every arrow that flies feels the attraction of earth.

Henry Wadsworth Longfellow

Jesus knew where he had come from, why he was here, and what he was supposed to accomplish. He came down from heaven, not to do his own will, but the will of the Father. That determination controlled every decision he made. As a result he was not distracted with trivia. He was never in a hurry, for he knew his Father would not give a task without the time to do it. Christ was not driven by crises, feeling he must heal everyone in Israel. He could say, "It is finished," even when many people were still bound by demands and twisted by disease. What mattered ultimately was not the number of people healed or fed, but whether the Father's will was being done. His clearly defined goals simplified his decisions.

Erwin W. Lutzer

Purpose is what gives life a meaning. . . . A drifting boat always drifts downstream.

Charles H. Parkhurst

More men fail through lack of purpose than through lack of talent.

William Ashley (Billy) Sunday

If you've nothing to shoot for you'll hit it every time.

John Richard Wimber

God

All-Knowing

The LORD searches every mind, and understands every plan and thought.

1 Chronicles 28:9 NRSV

O Lord, thou hast searched me, and known me. Thou knowest my downsitting and mine uprising, thou understandest my thought afar off. Thou compassest my path and my lying down, and art acquainted with all my ways. For there is not a word in my tongue but, lo, O Lord, thou knowest it altogether. Thou has beset me behind and before, and laid thine hand upon me. Such knowledge is too wonderful for me; it is high, I cannot attain unto it.

Psalm 139:1–6 KJV

Can you not buy two sparrows for a penny? And yet not one falls to the ground without your Father knowing. Why, every hair on your head has been counted.

Matthew 10:29–30 NJB

Nothing is hidden from God! He sees through everything, and we will have to tell him the truth.

Hebrews 4:13 CEV

What man is there who can comprehend that wisdom by which God knows all things, in such wise that neither what we call things past are past therein, nor what we call things future are therein looked for as coming, as though they were absent; but both past and future things together with those actually present are all present.

St. Augustine of Hippo

No masses of earth can block his vision as he looks over all. With one glance of his intelligence, he sees all that has been, that is, and that is to come.

Anicius Manlius Severinus Boethius

Almighty God, unto whom all hearts be open, all desires known, and from whom no secrets are hid: Cleanse the thoughts of our hearts by the inspiration of thy Holy Spirit, that we may perfectly love thee, and worthily magnify thy holy Name; through Christ our Lord. Amen.

Book of Common Prayer

Before God created the universe, he already had you in mind.

Erwin W. Lutzer

Nothing is too little to be ordered by our Father; nothing too little in which to see His hand; nothing which touches our souls too little to accept from Him; nothing too little to be done to Him.

Edward Bouverie Pusey

There is nothing round the corner which is beyond God's view.

J. Charles Stern

God dwells in eternity, but time dwells in God. He has already lived all our tomorrows as he has lived all our yesterdays.

Aiden Wilson (A.W.) Tozer

How unutterably sweet is the knowledge that our heavenly Father knows us completely. No talebearer can inform on us, no enemy can make an accusation stick; no forgotten skeleton can come tumbling out of some hidden closet to abash us and expose our past; no unsuspected weakness in our characters can come to light to turn God away from us, since he knew us utterly before we knew him and called us to himself in the full knowledge of everything that was against us.

Aiden Wilson (A.W.) Tozer

Anger of

The LORD is merciful and gracious, slow to anger and abounding in steadfast love. He will not always accuse, nor will he keep his anger forever.

Psalm 103:8–9 NRSV

Whoever puts his faith in the Son has eternal life. Whoever disobeys the Son will not see that life; God's wrath rests upon him.

John 3:36 REB

For the wrath of God is revealed from heaven against all ungodliness and unrighteousness of men, who hold the truth in unrighteousness.

Romans 1:18 KJV

On the day of judgment Jesus will save us from God's anger.

1 Thessalonians 1:10 CEV

God's anger, like the house that Samson pulled upon his own head, falls not upon us but when we pull it upon ourselves by sin.

Sir Richard Baker

The wrath of God is simply the rule of the universe that a man will reap what he sows, and that no one ever escapes the consequences of his sin. The wrath of God and the moral order of the universe are one and the same thing.

William Barclay

The wrath of God is as pure as the holiness of God. When God is angry he is perfectly angry. When he is displeased there is every reason he should be. We tend to think of anger as sin; but sometimes it is sinful not to be angry. It is unthinkable that God would not be purely and perfectly angry with sin.

Stuart Briscoe

The reality of God's wrath is as much a part of the biblical message as is God's grace.

Leighton Frederick Sandys Ford

As God's mercies are new every morning toward his people, so his anger is new every morning against the wicked.

Matthew Henry

God's wrath is his righteousness reacting against unrighteousness.

James Innell (J.I.) Packer

God's anger is not a passion but a principle—the eternal hatred of wrong, which corresponds with the eternal love of right, and which is only another aspect of love.

Arthur Tappan (A.T.) Pierson

Creator

See also Creation

In the beginning God created the heavens and the earth.

Genesis 1:1 CEV

The earth is the LORD's and all that is in it, the world, and those who live in it.

Psalm 24:1 NRSV

You created every part of me; you put me together in my mother's womb. I praise you because you are to be feared; all you do is strange and wonderful. I know it with all my heart. When my bones were being formed, carefully put together in my mother's womb, when I was growing in there in secret, you knew that I was there—you saw me before I was born. The days allotted to me had all been recorded in your book, before any of them ever began.

Psalm 139:13–16 GNB

Just as you do not know how the breath comes to the bones in the mother's womb, so you do not know the work of God, who makes everything.

Ecclesiastes 11:5 NRSV

Have you not known? Have you not heard? The LORD is the everlasting God, the Creator of the ends of the earth. He does not faint or grow weary; his understanding is unsearchable.

Isaiah 40:28 NRSV

Even those whom God allows to suffer should commit themselves to a Creator who is trustworthy, and go on doing good.

1 Peter 4:19 NJB

All created things are living in the Hand of God. The senses see only the action of the creatures; but faith sees in everything the action of God.

Jean Pierre de Caussade

Creativity is the basic attribute of God, identical with his uniqueness.

Hermann Cohen

The creation of things is executed by God not out of any necessity, whether of essence or of knowledge or of will, but out of a sheer freedom which is not moved—much less constrained—by anything external.

John Duns Scotus

God creates out of the absolute superabundance of his mercy and love.

Georges V. Florovsky

I saw three properties: the first is, that God made it; the second is, that God loveth it; the third is, that God keepeth it. But what beheld I therein? Verily the Maker, the Keeper, the Lover.

Julian of Norwich

The visible marks of extraordinary wisdom and power appear so plainly in all the works of creation that a rational creature who will but seriously reflect on them cannot miss the discovery of the Deity.

John Locke

The universe is not on the side of frugality; the stars were hurled, broadcast from the hand of God.

Donald Robert (Don) Marquis

The universe is a thought of God.

(Johann) Friedrich von Schiller

Such is the likeness of God, wholly given, spent and drained in that sublime self-giving which is the ground and source and origin of the universe.

W.H. Vanstone

To create requires infinite power. All the world cannot make a fly.

Thomas Watson

The Creator of the earth is the owner of it.

John Woolman

Faithfulness of

See also Faithfulness

Thy mercy, O Lord is in the heavens, and thy faithfulness reacheth unto the clouds.

Psalm 36:5 KJV

It is of the Lord's mercies that we are not consumed, because his compassions fail not. They are new every morning: great is thy faithfulness.

Lamentations 3:22–23 KJV

God is faithful; by him you were called into the fellowship of his Son, Jesus Christ our Lord.

1 Corinthians 1:9 NRSV

In God's faithfulness lies eternal security.

Corrie ten Boom

God is always like himself.

John Calvin

What more powerful consideration can be thought on to make us true to God, than the faithfulness and truth of God to us?

William Gurnall

Though men are false, God is faithful.

Matthew Henry

God's investment in us is so great he could not possibly abandon us.

Erwin W. Lutzer

Change and decay in all around I see; / O thou, who changest not, abide with me.

Henry Francis Lyte

God is faithful, and if we serve him faithfully, he will provide for our needs.

St. Richard of Chichester

Be still, my soul: the Lord is on thy side: / Bear patiently the cross of grief or pain; / Leave to thy God to order and provide; / In every change He faithful will remain. / Be still, my soul: thy best, thy heavenly Friend / Through thorny ways leads to a joyful end.

Katharina von Schlegel,
tr. Jane Laurie Borthwick

Consider seriously how quickly people change, and how little trust is to be had in them; and cleave fast unto God, who changeth not.

St. Teresa of Avila

Goodness of

See also Providence

O taste and see that the Lord is good: blessed is the man that trusteth in him.

Psalm 34:8 KJV

God is our refuge and strength, a very present help in trouble.

Psalm 46:1 NRSV

[Mary's "Magnificat"] My soul doth magnify the Lord, and my spirit hath rejoiced in God my Savior, for he hath regarded the lowliness of his hand-maiden. For behold from henceforth all generations shall call me blessed; for he that is mighty hath magnified me, and holy is his name. And his mercy is on them that fear him throughout all generations. He hath shewed strength with his arm, he hath scattered the proud in the imaginations of their hearts, he hath put down the mighty from their seat, and hath exalted the humble and meek. He hath filled the hungry with good things, and the rich he hath sent empty away. He remembering his mercy hath holpen his servant Israel, as he promised to our forefathers, Abraham and his seed, for ever.

Luke 1:46–55 BCP

Despiseth thou the riches of his goodness and forbearance and longsuffering; not knowing that the goodness of God leadeth thee to repentance?

Romans 2:4 KJV

The goodness of God knows how to use our disordered wishes and actions, often lovingly turning them to our advantage while always preserving the beauty of his order.

St. Bernard of Clairvaux

You are the garment which covers every nakedness. You feed the hungry in your sweetness.

St. Catherine of Siena

In his love he clothes us, enfolds and embraces us; that tender lover completely surrounds us, never to leave us. As I see it he is everything that is good.

Julian of Norwich

God is all that is good, in my sight, and the goodness that everything has is his.

Julian of Norwich

Think of how good God is! He gives us the physical, mental, and spiritual ability to work in his kingdom, and then he rewards us for doing it!

Erwin W. Lutzer

To the frightened, God is friendly; to the poor in spirit, he is forgiving; to the ignorant, considerate; to the weak, gentle; to the stranger, hospitable.

Aiden Wilson (A.W.) Tozer

God's goodness is the root of all goodness; and our goodness, if we have any, springs out of his goodness.

William Tyndale

Grace and Mercy of

See also Forgiveness; Grace; Mercy

I knew that you are a gracious God and merciful, slow to anger, and abounding in steadfast love, and ready to relent from punishing.

Jonah 4:2 NRSV

And of his fullness have all we received, and grace for grace. For the law was given by Moses, but grace and truth came by Jesus Christ.

John 1:16–17 KJV

For you know the grace of our Lord Jesus Christ, that though he was rich, yet for your sakes he became poor, so that you through his poverty might become rich.

2 Corinthians 8:9 NIV

In him we have redemption through his blood, the forgiveness of our trespasses, according to the riches of his grace that he lavished on us.

Ephesians 1:7–8 NRSV

For it is by God's grace that you have been saved through faith. It is not the result of your own efforts, but God's gift, so that no one can boast about it.

Ephesians 2:8 GNB

The grace of God does not find men fit for salvation, but makes them so.

St. Augustine of Hippo

Among the attributes of God, although they are all equal, mercy shines with even more brilliancy than justice.

Miguel de Cervantes

God tempers the cold to the shorn lamb.

Henri Estienne

There's a wideness in God's mercy, / Like the wideness of the sea; / There's a kindness in His justice, / Which is more than liberty. / For the love of God is broader / Than the measures of man's mind; / And the heart of the Eternal / Is most wonderfully kind.

Frederick William Faber

He giveth more grace when the burdens grow greater, / He sendeth more strength when the labors increase; / To added affliction he addeth his mercy, / To multiplied trials, his multiplied peace.

Annie Johnson Flint

Whoever falls from God's right hand is caught in his left.

Edwin Markham

When God's godliness cannot be seen, his mercy can be experienced.

Robert Harold Schuller

The grace of God is infinite and eternal. As it had no beginning, so it can have no end, and being an attribute of God, it is as boundless as infinitude.

Aiden Wilson (A.W.) Tozer

Grace is God himself, his loving energy at work within his Church and within our souls.

Evelyn Underhill

God is ever giving to His children, yet hath not the less. His riches are imparted, not impaired.

Thomas Watson

Greatness of

For I will proclaim the name of the LORD; ascribe greatness to our God!

Deuteronomy 32:3 NRSV

Lift up your heads, O ye gates; and be ye lift up, ye everlasting doors; and the King of glory shall come in. Who is this King of glory? The Lord strong and mighty, the Lord mighty in battle. Lift up your heads, O ye gates; even lift them up, ye everlasting doors; and the King of glory shall come in. Who is this King of glory? The Lord of hosts, he is the King of glory.

Psalm 24:7–10 KJV

Praise him for his mighty acts; praise him according to his excellent greatness.

Psalm 150:2 KJV

Lord, there is no one like you; you are mighty, and your name is great and powerful.

Jeremiah 10:6 GNB

Nothing is impossible for God!

Luke 1:7 CEV

Jesus rebuked the unclean spirit and cured the boy and gave him back to his father, and everyone was awestruck by the greatness of God.

Luke 9:42–43 NJB

What is impossible to God? Not that which is difficult to His power, but that which is contrary to His nature.

St. Ambrose

God is that, the greater than which cannot be conceived.

St. Anselm of Canterbury

My God, how wonderful Thou art! / Thy majesty how bright! / How beautiful Thy mercy-seat, / In depths of burning light! / How wonderful, how beautiful, / The sight of Thee must be, / Thine endless wisdom, boundless power, / And aweful purity!

Frederick William Faber

God is beyond our ken—infinite, immense, and his real greatness is known to himself alone. Our mind is too limited to understand him.

Marcus M. Felix

The world is charged with the grandeur of God.

Gerard Manley Hopkins

The world appears very little to a soul that contemplates the greatness of God.

Brother Lawrence

To him no high, no low, no great, no small, he fills, he bounds, connects, and equals all!

Alexander Pope

The imagery of the heavens as being two thousand million light-years in diameter is awesome when compared to the tiny earth, but trivial when compared to the imagery of the "hand that measured the heavens."

Fulton John Sheen

There is nothing little in God.

Charles Haddon Spurgeon

Hiddenness of

Truly you are a God who hides himself, O God and Savior of Israel.

Isaiah 45:15 NIV

Your iniquities have separated between you and your God, and your sins have hid his face from you, that he will not hear.

Isaiah 59:2 KJV

The kingdom of heaven is like treasure hidden in a field, which someone found and hid, then in his joy he goes and sells all that he has and buys that field.

Matthew 13:44 NRSV

God really does lie hidden and unknown beneath every person in need.

Leonardo Boff

A God who let us prove his existence would be an idol.

Dietrich Bonhoeffer

For silence is not God, nor speaking; fasting is not God, nor eating; solitude is not God, nor company; nor any other pairs of opposites. He is hidden between them and cannot be found by anything your soul does, but only by the desire of your heart.

The Cloud of Unknowing

The Christian must trust in a withdrawing God.

William Gurnall

The basic faith of Christianity is that the hidden God revealed himself in his world and in history in a very particular way. God became man. Jesus Christ is accepted in faith by Christians as both divine and human.

Michael Hollings

There may be a time when God will not be found, but no time wherein he must not be trusted.

Thomas Lye

Holiness of

See also Holiness

I brought you out of Egypt so that I could be your God. Now you must become holy, because I am holy.

Leviticus 11:45 CEV

There is no one holy like the Lord; there is no one besides you.

1 Samuel 2:2 NIV

Exalt ye the Lord our God, and worship at his footstool; for he is holy.

Psalm 99:5 KJV

In the year that King Uzziah died, I saw the Lord. He was sitting on his throne, high and exalted, and his robe filled the whole Temple. Round him flaming creatures were standing, each of which had six wings. Each creature covered its face with two wings, and its body with two, and used the other two for flying. They were calling out to each other: "Holy, holy, holy! The Lord Almighty is holy! His glory fills the world."

Isaiah 6:1–3 GNB

They [the four beasts] rest not day and night, saying, Holy, holy, holy, Lord God Almighty, which was, and is, and is to come.

Revelation 4:8 KJV

It is not the constant thought of their sins, but the vision of the holiness of God that makes the saints aware of their own sinfulness.

Anthony Bloom

Holiness in angels and saints is but a quality, but in God it is his essence.

Thomas Benton Brooks

There is a danger of forgetting that the Bible reveals, not first the love of God, but the intense, blazing holiness of God, with his love as the center of that holiness.

Oswald Chambers

A true love of God must begin with a delight in his holiness, and not with a delight in any other attribute; for no other attribute is truly lovely without this.

Jonathan Edwards

The pervasive sinfulness of man becomes evident when contrasted with the radiant holiness of God.

Richard J. Foster

Holy, holy, holy, Lord God Almighty! / All Thy works shall praise Thy Name, in earth and sky and sea; / Holy, holy, holy! merciful and mighty, / God in Three Persons, blessed Trinity!

Reginald Heber

No attribute of God is more dreadful to sinners than his holiness.

Matthew Henry

God is holy with an absolute holiness that knows no degrees, and this he cannot impart to his creatures. But there is a relative and contingent holiness which he shares with angels and seraphim in heaven and with redeemed men on earth as their preparation for heaven. This holiness God can and does impart to his children. He shares it with them by imputation and by impartation, and because he has made it available to them through the blood of the Lamb, he requires it of them.

Aiden Wilson (A.W.) Tozer

Infiniteness of

But will God indeed dwell on the earth? Behold, the heaven and heaven of heavens cannot contain thee; how much less this house that I have builded?

1 Kings 8:27 KJV

Lord, thou hast been our refuge from one generation to another. Before the mountains were brought forth, or ever the earth and the world were made: thou art God from everlasting, and world without end.

Psalm 90:1–2 BCP

Great is our Lord, and of great power: his understanding is infinite.

Psalm 147:5 KJV

Who can hide in secret places so that I cannot see them? says the LORD. Do I not fill heaven and earth? says the LORD.

Jeremiah 23:24 NRSV

Eternal Light, shine into our hearts; Eternal Goodness, deliver us from evil; Eternal Power, be thou our support; Eternal Wisdom, scatter our ignorance; Eternal Pity, have mercy upon us.

Alcuin of York

God is an infinite circle whose center is everywhere and whose circumference is nowhere.

St. Augustine of Hippo

He who sees the infinite in all things, sees God.

William Blake

We know that God is everywhere; but certainly we feel his presence most when his works are on the grandest scale spread before us; and it is in the unclouded night-sky, where his worlds wheel their silent course, that we sense clearest his infinitude, his omnipotence, his omnipresence.

Charlotte Brontë

As no place can be without God, so no place can compass and contain him.

Stephen Charnock

God cannot be grasped by the mind. If he could be grasped he would not be God.

Evagrius of Pontus

And I saw that there was an Ocean of Darkness and Death; but an infinite Ocean of Light and Love flowed over the Ocean of Darkness; and in that I saw the infinite love of God.

George Fox

I cannot tell where God begins, still less where he ends. But my belief is better expressed if I say there is no end to God's beginning.

André Gide

God is a sea of infinite substance.

St. John of Damascus

We know God not in his essence but by the magnificence of his creation and the action of his providence, which presents to us, as in a mirror, the reflection of his goodness, his wisdom and his infinite powers.

St. Maximus the Confessor

The attributes of God, though intelligible to us on their surface yet, for the very reason that they are infinite, transcend our comprehension, when they are dwelt upon, when they are followed out, and can only be received by faith.

John Henry Newman

How should finite comprehend infinite? We shall apprehend Him, but not comprehend Him.

Richard Sibbes

One who stands beside the sea sees the infinite ocean of the waters, but cannot grasp the extent of them, beholding only a part. So it is with one who is judged worthy to fix his gaze in contemplation on the infinite ocean of God's glory and behold him with the intelligence: he sees not how great God is, but only what the spiritual eyes of his soul can grasp.

Simeon the New Theologian

In God, time and eternity are one and the same thing.

Heinrich Suso

God's infinitude places him so far above our knowing that a lifetime spent in cultivating the knowledge of him leaves as much yet to learn as if we had never begun.

Aiden Wilson (A.W.) Tozer

Judgment of

See also Last Judgment

Surely you won't kill the innocent with the guilty. That's impossible! You can't do that. If you did, the innocent would be punished along with the guilty. That is impossible. The judge of all the earth has to act justly.

Genesis 18:25 GNB

The Lord shall endure for ever: he hath prepared his throne for judgment.

Psalm 9:7 KJV

In the same hour came forth fingers of a man's hand, and wrote over against the candlestick upon the plaister of the wall of the king's palace: and the king saw the part of the hand that wrote.

Daniel 5:5 KJV

He has set a day when he will judge the world's people with fairness. And he has chosen the man Jesus to do the judging for him. God has given proof of this to all of us by raising Jesus from death.

Acts 17:31 CEV

The day when, according to my gospel, God

will judge the secrets of human hearts through Christ Jesus.

Romans 2:16 REB

Then I saw a great white throne and the one who sat on it; the earth and the heaven fled from his presence, and no place was found for them. And I saw the dead, great and small, standing before the throne, and books were opened. Also another book was opened, the book of life. And the dead were judged according to their works, as recorded in the books. And the sea gave up the dead that were in it, Death and Hades gave up the dead that were in them, and all were judged according to what they had done.

Revelation 20:11–13 NRSV

If we judge ourselves, we will not be judged by God.

Bishop Jean Pierre Camus

The Lord is King! child of the dust, / The Judge of all the earth is just: / Holy and true are all His ways; / Let every creature speak His praise.

Josiah Conder

He has sounded forth the trumpet that shall never call retreat, / He is sifting out the hearts of men before his judgment seat.

Julia Ward Howe

God postpones the collapse and dissolution of the universe (through which the bad angels, the demons, and men would cease to exist), because of the Christian seed, which he knows to be the cause in nature of the world's preservation.

St. Justin Martyr

The judgment of God is the reaping which comes from sowing, and is evidence of the love of God, not proof of his wrath. The penalty of an evil harvest is not God's punishment; it is the consequence of defying the moral order which in love he maintains as the only environment in which maturity of fellowship and communion can be achieved.

Kirby Page

The judgment of God is going on wherever the word of God is being proclaimed; men are judging themselves, according to their acceptance or rejection of the Gospel.

Alan Richardson

God judges a man, not by the point he has reached, but by the way he is facing; not by distance, but by direction.

James Stewart

Justice of

See also Justice

The truth is, God would never do wrong, the Almighty does not pervert justice.

Job 34:12 REB

The LORD sits enthroned for ever, he has established his throne for judgment. He judges the world with righteousness; he judges the peoples with equity.

Psalm 9:7–8 NRSV

All who do evil are shameless, but the Lord does right and is always fair. With the dawn of each day, God brings about justice.

Zephaniah 3:5 CEV

If we confess our sins, he is faithful and just to forgive us our sins, and to cleanse us from all unrighteousness.

1 John 1:9 KJV

If his justice were such as could be adjudged just by human reckoning, it clearly would not be divine; it would in no way differ from human justice. But inasmuch as he is the one true God, wholly incomprehensible and inaccessible to man's understanding, it is reasonable, indeed inevitable, that his justice also should be incomprehensible.

Martin Luther

Sin and death are an adamantine chain and link that none can sever. Who shall separate that which God in his justice hath put together?

Richard Sibbes

Redemptive theology teaches that mercy does not become effective toward a man until justice has done its work.

Aiden Wilson (A.W.) Tozer

God's compassion flows out of his goodness and goodness without justice is not goodness. God spares us because he is good, but he could not be good if he were not just.

Aiden Wilson (A.W.) Tozer

Love of

See also God, Grace and Mercy of; Love

For as the heavens are high above the earth, so great is his steadfast love toward those who fear him.

Psalm 103:11 NRSV

O give thanks to the LORD, for he is good, for his steadfast love endures for ever.

Psalm 136:1 NRSV

For this is how God loved the world: he gave his only Son, so that everyone who believes in him may not perish but may have eternal life.

John 3:16 NJB

God has shown us how much he loves us—it was while we were still sinners that Christ died for us!

Romans 5:8 GNB

For I am convinced that neither death, nor life, nor angels, nor rulers, nor things present, nor things to come, nor powers, nor height, nor depth, nor anything else in all creation, will be able to separate us from the love of God in Christ Jesus our Lord.

Romans 8:38–39 NRSV

In this is love, not that we loved God but that he loved us and sent his Son to be the atoning sacrifice for our sins.

1 John 4:10 NRSV

God is love.

1 John 4:16 NRSV

God loves you as though you are the only person in the world, and he loves everyone the way he loves you.

St. Augustine of Hippo

We bless thee for our creation, preservation, and all the blessings of this life; but above all for thine inestimable love in the redemption of the world by our Lord Jesus Christ, for the means of grace, and for the hope of glory.

Book of Common Prayer

The person you are now, the person you have been, the person you will be—this person God has chosen as beloved.

William Countryman

God's love is always supernatural, always a miracle, always the last thing we deserve.

Robert Horn

There is no human wreckage, lying in the

ooze of the deepest sea of iniquity, that God's deep love cannot reach and redeem.

John Henry Jowett

Love is the most durable power in the world. This creative force, so beautifully exemplified in the life of Christ, is the most potent instrument available in mankind's quest for peace and security.

Martin Luther King Jr.

God's love is not drawn out by our lovableness, but wells up, like an artesian spring, from the depths of his nature.

Alexander Maclaren

We have a God who loves. That means that we have a God who suffers.

John Bertram (J.B.) Phillips

To say that God is love is to say that God is the living, active, dynamic, ceaselessly desiring reality who will not let go until he has won the free response of his creation.

Norman Pittenger

God does not love us because we are valuable. We are valuable because God loves us.

Fulton John Sheen

God soon turns from his wrath, but he never turns from his love.

Charles Haddon Spurgeon

It is certain that God cannot, will not, never did, reject a charitable man in his greatest need and in his most passionate prayers; for God himself is love, and every degree of charity that dwells in us is the participation of the Divine Nature.

Jeremy Taylor

Every existing thing is equally upheld in its existence by God's creative love. The friends

of God should love him to the point of merging their love into his with regard to all things here below.

Simone Weil

Love divine, all loves excelling, / Joy of heaven, to earth come down, / Fix in us Thy humble dwelling, / All Thy faithful mercies crown. / Jesus, Thou art all compassion, / Pure, unbounded love Thou art; / Visit us with Thy salvation, / Enter every trembling heart.

Charles Wesley

Mercy of, *see* God, Grace and Mercy of

Mystery of

There are some things that the Lord our God has kept secret; but he has revealed his Law, and we and our descendants are to obey it forever.

Deuteronomy 29:29 GNB

Can you fathom the mystery of God, or attain to the limits of the Almighty?

Job 11:7 REB

He made known to us the mystery of his will according to his good pleasure, which he purposed in Christ, to be put into effect when the times will have reached their fulfillment—to bring all things in heaven and on earth together under one head, even Christ.

Ephesians 1:9–10 NIV

The mystery which hath been hid from ages and from generations, but now is made manifest to his saints: To whom God would make known what is the riches of the glory of this mystery among the Gentiles; which is Christ in you, the hope of glory.

Colossians 1:26–27 KJV

As their hearts are joined together in love, they will be wonderfully blessed with complete understanding. And they will truly know Christ. Not only is he the key to God's mystery, but all wisdom and knowledge are hidden away in him.

Colossians 2:2–3 CEV

We can know what God is not, but we cannot know what he is.

St. Augustine of Hippo

God is the beyond in the midst of life.

Dietrich Bonhoeffer

God's richness is such that he can totally give himself to every man, can be there only for him—and likewise for a second and third, for millions and thousands of millions. That is the mystery of his infinity and inexhaustible richness.

Ladislaus Boros

God moves in a mysterious way / His wonders to perform; / He plants his footsteps in the sea, / And rides upon the storm.

William Cowper

Mystery is beyond human reason but it is not against reason.

Os Guinness

If the works of God were such as might be easily comprehended by human reason, they could not be called wonderful or unspeakable.

Thomas à Kempis

A comprehended God is no God at all.

Gerhard Tersteegen

God alone knows the depths and the riches of his Godhead, and divine wisdom alone can declare his secrets.

St. Thomas Aquinas

There is ever a beyond of mystery; for the more we know, the more we wonder.

George Tyrrell

Name of

Moses said to God, "If I come to the Israelites and say to them, 'The God of your ancestors has sent me to you,' and they ask me, 'What is his name?' what shall I say to them?" God said to Moses, "I AM WHO I AM . . . This is my name forever, and this my title for all generations."

Exodus 3:13–15 NRSV

You shall not misuse the name of the Lord your God, for the Lord will not hold anyone guiltless who misuses his name.

Exodus 20:7 NIV

The name of the Lord is a tower of strength, where the righteous may run for refuge.

Proverbs 18:10 REB

Our Father which art in heaven, Hallowed be thy name.

Matthew 6:9 KJV

Then God gave Christ the highest place and honored his name above all others. So at the name of Jesus everyone will bow down, those in heaven, on earth and under the earth.

Philippians 2:9–10 CEV

If our naming of God is distorted, our knowledge of God will be also.

Brian Wren

Personal Descriptions of

The eternal God is thy refuge, and underneath are the everlasting arms.

Deuteronomy 33:27 KJV

A father of the fatherless . . . is God in his holy habitation.

Psalm 68:5 KJV

As a father has compassion for his children, so the LORD has compassion for those who fear him.

Psalm 103:13 NRSV

The Lord answers, "Can a woman forget her own baby and not love the child she bore? Even if a mother should forget her child, I will never forget you."

Isaiah 49:15 GNB

For you are our father, though Abraham does not know us and Israel does not acknowledge us; you, O LORD, are our father, our Redeemer from of old is your name.

Isaiah 63:16 NRSV

As a mother comforts her child, so I will comfort you.

Isaiah 66:13 NRSV

When Israel was a child, I loved him, and out of Egypt I called my son. The more I called them, the more they went from me; and kept sacrificing to the Baals, and offering incense to idols. Yet it was I who taught Ephraim to walk. I took them up in my arms; but they did not know that I healed them. I led them with cords of human kindness, with bands of love. I was to them like those who lift infants to their cheeks. I bent down to them and fed them.

Hosea 11:1–4 NRSV

Our Father which art in heaven, Hallowed be thy name.

Matthew 6:9 KJV

I will welcome you and be your Father. You will be my sons and my daughters, as surely as I am God.

2 Corinthians 6:17–18 CEV

Once the soul has determined to be converted to the service of God, God nurtures her in spirit and caresses her, like a loving mother with her tender babe, warming it at her breasts, feeding it with nourishing milk and soft, sweet food, and carrying it in her arms and cherishing it.

St. John of the Cross

As truly as God is our Father, so truly is God our Mother . . . the power and greatness of fatherhood . . . the wisdom and lovingness of motherhood . . . the endless fulfilling of all true desires.

Julian of Norwich

Father-like, He tends and spares us, / Well our feeble frame He knows; / In His hands He gently bears us, / Rescues us from all our foes; / Praise Him! Praise Him! / Widely as His mercy flows.

Henry Francis Lyte

The heavenly Father has no spoiled children. He loves them too much to allow that.

Fred Mitchell

God is a kind Father. He sets us all in the places where He wishes us to be employed: and that employment is truly "Our Father's business."

John Ruskin

To speak of God as the Mother of Creation seems to me a beautiful image, entirely consistent with Christian faith in God who surpasses and contains all created things, yet expressing in a new way God's profound care for creation and involvement with it.

Brian Wren

Power of, *see* God, Greatness of; God, Infiniteness of; God, Sovereignty of

Presence of

The Lord replied, "My Presence will go with you, and I will give you rest."

Exodus 33:14 NIV

Where could I go to escape from you? Where could I get away from your presence? If I went up to heaven, you would be there; if I lay down in the world of the dead, you would be there. If I flew away beyond the east or lived in the farthest place in the west, you would be there to lead me, you would be there to help me. I could ask the darkness to hide me or the light round me to turn into night, but even darkness is not dark for you, and the night is as bright as the day. Darkness and light are the same to you.

Psalm 139:7–12 GNB

The eyes of the Lord are in every place, beholding the evil and the good.

Proverbs 15:3 KJV

God has done all this, so that we will look for him and reach out and find him. He isn't far from any of us.

Acts 17:27 CEV

Draw near to God, and he will draw near to you. Cleanse your hands, you sinners, and purify your hearts, you double-minded.

James 4:8 NRSV

How distant you are from my sight while I am present to your sight! You are wholly present everywhere and I do not see you.

St. Anselm of Canterbury

A sense of Deity is inscribed on every heart.

John Calvin

God is not an idea, or a definition that we have committed to memory, he is a presence which we experience in our hearts.

Louis Evely

The world is so empty if one thinks only of mountains, rivers and cities, but to know someone here and there who thinks and feels with us and who, though distant, is close to us in spirit, this makes the earth for us an inhabited garden.

Johann Wolfgang von Goethe

God is above, presiding; beneath, sustaining; within, filling.

Hildebert of Lavardin

God is as present as the air.

Michael Hollings

Be Thou my vision, O Lord of my heart; / Nought be all else to me, save that Thou art; / Thou my best thought, by day or by night, / Waking or sleeping, Thy presence my light.

Irish, tr. Mary Elizabeth Byrne

Once in my imagination I was taken down to the bed of the sea, and saw there green hills and dales that seemed to be clothed with moss, seaweed, and stones. And I understood that if a person firmly believes that God is always with man, then even if he is thrown into the depths of the sea, he will be preserved in body and soul, and will enjoy greater solace and comfort than all this world can offer.

Julian of Norwich

Though God be everywhere present, yet he is only present to thee in the deepest and most central part of the soul.

William Law

You need not cry very loud; he is nearer to us than we think.

Brother Lawrence

We may ignore, but we can nowhere evade, the presence of God. The world is crowded with him. He walks everywhere incognito.

Clive Staples (C.S.) Lewis

There is the fundamental thing, the most serious thing of all, that we are always in the presence of God.

David Martyn Lloyd-Jones

God is no White Knight who charges into the world to pluck us like distressed damsels from the jaws of dragons, or diseases. God chooses to become present to and through us. It is up to us to rescue one another.

Nancy Mairs

God, who is everywhere, never leaves us. Yet he seems sometimes to be present, sometimes absent. If we do not know him well, we do not realize that he may be more present to us when he is absent than when he is present.

Thomas Merton

Self-Existence of

God said unto Moses, I AM THAT I AM.

Exodus 3:14 KJV

For just as the Father has life in himself, so he has granted the Son also to have life in himself.

John 5:26 NRSV

By nothing that we can think or say can God be exalted.

Angela of Foligno

God is not for proof but proclamation; not for argument but acceptance.

Robert Horn

God does not belong to the class of existing things . . . not that he has no existence, but that he is above all existing things, nay even above existence itself.

St. John of Damascus

Since God is self-existent, he is not composed. There are in him no parts to be altered.

Aiden Wilson (A.W.) Tozer

Were every man on earth to become atheist, it could not affect God in any way. He is what he is in himself without regard to any other. To believe in him adds nothing to his perfections; to doubt him takes nothing away.

Aiden Wilson (A.W.) Tozer

God exists in himself and of himself. His being he owes to no one. His substance is indivisible. He has no parts but is single in his unitary being.

Aiden Wilson (A.W.) Tozer

Origin is a word that can apply only to things created. When we think of anything that has origin, we are not thinking of God. God is self-existent, while all created things necessarily originated somewhere at some time. Aside from God, nothing is self-caused.

Aiden Wilson (A.W.) Tozer

Sovereignty of

See also Kingdom of God

Job said: No one can oppose you, because you have the power to do what you want.

Job 42:1–2 CEV

Whatever the LORD pleases he does, in heaven and on earth, in the seas and all deeps.

Psalm 135:6 NRSV

The king's heart is in the hand of the Lord, as the rivers of water: he turneth it whithersoever he will.

Proverbs 21:1 KJV

In Christ we have also obtained an inheritance, having been destined according to the purpose of him who accomplishes all things according to his counsel and will.

Ephesians 1:11 NRSV

I am Alpha and Omega, the beginning and the ending.

Revelation 1:8 KJV

Our Lord and God! You are worthy to receive glory, honor and power. For you created all things, and by your will they were given existence and life.

Revelation 4:11 GNB

The sovereignty of God is that golden scepter in his hand by which he will make all bow, either by his word or by his works, by his mercies or by his judgments.

Thomas Benton Brooks

Nothing that is attempted in opposition to God can ever be successful.

John Calvin

I have lived a long time, Sir, and the longer I live the more convincing proofs I see of this truth—that God governs in the affairs of men.

Benjamin Franklin

Wherever God rules over the human heart as King, there is the kingdom of God established.

Paul W. Harrison

The Lord's presence is infinite, his brightness insupportable, his majesty aweful, his dominion boundless and his sovereignty incontestable.

Matthew Henry

God does not stop to consult us.

David Martyn Lloyd-Jones

Transcendence of

The Lord is high above all nations, and his glory above the heavens.

Psalm 113:4 KJV

For thus says the high and lofty one who inhabits eternity, whose name is Holy: I dwell in the high and holy place, and also with those who are contrite and humble in spirit.

Isaiah 57:15 NRSV

This God made the world and everything in it. He is Lord of heaven and earth, and he doesn't live in temples built by human hands. He doesn't need help from anyone. He gives life, breath, and everything else to all people.

Acts 17:24–25 CEV

God is within all things, but not included; outside all things, but not excluded; above all things but not beyond their reach.

St. Gregory I

Who am I, Lord, that I should presume to approach unto thee? Behold the Heaven of heavens cannot contain thee, and thou sayest, "Come ye all unto me."

Thomas à Kempis

We cannot grasp what God is, but only what he is not, and how other things are related to him.

St. Thomas Aquinas

Trinity

Hear, O Israel: the Lord our God, the Lord is one.

Deuteronomy 6:4 NIV

Go ye therefore, and teach all nations, baptizing them in the name of the Father, and of the Son, and of the Holy Ghost.

Matthew 28:19 KJV

The grace of the Lord Jesus Christ, and the love of God, and the fellowship of the Holy Spirit, be with you all.

2 Corinthians 13:14 REB

God the Father decided to choose you as his people, and his Spirit has made you holy. You have obeyed Jesus Christ and are sprinkled with his blood.

1 Peter 1:2 CEV

It is rashness to search, godliness to believe, safeness to preach, and eternal blessedness to know the Trinity.

Thomas Adams

The Trinity is a mystery which my faith embraces as revealed in the Word, but my reason cannot fathom.

John Arrowsmith

If asked to define the Trinity, we can only say that it is not this or that.

St. Augustine of Hippo

Among all things called One, the Unity of the Divine Trinity holds the first place.

St. Bernard of Clairvaux

How can plurality consist with unity, or unity with plurality? To examine the fact closely is rashness, to believe it is piety, to know it is life, and life eternal.

St. Bernard of Clairvaux

No wonder that the doctrine of the Trinity is inexplicable, seeing that the nature of God is incomprehensible. Our faith must assent to what our reason cannot comprehend, otherwise we can never be Christians.

Francis Crawford Burkitt

The distinction of persons is true only for our knowledge of God, not for his inner Being, which we cannot know.

Millar Burrows

The Trinity attributes to the Father those works of the Divinity in which power excels, to the Son those in which wisdom excels, and those in which love excels to the Holy Ghost.

John XXIII

The Creed confesses three persons as comprehended in one divine essence, each one, however, retaining his distinct personality ... to the Father we ascribe the work of creation; to the Son the work of redemption; to the Holy Spirit the power to forgive sins, to gladden, to strengthen, to transport from death to life eternal.

Martin Luther

God is revealed as the God of love, and henceforth every morally good act, that is, every act formed by charity, is a revelation of God. Every word of truth and love, every hand extended in kindness, echoes the inner life of the Trinity.

Gabriel Moran

For charity to be true, it requires more than one person; for it to be perfected, it requires a Trinity of persons.

Richard of St. Victor

Without belief in God's revelation the Trinity cannot be known at all; and even for believers it is incomprehensible in an exceptionally high degree, indeed in the highest degree. There it is a mystery in the truest, highest, most beautiful sense of the word.

M.J. Scheeben

The Holy Trinity, pervading all men from first to last, from head to foot, binds them all together.

Simeon the New Theologian

Love and faith are at home in the mystery of the Godhead. Let reason kneel in reverence outside.

Aiden Wilson (A.W.) Tozer

The Trinity is purely an object of faith, the plumbline of reason is too short to fathom this mystery; but where reason cannot wade, there faith must swim. . . . This sacred doctrine, though it be not against reason, yet is above reason.

Thomas Watson

Voice of

These words the Lord spake unto all your assembly in the mount out of the midst of the fire, of the cloud, and of the thick darkness, with a great voice: and he added no more.

Deuteronomy 5:22 KJV

And after the earthquake a fire; but the Lord was not in the fire: and after the fire a still small voice.

1 Kings 19:12 KJV

The voice of the LORD is over the waters; the God of glory thunders, the LORD, over mighty waters. The voice of the LORD is powerful; the voice of the LORD is full of majesty. The voice of the LORD breaks the cedars. . . . The voice of the LORD flashes forth flames of fire. The voice of the LORD shakes the wilderness; the LORD shakes the wilderness of Kadesh. The voice of the

LORD causes the oaks to whirl, and strips the forest bare; and in his temple all say, "Glory!"

Psalm 29:3–5, 7–9 NRSV

"Father, bring glory to your name!" Then a voice spoke from heaven, "I have brought glory to it, and I will do so again." The crowd standing there heard the voice, and some of them said it was thunder, while others said, "An angel spoke to him!"

John 12:28–29 GNB

We want God's voice to be clear but it is not. . . . We want it to be clear as day, but it is deep as night. It is deep and clear, but with a dark clarity like an x-ray. It reaches our bones.

Ernesto Cardenal

There is hardly ever a complete silence in our soul. God is whispering to us well nigh incessantly. Whenever the sounds of the world die out in the soul, or sink low, then we hear these whisperings of God. He is always whispering to us, only we do not always hear because of the noise, hurry, and distraction which life causes as it rushes on.

Frederick William Faber

It is true that the voice of God, having once fully penetrated the heart, becomes strong as the tempest and loud as the thunder; but before reaching the heart it is as weak as a light breath which scarcely agitates the air. It shrinks from noise, and is silent amid agitation.

St. Ignatius of Loyola

The voice of the subconscious argues with you, tries to convince you; but the inner voice of God does not argue, does not try to convince you. It just speaks and it is self-authenticating.

E. Stanley Jones

If you keep watch over your hearts, and listen for the voice of God and learn of him, in one short hour you can learn more from him than you could learn from man in a thousand years.

Johann Tauler

The voice of God is a friendly voice. No one need fear to listen to it unless he has already made up his mind to resist it.

Aiden Wilson (A.W.) Tozer

Breathe through the heats of our desire / Thy coolness and Thy balm; / Let sense be dumb—let flesh retire; / Speak through the earthquake, wind, and fire, / O still small voice of calm!

John Greenleaf Whittier

Will of

I delight to do your will, O my God, your law is within my heart.

Psalm 40:8 NRSV

Your kingdom come. Your will be done, on earth as it is in heaven.

Matthew 6:10 NRSV

It is not anyone who says to me, "Lord, Lord," who will enter the kingdom of Heaven, but the person who does the will of my Father in heaven.

Matthew 7:21 NJB

For I came down from heaven, not to do mine own will, but the will of him that sent me.

John 6:38 KJV

Conform no longer to the pattern of this present world, but be transformed by the renewal of your minds. Then you will be able to discern the will of God, and to know what is good, acceptable, and perfect.

Romans 12:2 REB

Do not be foolish, but understand what the will of the Lord is.

Ephesians 5:17 NRSV

Always be joyful and never stop praying. Whatever happens, keep thanking God because of Jesus Christ. This is what God wants you to do.

1 Thessalonians 5:16–18 CEV

The will of God is the measure of things.

St. Ambrose

There is no peace but in the will of God. God's will is our peace and there is no other peace. God's service is perfect freedom and there is no other freedom.

Fr. Andrew

Nothing, therefore, happens unless the Omnipotent wills it to happen: He either permits it to happen, or He brings it about Himself.

St. Augustine of Hippo

The ordaining of salvation for man and of man for salvation is the original and basic will of God, the ground and purpose of His will as Creator.

Karl Barth

No one may prefer his own will to the will of God, but in everything we must seek and do the will of God.

St. Basil the Great

The center of God's will is our only safety.

Betsie ten Boom

It we would avoid a senseless natural philosophy we must always start with this principle: that everything in nature depends upon the will of God, and that the whole course of nature is only the prompt carrying into effect of his orders.

John Calvin

There are no disappointments to those whose wills are buried in the will of God.

Frederick William Faber

All moral obligation resolves itself into the obligation of conformity to the will of God.

Charles Hodge

The great maker of the will is alive to carry out his own intentions.

Charles Haddon Spurgeon

God gives when he will, as he will, and to whom he will.

St. Teresa of Avila

Wisdom of

See also Holy Spirit; Jesus Christ

Our Lord, by your wisdom you made so many things: the whole earth is covered with your living creatures.

Psalm 104:24 CEV

Blessed be the name of God for ever and ever: for wisdom and might are his.

Daniel 2:20 KJV

To the only wise God through Jesus Christ be glory for endless ages! Amen.

Romans 16:27 REB

As a blind man has no idea of colors, so have we no idea of the manner by which the all-wise God perceives and understands all things.

Sir Isaac Newton

Immortal, invisible, God only wise, / In light inaccessible hid from our eyes, / Most blessed, most glorious, the Ancient of Days, / Almighty, victorious, thy great Name we praise.

Walter Chalmers Smith

He formed the stars, those heavenly flames, / He counts their numbers, calls their names; / His wisdom's vast, and knows no bounds, / A deep where all our thoughts are drowned.

Isaac Watts

God's sovereignty is not arbitrariness, as some misunderstand it, for God has his reasons, based on his infinite wisdom, which he does not always choose to reveal to us.

Spiros Zodhiates

Godlessness

The triumph of a wicked person is short-lived, the glee of one who is godless lasts but a moment!

Job 20:5 REB

The wrath of God is being revealed from heaven against all the godlessness and wickedness of men who suppress the truth by their wickedness.

Romans 1:18 NIV

Have nothing to do with godless philosophical discussions—they only lead further and further away from true religion.

2 Timothy 2:16 NJB

Nothing is more dangerous than associating with the ungodly.

John Calvin

God permits the wicked, but not forever.

Thomas Fuller

He that saith he will be good tomorrow, he saith he will be wicked today.

James Janeway

Searching for true happiness in the context of a godless life is like looking for a needle in a haystack that doesn't have any.

W.T. Purkiser

What wicked men do should not disturb the good man's tranquility.

Aiden Wilson (A.W.) Tozer

Golden Rule

See also Love, for Others

What you hate, do not do to anyone.

Tobit 4:15 NRSV

In everything do to others as you would have them do to you; for this is the law and the prophets.

Matthew 7:12 NRSV

The only thing you should owe to anyone is love for one another, for to love the other person is to fulfill the law.

Romans 13:8 NJB

For all the law is fulfilled in one word, even in this; Thou shalt love thy neighbor as thyself.

Galatians 5:14 KJV

To love our neighbor in charity is to love God in man.

St. Francis de Sales

It is easier to love humanity as a whole than to love one's neighbor.

Eric Hoffer

We have committed the Golden Rule to memory; let us now commit it to life.

Edwin Markham

The Golden Rule would reconcile capital and labor, all political contention and uproar, all selfishness and greed.

Joseph Parker

Good

See also God, Goodness of; Good Works; Virtues and Vices

God looked at what he had done. All of it was very good!

Genesis 1:31 CEV

Let love be without any pretense. Avoid what is evil; stick to what is good.

Romans 12:9 NJB

The fruit of the Spirit is . . . goodness.

Galatians 5:22 KJV

God himself would not permit evil in this world if good did not come of it.

St. Thomas Aquinas

He that is good is free, though he is a slave; he that is evil is a slave, though he be a king.

St. Augustine of Hippo

He who would do good to another must do it in Minute Particulars. General Good is the plea of the scoundrel, hypocrite, and flatterer.

William Blake

Genuine goodness is a matter of habitually acting and responding appropriately in each situation as it arises, moved always by the desire to please God.

The Cloud of Unknowing

He that returns a good for evil obtains the victory.

Thomas Fuller

Goodness is something so simple: always live for others, never to seek one's own advantage.

Dag Hammarskjöld

We cannot love good if we do not hate evil.

St. Jerome

Make a rule, and pray to God to help you to keep it, never, if possible to lie down at night without being able to say, I have made one human being at least a little wiser, a little happier, or a little better this day.

Charles Kingsley

An act of goodness, the least act of true goodness, is indeed the best proof of the existence of God.

Jacques Maritain

A good end cannot sanctify evil means; nor must we ever do evil that good may come of it.

William Penn

The fundamental idea of good is thus; that it consists in preserving life, in favoring it, in wanting to bring it to its highest value; and evil consists in destroying life, doing it injury, hindering its development.

Albert Schweitzer

Good is no good, but if it be not spend: God giveth good for none other end.

Edmund Spenser

To be good is to be in harmony with one's self.

Oscar Wilde

Good Friday, *see* Eucharist; Jesus Christ, Death of; Jesus Christ, Savior; Seven Last Words

Goodness, *see* Good; Holiness; Righteousness

Good Works

See also Good

Let your light so shine before men, that they may see your good works, and glorify your Father which is in heaven.

Matthew 5:16 KJV

How God anointed Jesus of Nazareth with the Holy Spirit and with power; how he went about doing good and healing all who were oppressed by the devil, for God was with him.

Acts 10:38 NRSV

We are God's handiwork, created in Christ Jesus for the life of good deeds which God designed for us.

Ephesians 2:10 REB

What good is it, my brothers and sisters, if you say you have faith but you do not have works? Can faith save you?

James 2:14 NRSV

To be active in works and unfaithful in heart is like raising a beautiful and lofty building on an unsound foundation. The higher the building, the greater the fall. Without the support of faith, good works cannot stand.

St. Ambrose

We do the works, but God works in us the doing of the works.

St. Augustine of Hippo

The confession of evil works is the first beginning of good works.

St. Augustine of Hippo

For faith without works cannot please, nor can good works without faith.

The Venerable Bede

It is faith alone that justifies, but the faith that justifies is not alone.

John Calvin

We are too fond of our own will. We want to be doing what we fancy mighty things, but the great point is to do small things, when called to them, in a right spirit.

Richard Cecil

One must not always think so much about what one should do, but rather what one should be. Our works do not ennoble us; but we must ennoble our works.

Meister Eckhart

You must live with people to know their problems, and live with God in order to solve them.

Peter Taylor Forsyth

Heaven will be filled with such as have done good works and hell with such as intended to do them.

Antonio Guevasa

The greatest pleasure I know is to do a good action by stealth, and to have it found out by accident.

Charles Lamb

True Christianity is love in action.

David O. McKay

How far that little candle throws his beams! So shines a good deed in a naughty world.

William Shakespeare

Do all the good you can, by all the means you can, in all the ways you can, to all the people you can, in all the places you can, as long as ever you can.

John Wesley

Gospel

See also Church, Mission and Ministry of; Evangelism; Witness

After John had been arrested, Jesus came into Galilee proclaiming the gospel of God: "The time has arrived; the kingdom of God is upon you. Repent, and believe the gospel."

Mark 1:14–15 REB

I have complete confidence in the gospel; it is God's power to save all who believe, first the Jews and also the Gentiles. For the gospel reveals how God puts people right with himself: it is through faith from beginning to end.

Romans 1:16–17 GNB

When I preach the gospel, I cannot boast, for I am compelled to preach. Woe to me if I do not preach the gospel!

1 Corinthians 9:16 NIV

For I handed on to you as of first importance what I in turn had received: that Christ died for our sins in accordance with the scriptures, and that he was buried, and that he was raised on the first day in accordance with the scriptures.

1 Corinthians 15:3–4 NRSV

Now I want to make it quite clear to you, brothers, about the gospel that was preached by me, that it was no human message. It was not from any human being that I received it, and I was not taught it, but it came to me through a revelation of Jesus Christ.

Galatians 1:11–12 NJB

That teaching is found in the gospel that was entrusted to me to announce, the Good News from the glorious and blessed God.

1 Timothy 1:11 GNB

Thanks be to the gospel, by means of which we also, who did not see Christ when He came into this world, seem to be with Him when we read His deeds.

St. Ambrose

Cry the gospel with your whole life.

Charles de Foucauld

The gospel reminds all men of an inescapable personal destiny in eternity, based on a conclusive decision in time.

Carl F.H. Henry

The gospel makes husbands better husbands, wives better wives, parents better parents, masters better masters, and servants better servants; in a word, I would not give a farthing for that man's religion whose cat and dog were not the better for it.

Rowland Hill

The gospel was not good advice but good news.

William Ralph Inge

Religions are man's search for God; the gospel is God's search for man. There are many religions, but one gospel.

E. Stanley Jones

The Gospel is open to all; the most respectable sinner has no more claim on it than the worst.

David Martyn Lloyd-Jones

The glory of the gospel is that when the Church is absolutely different from the world, she invariably attracts it.

David Martyn Lloyd-Jones

The gospel is neither a discussion nor a debate. It is an announcement.

Paul Stromberg Rees

Humble and self-forgetting we must be always, but diffident and apologetic about the gospel never.

James Stewart

Our reading of the gospel story can be and should be an act of personal communion with the living Lord.

William Temple

The Gospel is accessible to all. One can hear it any day at any hour of the day, and it seems childishly clear and simple. But which of us is child enough to understand it? It shines out like a lighted candle, but only those who have eyes to see can see. And however much of it is read and preached, its meaning, lke the meaning of every living thing, guards itself from those who have no ears to hear.

Lanza del Vasto

The gospel gives us different priorities from those of the popular culture and offers us a different agenda from that of the political economy.

Jim Wallis

There are two things to do about the Gospel—believe it and behave it.

Susanna Wesley

Gossip

See also Speech

Rash words are like sword thrusts, but the tongue of the wise brings healing.

Proverbs 12:18 NRSV

A perverse man stirs up dissension, and a gossip separates close friends.

Proverbs 16:28 NIV

Whoever gossips to you will gossip of you.

Anon.

Whispered insinuations are the rhetoric of the devil.

Johann Wolfgang von Goethe

A real Christian is a person who can give his pet parrot to the town gossip.

William Franklin (Billy) Graham

Gossip is always a personal confession either of malice or imbecility.

Josiah Gilbert Holland

Never listen to accounts of the frailties of others; and if anyone should complain to you of another, humbly ask him not to speak of him at all.

St. John of the Cross

We should have great peace if we did not busy ourselves with what others say and do.

Thomas à Kempis

Do not listen gleefully to gossip at your neighbor's expense or chatter to a person who likes to find fault.

Maximus the Confessor

If all men knew what each said of the other, there would not be four friends in the world.

Blaise Pascal

Believe nothing against another, but upon good authority; nor report what may hurt another, unless it be a greater hurt to others to conceal it.

William Penn

Rumor is a loud liar, like a snowball that gathers as it goeth.

John Trapp

Government and Politics

See also Rulers; Society

Give your servant [Solomon] a heart to understand how to govern your people, how to discern between good and evil, for how could one otherwise govern such a great people as yours?

1 Kings 3:9 NJB

Everyone must obey the state authorities, because no authority exists without God's permission, and the existing authorities have been put there by God.

Romans 13:1 GNB

Government originated as an ordinance of God. It is, in one sense, God's response to the nature of the people themselves. Whilst it cannot redeem the world or be used as a tool to establish the kingdom of God, civil government does set the boundaries for human behavior. The state is not a remedy for sin, but a means to restrain it.

Charles W. Colson

The foundation of our society and of our government rests so much on the teachings of the Bible that it would be difficult to support them if faith in these teachings should cease.

Calvin Coolidge

He who shall introduce into public affairs the principles of primitive Christianity will revolutionize the world.

Benjamin Franklin

The lesson of history tells us that no state or government devised by man can flourish forever.

William Franklin (Billy) Graham

God governs the world, and we have only to do our duty wisely and leave the issue to him.

John Jay

That government is best which governs the least, because its people discipline themselves.

Thomas Jefferson

We know that a separation of State and Church is a source of strength, but the conscience of our nation does not call for separation between men of State and faith in the Supreme Being.

Lyndon B. Johnson

Christian political action does not mean waiting for the orders of the bishop or campaigning under the banner of the Church; rather, it means bringing to politics a sense of Christian responsibility.

Franziskus Koenig

Man's capacity for justice makes democracy possible. His inclination to injustice makes democracy necessary.

(Karl Paul) Reinhold Niebuhr

Nothing is politically right which is morally wrong.

Daniel O'Connell

Men must be governed by God or they will be ruled by tyrants.

William Penn

One of the greatest delusions in the world is the hope that the evils in this world are to be cured by legislation.

Thomas Brackett Reed

Disbelief in Christianity is not so much to be dreaded as its acceptance with a complete denial of it in society and politics.

Mark Rutherford

No government can expect to be wholly at ease with the Church since the Church serves

the Kingdom which is not of this world.

Mark Santor

A Church which claims that the world is for Christ must be up to its neck in politics.

Donald Soper

If therefore, it is natural for man to live in the society of many, it is necessary that there exist among men some means by which the group may be governed. For where there are many men together, and each one is looking after his own interest, the group would be broken up and scattered unless there were also someone to take care of what appertains to the common weal.

St. Thomas Aquinas

It is impossible to rightly govern the world without God and the Bible.

George Washington

Grace

See also God, Grace and Mercy of; Jesus Christ, Love of; Law

With great power gave the apostles witness of the resurrection of the Lord Jesus: and great grace was upon them all.

Acts 4:33 KJV

All are justified by the free gift of his grace through being set free in Christ Jesus.

Romans 3:24 NJB

My grace is sufficient for thee: for my strength is made perfect in weakness.

2 Corinthians 12:9 KJV

For it is by grace you have been saved, through faith—and this not from yourselves, it is the gift of God.

Ephesians 2:8 NIV

No athlete is admitted to the contest of virtue, unless he has first been washed of all stains of sins and consecrated with the gift of heavenly grace.

St. Ambrose

Verily, here must the spirit rise to grace, or else neither the body nor it shall there rise to glory.

Lancelot Andrewes

I know nothing, except what everyone knows—if there when Grace dances, I should dance.

W.H. Auden

This grace of Christ without which neither infants nor adults can be saved, is not rendered for any merits, but is given gratis, on account of which it is also called grace.

St. Augustine of Hippo

Let grace be the beginning, grace the consummation, grace the crown.

The Venerable Bede

There is no such way to attain to a greater measure of grace as for a man to live up to the little grace he has.

Phillips Brooks

Grace is but glory begun, and glory is but grace perfected.

Jonathan Edwards

A state of mind that sees God in everything is evidence of growth in grace and a thankful heart.

Charles Grandison Finney

The doctrines of grace humble a man without degrading him, and exalt him without inflating him.

Charles Hodge

They travel lightly whom God's grace carries.

Thomas à Kempis

The law tells me how crooked I am. Grace comes along and straightens me out.

Dwight Lyman (D.L.) Moody

I am not what I might be, I am not what I ought to be, I am not what I wish to be, I am not what I hope to be; but I thank God I am not what I once was, and I can say with the great apostle, "By the grace of God I am what I am."

John Newton

Amazing grace! how sweet the sound / That saved a wretch like me; / I once was lost, but now am found; / Was blind, but now I see. / 'Twas grace that taught my heart to fear, / And grace my fears relieved; / How precious did that grace appear, / The hour I first believed!

John Newton

All men who live with any degree of serenity live by some assurance of grace.

(Karl Paul) Reinhold Niebuhr

Grace grows best in the winter.

Samuel Rutherford

Grace is love that cares and stoops and rescues.

John Stott

The grace of God is in my mind shaped like a key, that comes from time to time and unlocks the heavy doors.

Donald Swann

Grace strikes us when we are in great pain and restlessness. It strikes us when we walk through the dark valley of a meaningless and empty life. It strikes us when we feel that our separation is deeper than usual.

Paul Tillich

Gratitude, *see* Thankfulness and Thanksgiving

Greed

See also Covetousness; Possessions; Selfishness

A greedy man brings trouble to his family, but he who hates bribes will live.

Proverbs 15:27 NIV

He said to them, "Take care! Be on your guard against all kinds of greed; for one's life does not consist in the abundance of possessions."

Luke 12:15 NRSV

You can be quite certain that nobody who indulges in sexual immorality or impurity or greed—which is worshiping a false god—can inherit the kingdom of God.

Ephesians 5:5 NJB

Those who eat too much are just as guilty of sin as those who drink too much.

Joseph Caryl

Gluttony is an emotional escape, a sign something is eating us.

Peter De Vries

Bridle the appetite of gluttony and thou wilt with less difficulty restrain all other inordinate desires of animal nature.

Thomas à Kempis

Greed has three facets; love of things, love of fame, and love of pleasure; and these can be attacked directly with frugality, anonymity, and moderation.

Paul Martin

Nobody can fight properly and boldly for the faith if he clings to a fear of being stripped of earthly possessions.

St. Peter Damian

One of the weaknesses of our age is our apparent inability to distinguish our needs from our greeds.

Donald William Bradley Robinson

Grief

See also Bereavement; Loss; Sadness

Be merciful to me, O Lord, for I am in distress; my eyes grow weak with sorrow, my soul and my body with grief. My life is consumed by anguish and my years by groaning; my strength fails because of my affliction, and my bones grow weak.

Psalm 31:9–10 NIV

He is despised and rejected of men; a man of sorrows, and acquainted with grief: and we hid as it were our faces from him; he was despised, and we esteemed him not. Surely he hath borne our griefs, and carried our sorrows: yet we did esteem him stricken, smitten of God, and afflicted.

Isaiah 53:3–4 KJV

The LORD will be your everlasting light, and your days of mourning shall be ended.

Isaiah 60:20 NRSV

I will turn their mourning into joy, and will comfort them, and make them rejoice from their sorrow.

Jeremiah 31:13 KJV

Happy are those who mourn; God will comfort them!

Matthew 5:4 GNB

When he got up from prayer, he came to the disciples and found them sleeping because of grief.

Luke 22:45 NRSV

He that conceals his grief finds no remedy for it.

Anon.

In every pang that rends the heart, the Man of Sorrows has a part.

Michael Bruce

The true way to mourn the dead is to take care of the living who belong to them.

Edmund Burke

Passionate grief does not link us with the dead, but cuts us off from them.

Clive Staples (C.S.) Lewis

Deep is the plowing of grief! But often-times less would not suffice for the agriculture of God.

Thomas de Quincey

Grief can be your servant, helping you to feel more compassion for others who hurt.

Robert Harold Schuller

Be not hasty to offer advice to those who are bowed down with a weight of trouble. There is a sacredness in grief which demands our reverence; the very habitation of a mourner must be approached with awe.

Charles Simeon

The bitterest tears shed over graves are for words left unsaid and deeds left undone.

Harriet Beecher Stowe

We are healed of grief only when we express it to the full.

Charles R. Swindoll

Guidance

See also Holy Spirit, Guidance of

Make thy way plain before my face.

Psalm 5:8 BCP

He lets me rest in fields of green grass and leads me to quiet pools of fresh water. He gives me new strength. He guides me in the right paths, as he has promised.

Psalm 23:2–3 GNB

For this God is our God for ever and ever: he will be our guide even unto death.

Psalm 48:14 KJV

Put all your trust in the Lord and do not rely on your own understanding. At every step you take keep him in mind, and he will direct your path.

Proverbs 3:5–6 REB

Where there is no guidance, a nation falls, but in an abundance of counselors there is safety.

Proverbs 11:14 NRSV

If you spend yourselves on behalf of the hungry and satisfy the needs of the oppressed, then your light will rise in the darkness, and your night will become like the noonday. The Lord will guide you always; he will satisfy your needs in a sun-scorched land and will strengthen your frame.

Isaiah 58:10–11 NIV

[Zechariah's "Benedictus"] And thou, child, shall be called the Prophet of the Highest; for thou shalt go before the face of the Lord to prepare his ways, to give knowledge of salvation unto his people for the remission of their sins, through the tender mercy of our God, whereby the day-spring from on high hath visited us to give light to them that sit in darkness, and in the shadow of death, and to guide our feet into the way of peace.

Luke 1:76–79 BCP

When the Sprit of truth comes, he will guide you into all truth; for he will not speak on his own, but will speak whatever he hears, and he will declare to you the things that are to come.

John 16:13 NRSV

All the way my Savior leads me: / What have I to ask beside? / Can I doubt His tender mercy / Who through life has been my Guide? / Heavenly peace, divinest comfort, / Here by faith in Him to dwell! / For I know whate'er befall me, / Jesus doeth all things well.

Frances Jane van Alstyne

Open my eyes that I may see, / Incline my heart that I may desire, / Order my steps that I may follow / The way of your commandments.

Lancelot Andrewes

Thy way, not mine, O Lord, / However dark it be! / Lead me by Thine own hand, / Choose out the path for me.

Horatius Bonar

In me there is darkness, but with thee there is light. I am lonely, but thou leavest me not; I am feeble in heart, but thou leavest me not; I am restless, but with thee there is peace; In me there is bitterness, but with thee there is patience. Thy ways are past understanding, but though knowest the way for me.

Dietrich Bonhoeffer

God instructs the heart, not by ideas, but by pains and contradictions.

Jean Pierre de Caussade

If a sheep stray from his fellows, the shepherd sets his dog after it, not to devour it, but to bring it in again; even so our Heavenly Shepherd.

Daniel Cawdray

I know not the way God leads me, but well do I know my Guide.

Martin Luther

Who brought me hither will bring me hence; no other guide I seek.

John Milton

Lead kindly light, amid th'encircling gloom; lead thou me on. The night is dark, and I am far from home; lead thou me on. Keep thou my fear; I do not ask to see the distant scene—one step enough for me.

John Henry Newman

God's might to direct me, / God's power to protect me, / God's wisdom for learning, / God's eye for discerning, / God's ear for my hearing, / God's Word for my clearing.

St. Patrick

When God shuts a door, He opens a window.

John Ruskin

If God's will is your will and if He always has His way [with you] then you always have your way also.

Hannah Whitall Smith

God's promises of guidance are not given to save us the bother of thinking.

John R.W. Stott

Deep in your heart it is not guidance that you want as much as a guide.

John White

Guilt

See also Confession; Forgiveness; Repentance; Shame

Have mercy on me, O God, according to your steadfast love; according to your abundant mercy blot out my transgressions. Wash me thoroughly from my iniquity, and cleanse me from my sin. For I know my transgressions, and my sin is ever before me. Against you, you alone, have I sinned, and done what is evil in your sight, so that you are justified in your sentence and blameless when you pass judgment. Indeed, I was born guilty, a sinner when my mother conceived me.

Psalm 51:1–5 NRSV

Then one of the seraphs flew to me, holding in its hand a live coal which it had taken from the altar with a pair of tongs. With this it touched my mouth and said: "Look, this has touched your lips, your guilt has been removed and your sin forgiven."

Isaiah 6:6–7 NJB

Whosoever shall eat this bread, and drink this cup of the Lord, unworthily, shall be guilty of the body and blood of the Lord.

1 Corinthians 11:27 KJV

For whosoever shall keep the whole law, and yet offend in one point, he is guilty of all.

James 2:10 KJV

The act of sin may pass, and yet the guilt remain.

St. Thomas Aquinas

The purpose of being guilty is to bring us to Jesus. Once we are there, then its purpose is finished. If we continue to make ourselves guilty—to blame ourselves—then that is sin in itself.

Corrie ten Boom

Even as he who is troubled with a burning fever is hotter than he who is parched with

the sun; so is that man more troubled who hath a guilty conscience than a good man by all outward afflictions.

Daniel Cawdray

The terrors of God are the effects of guilt.

Stephen Charnock

You never lose the love of God. Guilt is the warning that temporarily you are out of touch.

Jack Dominion

Good works never erase guilt.

Erwin W. Lutzer

One of the most distressing signs of contemporary times is the denial of guilt.

Fulton John Sheen

A guilty mind can be eased by nothing but repentance; by which what was ill done, is revoked, and morally voided and undone.

Benjamin Whichcote

Happiness

See also Contentment; Joy; Laughter

Judah and Israel were as numerous as the sand by the sea; they ate and drank and were happy.

1 Kings 4:20 NRSV

Happy is that people, whose God is the Lord.

Psalm 144:15 KJV

Happy are those who know they are spiritually poor; the Kingdom of heaven belongs to them! Happy are those who mourn; God will comfort them! Happy are those who are humble; they will receive what God has promised! Happy are those whose greatest desire is to do what God requires; God will satisfy them fully! Happy are those who are merciful to others; God will be merciful to them! Happy are the pure in heart; they will see God! Happy are those who work for peace; God will call them his children! Happy are those who are persecuted because they do what God requires; the Kingdom of heaven belongs to them! Happy are you when people insult you and persecute you and tell all kinds of evil lies against you because you are my followers. Be happy and glad, for a great reward is kept for you in heaven. This is how the prophets who lived before you were persecuted.

Matthew 5:3–12 GNB

Is anyone happy? Let him sing songs of praise.

James 5:13 NIV

Heaven takes care that no man secures happiness by crime.

Vittorio Alfieri

Happiness is living by inner purpose, not by outer pressures. Happiness is a happening-with-God.

David Augsburger

Happy persons seldom think of happiness. They are too busy losing their lives in the meaningful sacrifices of service.

David Augsburger

Happiness consists in the attainment of our desires, and in our having only right desires.

St. Augustine of Hippo

Those who bring sunshine to the lives of others cannot keep it from themselves.

Sir James Matthew (J.M.) Barrie

Happiness is a mystery like religion, and should never be rationalized.

Gilbert Keith (G.K.) Chesterton

Happiness is the practice of the virtues.

Clement of Alexandria

Happy the ones, / and happy they alone, / they, who can call today their own: / They who, secure within, can say / "Tomorrow do your worst, / for I have lived today."

John Dryden

The happiest man is he who learns from nature the lesson of worship.

Ralph Waldo Emerson

Christians are the only people in the world who have anything to be happy about.

William Franklin (Billy) Graham

A cheerful look makes a dish a feast.

George Herbert

The supreme happiness of life is the conviction of being loved for yourself, or, more correctly, of being loved in spite of yourself.

Victor Hugo

Many persons have a wrong idea of what constitutes true happiness. It is not attained through self-gratification but through fidelity to a worthy purpose.

Helen Adams Keller

God cannot give us happiness and peace apart from himself, because it is not there. There is no such thing.

Clive Staples (C.S.) Lewis

My true happiness is to go and sin no more.

Robert Murray M'Cheyne

A happiness that is sought for ourselves alone can never be found: for a happiness that is diminished by being shared is not big enough to make us happy.

Thomas Merton

Happiness is neither within us only, or without us, it is the union of ourselves with God.

Blaise Pascal

Trust and obey! / For there's no other way / To be happy in Jesus / But to trust and obey.

John Henry Sammis

Happiness is a great love and much serving.

Olive Schreiner

To forget oneself is to be happy.

Robert Louis Stevenson

The happiness of a man in this life does not consist in the absence but in the mastery of his passions.

Alfred, Lord Tennyson

There are two things to do about the Gospel—believe it and behave it.

Susanna Wesley

Hardness of Heart, *see* Stubbornness

Harvest

As long as the earth remains, there will be planting and harvest, cold and heat; winter and summer, day and night.

Genesis 8:22 CEV

Let the nations praise you, God, let all the nations praise you. The earth has yielded its produce; God, our God has blessed us.

Psalm 67:5–6 NJB

The harvest is past, the summer is ended, and we are not saved.

Jeremiah 8:20 NRSV

The harvest truly is plenteous, but the laborers are few; Pray ye therefore the Lord of the harvest, that he will send forth laborers into his harvest.

Matthew 9:37 KJV

Let us not grow weary in doing what is right, for we will reap at harvest time, if we do not give up.

Galatians 6:9 NRSV

No discipline seems pleasant at the time, but painful. Later on, however, it produces a harvest of righteousness and peace for those who have been trained by it.

Hebrews 12:11 NIV

Even so, Lord, quickly come, / To Thy final harvest-home: / Gather Thou Thy people in, / Free from sorrow, free from sin; / There, forever purified, / In Thy presence to abide; / Come, with all Thine angels come, / Raise the glorious harvest-home.

Henry Alford

The seed of God is in us. Given an intelligent and hard-working farmer, it will thrive and grow up to God, whose seed it is; and accordingly its fruits will be God-nature. Pear seeds grow into pear trees, nut seeds into nut trees, and God seeds into God.

Meister Eckhart

Harvest time is always the ever-present now!

William Franklin (Billy) Graham

Sow a thought and you reap an action; sow an action and you reap a habit; sow a habit and you reap a character; sow a character and you reap a destiny.

William James

The trivial round, the common task, Would furnish all we ought to ask; Room to deny ourselves: a road To bring us, daily, nearer God.

John Keble

God's seed will come to God's harvest.

Samuel Rutherford

Hatred

Better is a dinner of vegetables where love is than a fatted ox and hatred with it.

Proverbs 15:17 NRSV

You will then be handed over for punishment and execution; all nations will hate you for your allegiance to me.

Matthew 24:9 REB

If the world hate you, ye know that it hated me before it hated you. If ye were of the world, the world would love his own: but because ye are not of the world, but I have chosen you out of the world, therefore the world hateth you.

John 15:18–19 KJV

Anyone who hates his brother is a murderer, and you are well aware that no murderer has eternal life remaining in him.

1 John 4:15 NJB

One of the reasons people cling to their hates so stubbornly is because they seem to sense, once hate is gone, that they will be forced to deal with pain.

James Arthur Baldwin

Hatred rarely does any harm to its object. It is the hater who suffers. His soul is warped and his life poisoned by dwelling on past injuries or projecting schemes of revenge.

Rancor in the bosom is the foe of personal happiness.

Lord Beaverbrook

O love of God, how deep and great. Far deeper than man's deepest hate.

Corrie ten Boom

How could we be filled with hatred, if we live night and day in God who is love?

Dom Helder Câmara

Hatred is like fire; it makes even light rubbish deadly.

George Eliot

Hatred is like burning down your own house to get rid of a rat.

Harry Emerson Fosdick

The important thing is not to oneself be poisoned. Now, hatred poisons.

André Gide

Hatred and bitterness can never cure the disease of fear; only love can do that. Hatred paralyzes life; love releases it. Hatred confuses life; love harmonizes it. Hatred darkens life; love illumines it.

Martin Luther King Jr.

If I hate or despise any one man in the world, I hate something which God cannot hate, and despise that which he loves.

William Law

Healing

See also Health and Wholeness; Illness; Suffering

Bless the LORD, O my soul, and do not forget all his benefits—who forgives all your iniquity, who heals all your diseases.

Psalm 103:2–3 NRSV

He was pierced for our transgressions, he was crushed for our iniquities; the punishment that brought us peace was upon him, and by his wounds we are healed.

Isaiah 53:5 NIV

Is there no balm in Gilead?

Jeremiah 8:22 KJV

Honor physicians for their services, for the Lord created them; for their gift of healing comes from the Most High, and they are rewarded by the king. The skill of physicians makes them distinguished, and in the presence of the great they are admired. The Lord created medicines out of the earth, and the sensible will not despise them.

Ecclesiasticus 38:1–4 NRSV

Jesus went about all Galilee, teaching in their synagogues, and preaching the gospel of the kingdom, and healing all manner of sickness and all manner of disease among the people.

Matthew 4:23 KJV

If you are sick, ask the church leaders to come and pray for you. Ask them to put olive oil on you in the name of the Lord. If you have faith when you pray for sick people, they will get well. The Lord will heal them, and if they have sinned he will forgive them. If you have sinned, you should tell each other what you have done. Then you can pray for one another and be healed. The prayer of an innocent person is powerful, and it can help a lot.

James 5:14–16 CEV

The good Instructor, the Wisdom, the Word of the Father, who made man, cares for the whole nature of his creature. The all-sufficient Physician of humanity, the Savior, heals both our body and soul, which are the proper man.

Clement of Alexandria

The temperature of the spiritual life of the Church is the index of her power to heal.

Evelyn Frost

Healing is one of the most striking manifestations of the redemption of our bodies which salvation will bring, but it is an anticipation graciously and mysteriously vouchsafed to some and, equally graciously and mysteriously, withheld from others.

John Gunstone

Sometimes the Lord disturbs the waters before sending His healing angel.

Fr. John Harper

Inner healing is simply this: Jesus can take the memories of our past and heal them. And fill with his love all these places in us that have been empty for so long, once they have been healed and drained of the poison of past hates and resentment.

Francis MacNutt

In healing one can concentrate on either of two attributes; the power of God or the love of God. In every healing there is a manifestation of both.

Francis MacNutt

There is medicine in the Bible for every sin-sick soul, but every soul does not need the same medicine.

Reuben Archer (R.A.) Torrey

Inner healing is concerned to bring to light the causes of the inner pain; to help the sufferer to interpret them correctly; and to release the person from the emotional grip of the past.

John Townroe

Health and Wholeness

See also Healing

Good people will prosper like palm trees, and they will grow strong like the cedars of Lebanon. They will take root in your house, Lord God, and they will do well. They will be like trees that stay healthy and fruitful, even when they are old.

Psalm 92:12–14 CEV

Pleasant words are as an honeycomb, sweet to the soul, and health to the bones.

Proverbs 16:24 KJV

A cheerful heart is a good medicine, but a downcast spirit dries up the bones.

Proverbs 17:22 NRSV

He said unto her, Daughter, be of good comfort: thy faith hath made thee whole; go in peace.

Luke 8:48 KJV

Take care of your health, that it may serve you to serve God.

St. Francis de Sales

The secret of the physical well-being of the Christian is the vitality of the divine life welling up within by virtue of his incorporation into Christ.

Evelyn Frost

Even a cursory reading of the New Testament leaves a convincing impression that Jesus was typically Hebrew in his view of man: he did not divide man into body and soul, but he saw him as a whole person.

Francis MacNutt

Do the best you can, without straining yourself too much and too continuously, and leave the rest to God. If you strain yourself too much you'll have to ask God to patch you up. And for all you know, patching you up may take time that it was planned to use some other way.

Donald Robert (Don) Marquis

The refusal to forgive and be forgiven lies at the root of a great deal of sickness. Like a root it is as often as not hidden. For true health we have to forgive God, others, and ourselves.

Philip Pare

The terms for salvation in many languages are derived from roots like *salvus, saos, whole, heil,* which all designate health, the opposite of disintegration and disruption. Salvation is healing in the ultimate sense; it is final, cosmic, and individual healing.

Paul Tillich

To be "whole" is to be spiritually, emotionally, and physically healthy. Jesus lived in perfect wholeness.

Colin Urquhart

Be careful to preserve your health. It is a trick of the devil, which he employs to deceive good souls, to incite them to do more than they are able, in order that they may no longer be able to do anything.

St. Vincent de Paul

Look at your health; and if you have it, praise God, and value it next to a good conscience.

Izaak Walton

Heart

See also Purity

The LORD said to Samuel, "Do not look on his appearance or on the height of his stature, because I have rejected him; for the LORD does not see as mortals see; they look on the outward appearance, but the LORD looks on the heart."

1 Samuel 16:7 NRSV

Create a pure heart in me, O God, and put a new and loyal spirit in me.

Psalm 51:10 GNB

Above all else, guard your heart, for it is the wellspring of life.

Proverbs 4:23 NIV

Who can understand the human heart? There is nothing else so deceitful; it is too sick to be healed. I, the Lord, search the minds and test the hearts of men. I treat each of them according to the way they live, according to what they do.

Jeremiah 17:9–10 GNB

A new heart also will I give you, and a new spirit will I put within you: and I will take away the stony heart out of your flesh, and I will give you an heart of flesh.

Ezekiel 36:26 KJV

Blessed are the pure in heart: for they shall see God.

Matthew 5:8 KJV

For where your treasure is, there will your heart be also.

Matthew 6:21 KJV

Then Jesus called the crowd to him and said to them, "Listen and understand! It is not what goes into your mouth that makes you ritually unclean; rather, what comes out of it makes you unclean. . . . Anything that goes into your mouth goes into your stomach and then on out of your body. But the things that come out of the mouth come from the heart, and these are the things that make you ritually unclean. For from your heart come the evil ideas which lead you to kill, commit adultery, and do other immoral things; to rob, lie, and slander others. These are the things that make you unclean.

"But to eat without washing your hands as they [the Pharisees and teachers of the Law] say you should—this doesn't make you unclean."

Matthew 15:10–11, 17–20 GNB

For from within, out of men's hearts, come evil thoughts, sexual immorality, theft, murder, adultery, greed, malice, deceit, lewdness, envy, slander, arrogance and folly.

Mark 7:21–22 NIV

"Let anyone who is thirsty come to me! Let anyone who believes in me come and drink! As scripture says, 'From his heart shall flow streams of living water.'"

John 7:37–38 NJB

To my God, a heart of flame; to my fellow men, a heart of love; to myself, a heart of steel.

St. Augustine of Hippo

The heart is as divine a gift as the mind; and to neglect it in the search for God is to seek ruin.

Robert Hugh Benson

Let us learn to cast our hearts into God.

St. Bernard of Clairvaux

The "heart" in the biblical sense is not the

inward life, but the whole man in relation to God.

Dietrich Bonhoeffer

There is only one being who can satisfy the last aching abyss of the human heart, and that is the Lord Jesus Christ.

Oswald Chambers

Plato located the soul of man in the head; Christ located it in the heart.

St. Jerome

I am more afraid of my own heart than of the pope and all his cardinals.

Martin Luther

The heart has its reasons, which reason knows not, as we feel in a thousand instances.

Blaise Pascal

The capital of Heaven is the heart in which Jesus Christ is enthroned as King.

Sadhu Sundar Singh

O for a heart to praise my God, / A heart from sin set free; / A heart that always feels Thy blood / So freely shed for me; / A heart resigned, submissive, meek, / My great Redeemer's throne, / Where only Christ is heard to speak, / Where Jesus reigns alone.

Charles Wesley

Put everything you have into the care of your heart, for it determines what your life amounts to.

Dallas Willard

Heaven

See also Hell

Whom have I in heaven but you? And earth has nothing I desire besides you.

Psalm 73:25 NIV

Our Father which art in heaven, Hallowed be thy name. Thy kingdom come. Thy will be done on earth, as it is in heaven.

Matthew 6:9–10 KJV

In my Father's house there are many dwelling places. If it were not so, would I have told you that I go to prepare a place for you? And if I go and prepare a place for you, I will come again and will take you to myself, so that where I am, there you may be also.

John 14:2–3 NRSV

What God has planned for people who love him is more than eyes have seen or ears have heard. It has never even entered our minds!

1 Corinthians 2:9 CEV

I saw a new heaven and a new earth. The first heaven and the first earth had disappeared, and so had the sea.

Revelation 21:1 CEV

The throne of God and of the Lamb will be in the city, and his servants will worship him. They will see his face, and his name will be written on their foreheads. There shall be no more night, and they will not need lamps or sunlight, because the Lord God will be their light, and they will rule as kings for ever and ever.

Revelation 22:3–5 GNB

The gates of heaven are so easily found when we are little, and they are always standing open to let children wander in.

Sir James Matthew (J.M.) Barrie

Heaven will be the endless portion of every man who has heaven in his soul.

Henry Ward Beecher

In one little moment, short as it is, heaven may be lost.

The Cloud of Unknowing

The main object of religion is not to get a man into heaven, but to get heaven into him.

Thomas Hardy

If you are a Christian, you are not a citizen of this world trying to get to heaven; you are a citizen of heaven making your way through this world.

Vance Havner

Our duty as Christians is always to keep heaven in our eye and earth under our feet.

Matthew Henry

It is certain that all that will go to heaven hereafter begin their heaven now, and have their hearts there.

Matthew Henry

It is since Christians have largely ceased to think of the other world that they have become so ineffective in this. Aim at heaven and you will get earth thrown in: aim at earth and you will get neither.

Clive Staples (C.S.) Lewis

If one man should suffer all the sorrows of all the saints in the world, yet they are not worth one hour's glory in heaven.

St. John Chrysostom

Joy is the serious business of heaven.

Clive Staples (C.S.) Lewis

I would not give one moment of heaven for all the joys and riches of the world, even if it lasted for thousands and thousands of years.

Martin Luther

Take all the pleasures of all the spheres, / And multiply each through endless years / One minute of heaven is worth them all.

Thomas V. Moore

Earth has no sorrow that heaven cannot heal.

Thomas V. Moore

When I get to heaven, I shall see three wonders there—the first wonder will be to see any people there whom I did not expect to see; the second wonder will be to miss many people whom I did expect to see; and the third and greatest wonder of all will be to find myself there.

John Newton

Heaven will chiefly consist in the enjoyment of God.

William S. Plummer

In that sweet by and by we shall meet on that beautiful shore.

Ira David Sankey

There are no crown-wearers in heaven that were not cross-bearers here below.

Charles Haddon Spurgeon

Heaven must be in thee before thou canst be in heaven.

George Swinnock

Heaven is not a space overhead to which we lift our eyes; it is the background of our existence, the all-encompassing lordship of God within which we stand.

Helmut Thielicke

I'll praise my Maker while I've breath, / And when my voice is lost in death, / Praise shall employ my nobler powers; / My days of praise shall ne'er be past, / While life, and thought, and being last, / Or immortality endures.

Isaac Watts

Finish then Thy new creation, / Pure and spotless may we be; / Let us see Thy great salvation, / Perfectly restored in Thee; / Changed from glory into glory, / Till in heaven we take our place, / Till we cast our crowns before Thee, / Lost in wonder, love, and praise.

Charles Wesley

No man may go to heaven who hath not sent his heart thither before.

Thomas Wilson

Hell

See also Heaven

Then he will say to those on his left hand, "Go away from me, with your curse upon you, to the eternal fire prepared for the devil and his angels." . . . And they will go away to eternal punishment, and the upright to eternal life.

Matthew 25:41, 46 NJB

In flaming fire taking vengeance on them that know not God, and that obey not the gospel of our Lord Jesus Christ: Who shall be punished with everlasting destruction from the presence of the Lord, and from the glory of his power.

2 Thessalonians 1:8–9 KJV

Anyone whose name was not found written in the book of life was thrown into the lake of fire.

Revelation 20:15 NRSV

If you insist on having your own way, you will get it. Hell is the enjoyment of your own way forever. If you really want God's way with you, you will get it in heaven.

Dante Alighieri

Hell is paved with good intentions and roofed with lost opportunities.

Anon.

Each man's sin is the instrument of his punishment, and his iniquity is turned into his torment.

St. Augustine of Hippo

The pain of punishment will be without the fruit of penitence; weeping will be useless, and prayer ineffectual. Too late they will believe in eternal punishment who would not believe in eternal life.

St. Cyprian

Hell is truth seen too late—duty neglected in its season.

Tryon Edwards

God will never send anybody to hell. If man goes to hell, he goes by his own free choice. Hell was created for the devil and his angels, not for man. God never meant that man should go there.

William Franklin (Billy) Graham

The love of God, with arms extended on a cross, bars the way to hell. But if that love is ignored, rejected, and finally refused, there comes a time when love can only weep while man pushes past into the self-chosen alienation which Christ went to the cross to avert.

Michael Green

Men are not in hell because God is angry with them; they are in wrath and darkness because they have done to the light, which infinitely flows forth from God, as that man does to the light of the sun who puts out his own eyes.

William Law

It does not matter how small the sins are provided that their cumulative effect is to edge the man away from the light out into nothing. Murder is no better than cards, if cards do the trick. Indeed, the safest road to hell is the gradual one—the gentle slope, soft under foot, without sudden turnings, without signposts.

Clive Staples (C.S.) Lewis

The one principle of hell is "I am my own."

George MacDonald

There are two ways of going to hell; one is to walk into it with your eyes open . . . the other is to go down by the steps of little sins.

John Charles Ryle

It will be hell to a man to have his now voluntary choice confirmed, and made unchangeable.

Charles Haddon Spurgeon

Hell is the highest reward that the devil can offer you for being a servant of his.

William Ashley (Billy) Sunday

The anguish of hell is the anguish of knowing—eternally—that you could have chosen differently, but didn't.

John White

Helplessness, *see* Weakness

Heresy

See also Orthodoxy

Now I beseech you, brethren, mark them which cause divisions and offenses contrary to the doctrine which ye have learned; and avoid them.

Romans 16:17 KJV

If someone disputes what you teach, then after a first and a second warning, have no more to do with him: you will know that anyone of that sort is warped and is self-condemned as a sinner.

Titus 3:10–11 NJB

There were also false prophets among the people, just as there will be false teachers among you. They will secretly introduce destructive heresies, even denying the sovereign Lord who bought them—bringing swift destruction on themselves.

2 Peter 2:1 NJB

An error is the more dangerous in proportion to the degree of truth which it contains.

Henri-Frédéric Amiel

We should detest and prohibit in heretics not those common beliefs in which they are with us and not against us, but those divisions of peace contrary to truth by which they are against us and do not follow.

The Venerable Bede

The heretic is not a man who loves truth too much; no man can love truth too much. The heretic is a man who loves his truth more than truth itself. He prefers the half-truth that he has found to the whole truth which humanity has found.

Gilbert Keith (G.K.) Chesterton

Heresy is the school of pride.

George Herbert

Heresy may be easier kept out than shook off.

George Herbert

In reading ecclesiastical history, when I was an Anglican, it used to be forcibly brought home to me how the initial error of what afterwards became heresy was the urging forward some truth against the prohibition of authority at an unseasonable time.

John Henry Newman

Church members who deny in fact their responsibility for the needy in any part of the world are just as much guilty of heresy as those who deny this or that article of the faith.

Willem Adolf Visser 't Hooft

Holiness

See also God, Holiness of; Jesus, Perfection of; Holy Spirit and Sanctification

O worship the Lord in the beauty of holiness: fear before him, all the earth.

Psalm 96:9 KJV

And one [seraphim] cried unto another, and said, Holy, holy, holy, is the Lord of hosts: the whole earth is full of his glory.

Isaiah 6:3 KJV

Since we have these promises, beloved, let us cleanse ourselves from every defilement of body and of spirit, making holiness perfect in the fear of God.

2 Corinthians 7:1 NRSV

Seek peace with all people, and the holiness without which no one can ever see the Lord.

Hebrews 12:14 NJB

Real holiness has a fragrance about it which is its own.

Fr. Andrew

For everything that lives is holy, life delights in life.

William Blake

All holiness is God's holiness in us: it is a holiness that is participation and, in a certain way, more than participation, because we participate in what we can receive from God, we become a revelation of that which transcends us. Being a limited light, we reveal the Light.

Anthony Bloom

The destined end of man is not happiness, nor health, but holiness. God's one aim is the production of saints.

Oswald Chambers

Sanctify yourself and you will sanctify society.

St. Francis of Assisi

There is no true holiness without humility.

Thomas Fuller

"Be ye holy" is the great and fundamental law of our religion.

Matthew Henry

Holiness is the only evidence of election.

Charles Hodge

The essence of true holiness consists in conformity to the nature and will of God.

Samuel Lucas

There may be living and habitual conversation in heaven, under the aspect of the most simple, ordinary life. Let us always remember that holiness does not consist in doing uncommon things, but in doing everything with purity of heart.

Henry Edward Manning

A holy life will produce the deepest impression. Lighthouses blow no horns; they only shine.

Dwight Lyman (D.L.) Moody

Holiness is not inability to sin, but ability not to sin.

George Campbell Morgan

Holiness is a state of soul in which all the powers of the body and mind are consciously given up to God.

Phoebe Palmer

Holiness is the sanctification of ordinary life.

Maggie Ross

Holiness is the visible side of salvation.

Charles Haddon Spurgeon

I would . . . suggest that some form of suffering is virtually indispensable to holiness.

John R. W. Stott

Holiness consists of doing the will of God with a smile.

Mother Teresa

You must be holy in the way God asks you to be holy. God does not ask you to be a Trappist monk or a hermit. He wills that you sanctify the world and your everyday life.

St. Vincent Pallotti

Holiness is not the laborious acquisition of virtue from without, but the expression of the Christ-life from within.

John William Charles (J.W.C.) Wand

Holy Spirit

See also Fruitfulness; Pentecost; Soul and Spirit

And Regeneration

See also New Birth

I will give you a new heart and put a new spirit in you: I will remove from you your heart of stone and give you a heart of flesh. And I will put my Spirit in you and move you to follow my decrees and be careful to keep my laws.

Ezekiel 36:26–27 NIV

Jesus answered, Verily, verily, I say unto thee, Except a man be born of water and of the Spirit, he cannot enter into the kingdom of God. That which is born of the flesh is flesh, and that which is born of the Spirit is spirit.

John 3:5–6 KJV

You show that you are a letter of Christ, prepared by us, written not with ink but with the Spirit of the living God, not on tablets of stone but on tablets of human hearts.

2 Corinthians 3:3 NRSV

He saved us, not because of righteous things we had done, but because of his mercy. He saved us through the washing of rebirth and renewal by the Holy Spirit, whom he poured out on us generously through Jesus Christ our Savior.

Titus 3:5–6 NIV

Repentance is a change of the mind and regeneration is a change of the man.

Thomas Adams

I should as soon attempt to raise flowers if there were no atmosphere, or produce fruits if there were neither light nor heat, as to regenerate men if I did not believe there was a Holy Ghost.

Henry Ward Beecher

What takes place is an explosion on the inside (a literal explosion, not a theoretical one) that opens all the doors that have been closed and life becomes larger; there is the incoming of a totally new point of view.

Oswald Chambers

Regeneration is a single act, complete in itself, and never repeated; conversion, as the beginning of holy living, is the commencement of a series, constant, endless, and progressive.

Archibald Alexander (A.A.) Hodge

Every time we say "I believe in the Holy Spirit" we mean that we believe there is a living God able and willing to enter human personality and change it.

John Bertram (J.B.) Phillips

Regeneration is essentially a changing of the fundamental taste of the soul. By taste we mean the direction of man's love, the bent of his affection, the trend of his will.

Augustus Hopkins Strong

And Sanctification

See also Holiness

For if you live according to the sinful nature, you will die; but if by the Spirit you put to death the misdeeds of the body, you will live, because those who are led by the Spirit of God are sons of God. For you did not receive a spirit that makes you a slave again to fear, but you received the Spirit of sonship. And by him we cry, "Abba, Father." The Spirit himself testifies with our spirit that we are God's children.

Romans 8:13–16 NIV

Such were some of you: but ye are washed, but ye are sanctified, but ye are justified in the name of the Lord Jesus, and by the Spirit of our God.

1 Corinthians 6:11 KJV

But the fruit of the Spirit is love, joy, peace, patience, kindness, goodness, faithfulness, gentleness and self-control.

Galatians 5:22–23 NIV

But we must always give thanks to God for you, brothers and sisters beloved by the Lord, because God chose you as the first fruits for salvation through sanctification by the Spirit and through belief in the truth.

2 Thessalonians 2:13 NRSV

Who have been chosen according to the foreknowledge of God the Father, through the sanctifying work of the Spirit, for obedience to Jesus Christ and sprinkling by his blood: Grace and peace be yours in abundance.

1 Peter 1:2 NIV

Are we prepared for what sanctification will do? It will cost an intense narrowing of all our interests on earth and an immense broadening of our interest in God.

Oswald Chambers

To live the sanctified life we must choose to be holy. Sanctification is a life of Christ-centered choices, made evident in loving obedience to God.

Mel E. De Peal

Breathe on me, Breath of God, / Till I am wholly Thine; / Until this earthly part of me / Glows with Thy fire divine.

Edwin Hatch

When God works in us, the will, being changed and sweetly breathed upon by the

Spirit of God, desires and acts, not from compulsion, but responsively.

Martin Luther

Holiness is inwrought by the Holy Spirit, not because we have suffered, but because we have surrendered.

Richard Shelley Taylor

Gifts of, *see* Spiritual Gifts

Guidance of

See also Guidance

My Spirit remains among you. Do not fear.

Haggai 2:5 NIV

The Spirit shows what is true and will come and guide you into the full truth. The Spirit doesn't speak on his own. He will tell you only what he has heard from me, and he will let you know what is going to happen.

John 16:13 CEV

It seemed good to the Holy Spirit and to us not to burden you with anything beyond the following requirements. . . .

Acts 15:28 NIV

They traveled through the region of Phrygia and Galatia because the Holy Spirit did not let them preach the message in the province of Asia. When they reached the border of Mysia, they tried to go into the province of Bithynia, but the Spirit of Jesus did not allow them.

Acts 16:6–7 GNB

For as many as are led by the Spirit of God, they are the sons of God.

Romans 8:14 KJV

God is an ever-present Spirit guiding all that happens to a wide and holy end.

David Hume

The Holy Spirit expects us to take seriously the answers he has already provided, the light he has already shed; and he does not expect us to plead for things that have already been denied.

Paul E. Little

If the Holy Spirit guides us at all, he will do it according to the Scriptures, and never contrary to them.

George Müller

No generation can claim to have plumbed to the depths the unfathomable riches of Christ. The Holy Spirit has promised to lead us step by step into the fullness of truth.

Leon Joseph Suenens

Indwelling of

A new heart I will give you, and a new spirit I will put within you; and I will remove from your body the heart of stone and give you a heart of flesh. I will put my spirit within you, and make you follow my statutes and be careful to observe my ordinances.

Ezekiel 36:26–27 NRSV

The Spirit of truth; whom the world cannot receive, because it seeth him not, neither knoweth him: but ye know him; for he dwelleth with you, and shall be in you.

John 14:17 KJV

That good thing which was committed unto thee keep by the Holy Ghost which dwelleth in us.

2 Timothy 1:14 KJV

What else are the laws of God written in our hearts but the very presence of the Holy Ghost?

St. Augustine of Hippo

The indwelling of God is this—to hold God ever in memory, His shrine established within us.

St. Basil the Great

When the Spirit of God comes into a man, he gives him a worldwide outlook.

Oswald Chambers

The Holy Spirit cannot be located as a guest in a house. He invades everything.

Oswald Chambers

Watches, cars, and Christians can all look chromed and shiny. But watches don't tick, cars don't go, and Christians don't make a difference without insides. For a Christian, that's the Holy Spirit.

Tim Downs

The gift of the Holy Spirit closes the gap between the life of God and ours. When we allow the love of God to move in us, we can no longer distinguish ours and his; he becomes us, he lives in us. It is the first fruits of the Spirit, the beginning of our being made divine.

Austin Farrer

All the Holy Spirit's influences are heaven begun, glory in the seed and bud.

Matthew Henry

All His glory and beauty comes from within, and there He delights to dwell. His visits there are frequent, His conversations sweet, His comforts refreshing, His peace passing all understanding.

Thomas à Kempis

To be controlled by the Spirit means that we are not controlled by what happens on the outside but by what is happening on the inside.

Erwin W. Lutzer

In every man there is something of the Universal Spirit, strangely limited by that which is finite and personal, but still there. Occasionally it makes itself known in a word, a look or gesture, and then becomes one with the stars and sea.

Mark Rutherford

One person works upon another person from outside inwards, but God alone comes to us from within outwards.

Jan van Ruysbroeck

Come down, O Love divine / Seek Thou this soul of mine, / And visit it with Thine own ardor glowing; / O Comforter, draw near, / Within my heart appear, / And kindle it, Thy holy flame bestowing.

Bianco da Siena

Power of

See also Power

"Not by might nor by power, but by my Spirit" says the Lord Almighty.

Zechariah 4:6 NIV

I indeed baptize you with water unto repentance: but he that cometh after me is mightier than I, whose shoes I am not worthy to bear: he shall baptize you with the Holy Ghost, and with fire.

Matthew 3:11 KJV

Then Jesus, filled with the power of the Spirit, returned to Galilee, and a report about him spread through all the surrounding country.

Luke 4:14 NRSV

Behold I send the promise of my Father upon you: but tarry ye in the city of Jerusalem, until ye be endued with power from on high.

Luke 24:49 KJV

When the Holy Spirit comes upon you, you will be filled with power, and you will be witnesses for me in Jerusalem, in all Judea and Samaria, and to the ends of the earth.

Acts 1:8 GNB

May the God of hope fill you with all joy and peace in your faith, so that in the power of the Holy Spirit you may be rich in hope.

Romans 15:13 NJB

My message and my preaching were not with wise and persuasive words, but with a demonstration of the Spirit's power.

1 Corinthians 2:4 NIV

And I believe in the Holy Ghost, The Lord and giver of life, Who proceedeth from the Father and Son, Who with the Father and the Son together is worshiped and glorified, Who spake by the Prophets.

Book of Common Prayer

Without the power of the Holy Spirit all human efforts, methods, and plans are as futile as attempting to propel a boat by puffing at the sails with our own breath.

D.M. Dawson

The Spirit-filled life is no mystery revealed to a select few, no goal difficult of attainment. To trust and to obey is the substance of the whole matter.

Victor Raymond Edman

The Holy Spirit descended upon me in a manner that seemed to go through me, body and soul. I could feel the impression like a wave of electricity going through and through me. Indeed, it seemed to come in waves and waves of liquid love . . . like the very breath of God . . . it seemed to fan me like immense wings.

Charles Grandison Finney

I sincerely believe that any man preaching a simple Gospel message in the power of the Spirit can expect results if he is speaking to unconverted people.

William Franklin (Billy) Graham

O Breath of life, come sweeping through us, / Revive your church with life and power; / O Breath of life, come, cleanse, renew us / And fit your church to meet this hour.

Elizabeth A.P. Head

The word "Comforter" as applied to the Holy Spirit needs to be translated by some vigorous term. Literally, it means "with strength." Jesus promised His followers that "The Strengthener" would be with them forever. This promise is no lullaby for the fainthearted. It is a blood transfusion for courageous living.

E. Paul Hovey

Seek Him! Seek Him! What can we do without Him? Seek Him! Seek Him always. But go beyond seeking Him; expect Him. Do you expect anything to happen to you when you get up to preach in a pulpit? . . . Seek this power, expect this power, yearn for this power; and when this power comes, yield to Him. Do not resist. Forget all about your sermon if necessary. Let him loose you, let Him manifest His power in you and through you.

David Martyn Lloyd-Jones

Holy Spirit, power divine, / Fill and nerve this will of mine; / By Thee may I strongly live, / Bravely bear, and nobly strive.

Samuel Longfellow

The Spirit's control will replace sin's control. His power is greater than the power of all your sin.

Erwin W. Lutzer

No man can do the work of God until he has the Holy Spirit and is endued with power. It is impossible to preach the Gospel save in the power of the Spirit.

George Campbell Morgan

Only Jesus Christ by His Holy Spirit can open blind eyes, give life to the dead, and rescue slaves from Satanic bondage.

John R.W. Stott

Sin against

I tell you, every sin and blasphemy will be forgiven men, but the blasphemy against the Spirit will not be forgiven. Anyone who speaks a word against the Son of Man will be forgiven, but anyone who speaks against the Holy Spirit will not be forgiven, either in this age or in the age to come.

Matthew 12:31–32 NIV

Peter said to him, "Ananias, why did you let Satan take control of you and make you lie to the Holy Spirit by keeping part of the money you received for the property?"

Acts 5:3 GNB

You stubborn people, with uncircumcised hearts and ears. You are always resisting the Holy Spirit, just as your ancestors used to do.

Acts 7:51 NJB

Grieve not the holy Spirit of God, whereby ye are sealed unto the day of redemption.

Ephesians 4:30 KJV

Do not quench the Spirit.

1 Thessalonians 5:19 NRSV

Fire is quenched by pouring on water or by withdrawing fuel; so the Spirit is quenched by living on sin, which is like pouring water on a fire; or by not improving our gifts and graces, which is like withdrawing fuel from the hearth.

Thomas Manton

Witness of

We are witnesses to these things, and so is the Holy Spirit whom God has given to those who obey him.

Acts 5:32 NRSV

What you received was not the spirit of slavery to bring you back into fear; you received the Spirit of adoption, enabling us to cry out, "Abba, Father!" The Spirit himself joins with our spirit to bear witness that we are children of God.

Romans 8:15–16 NJB

I am speaking the truth in Christ—I am not lying; my conscience confirms it by the Holy Spirit.

Romans 9:1 NRSV

If we obey God's commandments, we will stay one in our hearts with him, and he will stay one with us. The Spirit that he has given us is proof that we are one with him.

1 John 3:24 CEV

This is the one who came by water and blood—Jesus Christ. He did not come by water only, but by water and blood. And it is the Spirit who testifies, because the Spirit is the truth. For there are three that testify: the Spirit, the water and the blood; and the three are in agreement.

1 John 5:6 NIV

The Holy Spirit is no skeptic, and the things he has written in our hearts are not doubts or opinions, but assertions—surer and more certain than sense or life itself.

Martin Luther

God will not give us the Holy Spirit to enable us to gain celebrity or to procure a name or to live an easy, self-controlled life. The Spirit's passion is the glory of the Lord Jesus and [the Spirit] can make His abode [only] with those who are willing to be at one with Him in this.

Frederick Brotherton (F.B.) Meyer

There is not a better evangelist in the world than the Holy Spirit.

Dwight Lyman (D.L.) Moody

The Holy Spirit is God the evangelist.

James Innell (J.I.) Packer

Biblically, the Holy Spirit means the militant presence of the Word of God inhering in the life of the whole of creation. Biblically, the Holy Spirit is the Word of God at work both historically and existentially, acting incessantly and pervasively to renew the integrity of life in this world.

William Stringfellow

O love divine, how sweet Thou art! / When shall I find my willing heart / All taken up by Thee? / I thirst, I faint, I die to prove / The greatness of redeeming love, / The love of Christ to me.

Charles Wesley

Homes

A man away from his home is like a bird away from its nest.

Proverbs 27:8 GNB

Jesus said to him, "Foxes have holes, and birds of the air have nests; but the Son of Man has nowhere to lay his head."

Matthew 8:20 NRSV

Jesus told him: You can be sure that anyone who gives up homes or brothers or sisters or mother or father or children or land for me and for the good news will be rewarded. In this world they will be given a hundred times as many houses and brothers and sisters and mothers and children and pieces of land, though they will also be mistreated. And in the world to come, they will have eternal life.

Mark 10:29–30 CEV

As Jesus and his disciples were on their way, he came to a village where a woman named Martha opened her home to him.

Luke 10:38 NIV

Day by day, as they spent much time together in the temple, they broke bread at home and ate their food with glad and generous hearts.

Acts 2:46 NRSV

To this very hour we go hungry and thirsty, we are in rags, we are brutally treated, we are homeless.

1 Corinthians 4:11 NIV

The home must be in accord with the Church, that all harmful influences be withheld from the souls of children. Where there is true piety in the home, purity of morals reigns supreme.

The Curé d'Ars

A home is no home unless it contains food and fire for the mind as well as for the body.

Margaret Fuller

He is the happiest, be he king or peasant, who finds peace in his home.

Johann Wolfgang von Goethe

The Christian home is the Master's workshop where the process of character-molding is silently, lovingly, faithfully, and successfully carried on.

Richard Monckton Milnes

Home is where life makes up its mind. It is there—with fellow family members—we hammer out our convictions on the anvil of relationships. It is there we cultivate the valuable things in life, like attitudes, memories, beliefs, and most of all, character.

Charles R. Swindoll

Home is a mighty test of character. What you are at home you are everywhere, whether you demonstrate it or not.

Thomas De Witt Talmage

Christ moves among the pots and pans.

St. Teresa of Avila

Happiness is to be found only in the home where God is loved and honored, where each one loves, and helps, and cares for the others.

Theophane Vénard

Homosexuality, *see* Sex and Sexuality

Honesty

See also Deceit; Falsehood; Integrity

You shall not cheat in measuring length, weight, or quantity. You shall have honest balances, honest weights, an honest ephah, and an honest hin: I am the LORD your God, who brought you out of the land of Egypt.

Leviticus 19:35–36 NRSV

Whoever returns an honest answer, plants a kiss on the lips.

Proverbs 24:26 NJB

Those seeds that fell on good ground are the people who listen to the message and keep it in good and honest hearts. They last and produce a harvest.

Luke 8:15 CEV

How desperately difficult it is to be honest with oneself. It is much easier to be honest with other people.

Edward White Benson

Make yourself a seller when you are buying, and a buyer when you are selling, and then you will sell and buy justly.

St. Francis de Sales

Honesty is the first chapter of the book of wisdom.

Thomas Jefferson

Friends, if we be honest with ourselves, we shall be honest with each other.

George MacDonald

An honest man's the noblest work of God.

Alexander Pope

Honesty has a beautiful and refreshing simplicity about it. No ulterior motives. No hidden meanings. An absence of hypocrisy, duplicity, political games, and verbal superficiality. As honesty and real integrity characterize our lives, there will be no need to manipulate others.

Charles R. Swindoll

I hope I shall possess firmness and virtue enough to maintain what I consider the most enviable of all titles, the character of an honest man.

George Washington

Honesty is the best policy; but he who is governed by that maxim is not an honest man.

Richard Whately

Hope

See also Despair

Hope deferred makes the heart sick, but a desire fulfilled is a tree of life.

Proverbs 13:12 NRSV

For we are saved by hope: but hope that is seen is not hope: for what a man seeth, why doth he yet hope for? But if we hope for that we see not, then do we with patience wait for it.

Romans 8:24–25 KJV

Meanwhile these three remain: faith, hope, and love; and the greatest of these is love.

1 Corinthians 13:13 GNB

Be alert and think straight. Put all your hope in how kind God will be to you when Jesus Christ appears.

1 Peter 1:13 CEV

There is not a heart but has its moments of longing, yearning for something better, nobler, holier than it knows how.

Henry Ward Beecher

Other men see only a hopeless end, but the Christian rejoices in an endless hope.

Gilbert Brenken

Hope can see heaven through the thickest clouds.

Thomas Benton Brooks

What oxygen is to the lungs, such is hope for the meaning of life.

Heinrich Emil Brunner

Optimism means faith in men, in their human potential; hope means faith in God and in His omnipotence.

Carlo Carretto

Hope is the power of being cheerful in circumstances which we know to be desperate.

Gilbert Keith (G.K.) Chesterton

If you do not hope, you will not find out what is beyond your hopes.

Clement of Alexandria

To live without hope is to cease to live.

Fyodor Dostoevsky

Hope is a dimension of the spirit. It is not outside us, but within us. When you lose it, you must seek it again WITHIN YOURSELF and in people around you—and not in objects or even in events.

Václav Havel

Hope is itself a species of happiness, and, perhaps, the chief happiness which the world affords.

Samuel Johnson

Never cease loving a person and never give up hope for him, for even the Prodigal Son who had fallen most low could still be saved. The bitterest enemy and also he who was your friend could again be your friend; love that has grown cold can kindle again.

Søren Kierkegaard

We must accept finite disappointment, but we must never lose infinite hope.

Martin Luther King Jr

Everything that is done in the world is done by hope.

Martin Luther

Hope is the struggle of the soul, breaking loose from what is perishable, and attesting her eternity.

Herman Melville

In hope we count on the possibilities of the future and we do not remain imprisoned in the institutions of the past.

Jürgen Moltmann

Hope springs eternal in the human breast.

Alexander Pope

The future belongs to those who belong to God. This is hope.

W.T. Purkiser

I am a man of hope, not for human reasons, nor from any natural optimism, but because I believe the Holy Spirit is at work in the Church and in the world even when His name remains unheard.

Leon Joseph Suenens

Hospitality

When I was hungry, you gave me something to eat, and when I was thirsty, you gave me something to drink. When I was a stranger, you welcomed me.

Matthew 25:35 CEV

Share with God's people who are in need. Practice hospitality.

Romans 12:13 NIV

Do not neglect to show hospitality to strangers, for by doing that some have entertained angels without knowing it.

Hebrews 13:2 NRSV

Who practices hospitality entertains God himself.

Anon.

Hospitality is one form of worship.

Anon.

The Christian should offer his brethren simple and unpretentious hospitality.

St. Basil the Great

Hospitality is threefold: for one's family, this of necessity; for strangers, this of courtesy; for the poor, this is charity.

Thomas Fuller

Hospitality is a test for godliness because those who are selfish do not like strangers (especially needy ones) to intrude upon their private lives. They prefer their own friends who share their life-style. Only the humble have the necessary resources to give of themselves to those who could never give of themselves in return.

Erwin W. Lutzer

To give our Lord a perfect hospitality, Mary and Martha must combine.

St. Teresa of Avila

Human Nature

See also Sin; Sinful Nature

I know of nothing good living in me—in my natural self, that is—for though the will to do what is good is in me, the power to do it is not: the good thing I want to do, I never do; the evil thing which I do not want—that is what I do. But every time I do what I do not want to, then it is not myself acting, but the sin that lives in me. So I find this rule: that for me, where I want to do nothing but good, evil is close at my side.

Romans 7:18–21 NJB

Live by the Spirit, I say, and do not gratify the desires of the flesh. For what the flesh desires is opposed to the Spirit, and what the Spirit desires is opposed to the flesh; for these are opposed to each other, to prevent you from doing what you want.

Galatians 5:16–17 NRSV

Put to death, therefore, whatever belongs to your earthly nature: sexual immorality, impurity, lust, evil desires and greed, which is idolatry. Because of these the wrath of God is coming.

Colossians 3:5–6 NIV

Since all the children share the same human nature, he too shared equally in it, so that by his death he could set aside him who held the power of death, namely the devil, and set free all those who had been held in slavery all their lives by the fear of death.

Hebrews 2:14–15 NJB

The most profound essence of my nature is that I am capable of receiving God.

St. Augustine of Hippo

Human action can be modified to some extent, but human nature cannot be changed.

Abraham Lincoln

Left to itself, human nature tends to death, and utter apostasy from God, however plausible it may look externally.

John Henry Newman

You can learn more about human nature by reading the Bible than by living in New York.

William Lyon Phelps

Man is a peculiar, puzzling paradox, groping for God and hoping to hide from Him at the selfsame time.

William Arthur Ward

Human Rights

See also Justice

Defend the cause of the weak and fatherless; maintain the rights of the poor and oppressed. Rescue the weak and needy; deliver them from the hand of the wicked.

Psalm 82:3–4 NIV

Speak out for those who cannot speak, for the rights of all the destitute. Speak out, judge righteously, defend the rights of the poor and needy.

Proverbs 31:8–9 NRSV

Woe to those who enact unjust decrees, who compose oppressive legislation to deny justice to the weak and to cheat the humblest of my people of fair judgment, to make widows their prey and to rob the orphan.

Isaiah 10:1–2 NJB

Either no member of the human race has any natural rights or they all have the same; and anyone who votes against the rights of another, of whatever religion, color, or sex, has from that moment denied his own.

Marquis de Condorcet

Wherever there is a human being, I see God-given rights inherent in that being, whatever may be the sex or complexion.

William Lloyd Garrison

I am the inferior of any man whose rights I trample under foot.

Robert Green Ingersoll

They have rights who dare maintain them.

James Russell Lowell

Government laws are needed to give us civil rights and God is needed to make us civil.

Ralph Washington Sockman

Humanity

See also Jesus Christ, Humanity of; Peace, between People and Nations

God said, "Now we will make humans, and they will be like us. We will let them rule the fish, the birds, and all other living creatures." So God created humans to be like himself: he made men and women. God gave them his blessing and said: "Have a lot of children! Fill the earth with people and bring it under your control. Rule over the fish in the ocean, the birds in the sky, and every animal on the earth."

Genesis 1:26–27 CEV

What are human beings that you are mindful of them, mortals that you care for them? Yet you have made them a little lower than God, and crowned them with glory and honor. You have given them dominion over the works of your hands; you have put all things under their feet, all sheep and oxen, and also the beasts of the field, the birds of the air, and the fish of the sea, whatever passes along the paths of the seas.

Psalm 8:4–8 NRSV

Man is like a thing of nought: his time passeth away like a shadow.

Psalm 144:4 BCP

All go to the same place; all came from the dust, and to the dust all return.

Ecclesiastes 3:20 REB

Our humanity were a poor thing were it not for the divinity that stirs within us.

Francis Bacon

We are mirrors of God, created to reflect Him.

Even when the water is not calm, it reflects the sky.

Ernesto Cardenal

Our Lord says to every living soul, "I became man for you. If you do not become God for me, you do me wrong."

Meister Eckhart

The only ultimate reason why man as man has individual significance is that Christ died for him.

Lord George Fielden MacLeod

Only love enables humanity to grow, because love engenders life and it is the only form of energy that lasts forever.

Michael Quoist

Made in God's image, man was made to be great, he was made to be beautiful, and he was made to be creative in life and art. But his rebellion has led him into making himself into nothing but a machine.

Francis August Schaeffer

Man still stands in the image of God— twisted, broken, abnormal, but still the image-bearer of God.

Francis August Schaeffer

What is the chief end of man? To glorify God and to enjoy him for ever.

The Shorter Catechism

We must not reject man in favor of God, nor reject God in favor of man; for the glory of God is man alive, supremely in Christ.

Leon Joseph Suenens

We are, because God is.

Emanuel Swedenborg

Man is God's risk.

Philip Yancey

Humility

See also Jesus Christ, Humility of; Modesty; Pride

But this is the one to whom I will look, to the humble and contrite in spirit, who trembles at my word.

Isaiah 66:2 NRSV

Seek the Lord, all in the land who live humbly, obeying his laws; seek righteousness, seek humility; it may be that you will find shelter on the day of the Lord's anger.

Zephaniah 2:3 REB

God blesses those people who depend only on him. They belong to the kingdom of heaven!

Matthew 6:3 CEV

Therefore, whoever humbles himself like this child is the greatest in the kingdom of heaven.

Matthew 18:4 NIV

For all who exalt themselves will be humbled, and those who humble themselves will be exalted.

Luke 14:11 NRSV

And lest I should be exalted above measure through the abundance of the revelations, there was given to me a thorn in the flesh, the messenger of Satan to buffet me, lest I should be exalted above measure.

2 Corinthians 12:7 KJV

[Christ Jesus] being found in human form, he humbled himself and became obedient to the point of death—even death on a cross.

Philippians 2:7–8 NRSV

All of you be subject one to another, and be clothed with humility: for God resisteth the proud, and giveth grace to the humble. Humble yourselves therefore under the mighty hand of God, that he may exalt you in due time.

1 Peter 5:5–6 KJV

For those who would learn God's ways, humility is the first thing, humility is the second, humility is the third.

St. Augustine of Hippo

The first degree of humility is obedience without delay.

St. Benedict

The true way to be humble is not to stoop until you are smaller than yourself, but to stand at your real height against some higher nature that will show you what the real smallness of your greatness is.

Phillips Brooks

He who knows himself best esteems himself least.

Henry G. Brown

He that is down need fear no fall, he that is low no pride.

John Bunyan

To be a saint does not mean never to sin. It means to start again with humility and joy after each fall.

Dom Helder Câmara

Humility is nothing else but a true knowledge and awareness of oneself as one really is.

The Cloud of Unknowing

See what you lack and not what you have, for that is the quickest path to humility.

The Cloud of Unknowing

Nothing sets a person so much out of the devil's reach as humility.

Jonathan Edwards

The only wisdom we can hope to acquire is the wisdom of humility.

Thomas Stearns (T.S.) Eliot

He who stays not in his littleness, loses his greatness.

St. Francis de Sales

I shall recommend humility to you as highly proper to be made the constant subject of your devotions, earnestly desiring you to think no day safe, or likely to end well, in which you have not called upon God to carry you through the day, in the exercise of a meek and lowly spirit.

William Law

I used to think that God's gifts were on shelves one above the other and that the taller we grew in Christian character the more easily we could reach them. I now find that God's gifts are on shelves one beneath the other and that it is not a question of growing taller but of stooping lower.

Frederick Brotherton (F.B.) Meyer

Unless you humble yourself before [God] in the dust, and confess before Him your iniquities and sins, the gate of heaven, which is open for sinners saved by grace, must be shut against you forever.

Dwight Lyman (D.L.) Moody

The Body of Christ is the fundamental resonance of humility, of self-giving, that is,

sacrificial *kenosis* that leads to creation and re-creation, no matter in what sphere. It is the cohesion of creation.

Maggie Ross

If you are humble, nothing will touch you, neither praise nor disgrace, because you know what you are.

Mother Teresa

A fault which humbles a man is of more use to him than a good action which puffs him up.

Thomas Wilson

Humor, *see* Laughter

Hunger and Thirst

Ho, everyone who thirsts, come to the waters; and you that have no money, come, buy and eat! Come, buy wine and milk without money and without price.

Isaiah 55:1 NRSV

Blessed are they which do hunger and thirst after righteousness: for they shall be filled.

Matthew 5:6 KJV

No one who drinks the water that I shall give will ever be thirsty again: the water that I shall give will become a spring of water within, welling up for eternal life.

John 4:14 NJB

Jesus said to them, "I am the bread of life. Whoever comes to me will never be hungry, and whoever believes in me will never be thirsty."

John 6:35 REB

They will hunger no more, and thirst no more; the sun will not strike them, nor any scorching heat; for the Lamb at the center of the throne will be their shepherd, and he will guide them to springs of the water of life, and God will wipe away every tear from their eyes.

Revelation 7:16–17 NRSV

There is no reason that the senseless Temples of God should abound in riches, and the living Temples of the Holy Spirit starve for hunger.

Ethelwold

"I am your life," says the Lord, "your bread, your source. If you drink of this water you'll never thirst, if you eat of this bread you will live forever." I suffer from spiritual malnutrition.

Michel Quoist

If we fail to feed the needy, we do not have God's love, no matter what we say. Regardless of what we do or say at 11 AM on a Sunday morn, affluent people who neglect the poor are not the people of God.

Ronald J. Sider

The greatest threat to this nation [the United States] and the stability of the entire world is hunger. It's more explosive than all the atomic weaponry possessed by the big powers. Desperate people do desperate things, and remember that nuclear fission is now in the hands of even developing nations.

Ronald J. Sider

In the Lord's Prayer the first petition is for daily bread. No one can worship God or love his neighbor on an empty stomach.

(Thomas) Woodrow Wilson

Husbands and Wives

See also Adam and Eve; Marriage; Men and Manhood; Women and Womanhood

Therefore a man leaves his father and his mother and clings to his wife, and they become one flesh.

Genesis 2:24 NRSV

A helpful wife is a jewel for her husband, but a shameless wife will make his bones rot.

Proverbs 12:4 CEV

A capable wife who can find? She is far more precious than jewels.

Proverbs 31:10 NRSV

Submit yourselves to one another because of your reverence for Christ.

Ephesians 5:21 GNB

Christian husband! Imitate St. Joseph by beginning your day's work with God, and ending it for Him. Cherish those belonging to you as the holy foster father did Jesus, and be their faithful protector.

The Curé d'Ars

You'll never see perfection in your mate, nor will he or she find it in you.

James Dobson

The best thing a woman can do for her husband is to make it easy for him to do the will of God.

Elisabeth Elliot

Husbands who have the courage to be tender, enjoy marriages that mellow through the years.

Brendan Francis

A wife is not to be chosen by the eye only. Choose a wife rather by your ear than your eye.

Thomas Fuller

The best advice I can give to unmarried girls

is to marry someone you don't mind adjusting to.

Ruth Bell Graham

To make a good husband, make a good wife.

John Heywood

We don't naturally grow together and love each other more. We tend to grow apart, to grow distant. So we have to work hard at marriage. It's the most fun work in the world, but still it's work.

Anne Ortlund

She is but half a wife who is not a friend.

William Penn

Hypocrisy

See also Falsehood

They do but flatter with their lips, and dissemble in their double heart.

Psalm 12:2 BCP

So whenever you give alms, do not sound a trumpet before you, as the hypocrites do in the synagogues and in the streets, so that they may be praised by others. Truly I tell you, they have received their reward. . . . And whenever you pray, do not be like the hypocrites; for they love to stand and pray in the synagogues and at the street corners, so that they may be seen by others. Truly I tell you, they have received their reward. . . . And whenever you fast, do not look dismal, like the hypocrites, for they disfigure their faces so as to show others that they are fasting. Truly I tell you, they have received their reward.

Matthew 6:2, 5, 16 NRSV

You hypocrite, first take the plank out of your own eye, and then you will see clearly to remove the speck from your brother's eye.

Matthew 7:5 NIV

You hypocrites! Isaiah was right when he prophesied about you: "These people honor me with their lips, but their hearts are far from me. They worship me in vain; their teachings are but rules taught by men."

Matthew 15:7–9 NIV

How terrible for you, teachers of the Law and Pharisees! You hypocrites! You clean the outside of your cup and plate, while the inside is full of what you have gotten by violence and selfishness. Blind Pharisee! Clean what is inside the cup first, and then the outside will be clean too!

Matthew 23:25–26 GNB

Even though they [people in the last days] will make a show of being religious, their religion won't be real. Don't have anything to do with such people.

2 Timothy 3:5 CEV

He who beats his heart, but does not mend his ways, does not remove his sins but hardens them.

St. Augustine of Hippo

An apple, if it be rotten at the core, though it have a fair and shining outside, yet rottenness will not stay long, but will taint the outside also . . . hypocrisy will discover itself in the end.

John Bond

It is no fault of Christianity if a hypocrite falls into sin.

St. Jerome

Gladly we desire to make other men perfect but we will not amend our own fault.

Thomas à Kempis

Hypocrisy is the homage which vice pays to virtue.

François, Duc de La Rochefoucauld

Solemn prayers, rapturous devotions, are but repeated hypocrisies unless the heart and mind be conformable to them.

William Law

God is not deceived by externals.

Clive Staples (C.S.) Lewis

Men never do evil so completely and cheerfully as when they do it from religious conviction.

Blaise Pascal

Hypocrites in the church? Yes, and in the lodge, and at home. Don't hunt through the church for a hypocrite. Go home and look in the glass. Hypocrites? Yes. See that you make the number one less.

William Ashley (Billy) Sunday

I cannot believe that a man is on the road to heaven when he is habitually performing the kind of deeds that would logically indicate that he ought to be on his way to hell.

Aiden Wilson (A.W.) Tozer

Ideals, *see* Perfection

Idleness, *see* Laziness

Idolatry

See also Worship

Do not worship any god except me. Do not make idols that look like anything in the sky or on earth or in the ocean under the earth. Don't bow down and worship idols. I am the Lord your God, and I demand all your love.

Exodus 20:3–5 CEV

Their wooden gods overlaid with gold and silver are like a scarecrow in a field of cucumbers—protecting nothing.

Letter of Jeremiah 6 NJB

The acts of the sinful nature are obvious . . . idolatry.

Galatians 5:19–20 NIV

Little children, keep yourselves from idols.

1 John 5:21 KJV

The Church is society's permanent rampart against idolatry. This is the ultimate, in a sense it is the only, sin, the root of all disorder.

St. Aelred

Thus does the world forget You, its Creator, and falls in love with what You have created instead of with You.

St. Augustine of Hippo

Whenever we take what God has done and put it in the place of himself, we become idolaters.

Oswald Chambers

Idolatry: trusting people, possessions, and positions to do for me what only God can do.

Bill Gothard

A man's god is that for which he lives, for which he is prepared to give his time, his energy, his money, that which stimulates him and rouses him, excites, and enthuses him.

David Martyn Lloyd-Jones

We easily fall into idolatry, for we are inclined to it by nature; and coming to us by inheritance, it seems pleasant.

Martin Luther

Idolatry is not only the adoration of images . . . but also trust in one's own righteousness, works, and merits, and putting confidence in riches and power.

Martin Luther

When we invent our own ideas of God, we simply create him in our own image.

Kenneth F.W. Prior

It's easy to get attached to idols, good things inappropriately adored. But when you have Jesus in the center of a room, everything else only junks up the décor.

Charles R. Swindoll

When men have gone so far as to talk as though their idols have come to life, it is time that someone broke them.

Richard Henry Tawney

Whatever a man seeks, honors, or exalts more than God, this is the god of idolatry.

William Bernard Ullathorne

All pride is idolatry.

John Wesley

Patriarchal Christianity is in danger of worshipping an idol.

Brian Wren

Ignorance

Then Job answered the LORD: "I know that you can do all things, and that no purpose of yours can be thwarted. 'Who is this that hides counsel without knowledge?' Therefore I have uttered what I did not understand, things too wonderful for me, which I did not know."

Job 42:1–3 NRSV

Gather together, come, draw near, you survivors of the nations, who in ignorance carry wooden idols in procession, praying to a god that cannot save.

Isaiah 45:20 REB

We should not think that the divine being is like gold or silver or stone—an image made by man's design and skill. In the past God overlooked such ignorance, but now he commands all people everywhere to repent.

Acts 17:29–30 NIV

Like obedient children, do not be conformed to the desires that you formerly had in ignorance.

1 Peter 1:14 NRSV

Ignorance is not innocence but sin.

Robert Browning

He that knows nothing will believe anything.

Thomas Fuller

A young Levite once remarked to his professor, "God can dispense with my learning." "Yes" was the reply, "but He has still less need of your ignorance."

James Gibbons

The more we know, the more we see of our own ignorance.

Matthew Henry

It is worse still to be ignorant of your ignorance.

St. Jerome

The modern attitude is, "Father, forgive us for we know not what we are doing—and please don't tell us!"

Erwin W. Lutzer

Conviction of ignorance is the doorstep to the temple of wisdom.

Charles Haddon Spurgeon

Ignorance is the mother of superstition, not of devotion.

Augustus Hopkins Strong

Illness

See also Healing; Suffering

Bless the LORD, O my soul, and do not forget all his benefits—who forgives all your iniquity, who heals all your diseases.

Psalm 103:2–3 NRSV

When he had called unto him his twelve disciples, he gave them power against unclean spirits, to cast them out, and to heal all manner of sickness and all manner of disease.

Matthew 10:1 KJV

The talk about him spread ever wider, so that great crowds kept gathering to hear him and to be cured of their ailments.

Luke 5:15 REB

All diseases of Christians are to be ascribed to demons.

St. Augustine of Hippo

Before all things and above all things, care must be taken of the sick, so that they may be served in very deed as Christ himself. . . . But let the sick on their part consider that they are being served for the honor of God, and not provoke their brethren who are serving them by their unreasonable demands. Yet they should be patiently borne with, because from such as these is gained a more abundant reward.

St. Benedict

Long illnesses are good schools of mercy for those who tend the sick, and of loving patience for those who suffer.

Bishop Jean Pierre Camus

If people learned to team up with God, the human race would soon be able to throw off the 50 percent of its ailments that medical authorities admit are psychological.

George W. Crance

To have a curable illness and to leave it untreated except for prayer is like sticking your hand in a fire and asking God to remove the flame.

Sandra L. Douglas

Before you can cure the diseases of the body, you must cure the diseases of the soul—greed, ignorance, prejudice, and intolerance.

Paul Ehrlich

A bodily disease, which we look upon as whole and entire within itself may, after all, be but a symptom of some ailment in the spiritual part.

Nathaniel Hawthorne

If cures were to be found for every illness ever known, it would make no essential difference. We should be sick, mad and blind as long as we allowed ourselves to be wholly preoccupied with the hopes and desires of this world.

Malcolm Muggeridge

Imagination

God saw that the wickedness of man was great in the earth, and that every imagination of the thoughts of his heart was only evil continually.

Genesis 6:5 KJV

All day long I have held out my hands to an obstinate people, who walk in ways not good, pursuing their own imaginations.

Isaiah 65:2 NIV

Since we are God's offspring, we ought not to think that the deity is like gold, or silver, or stone, an image formed by the art and imagination of mortals.

Acts 17:29 NRSV

The weapons with which we do battle are not those of human nature, but they have the power, in God's cause, to demolish fortresses. It is ideas that we demolish, every presumptuous notion that is set up against the knowledge of God, and we bring every thought into captivity and obedience to Christ.

2 Corinthians 10:4–5 NJB

This is imagination: the power to see the grass grow, to feel the toothache of a child, to shudder at the fall of a bird, to thrill with fear at a blood red sunset, to agonize with Jeremiah over truth frustrated by circumstance, to stand with David beneath the balsam trees and hear God pass by, to sing with John in exile, and with ten thousand times ten thousand and thousands of thousands, "Worthy is the Lamb that was slain."

Anon.

The primary imagination I hold to be the living power and prime agent of all human perception, and as a repetition in the finite mind of the eternal act of creation in the infinite I AM.

Samuel Taylor Coleridge

A stand can be made against invasion by an army; no stand can be made against invasion by an idea.

Victor Hugo

Where there is no imagination there is cruelty, selfishness, death. Christ . . . taught us to look on other people imaginatively, not as though they were ciphers in a statistical abstract.

Robert Staughton Lynd

Men often mistake their imagination for the prompting of their heart, and believe they are converted the moment they think of conversion.

Blaise Pascal

Always be on your guard against your imagination. How many lions it creates in paths, and so easily! And we suffer so much if we do not turn a deaf ear to its tales and suggestions.

George Porter

We sin against our dearest, not because we do not love but because we do not imagine.

John Watson

Imagination and fiction make up more than three-quarters of our real life. Rare indeed are the true contacts with good and evil.

Simone Weil

Immortality

Some people keep on doing good, and seek glory, honor, and immortal life; to them God will give eternal life.

Romans 2:7 GNB

Do not be deceived; God is not mocked, for you reap whatever you sow. If you sow to your own flesh, you will reap corruption from the flesh; but if you sow to the Spirit, you will reap eternal life from the Spirit.

Galatians 6:7–8 NRSV

He [our Savior Christ Jesus] has abolished death, and he has brought to light immortality and life through the gospel.

2 Timothy 1:10 NJB

We are not made to rest in this world. It is not our true native land.

Fr. Andrew

No man is prosperous whose immortality is forfeited. No man is rich to whom the grave brings eternal bankruptcy. No man is happy upon whose path there rests but a momentary glimmer of light, shining out between clouds that are closing over him in darkness forever.

Henry Ward Beecher

There is surely a piece of divinity in us, something that was before the elements, and owes no homage unto the sun.

Sir Thomas Browne

Christ gave us proof of immortality, and yet it would hardly seem necessary that one should rise from the dead to convince us that the grave is not the end. To every created thing God has given a tongue that proclaims a resurrection. If the Father deigns to touch with divine power the cold and pulseless heart of the buried acorn and to make it burst forth from its prison walls, will He leave neglected in the earth the soul of man, made in the image of his Creator?

William Jennings Bryan

There is only one way I can get ready for immortality, and that is love this life, and live it bravely and cheerfully and as faithfully as I can.

Henry van Dyke

Our dissatisfaction with any other solution is the blazing evidence of immortality.

Ralph Waldo Emerson

We cannot resist the conviction that this world is for us only the porch of another and more magnificent temple of the Creator's majesty.

Frederick William Faber

I believe that man will not merely endure; he will prevail. He is immortal, not because he alone among creatures has an inexhaustible voice, but because he has a soul, a spirit capable of compassion and sacrifice and endurance.

William Faulkner

Surely God would not have created such a being as man . . . to exist only for a day! No, no, man was made for immortality.

Abraham Lincoln

I am immortal until the will of God for me is accomplished.

David Livingstone

Beyond this vale of tears there is a life above / Unmeasured by the flight of years / And all that life is love.

James Montgomery

You can't die, for you are linked to the permanent life of God through Jesus Christ.

John Bertram (J.B.) Phillips

In the midst of finitude to be at one with the Infinite and in every moment to be eternal is the immortality of religion.

Friedrich Schleiermacher

None but God can satisfy the longings of an immortal soul; that as the heart was made for Him, so He only can fill it.

Richard Chenevix Trench

The wicked have a never-dying worm and the godly a never-fading crown.

Thomas Watson

Not in utter nakedness, / But trailing clouds of glory do we come / From God, who is our home.

William Wordsworth

He sins against this life, who slights the next.

Edward Young

Incarnation, *see* Jesus Christ, Incarnation

Injustice

See also Justice; Oppression

You will not be unjust in administering justice. You will neither be partial to the poor nor be overawed by the great, but will administer justice to your fellow-citizen justly.

Leviticus 19:15 NJB

Now, let the fear of the LORD be upon you; take care what you do, for there is no perversion of justice with the LORD our God, or partiality, or taking of bribes.

2 Chronicles 19:7 NRSV

How long will you judge unjustly and show partiality to the wicked? Give justice to the weak and the orphan; maintain the right of the lowly and the destitute.

Psalm 82:2 NRSV

A wicked person produces a bribe from under his cloak to pervert the course of justice.

Proverbs 17:23 REB

Is not this the kind of fasting I have chosen: to loose the chains of injustice and untie the cords of the yoke, to set the oppressed free and break every yoke?

Isaiah 58:6 NIV

Rather suffer an injustice than commit one.

Anon.

There is no greater opportunity to influence our fellowman for Christ than to respond with love when we have been unmistakably wronged. Then the difference between Christian love and the values of the world are most brilliantly evident.

James Dobson

Injustice anywhere is a threat to justice everywhere. We are caught in an inescapable network of mutuality tied in a single garment of destiny.

Martin Luther King Jr.

If the Christian tries to spread the good news of salvation though Jesus Christ, he should also join in the fight against social injustice and political oppression.

John R.W. Stott

God's justice guarantees that ultimately all that is unfair will be dealt with. . . . In his time and in his own way he will deal with both the injustice and those who have been unjust.

Joseph Stowell

Every time that there arises from the depths of a human heart the childish cry which Christ himself could not restrain, "Why am I being hurt?" then there is certainly injustice.

Simone Weil

Innocence

See also Guilt

I wash my hands in innocence, and go about your altar, O Lord, proclaiming aloud your praise and telling of all your wonderful deeds.

Psalm 26:6–7 NIV

Keep innocence, and take heed unto the thing that is right: for that shall bring a man peace at the last.

Psalm 37:36–38 BCP

To acquit the guilty and to condemn the innocent—both are abominable to the Lord.

Proverbs 17:15 REB

All crooks are liars, but anyone who is innocent will do right.

Proverbs 21:8 CEV

When Pilate saw that he could do nothing, but rather that a riot was beginning, he took some water and washed his hands before the crowd, saying, "I am innocent of this man's blood; see to it yourselves."

Matthew 27:24 NRSV

The virtue of innocence is regarded as foolishness by the wise of the world. Anything done out of innocence they doubtless consider stupid; and whatever is approved by truth, by the wordly wise will be called folly.

St. Gregory I

Hold fast to simplicity of heart and innocence. Yes, be as babes who do not know the wickedness that destroys grown people's lives.

Hermas

Innocence comes in contact with evil and doesn't know it; it baffles temptation; it is protected where no one else is.

Basil W. Maturin

What hope is there for innocence if it is not recognized?

Simone Weil

Integrity

See also Honesty

Let integrity and uprightness preserve me; for I wait on thee.

Psalm 25:21 KJV

David shepherded them with integrity of heart; with skillful hands he led them.

Psalm 78:72 NIV

Show yourself in all respects a model of good works, and in your teaching show integrity.

Titus 2:7 NRSV

Resolve to be thyself: and know, that he who finds himself, loses his misery.

Matthew Arnold

Live so that the preacher can tell the truth at your funeral.

K. Beckstrom

He is rich or poor according to what he is, not according to what he has.

Henry Ward Beecher

Be what thou seemest! Live thy creed!

Horatius Bonar

Integrity of heart is indispensable.

John Calvin

My worth to God in public is what I am in private.

Oswald Chambers

When a Christian jealously guards his secret life with God, his public life will take care of itself.

Oswald Chambers

Take care not knowingly to do or say anything which, if everyone were to know of it, you could not own, and say, "Yes, that is what I did or what I said."

Louis IX of France

More depends on my walk than my talk.

Dwight Lyman (D.L.) Moody

[Jesus] knows we are sinners and there will be people that we do not like and that do not like us. The issue as a Christian is not to pretend that we love everything that moves and breathes. That would be phony and hypocritical. Jesus does not tell us to pretend they are friends either. Rather he asks that we acknowledge the fact that they are enemies without pretense and yet respond to them with love, not hate, or bitterness.

Rebecca Manley Pippert

Integrity is the first step to true greatness.

Charles Simmons

Intercession, *see* Prayer, Intercession

Jealousy

See also Envy

For thou shalt worship no other god: for the Lord, whose name is Jealous, is a jealous God.

Exodus 34:14 KJV

Wrath is cruel, anger is overwhelming, but who is able to stand before jealousy?

Proverbs 27:4 NRSV

Love is as strong as death, its jealousy unyielding as the grave. It burns like blazing fire, like a mighty flame.

Song of Songs 8:6 NIV

A jealous ear hears all things.

Wisdom of Solomon 1:10 NRSV

Love is kind and patient, never jealous, boastful, proud, or rude.

1 Corinthians 13:4–5 CEV

Jealousy is a terrible thing. It resembles love, only it is precisely love's contrary. Instead of wishing for the welfare of the object loved, it desires the dependence of that object upon

itself, and its own triumph. Love is the forgetfulness of self; jealousy is the most passionate form of egotism, the glorification of a despotic, exacting, and vain ego, which can neither forget nor subordinate itself. The contrast is perfect.

Henri-Frédéric Amiel

Of all the passions, jealousy is that which exacts the hardest service, and pays the bitterest wages. Its service is—to watch the success of our enemy; its wages—to be sure of it.

Charles Caleb Colton

Jealousy, the jaundice of the soul.

John Dryden

In jealousy there is more self-love than love.

François, Duc de La Rochefoucauld

The jealous are troublesome to others; a torment to themselves.

William Penn

O, beware, my lord, of jealousy; / It is the green-ey'd monster which doth mock / The meat it feeds on.

William Shakespeare

Moral indignation is jealousy with a halo.

Herbert George (H.G.) Wells

Jesus Christ

See also God; Word of God

Ascension of

Jesus saith unto her, Touch me not; for I am not yet ascended to my Father: but go to my brethren, and say unto them, I ascend unto my Father, and your Father; and to my God, and your God.

John 20:17 KJV

When he had said this, as they were watching, he was lifted up, and a cloud took him out of their sight.

Acts 1:9 NRSV

I want you to know about the great and mighty power that God has for us followers. It is the same wonderful power he used when he raised Christ from death and let him sit at his right side in heaven. There Christ rules over all forces, authorities, powers and rulers. He rules over all beings in this world and will rule in the future world as well. God has put all things under the power of Christ, and for the good of the church he has made him the head of everything.

Ephesians 1:19–22 CEV

Jesus departed from our sight that he might return to our hearts. He departed, and behold, he is here.

St. Augustine of Hippo

As sign and wonder this exaltation is a pointer to the revelation that occurred in His resurrection, of Jesus Christ as the heart of all powers in heaven and earth.

Karl Barth

At his ascension our Lord entered heaven, and he keeps the door open for humanity to enter.

Oswald Chambers

The ascension placed Jesus Christ back in the glory which he had with the Father before the world was. The ascension, not the resurrection, is the completion of the transfiguration.

Oswald Chambers

The ascension of Christ is his liberation from all restriction of time and space. It does not represent his removal from the earth, but his constant presence everywhere on earth.

William Temple

Authority of

When Jesus had finished saying these things, the crowds were amazed at his teaching, because he taught as one who had authority, and not as their teachers of the law.

Matthew 7:28–29 NIV

"But so that you may know that the Son of Man has authority on earth to forgive sins . . ." Then he said to the paralytic, "Get up, take your mat and go home." And the man got up and went home.

Matthew 9:6–7 NIV

Jesus came and said to them, "All authority in heaven and on earth has been given to me."

Matthew 28:18 NRSV

If you accept the authority of Jesus in your life, then you accept the authority of His words.

Colin Urquhart

Birth of

See also Christmas; Jesus Christ, Incarnation

She shall bring forth a son, and thou shalt call his name Jesus: for he shall save his people from their sins. Now all this was done, that it might be fulfilled which was spoken of the Lord by the prophet, saying, Behold a virgin shall be with child, and shall bring forth a son, and they shall call his name Emmanuel, which being interpreted is, God with us.

Matthew 1:21–23 KJV

She gave birth to her firstborn son and wrapped him in bands of cloth, and laid him in a manger, because there was no place for them in the inn.

Luke 2:7 NRSV

When the time was right, God sent his Son, and a woman gave birth to him.

Galatians 4:4 CEV

O holy Child of Bethlehem, / Descend to us, we pray; / Cast out our sin, and enter in; / Be born in us today. / We hear the Christmas angels / The great glad tidings tell; / O come to us, abide with us, / Our Lord Immanuel.

Phillips Brooks

Great little one! / Whose all-embracing birth / Lifts Earth to Heaven, / Stoops Heaven to Earth.

Richard Crashaw

At Bethlehem God became man to enable men to become the sons of God.

Clive Staples (C.S.) Lewis

Silent night! holy night! / Son of God, love's pure light. / Radiant beams from Thy holy face, / With the dawn of redeeming grace, / Jesus, Lord, at Thy birth.

Joseph Mohr

The coming of Jesus into the world is the most stupendous event in human history.

Malcolm Muggeridge

The coming of Christ by way of a Bethlehem manger seems strange and stunning. But when we take him out of the manger and invite him into our hearts, then the meaning unfolds and the strangeness vanishes.

Neil C. Strait

Compassion of

See also Compassion

He will not snap off a broken reed, nor snuff out a smouldering wick, until he leads justice on to victory.

Matthew 12:20 REB

Filled with compassion, Jesus reached out his hand and touched the man. "I am willing," he said, "Be clean!"

Mark 1:41 NIV

As he went ashore, he saw a great crowd; and he had compassion for them, because they were like sheep without a shepherd.

Mark 6:34 NRSV

When the Lord saw her, his heart was filled with pity for her, and he said to her, "Don't cry."

Luke 7:13 GNB

Therefore, since we have a great high priest who has gone through the heavens, Jesus the Son of God, let us hold firmly to the faith we profess. For we do not have a high priest who is unable to sympathize with our weaknesses, but we have one who has been tempted in every way, just as we are—yet was without sin. Let us then approach the throne of grace with confidence, so that we may receive mercy and find grace to help us in our time of need.

Hebrews 4:14–16 NIV

With infinite love and compassion our Lord understood the human predicament. He had deep empathy with people; he saw their needs, their weaknesses, their desires, and their hurt. He understood and was concerned for people. Every word he spoke was uttered because he saw a need for that word in some human life. His concern was always to uplift and never to tear down, to heal and never hurt, to save and not condemn.

Charles L. Allen

Christ is the ocean, in which every drop is infinite compassion. He is the mountain towering above the mountains, in which every grain is God's own goodness.

Henry Law

Though our Savior's passion is over, his compassion is not.

William Penn

Death of

See also Cross; Seven Last Words

He was despised and rejected by men, a man of sorrows, and familiar with suffering. Like one from whom men hide their faces he was despised, and we esteemed him not. Surely he took up our infirmities and carried our sorrows, yet we considered him stricken by God, smitten by him, and afflicted. But he was pierced for our transgressions, he was crushed for our iniquities; the punishment that brought us peace was upon him, and by his wounds we are healed. We all, like sheep, have gone astray, each of us has turned to his own way; and the Lord has laid on him the iniquity of us all. He was oppressed and afflicted, yet he did not open his mouth; he was led like a lamb to the slaughter, and as a sheep before her shearers is silent, so he did not open his mouth.

Isaiah 53:3–7 NIV

Then Jesus cried again with a loud voice and breathed his last. At that moment the curtain of the temple was torn in two, from top to bottom. The earth shook, and the rocks were split. The tombs also were opened, and many bodies of the saints who had fallen asleep were raised.

Matthew 27:50–52 NRSV

For when we were still helpless, Christ died for the wicked at the time that God chose. It

is a difficult thing for someone to die for a righteous person. It may even be that someone might dare to die for a good person. But God has shown us how much he loves us— it was while we were still sinners that Christ died for us!

Romans 5:6–8 GNB

For I delivered unto you first of all that which I also received, how that Christ died for our sins according to the scriptures.

1 Corinthians 15:3 KJV

And having disarmed the powers and authorities, he [God] made a public spectacle of them, triumphing over them by the cross.

Colossians 2:15 NIV

We are people of flesh and blood. That is why Jesus became one of us. He died to destroy the devil, who had power over death. But he also died to rescue all of us who live each day in fear of dying.

Hebrews 2:14–15 CEV

There is a green hill far away, / Outside a city wall, / Where the dear Lord was crucified, / Who died to save us all.

Cecil Frances Alexander

No man took His life; He laid it down of Himself.

Robert Hugh Benson

To know Jesus and Him crucified is my philosophy, and there is none higher.

St. Bernard of Clairvaux

Bearing shame and scoffing rude, / In my place condemned He stood; / Sealed my pardon with His blood: / Hallelujah, what a Savior!

Philipp Paul Bliss

Crown Him with many crowns, / The Lamb upon His throne; / Hark! how the heavenly anthem drowns / All music but its own. / Awake, my soul and sing / Of Him who died for thee, / And hail Him as thy chosen King / Through all eternity.

Matthew Bridges, Godfrey Thring

There is something in Calvary that passes our understanding, and the words about the Precious Blood should never be read or sung except on the knees of our spirit.

Amy Wilson Carmichael

For the sake of each of us he laid down his life—worth no less than the universe. He demands of us in return our lives for the sake of each other.

Clement of Alexandria

Sin could not die, unless Christ died; Christ could not die without being made sin; nor could He die, but sin must die with Him.

Elisha Coles

O make me understand it, / Help me to take it in, / What it meant to Thee, the Holy One, / To bear away my sin.

Katharine Agnes May Kelly

Christ died to save us, not from suffering, but from ourselves; not from injustice, far less than justice, but from being unjust. He died that we might live—but live as he lives, by dying as he died who died to himself.

George MacDonald

The symbol of the cross in the church points to the God who was crucified not between two candles on an altar, but between two thieves in the place of the skull, where the outcasts belong, outside the gates of the city. It does not invite thought but a change of mind. It is a symbol which therefore leads out

of the church and out of religious longing into the fellowship of the oppressed and abandoned. On the other hand, it is a symbol which calls the oppressed and godless into the church and through the church into the fellowship of the crucified God.

Jürgen Moltmann

Calvary is the key to an omnipotence which works only and always through sacrificial love.

(Arthur) Michael Ramsey

It we would live aright it must be by the contemplation of Christ's death.

Charles Haddon Spurgeon

Well might the sun in darkness hide, / And shut his glories in, / When God, the mighty Maker, died / For man, the creature's sin.

Isaac Watts

Christ did not die a martyr. He died— infinitely more humbly—a common criminal.

Simone Weil

Divinity of

In the beginning was the Word, and the Word was with God, and the Word was God. The same was in the beginning with God.

John 1:1–2 KJV

The leaders wanted to kill Jesus for two reasons. First, he had broken the law of the Sabbath. But even worse, he had said that God was his Father, which made him equal with God.

John 5:18 CEV

Thomas replied, "My Lord and my God!"

John 20:28 NJB

Who, being in very nature God, did not

consider equality with God something to be grasped.

Philippians 2:6 NIV

Of the Son he says, "Your throne, O God, is for ever and ever, and the righteous sceptre is the sceptre of your kingdom."

Hebrews 1:8 NRSV

As the print of the seal on the wax is the express image of the seal itself, so Christ is the express image—the perfect representation—of God.

St. Ambrose

The Son is the Image of the invisible God. All things that belong to the Father He expresses as the Image; all things that are the Father's He illumines as the splendor of His glory and manifests to us.

St. Ambrose

If Jesus Christ is not true God, how could he *help* us? If he is not true man, how could he help *us*?

Dietrich Bonhoeffer

I consider the Gospels to be thoroughly genuine; for in them there is the effective reflection of a sublimity which emanated from the Person of Christ; and this is as Divine as ever the divine appeared on earth.

Johann Wolfgang von Goethe

He suffered not as God, but He suffered who was God.

John Owen

Example of

Take my yoke upon you, and learn from me, for I am gentle and humble-hearted; and you will find rest for your souls.

Matthew 11:29 REB

You call me your teacher and Lord, and you should, because that is who I am. And if your Lord and teacher has washed your feet, you should do the same for each other. I have set the example, and you should do for each other exactly what I have done for you.

John 13:13–15 CEV

Take me as your pattern, just as I take Christ for mine.

1 Corinthians 11:1 NJB

Your attitude should be the same as that of Christ Jesus: Who, being in very nature God, did not consider equality with God something to be grasped, but made himself nothing, taking the very nature of a servant, and being found in appearance as a man, he humbled himself and became obedient to death—even death on a cross.

Philippians 2:5–8 NIV

To this you were called, because Christ suffered for you, leaving you an example, that you should follow in his steps. "He committed no sin, and no deceit was found in his mouth." When they hurled their insults at him, he did not retaliate; when he suffered, he made no threats. Instead, he entrusted himself to him who judges justly. He himself bore our sins in his body on the tree, so that we might die to sins and live for righteousness; by his wounds you have been healed. For you were like sheep going astray, but now you have returned to the Shepherd and Overseer of your souls.

1 Peter 2:21–25 NIV

When we are right with God, he gives us our desires and aspirations. Our Lord had only one desire, and that was to do the will of his Father, and to have this desire is characteristic of a disciple.

Oswald Chambers

Our Lord lived his life . . . to give the normal standard for our lives.

Oswald Chambers

There is no detour to holiness. Jesus came to the resurrection through the cross, not around it.

Leighton Frederick Sandys Ford

Christ was willing to suffer; do you dare to complain? Christ had enemies and detractors; so you want everyone to be your friend and benefactor?

Thomas à Kempis

Are you laying a feather bed for me, no that shall not be. / My Lord was stretched on a hard and painful tree.

Brother Lawrence

In his life Christ is an example showing us how to live; in his death, he is a sacrifice satisfying for our sins; in his resurrection, a conqueror; in his ascension, a king; in his intercession a high priest.

Martin Luther

Example moves the world more than doctrine.

Henry Miller

Humanity of

The Word became flesh and made his dwelling among us.

John 1:14 NIV

Jacob's well was there, and Jesus, tired as he was from the journey, sat down by the well.

John 4:6 NIV

Jesus wept.

John 11:35 NIV

He emptied himself, taking the form of a slave, becoming as human beings are; and being in every way like a human being, he was humbler yet, even to accepting death, death on a cross.

Philippians 2:7–8 NJB

Since the children, as he calls them, are people of flesh and blood, Jesus himself became like them and shared their human nature. He did this so that through his death he might destroy the Devil, who has the power over death, and in this way set free those who were slaves all their lives because of their fear of death. For it is clear that it is not the angels that he helps. Instead, as the scripture says, "He helps the descendants of Abraham." This means that he had to become like his brothers in every way, in order to be their faithful and merciful High Priest in his service to God, so that the people's sins would be forgiven. And now he can help those who are tempted, because he himself was tempted and suffered.

Hebrews 2:14–18 GNB

By this you know the Spirit of God: every spirit that confesses that Jesus Christ has come in the flesh is from God.

1 John 4:2 NRSV

He became what we are that he might make us what he is.

St. Athanasius of Alexandria

Christ as God is the fatherland where we are going. Christ as man is the way by which we go.

St. Augustine of Hippo

If Jesus Christ is not true God, how could he *help* us? If he is not true man, how could he help *us*?

Dietrich Bonhoeffer

God clothed himself in a vile man's flesh so he might be weak enough to suffer.

John Donne

By a Carpenter mankind was created and made, and by a Carpenter meet it was that man should be repaired.

Desiderius Erasmus

The mystery of the humanity of Christ, that he sunk himself into our flesh, is beyond all human understanding.

Martin Luther

God's only Son doth hug humanity into his very person.

Edward Taylor

Christ took our flesh upon him that he might take our sins upon him.

Thomas Watson

Humility of

See also Humility

Take my yoke upon you, and learn from me; for I am gentle and humble in heart, and you will find rest for your souls.

Matthew 11:29 NRSV

It was just before the Passover Feast. Jesus knew that the time had come for him to leave this world and go to the Father. Having loved his own who were in the world, he now showed them the full extent of his love. The evening meal was being served, and the devil had already prompted Judas Iscariot, son of Simon, to betray Jesus. Jesus knew that the Father had put all things under his power, and that he had come from God and was returning to God; so he got up from the meal, took off his outer clothing, and wrapped a towel round his waist. After that, he poured water into a basin and began to wash his disciples' feet, drying them with the towel that was wrapped around him.

John 13:1–5 NIV

For you know the grace of our Lord Jesus Christ, that though he was rich, yet for your sakes he became poor, so that you through his poverty might become rich.

2 Corinthians 8:9 NIV

Do nothing from selfish ambition or conceit, but in humility regard others as better than yourselves.

Philippians 2:3 NRSV

Jesus Christ served others first; he spoke to those to whom no one spoke; he dined with the lowest members of society; he touched the untouchable. He had no throne, no crown, no bevy of servants or armored guards. A borrowed manger and a borrowed tomb framed his early life.

Charles W. Colson

Christ ceased not to be a King because He was like a servant, nor to be a lion because He was like a lamb, nor to be God because He was made man, nor to be a judge because He was judged.

Henry Smith

If you are looking for an example of humility, look at the cross.

St. Thomas Aquinas

Because Jesus Christ came to the world clothed in humility, he will always be found among those who are clothed with humility. He will be found among the humble people.

Aiden Wilson (A.W.) Tozer

Incarnation

See also Jesus Christ, Birth of

All this took place to fulfill what the Lord had said through the prophet: "The virgin will be with child and will give birth to a son, and they will call him Immanuel"—-which means, "God with us."

Matthew 1:22–23 NIV

The Word became flesh, he lived among us, and we saw his glory, the glory that he has from the Father as the only Son of the Father, full of grace and truth.

John 1:14 NJB

Christ Jesus: Who, being in very nature God, did not consider equality with God something to be grasped, but made himself nothing, taking the very nature of a servant, being made in human likeness. And being found in appearance as a man, he humbled himself and became obedient to death—even death on a cross!

Philippians 2:5–8 NIV

Here is the great mystery of our religion: Christ came as a human. The Spirit proved that he pleased God, and he was seen by angels. Christ was preached to the nations. People in this world put their faith in him, and he was taken up to glory.

1 Timothy 3:16 CEV

Christ became what we are that he might make us what he is.

St. Athanasius of Alexandria

He became human that we might become divine; he revealed himself in a body that we might understand the unseen Father; he endured man's insults that we might inherit immortality.

St. Athanasius of Alexandria

The one thoroughly laid down and safe way to avoid all going wide of the truth is the doctrine of the Incarnation—that one and the same person is God and man; as God, the end of our going; as man, the way we are to go.

St. Augustine of Hippo

The fact of Jesus' coming is the final and unanswerable proof that God cares.

William Barclay

Very God of very God, Begotten, not made, Being of one substance with the Father, By whom all things were made: Who for us men and for our salvation came down from heaven.

Book of Common Prayer

The incarnation is the pattern for all evangelism. Jesus Christ was totally in the world yet totally uncontaminated by it.

Everett L. Cattell

The Word of God became man that you also may learn from a man how a man becomes a God.

Clement of Alexandria

If Jesus Christ is God incarnate, no fuller disclosure of God in terms of manhood than is given in his person is conceivable or possible.

St. Irenaeus

God of God, / Light of Light, / Lo, he abhors not the Virgin's womb; / Very God, / Begotten, not created.

Latin, tr. Frederick Oakeley

God became man to turn creatures into sons; not simply to produce better men of the old kind but to produce a new kind of man.

Clive Staples (C.S.) Lewis

The Incarnation is the most stupendous event which ever can take place on earth, and after it henceforth, I do not see how we can scruple at any miracle on the mere ground of it being unlikely to happen.

John Henry Newman

The Incarnation is the place where hope contends with fear.

Kathleen Norris

The greatness of God was not cast off, but the slightness of human nature was put on.

St. Thomas Aquinas

In order that the body of Christ might be shown to be a real body, he was born of a woman; but in order that his Godhead might be made clear he was born of a virgin.

St. Thomas Aquinas

Christ, by highest heaven adored, / Christ, the Everlasting Lord, / Late in time behold Him come, / Offspring of a virgin's womb. / Veiled in flesh the Godhead see! / Hail the incarnate Deity! / Pleased as Man with man to dwell, / Jesus, our Immanuel. / Hark! the herald angels sing / Glory to the new-born King.

Charles Wesley

I find it much easier to accept the fact of God incarnating in Jesus of Nazareth than in the people who attend my local church and in me. Yet that is what we are asked to believe; that is how we are asked to live. Jesus played his part and then left. Now it is up to us, the body of Christ.

Philip Yancey

Kingship of

See also Kingdom of God

Rejoice greatly, O daughter of Zion; shout, O daughter of Jerusalem: behold, thy King cometh unto thee: he is just, and having salvation; lowly, and riding upon an ass, and upon a colt the foal of an ass.

Zechariah 9:9 KJV

Jesus said, "My kingdom is not of this world. If it were, my servants would fight to prevent my arrest by the Jews. But now my kingdom is from another place." "You are a king, then!" said Pilate. Jesus answered, "You are right in saying I am a king. In fact, for this reason I was born, and for this I came into the world, to testify to the truth."

John 18:36–37 NIV

Pilate also had an inscription written and put on the cross. It read, "Jesus of Nazareth, the King of the Jews" . . . Then the chief priests of the Jews said to Pilate, "Do not write, 'The King of the Jews,' but, 'This man said, I am King of the Jews,'"

John 19:19, 21 NRSV

For he must reign until he has put all his enemies under his feet.

1 Corinthians 15:25 NRSV

Then the seventh angel blew his trumpet, and there were loud voices in heaven, saying, "The kingdom of the world has become the kingdom of our Lord and of his Messiah, and he will reign forever and ever."

Revelation 11:15 NRSV

Christ is not valued at all unless he be valued above all.

St. Augustine of Hippo

Jesus Christ will be Lord of all or he will not be Lord at all.

St. Augustine of Hippo

Though Christ's coat was once divided, He will never suffer His crown to be divided.

Thomas Benton Brooks

We must not have Christ Jesus, the Lord of Life, put any more in the stable amongst the horses and asses, but he must now have the best chamber.

George Fox

Tomorrow's history has already been written—at the name of Jesus every knee must bow.

Paul E. Kauffman

Crown the Savior! angels, crown Him! / Rich the trophies Jesus brings; / In the seat of power enthrone Him, / Whilst the vault of heaven rings: / Crown Him! Crown Him! / Crown the Savior King of kings!

Thomas Kelly

There's not a thumb's breadth of this universe about which Jesus Christ does not say, "It is mine."

Abraham Kuyper

Such as will not have Christ to be their King to rule over them shall never have his blood to save them.

Thomas Watson

Love of

See also Love

O Jerusalem, Jerusalem, which killest the prophets, and stonest them that are sent unto thee; how often would I have gathered thy children together, as a hen doth gather her brood under her wings, and ye would not!

Luke 13:34 KJV

No one can have greater love than to lay down his life for his friends.

John 15:13 NJB

I pray that you may have the power to comprehend, with all the saints, what is the breadth and length and height and depth, and to know the love of Christ that surpasses

knowledge, so that you may be filled with all the fullness of God.

Ephesians 3:18–19 NRSV

Let love be your guide. Christ loved us and offered his life for us as a sacrifice that pleases God.

Ephesians 5:2 CEV

Hereby perceive we the love of God, because he laid down his life for us: and we ought to lay down our lives for the brethren.

1 John 3:16 KJV

My song is love unknown, / My Savior's love to me, / Love to the loveless shown, / That they might lovely be. / O who am I, / That for my sake / My Lord should take / Frail flesh, and die?

Samuel Crossman

Lord Jesus Christ, Son of God, have mercy on me, a sinner.

The Jesus Prayer

When men are animated by the love of Christ they feel united, and the needs, sufferings and joys of others are felt as their own.

John XXIII

We are never nearer Christ than when we find ourselves lost in a holy amazement at His unspeakable love.

John Owen

In our fluctuations of feeling, it is well to remember that Jesus admits no change in his affections; your heart is not the compass Jesus saileth by.

Samuel Rutherford

The distinguishing mark of a Christian is his confidence in the love of Christ, and the yielding of his affections to Christ in return.

Charles Haddon Spurgeon

Jesus loves me, this I know, / For the Bible tells me so: / Little ones to Him belong, / They are weak, but He is strong. / Yes, Jesus loves me, / Yes, Jesus loves me, / Yes, Jesus loves me, / The Bible tells me so.

Anna Bartlett Warner

Messiah

He saith unto them, But whom say ye that I am? And Simon Peter answered and said, Thou art the Christ, the Son of the living God.

Matthew 16:15–16 KJV

The first thing Andrew did was to find his brother and say to him, "We have found the Messiah"—which means the Christ—and he took Simon to Jesus.

John 1:41–42 NJB

The woman said to him, "I know that Messiah is coming" (who is called Christ). "When he comes, he will proclaim all things to us." Jesus said to her, "I am he, the one who is speaking to you."

John 4:25–26 NRSV

But these are written that you may believe that Jesus is the Christ, the Son of God, and that by believing you may have life in his name.

John 20:31 NIV

Following his usual practice Paul went to their meetings; and for the next three Sabbaths he argued with them, quoting texts of scripture which he expounded and applied to show that the Messiah had to suffer and rise from the dead. "And this Jesus," he said, "whom I am proclaiming to you is the Messiah."

Acts 17:2–3 REB

Miracles of

See also Miracles

Jesus went throughout Galilee, teaching in their synagogues and proclaiming the good news of the kingdom and curing every disease and every sickness among the people. So his fame spread throughout all Syria, and they brought to him all the sick, those who were afflicted with various diseases and pains, demoniacs, epileptics and paralytics, and he cured them.

Matthew 4:23–24 NRSV

He stood up and rebuked the winds and the sea, and there was a great calm. They were astounded and said, "Whatever kind of man is this, that even the winds and the sea obey him?"

Matthew 8:26–27 NJB

He took the five loaves and the two fish, looked up to heaven, and gave thanks to God. He broke the loaves and gave them to the disciples, and the disciples gave them to the people. Everyone ate and had enough. Then the disciples took up twelve baskets full of what was left over. The number of men who ate was about five thousand, not counting the women and children.

Matthew 14:19–21 GNB

This was Jesus' first miracle, and he did it in the village of Cana in Galilee. There Jesus showed his glory, and his disciples put their faith in him.

John 2:11 CEV

He cried with a loud voice, Lazarus, come forth. And he that was dead came forth, bound hand and foot with graveclothes: and his face was bound about with a napkin. Jesus saith unto them, Loose him, and let him go.

John 11:43–44 KJV

The miracles of Jesus were the ordinary works of his Father, wrought small and swift that we might take them in.

George MacDonald

The healing acts of Jesus were themselves a message that he had come to set men free.

Francis MacNutt

Mission of

See also Church, Mission and Ministry of

The Son of Man did not come to be served, but to serve, and to give his life as a ransom for many.

Matthew 20:28 NIV

The Spirit of the Lord is upon me, because he has anointed me to bring good news to the poor. He has sent me to proclaim release to the captives and recovery of sight to the blind, to let the oppressed go free, to proclaim the year of the Lord's favor.

Luke 4:18–19 NRSV

I am come a light into the world, that whosoever believeth on me should not abide in darkness. And if any man hear my words, and believe not, I judge him not: for I came not to judge the world, but to save the world.

John 12:46–47 KJV

Here is a trustworthy saying that deserves full acceptance: Christ Jesus came into the world to save sinners—of whom I am the worst.

1 Timothy 1:15 NIV

This was the purpose of the appearing of the Son of God, to undo the work of the devil.

1 John 3:8 NJB

If people ask, "Why did he not appear by means of other parts of creation, and use some nobler instrument, as the sun or moon or stars or fire or air, instead of man merely?" let them know that the Lord came not to make a display, but to teach and heal those who were suffering.

St. Athanasius of Alexandria

Jesus Christ's outward life was densely immersed in the things of the world, yet he was inwardly disconnected. The one irresistible purpose of his life was to do the will of his Father.

Oswald Chambers

Jesus came to save persons, not just souls. He came to help the suffering in whatever way they were suffering. Sickness of the body was part of the kingdom of Satan he had come to destroy.

Francis MacNutt

A radical revolution, embracing even nature itself, was the fundamental idea of Jesus.

Joseph Ernst Renan

We shall never understand anything of our Lord's preaching and ministry unless we continually keep in mind what exactly and exclusively his errand was in this world. Sin was his errand in this world, and it was his only errand. He would never have been in this world, either preaching or doing anything else, but for sin. He could have done everything else for us without coming down into this world at all; everything else but take away our sin.

Alexander Whyte

Perfection of

See also Perfection

Judas had betrayed Jesus, but when he learned that Jesus had been sentenced to death, he was sorry for what he had done. He returned the thirty silver coins to the chief priests and leaders and said, "I have sinned by betraying a man who has never done anything wrong."

Matthew 27:3–4 CEV

For he hath made him to be sin for us, who

knew no sin, that we might be made the righteousness of God in him.

2 Corinthians 5:21 KJV

In bringing many sons to glory, it was fitting that God, for whom and through whom everything exists, should make the author of their salvation perfect through suffering.

Hebrews 2:10 NIV

How much greater is the power of the blood of Christ; through the eternal Spirit he offered himself without blemish to God.

Hebrews 9:14 REB

The Transfiguration was the "Great Divide" in the life of our Lord. He stood there in the perfect, spotless holiness of his manhood; then he turned his back on the glory and came down from the Mount to be identified with sin.

Oswald Chambers

I believe there is no one lovelier, deeper, more sympathetic and more perfect than Jesus— not only is there no one else like him, but there could never be anyone like him.

Fyodor Dostoevsky

The most perfect being who has ever trod the soil of this planet was called the Man of Sorrows.

James Anthony Froude

No critic of Jesus has ever been taken seriously. His life was the epitome of virtue.

Richard Christian Halverson

Jesus perfectly lived what he perfectly taught.

Herman H. Horne

If you check out the life of Jesus you will discover what made him perfect. He did not attain a state of perfection by carrying around in his pocket a list of rules and regulations, or by seeking to conform to the cultural mores of his time. He was perfect because he never made a move without his Father.

Thomas Skinner

Prayers of

See also Seven Last Words

My Father, if it is possible, let this cup pass from me; yet not what I want but what you want.

Matthew 26:39 NRSV

O my Father, if this cup may not pass away from me, except I drink it, thy will be done.

Matthew 26:42 KJV

It came to pass, that, as he was praying in a certain place, when he ceased, one of his disciples said unto him, Lord, teach us to pray, as John also taught his disciples. And he said unto them, When ye pray, say, Our Father which art in heaven, Hallowed be thy name. Thy kingdom come. Thy will be done, as in heaven, so in earth. Give us day by day our daily bread. And forgive us our sins; for we also forgive every one that is indebted to us. And lead us not into temptation; but deliver us from evil.

Luke 11:1–4 KJV

Simon, Simon! Listen! Satan has received permission to test all of you, to separate the good from the bad, as a farmer separates the wheat from the chaff. But I have prayed for you, Simon, that your faith will not fail. And when you turn back to me, you must strengthen your brothers.

Luke 22:31–32 GNB

He withdrew from them about a stone's throw, knelt down, and prayed, "Father, if you are willing, remove this cup from me;

yet, not my will but yours be done." Then an angel from heaven appeared to him and gave him strength. In his anguish he prayed more earnestly, and his sweat became like great drops of blood falling down on the ground.

Luke 22:41–44 NRSV

Father, the hour has come; glorify your Son so that the Son may glorify you, since you have given him authority over all people, to give eternal life to all whom you have given him. And this is eternal life, that they may know you, the only true God, and Jesus Christ whom you have sent. I glorified you on earth by finishing the work that you gave me to do. So now, Father, glorify me in your own presence with the glory that I had in your presence before the world existed.

John 17:1–5 NRSV

I pray not only for these but also for those who through their teaching will come to believe in me. May they all be one, just as, Father, you are in me and I am in you, so that they also may be in us, so that the world may believe it was you who sent me.

John 17:20–21 NJB

During the days of Jesus' life on earth, he offered up prayers and petitions with loud cries and tears to the one who could save him from death, and he was heard because of his reverent submission.

Hebrews 5:7 NIV

He [Jesus] is able to save completely those who come to God through him, because he always lives to intercede for them.

Hebrews 7:25 NIV

I do not think that prayer is ever evasion, that prayer saves us from having to face things that we do not want to face and that are going to hurt if we face them. Jesus in Gethsemane discovered that there was no evasion of the cross.

William Barclay

What deep mysteries, my dearest brothers, are contained in the Lord's Prayer! How many and great they are! They are expressed in a few words but they are rich in spiritual powers so that nothing is left out; every petition and prayer we have to make is included. It is a compendium of heavenly doctrine.

St. Cyprian

The "Our Father" is a very personal prayer which nevertheless brings those praying closely together in the opening words. It is a very simple prayer of petition, but wholly concentrated on essentials, on God's cause which appears to be inextricably linked with man's cause.

Hans Küng

The Lord's Prayer is the prayer above all prayers. It is a prayer which the most high Master taught us, wherein are comprehended all spiritual and temporal blessings, and the strongest comforts in all trials, temptations, and troubles, even in the hour of death.

Martin Luther

If I could hear Christ praying for me in the next room, I would not fear a million enemies. Yet the distance makes no difference; he is praying for me!

Robert Murray M'Cheyne

The Lord's Prayer may be committed to memory quickly, but it is slowly learnt by heart.

John Frederick Denison Maurice

Priesthood of

See also Priests and Priesthood

Through our Lord Jesus Christ . . . we have gained access by faith into this grace in which we now stand.

Romans 5:1–2 NIV

Now in Christ Jesus ye who sometimes were far off are made nigh by the blood of Christ . . . For through him we both have access by one Spirit unto the Father.

Ephesians 2:13, 18 KJV

For there is one God and one mediator between God and men, the man Christ Jesus.

1 Timothy 2:5 KJV

For we have a great High Priest who has gone into the very presence of God—Jesus, the Son of God. Our High Priest is not one who cannot feel sympathy for our weaknesses. On the contrary, we have a High Priest who was tempted in every way that we are, but did not sin.

Hebrews 4:14–15 GNB

Because Jesus lives for ever, he has a permanent priesthood. Therefore he is able to save completely those who come to God through him, because he always lives to intercede for them. Such a high priest meets our need—one who is holy, blameless, pure, set apart from sinners, exalted above the heavens.

Hebrews 7:24–26 NIV

We have, then, my brothers, complete freedom to go into the Most Holy Place by means of the death of Jesus. He opened for us a new way, a living way, through the curtain—that is, through his own body. We have a great priest in charge of the house of God. So let us come near to God with a sincere heart and a sure faith, with hearts that have been purified from a guilty conscience and with bodies washed with clean water.

Hebrews 10:19–22 GNB

The system of human mediation falls away in the advent to our souls of the living Christ. Who wants stars, or even the moon, after the sun is up?

A.B. Cave

Christ has taken our nature into heaven to represent us, and has left us on earth with his nature to represent him.

John Newton

Christ's intercession in heaven is a kind of powerful remembrance of His people, and of all their concerns, managed with state and majesty: not as a suppliant at the footstool, but as a crowned prince on the throne, at the right hand of the Father.

Robert Traill

Prophethood of

See also Prophets and Prophecy

Instead, he [the Lord your God] will send you a prophet like me from among your own people, and you are to obey him.

Deuteronomy 18:15 GNB

The multitude said, This is Jesus the prophet of Nazareth of Galilee.

Matthew 21:11 KJV

Everyone was filled with awe and glorified God saying, "A great prophet has risen up among us; God has visited his people."

Luke 7:16 NJB

Jesus of Nazareth, who was a prophet mighty in deed and word before God and all the people.

Luke 24:19 NRSV

Jesus is the prophet of the loser's not the victor's camp, the one who proclaims that the first will be last, that the weak are the strong, and the fools are the wise.

Malcolm Muggeridge

Resurrection of

See also Easter

He is not here: for he is risen, as he said. Come, see the place where the Lord lay.

Matthew 28:6 KJV

This Jesus God raised up, and of that all of us are witnesses.

Acts 2:32 NRSV

For he has fixed a day in which he will judge the whole world with justice by means of a man he has chosen. He has given proof of this to everyone by raising that man from death!

Acts 17:31 GNB

So by our baptism into his death we were buried with him, so that as Christ was raised from the dead by the Father's glorious power, we too should begin living a new life. If we have been joined to him by dying a death like his, so we shall be by a resurrection like his.

Romans 6:4–5 NJB

Christ died for our sins according to the Scriptures, that he was buried, that he was raised on the third day according to the Scriptures, and that he appeared to Peter, and then to the Twelve. After that, he appeared to more than five hundred of the brothers at the same time, most of whom are still living, though some have fallen asleep. Then he appeared to James, then to all the apostles, and last of all he appeared to me also, as to one abnormally born.

1 Corinthians 15:3–8 NIV

I am he that liveth, and was dead; and, behold, I am alive for evermore, Amen; and have the keys of hell and of death.

Revelation 1:18 KJV

Jesus' resurrection makes it impossible for man's story to end in chaos—it has to move inexorably toward light, toward life, toward love.

Carlo Carretto

Christ has turned all our sunsets into dawns.

Clement of Alexandria

The resurrection is not a miracle like any other. It is a unique manifestation within this world of the transition God makes for us out of this way of being into another.

Austin Farrer

Jesus lives! Thy terrors now / Can, O death, no more appal us; / Jesus lives! by this we know / Thou, O grave, canst not enthral us. / Hallelujah!

Christian Furchtegott Gellert,
tr. Frances Elizabeth Cox

Jesus has forced open a door that had been locked since the death of the first man. He has met, fought, and beaten the King of Death. Everything is different because he has done so.

Clive Staples (C.S.) Lewis

The birth and rapid rise of the Christian Church remain an unsolved enigma for any historian who refuses to take seriously the only explanation offered by the Church itself.

Charles F.D. Moule

Ghosts, apparitions, and various psychological hallucinations may do a lot of things, but they don't fire up the charcoal grill and cook fish for breakfast.

Pheme Perkins

No resurrection. No Christianity.

(Arthur) Michael Ramsey

Christianity is in its very essence a resurrection religion. The concept of resurrection lies at its heart. If you remove it, Christianity is destroyed.

John R.W. Stott

If Christ be not risen, the dreadful consequence is not that death ends life, but that we are still in our sins.

Geoffrey Anketell Studdert-Kennedy

The Gospels do not explain the resurrection; the resurrection explains the Gospels. Belief in the resurrection is not an appendage to the Christian faith; it is the Christian faith.

John S. Whale

Without the resurrection, at the name of Jesus every knee would not bow; more likely, people would say, "Jesus who?"

John Young

Savior

See also Cross; Salvation

She shall bring forth a son, and thou shalt call his name Jesus: for he shall save his people from their sins.

Matthew 1:21 KJV

For God did not send his Son into the world to be its judge, but to be its savior.

John 3:17 GNB

We no longer believe just because of what you said; now we have heard for ourselves, and we know that this man really is the Savior of the world.

John 4:42 NIV

There is salvation in no one else, for there is no other name under heaven given among mortals by which we must be saved.

Acts 4:12 NRSV

By his own right hand God has now raised him up to be leader and Savior, to give repentance and forgiveness of sins through him to Israel.

Acts 5:31 NJB

Christ our Savior defeated death and brought us the good news. It shines like a light and offers life that never ends.

2 Timothy 1:10 CEV

We have seen and testify that the Father has sent his Son to be the Savior of the world.

1 John 4:14 NIV

The cross of Jesus Christ and his baptism express the same thing. Our Lord was not a martyr; he was not merely a good man; he was God Incarnate. He came down to the lowest reach of creation in order bring back the whole human race to God, and in order to do this he must take upon him, as representative man, the whole massed sin of the race.

Oswald Chambers

There are as many paths to Christ as there are feet to tread them, but there is only one way to God.

A. Lindsay Glegg

Jesus Christ is God's everything for man's total needs.

Richard Christian Halverson

I remember two things; that I am a great sinner and that Christ is a great Savior.

John Newton

Jesus was in a garden, not of delight as the first Adam, in which he destroyed himself and the whole human race, but in one of agony, in which he saved himself and the whole human race.

Blaise Pascal

Verbally in Scripture, visually in sacrament, Jesus Christ is set forth as the only Savior of sinners.

John R.W. Stott

Christ's blood has value enough to redeem the whole world, but the virtue of it is applied only to such as believe.

Thomas Watson

O for a thousand tongues to sing / My great Redeemer's praise, / The glories of my God and King, / The triumphs of His grace!

Charles Wesley

Second Coming of

I tell you, From now on you will see the Son of Man seated at the right hand of Power and coming on the clouds of heaven.

Matthew 26:64 NRSV

Why are you men from Galilee standing here and looking up into the sky? Jesus has been taken into heaven. But he will come back in the same way that you have seen him go.

Acts 1:11 CEV

For whenever you eat this bread and drink this cup, you proclaim the Lord's death until he comes.

1 Corinthians 11:26 NIV

What we are teaching you now is the Lord's teaching: we who are alive on the day the Lord comes will not go ahead of those who have died. There will be the shout of command, the archangel's voice, the sound of

God's trumpet, and the Lord himself will come down from heaven. Those who have died believing in Christ will rise to life first; then we who are living at that time will be gathered up along with them in the clouds to meet the Lord in the air. And so we will always be with the Lord.

1 Thessalonians 4:15–17 GNB

Look, he is coming with the clouds and every eye will see him, even those who pierced him; and all the peoples of the earth will mourn because of him. So shall it be. Amen!

Revelation 1:7 NIV

He who loves the coming of the Lord is not he who affirms it is far off, nor is it he who says it is near. It is he who, whether it be far or near, awaits it with sincere faith, steadfast hope, and fervent love.

St. Augustine of Hippo

There are three distinct comings of the Lord of which I know; His coming to men; His coming into men; and His coming against men.

St. Bernard of Clairvaux

We are not a post-war generation; but a pre-peace generation. Jesus is coming.

Corrie ten Boom

Christ hath told us He will come, but not when, that we might never put off our clothes, or put out the candle.

William Gurnall

In the first advent God veiled his divinity to prove the faithful; in the second advent he will manifest his glory to reward their faith.

St. John Chrysostom

I hope that the day is near at hand when the advent of the great God will appear, for all things everywhere are boiling, burning, moving, falling, sinking, groaning.

Martin Luther

Christ designed that the day of his coming should be hid from us, that being in suspense, we might be as it were upon the watch.

Martin Luther

If Christ were coming again tomorrow, I would plant a tree today.

Martin Luther

The primitive church thought more about the Second Coming of Jesus Christ than about death or about heaven. The early Christians were looking not for a cleft in the ground called a grave but for a cleavage in the sky called Glory. They were watching not for the undertaker but for the uppertaker.

Alexander Maclaren

The fact that Jesus Christ is to come again is not a reason for star-gazing, but for working in the power of the Holy Ghost.

Charles Haddon Spurgeon

Teaching of

See also Kingdom of God

Now when Jesus had finished saying these things, the crowds were astounded at his teaching, for he taught them as one having authority, and not as their scribes.

Matthew 7:28–29 NRSV

He taught them many things by parables, and in his teaching said. . . .

Mark 4:2 NIV

Jesus answered, "What I teach is not my own teaching, but it comes from God, who sent me."

John 7:16 GNB

"I give you a new commandment, that you love one another. Just as I have loved you, you also should love one another."

John 13:34 NRSV

If Jesus Christ is only a teacher, then all he can do is to tantalize us, to erect a standard we cannot attain to; but when we are born again of the Spirit of God, we know that he did not come only to teach us, he came to make us what he teaches we should be.

Oswald Chambers

Everything Jesus Christ taught was contrary to common sense. Not one thing in the Sermon on the Mount is common sense. The basis of Christianity is neither common sense nor rationalism.

Oswald Chambers

Certainly, no revolution that has ever taken place in society can be compared to that which has been produced by the words of Jesus Christ.

Mark Hopkins

Had the doctrines of Jesus been preached always as pure as they came from his lips, the whole civilized world would now have been Christian.

Thomas Jefferson

The discrepancy between the depth, sincerity and, may I say, shrewdness of Christ's moral teaching and the rampant megalomania which must lie behind his theological teaching unless he is indeed God, has never been got over.

Clive Staples (C.S.) Lewis

The essential teachings of Jesus . . . were literally revolutionary and will always remain so if they are taken seriously.

Herbert J. Muller

We will never understand the full meaning of Jesus' richly varied ministry unless we see how the many things are rooted in the one thing: listening to the Father in the intimacy of perfect love. When we see this, we will also realize the goal of Jesus' ministry is nothing less than to bring us into this most intimate community.

Henri J.M. Nouwen

There is no discovery of the truth of Christ's teaching, no unanswerable inward endorsement of it, without committing oneself to his way of life.

John Bertram (J.B.) Phillips

The teachings of Christ alone can solve our personal difficulties and the world's problems. Every man is a miniature world. Christ enters that world to heal its wounds. We know that all the various schemes of world reconstruction from the beginning of history to our time have failed. Christ's method of making a better world by making better men alone succeeds.

Max I. Reich

Jesus differs from all other teachers; they reach the ear, but he instructs the heart; they deal with the outward letter, but he imparts an inward taste for the truth.

Charles Haddon Spurgeon

You never get to the end of Christ's words. There is something in them always behind. They pass into proverbs; they pass into laws; they pass into doctrines; they pass into consolations; but they never pass away, and after all the use that is made of them they are still not exhausted.

Arthur Penrhyn Stanley

When I came to believe in Christ's teaching, I ceased desiring what I had wished for before. The direction of my life, my desires, became different. What was good and bad had changed places.

Count Leo Tolstoy

I believe Christ's teaching; and this is what I believe. I believe that my welfare in the world will only be possible when all men fulfill Christ's teaching.

Count Leo Tolstoy

Journeys

See also Pilgrimage

Do not enter the path of the wicked, and do not walk in the way of evildoers. . . . But the path of the righteous is like the light of dawn, which shines brighter and brighter until full day.

Proverbs 4:14, 18 NRSV

Enter through the narrow gate; for the gate is wide and the road is easy that leads to destruction, and there are many who take it. For the gate is narrow and the road is hard that leads to life, and there are few who find it.

Matthew 7:13–14 NRSV

During my many travels, I have been in danger from rivers, robbers, my own people, and foreigners. My life has been in danger in cities, in deserts, at sea, and with people who only pretended to be the Lord's followers.

2 Corinthians 11:26 CEV

A person who does not travel is like a man who reads only one page of a book.

St. Augustine of Hippo

The Godward journey is a journey on which every individual is launched, all unknowingly, at birth.

Christopher Bryant

Traveling is almost like talking with men of other centuries.

> *René Descartes*

The longest journey is the journey inward.

> *Dag Hammarskjöld*

Journeying is more / Than reaching destinations. / Journeying is more.

> *Jean Fox Holland*

Travel suddenly opens the windows of the soul to the reality of God in other people.

> *Eric James*

Lord Jesus Christ, the Way by which we travel; show me thyself, the Truth that we must walk in; and be in me the Life that lifts up to God, our journey's ending.

> *Frederick B. MacNutt*

Wealth I ask not; hope nor love, / Nor a friend to know me; / All I seek, the heaven above / And the road below me.

> *Robert Louis Stevenson*

To travel hopefully is a better thing than to arrive, and the true success is to labor.

> *Robert Louis Stevenson*

Joy

See also Happiness

You show me the path of life. In your presence there is fullness of joy; in your right hand are pleasures for evermore.

> *Psalm 16:11 NRSV*

The ransomed of the Lord shall return, and come to Zion with songs and everlasting joy upon their heads: they shall obtain joy and gladness, and sorrow and sighing shall flee away.

> *Isaiah 35:10 KJV*

Although the fig tree shall not blossom, neither shall fruit be in the vines; the labor of the olive shall fail, and the fields shall yield no meat; the flock shall be cut off from the fold, and there shall be no herd in the stalls: Yet I will rejoice in the Lord, I will joy in the God of my salvation.

> *Habakkuk 3:17–18 KJV*

At that time Jesus, full of joy through the Holy Spirit, said, "I praise you, Father, Lord of heaven and earth, because you have hidden these things from the wise and learned, and revealed them to little children. Yes, Father, for this was your good pleasure."

> *Luke 10:21 NIV*

Ask and you will receive, and your joy will be complete.

> *John 16:24 NIV*

The Spirit produces . . . joy.

> *Galatians 5:22 GNB*

Rejoice in the Lord always; again I will say, Rejoice.

> *Philippians 4:4 NRSV*

Praise the Lord! Praise the Lord! Let the earth hear His voice! / Praise the Lord, praise the Lord! Let the people rejoice! / O come to the Father through Jesus the Son: / And give Him the glory! Great things He hath done!

> *Frances Jane van Alstyne*

He who binds himself to joy / Doth the winged life destroy but he who kisses the joy as it flies / Lives in Eternity's sunrise.

> *William Blake*

Joy is the most infallible sign of the presence of God.

> *Leon Bloy*

We are all strings in the concert of his joy.

Jacob Böhme

The joy that Jesus gives is the result of our disposition being at one with his own.

Oswald Chambers

Happiness depends on what happens; joy does not.

Oswald Chambers

To rejoice at another person's joy is like being in heaven.

Meister Eckhart

When I think upon my God, my heart is so full of joy that the notes dance and leap from my pen; and since God has given me a cheerful heart, it will be pardoned me that I serve Him with a cheerful spirit.

Franz Joseph Haydn

Life need not be easy to be joyful. Joy is not the absence of trouble but the presence of Christ.

William Van der Hoven

When I met Christ, I felt that I had swallowed sunshine.

E. Stanley Jones

You will always have joy in the evening if you spend the day fruitfully.

Thomas à Kempis

Joy is the serious business of heaven.

Clive Staples (C.S.) Lewis

Joy is never in our power, and pleasure is. I doubt whether anyone who has tasted joy would ever, if both were in his power, exchange it for all the pleasure in the world.

Clive Staples (C.S.) Lewis

Joy is peace dancing and peace is joy at rest.

Frederick Brotherton (F.B.) Meyer

Happiness is caused by things that happen around me, and circumstances will mar it; but joy flows right on through trouble; joy flows on through the day; joy flows in the night as well as in the day; joy flows through persecution and opposition. It is an unceasing fountain bubbling up in the heart; a secret spring the world can't see and doesn't know anything about. The Lord gives his people perpetual joy when they walk in obedience to him.

Dwight Lyman (D.L.) Moody

Savior, if of Zion's city I, through grace, a member am, / Let the world deride or pity, I will glory in thy name: / Fading is the worldling's pleasure, all his boasted pomp and show; / Solid joys and lasting treasure none but Zion's children know.

John Newton

The surest mark of a Christian is not faith, or even love, but joy.

Samuel Moor Shoemaker

A joyful heart is the normal result of a heart burning with love.

Mother Teresa

No one can live without delight, and that is why a man deprived of spiritual joy goes over to carnal pleasure.

St. Thomas Aquinas

Joy is the emotional expression of the courageous Yes to one's being.

Paul Tillich

This is the secret of joy. We shall no longer strive for our own way; but commit ourselves, easily and simply, to God's way, acquiesce in his will and in so doing find our peace.

Evelyn Underhill

Judging Others

See also Tolerance

Judge not, that ye be not judged. For with what judgment ye judge, ye shall be judged: and with what measure ye mete, it shall be measured to you again.

Matthew 7:1–2 KJV

Do you, my friend, pass judgment on others? You have no excuse at all, whoever you are. For when you judge others and then do the same things which they do, you condemn yourself.

Romans 2:1 GNB

Why dost thou judge thy brother? or why dost thou set at nought thy brother? for we shall all stand before the judgment seat of Christ. . . . So then every one of us shall give an account of himself to God. Let us not therefore judge one another any more: but judge this rather, that no man put a stumbling block or an occasion to fall in his brother's way.

Romans 14:10, 12–13 KJV

Who judges others condemns himself.

Anon.

Anybody who has once been horrified by the dreadfulness of his own sin that nailed Jesus to the cross will no longer be horrified by even the rankest sins of a brother.

Dietrich Bonhoeffer

No man can justify censure or condemn another, because indeed no man truly knows another.

Sir Thomas Browne

When it seems that God shows us the faults of others, keep on the safer side. It may be that thy judgment is false.

St. Catherine of Siena

You will not become a saint through other people's sins.

Anton Pavlovich Chekhov

The business of finding fault is very easy, and that of doing better very difficult.

St. Francis de Sales

The Lord knows those who are His. He will determine the saved and the unsaved, and will never ask any man's opinion. So let's not give one.

Virgil Hurley

Prejudice, not being founded on reason, cannot be removed by argument.

Samuel Johnson

How rarely we weigh our neighbor in the same balance in which we weigh ourselves.

Thomas à Kempis

Stoning prophets is poor work.

Harold St. John

A desire to disgrace others never sprang from grace.

George Swinnock

Do not think of the faults of others but of what is good in them and faulty in yourself.

St. Teresa of Avila

A man's judgment of another depends more on the judging and on his passions than on the one being judged and his conduct.

Paul Tournier

Judgment, *see* God, Judgment of; Last Judgment

Justice

See also God, Justice of; Injustice

Justice, and only justice, you shall pursue, so that you may live and occupy the land that the LORD your God is giving you.

Deuteronomy 16:20 NRSV

And he shall judge among the nations, and shall rebuke many people: and they shall beat their swords into plowshares, and their spears into pruninghooks: nation shall not lift up sword against nation, neither shall they learn war any more.

Isaiah 2:4 KJV

Let justice flow like water, and uprightness like a never-failing stream!

Amos 5:24 NJB

The Lord God has told us what is right and what he demands: "See that justice is done, let mercy be your first concern, and humbly obey your God."

Micah 6:8 CEV

The rule of justice is plain, namely, that a good man ought not to swerve from the truth, not to inflict any unjust loss on anyone, nor to act in any way deceitfully or fraudulently.

St. Ambrose

Let justice be done though the world perish.

St. Augustine of Hippo

To acknowledge another man's right to be himself, not to resemble me, is the fundamental act of justice, which alone will make it possible for us to look at a man without trying to see and recognize ourselves in him, but to recognize and beyond yet within him, to discern the Image of the Lord.

Anthony Bloom

Jesus will continue to be condemned to death so long as we do not establish the human and historical conditions that will allow justice to flower and right to flourish. And without justice and right, the kingdom of God will not be established.

Leonardo Boff

The pearl of justice is found in the heart of mercy.

St. Catherine of Siena

Peace is more important than all justice: and peace was not made for the sake of justice, but justice for the sake of peace.

Martin Luther

If you love the justice of Jesus Christ more than you fear human judgment, then you will seek to do compassion.

Mechtilde of Magdeburg

Justice and power must be brought together, so that whatever is just may be powerful, and whatever is powerful may be just.

Blaise Pascal

No human actions ever were intended by the Maker of men to be guided by balances of expediency, but by balances of justice.

John Ruskin

The preaching of the Gospel and its acceptance imply a social revolution whereby the hungry are fed and justice becomes the right of all.

Leon Joseph Suenens

In times when the government imprisons any unjustly, the true place for a just man is also the prison.

Henry David Thoreau

The sheer act of making the truth public is a form of justice.

Desmond Tutu

Justification

See also Righteousness; Salvation; Sanctification

And he [Abram] believed in the Lord; and he counted it to him for righteousness.

Genesis 15:6 KJV

Happy are those whose transgression is forgiven, whose sin is covered. Happy are those to whom the LORD imputes no iniquity, and in whose spirit there is no deceit.

Psalm 32:1–2 NRSV

All are justified by the free gift of his grace through being set free in Christ Jesus.

Romans 3:24 NJB

He was delivered over to death for our sins and was raised to life for our justification.

Romans 4:25 NIV

Knowing that a man is not justified by the works of the law, but by the faith of Jesus Christ . . . for by the works of the law shall no flesh be justified.

Galatians 2:16 KJV

We must first be made good before we can do good; we must first be made just before our works can please God.

Hugh Latimer

The doctrine of justification is the foundation that supports all of the other benefits we receive from Christ.

Erwin W. Lutzer

Justification takes place in the mind of God and not in the nervous system of the believer.

C.I. Schofield

He hideth our unrighteousness with His righteousness. He covereth our disobedience with His obedience. He shadoweth our death with His death, that the wrath of God cannot find us.

Henry Smith

The whole doctrine of justification by faith hinges, for me, on my painfully reluctant realization that my Father is not going to be more pleased with me when I am good than when I am bad. He accepts me and delights in me as I am. It is ridiculous of him, but that is how it is between us.

John V. Taylor

The courage to be is the courage to accept oneself as accepted in spite of being unacceptable . . . this is the genuine meaning of the Paulinian–Lutheran doctrine of justification by faith.

Paul Tillich

God does not justify us because we are worthy, but by justifying us makes us worthy.

Thomas Watson

Kindness

See also Compassion; Golden Rule; Love, for Others; Neighbors

Whoever is kind to the poor lends to the LORD, and will be repaid in full.

Proverbs 19:17 NRSV

Love ye your enemies, and do good, and lend, hoping for nothing again; and your reward shall be great, and ye shall be the children of the Highest: for he is kind unto the unthankful and to the evil.

Luke 6:35 KJV

Do you despise the riches of his kindness and forbearance and patience? Do you not realize that God's kindness is meant to lead you to repentance?

Romans 2:4 NRSV

Love is patient, love is kind.

1 Corinthians 13:4 NIV

The Spirit produces . . . kindness.

Galatians 5:22 GNB

The best exercise for strengthening the heart is reaching down and lifting people up.

Ernest Blevins

The greatest thing a man can do for his Heavenly Father is to be kind to some of His other children.

Henry Drummond

Kind words are the music of the world. They have a power which seems to be beyond natural causes, as though they were some angel's sons which had lost its way and come to earth.

Frederick William Faber

Kindness has converted more sinners than zeal, eloquence, and learning.

Frederick William Faber

Nobody is kind to only one person at one, but to many persons in one.

Frederick William Faber

Kindness is the golden chain by which society is bound together.

Johann Wolfgang von Goethe

Wise sayings often fall on barren ground; but a kind word is never thrown away.

Sir Arthur Helps

There is no law which lays it down that you must smile! But you can make a gift of your smile; you can be the heaven of kindness in your family.

John Paul II

Kindness is loving people more than they deserve.

Joseph Joubert

The sun makes ice melt; kindness causes misunderstanding, mistrust, and hostility to evaporate.

Albert Schweitzer

Be the living expression of God's kindness: kindness in your face, kindness in your eyes, kindness in your smile, kindness in your warm greeting.

Mother Teresa

Be kind. Remember that everyone you meet is fighting a hard battle.

Harry Thompson

That best portion of a good man's life, / His little, nameless, unremembered acts / Of kindness and of love.

William Wordsworth

Kingdom of God

See also God, Sovereignty of; Jesus Christ, Kingship of

Strive first for the kingdom of God and his righteousness, and all these things will be given to you as well.

Matthew 6:33 NRSV

Then the King will say to those on his right, "Come, you who are blessed by my Father; take your inheritance, the kingdom prepared for you since the creation of the world."

Matthew 25:34 NIV

Anyone who will not receive the kingdom of God like a little child will never enter it.

Mark 10:15 NIV

The kingdom of God is among you.

Luke 17:21 REB

I tell you for certain that you must be born from above before you can see God's kingdom.

John 3:3 CEV

Ten million roots are pumping in the streets: do you hear them? Ten million buds are forming in the axils of the leaves: do you hear the sound of the saw or the hammer? All next summer is at work in the world, but is unseen by us. And so "the kingdom of God comes not with observation."

Henry Ward Beecher

Wherever the bounds of beauty, truth, and goodness are advanced there the kingdom comes.

(Frederick) Donald Coggan

The kingdom of God is a kingdom of paradox, where through the ugly defeat of a cross, a holy God is utterly glorified. Victory comes through defeat; healing through brokenness; finding self through losing self.

Charles W. Colson

The entrance fee into the kingdom of God is nothing; the annual subscription is all we possess.

Henry Drummond

To want all that God wants, always to want it, for all occasions and without reservations, this is the kingdom of God which is all within.

François de la Mothe Fénelon

Wherever God rules over the human heart as King, there is the kingdom of God established.

Paul W. Harrison

The healing of the sick in His name is as much a part of the proclamation of the Kingdom as the preaching of the Good News of Jesus Christ.

Lambeth Conference 1978 Resolution 8

The kingdom of God has come into the world and the powers of the age to come are operative even in the age that now is.

Peter Lewis

The kingdom of God is simply God's power enthroned in our hearts. Faith in the kingdom of God is what makes us light of heart and what Christian joy is all about.

John Main

The core of all that Jesus teaches about the kingdom is the immediate apprehension and acceptance of God as King in his own life.

T.W. Mason

The more seriously we take the future promise of God's kingdom, the more unbearable will be the contradictions of that promise which we meet in the present.

Jürgen Moltmann

In the Gospel, Jesus is *autobasileia*, the kingdom himself.

Origen of Alexandria

Before we can pray, "Thy kingdom come," we must be willing to pray, "My kingdom go."

Alan Redpath

If you do not wish for His kingdom, don't pray for it. But if you do, you must do more than pray for it; you must work for it.

John Ruskin

There is no structural organization of society which can bring about the coming of the kingdom of God on earth, since all systems can be perverted by the selfishness of man.

William Temple

Power in complete subordination to love—that is something like a definition of the kingdom of God.

William Temple

The only significance of life consists in helping to establish the kingdom of God; and this can be done only by means of the acknowledgment and profession of the truth by each one of us.

Count Leo Tolstoy

Knowing God

See also Knowledge

Be still, and know that I am God; I will be exalted among the nations, I will be exalted in the earth.

Psalm 46:10 NIV

Let us know, let us press on to know the LORD; his appearing is as sure as the dawn; he will come to us like the showers, like the spring rains that water the earth.

Hosea 6:3 NRSV

All things have been committed to me by my Father. No one knows the Son except the Father, and no one knows the Father except the Son and those to whom the Son chooses to reveal him.

Matthew 11:27 NIV

I am the good shepherd. As the Father knows me and I know the Father, in the same way I know my sheep and they know me. And I am willing to die for them.

John 10:14–15 GNB

This is life eternal, that they might know thee the only true God, and Jesus Christ, whom thou hast sent.

John 17:3 KJV

But now that you know God—or rather are known by God—how is it that you are turning back to those weak and miserable principles? Do you wish to be enslaved by them all over again?

Galatians 4:9 NIV

May you come to know his love—although it can never be fully known—and so be completely filled with the very nature of God.

Ephesians 3:19 GNB

Nothing is as wonderful as knowing Christ Jesus my Lord. I have given up everything else and count it all as garbage. All I want is Christ and to know that I belong to him.

Philippians 3:8–9 CEV

For this reason we have always prayed for you, ever since we heard about you. We ask God to fill you with the knowledge of his will, with all the wisdom and understanding that his Spirit gives. Then you will be able to live as the Lord wants and will always do what pleases him. Your lives will produce all kinds of good deeds, and you will grow in your knowledge of God.

Colossians 1:9–10 GNB

Hereby do we know that we know him, if we keep his commandments.

1 John 2:3 KJV

The evidence of knowing God is obeying God.

Eric Alexander

Those persons who best know God are those who least presume to speak of him.

Angela of Foligno

Eternal God, the light of the minds that know you, the joy of the hearts that love you and the strength of the wills that serve you; grant us so to know you, that we may truly love you, and so to love you that we may fully serve you, whom to serve is perfect freedom.

St. Augustine of Hippo

You may know God, but not comprehend him.

Richard Baxter

There is but one thing in the world really worth pursuing—the knowledge of God.

Robert Hugh Benson

It is in silence that God is known, and through mysteries that he declares himself.

Robert Hugh Benson

We should always approach God knowing that we do not know him. We must approach the unsearchable, mysterious God who reveals himself as he chooses; whenever we come to him, we are before a God we do not yet know.

Anthony Bloom

God cannot be found by thought; he can only be known through his own manifestation of himself, and in this he shows himself to be the absolute mystery, who can be understood only through his own self-revelation.

Heinrich Emil Brunner

It takes all time and eternity to know God.

Oswald Chambers

Although we cannot have knowledge of God, we can love him: by love he may be touched and embraced, by thought, never.

The Cloud of Unknowing

No one can know God who has not first known himself. Go to the depths of the soul, the secret place of the Most High, to the roots, to the heights; for all that God can do is focused there.

Meister Eckhart

A little knowledge of God is worth a lot more than a great deal of knowledge about him.

James Innell (J.I.) Packer

God alone knows the depth and the riches of His Godhead, and divine wisdom alone can declare His secrets.

St. Thomas Aquinas

We can no more find a method for knowing God than for making God, because the knowledge of God is God himself dwelling in the soul. The most we can do is to prepare for his entry, to get out of his way, to remove the barriers, for until God acts in us there is nothing positive that we can do in this direction.

Alan W. Watts

Knowledge

See also Education; Knowing God; Wisdom

But of the tree of the knowledge of good and evil, thou shalt not eat of it: for in the day that thou eatest thereof thou shalt surely die.

Genesis 2:17 KJV

They will not hurt or destroy on all my holy mountain; for the earth will be full of the knowledge of the LORD as the waters cover the sea.

Isaiah 11:9 NRSV

Knowledge makes us proud of ourselves, while love makes us helpful to others.

1 Corinthians 8:1 CEV

For this cause we also, since the day we heard it, do not cease to pray for you, and to desire that ye might be filled with the knowledge of his will in all wisdom and spiritual understanding; That ye might walk worthy of the Lord unto all pleasing, being fruitful . . . in the knowledge of God.

Colossians 1:9–10 KJV

There is no true knowing without doing.

Anon.

Let me know myself, O God, that I may know thee.

St. Augustine of Hippo

Let knowledge be applied to a kind of scaffolding, making it possible for the edifice of charity to rise, to endure for ever, even when knowledge is done away with.

St. Augustine of Hippo

The only way to know is to will to do God's will.

Oswald Chambers

A man may be theologically knowing and spiritually ignorant.

Stephen Charnock

Fruitless the wisdom of him who has no knowledge of himself.

Desiderius Erasmus

It is in the matter of knowledge that a man is most haunted with a sense of inevitable limitation.

Joseph Farrell

A humble knowledge of yourself is a surer way to God than an extensive search after knowledge.

Thomas à Kempis

All men naturally desire to know, but what doth knowledge avail without the fear of God?

Thomas à Kempis

All knowledge is sterile which does not lead to action and end in charity.

Désiré Joseph Mercier

We must make up our minds to be ignorant of much, if we would know anything.

John Henry Newman

I do not know what I may appear to the world, but to myself I seem to have been only like a boy playing on the sea-shore, and diverting myself in now and then finding a smoother pebble or a prettier shell than ordinary, whilst the great ocean of truth lay all undiscovered before me.

Sir Isaac Newton

What use is deeper knowledge if we have shallower hearts?

Leonard Ravenhill

A thorough knowledge of the Bible is worth more than a college education.

Theodore Roosevelt

To be proud of learning is the greatest ignorance.

Jeremy Taylor

A scrap of knowledge about sublime things is worth more than any amount about trivialities.

St. Thomas Aquinas

Many a man's knowledge is a torch to light him to hell.

Thomas Watson

Beware you be not swallowed up in books! An ounce of love is worth a pound of knowledge.

John Wesley

Land, *see* Environment; God, Creator

Last Judgment

See also God, Judgment of

When the Son of Man comes as King and all the angels with him, he will sit on his royal throne, and the people of all the nations will be gathered before him. Then he will divide them into two groups, just as a shepherd separates the sheep from the goats. He will put the righteous people at his right and the others at his left.

Matthew 25:31–33 GNB

For he [God] has set a day when he will judge the world with justice by the man he has appointed. He has given proof of this to all men by raising him from the dead.

Acts 17:31 NIV

For we must all appear before the judgment seat of Christ; that every one may receive the things done in his body, according to that he hath done, whether it be good or bad.

2 Corinthians 5:10 KJV

It is appointed for mortals to die once, and after that the judgment.

Hebrews 9:27 NRSV

I saw a great white throne with someone sitting on it. Earth and heaven tried to run away, but there was no place for them to go. I also saw all the dead people standing in front of that throne. Every one of them was there, no matter who they had once been. Several books were opened and then the book of life was opened. The dead were judged by what those books said they had done. The sea gave up the dead people who were in it, and death and its kingdom also gave up their dead. Then everyone was judged by what they had done. Afterwards, death and its kingdom were thrown into the lake of fire. This is the second death. Anyone whose name wasn't written in the book of life was thrown into the lake of fire.

Revelation 20:11–15 CEV

Nothing has contributed more powerfully to wean me from all that held me down to earth than the thought, constantly dwelt upon, of death and of the last judgment.

St. Augustine of Hippo

It may be that the day of judgment will dawn tomorrow; in that case, we shall gladly stop working for a better future. But not before.

Dietrich Bonhoeffer

Foolish men imagine that because judgment for an evil thing is delayed, there is no justice, but only accident here below. Judgment for an evil thing is many times delayed some day or two, some century or two, but it is sure as life, it is sure as death!

Thomas Carlyle

If we are believers in Jesus Christ we have already come through the storm of judgment. It happened at the cross.

William Franklin (Billy) Graham

Those who will not deliver themselves into the hand of God's mercy cannot be delivered out of the hand of his justice.

Matthew Henry

Fools measure actions after they are done, by the event; wise men beforehand, by the rules of reason and right. The former look to the end to judge of the act. Let me look to the act, and leave the end to God.

Richard Hill

Truly at the day of judgment we shall not be examined on what we have read, but what we have done; not how well we have spoken, but how religiously we have lived.

Thomas à Kempis

Death and what is beyond it will show who is wise and who is a fool.

William S. Plummer

Laughter

See also Happiness

Sarah said, "God has made me laugh. Now everyone will laugh with me."

Genesis 21:6 CEV

Even in laughter the heart is sad, and the end of joy is grief.

Proverbs 14:13 NRSV

A time to weep and a time to laugh, a time to mourn and a time to dance.

Ecclesiastes 3:4 NIV

For like the crackling of thorns under a pot, so is the laughter of fools; this also is vanity.

Ecclesiastes 7:6 NRSV

Blessed are ye that weep now: for ye shall laugh. . . . Woe unto you that laugh now! For ye shall mourn and weep.

Luke 6:21, 25 KJV

Keep company with the more cheerful sort of the godly; there is no mirth like the mirth of believers.

Richard Baxter

Mirth is the sweet wine of human life. It should be offered sparkling with zestful life unto God.

Henry Ward Beecher

Laughter and weeping are the two intensest forms of human emotion, and these profound wells of human emotion are to be consecrated to God.

Oswald Chambers

No mind is thoroughly well organized that is deficient in a sense of humor.

Samuel Taylor Coleridge

Laughter adds richness, texture, and color to otherwise ordinary days. It is a gift, a choice, a discipline, and an art.

Tim Hansel

Laugh and grow strong.

St. Ignatius of Loyola

One must laugh before one is happy, or one may die without ever laughing at all.

Jean de La Bruyère

Shared laughter creates a bond of friendship. When people laugh together, they cease to be young and old, master and pupils, worker and driver. They have become a single group of human beings, enjoying their existence.

William Grant Lee

If you're not allowed to laugh in heaven, I don't want to go there.

Martin Luther

It is the soul that is not yet sure of its God that is afraid to laugh in His presence.

George MacDonald

Laughter is able to mediate between the infinite magnitude of our tasks and the limitation of our strengths.

Jürgen Moltmann

Laughter is the most beautiful and beneficial therapy God ever granted humanity.

Charles R. Swindoll

It is often just as sacred to laugh as it is to pray.

Charles R. Swindoll

It is a splendid thing to laugh inwardly at yourself. It is the best way of regaining your good humor and of finding God without further anxiety.

Henri de Tourville

Humor will never destroy anything that is genuine. All it can do is puncture balloons.

Kenneth L. Wilson

Law

See also Grace; Ten Commandments

The Law of the Lord is perfect, reviving the soul. The statutes of the Lord are trustworthy, making wise the simple.

Psalm 19:7 NIV

Don't suppose that I came to do away with the Law and the Prophets. I did not come to do away with them, but to give them their full meaning.

Matthew 5:17 CEV

For the law was given by Moses, but grace and truth came by Jesus Christ.

John 1:17 KJV

Thus, condemnation will never come to those who are in Christ Jesus, because the law of the Spirit which gives life in Christ Jesus has set you free from the law of sin and death. What the Law could not do because of the weakness of human nature, God did, sending his own Son in the same human nature as any sinner to be a sacrifice for sin, and condemning sin in that human nature. This was so that the Law's requirements might be fully satisfied in us as we direct our lives not by our natural inclinations but by the Spirit.

Romans 8:1–4 NJB

Love does no wrong to a neighbor, therefore, love is the fulfilling of the law.

Romans 13:10 NRSV

For this is the covenant that I will make with the house of Israel after those days, saith the Lord; I will put my laws into their mind, and write them in their hearts: and I will be to them a God, and they shall be to me a people.

Hebrews 8:10 KJV

The law, though it have no power to condemn us, hath power to command us.

Thomas Adams

The law sends us to the gospel, that we may be justified, and the gospel sends us to the law again to inquire what is our duty, being justified.

Samuel Bolton

He who makes the law his standard is obligated to perform all its precepts, for to break one commandment is to break the law. He who lives by faith and love is not judged on that basis, but by a standard infinitely higher and at the same time more attainable.

Joseph Fletcher

Moral law is more than a test, it is for man's own good. Every law that God has given has been for man's benefit. If man breaks it, he is not only rebelling against God, he is hurting himself.

William Franklin (Billy) Graham

Law says "Do," grace says "Done."

John Henry Jowett

Legalism is self-righteousness. It is the belief that God is satisfied with our attempt to obey a moral code.

Erwin W. Lutzer

The law reflects God's holiness; it is a plumbline that shows us that we are crooked.

Erwin W. Lutzer

The law tells me how crooked I am. Grace comes along and straightens me out.

Dwight Lyman (D.L.) Moody

The essence of the ethics of Jesus is not law, but a relationship of persons to God.

(Arthur) Michael Ramsey

Law never made men a whit more just.

Henry David Thoreau

Laziness

See also Work

Go to the ant, thou sluggard; consider her ways, and be wise.

Proverbs 6:6 KJV

If you are lazy, you will meet difficulty everywhere, but if you are honest, you will have no trouble.

Proverbs 15:19 GNB

Our friends, we command you in the name of our Lord Jesus Christ to keep away from all believers who are living a lazy life and who do not follow the instructions that we gave them. You yourselves know very well that you should do just what we did. We were not lazy when we were with you. We did not accept anyone's support without paying for it. Instead, we worked and toiled; we kept working day and night so as not to be an expense to any of you.

2 Thessalonians 3:6–8 GNB

We do not want you to become lazy, but to imitate those who through faith and patience inherit what has been promised.

Hebrews 6:12 NIV

Idleness is the enemy of the soul.

St. Benedict

Our laziness after God is our crying sin . . . no man gets God who does not follow hard after him.

Edward M. Bounds

Sloth, like rust, consumes faster than labor wears.

Benjamin Franklin

Laziness travels so slowly that poverty soon overtakes him.

Benjamin Franklin

The way to be nothing is to do nothing.

Nathaniel Howe

Find some work for your hands to do, so that Satan may never find you idle.

St. Jerome

If I rest, I rust.

Martin Luther

Some temptations come to the industrious, but all temptations attack the idle.

Charles Haddon Spurgeon

Iron rusts from disuse; stagnant water loses its purity, and in cold weather becomes frozen; even so does inaction sap the vigors of the mind.

Leonardo da Vinci

For Satan finds some mischief still / For idle hands to do.

Isaac Watts

Leadership

See also Church, Leaders of

The LORD said to Moses, "Send men to spy out the land of Canaan, which I am giving to the Israelites; from each of their ancestral tribes you shall send a man, every one a leader among them."

Numbers 13:1–2 NRSV

[to the Shepherds of Israel] You have not strengthened the weak, you have not healed the sick, you have not bound up the injured, you have not brought back the strayed, you have not sought the lost, but with force and harshness you have ruled them.

Ezekiel 34:4–5 NRSV

Let them alone; they are blind guides of the blind.

Matthew 15:14 NRSV

There is a true saying: If a man is eager to be a church leader, he desires an excellent work.

1 Timothy 3:1 GNB

Do not lord it over those in your charge, but be examples to the flock.

1 Peter 5:3 NRSV

Leaders are ordinary people with extraordinary determination.

Anon.

"For you, I am Bishop," said St. Augustine to his people, "but with you, I am a Christian. The first is an office accepted, the second a grace received; one a danger, the other safety. If then I am gladder by far to be redeemed with you than I am to be placed over you, I shall, as the Lord commanded, be more completely your servant."

St. Augustine of Hippo

The church is looking for better methods; God is looking for better men.

Edward M. Bounds

The lure of power can separate the most resolute of Christians from the true nature of Christian leadership, which is service to others. It's difficult to stand on a pedestal and wash the feet of those below.

Charles W. Colson

A good leader takes a little more than his share of blame; a little less than his share of credit.

Arnold H. Glasgow

Whoever is sent by the Master to run his house, we ought to receive him as we would receive the Master himself. It is obvious, therefore, that we ought to regard the bishop as we would the Lord himself.

St. Ignatius of Antioch

One of the marks of true greatness is the ability to develop greatness in others.

J.C. Macaulay

Leadership is a serving relationship that has the effect of facilitating human development.

Ted Ward

Learning, *see* Education

Lending, *see* Debt

Lent, *see* Desert; Self-Denial

Life

See also Death

The LORD God formed man from the dust of the ground, and breathed into his nostrils the breath of life; and the man became a living being.

Genesis 2:7 NRSV

For whoever finds me [wisdom] finds life and receives favor from the Lord.

Proverbs 8:35 NIV

There is no new thing under the sun.

Ecclesiastes 1:9 KJV

He that findeth his life shall lose it: and he that loseth his life for my sake shall find it.

Matthew 10:39 KJV

The thief cometh not, but for to steal, and to kill, and to destroy: I am come that they might have life, and that they might have it more abundantly.

John 10:10 KJV

For what is life? To me, it is Christ. Death, then, will bring more.

Philippians 1:21 GNB

Now a word with all who say, "Today or the next day we will go off to such and such a town and spend a year there trading and making money." Yet you have no idea what tomorrow will bring. What is your life after all? You are no more than a mist, seen for a little while and then disappearing. What you ought to say is: "If it be the Lord's will, we shall live to do so and so."

James 4:13–15 REB

Whoever has the Son has life, and whoever has not the Son of God has not life.

1 John 5:12 NJB

The man who has no inner life is the slave to his surroundings.

Henri-Frédéric Amiel

The present life of men on earth, O king, as compared with the whole length of time which is unknowable to us, seems to me to be like this: as if, when you are sitting at dinner with your chiefs and ministers in wintertime . . . one of the sparrows from outside flew very quickly through the hall; as if it came in one door and soon went out through another. In that actual time it is indoors it is not touched by the winter's storm; but yet the tiny period of calm is over in a moment, and having come out of the winter it soon returns to the winter and slips out of your sight. Man's life appears to be more or less like this; and of what may follow it, or what preceded it, we are absolutely ignorant.

The Venerable Bede

In the midst of life we are in death.

Book of Common Prayer

How can we understand life, when it is the will of God, and as such, far grander in design that we could ever imagine?

Catherine Bramwell Booth

You will find as you look back on your life that the moments when you have really lived are the moments when you have done things in the spirit of love.

Henry Drummond

One person who has mastered life is better than a thousand persons who have mastered only the contents of books, but no one can get anything out of life without God.

Meister Eckhart

The Christian life is not a way "out," but a way "through" life.

William Franklin (Billy) Graham

The whole of human life is but a single day, to those who labor with law.

Gregory of Nazianzus

Nothing is trivial here if heaven looks on.

Vance Havner

It ought to be the business of every day to prepare for our last day.

Matthew Henry

The great use of life is to spend it for something that outlasts it.

William James

I will not just live my life. I will not just spend my life. I will invest my life.

Helen Adams Keller

Make sure the thing you are living for is worth dying for.

Charles Mayes

If you wish to be fully alive you must develop a sense of perspective. Life is infinitely greater than this trifle your heart is attached to and which you have given the power to so upset you.

Anthony de Mello

We are all making a crown for Jesus out of these daily lives of ours, either a crown of golden, divine love, studded with gems of sacrifice and adoration, or a thorny crown, filled with the cruel briars of unbelief, of selfishness, and sin, and placing it upon his brow.

Aimee Semple McPherson

Let God have your life; he can do more with it than you can.

Dwight Lyman (D.L.) Moody

Life is filled with meaning as soon as Jesus Christ enters into it.

Bishop Stephen Charles Neill

Fear not that your life shall come to an end, but rather that it shall never have a beginning.

John Henry Newman

Live to explain thy doctrine by thy life.

Matthew Prior

Life is learning to love, and most of us have merely begun when we die. This is the main reason why many of us long for and expect another life.

Cicely Saunders

To believe in God means to take sides with life and to end our alliance with death. It means to stop killing and wanting to kill, and to do battle with apathy which is so akin to killing.

Dorothee Soelle

Life can be worth the energy it takes to live it only if it is governed by something that is stronger than death.

J. Neville Ward

Take care of your life; and the Lord will take care of your death.

George Whitefield

Ask the Lord to make your life a glory to him, a menace to the devil, a strength to your church, and a witness to the world.

Frederick P. Wood

Though nothing can bring back the hour / Of splendor in the grass, of glory in the flower; / We will grieve not, rather find / Strength in what remains behind.

William Wordsworth

The world is too much with us; late and soon, / Getting and spending, we lay waste our powers. / Little we see in Nature that is ours.

William Wordsworth

Light

See also Darkness

Then God commanded, "Let there be light" —and light appeared.

Genesis 1:3 GNB

The people that walked in darkness have seen a great light: they that dwell in the land of the shadow of death, upon them hath the light shined.

Isaiah 9:2 KJV

Ye are the light of the world. A city that is set on a hill cannot be hid. Neither do men light a candle, and put it under a bushel, but on a candlestick; and it giveth light unto all that are in the house. Let your light so shine before men, that they may see your good works, and glorify your Father which is in heaven.

Matthew 5:14–16 KJV

This is the verdict: Light has come into the world, but men loved darkness instead of light because their deeds were evil. Everyone who does evil hates the light, and will not come into the light for fear that his deeds will be exposed. But whoever lives by the truth comes into the light, so that it may be seen plainly that what he has done has been done through God.

John 3:19–21 NIV

This then is the message which we have heard of him, and declare unto you, that God is light, and in him is no darkness at all.

1 John 1:5 KJV

I do not pretend to see light, but I do see gleams, and I know I am right to follow those gleams.

Fr. Andrew

Light even though it passes through pollution, is not polluted.

St. Augustine of Hippo

Eternal Light! Eternal Light! / How pure the soul must be, / When, placed within Thy searching sight, / It shrinks not, but with calm delight / Can live and look on Thee.

Thomas Binney

Light has been made so that human beings, who share in the nature of both higher and lower beings, may be able to support themselves by working hard during the day, remembering the pleasure of the everlasting light they have lost. Night has been made so that they may rest their bodies with the intention of reaching that place where there is neither night nor toil, but rather eternal day and everlasting glory.

St. Bridget of Sweden

The Lord does not shine upon us, except when we take his Word as our light.

John Calvin

In darkness there is no choice. It is light than enables us to see the differences between things; and it is Christ who gives us light.

Augustus W. Hare

Some Christians are like candles: they glow with a warmth that draws people to them. Then again, you have the flashlight sort of believers who seem to be able to look right through you. Christians with the gift of teaching remind me of reliable, steady light bulbs—dispelling darkness, showing things for what they truly are. Then there are the laser-types, cutting right through the tom-foolery and getting things done. Searchlight people have a way of leading others out of darkness and guiding and directing them back to safety.

Joni Eareckson Tada

There are two ways of spreading light; to be a candle, or the mirror that reflects it.

Edith Newbold Wharton

Listening

The Lord came and stood there, and called as he had before, "Samuel! Samuel!" Samuel answered, "Speak; your servant is listening."

1 Samuel 3:10 GNB

Guard your steps when you go to the house of God; to draw near to listen is better than the sacrifice offered by fools.

Ecclesiastes 5:1 NRSV

He that hath ears to hear, let him hear.

Matthew 11:15 KJV

My dear friends, you should be quick to listen and slow to speak or to get angry.

James 1:19 CEV

A good listener is popular everywhere. Not only that, but after a while he knows something too.

Bennie Bargen

Man has been given two ears and only one tongue that he might listen twice as much as he speaks.

Walter Colton

Half an hour's listening is essential except when you are very busy. Then a full hour is needed.

St. Francis de Sales

Love's finest speech is without words.

Hadewijch of Brabant

Master, speak! Thy servant heareth, / Waiting for Thy gracious word, / Longing for Thy voice that cheereth, / Master, let it now be heard. / I am listening, Lord, for Thee; / What hast Thou to say to me?

Frances Ridley Havergal

God is a great listener. Out of his silent being he is with us silently, he speaks to us silently, he asks us to learn the response which comes from the deep part of our being. He asks us to learn from him how to listen.

Michael Hollings

Most people have the best of intentions, but they are not secure enough to express love by listening in depth when others express some idea or intention that they believe is wrong.

Morton T. Kelsey

One of the best ways to demonstrate God's love is to listen to people.

Bruce Larsen

Before we can hear the Divine Voice we must shut out all other voices, so that we may be able to listen, to discern its faintest whisper. The most precious messages are those which are whispered.

Mark Rutherford

The first duty of love is to listen.

Paul Tillich

Be not only attentive in hearing, but retentive after hearing.

Thomas Watson

Loneliness

See also Sadness

Then the Lord God said, "It is not good that the man should be alone; I will make him a helper as his partner."

Genesis 2:18 NRSV

He [Elijah] answered, "Lord God Almighty, I have always served you—you alone. But the people of Israel have broken their covenant with you, torn down your altars, and killed all your prophets. I am the only one left—and they are trying to kill me."

1 Kings 19:14 GNB

God has turned relatives and friends against me, and I am forgotten. My guests and my servants consider me a stranger, and when I call my servants, they pay no attention. My breath disgusts my wife; everyone in my family turns away.

Job 19:13–17 CEV

God sets the lonely in families.

Psalm 68:6 NIV

About the ninth hour Jesus cried with a loud voice, saying, Eli, Eli, lama sabachthani? That is to say, My God, my God, why hast thou forsaken me?

Matthew 27:46 KJV

A man with God is always in the majority.

John Knox

We are born helpless. As soon as we are fully conscious we discover loneliness. We need others physically, emotionally, intellectually; we need them if we are to know anything, even ourselves.

Clive Staples (C.S.) Lewis

Loneliness is the first thing which God's eye named not good.

John Milton

People are lonely because they build walls instead of bridges.

Joseph Fort Newton

The man who lives by himself and for himself is apt to be corrupted by the company he keeps.

Charles Henry Parkhurst

Christ understands loneliness; he's been through it.

Paul Stromberg Rees

Loneliness and the feeling of being uncared for and unwanted are the greatest poverty.

Mother Teresa

The world's greatest tragedy is unwantedness; the world's greatest disease is loneliness.

Mother Teresa

He himself was forsaken that none of his children might ever need to utter his cry of loneliness.

Bishop John Heyl (J.H.) Vincent

It is better to be alone than in bad company.

George Washington

The soul hardly ever realizes it, but whether he is a believer or not, his loneliness is really a homesickness for God.

Hubert van Zeller

Longing for God

See also Seeking God; Soul and Spirit

As a deer longs for flowing streams, so my soul longs for you, O God. My soul thirsts for God, for the living God. When shall I come and behold the face of God?

Psalm 42:1–2 NRSV

My soul longeth, yea, even fainteth for the courts of the Lord: my heart and my flesh crieth out for the living God.

Psalm 84:2 KJV

With all my heart I long for you in the night, at dawn I seek for you; for when your laws prevail on earth, the inhabitants of the world learn what justice is.

Isaiah 26:9 REB

In this earthly state we do indeed groan, longing to put on our heavenly home over the present one.

2 Corinthians 5:2 NJB

O Lord our God, grant us grace to desire thee with our whole heart; so that desiring, we may seek, and seeking, find thee; and so finding thee, may love thee, and loving thee, may hate those sins from which thou hast redeemed us. Amen.

St. Anselm of Canterbury

I beg you to come into my heart, for by inspiring it to long for you, you make it ready to receive you.

St. Augustine of Hippo

Lord, of thy goodness, give me thyself.

Augustine Baker

We taste thee, O thou living bread, / And long to feast upon thee still; / We drink of thee, the fountain-head, / And thirst our souls from thee to fill. / Our restless spirits yearn for thee, / Where'er our changeful lot is cast; / Glad when thy gracious smile we see, / Blest when our faith can hold thee fast.

St. Bernard of Clairvaux

Lord, enfold me in the depths of your heart; and there, hold me, refine, purge, and set me on fire, raise me aloft, until my own self knows utter annihilation.

Pierre Teilhard de Chardin

My spirit has become dry because it forgets to feed on you.

St. John of the Cross

Many of us are not thirsty for God because we have quenched our thirst at other fountains!

Erwin W. Lutzer

Lord, you are my lover, / My longing, / My flowing stream, my sun, / And I am your reflection.

Mechtilde of Magdeburg

If there is anything in your life more demanding than your longing after God, then you will never be a Spirit-filled Christian.

Aiden Wilson (A.W.) Tozer

If there is a man anywhere who is hungering for God and is not filled, then the Word of God is broken. We are as full as we want to be.

Aiden Wilson (A.W.) Tozer

O Thou who camest from above / The pure celestial fire to impart, / Kindle a flame of sacred love / On the mean altar of my heart!

Charles Wesley

Lord's Prayer, *see* Jesus Christ, Prayers of

Lord's Supper, *see* Eucharist

Loss

See also Bereavement; Grief; Sadness

For those who want to save their life will lose it, and those who lose their life for my sake will find it.

Matthew 16:25 NRSV

Yet whatever gains I had, these I have come to regard as loss because of Christ. More than that, I regard everything as loss because of the surpassing value of knowing Jesus Christ my Lord.

Philippians 3:7–8 NRSV

He loses nothing who loses not God.

Anon.

Heaven will pay for any loss we may suffer to gain it; but nothing can pay for the loss of heaven.

Richard Baxter

I can afford to lose everything except the touch of God on my life.

William Cantelon

Watergate caused my world to crack around me and sent me to prison. I lost the mainstay of my existence—the awards, the six-figure income and lifestyle to match, a position of power at the right hand of the President of the United States. But only when I lost them did I find a far greater gain: knowing Christ.

Charles W. Colson

When you feel that all is lost, sometimes the greatest gain is ready to be yours.

Thomas à Kempis

Our Heavenly Father never takes anything from His children unless He means to give them something better.

George Müller

They lose nothing who gain Christ.

Samuel Rutherford

Never look at what you have lost; look at what you have left.

Robert Harold Schuller

Love

See also God, Love of; Jesus Christ, Love of

For God

See also Adoration; Praise; Worship

You shall love the LORD your God with all your heart, and with all your soul, and with all your might.

Deuteronomy 6:5 NRSV

If you love me, you will do what I have said, and my Father will love you. I will also love you and show you what I am like.

John 14:21 CEV

We know that all things work together for good to them that love God, to them who are the called according to his purpose.

Romans 8:28 KJV

If we have all we need and see one of our own people in need, we must have pity on that person, or else we cannot say we love God.

1 John 3:17 CEV

I would hate my own soul if I did not find it loving God.

St. Augustine of Hippo

An old woman can love God better than a doctor of theology can.

St. Bonaventure

Give me such love for God and men, as will blot out all hatred and bitterness.

Dietrich Bonhoeffer

Love for God and obedience to God are so completely involved in each other that any one of them implies the other too.

F.F. Bruce

The reason why God's servants love creatures so much is that they see how much Christ loves them, and it is one of the properties of love to love what is loved by the person we love.

St. Catherine of Siena

By love he may be gotten and holden, but by thought never.

The Cloud of Unknowing

Virtue is nothing else than an ordered and measured affection directed towards God for his sake alone.

The Cloud of Unknowing

Charity means nothing else but to love God for himself above all creatures, and to love one's fellowmen for God's sake as one loves oneself.

The Cloud of Unknowing

Love for God is ecstatic, making us go out from ourselves: it does not allow the lover to belong any more to himself, but he belongs only to the Beloved.

St. Dionysios the Areopagite

A true love of God must begin with a delight in his holiness, and not with a delight in any other attribute; for no other attribute is truly lovely without this.

Jonathan Edwards

God can do everything except compel a man to love him.

Paul Evdokimov

We are shaped and fashioned by what we love.

Johann Wolfgang von Goethe

Love unites the soul with God: and the more love the soul has the more powerfully it enters into God and is centered on him.

St. John of the Cross

A man's spiritual health is exactly proportional to his love for God.

Clive Staples (C.S.) Lewis

Let us make God the beginning and end of our love, for he is the fountain from which all good things flow and into him alone they flow back. Let him therefore be the beginning of our love.

Richard Rolle of Hampole

Love of the creature toward the Creator must include obedience or it is meaningless.

Francis August Schaeffer

Only through love can we attain communion with God.

Albert Schweitzer

Our love for God is tested by the question of whether we seek him or his gifts.

Ralph Washington Sockman

Love of God is the root, love of our neighbor the fruit of the Tree of Life. Neither can exist without the other, but the one is cause and the other effect.

William Temple

By love alone is God enjoyed, by love alone delighted in, by love alone approached and admired. His nature requires love. The law of nature commands thee to love him: the law of his nature, and the law of thine.

Thomas Traherne

For Others

See also Church, Mission and Ministry of; Compassion; Golden Rule; Kindness; Neighbors

But I say to you that listen, Love your enemies, do good to those who hate you. . . . If you love those who love you, what credit is that to you? For even sinners love those who love them.

Luke 6:27, 32 NRSV

I give you a new commandment, that you love one another. Just as I have loved you, you also should love one another. By this everyone will know that you are my disciples, if you have love for one another.

John 13:34–35 NRSV

Though I command languages both human and angelic—if I speak without love, I am no more than a gong booming or a cymbal clashing. And though I have the power of prophecy, to penetrate all mysteries and knowledge, and though I have all the faith necessary to move mountains—if I am without love, I am nothing. Though I should give away to the poor all that I possess, and even give up my body to be burned—if I am without love, it will do me no good whatever. Love is always patient and kind: love is never jealous; love is not boastful or conceited, it is never rude and never seeks its own

advantage, it does not take offense or store up grievances. Love does not rejoice at wrongdoing, but finds its joy in the truth. It is always ready to make allowances, to trust, to hope and to endure whatever comes. Love never comes to an end.

1 Corinthians 13:1–8 NJB

The Spirit produces . . . love.

Galatians 5:22 GNB

Above all, maintain constant love for one another, for love covers a multitude of sins.

1 Peter 4:8 NRSV

No one has ever seen God; if we love one another, God lives in us, and his love is perfected in us.

1 John 4:12 NRSV

If anyone says, "I love God," yet hates his brother, he is a liar. For anyone who does not love his brother, whom he has seen, cannot love God, whom he has not seen. And he has given us this command: Whoever loves God must also love his brother.

1 John 4:20–21 NIV

He who is filled with love is filled with God himself.

St. Augustine of Hippo

"Pour into our hearts to the attitude of your love." Pour it in: become yourself one flowing for us, for your flowing does not carry us to you. Be rain in our dryness; be a river through our landscape so that it might have in you its center as well as the cause of its growing and bearing fruit.

Hans urs von Balthasar

Love seeketh not itself to please, / Nor for itself hath any care, / But for another gives its ease, / And builds a Heaven in Hell's despair.

William Blake

He who loves his fellow man is loving God the best he can.

Alice Cary

Only love can bring individual beings to their perfect completion as individuals because only love takes possession of them and unites them by what lies deepest within them.

Pierre Teilhard de Chardin

It is impossible to love Christ without loving others in proportion as these others are moving towards Christ. And it is impossible to love others in a spirit of broad human communion without moving nearer to Christ.

Pierre Teilhard de Chardin

Charity means nothing else but to love God for himself above all creatures, and to love one's fellowmen for God's sake as one loves oneself.

The Cloud of Unknowing

Remember that the ones you love in your heart are but guests in your soul.

Jim Cotter

We cannot love God unless we love each other, and to love we must know each other.

Dorothy Day

No man can be a Christian who is unconcerned for the salvation of others.

Richard Burdon Haldane

Love is the only force capable of transforming an enemy into a friend.

Martin Luther King Jr.

Love is infallible; it has no errors, for errors are the want of love.

William Law

Condescend to all weaknesses and infirmities of your fellow creatures, cover their frailties, love their excellencies, encourage their virtues, relieve their wants, rejoice in their friendship, overlook their unkindness, forgive their malice, and condescend to do the lowest offices to the lowest of mankind.

William Law

Faith like light, should always be simple, and unbending; while love, like warmth, should beam forth on every side, and bend to every necessity of our brethren.

Martin Luther

To know ourselves loved is to have the depths of our own capacity to love opened up.

John Main

Blessed is the man who can love all men especially.

Maximus the Confessor

True charity means returning good for evil—always.

Mary Mazzarello

It is only inasmuch as you see someone else as he or she really is here and now, and not as they are in your memory or your desire or in your imagination or projection, that you can truly love them.

Anthony de Mello

Love seeks one thing only: the good of the one loved. It leaves all the other secondary effects to take care of themselves.

Thomas Merton

Love is an action, an activity. It is not a feeling.

M. Scott Peck

The measure of our love for others can largely be determined by the frequency and earnestness of our prayers for them.

Aiden Wilson (A.W.) Pink

He who has charity is far from all sin.

St. Polycarp

When a man sees that his neighbor hates him, then he must love him more than he did before to fill up the gap.

Rabbi Rafeal

Charity is that with which no man is lost, and without which no man is saved.

St. Robert Bellarmine

Can a man love God while ignoring the need of his brother?

Frances J. Roberts

Let me not to the marriage of true minds / Admit impediments. Love is not love / Which alters when it alteration finds, / Or bends with the remover to remove. / O no! it is an ever-fixed mark, / That looks on tempests and is never shaken.

William Shakespeare

I have found the paradox that if I love until it hurts, then there is no hurt, but only more love.

Mother Teresa

It is not a matter of thinking a great deal but of loving a great deal, so do whatever arouses you most to love.

Mother Teresa

Love is the only spiritual power that can overcome the self-centeredness that is inherent in being alive. Love is the thing that makes life possible or, indeed, tolerable.

Arnold Joseph Toynbee

His love enableth me to call every country my country, and every man my brother.

Daniel Wheeler

For Self

See also Selfishness

The man who loves his life will lose it, while the man who hates his life in this world will keep it for eternal life.

John 12:25 NIV

Let each of you look not to your own interests, but to the interests of others.

Philippians 2:4 NRSV

Self–admiration is the death of the soul. To admire ourselves as we are is to have no wish to change. And with those who don't want to change, the soul is dead.

William Barclay

Love is pure when self is slain.

Harold R. Crosser

Self-love is cunning, it pushes and insinuates itself into everything, while making us believe it is not there at all.

St. Francis de Sales

You have an ego—a consciousness of being an individual. But that doesn't mean that you are to worship yourself, to think constantly about yourself, and to live entirely for yourself.

William Franklin (Billy) Graham

The love of liberty is the love of others; the love of power is the love of ourselves.

William Hazlitt

Love is swift, sincere, pious, pleasant, gentle, strong, patient, faithful, prudent, longsuffering, manly, and never seeking her own: for wheresoever a man seeketh his own, there he falleth from love.

Thomas à Kempis

All the sin of heathendom, all the sin of Christendom, is but the outgrowth of the one root—God dethroned, self enthroned in the heart of man.

Andrew Murray

If I am half-full of myself, there is no way I can be full of God.

Richard Owen Roberts

Love, Sexual, *see* Sex and Sexuality

Loyalty

See also Faithfulness

Ruth said, Entreat me not to leave thee, or to return from following after thee: for whither thou goest, I will go; and where thou lodgest, I will lodge: thy people shall be my people, and thy God my God.

Ruth 1:16 KJV

Their hearts were not loyal to him, they were not faithful to his covenant.

Psalm 78:37 NIV

By loyalty and faithfulness iniquity is atoned for, and by the fear of the LORD one avoids evil.

Proverbs 16:6 NRSV

You cannot be a slave of two masters; you will hate one and love the other; you will be loyal to one and despise the other. You cannot serve both God and money.

Matthew 6:24 GNB

To have no loyalty is to have no dignity and in the end no manhood.

Peter Taylor Forsyth

Loyalty that will do anything, that will endure anything, that will make the whole being consecrate to Him, is what Christ wants. Anything else is not worthy of Him.

Burdett Hart

It is not best to swap horses while crossing the river.

Abraham Lincoln

Loyalty means not that I am you, or that I agree with everything you say or that I believe you are always right. Loyalty means that I share a common ideal with you and that regardless of minor differences we fight for it, shoulder to shoulder, confident in one another's good faith, trust, constancy, and affection.

Karl (Augustus) Menninger

Loyalty is so fierce and contagious an energy that it is safe only when the object of it is something that we can love or worship when we are alone.

William L. Sullivan

Lying, *see* Deceit; Dishonesty; Falsehood

Mankind, *see* Humanity

Marriage

See also Husbands and Wives; Parents; Sex and Sexuality

The Lord God said, "It is not good for the man to be alone. I will make a helper suitable for him."

Genesis 2:18 NIV

For this reason a man shall leave his father and mother and be joined to his wife, and the two shall become one flesh. So they are no longer two, but one flesh. Therefore what God has joined together, let no one separate.

Matthew 19:5–6 NRSV

Have respect for marriage. Always be faithful to your partner, because God will punish anyone who is immoral or unfaithful in marriage.

Hebrews 13:4 CEV

As God by creation made two of one, so again by marriage He made one of two.

Thomas Adams

Marriage is our last, best chance to grow up.

Joseph Barth

Dearly beloved, we are gathered together here in the sight of God, and in the face of this Congregation, to join together this man and this woman in holy Matrimony; which is an honorable estate, instituted of God.

Book of Common Prayer

To have and to hold from this day forward, for better for worse, for richer for poorer, in sickness and in health, to love and to cherish, till death us do part, according to God's holy ordinance; and thereto I plight thee my troth.

Book of Common Prayer

To love, cherish, and to obey.

Book of Common Prayer

Those whom God hath joined together let no man put asunder.

Book of Common Prayer

Success in marriage is more than finding the right person; it is a matter of being the right person.

Rabbi B.R. Brickner

[Marriage] was ordained for the mutual society, help, and comfort, that the one ought to have of the other, both in prosperity and adversity.

Thomas Cranmer

The state of marriage is one that requires more virtue and constancy than any other, it is a perpetual exercise of mortification.

St. Francis de Sales

A successful marriage demands a divorce; a divorce from your own self-love.

Paul Frost

There is no more lovely, friendly, or charming, relationship, communion, or company, than a good marriage.

Martin Luther

One plus one equals one may not be an accurate mathematical concept, but it is an accurate description of God's intention for the marriage relationship.

Wayne Mack

God is the witness to every marriage ceremony, and will be the witness to every violation of its vows.

Thomas V. Moore

Successful marriage is always a triangle, a man, a woman, and God.

Cecil Myers

Every man who is happily married is a successful man, even if he has failed in everything else.

William Lyon Phelps

A happy marriage is the union of two good forgivers.

Robert Quillen

One of the great similarities between Christianity and marriage is that, for Christians, they both get better as we get older.

Jean Rees

Marriage is like twirling a baton, turning handsprings, or eating with chopsticks; it looks so easy till you try it.

Helen Rowland

Martyrs and Martyrdom

See also Witness

For your sake we are being massacred all day long, treated as sheep to be slaughtered.

Psalm 44:22 NJB

When the blood of your martyr Stephen was shed, I stood there giving my approval.

Acts 22:20 NIV

And when he had opened the fifth seal, I saw under the altar the souls of them that were slain for the word of God, and for the testimony which they held: And they cried with a loud voice, saying, How long, O Lord, holy and true, dost thou not judge and avenge our blood on them that dwell on the earth?

Revelation 6:9–10 KJV

They have conquered him by the blood of the Lamb and by the word of their testimony, for they did not cling to life even in the face of death.

Revelation 12:11 NRSV

The martyrs were bound, imprisoned, scourged, racked, burnt, rent, butchered— and they multiplied.

St. Augustine of Hippo

The noble army of Martyrs.

Book of Common Prayer

The Lord knows I go up this ladder [to be hung as a martyr] with less fear, confusion, or perturbation of mind than ever I entered a pulpit to preach.

Donald Cargill

Let others wear the martyr's crown; I am not worthy of this honor.

Desiderius Erasmus

Live as though you may die a martyr's death.

Charles de Foucauld

He that will not live a saint cannot die a martyr.

Thomas Fuller

God sometimes raises up many faithful ministers out of the ashes of one.

Matthew Henry

Most joyfully will I confirm with my blood that truth which I have written and preached.

Jan Hus

Fire and cross and battling with wild beasts, their clawing and tearing, the breaking of bones and mangling of members, the grinding of my whole body, the wicked torments of the devil—let them assail me, so long as I get to Jesus Christ.

St. Ignatius of Antioch

The tyrant dies and his rule ends, the martyr dies and his rule begins.

Søren Kierkegaard

James the brother of Jesus and James the son of Zebedee preach and are killed by mobs in Jerusalem; Matthew is slain with a sword in Ethiopia; Philip is hanged in Phrygia; Bartholomew flayed alive in Armenia; Andrew is crucified in Achaia; Thomas is run through with a lance in East India; Thaddeus is shot to death with arrows; a cross goes up in Persia for Simon the Zealot; and another in Rome for Peter; Matthias is beheaded. Only John escapes a martyr's grave.

Frank S. Mead

The martyrs shook the powers of darkness with the irresistible power of weakness.

John Milton

No one is a martyr for a conclusion, no one is a martyr for an opinion; it is faith that makes martyrs.

John Henry Newman

Some ministers would make good martyrs. They are so dry, they would burn well.

Charles Haddon Spurgeon

The blood of the martyrs is the seed of the Church.

Quintus Tertullian

Love makes the whole difference between an execution and martyrdom.

Evelyn Underhill

Mary, the Mother of Jesus

Mary said, "I am the Lord's servant! Let it happen as you have said."

Luke 1:26–35, 38 CEV

Mary said, "My soul magnifies the Lord, and my spirit rejoices in God my Savior, for he has looked with favor on the lowliness of his servant. Surely, from now on all generations will call me blessed; for the Mighty One has done great things for me, and holy is his name."

Luke 1:46–49 NRSV

Mary treasured up all these things and pondered them in her heart.

Luke 2:19 NIV

Near the cross of Jesus stood his mother, his mother's sister, Mary the wife of Clopas, and Mary Magdalene. When Jesus saw his mother there, and the disciple whom he loved standing near by, he said to his mother, "Dear woman, here is your son," and to the disciple, "Here is your mother." From that time on, this disciple took her into his home.

John 19:25–27 NIV

Hail Mary, full of grace, the Lord is with thee: Blessed art thou among women, and blessed is the fruit of thy womb, Jesus.

Anon.

Had Mary been filled with reason there'd have been no room for the child.

Madeleine L'Engle

The feast we call "Annunciatio Mariae," when the angel came to Mary and brought her the message from God, may be fitly called the Feast of Christ's Humanity, for then began our deliverance.

Martin Luther

Since God has revealed very little to us about Mary, men who know nothing of who and what she was only reveal themselves when they try to add something to what God has told us about her.

Thomas Merton

Mary's humble acceptance of the divine will is the starting point of the story of the redemption of the human race from sin.

Alan Richardson

The poverty of Mary, living out her unseen, humble, and quite ordinary existence and sharing life with common humanity in an insignificant little village, is altogether the sign of the grace and glory of the Lord's greatness.

Max Thurian

Masculinity, *see* Men and Manhood

Maturity

See also Perfection; Spiritual Growth

The gifts he gave were that some would be apostles, some prophets, some evangelists, some pastors and teachers, to equip the saints for the work of ministry, for building up the body of Christ, until all of us come to the unity of the faith and of the knowledge of the Son of God, to maturity, to the measure of the full stature of Christ.

Ephesians 4:11–13 NRSV

All of us who are spiritually mature should have this same attitude. But if some of you have a different attitude, God will make this clear to you.

Philippians 3:15 GNB

It is he whom we proclaim, warning everyone and teaching everyone in all wisdom, so that we may present everyone mature in Christ.

Colossians 1:28 NRSV

God never destroys the work of his own hands, he removes what would pervert it, that is all. Maturity is the stage where the whole life has been brought under the control of God.

Oswald Chambers

Honesty consists of the unwillingness to lie to others; maturity, which is equally hard to attain, consists of the unwillingness to lie to oneself.

Sydney J. Harris

Spiritual maturity comes, not by erudition, but by compliance with the known will of God.

D.W. Lambert

Age is not all decay; it is the ripening, the swelling, of the fresh life within, that withers and bursts the husk.

George MacDonald

Maturity begins to grow when you can sense your concern for others outweighing your concern for yourself.

John MacNaughton

Blisters are a painful experience, but if you get enough blisters in the same place, they will eventually produce a callus. That is what we call maturity.

Herbert Miller

Poverty of mind as a spiritual attitude is a growing willingness to recognize the incomprehensibility of the mystery of life. The more mature we become the more we will be able to give up our inclination to grasp, catch, and comprehend the fullness of life and the more we will be ready to let life enter into us.

Henri J.M. Nouwen

He is only advancing in life, whose heart is getting softer, his blood warmer, his brain quicker, and his spirit entering into living peace.

John Ruskin

Growth is not the product of effort, but of life.

Augustus Hopkins Strong

One of the marks of spiritual maturity is the quiet confidence that God is in control . . . without the need to understand why he does what he does.

Charles R. Swindoll

In this world, things that are naturally to endure for a long time, are the slowest in reaching maturity.

St. Vincent de Paul

Let's learn to grow up before we grow old.

John Richard Wimber

If there is anything that characterizes Christian maturity, it is the willingness to become a beginner again for Jesus.

John Richard Wimber

Meditation and Contemplation

See also Bible; Mystics and Mysticism; Prayer; Quiet and Stillness

Happy are those who do not follow the advice of the wicked, or take the path that sinners tread, or sit in the seat of scoffers; but their delight is in the law of the LORD, and on his law they meditate day and night.

Psalm 1:1–2 NRSV

Let me understand the teaching of your precepts; then I will meditate on your wonders.

Psalm 119:27 NIV

I remember the days of old, I think about all your deeds, I meditate on the works of your hands.

Psalm 143:5 NRSV

I don't say anything to God. I just sit there and look at him and let him look at me.

Anon. (19ᵗʰ century peasant)

Place your mind before the mirrors of eternity! Place your soul in the brilliance of glory. Place your heart in the figure of the divine substance and transform your whole being into the magic of the Godhead Itself through contemplation.

St. Clare of Assisi

The higher part of contemplation is wholly caught up in darkness and in this cloud of unknowing, with an outreaching of love and a blind groping for the naked being of God, himself and him alone.

The Cloud of Unknowing

Meditate daily on the words of your Creator. Learn the heart of God in the words of God, that your soul may be kindled with greater longings for heavenly joys.

St. Gregory I

At its highest peak prayer become contemplation. Here it is wordless. It is a merging of the human consciousness with the Divine.

Bede Griffiths

The longest journey is the journey inward. . . . The road to holiness necessarily passes through the world of action.

Dag Hammarskjöld

It is easier to go six miles to hear a sermon, than to spend one quarter of an hour in meditating on it when I come home.

Philip Henry

Seek in reading and thou shalt find in meditation; knock in prayer and it shall be opened to thee in contemplation.

St. John of the Cross

Contemplation is nothing else but a secret, peaceful, and loving infusion of God, which, if admitted, will set the soul on fire with the Spirit of love.

St. John of the Cross

Meditation is the devotional practice of pondering the words of a verse, or verses of Scripture, allowing the Holy Spirit to take the written word and apply it as the living word to the inner being.

Campbell McAlpine

The all-important aim in Christian meditation is to allow God's mysterious and silent presence within us to become more and more not only a reality, but the reality in our lives; to let it become that reality which gives meaning and shape and purpose to everything we do; to everything we are.

John Main

Devout meditation on the Word is more important to soul-health even than prayer. It is more needful for you to hear God's words than that God should hear yours, though the one will always lead to the other.

Frederick Brotherton (F.B.) Meyer

[Meditation is] holding the word of God in the mind until it has affected every area of one's life and character.

Andrew Murray

Meditation is the activity of calling to mind, and thinking over, and dwelling on, and applying to oneself, the various things that one knows about the works and ways and purposes and promises of God.

James Innell (J.I.) Packer

The way through to the vision of the Son of Man and the knowledge of God, which is the heart of contemplative prayer, is by unconditional love of thy neighbor, or the nearest Thou to hand.

Bishop John Arthur Thomas Robinson

God in the depths of us receives God who comes to us; it is God contemplating God.

Jan van Ruysbroeck

Be pure, still, learn to yield, and climb to darkest heights: / Then you will come o'er all to contemplate your God.

Angelus Silesius

Breathing, meditation, contemplation—these are all attempts of the soul to "make an exit out of the world, out of the flesh, out of all mental objects, then finally out of myself, that is, out of one's own will," attempts to make the dominant "I" smaller, to become "I-less," so that we can come to ourselves.

Dorothee Soelle

Contemplation is a gift of God which is not necessary for salvation nor for earning our eternal reward, nor will anyone require you to possess it.

St. Teresa of Avila

The acts of contemplation are four; to seek after God, to find Him, to feel His sacred touch in the soul, and to be united with Him and to enjoy Him.

William Bernard Ullathorne

Proficiency in meditation lies not in thinking much, but in loving much. It is a way of seeking the divine companionship, the "closer walk." Thus it is that meditation has come to be called "the mother of love."

Richardson Wright

To ears which have been trained to wait upon God in silence, and in the quietness of meditation and prayer, a very small incident, or a word, may prove to be a turning point in our lives, and a new opening for his love to enter our world, to create and to redeem.

Olive Wyon

Meekness

See also Gentleness; Humility

Now the man Moses was very meek, above all the men which were upon the face of the earth.

Numbers 12:3 KJV

The meek shall inherit the land, and delight in abundant prosperity.

Psalm 37:11 NRSV

Blessed are the meek: for they shall inherit the earth.

Matthew 5:5 KJV

Take my yoke upon you, and learn of me; for I am meek and lowly in heart: and ye shall find rest unto your souls.

Matthew 11:29 KJV

If you should ask me concerning the precepts of the Christian religion, I should answer you: nothing but humility.

St. Augustine of Hippo

Meekness is love at school, at the school of Christ. It is the disciple learning to know, and fear, and distrust himself, and learning of him who is meek and lowly of heart, and so finding rest to his soul.

James Hamilton

If thou have any good things believe better things of others, that thou may keep thy meekness.

Thomas à Kempis

Meek endurance and meek obedience, the accepting of his dealings, of whatever complexion they are and however they may tear and desolate our hearts, without murmuring, without sulking, without rebellion or resistance, is the deepest conception of the meekness that Christ pronounced blessed.

Alexander Maclaren

Spread abroad the name of Jesus in humility and with a meek heart; show him your feebleness, and he will become your strength.

Thomas Merton

Meekness is not weakness. It is power under control.

Warren W. Wiersbe

Meekness is the mark of a man who has been mastered by God.

Geoffrey B. Wilson

Memories, *see* Remembrance

Men and Manhood

See also Adam and Eve; Fathers and Fatherhood; Husbands and Wives

To the man he said, "Because you have listened to the voice of your wife, and have eaten of the tree about which I commanded you, 'You shall not eat of it,' cursed is the ground because of you; in toil you shall eat of it all the days of your life."

Genesis 3:17 NRSV

As the man is, so is his strength.

Judges 8:21 NRSV

A faith in God that is identified only with masculine traits is incompatible with Christian revelation.

Maria Clara Bingemer

Men's men: gentle or simple, they're much of a muchness.

George Eliot

I know a man who, when he saw a woman of striking beauty, praised the Creator for her. The sight of her lit within him the love of God.

St. John Climacus

Lord, save me from being a wicked old man.

George Müller

I see in Jesus a compelling picture of male sexual wholeness, of creative masculinity, and of the redemption of manhood from both oppressiveness and superficiality.

James Nelson

Masculinity is a problem for Christian theology and ought to be felt as such.

Brian Wren

Mercy

See also Forgiveness; God, Grace and Mercy of; Grace

The Lord has heard my cry for mercy; the Lord accepts my prayer.

Psalm 6:9 NIV

Have mercy upon me, O God, according to thy lovingkindness: according unto the multitude of thy tender mercies blot out my transgressions.

Psalm 51:1 KJV

It is of the Lord's mercies that we are not consumed, because his compassions fail not. They are new every morning: great is thy faithfulness.

Lamentations 3:22–23 KJV

Blessed are the merciful, for they will receive mercy.

Matthew 5:7 NRSV

The tax collector stood some distance away, not daring even to raise his eyes to heaven; but he beat his breast and said, "God, be merciful to me, a sinner."

Luke 18:13 NJB

God's mercy is so abundant, and his love for us is so great, that while we were spiritually dead in our disobedience he brought us to life with Christ. It is by God's grace that you have been saved.

Ephesians 2:4–5 GNB

He that demands mercy and shows none ruins the bridge over which he himself is to pass.

Thomas Adams

Mercy also, is a good thing, for it makes men perfect, in that it imitates the perfect Father. Nothing graces the Christian soul as much as mercy.

St. Ambrose

Two works of mercy set a man free; forgive and you will be forgiven, and give and you will receive.

St. Augustine of Hippo

The more godly any man is, the more merciful that man will be.

Thomas Benton Brooks

We are going to meet unmerciful good people and unmerciful bad people, unmerciful institutions, unmerciful organizations, and we shall have to go through the discipline of being merciful to the merciless.

Oswald Chambers

Mercy imitates God and disappoints Satan.

St. John Chrysostom

Mercies are such gifts as advance our debts.

William Secker

If we refuse mercy here, we shall have justice in eternity.

Jeremy Taylor

A debtor to mercy alone, / Of covenant mercy I sing; / Nor fear, with Thy righteousness on, / My person and offering to bring; / The terrors of law and of God / With me can have nothing to do; My Savior's obedience and blood / Hide all my transgressions from view.

Augustus Montague Toplady

Messiah, *see* Jesus Christ, Messiah

Mind

See also Peace, of Mind; Thoughts and Thinking

Thou wilt keep him in perfect peace, whose mind is stayed on thee: because he trusteth in thee.

Isaiah 26:3 KJV

Do not be conformed to this world, but be transformed by the renewing of your minds, so that you may discern what is the will of God.

Romans 12:2 NRSV

As the scripture says, "Who knows the mind of the Lord? Who is able to give him advice?" We, however, have the mind of Christ.

1 Corinthians 2:16 GNB

Let the same mind be in you that was in Christ Jesus, who, though he was in the form of God, did not regard equality with God as something to be exploited, but emptied himself, taking the form of a slave, being born in human likeness. And being found in human form, he humbled himself and became obedient to the point of death—even death on a cross.

Philippians 2:5–8 NRSV

The point of having an open mind, like having an open mouth, is to close it on something solid.

Gilbert Keith (G.K.) Chesterton

There is no salvation save in truth, and the royal road of truth is by the mind.

Martin Cyril D'Arcy

To the quiet mind all things are possible. What is the quiet mind? A quiet mind is one which nothing weighs on, nothing worries, which, free from ties and from all self-seeking, is wholly merged into the will of God and dead to its own.

Meister Eckhart

The human mind is so constructed that it resists vigor and yields to gentleness.

St. Francis de Sales

My mind is the central control area of my personality, and sanctification is the mind coming more and more under the Holy Spirit's control.

David Jackman

Let us never forget that the message of the Bible is addressed primarily to the mind, to the understanding.

David Martyn Lloyd-Jones

The mind is its own place, and in itself can make a heaven of hell, a hell of heaven.

John Milton

Almighty God influences us and works in us, through our minds, not without them, or in spite of them.

John Henry Newman

No one would allow garbage at his table, but many allow it served into their minds.

Fulton John Sheen

Untilled ground, however rich, will bring forth thistles and thorns; so also the mind of man.

St. Teresa of Avila

The mind is good—God put it there. He gave us our heads and it was not his intention that our heads would function just as a place to hang a hat.

Aiden Wilson (A.W.) Tozer

Ministry, *see* Church, Leaders of; Church, Mission and Ministry of

Miracles

See also Jesus Christ, Miracles of

Lord God of Israel, we praise you. Only you can work miracles.

Psalm 72:18 CEV

He sent signs and wonders into your midst, O Egypt, against Pharaoh and all his servants.

Psalm 135:9 NRSV

Now while he was in Jerusalem at the Passover Feast, many people saw the miraculous signs he was doing and believed in his name.

John 2:23 NIV

"Unless you people see miraculous signs and wonders," Jesus told him, "you will never believe." The royal official said, "Sir, come down before my child dies." Jesus replied, "You may go. Your son will live." . . . This was the second miraculous sign that Jesus performed, having come from Judea to Galilee.

John 4:48–50, 54 NIV

Believe me when I say that I am in the Father and the Father is in me; or at least believe on the evidence of the miracles themselves. I tell you the truth, anyone who has faith in me will do what I have been doing. He will do even greater things than these, because I am going to the Father.

John 14:11–12 NIV

There were indeed many other signs that Jesus performed in the presence of his disciples, which are not recorded in this book. Those written here have been recorded in order that you may believe that Jesus is the Christ, the Son of God, and that through this faith you may have life by his name.

John 20:30–31 REB

I will shew wonders in heaven above, and signs in the earth beneath; blood, and fire, and vapor of smoke: The sun shall be turned into darkness, and the moon into blood, before that great and notable day of the Lord come.

Acts 2:19–20 KJV

Reach out your hand to heal, and grant that wonders and miracles may be performed through the name of your holy Servant Jesus.

Acts 4:30 GNB

All the marks characteristic of a true apostle have been at work among you: complete perseverance, signs, marvels, demonstrations of power.

2 Corinthians 12:12 NJB

God himself confirmed their witness with signs and marvels and miracles of all kinds, and by distributing the gifts of the Holy Spirit in the various ways he wills.

Hebrews 2:4 NJB

It is only two years ago that the keeping of records was begun here in Hippo, and already, at this writing, we have nearly seventy attested miracles.

St. Augustine of Hippo

Miracles are not contrary to nature but only contrary to what we know about nature.

St. Augustine of Hippo

I should not be Christian but for the miracles.

St. Augustine of Hippo

A miracle is not the breaking of the laws of the fallen world, it is the re-establishment of the laws of the kingdom.

Anthony Bloom

You can't separate God and miracles, but you must be able to interpret and proclaim both in a "non-religious" sense.

Dietrich Bonhoeffer

A miracle in the sense of the New Testament is not so much a breach of the laws of nature, but rather a remarkable or exceptional occurrence which brought an undeniable sense of the presence and power of God.

Charles Harold (C.H.) Dodd

Miracles are the great bell of the universe, which draws men to God's sermon.

John Foster

The divine art of miracle is not an art of suspending the pattern to which events confirm, but of feeding new events into that pattern.

Clive Staples (C.S.) Lewis

I had rather obey than work miracles.

Martin Luther

We are not to require "signs," but we are to regard signs. They are not given to produce faith, but to inform faith.

Ian MacPherson

A miracle is a law-abiding event by which God accomplishes his redemptive purposes through the release of energies which belong to a plane of being higher than any with which we are normally familiar.

Leslie Weatherhead

Mission, *see* Church, Mission and Ministry of; Evangelism; Jesus Christ, Mission of

Modesty

See also Humility

Let another praise you and not your own mouth—a stranger, and not your own lips.

Proverbs 27:2 NRSV

Let us learn to lay upon ourselves the restraint of modesty.

John Calvin

To affect obscurity or submission is base and suspicious; but that man, whose modesty presents him mean to his own eyes and lowly to others, is commonly secretly rich in virtue. Give me rather a low fulness than an empty advancement.

Joseph Hall

Modesty is the badge of wisdom.

Matthew Henry

Guard your eyes, since they are the windows through which sin enters into the soul. Never look curiously on those things which are contrary to modesty, even slightly.

St. John Bosco

Modesty is to merit what shade is to figures in a picture; it gives it strength and makes it stand out.

Jean de La Bruyère

Modesty in human beings is praised because it is not a matter of nature, but of will.

Lactantius

We have plenty of people nowadays who could not kill a mouse without publishing it in the Gospel Gazette. Samson killed a lion and said nothing about it; the Holy Spirit finds modesty so rare that he takes care to record it. Say much of what the Lord has done for you, but say little of what you have done for the Lord.

Charles Haddon Spurgeon

Money

See also Possessions; Wealth

One scatters money around, yet only adds to his wealth, another is excessively mean, but only grows the poorer.

Proverbs 11:24 NJB

No one who loves money can ever have enough, and no one who loves wealth enjoys any return from it.

Ecclesiastes 5:10 REB

Do not store up riches for yourselves here on earth, where moths and rust destroy, and robbers break in and steal. Instead, store up riches for yourselves in heaven, where moths and rust cannot destroy, and robbers cannot break in and steal. For your heart will always be where your riches are.

Matthew 6:19–21 GNB

No slave can serve two masters; for a slave will either hate the one and love the other, or be devoted to the one and despise the other. You cannot serve God and wealth.

Luke 16:13 NRSV

Don't fall in love with money. Be satisfied with what you have. The Lord has promised that he will not leave us or desert us.

Hebrews 13:5 CEV

For the love of money is a root of all kinds of evil. Some people, eager for money, have wandered from the faith and pierced themselves with many griefs.

1 Timothy 6:10 NIV

Money is like muck, no good except it be spread.

Francis Bacon

If you would know what the Lord God thinks of money, you have only to look at those to whom he gives it.

Maurice Baring

Jesus talked a great deal about money and the problems it causes man—in fact, one-fifth of all Jesus had to say was about money.

William Franklin (Billy) Graham

If a person gets his attitude toward money straight, it will help straighten out almost every other area in his life.

William Franklin (Billy) Graham

Take my silver and my gold, / Not a mite would I withhold; / Take my intellect, and use / Every power as Thou shalt choose.

Frances Ridley Havergal

Honor and profit lie not all in one sack.

George Herbert

Money can buy the husk of many things, but not the kernel. It brings you food, but not appetite; medicine, but not health; acquaintances, but not friends; servants, but not faithfulness; days of joy, but not peace and happiness.

Henrik Ibsen

God pity the nation whose factory chimneys rise higher than her church spires.

John Kelman

Money is emphasized in Scripture simply because our temptation to love it is inexplicably powerful.

Erwin W. Lutzer

If a man's religion does not affect his use of money, that man's religion is vain.

Hugh Martin

God demands the tithe, deserves the offerings, defends the savings, and directs the expenses.

Stephen Olford

Money has never yet made anyone rich.

Seneca

Nothing that is God's is obtainable by money.

Quintus Tertullian

When I have any money, I get rid of it as quickly as possible, lest it find a way into my heart.

John Wesley

Monotony

The rabble among them had a strong craving; and the Israelites also wept again, and said, "If only we had meat to eat! We remember the fish we used to eat in Egypt for nothing, the cucumbers, the melons, the leeks, the onions, and the garlic; but now our strength is dried up, and there is nothing at all but this manna to look at."

Numbers 11:4–6 NRSV

Life is not lost by dying! Life is lost minute by minute, day by dragging day, in all the thousand, small, uncaring ways.

Stephen Vincent Benét

Do you want to grow in virtue, to serve God, to love Christ? Well, you will grow, and attain to these things if you will make them a slow and sure, plodding, mountain ascent; if you are willing to have to camp for weeks or months in spiritual desolation, darkness, and emptiness at different stages in your march and growth. All demand for constant light, all attempt at eliminating the cross and trial, is so much soft folly and puerile trifling.

Baron Friedrich von Hügel

The trivial round, the common task, / Would furnish all we ought to ask; / Room to deny ourselves; a road / To bring us, daily, nearer God.

John Keble

The most bored people in life are not the underprivileged but the overprivileged.

Fulton John Sheen

The test of a vocation is the love of the drudgery it involves.

Logan Pearsall Smith

Nor greeting where no kindness is, nor all / The dreary intercourse of daily life, / Shall e'er prevail against us, or disturb / Our cheerful faith, that all which we behold / Is full of blessings.

William Wordsworth

Morality, *see* Right and Wrong

Mothers and Motherhood

See also Fathers and Fatherhood; God, Personal Description of; Husbands and Wives; Mary, Mother of Jesus; Parents

Adam called his wife's name Eve; because she was the mother of all living.

Genesis 3:20 KJV

He settles the barren woman in her home as a happy mother of children.

Psalm 113:9 NIV

When Elizabeth heard Mary's greeting, the child leaped in her womb. And Elizabeth was filled with the Holy Spirit.

Luke 1:41 NRSV

The mother's heart is the child's schoolroom.

Henry Ward Beecher

My love for you makes me desire your highest good. How can love desire less? Anything that desires less is selfishness, not love. You may have others who will be more demonstrative but never who will love you more unselfishly than your mother or who will be willing to do or bear more for your good.

Catherine Bramwell Booth

The commonest fallacy among women is that simply having children makes one a mother —which is as absurd as believing that having a piano makes one a musician.

Sydney J. Harris

The woman who creates and sustains a home and under whose hands children grow up to be strong and pure men and women, is a creator second only to God.

Helen Maria Fiske Hunt Jackson

No man is poor who has had a godly mother.

Abraham Lincoln

Son, for mine own part, I have no further delight in anything in this life. What I do here any longer, and to what end I am here, I know not, now that my hopes in this world are accomplished. One thing there was for which I desired to linger for a while in this life—that I might see thee a Catholic Christian before I died. My God hath done this for me, and

more; since I now see thee despising earthly happiness, and become his servant: what then do I here?

St. Monica

The loveliest masterpiece of the heart of God is the heart of a mother.

St. Thérèse of Lisieux

I learned more about Christianity from my mother than from all the theologians of England.

John Wesley

Motives

You, my son Solomon, acknowledge the God of your father, and serve him with wholehearted devotion and with a willing mind, for the Lord searches every heart and understands every motive behind the thoughts.

1 Chronicles 28:9 NIV

A person's whole conduct may be right in his own eyes, but the Lord weighs up his motives.

Proverbs 21:2 REB

You do not have what you want because you do not ask God for it. And when you ask, you do not receive it, because your motives are bad; you ask for things to use for your own pleasures.

James 4:2–3 GNB

What horror has the world come to when it uses profit as the prime incentive in human progress, and competition as the supreme law of economics?

Dom Helder Passoa Câmara

God looks at the intention of the heart rather than the gifts He is offered.

Bishop Jean Pierre Camus

Jesus offends men because he lays emphasis on the unseen life, because he speaks of motives rather than of actions.

Oswald Chambers

What makes life dreary is absence of motive. What makes life complicated is multiplicity of motive. What makes life victorious is singleness of motive.

George Eliot

Christianity is a religion of motives—ways of acting and reasons for acting, more than actions.

Frederick William Faber

One of the most excellent intentions that we can possibly have in all our actions, is to do them because our Lord did them.

St. Francis de Sales

Man sees your actions, but God your motives.

Thomas à Kempis

Man beholds the face, but God looks upon the heart. Man considers the actions, but God weighs the intentions.

Thomas à Kempis

Right intention is to the actions of a man what the soul is to the body, or the root to the tree.

Jeremy Taylor

It is not what a man does that determines whether his work is sacred or secular, it is why he does it.

Aiden Wilson (A.W.) Tozer

Mourning, *see* Bereavement; Grief; Loss

Music

Hear, O kings; give ear, O princes; to the LORD

I will sing, I will make melody to the LORD, the God of Israel.

Judges 5:3 NRSV

Whenever the evil spirit sent by God came on Saul, David would get his harp and play it. The evil spirit would leave, and Saul would feel better and be all right again.

1 Samuel 16:23 GNB

Praise ye the Lord. Praise God in his sanctuary: praise him in the firmament of his power. Praise him for his mighty acts: praise him according to his excellent greatness. Praise him with the sound of the trumpet: praise him with the psaltery and harp. Praise him with the timbrel and dance: praise him with stringed instruments and organs. Praise him upon the loud cymbals: praise him upon the high sounding cymbals. Let every thing that hath breath praise the Lord. Praise ye the Lord.

Psalm 150:1–6 KJV

Break into song for my God, to the tambourine, sing in honor of the Lord, to the cymbal, let psalm and canticle mingle for him, extol his name, invoke it!

Judith 16:1 NJB

Speak to one another with psalms, hymns and spiritual songs. Sing and make music in your heart to the Lord.

Ephesians 5:19 NIV

The hymnal of the church is a reflection of its theology.

Milton S. Agnew

Music exalts each joy, allays each grief. / Expels diseases, softens every pain. / Subdues the rage of poison and the plague.

John Armstrong

Of all earthly music that which reaches far-thest into heaven is the beating of a truly lov-ing heart.

Henry Ward Beecher

What is to reach the heart must come from above; if it does not come from thence, it will be nothing but notes, body without spirit.

Ludwig van Beethoven

Music strikes in me a deep fit of devotion, and a profound contemplation on the First Composer. There is something in it of Divin-ity more than the ear discovers.

Sir Thomas Browne

So is music an asylum. It takes us out of the actual and whispers to us dim secrets that startle our wonder as to who we are, and for what, whence, and whereto, all the great interrogatories, like questioning angels, float in on its waves of sound.

Ralph Waldo Emerson

When I think upon my God, my heart is so full of joy that the notes dance and leap from my pen; and since God has given me a cheer-ful heart, it will be pardoned me that I serve him with a cheerful spirit.

Franz Joseph Haydn

Music is God's best gift to man. The only art of heaven given to earth, the only art of earth we take to heaven.

Letitia Elizabeth Landon

Next to theology I give to music the highest place and honor. Music is the art of the prophets, the only art that can calm the agi-tations of the soul; it is one of the most mag-nificent and delightful presents God has given us.

Martin Luther

Music is one of the greatest gifts God has given us: it is divine and therefore Satan is its enemy. For with its aid many dire tempta-tions are overcome; the devil does not stay where music is.

Martin Luther

O Music! thou bringest the receding waves of eternity nearer to the weary soul of man as he stands upon the shore and longs to cross over!

Johann Paul Friedrich Richter

The man that hath no music in himself, / Nor is not mov'd with concord of sweet sounds, / Is fit for treasons, strategems, and spoils.

William Shakespeare

Church music should not be for entertain-ment, but a worship experience that lifts us to the portals of heaven and leaves us think-ing of the greatness and goodness of God.

Alice Tucker

Mystics and Mysticism

See also Meditation and Contemplation

I know a man in Christ who fourteen years ago was caught up to the third heaven. Whether it was in the body or out of the body I do not know—God knows.

2 Corinthians 12:2 NIV

In order to arrive at that which thou know-est not, thou must go by a way that thou knowest not, in order to arrive at that which thou possesseth not.

St. John of the Cross

One of the greatest paradoxes of the mystical life is this: that a man cannot enter into the deepest center of himself and pass through that center into God, unless he is able to pass entirely out of himself and empty himself and give himself to other people in the purity of a selfless love.

Thomas Merton

Any profound view of the world is mysticism, in that it brings men into a spiritual relation with the Infinite.

Albert Schweitzer

Mysticism is the name of that organic process which involves the perfect consummation of the love of God.

Evelyn Underhill

Nations and Nationhood

See also Peace, between People and Nations; Race and Racism

Blessed is the nation whose God is the Lord.

Psalm 33:12 KJV

Righteousness exalts a nation, but sin is a reproach to any people.

Proverbs 14:34 NRSV

When good people in any country cease their vigilance and struggle, then evil men prevail.

Pearl S. Buck

The strength of a country is the strength of its religious convictions.

Calvin Coolidge

The spectacle of a nation praying is more awe-inspiring than the explosion of an atom bomb. The force of prayer is greater than any possible combination of man-controlled powers because prayer is man's greatest means of tapping the infinite resources of God.

J. Edgar Hoover

With malice toward none; with charity for all; with firmness in the right, as God gives us to see the right, let us strive on to finish the work we are in; to bind up the nation's wounds; to care for him who shall have borne the battle, and for his widow and his orphan—to do all which may achieve and cherish a just and lasting peace among ourselves and with all nations.

Abraham Lincoln

I recognize the sublime truth announced in the Holy Scriptures and proven by all history that those nations only are blest whose God is the Lord.

Abraham Lincoln

Neighbors

See also Compassion; Golden Rule; Kindness; Love, for Others

You shall not bear false witness against your neighbor. You shall not covet your neighbor's house; you shall not covet your neighbor's wife, or male or female slave, or ox, or donkey, or anything that belongs to your neighbor.

Exodus 20:16–17 NRSV

If you are in trouble, don't ask a relative for help; a nearby neighbor can help you more than relatives who are far away.

Proverbs 27:10 GNB

Love the Lord your God with all your heart, and with all your soul, with all your strength, and with all your mind; and your neighbor as yourself.

Luke 10:27 REB

He asked Jesus, "And who is my neighbor?" In reply Jesus said: "A man was going down from Jerusalem to Jericho, when he fell into the hands of robbers. They stripped him of his clothes, beat him and went away leaving him half dead. A priest happened to be going down the same road, and when he saw the man, he passed by on the other side. So too, a Levite, when he came to the place and saw him, passed by on the other side. But a Samaritan, as he traveled, came where the man was; and when he saw him, he took pity on him. He went to him and bandaged his wounds, pouring on oil and wine. Then he put the man on his own donkey, and took him to an inn and took care of him. The next day he took out two silver coins and gave them to the innkeeper, 'Look after him,' he said, 'and when I return, I will reimburse you for any extra expense you may have.' Which of these three do you think was a neighbor to the man who fell into the hands of robbers?" The expert in the law replied, "The one who had mercy on him." Jesus told him, "Go and do likewise."

Luke 10:29–37 NIV

For all the law is fulfilled in one word, even in this; Thou shalt love thy neighbor as thyself.

Galatians 5:14 KJV

If you want your neighbor to know what Christ will do for him, let the neighbor see what Christ has done for you.

Anon.

He alone loves the Creator perfectly who manifests pure love for his neighbor.

The Venerable Bede

If my heart is right with God, every human being is my neighbor.

Oswald Chambers

He who withholds but a pennyworth of worldly goods from his neighbor, knowing

him to be in need of it, is a robber in the sight of God.

Meister Eckhart

Your neighbor is the man who needs you.

Elbert Green Hubbard

If you truly love God, you will love your neighbor. It does not make any difference if he loves you or not.

Thomas A. Judge

It is His long-term policy, I fear, to restore to them a new kind of self-love—a charity and gratitude for all selves including their own; when they have really learned to love their neighbors as themselves, they will be allowed to love themselves as their neighbors.

Clive Staples (C.S.) Lewis

The love of our neighbor is the only door out of the dungeon of self.

George MacDonald

Your neighbor is the man who is next to you at the moment, the man with whom any business has brought you into contact.

George MacDonald

Though we do not have our Lord with us in bodily presence, we have our neighbor, who, for the ends of love and loving service, is as good as our Lord himself.

St. Teresa of Avila

If you dislike war, respect your neighbor. And cherish the man who comes from afar. Venerate the distance in him. Distance is like allusion to the infinite. Love the man in your neighbor. Love God in the man who comes from afar.

Lanza del Vasto

Love for our neighbor consists of three things: to desire the greater good of everyone;

to do what good we can when we can; to bear, excuse and hide others' faults.

Jean Viannes

Looking through the wrong end of a telescope is an injustice to the astronomer, to the telescope, and to the stars: likewise, looking at our neighbor's faults instead of his attributes gives us an incorrect conception of ourselves, our neighbor, and our God.

William Arthur Ward

New Beginnings

See also New Birth

Remember ye not the former things, neither consider the things of old. Behold, I will do a new thing; now it shall spring forth; shall ye not know it? I will even make a way in the wilderness, and rivers in the desert.

Isaiah 43:18–19 KJV

The one who was seated on the throne said, "See, I am making all things new."

Revelation 21:5 NRSV

All glory comes from daring to begin.

Anon.

He that will not apply new remedies must expect new evils: for time is the greatest innovator.

Francis Bacon

No man is an island, entire of itself; every man is a piece of the Continent, a part of the main.

John Donne

Another year is dawning; dear Father, let it be, / In working or in waiting, another year with thee. / Another year of progress, another year of praise, / Another year of proving thy presence all the days. / Another year of service, of witness for thy love; / Another year of training for holier work above. / Another year is dawning, dear Father, let it be, / On earth, or else in heaven, another year for thee.

Frances Ridley Havergal

If well thou hast begun, go on foreright; / It is the end that crowns us, not the fight.

Robert Herrick

I suppose when we take on January 1 the world will look the same. But there is a reminder of the Resurrection at the start of each new year, each new decade. That's why I also like sunrises, Mondays, and new seasons. God seems to be saying, "With me you can always start afresh."

Ada Lum

You can never change the past. But by the grace of God, you can win the future. So remember those things which will help you forward, but forget those things which will only hold you back.

Richard C. Woodsome

New Birth

See also Conversion; Holy Spirit, and Regeneration; Renewal

No one can see the kingdom of God unless he has been born again.

John 3:3 REB

He saved us, not because of righteous things we had done, but because of his mercy. He saved us through the washing of rebirth and renewal by the Holy Spirit.

Titus 3:5 NIV

You have been born anew, not of perishable but of imperishable seed, through the living and enduring word of God.

1 Peter 1:23 NRSV

I remember this, that everything looked new to me . . . the fields, the cattle, the trees, I was like a new man in a new world.

Billy Bray

The first time we're born, as children, human life is given to us; and when we accept Jesus as our Savior, it's a new life. That's what "born again" means.

(James Earl) Jimmy Carter

It is impossible for us to be the children of God naturally, to love our enemies, to forgive, to be holy, to be pure, and it is certainly impossible for us to follow God naturally; consequently the fundamental fact to recognize is that we must be born again.

Oswald Chambers

In new birth God does three impossible things; the first is to make a man's past as though it had never been; the second, to make a man all over again; and the third, to make a man as certain of God as God is of himself.

Oswald Chambers

You must be born again. This is not a command, it is a foundation fact. The characteristic of the new birth is that I yield myself so completely to God that Christ is formed in me.

Oswald Chambers

If you are never born again, you will wish you had never been born at all.

Derek Cleave

Your whole nature must be re-born, your passions, and your affections, and your aims,

and your conscience, and your will must all be bathed in a new element and reconsecrated to your Maker and, the last not the least, your intellect.

John Henry Newman

When the wheels of a clock move within, the hands on the dial will move without. When the heart of a man is sound in conversion, then the life will be fair in profession.

William Secker

Every generation needs re-generation.

Charles Haddon Spurgeon

Christian experience is not so much a matter of imitating a leader as accepting and receiving a new quality of life, a life infinitely more profound and dynamic and meaningful than human life without Christ.

H.A. Williams

New Creation

See also Heaven

For, behold, I create new heavens and a new earth and the former shall not be remembered, nor come into mind.

Isaiah 65:17 KJV

So if anyone is in Christ, there is a new creation: everything old has passed away; see, everything has become new!

2 Corinthians 5:17 NRSV

And I saw a new heaven and a new earth: for the first heaven and the first earth were passed away.

Revelation 21:1 KJV

And I saw the holy city, the new Jerusalem, coming down out of heaven from God, prepared as a bride adorned for her husband. And I heard a loud voice from the throne saying, "See, the home of God is among mortals. He will dwell with them; they will be his peoples, and God himself will be with them; he will wipe every tear from their eyes. Death will be no more; mourning and crying and pain will be no more, for the first things have passed away." And the one who was seated on the throne said, "See, I am making all things new."

Revelation 21:2–5 NRSV

We are told to sing to the Lord a new song. A new man knows a new song. A song is a thing of joy and, if we think of it, a thing to love. So the man who has learned to love a new life has learned to sing a new song. For a new man, a new song and the new Testament all belong to the same kingdom.

St. Augustine of Hippo

That's what we're here for: to make the world new. We know what to do: seek justice, love mercy, walk humbly, treat every person as though she were yourself. These are not complicated instructions. It's much harder to decipher the directions for putting together a child's tricycle than it is to understand these.

Nancy Mairs

Christianity is not a system of doctrine but a new creature.

John Newton

The people of God are not merely to mark time, waiting for God to step in and set right all that is wrong. Rather, they are to model the new heaven and new earth, and by so doing awaken longings for what God will someday bring to pass.

Philip Yancey

New Jerusalem, *see* Heaven

Obedience

See also Commitment; God, Will of

If you faithfully obey the Lord your God by diligently observing all his commandments which I lay on you this day, then the Lord your God will raise you high above all nations of the earth, and the following blessings will all come and light on you, because you obey the Lord your God.

Deuteronomy 28:1–2 REB

Samuel said, "Has the LORD as great delight in burnt offerings and sacrifices, as in obedience to the voice of the LORD? Surely, to obey is better than sacrifice, and to heed than the fat of rams."

1 Samuel 15:22 NRSV

Not everyone who calls me their Lord will get into the kingdom of heaven. Only the ones who obey my Father in heaven will get in.

Matthew 7:21 CEV

If you love me, you will obey my commandments.

John 14:15 GNB

Peter and the other apostles replied: "We must obey God rather than men! The God of our fathers raised Jesus from the dead— whom you had killed by hanging him on a tree. God exalted him to his own right hand as Prince and Savior that he might give repentance and forgiveness of sins to Israel. We are witnesses of these things, and so is the Holy Spirit, whom God has given to those who obey him."

Acts 5:29–32 NIV

Though he were a Son, yet learned he obedience by the things which he suffered.

Hebrews 5:8 KJV

But be ye doers of the word, and not hearers only.

James 1:22 KJV

The evidence of knowing God is obeying God.

Eric Alexander

I can say from experience that 95% of knowing the will of God consists in being prepared to do it before you know what it is.

Donald Grey Barnhouse

All true knowledge of God is born out of obedience.

John Calvin

The best measure of a spiritual life is not its ecstasies but its obedience.

Oswald Chambers

It is a vain thought to flee from the work that God appoints us, for the sake of finding a greater blessing, instead of seeking it where alone it is to be found—in loving obedience.

George Eliot

Obedience to God is the most infallible evidence of sincere and supreme love to him.

Nathanael Emmons

Holy obedience puts to shame all natural and selfish desires. It mortifies our lower nature and makes it obey the Spirit and our fellow men.

St. Francis of Assisi

God will not thank thee for doing that which he did not set thee about.

William Gurnall

The surest evidence of our love to Christ is obedience to the laws of Christ. Love is the root, obedience is the fruit.

Matthew Henry

God is not otherwise to be enjoyed than as he is obeyed.

John Howe

No man securely commands but he who has learned to obey.

Thomas à Kempis

Every duty, even the least duty, involves the whole principle of obedience. And little duties make the will dutiful, that is supple and prompt to obey. Little obediences lead into great.

Thomas à Kempis

It is so hard to believe because it is so hard to obey.

Søren Kierkegaard

Obedience is the key to every door.

George MacDonald

Obedience means marching right on whether we feel like it or not. Many times we go against our feelings. Faith is one thing, feeling is another.

Dwight Lyman (D.L.) Moody

Justice is the insurance we have on our lives, and obedience is the premium we pay for it.

William Penn

Anyone who obeys Christ by making Christ's submission to God the basis of one's own life will be saved from bondage to Satan and from fear of death.

Mark Searle

Every revelation of God is a demand, and the way to knowledge of God is by obedience.

William Temple

Obstinacy, *see* Stubbornness

Occult

See also Demons; Disobedience; Rebellion

No one shall be found among you who makes a son or daughter pass through fire, or who practices divination, or is a soothsayer, or an auger, or a sorcerer, or one who casts spells, or who consults ghosts or spirits, or who seeks oracles from the dead. For whoever does these things is abhorrent to the LORD.

Deuteronomy 18:10–12 NRSV

Saul died because he was unfaithful to the Lord. . . . [H]e tried to find guidance by consulting the spirits of the dead instead of consulting the Lord. So the Lord killed him and gave control of the kingdom to David son of Jesse.

1 Chronicles 10:13–14 GNB

Many of those who had practiced magic brought their books together and burned them in public.

Acts 19:19 GNB

The acts of the sinful nature are obvious . . . witchcraft . . .

Galatians 5:19–20 NIV

Among you the idols are being abolished. . . . [W]e, calling on the name of Christ crucified, chase away all the demons you fear as gods. Where the sign of the cross occurs, magic loses its power, and sorcery has no effect.

St. Antony of Egypt

To deny the possibility, nay, actual existence, of witchcraft and sorcery, is . . . to contradict the revealed word of God.

Sir William Blackstone

Reject absolutely all divination, fortune-telling, sacrifices to the dead, prophecies in groves or by fountains, amulets, incantations, sorcery (that is wicked enchantments), and all those sacrilegious practices which used to go on in your country.

Gregory III

Old Age

See also Youth

Rise in the presence of gray hairs, give honor to the aged, and fear your God. I am the Lord.

Leviticus 19:32 REB

Cast me not off in the time of old age; forsake me not when my strength faileth.

Psalm 71:9 KJV

The days of our life are seventy years, or perhaps eighty, if we are strong; even then their span is only toil and trouble; they are soon gone, and we fly away.

Psalm 90:10 NRSV

Remember your creator in the days of your youth, before the days of trouble come, and the years draw near when you will say, "I have no pleasure in them"; before the sun and the light and the moon and the stars are darkened and the clouds return with the rain; in the day when the guards of the house tremble, and the strong men are bent, and the women who grind cease working because they are few, and those who look through the windows see dimly; when the doors on the street are shut, and the sound of the grinding is low, and one rises up at the sound of a bird, and all the daughters of song are brought low; when one is afraid of heights, and terrors are in the road; the almond tree blossoms, the grasshopper drags itself along and desire fails; because all must go to their eternal home, and the mourners will go about the streets; before the silver cord is snapped, and the golden bowl is broken, and the pitcher is broken at the fountain, and the wheel broken at the cistern, and the dust returns to the earth as it was, and the breath returns to God who gave it.

Ecclesiastes 12:1–7 NRSV

Grant that she [Sarah] and I [Tobias] may find mercy and that we may grow old together.

Tobit 8:7 NRSV

To know how to grow old is the master work of wisdom and one of the most difficult chapters in the great art of living.

Henri-Frédéric Amiel

Old age comes from God, old age leads on to God, old age will not touch me only so far as He wills.

Pierre Teilhard de Chardin

The years teach much which the days never knew.

Ralph Waldo Emerson

Now that life is almost at an end for us, the light into which we shall enter at our death begins to shine and to show us what are realities and what are not.

Charles de Foucauld

You don't grow old; when you cease to grow, you are old.

Charles Judson Herrick

Winter is on my head, but eternal spring is in my heart.

Victor Hugo

In the evening of our lives we shall be examined in love.

St. John of the Cross

There is a wicked inclination in most people to suppose an old man decayed in his intellects. If a young or middle-aged man, when leaving a company, does not recollect where he laid his hat, it is nothing; but if the same inattention is discovered in an old man, people will shrug up their shoulders, and say, "His memory is going."

Samuel Johnson

The evening of a well spent life brings its lamps with it.

Joseph Joubert

It is better to show up for work in the kingdom of heaven at sunset than not to show up at all!

Erwin W. Lutzer

Age is not all decay; it is the ripening, the swelling of the fresh life within, that withers and bursts the husk.

George MacDonald

Strength has ever to be made perfect in weakness, and old age is one of the weaknesses in which it is perfected.

George MacDonald

In old age faith seems to be the most marvelous possession anyone can have.

Malcolm Muggeridge

Opportunity

See also Choices; Decisions

As we have therefore opportunity, let us do good unto all men, especially unto them who are of the household of faith.

Galatians 6:10 KJV

Be careful, then, how you live—not as unwise but as wise, making the most of every opportunity, because the days are evil.

Ephesians 5:15–16 NIV

Be wise in the way you act towards those who are not believers, making good use of every opportunity you have.

Colossians 4:5 GNB

A wise man will make more opportunities than he finds.

Francis Bacon

Man's extremity is God's opportunity.

John Flavel

To improve the golden moment of opportunity, and catch the good that is within our reach, is the great art of life.

Samuel Johnson

Problems are opportunities in work clothes.

Henry J. Kaiser

When one door of happiness closes, another opens; but often we look so long at the closed door that we do not see the one which has been opened for us.

Helen Adams Keller

Opportunities are usually disguised as hard work, so most people don't recognize them.

Ann Landers

Throughout the whole [New Testament] there runs the conviction that the time looked forward to by the prophets has in fact arrived in history with the advent of Jesus Christ. The time of Jesus is *kairos*—a time of opportunity. To embrace the opportunity means salvation; to neglect it, disaster. There is no third course.

John Marsh

I expect to pass through life but once. If therefore there be any kindness I can show, or any good thing that I can do to any fellow being, let me do it now, and not defer or neglect it, as I shall not pass this way again.

William Penn

Now is the watchword of the wise.

Charles Haddon Spurgeon

We are all faced with a series of great opportunities brilliantly disguised as impossible situations.

Charles R. Swindoll

To recognize opportunity is the difference between success and failure.

Charles R. Swindoll

Oppression

See also Cruelty; Injustice; Persecution; Poverty

Do not mistreat or oppress a foreigner; remember that you were foreigners in Egypt.

Exodus 22:21 GNB

The LORD works vindication and justice for all who are oppressed.

Psalm 103:6 NRSV

Learn to do good; seek justice, rescue the oppressed, defend the orphan, plead for the widow.

Isaiah 1:17 NRSV

He was oppressed and afflicted, yet he did not open his mouth; he was led like a lamb to the slaughter, and as a sheep before her shearers is silent, so he did not open his mouth. By oppression and judgment he was taken away.

Isaiah 53:7–8 NIV

Oppress not the widow, nor the fatherless, the stranger, nor the poor; and let none of you imagine evil against his brother in your heart.

Zechariah 7:10 KJV

God chose the poor people of this world to be rich in faith and to possess the kingdom which he promised to those who love him. But you dishonor the poor! Who are the ones who oppress you and drag you before the judges? The rich! They are the ones who speak evil of that good name which has been given to you.

James 2:5–7 GNB

The oppressed must realize that they are fighting not merely for freedom from hunger, but for . . . freedom to create and to construct, to wonder and to venture.

Paolo Friere

Freedom is never voluntarily given by the oppressor; it must be demanded by the oppressed.

Martin Luther King Jr.

We cannot be free men if this is, by our national choice, to be a land of slavery. Those who deny freedom to others, deserve it not for themselves.

Abraham Lincoln

Poor and oppressed people have faces, and we are required to look squarely into them. We can't love what we won't experience.

Nancy Mairs

Don't put people down—unless it's on your prayer list.

Stan Michalski

So long as people believe in the Yahweh of deliverance, the world will not be safe from Yahweh the conqueror. But perhaps, if they are true to their struggle, people will be able to achieve what Yahweh's chosen people in the past have not: a society of people delivered from oppression who are not so afraid of becoming victims again that they become oppressors themselves.

Robert Allen Warrior

I have learned that assistance given to the weak makes the one who gives it strong; and that oppression of the unfortunate makes one weak.

Booker T. Washington

Christianity assumes her true character . . . when she takes under protection those poor degraded beings on whom philosophy looks down with disdain.

William Wilberforce

Optimism, *see* Hope

Ordination

See also Church, Leaders of

You shall put them [the vestments for the priesthood] on your brother Aaron, and on his sons with him, and shall anoint them and ordain them and consecrate them, so that they may serve me as priests.

Exodus 28:41 NRSV

These men were brought to the apostles. Then the apostles prayed and placed their hands on the men to show that they had been chosen to do this work.

Acts 6:6 CEV

When they had ordained them elders in every church, and had prayed with fasting, they commended them to the Lord.

Acts 14:23 KJV

He cannot have the ordination of the Church who does not hold the unity of the Church.

St. Cyprian

None is a Christian minister who has not been ordained by the laying on of unseen hands.

Richard Glover

A man should only enter the Christian ministry if he cannot stay out of it.

David Martyn Lloyd-Jones

The way appointed by Christ for the calling of any person, fitted and gifted by the Holy Ghost, unto the Office of Pastor, Teacher, or Elder in the Church, is that he be chosen there unto by the common suffrage of the Church itself.

The Savoy Declaration

I cannot recall, in any of my reading, a single instance of a prophet who applied for the job.

Aiden Wilson (A.W.) Tozer

Orthodoxy

See also Heresy; Teachers and Teaching

Now I would remind you brothers and sisters, of the good news that I proclaimed to you, which you in turn received, in which also you stand, through which also you are being saved, if you hold firmly to the message that I proclaimed to you—unless you have come to believe in vain. For I handed on to you as of first importance what I in turn had received: that Christ died for our sins in accordance with the scriptures . . .

1 Corinthians 15:1–3 NRSV

So then, brothers and sisters, stand firm and fast to the traditions that you were taught by us, either by word of mouth, or by our letter.

2 Thessalonians 2:15 NRSV

Hold to the standard of sound teaching that you have heard from me, in the faith and love that you are in Jesus Christ.

2 Timothy 1:13–14 NRSV

We should not conform with human traditions to the extent of setting aside the command of God.

St. Basil the Great

It is not that doing is unimportant. It is rather that right doing springs from right being.

Robert Llewelyn

Any teaching which does not square with the Scriptures is to be rejected even if it shows miracles every day.

Martin Luther

At every point right living begins with right thinking.

Bruce J. Milne

Biblical orthodoxy without compassion is surely the ugliest thing in the world.

Francis August Schaeffer

Pain, *see* Suffering

Paradise

See also Heaven

He [the other criminal] said to Jesus, "Remember me when you come into power!" Jesus replied, "I promise that today you will be with me in paradise."

Luke 23:42–43 CEV

How that he was caught up into paradise, and heard unspeakable words, which it is not lawful for a man to utter.

2 Corinthians 12:4 KJV

To him who overcomes, I will give the right to eat from the tree of life, which is in the paradise of God.

Revelation 2:7 NIV

In our first paradise in Eden there was a way to go out but no way to go in again. But as for the heavenly paradise, there is a way to go in, but no way to go out again.

Richard Baxter

She is an all-pure soul who cannot love the paradise of God, but only the God of paradise.

St. Francis de Sales

One breath of paradise will extinguish all the adverse winds of earth.

Aiden Wilson (A.W.) Pink

Parents and Parenthood

See also Children; Families; Fathers and Fatherhood; Mothers and Motherhood

Hear, my child, your father's instruction, and do not reject your mother's teaching; for they are a fair garland for your head, and pendants for your neck.

Proverbs 1:8–9 NRSV

A wise son maketh a glad father: but a foolish son is the heaviness of his mother.

Proverbs 10:1 KJV

Grandparents are proud of their grandchildren, and children should be proud of their parents.

Proverbs 17:6 CEV

Jesus went back with them to Nazareth, where he was obedient to them. His mother treasured these things in her heart. Jesus grew both in body and in wisdom, gaining favor with God and people.

Luke 2:51–52 GNB

"Honor your father and mother"—this is the first commandment with a promise: "so that it may be well with you and you may live long on the earth."

Ephesians 6:2–3 NRSV

We never know the love of the parent until we become parents ourselves.

Henry Ward Beecher

Thirty years of our Lord's life are hidden in these words of the gospel: "He was subject unto them."

Jacques Bénigne Bossuet

Let every Christian father and mother understand, when their child is three years old, that they have done more than half of all they will ever do for his character.

Horace Bushnell

What we desire our children to become, we must endeavor to be before them.

Andrew Combe

Don't let these parenting years get away from you. Your contributions to your children and grandchildren could rank as your greatest accomplishments in life.

James Dobson

The parent must convince himself that discipline is not something he does to the child; it is something he does for the child.

James Dobson

Ideal parenting is modeled after the relationship between God and man.

James Dobson

Parents have little time for children and a great vacuum has developed and into that vacuum is going to move some kind of ideology.

William Franklin (Billy) Graham

No man or woman ever had a nobler challenge or a higher privilege than to bring up a child for God and whenever we slight that privilege or neglect that ministry for anything else, we live to mourn it in heartache and grief.

Vance Havner

What greater work is there than training the mind and forming the habits of the young?

St. John Chrysostom

Parents generally pay vigilant attention to the type of friends with whom their children associate, but do not exercise a similar vigilance regarding the ideas which the radio, the television, records, papers and comics carry into the "protected" and "safe" intimacy of their homes.

John Paul II

Half the world's sorrows comes from the unwisdom of parents.

Mary Slessor

Do not try to produce an ideal child; it would find no fitness in this world.

Herbert Spencer

Every word and deed of a parent is a fiber woven into the character of a child, which ultimately determines how that child fits into the fabric of society.

David Wilkerson

Children can forgive their parents for being wrong, but weakness sends them elsewhere for strength.

Leontine Young

Past

See also Remembrance

Do not remember against us the iniquities of our ancestors; let your compassion come speedily to meet us, for we are brought very low.

Psalm 79:8 NRSV

Review the past for me, let us argue the matter together; state the case for your innocence.

Isaiah 43:26 NIV

The harvest is past, the summer is ended, and we are not saved.

Jeremiah 8:20 NRSV

I will restore to you the years that the locust hath eaten.

Joel 2:25 KJV

From now on, then, you must live the rest of your earthly lives controlled by God's will and not by human desires. You have spent enough time in the past doing what the heathen like to do.

1 Peter 4:2–3 GNB

There is no past we can bring back by longing for it. There is only an eternal now that builds and creates out of the past something new and better.

Johann Wolfgang von Goethe

The past cannot be changed, but our response to it can be.

Erwin W. Lutzer

In Christ we can move out of our past into a meaningful present and a breathtaking future.

Erwin W. Lutzer

The past cannot be changed; the future is still in your power.

Hugh Lawson White

The past is never completely lost, however extensive the devastation. Your sorrows are the bricks and mortar of a magnificent temple. What you are today and what you will be tomorrow are because of what you have been. Your faith of yesterday is built into your faith today.

Gordon Wright

Pastor, *see* Church, Leaders of

Pastoral Care

See also Caring; Church, Leaders of

The Lord is my shepherd; I shall not want. He maketh me to lie down in green pastures: he leadeth me beside the still waters. He restoreth my soul: he leadeth me in the paths of righteousness for his name's sake. Yea, though I walk through the valley of the shadow of death, I will fear no evil: for thou art with me; thy rod and thy staff they comfort me. Thou preparest a table before me in the presence of mine enemies: thou anointest my head with oil; my cup runneth over. Surely goodness and mercy shall follow me all the days of my life: and I will dwell in the house of the Lord for ever.

Psalm 23:1–6 KJV

Woe to the shepherds of Israel who only take care of themselves! Should not shepherds take care of the flock? You eat the curds, clothe yourselves with the wool and slaughter the choice animals, but you do not take care of the flock. You have not strengthened the weak or healed the sick or bound up the injured. You have not brought back the strays or searched for the lost. You have ruled them harshly and brutally.

Ezekiel 34:2–4 NIV

He [Jesus] saith unto him [Simon Peter], Feed my lambs.

John 21:15 KJV

Brothers, if someone is caught in a sin, you who are spiritual should restore him gently. But watch yourself, or you may also be tempted.

Galatians 6:1 NIV

But we were gentle among you, even as a nurse cherisheth her children.

1 Thessalonians 2:7 KJV

As you know, we treated every one of you as a father treats his children, urging you, encouraging you and appealing to you to live a life worthy of God, who calls you into his kingdom and his glory.

1 Thessalonians 2:11–12 NJB

This is how we can faithfully serve the Lord: we should in an orderly manner elect and install ministers from every level of society. The aim is to have those who are trusted and loved by all, who are also gifted and zealous for this ministry and for true pastoral care. . . . That way the five tasks of pastoral care will be performed: to seek and to find all the lost; to bring back those that are scattered; to heal the wounded; to strengthen the sickly; to protect the healthy and to put them to pasture.

Martin Bucer

Like a farmer tending a sound tree, untouched by ax or fire because of its fruit, I want not only to serve you good people in the body, but also to give my life for your well-being.

St. Eusebius of Vercelli

When a Christian minister becomes primarily a moralist he is creating insuperable difficulties in the way of pastoral dialogue. He remains a religious man, but he has ceased to be a Christian.

Frank Lake

Pastoring is finding out where somebody is in the process of Christian maturity, and leading them to the next phase.

John Richard Wimber

Patience

See also Diligence; Endurance; Waiting

Be still before the LORD, and wait patiently for him; do not fret over those who prosper in their way, over those who carry out evil devices.

Psalm 37:7 NRSV

Let your hope keep you joyful, be patient in your troubles, and pray at all times.

Romans 12:12 GNB

The fruit of the Spirit is . . . patience.

Galatians 5:22 NIV

My friends, be patient until the Lord returns. Think of farmers who wait patiently for the spring and summer rains to make their valuable crops grow. Be patient like those farmers and don't give up. The Lord will soon be here!

James 5:7–8 CEV

Patience is the companion of wisdom.

St. Augustine of Hippo

Patience means waiting without anxiety.

St. Francis de Sales

Be patient with everyone, but above all with yourself. I mean, do not be disturbed because of your imperfections, and always rise up bravely from a fall.

St. Francis de Sales

Be patient toward all that is unsolved in your heart.

Dag Hammarskjöld

Though God take the sun out of heaven, yet we must have patience.

George Herbert

At the least bear patiently, if thou canst not joyfully.

Thomas à Kempis

He who possesses patience, possesses himself.

Raymond Lull

Teach us, O Lord, the disciplines of patience, for to wait is often harder than to work.

Peter Marshall

Patience and diligence, like faith, remove mountains.

William Penn

To climb steep hills / Requires slow pace at first.

William Shakespeare

On every level of life from housework to heights of prayer, in all judgment and all efforts to get things done, hurry and impatience are sure marks of an amateur.

Evelyn Underhill

Patience with ourselves is duty for Christians and the only humility. For it means patience with a growing creature who God has taken in hand and whose completion he will effect in his own time and way.

Evelyn Underhill

Paul

Are they Hebrews? so am I. Are they Israelites? so am I. Are they the seed of Abraham? so am I. Are they ministers of Christ? (I speak as a fool) I am more; in labors more abundant, in stripes above measure, in prisons more frequent, in death oft. Of the Jews five times received I forty stripes save one. Thrice was I beaten with rods, once was I stoned, thrice I suffered shipwreck, a night and a day I have been in the deep; In journeyings often, in perils of waters, in perils of robbers, in perils by mine own countrymen, in perils by the heathen, in perils in the city, in perils in the wilderness, in perils in the sea, in perils among false brethren; In weariness and painfulness, in watchings often, in hunger and thirst, in fastings often, in cold and nakedness. Beside those things that are without, that which cometh upon me daily, the care of all the churches.

2 Corinthians 11:22–28 KJV

Bear in mind that our Lord's patience means salvation, just as our dear brother Paul also wrote to you with the wisdom that God gave him. He writes the same way in all his letters, speaking in them of these matters. His letters contain some things that are hard to understand, which ignorant and unstable people distort, as they do the other Scriptures, to their own destruction.

2 Peter 3:15–16 NIV

Because of what he grasped and taught, the church passed the frontiers of Palestine and left Judaism behind. Because of what he did, the church survived the collapse of Rome and lived on through the dark ages. Because of what he experienced and movingly told and courageously argued out, the revelation that he had in Christ was translated, expounded, and established as a world faith.

Anon.

The epistles of Paul show us the elder brother of the parable, broken down by the Father's love, now leaving home and its secure delights to go out into far countries— Cyprus, Pisidia, Macedonia, Greece, Rome— to seek out those brothers who still lingered among the husks and the swine.

Charles Harold (C.H.) Dodd

Paul thunders, and lightens, and speaks sheer flame.

Desiderius Erasmus

Paul's preaching usually ended in a riot or in a revival.

Orin Philip Gifford

An exceptional man, the maker of an epoch.

Terrot Reaveley (T.R.) Glover

A man of little stature, thin-haired upon the head, crooked in the legs, of good state of body, with eyebrows joining and a nose somewhat crooked; full of grace, for sometimes he appeared like a man, and sometimes had the face of an angel.

Paul and Thecla

Peace

Between People and Nations

Pray for the peace of Jerusalem: they shall prosper that love thee.

Psalm 122:6 KJV

The wolf also shall dwell with the lamb, and the leopard shall lie down with the kid; and the calf and the young lion and the fatling together; and a little child shall lead them.

Isaiah 11:6 KJV

Blessed are the peacemakers: they shall be recognized as children of God.

Matthew 5:9 NJB

Don't think that I came to bring peace to the earth! I came to bring trouble, not peace.

Matthew 10:34 CEV

If it is possible, so far as it depends on you, live peaceably with all.

Romans 12:18 NRSV

For he is himself our peace. Gentiles and Jews, he has made the two one, and in his own body of flesh and blood has broken down the barrier of enmity which separated them; for he annulled the law with its rules and regulations, so as to create out of the two a single new humanity in himself, thereby making peace. This was his purpose, to reconcile the two in a single body to God through the cross, by which he killed the enmity. So he came and proclaimed the good news: peace to you who were far off, and peace to those who were near; for through him we both alike have access to the Father in the one Spirit.

Ephesians 2:14–18 REB

A harvest of righteousness is sown in peace for those who make peace.

James 3:18 NRSV

O God of many names / Lover of all nations / We pray for peace / In our hearts / In our homes / In our nations / In our world. / The peace of your will / The peace of our need.

George Appleton

Give peace in our time, O Lord.

Book of Common Prayer

If we will have peace without a worm in it, lay we the foundations of justice and good will.

Oliver Cromwell

Lord, make me an instrument of your peace. Where there is hatred, let me sow love. Where there is injury, pardon. Where there is discord, vision. Where there is doubt, faith. Where there is despair, hope. Where there is darkness, light. Where there is sadness, joy.

St. Francis of Assisi

Peace is not made at the council tables, or by treaties, but in the hearts of men.

Herbert Hoover

Only a world that is truly human can be a world that is peaceful and strong.

John Paul II

All men desire peace, but very few desire those things that make for peace.

Thomas à Kempis

First keep yourself in peace, and then you will be able to pacify others. A peaceable man does more good than a learned one.

Thomas à Kempis

The springs of human conflict cannot be eradicated through institutions, but only through the reform of the individual human being.

Douglas MacArthur

In God alone can man meet man.

George MacDonald

Where people are praying for peace the cause of peace is being strengthened by their very act of prayer, for they are themselves becoming immersed in the spirit of peace.

John Macquarrie

If we wish to have true peace, we must give it a soul. The soul of peace is love, which for us believers comes from the love of God and expresses itself in love for men.

Paul VI

Reconciliation is not weakness or cowardice. It demands courage, mobility, generosity, sometimes heroism, an overcoming of oneself rather than of one's adversary.

Paul VI

Of Mind

See also Acceptance; Contentment

Peace I leave with you, my peace I give unto you: not as the world giveth, give I unto you. Let not your heart be troubled, neither let it be afraid.

John 14:27 KJV

To set the mind on the flesh is death, but to set the mind on the Spirit is life and peace.

Romans 8:6 NRSV

The peace of God, which transcends all understanding, will guard your hearts and your minds in Christ Jesus.

Philippians 4:7 NIV

Peace rules the day when Christ rules the mind.

Anon.

Order your soul; reduce your wants; live in charity; associate in Christian community; obey the laws; trust in Providence.

St. Augustine of Hippo

If the basis of peace is God, the secret of peace is trust.

J.N. Figgis

Great tranquility of heart is his who cares for neither praise not blame.

Thomas à Kempis

My son, now will I teach thee the way of peace and inward liberty. Be desirous to do the will of another rather than thine own. Choose always to have less rather than more. Seek always the lowest place and to be inferior to everyone. Wish always, and pray, that the will of God may be wholly fulfilled in thee.

Thomas à Kempis

Dale Carnegie knew the techniques for "positive thinking" and "self confidence." He could even teach people to overcome worry with his techniques, but in the end, peace eluded him and he committed suicide. In a world filled with causes for worry and anxiety, we need something tougher than "positive thinking" or even "possibility thinking." We need the peace of God standing guard over our hearts and minds.

Jerry W. McCant

When peace, like a river, attendeth my way, / When sorrows, like sea-billows, roll, / Whatever my lot, Thou hast taught me to say, / It is well, it is well with my soul.

Horatio Gates Spafford

"Seek ye first the rule of God," the Master says. And after that? The key that one needs for one's peace is in the heart. There can be no personal freedom where there is not an initial personal surrender.

Howard Thurman

Forgiving those who hurt us is the key to personal peace.

G. Weatherley

Peace comes not by establishing a calm outward setting so much as by inwardly surrendering to whatever the setting.

Hubert van Zeller

With God

Thou wilt keep him in perfect peace, whose mind is stayed on thee: because he trusteth in thee.

Isaiah 26:3 KJV

Therefore, since we are justified by faith, we have peace with God through our Lord Jesus Christ.

Romans 5:1 NRSV

The fruit of the Spirit is . . . peace.

Galatians 5:22 NIV

O God, from whom all holy desires, all good counsels, and all just works do proceed: Give unto thy servants that peace which the world cannot give.

Book of Common Prayer

The peace of God, which passeth all understanding, keep your hearts and minds in the knowledge and love of God, and of his Son Jesus Christ our Lord: And the blessing of God Almighty, the Father, the Son, and the Holy Ghost, be amongst you and remain with you always.

Book of Common Prayer

O my God, Trinity whom I adore, let me entirely forget myself that I may abide in you, still and peaceful as if my soul were already in eternity; let nothing disturb my peace nor separate me from you, O my unchanging God, but that each moment may take me further into the depths of your mystery.

Elizabeth of the Trinity

Peace is not arbitrary. It must be based upon definite facts. God has all the facts on his side; the world does not. Therefore God, and not the world, can give peace.

William Franklin (Billy) Graham

What peace can they have who are not at peace with God?

Matthew Henry

There may be those on earth who dress better or eat better, but those who enjoy the peace of God sleep better.

L. Thomas Holdcroft

Always long and pray that the will of God may be fully realized in your life. You will find that the man who does this walks in the land of peace and quietness.

Thomas à Kempis

Peace does not mean the end of all our striving. / Joy does not mean the drying of our tears; / Peace is the power that comes to souls arriving / Up to the light where God Himself appears.

G.A. Studdert Kennedy

Emotional peace and calm come after doing God's will and not before.

Erwin W. Lutzer

A great many people are trying to make peace, but that has already been done. God has not left it for us to do; all we have to do is to enter into it.

Dwight Lyman (D.L.) Moody

Finding God, you have no need to seek peace, for he himself is your peace.

Frances J. Roberts

Where there is peace, God is.

Walt Whitman

Drop Thy still dews of quietness / Till all our strivings cease; / Take from our souls the strain and stress, / And let our ordered lives confess / The beauty of Thy peace.

John Greenleaf Whittier

Penitence, *see* Repentance

Pentecost

See also Holy Spirit, Power of

And it shall come to pass afterward, that I will pour out my spirit upon all flesh; and your sons and your daughters shall prophesy, your old men shall dream dreams, your young men shall see visions: And also upon the servants and upon the handmaids in those days will I pour out my spirit.

Joel 2:28–29 KJV

When the day of Pentecost came, all the believers were gathered together in one place. Suddenly there was a noise from the sky which sounded like a strong wind blowing, and it filled the whole house where they were sitting. Then they saw what looked like tongues of fire which spread out and touched each person there. They were all filled with the Holy Spirit and began to talk in other languages, as the Spirit enabled them to speak.

Acts 2:1–4 GNB

The question on Pentecost is not whether God is blessing our own plans and programs but whether we are open to the great opportunities to which his Spirit calls us.

Corrie ten Boom

To the Church, Pentecost brought light, power, joy. There came to each illumination of mind, assurance of heart, intensity of love, fullness of power, exuberance of joy. No one needed to ask if they had received the Holy Ghost. Fire is self-evident. So is power!

Samuel Chadwick

Before Pentecost the disciples found it hard to do easy things; after Pentecost they found it easy to do hard things.

Adoniram Judson (A.J.) Gordon

The coming of the Holy Spirit at Pentecost was an advent similar in nature and nearly, if not equally, as important as Christ's coming to earth.

Maurice R. Irvin

If Pentecost is not repeated neither is it retracted. . . . This is the era of the Holy Spirit.

John Murray

Before Christ sent the church into the world, he sent the Spirit into the church. The same order must be observed today.

John R.W. Stott

In one sense, Pentecost can never happen again. In another sense, it may always be happening, since we live in the age of the Spirit.

Arthur Skevington Wood

Perfection

See also Jesus Christ, Perfection of

The law of the LORD is perfect, reviving the soul.

Psalm 19:7 NRSV

Be perfect, therefore, as your heavenly Father is perfect.

Matthew 5:48 NIV

By virtue of that one single offering, he has achieved the eternal perfection of all who are sanctified.

Hebrews 10:14 NJB

If thou shouldst say, "It is enough I have reached perfection," all is lost, since it is the function of perfection to make one know one's imperfections.

St. Augustine of Hippo

Good family, athletic prowess, a handsome face, tall stature, the esteem of others, control over others—none of these are important to us or fit matter for our prayers; we do not pay court to those who can boast of them. Our ideals are far higher than that.

St. Basil the Great

No man can advance three paces on the road to perfection unless Jesus Christ walks beside him.

Robert Hugh Benson

The Bible holds up before us ideals that are within sight of the weakest and the lowliest, and yet so high that the best and the noblest are kept with their faces turned ever upward.

William Jennings Bryan

If we put an absurdly high ideal before us, it ceases to be an ideal at all, because we have no idea of acting upon it.

Frederick William Faber

It is only imperfection that complains of what is imperfect. The more perfect we are, the more gentle and quiet we become toward the defects of others.

François de la Mothe Fénelon

Did Christ finish his work for us? Then there can be no doubt but he will also finish his work in us.

John Flavel

We must not be disturbed at our imperfections, since for us perfection consists in fighting against them.

St. Francis de Sales

True perfection consists . . . in having but one fear, the loss of God's friendship.

St. Gregory of Nyssa

That soul is perfect which is guided habitually by the instinct of the Holy Spirit.

Isaac Thomas Hecker

We shall never come to the perfect man till we come to the perfect world.

Matthew Henry

Rightfulness has two qualities; it is right, and it is full. Such are all the works of God. They lack neither mercy nor grace, for they are altogether right, and nothing is lacking in them.

Julian of Norwich

Give yourself to God without reserve; in singleness of heart, meeting everything that every day brings forth, as something that comes from God, and is to be received and gone through by you, in such a heavenly use of occurrences. This is an attainable degree of perfection.

William Law

God demands perfection from his creatures, but if they will ever have it, he himself must supply it. We need not be concerned about how high God's standard is, as long as he meets it for us.

Erwin W. Lutzer

It is right to be contented with what we have but never with what we are.

Sir James Mackintosh

Ideals are like the stars—we never reach them, but like the mariners of the sea we chart our course by them.

Carl Schurz

Perfection is being, not doing; it is not to effect an act but to achieve a character.

Fulton John Sheen

Perfection never exists apart from imperfection, just as good health cannot exist without our feeling effort, fatigue, hunger or thirst, heat or cold; yet none of those prevent the enjoyment of good health.

Henri de Tourville

Christian perfection is loving God with all our heart, mind, soul, and strength. This implies that no wrong frame of mind, nothing contrary to love, remains in the soul; and that all the thoughts, words, and actions, are governed by pure love.

John Wesley

The Christian ideal . . . is not that of a number of "integrated" individuals, concerned about their own spiritual progress, but of growth into Christ, as members of the Body of Christ, in which we all live by the same Life, which flows through the Body and animates us all.

Olive Wyon

Persecution

See also Martyrs and Martyrdom; Oppression

Blessed are they which are persecuted for righteousness' sake: for theirs is the kingdom of heaven. Blessed are ye, when men shall revile you, and persecute you, and shall say all manner of evil against you falsely, for my sake. Rejoice, and be exceed-

ing glad: for great is your reward in heaven: for so persecuted they the prophets which were before you.

Matthew 5:10–12 KJV

Bless your persecutors; never curse them, bless them.

Romans 12:14 NJB

All who want to live a godly life in Christ Jesus will be persecuted.

2 Timothy 3:12 NRSV

It much more concerned us, to be sure that we deserved not suffering, than that we be delivered from it.

Richard Baxter

Prosperity has often been fatal to Christianity, but persecution never.

Amish Bishop

Opposition may become sweet to a man when he has christened it persecution.

George Eliot

Persecution is one of the surest signs of the genuineness of our Christianity.

Benjamin E. Fernando

Crushing the Church is like smashing the atom: divine energy of high quality is released in enormous quantity and with miraculous effects.

Benjamin E. Fernando

Christ's followers cannot expect better treatment in the world than their Master had.

Matthew Henry

It is preferable to have the whole world against thee, than Jesus offended with thee.

Thomas à Kempis

If you were not strangers here the dogs of the world would not bark at you.

Samuel Rutherford

Progress toward the welfare of mankind is made not by the persecutors but by the persecuted . . . Only goodness, meeting evil and not infected by it, conquers evil.

Count Leo Tolstoy

Perseverance

See also Endurance

Everyone will hate you because of me. But whoever holds out to the end will be saved.

Mark 13:13 GNB

We also rejoice in our sufferings, because we know that suffering produces perseverance; perseverance, character; and character, hope.

Romans 5:3–4 NIV

Let us run with perseverance the race that is set before us.

Hebrews 12:1 NRSV

The testing of your faith produces perseverance, and perseverance must complete its work so that you will become fully developed, complete, not deficient in any way.

James 1:3–4 NJB

We are undefeated as long as we keep on trying, as long as we have some source of movement within ourselves and are not just moved by outside forces, as long as we retain the freedom of right decision and action, whatever the circumstances.

George Appleton

Genius, that power that dazzles mortal eyes, / Is oft but perseverance in disguise.

Henry Austin

When a train goes through a tunnel and it gets dark, you don't throw away your ticket and jump off. You sit still and trust the engineer.

Corrie ten Boom

Every noble work is at first impossible.

Thomas Carlyle

He that perseveres makes every difficulty an advancement and every contest a victory.

Charles Caleb Colton

There must be a beginning of any great matter, but the continuing unto the end until it be thoroughly finished yields the true glory.

Francis Drake

A tree is shown by its fruits, and in the same way those who profess to belong to Christ will be seen by what they do. For what is needed is not mere present professions, but perseverance to the end in the power of faith.

St. Ignatius of Antioch

Great works are performed not by strength but by perseverance.

Samuel Johnson

The perseverance of the saints is only possible because of the perseverance of God.

J. Oswald Sanders

The will to perseverance is often the difference between failure and success.

David Sarnoff

By perseverance the snail reached the ark.

Charles Haddon Spurgeon

No one is wise, no one is faithful, no one excels in dignity, but the Christian: and no one is a Christian but he who perseveres even to the end.

Quintus Tertullian

Pessimism, *see* Despair

Petition, *see* Prayer, Petition

Pilgrimage

See also Journeys

Blessed are those whose strength is in you, who have set their hearts on pilgrimage.

Psalm 84:5 NIV

I will rejoice over the creation of the righteous, over their pilgrimage also, and their salvation, and their receiving their reward.

2 Esdras 8:39 RSV

These all died in faith, not having received the promises, but have seen them afar off, and were persuaded of them, and embraced them, and confessed that they were strangers and pilgrims on the earth.

Hebrews 11:13 KJV

When you walk with God, you get where he's going.

Anon.

The strength of a man consists in finding out which way God is going, and going that way too.

Henry Ward Beecher

In the spiritual journey we travel through the night toward the day. We walk not in the bright sunshine of total certainty but through the darkness of ignorance, error, muddle and uncertainty. We make progress in the journey as we grow in faith.

Christopher Bryant

He who would valiant be / 'Gainst all disaster, / Let him in constancy / Follow the Master. / There's no discouragement / Shall make

him once relent / His first avowed intent / To be a pilgrim.

John Bunyan

He who believes himself to be far advanced in the spiritual life has not even made a good beginning.

Bishop Jean Pierre Camus

The pilgrim who spends all his time counting his steps will make little progress.

Bishop Jean Pierre Camus

This world nis but a thurghfare ful of wo, / And we ben pilgrimes, passinge to and fro; / Deeth is an ende of every worldly sore.

Geoffrey Chaucer

God counseled Abraham to leave his own country and go in pilgrimage into the land which God has shown him, that is, the "Land of Promise." . . . Now the good counsel which God enjoined here on the father of the faithful is incumbent on all the faithful, that is, to leave their country and their land, their wealth and their worldly delight, for the sake of the Lord of the elements, and go in perfect pilgrimage in imitation of him.

St. Columba

The road is long and hard and difficult. Never be afraid. You won't be if you understand where you are and why you are there.

Catherine de Heuck Doherty

Every man has two journeys to make through life. There is the outer journey, with its various incidents and the milestones. . . . There is also an inner journey, a spiritual Odyssey, with a secret history of its own.

William Ralph Inge

We should be low and lovelike and lean each

man to the other. And patient as pilgrims, for pilgrims are we all.

William Langland

Our Father refreshes us on the journey with some pleasant inns but will not encourage us to mistake them for home.

Clive Staples (C.S.) Lewis

Long is the way / And hard, that out of hell leads up to light.

John Milton

Guide me, O Thou great Jehovah, / Pilgrim through this barren land; / I am weak, but Thou art mighty, / Hold me with Thy powerful hand; / Bread of heaven, / Feed me now and evermore.

William Williams

Pity

See also Compassion

He has pity on the weak and the needy, and saves the lives of the needy.

Psalm 72:13 NRSV

He that hath pity upon the poor lendeth unto the Lord.

Proverbs 19:17 KJV

Jesus got out of the boat, and when he saw the large crowd, his heart was filled with pity for them, and he healed their sick.

Matthew 14:14 GNB

Jesus felt pity for them [two blind men] and touched their eyes, and at once their sight returned and they followed him.

Matthew 20:34 NJB

A Samaritan, as he traveled, came where the

man was; and when he saw him, he took pity on him.

Luke 10:33 NIV

When a man suffers himself, it is called misery; when he suffers in the suffering of another, it is called pity.

St. Augustine of Hippo

Justice seeks out the merits of the case, but pity only regards the need.

St. Bernard of Clairvaux

More helpful than all wisdom is one draught of simple human pity that will not forsake us.

George Eliot

He that pities another remembers himself.

George Herbert

Pleasure

See also Happiness; Joy

You show me the path of life. In your presence there is fullness of joy; in your right hand are pleasures forevermore.

Psalm 16:11 NRSV

He that loveth pleasure shall be a poor man: he that loveth wine and oil shall not be rich.

Proverbs 21:17 KJV

The seeds that fell among the thornbushes are also people who hear the message. But they are so eager for riches and pleasures that they never produce anything.

Luke 8:14 CEV

For people [in the last days] will be . . . lovers of pleasure rather than lovers of God.

2 Timothy 3:2, 4 NRSV

Nothing can permanently please, which does not contain in itself the reason why it is so, and not otherwise.

Samuel Taylor Coleridge

Pleasure is very seldom found where it is sought; our brightest blazes of gladness are commonly kindled by unexpected sparks.

Samuel Johnson

The greatest pleasure I know is to do a good action by stealth and to have it found out by accident.

Charles Lamb

Pleasure-seeking is a barren business; happiness is never found till we have the grace to stop looking for it, and to give our attention to persons and matters external to ourselves.

James Innell (J.I.) Packer

We tire of those pleasures we take, but never of those we give.

John Petit-Senn

The only path to pleasure is in pleasing God.

Richard Owen Roberts

Soft pleasures harden the heart.

Thomas Watson

Leisure and I have parted company. I am resolved to be busy till I die.

John Wesley

We never better enjoy ourselves than when we most enjoy God.

Benjamin Whichcote

Politics, *see* Government and Politics

Pollution, *see* Environment

Possessions

See also Money; Wealth

When God gives any man wealth and possessions, and enables him to enjoy them, to accept his lot and be happy in his work—this is a gift of God.

Ecclesiastes 5:19 NIV

Take care! Be on your guard against all kinds of greed; for one's life does not consist in the abundance of possessions.

Luke 12:15 NRSV

Sell your possessions and give to those in need. Get yourselves purses that do not wear out, treasure that will not fail you, in heaven where no thief can reach it and no moth destroy it.

Luke 12:33 NJB

For we brought nothing into this world, and it is certain we can carry nothing out.

1 Timothy 6:7 KJV

If we have God in all things while they are ours, we shall have all things in God when they are taken away.

Anon.

Theirs is an endless road, a hopeless maze, who seek for goods before they seek for God.

St. Bernard of Clairvaux

A man there was, though some did count him mad; the more he cast away the more he had.

John Bunyan

It is not the fact that a man has riches which keeps him from the kingdom of heaven, but the fact that riches have him.

John Caird

It is easier to renounce worldly possessions than it is to renounce the love of them.

Walter Hilton

Lives based on having are less free than lives based either on doing or on being.

William James

Material abundance without character is the surest way to destruction.

Thomas Jefferson

Riches are not forbidden, but the pride of them is.

St. John Chrysostom

I will place no value on anything I have or may possess, except in relation to the kingdom of Christ.

David Livingstone

Nobody can fight properly and boldly for the faith if he clings to fear of being stripped of earthly possessions.

St. Peter Damian

Be sure, as long as worldly fancies you pursue, you are a hollow man—a pauper lives in you.

Angelus Silesius

So we, who are united in mind and soul, have no hesitation about sharing property. All is common among us—except our wives.

Quintus Tertullian

Poverty

See also Hunger and Thirst; Wealth

If there be among you a poor man of one of thy brethren within any of thy gates in thy land which the Lord thy God giveth thee, thou shalt not harden thine heart, nor shut thine hand from thy poor brother.

Deuteronomy 15:7 KJV

Those who oppress the poor insult their Maker, but those who are kind to the needy honor him.

Proverbs 14:31 NRSV

Blessed are the poor in spirit: for theirs is the kingdom of heaven.

Matthew 5:3 KJV

You will always have the poor with you, but you won't always have me.

Matthew 26:11 CEV

Poverty is the load of some, and wealth is the load of others, perhaps the great load of the two. Bear the load of your neighbor's poverty, and let him bear with you the load of your wealth. You lighten your load by lightening his.

St. Augustine of Hippo

The man who is poor in spirit is the man who has realized that things mean nothing, and that God means everything.

William Barclay

No man should praise poverty but he who is poor.

St. Bernard of Clairvaux

He who wants anything from God must approach him with empty hands.

Robert C. Cunningham

The greatest of men must turn beggars when they have to do with Christ.

Matthew Henry

The worst poverty today is the poverty of not having spiritual values in life.

George Basil Hume

He is rich enough who is poor with Christ.

St. Jerome

World poverty is a hundred million mothers weeping . . . because they cannot feed their children.

Ronald J. Sider

Many a man becomes empty-handed because he does not know the art of distribution.

Charles Haddon Spurgeon

We choose to be poor for love of God. In the service of the poorest of the poor, we are feeding the hungry Christ, clothing the naked Christ, taking care of the sick Christ, and giving shelter to the homeless Christ.

Mother Teresa

The poor come to all of us in many forms. Let us be sure that we never turn our backs on them, wherever we may find them. For when we turn our backs on the poor, we turn them on Jesus Christ.

Mother Teresa

God does not dwell in a heart that's confined, / And a heart is only as big as the love that it holds: / In the great heart of Poverty / God has room to dwell.

Jacapone da Todi

The poor man, rich in faith, who toils for the love of God and is generous of the little fruit of his labors, is much nearer to Heaven than the rich man who spends a fortune in goods and works from no higher motive than his natural inclination to benevolence.

William Bernard Ullathorne

I am mended by my sickness, enriched by my poverty, and strengthened by my weakness.

Abraham Wright

Power

See also Authority; Holy Spirit, Power of; Weakness

But to all who received him, who believed in his name, he gave power to become children of God.

John 1:12 NRSV

I see no reason to be ashamed of the gospel; it is God's power for the salvation of everyone who has faith—Jews first, but Greeks as well.

Romans 1:16 NJB

We have this treasure in clay jars, so that it may be made clear that this extraordinary power belongs to God and does not come from us.

2 Corinthians 4:7 NRSV

How very great is his power at work in us who believe. This power working in us is the same as the mighty strength which he used when he raised Christ from death and seated him at his right side in the heavenly world.

Ephesians 1:19–20 GNB

Now to him who is able to do immeasurably more than all we ask or imagine, according to his power that is at work within us, to him be glory in the church and in Christ Jesus throughout all generations, for ever and ever! Amen.

Ephesians 3:20–21 NIV

I can do all things through Christ which strengtheneth me.

Philippians 4:13 KJV

Power tends to corrupt, and absolute power corrupts absolutely.

John Acton

When God is our strength, it is strength indeed; when our strength is our own, it is only weakness.

St. Augustine of Hippo

Biblically speaking, healing is never accomplished by the powerful, but those in command. Indeed the Bible underscores the illness of wrong power, the spirit of control, of ego run amok.

Daniel Berrigan

Nearness to Christ, intimacy with him, assimilation to his character—these are the elements of a ministry of power.

Horatius Bonar

The greatness of a man's power is the measure of his surrender.

William Booth

We are the wire, God is the current. Our only power is to let the current pass through us.

Carlo Carretto

There is one source of power that is stronger than every disappointment, bitterness, or ingrained mistrust, and that power is Jesus Christ, who brought forgiveness and reconciliation to the world.

John Paul II

You become stronger only when you become weaker. When you surrender your will to God, you discover the resources to do what God requires.

Erwin W. Lutzer

When a man has no strength, if he leans on God, he becomes powerful.

Dwight Lyman (D.L.) Moody

When God wants to move a mountain, he does not take a bar of iron, but he takes a little worm. The fact is, we have too much strength. We are not weak enough. It is not our strength that we want. One drop of God's strength is worth more than all the world.

Dwight Lyman (D.L.) Moody

The same power that brought Christ back from the dead is operative within those who are Christ's. The resurrection is an ongoing thing.

Leon Lamb Morris

The silent power of a consistent life.

Florence Nightingale

What makes the temptation of power so seemingly irresistible? Maybe it's that power offers an easy substitute for the hard task of love. It seems easier to be God than to love God, easier to control people than to love people, easier to own life than to love life.

Henri J.M. Nouwen

It is the combination of power and love which Christians call the spirit . . . which empowers us to shape our common future for the good of all.

Anne Primavesi

We live by our Lord's own power; but we can only live by His power in proportion as we give ourselves to be in His crucifixion.

Gilbert Shaw

The power of God's reign is not exhibitionistic. It is self-effacing, self-concealing. That power, like the leaves buried inside the mass of dough, is a fermentative power in the depth of humanity, in the womb of God's creation. It is the power of compassion. It is the power of the cross.

Choan-Seng Song

Praise

See also Doxologies; Prayer, Adoration; Thankfulness and Thanksgiving; Worship

Then Moses and the Israelites sang this song to the LORD: "I will sing to the LORD, for he has triumphed gloriously; horse and rider he has thrown into the sea. The LORD is my strength and my might, and he has become my salvation; this is my God, and I will praise him, my father's God, and I will exalt him."

Exodus 15:1–2 NRSV

He is thy praise, and he is thy God, that hath done for thee these great and terrible things, which thine eyes have seen.

Deuteronomy 10:21 KJV

Sing unto the Lord a new song: sing praises lustily unto him with a good courage.

Psalm 33:3 BCP

I will bless the LORD at all times; his praise shall continually be in my mouth.

Psalm 34:1 NRSV

Shout for joy to the Lord, all the earth. Worship the Lord with gladness; come before him with joyful songs. Know that the Lord is God. It is he who made us, and we are his; we are his people, the sheep of his pasture. Enter his gates with thanksgiving and his courts with praise; give thanks to him and praise his name.

Psalm 100:1–4 NIV

Let us now praise famous men, our fathers in their generations.

Ecclesiasticus 44:1 RSV

By him therefore let us offer the sacrifice of praise to God continually, that is, the fruit of our lips giving thanks to his name.

Hebrews 13:15 KJV

After this I heard what sounded like the roar of a large crowd of people in heaven, saying, "Praise God! Salvation, glory, and power belong to our God! True and just are his judgments!" . . . Again they shouted, "Praise God!" . . . The twenty–four elders and the four living creatures fell down and worshipped God, who was seated on the throne. They said, "Amen, Praise God!"

Revelation 19:1–4 GNB

You awaken us to delight in your praise; for you have made us for yourself, and our hearts are restless until they find their rest in you.

St. Augustine of Hippo

Fill Thou my life, O Lord my God, / In every part with praise, / That my whole being may proclaim / Thy being and Thy ways.

Horatius Bonar

Men in general praise God in such a manner that he scarcely obtains the tenth part of his due.

John Calvin

To the ear of God everything he created makes exquisite music, and man joined in the paean of praise until he fell, then there came in the frantic discord of sin. The realization of redemption brings man by way of the minor note of repentance back into tune with praise again.

Oswald Chambers

Be not afraid of saying too much in the praises of God; all the danger is of saying too little.

Matthew Henry

You don't learn to praise in a day, especially since you may have been complaining for years! New habits take time to develop. But you can begin today, and practice tomorrow, and the next day, until it becomes part of you.

Erwin W. Lutzer

Praise, my soul, the King of Heaven, / To His feet thy tribute bring.

Henry Francis Lyte

He who does not praise God while here on earth shall in eternity be dumb.

Jan van Ruysbroeck

Prayer

See also Jesus Christ, Prayers of; Meditation and Contemplation; Spiritual Warfare

Adoration

See also Adoration

Thou, even thou, art Lord alone; thou hast made heaven, the heaven of heavens, with all their host, the earth, and all things that are therein, the seas, and all that is therein, and thou preservest them all; and the host of heaven worshippeth thee. Thou art the Lord.

Nehemiah 9:6–7 KJV

I had said in my alarm, "I am driven far from your sight." But you heard my supplications when I cried out to you for help. Love the LORD, all you his saints.

Psalm 31:22–23 NRSV

I love the Lord, for he has heard me and listened to my prayer.

Psalm 116:1 REB

Remember, O Lord; make thyself known in this time of our affliction, and give me courage, O King of the gods and Master of all dominion!

Additions to Esther 14:12 RSV

Day and night without ceasing they [the four living creatures] sing, "Holy, holy, holy, the Lord God Almighty, who was and is and is to come." And whenever the living creatures give glory and honor and thanks to the one who is seated on the throne, who lives forever and ever, the twenty-four elders fall before the one who is seated on the throne and worship the one who lives forever and ever; they cast their crowns before the throne, singing, "You are worthy, our Lord and God, to receive glory and honor and power, for you created all things and by your will they existed and were created."

Revelation 4:8–11 NRSV

Therefore with Angels, and Archangels, and with all the company of heaven, we laud and magnify thy glorious Name; evermore praising thee, and saying: Holy, holy, holy, Lord God of hosts, heaven and earth are full of thy glory: Glory be to thee, O Lord most High. Amen.

Book of Common Prayer

Glory be to the Father, and to the Son: and to the Holy Ghost.

Book of Common Prayer

Adoration is the highest form of prayer.

Louis Cassels

You are not drawn to God primarily for your own benefit but for his.

Gonville ffrench-Beytagh

If you love God you cannot be at a loss for something to say to him, something for your heart to pour out before him, which his grace has already put there.

Matthew Henry

No one can say his prayers are poor prayers when he is using the language of love.

John Maillard

In prayer . . . the perfections of God, and especially his mercies in our redemption, should occupy our thoughts as much as our sins; our obligation to him as much as our departure from him.

Hannah More

Answers to

This poor soul cried, and was heard by the LORD, and was saved from every trouble.

Psalm 34:6 NRSV

Three times I begged the Lord to make this suffering go away. But he replied, "My kindness is all you need. My power is strongest when you are weak."

2 Corinthians 12:8–9 CEV

A good man's prayer is very powerful and effective.

James 5:16 REB

God will always answer our prayers; but he will answer them in his way, and his way will be the way of perfect love. Often if he answered our prayer, as we at the moment desire, it would be the worst thing possible for us, for in our ignorance we often ask for gifts which would be our ruin.

William Barclay

Never make the blunder of trying to forecast the way God is going to answer your prayer.

Oswald Chambers

"Does God always answer prayer?" the cardinal was asked. "Yes," he said, "and sometimes the answer is 'No.'"

Alistair Cooke

Prayer's perplexities are most often camouflaged discoveries, there for the making.

Donald Cranefield

Keep praying, but be thankful that God's answers are wiser than your prayers!

William Culbertson

God has not always answered my prayers. If he had, I would have married the wrong man—several times!

Ruth Bell Graham

God answers only the requests which he inspires.

Ralph A. Herring

There is a communion with God that asks for nothing, yet asks for everything. . . . He who seeks the Father more than anything he can give is likely to have what he asks, for he is not likely to ask amiss.

George MacDonald

The great tragedy of life is not unanswered prayer but unoffered prayer.

Frederick Brotherton (F.B.) Meyer

We should be glad that God makes us wait for mercy. A great part of our sanctification is waiting for answer to our prayers.

Humphrey Mildred

I live in the spirit of prayer. I pray as I walk about, when I lie down, and when I rise up. And the answers are always coming.

George Müller

All my discoveries have been made in answer to prayer.

Sir Isaac Newton

When I pray, coincidences happen, and when I do not, they don't.

William Temple

The chief purpose of prayer is that God may be glorified in the answer.

Reuben Archer (R.A.) Torrey

Prayer changes things? No! Prayer changes people and people change things.

Paul Tournier

Attitudes in

When you are praying, do not heap up empty phrases as the Gentiles do; for they think that they will be heard because of their many words. Do not be like them, for your Father knows what you need before you ask him.

Matthew 6:7–8 NRSV

Let us therefore come boldly unto the throne of grace, that we may obtain mercy, and find grace to help in time of need.

Hebrews 4:16 KJV

Without faith it is impossible to please him: for he that cometh to God must believe that he is, and that he is a rewarder of them that diligently seek him.

Hebrews 11:6 KJV

The best prayer is not that which feels most, but that which gives most.

Fr. Andrew

The mind is not perfectly at prayer until the one praying does not think of himself or know he is praying.

St. Antony of Egypt

Unless the prayer which you intend to offer to God is important and meaningful to you first, you will not be able to present it to the Lord. If you are inattentive to the words you pronounce, if your heart does not respond to them, or if your life is not turned to the same direction as your prayer, it will not reach out Godwards.

Anthony Bloom

Is prayer your steering wheel or your spare tire?

Corrie ten Boom

When thou prayest, rather let thy heart be without words than thy words be without heart.

John Bunyan

The best prayers have often more groans than words.

John Bunyan

Prayer takes place in the heart, not in the head.

Carlo Carretto

Build yourself a cell in your heart and retire there to pray.

St. Catherine of Siena

Teach me to pray, pray thou thyself in me.

François de la Mothe Fénelon

Prayer allows us a direct relationship with the one person who can save us from the evil that invades our hearts.

James Houston

No one should give the answer that it is impossible for a man occupied with worldly cares to pray always. You can set up an altar to God in your mind by means of prayer. And so it is fitting to pray at your trade, on a journey, standing at a counter, or sitting at your handicraft.

St. John Chrysostom

Great talent is a gift of God, but it is a gift which is by no means necessary in order to pray well. This gift is required in order to converse well with men; but it is not necessary in order to speak well with God. For that, one needs good desires, and nothing more.

St. John of the Cross

Hold yourself in prayer before God, like a dumb or paralytic beggar at a rich man's gate:

let it be your business to keep your mind in the presence of God.

Brother Lawrence

Prayer is like watching for the kingfisher. All you can do is Be where he is likely to appear, and Wait.

Ann Lewin

Although posture is not important, I find that I am able to express my dependence better on my knees, a sign of our helplessness apart from the divine enablement.

Erwin W. Lutzer

The worth of a prayer is not gauged by its dimensions.

Robert Murray M'Cheyne

For every one look within, take ten looks at Christ.

Robert Murray M'Cheyne

What a man is on his knees before God, that he is—no more, and no less.

Robert Murray M'Cheyne

If a man's deeds are not in harmony with his prayer, he labors in vain.

Moses (Desert Father)

Lord, help me to say "yes."

Michel Quoist

We should believe that nothing is too small to be named before God. What should we think of the patient who told his doctor he was ill, but never went into particulars?

John Charles Ryle

To pray effectively we must want what God wants—that and that only is to pray in the will of God.

Aiden Wilson (A.W.) Tozer

To an effectual prayer there must concur the intention of the mind and the affections of the heart; else it is not praying but parrotting.

John Trapp

Jesus, my strength, my hope, / On Thee I cast my care, / With humble confidence look up, / And know Thou hear'st my prayer. / Give me on Thee to wait, / Till I can all things do, / On Thee, almighty to create, / Almighty to renew.

Charles Wesley

Confession

See also Confession

Have mercy on me, O God, according to your steadfast love; according to your abundant mercy blot out my transgressions. Wash me thoroughly from my iniquity, and cleanse me from my sin. For I know my transgressions, and my sin is ever before me. Against you, you alone, have I sinned, and done what is evil in your sight, so that you are justified in your sentence and blameless when you pass judgment.

Psalm 51:1–4 NRSV

If we confess our sins, he is faithful and just to forgive us our sins, and to cleanse us from all unrighteousness.

1 John 1:9 KJV

Dearly beloved brethren, the Scripture moveth us in sundry places to acknowledge and confess our manifold sins and wickedness.

Book of Common Prayer

We acknowledge and bewail our manifold sins and wickedness, Which we from time to time most grievously have committed, By thought, word, and deed, Against thy Divine

Majesty, Provoking most justly thy wrath and indignation.

Book of Common Prayer

Prayer is not designed for the furnishing of God with the knowledge of what we need, but it is designed as a confession to him of our sense of need.

Aiden Wilson (A.W.) Pink

The way to cover our sin is to uncover it by confession.

Richard Sibbes

Definitions of

Give rest to the weary, visit the sick, support the poor; for this also is prayer.

Aphrahat

To wish to pray is a prayer in itself.

Georges Bernanos

To pray is to sit open-handed before God.

Peter G. van Breeman

Prayer is the sum of our relationship with God. We are what we pray. The degree of our faith is the degree of our prayer. Our ability to love is our ability to pray.

Carlo Carretto

Prayer is conversation with God.

Clement of Alexandria

Prayer is happy company with God.

Clement of Alexandria

Really to pray is to stand to attention in the presence of the King and to be prepared to take orders from Him.

(Frederick) Donald Coggan

Prayer is the application of the heart to God, and the internal exercise of love.

Samuel Taylor Coleridge

Is not prayer precisely of itself peace, silence, strength, since it is a way of being with God?

Jacques Ellul

To pray . . . is to desire; but it is to desire what God would have us desire. He who desires not from the bottom of his heart, offers a deceitful prayer.

François de la Mothe Fénelon

To pray is to change. Prayer is the central avenue God uses to transform us.

Richard J. Foster

Prayer is the rope that pulls God and man together. But it doesn't pull God down to us; it pulls us up to him.

William Franklin (Billy) Graham

Prayer is the application of the heart to God, and the internal exercise of love.

Jeanne Guyon

To pray is nothing more than to lie in the sunshine of his grace.

O. Hallesby

Prayer is a summit meeting in the throne room of the universe.

Ralph A. Herring

Prayer is the breath of the new-born soul, and there can be no Christian life without it.

Rowland Hill

Certain thoughts are prayers. There are moments when, whatever be the attitude of the body, the soul is on its knees.

Victor Hugo

Prayer is the breathing of the soul.

John of Kronstadt

To pray is to open oneself to the possibility of sainthood, to the possibility of becoming set on fire by the Spirit.

Kenneth Leech

Prayer is a strong wall and fortress of the church; it is a good Christian weapon.

Martin Luther

Prayer is the sweat of the soul.

Martin Luther

The purpose of all prayer is to find God's will and to make that will our prayer.

Catherine Wood Marshall

For what is prayer in the last analysis? It is a conscious spreading out of my helplessness before God.

Al Martin

Prayer is none other but the revelation of the will or mind of God.

John Saltmarsh

Prayer enlarges the heart until it is capable of containing God's gift of himself.

Mother Teresa

The pulse of prayer is praise. The heart of prayer is gratitude. The voice of prayer is obedience. The arm of prayer is service.

William Arthur Ward

Prayer opens up the old wound which hasn't healed right, eases in the ointment and helps it to heal at last.

Tom Wright

Prayer is God being God in me being me.

Tom Wright

Encouragements to

Before they call, I will answer, and while they are yet speaking, I will hear.

Isaiah 65:24 KJV

Whenever you pray, go into your room and shut the door and pray to your Father who is in secret; and your Father who sees in secret will reward you.

Matthew 6:6 NRSV

Your Father already knows what you need before you ask him. This then, is how you should pray: "Our Father in heaven . . ."

Matthew 6:8–9 GNB

Jesus told his disciples a story about how they should keep on praying and never give up.

Luke 18:1 CEV

In certain ways we are weak, but the Spirit is here to help us. For example, when we don't know what to pray for, the Spirit prays for us in ways that cannot be put into words.

Romans 8:26 CEV

Consequently he is able for all time to save those who approach God through him, since he always lives to make intercession for them.

Hebrews 7:25 NRSV

He [Jesus] is able for all time to save those who approach God through him, since he always lives to make intercession for them.

Hebrews 7:25 NRSV

Let not our prayers die while our Intercessor lives.

Anon.

Prayer is not wrestling with God's reluctance to bless us; it is laying hold of his willingness to do so.

John Blanchard

Prayer is a shield to the soul, a sacrifice to God, and a scourge to Satan.

John Bunyan

The degree of our faith is the degree of our prayer. The strength of our hope is the strength of our prayer. The warmth of our charity is the warmth of our prayer.

Carlo Carretto

Pray as you can, and do not try to pray as you can't.

John Chapman

God wants us to pray, and will tell us how to begin where we are.

The Cloud of Unknowing

There is no place like the feet of Jesus for resolving the problems that perplex our hearts.

G.B. Duncan

If you pray truly, you will feel within yourself a great assurance: and the angels will be your companion.

Evagrius of Pontus

The man who kneels to God can stand up to anything.

Louis H. Evans

Talk to him in prayer of all your wants, your troubles, even of the weariness you feel in serving him. You cannot speak too freely, too trustfully, of him.

François de la Mothe Fénelon

A good prayer, though often used, is still fresh and fair in the eyes and ears of heaven.

Thomas Fuller

Prayer should be the key of the day and the lock of the night.

Thomas Fuller

The greatest thing anyone can do for God and for man is to pray.

Samuel Dickey (S.D.) Gordon

Perfume all your actions with the life-giving breath of prayer.

John XXIII

Pray inwardly, even if you do not enjoy it. It does good though you feel nothing, even though you think you are doing nothing.

Julian of Norwich

He who has learned to pray has learned the greatest secret of a holy and a happy life.

William Law

Prayer is the most important thing in my life. If I should neglect prayer for a single day, I should lose a great deal of the fire of faith.

Martin Luther

We talk about heaven being so far away. It is within speaking distance to those who belong there.

Dwight Lyman (D.L.) Moody

It is because God has promised certain things that we can ask for them with the full assurance of faith.

Aiden Wilson (A.W.) Pink

The world may doubt the power of prayer. But the saints know better.

Gilbert Shaw

Hindrances to

If I had cherished iniquity in my heart, the LORD would not have listened.

Psalm 66:18 NRSV

Whoso stoppeth his ears at the cry of the poor, he also shall cry himself, but shall not be heard.

Proverbs 21:13 KJV

The prayer must be made with faith, and no trace of doubt.

James 1:6 NJB

Anyone who has ever tried to formulate a private prayer in silence, and in his own heart, will know what I mean by diabolical interference. The forces of evil are in opposition to the will of God. And the nearer a man approaches God's will, the more apparent and stronger and more formidable this opposition is seen to be. It is only when we are going in more or less the same direction as the devil that we are unconscious of any opposition at all.

David Bolt

Nothing whatsoever can atone for the neglect of praying.

Edward M. Bounds

Hurry is the death of prayer.

Samuel Chadwick

Beware of placing the emphasis on what prayer costs us; it cost God everything to make it possible for us to pray.

Oswald Chambers

The biggest problem in prayer is now to "let go and let God."

Glenn Clark

Cold prayers, like cold suitors, are seldom effective in their aims.

Jim Elliot

None can pray well but he that lives well.

Thomas Fuller

I am convinced that the most outstanding enemy in prayer is the lack of knowledge of what we are in Christ, and of what he is in us, and what he did for us, and of our standing and legal rights before the throne.

E.W. Kenyon

Beware in your prayer above everything of limiting God, not only by unbelief but by fancying that you know what he can do.

Andrew Murray

The self-sufficient do not pray, the self-satisfied will not pray, the self-righteous cannot pray.

Leonard Ravenhill

Many people pray for things that can only come by work and work for things that can only come by prayer.

William Edwyn Robert Sangster

Yank some of the groans out of your prayers, and shove in some shouts.

William Ashley (Billy) Sunday

When we become too glib in prayer we are almost certainly talking to ourselves.

Aiden Wilson (A.W.) Tozer

Importance of

Stay awake, and pray that you may be spared the test. The spirit is willing, but the flesh is weak.

Matthew 26:41 REB

When he had entered the house, his disciples asked him privately, "Why could we not cast it out?" He said to them, "This kind can come out only through prayer."

Mark 9:28–29 NRSV

The effectual fervent prayer of a righteous man availeth much.

James 5:16 KJV

Pray as though everything depended on God. Work as though everything depended on you.

St. Augustine of Hippo

Seven days without prayer makes one weak.

Allen E. Bartlett

We need more Christians for whom prayer is the first resort, not the last.

John Blanchard

God shapes the world by prayer.

Edward M. Bounds

You can do more than pray, after you have prayed, but you cannot do more than pray until you have prayed.

John Bunyan

The one concern of the devil is to keep the saints from praying. He fears nothing from prayerless studies, prayerless work, prayerless religion. He laughs at our toil, he mocks at our wisdom, but he trembles when we pray.

Samuel Chadwick

It is not that prayer changes God, or awakens in him purposes of love and compassion that he has not already felt. No, it changes us, and therein lies its glory and its purpose.

Hannah Hurnard

To know how to speak to God is more important than knowing how to speak to men.

Andrew Murray

In every prayer an angel waits for us, since every prayer changes the one who prays.

Dorothy Soelle

Prayer meetings are the throbbing machinery of the Church.

Charles Haddon Spurgeon

It is significant that there is no record of the Lord teaching his disciples how to preach; but he took time to teach them how to pray and how not to pray.

L.A.T. Van Dooren

I have so much to do that I must spend several hours in prayer before I am able to do it.

John Wesley

Intercession

Who is to condemn? It is Christ Jesus, who died, yes, who was raised, who is at the right hand of God, who indeed intercedes for us.

Romans 8:34 NRSV

Please help us by praying for us. Then many people will give thanks for the blessings we receive in answer to all these prayers.

2 Corinthians 1:11 CEV

I exhort therefore, that, first of all, supplications, prayers, intercessions, and giving of thanks, be made for all men; For kings, and for all that are in authority; that we may lead a quiet and peaceable life in all godliness and honesty.

1 Timothy 2:1–2 KJV

Do not let us fail one another in interest, care, and practical help; but supremely we must not fail one another in prayer.

Michael Baughen

It is love which gives things their value. It makes sense of the difficulty of spending hours and hours on one's knees praying whilst so many men need looking after in the world.

Carlo Carretto

Jesus Christ carries on intercession for us in heaven; the Holy Ghost carries on intercession in us on earth; and we the saints have to carry on intercession for all men.

Oswald Chambers

When we are linked by the power of prayer, we hold each other's hand, as it were, while we walk along a slippery path.

St. Gregory I

An intercessor means one who is in such vital contact with God and with his fellowmen that he is like a live wire closing the gap between the saving power of God and the sinful men who have been cut off from that power.

Hannah Hurnard

We need less traveling by jet planes from congress to congress . . . but more kneeling and praying and pleading to God to have mercy upon us, more crying to God to arise and scatter his enemies and make himself known.

David Martyn Lloyd-Jones

I have benefited by praying for others; for by making an errand to God for them I have gotten something for myself.

Samuel Rutherford

The impulse to prayer, within our hearts, is evidence that Christ is urging our claims in heaven.

Augustus Hopkins Strong

Petition

So we fasted and petitioned our God for this, and he listened to our entreaty.

Ezra 8:23 NRSV

Do not be anxious about anything, but in everything, by prayer and petition, with thanksgiving, present your requests to God.

Philippians 4:6 NIV

In the course of his earthly life he offered up prayers and petitions, with loud cries and tears, to God who was able to deliver him from death. Because of his devotion his prayer was heard.

Hebrews 5:7 REB

Prayer is the little implement / Through which men reach / Where presence is denied them.

Emily Dickinson

Your needs are absolutely guaranteed by the most stringent of warranties, in the plainest, truest words! Knock, seek; ask. But you must read the fine print. "Not as the world giveth, give I unto you."

Annie Dillard

Most high glorious God, enlighten the darkness of my heart and give me, Lord, a correct faith, a certain hope, a perfect charity, sense and knowledge, so that I may carry out Your holy and true command.

St. Francis of Assisi

The reason we must ask God for things he already intends to give us is that he wants to teach us dependence, especially our need for himself.

Erwin W. Lutzer

Anything large enough for a wish to light upon is large enough to hang a prayer on.

George MacDonald

Whether we like it or not, asking is the rule of the Kingdom.

Charles Haddon Spurgeon

Large asking and large expectation on our part honor God.

A.L. Stone

Only one petition in the Lord's Prayer has any condition attached to it; it is the petition for forgiveness.

William Temple

God of all goodness, grant us to desire ardently, to seek wisely, to know surely, and to accomplish perfectly Thy holy will, for the glory of Thy name.

St. Thomas Aquinas

Thanksgiving

See also Thankfulness and Thanksgiving

O come, let us sing unto the Lord: let us make a joyful noise to the rock of our salvation. Let us come before his presence with thanksgiving, and make a joyful noise unto him with psalms. For the Lord is a great God, and a great King above all gods.

Psalm 95:1–3 KJV

O praise the Lord, for it is a good thing to sing praises unto our God: yea, a joyful and pleasant thing it is to be thankful.

Psalm 147:1 BCP

One act of thanksgiving when things go wrong with us is worth a thousand thanks when things are agreeable to our inclination.

John of Avila

Prayer is a state of continual gratitude.

John of Kronstadt

We should spend as much time in thanking God for His benefits as we do in asking Him for them.

St. Vincent de Paul

Now thank we all our God, / With hearts, and hands, and voices; / Who wondrous things hath done, / In whom His world rejoices; / Who, from our mothers' arms, / Hath blessed us on our way / With countless gifts of love, / And still is ours today.

Martin Rinkart, tr. Catherine Winkworth

Preaching

See also Sermons

How beautiful upon the mountains are the feet of the messenger who announces peace, who brings good news, who announces salvation, who says to Zion, "Your God reigns."

Isaiah 52:7 NRSV

Repentance and forgiveness of sins will be preached in his name to all nations, beginning at Jerusalem.

Luke 24:47 NIV

How then shall they call on him in whom they have not believed? And how shall they believe in him of whom they have not heard? And how shall they hear without a preacher? And how shall they preach, except they be sent? As it is written, How beautiful are the feet of them that preach the gospel of peace, and bring glad tidings of good things!

Romans 10:14–15 KJV

For after that in the wisdom of God the world by wisdom knew not God, it pleased God by the foolishness of preaching to save them that believe. For the Jews require a sign, and the Greeks seek after wisdom: But we preach Christ crucified, unto the Jews a stumblingblock, and unto the Greeks foolishness; But unto them which are called, both Jews and Greeks, Christ the power of God, and the wisdom of God.

1 Corinthians 1:21–24 KJV

I don't have any reason to brag about preaching the good news. Preaching is something God told me to do, and if I don't do it, I am doomed.

1 Corinthians 9:16 CEV

I solemnly urge you to preach the message, to insist upon proclaiming it (whether the time is right or not), to convince, reproach, and encourage, as you teach with all patience.

2 Timothy 4:1–2 GNB

I preached as never sure to preach again, and as a dying man to dying men.

Richard Baxter

Preaching is truth through personality.

Phillips Brooks

The preaching moment is the moment for the gift of God's life in the midst of our tired alienation.

Walter Brueggemann

I preached what I did feel, what I smartingly did feel.

John Bunyan

Preaching is the public exposition of Scripture by the man sent from God, in which God himself is present in judgment and in grace.

John Calvin

To love to preach is one thing—to love those to whom we preach quite another.

Richard Cecil

He preaches well who lives well. That's all the divinity I know.

Miguel de Cervantes

I had rather be fully understood by ten than admired by ten thousand.

Jonathan Edwards

I go out to preach with two propositions in mind. First, every person ought to give his life to Christ. Second, whether or not anyone else gives him his life, I will give him mine.

Jonathan Edwards

It is no use walking anywhere to preach unless we preach as we walk.

St. Francis of Assisi

Preach the gospel at all times; if necessary, use words.

St. Francis of Assisi

The test of a preacher is that his congregation goes away saying, not "What a lovely sermon!" but "I will do something."

St. Francis de Sales

There are those who laudably desire the office of preaching, whereas others no less laudably are driven to it by compulsion.

St. Gregory I

A man cannot really preach until preach he must. If he can do something else, he probably should!

Vance Havner

Preaching is theology coming through a man who is on fire.

David Martyn Lloyd-Jones

When I preach I regard neither doctors nor magistrates, of whom I have above forty in my congregation; I have all my eyes on the servant maids and on the children. And if the learned men are not well pleased with what they hear, well, the door is open.

Martin Luther

He that has but one word of God before him, and out of that word cannot make a sermon, can never be a preacher.

Martin Luther

I preach as though Christ was crucified yesterday, rose from the dead today, and was coming back tomorrow.

Martin Luther

My grand point in preaching is to break the hard heart and to heal the broken one.

John Newton

True preaching is the sweating of blood.

Joseph Parker

No man ought to be in a Christian pulpit who fears man more than God.

William Still

Give me one hundred preachers who fear nothing but sin and desire nothing but God, and I care not a straw whether they be clergymen or laymen, such alone will shake the gates of hell and set up the Kingdom of God upon earth.

John Wesley

Preach not because you have to say something, but because you have something to say.

Richard Whately

To preach more than half an hour, a man should be an angel and have angels for hearers.

George Whitefield

If we do not possess a positive appetite for the Word, then we are not meant to be preachers. For it is not anything other than the Word that we are called to preach.

Arthur Skevington Wood

Predestination

See also Election

Before I formed you in the womb I knew you, and before you were born I consecrated you;

I appointed you a prophet to the nations.

Jeremiah 1:5 NRSV

For whom he did foreknow, he also did predestinate to be conformed to the image of his Son, that he might be the firstborn among many brethren. Moreover whom he did predestinate, them he also called: and whom he called, them he also justified: and whom he justified, them he also glorified.

Romans 8:29–30 KJV

For he chose us in him before the creation of the world to be holy and blameless in his sight. In love he predestined us to be adopted as his sons through Jesus Christ, in accordance with his pleasure and will.

Ephesians 1:4–5 NIV

God predestines every man to be saved. The devil predestines every man to be damned. Man has the casting vote.

Anon.

God chose us in Christ before the foundations of the world, predestinating us to the adoption of children, not because we were going to be ourselves holy and immaculate, but He chose and predestinated us that we might be so.

St. Augustine of Hippo

This is the predestination of saints, namely the foreknowledge and planning of God's kindnesses, by which they are most surely delivered. As for the rest, where are they left by God's righteous judgment save in the mass of perdition?

St. Augustine of Hippo

In the wounds of Christ alone is predestination found and understood.

Martin Luther

By the decree of God, for the manifestation of His glory, some men and angels are predestinated unto everlasting life, and other foreordained to everlasting death.

Westminster Confession of Faith

Let a man go to the grammar school of faith and repentance before he goes to the university of election and predestination.

George Whitefield

Pregnancy, *see* Birth

Prejudice, *see* Judging Others; Race and Racism

Pride

See also Humility

Pride goes before destruction, and a haughty spirit before a fall.

Proverbs 16:18 NRSV

Whoever shall exalt himself shall be abased; and he that shall humble himself shall be exalted.

Matthew 23:12 KJV

Do not be proud, but be ready to mix with humble people. Do not keep thinking how wise you are.

Romans 12:16 REB

Pride is the perverse desire of height.

St. Augustine of Hippo

Pride is the ground in which all the other sins grow, and the parent from which all the other sins come.

William Barclay

It is our self-importance, not our misery, that gets in His way.

Daniel Considine

You can have no greater sign of a confirmed pride than when you think you are humble enough.

William Law

A proud man is always looking down on things and people; and, of course, as long as you're looking down, you can't see something that's above you.

Clive Staples (C.S.) Lewis

Pride not only withdraws the heart from God, but lifts it up against God.

Thomas Manton

God sends no one away empty except those who are full of themselves.

Dwight Lyman (D.L.) Moody

Let me give you the history of pride in three small chapters. The beginning of pride was in heaven. The continuance of pride is on earth. The end of pride is in hell. This history shows how unprofitable it is.

Richard Newton

The most serious sin is one of thought, the sin of pride.

Paul VI

Of all the causes which conspire to blind / Man's erring judgment, and misguide the mind. / What the weak head with strongest bias rules. / Is Pride, the never-failing vice of fools.

Alexander Pope

Pride is the idolatrous worship of ourselves, and that is the national religion of hell.

Alan Redpath

Be not proud of race, face, place, or grace.

Charles Haddon Spurgeon

To consider oneself worthy of consideration and to behave with self-assurance and self-importance is to simply forget God.

Lanza del Vasto

Priests and Priesthood

See also Jesus Christ, Priesthood of

Since, then, we have a great high priest who has passed through the heavens, Jesus, the Son of God, let us hold fast to our confession. For we do not have a high priest who is unable to sympathize with our weaknesses, but we have one who in every respect has been tested as we are, yet without sin.

Hebrews 4:14–15 NRSV

Now you are living stones that are being used to build a spiritual house. You are also a group of holy priests, and with the help of Jesus Christ, you will offer sacrifices that please God. . . . You are God's chosen and special people. You are a group of royal priests and a holy nation.

1 Peter 2:5, 9 CEV

If her priests are saints, what good they are able to do! But whatever they are, never speak against them.

The Curé d'Ars

The most high and infinitely good God has not granted to angels the power with which he has invested priests.

St. John Chrysostom

Every day bring God sacrifices and be the priest in this reasonable service, offering thy body and the virtue of thy soul.

St. John Chrysostom

All Christians whatsoever belong to the "religious" class; there is no difference between them except as they do different work. . . . Baptism makes us all priests. . . . Those who exercise secular authority have all been baptized like the rest of us; therefore they are priests and bishops.

Martin Luther

A priest ought to be in no place where his Master would not go, nor employed in anything which his Master would not do.

Henry Edward Manning

Prisoners

See also Bondage

Let the sighing of the prisoner come before thee; according to the greatness of thy power preserve thou those that are appointed to die.

Psalm 79:11 KJV

I, Paul . . . a prisoner of Christ Jesus.

Philemon 1:9 NRSV

Remember the Lord's people who are in jail and be concerned for them. Don't forget those who are suffering but imagine that you are there with them.

Hebrews 13:3 CEV

During these years, in sheer terror we may sometimes have felt as though we were falling into the bottomless abyss. . . . But there is a Power that sustains us; we are borne up by God the Father's everlasting arms. . . . It is the tenth week now that I wait for the opening of my prison door; and looking back and around I am amazed at the good cheer that I have felt for weeks . . . an answer to so many prayers.

Anon.

I can say, as did Solzhenitsyn, bless you, prison, for having been in my life. For there

I caught a glimpse of God's view of his world and his passion for justice and righteousness.

Charles W. Colson

If anyone wants a confirmation of the truth of Christianity, let him go and read the scriptures in prisons to poor sinners; you there see how the gospel is exactly adapted to the fallen condition of man.

Elizabeth Fry

Privilege, *see* Responsibility

Promises

Offer to God a sacrifice of thanksgiving, and pay your vows to the Most High.

Psalm 50:14 NRSV

Don't fall into the trap of making promises to God before you think!

Proverbs 20:25 CEV

Christ says "Yes" to all of God's promises. That's why we have Christ to say "Amen" for us to the glory of God.

2 Corinthians 1:20 CEV

He has given us . . . his precious and very great promises, so that through them you may escape from the corruption that is in the world because of lust, and may become participants of the divine nature.

2 Peter 1:4 NRSV

The Lord is not being slow in carrying out his promises, as some people think he is; rather is he being patient with you, wanting nobody to be lost and everybody to be brought to repentance.

2 Peter 3:9 NJB

The promises of God are just as good as ready money any day.

Billy Bray

We cannot rely on God's promises without obeying his commandments.

John Calvin

It is better to run the risk of being considered indecisive, better to be uncertain and not promise, than to promise and not fulfill.

Oswald Chambers

God has never promised to solve our problems. He has not promised to answer our questions. . . . He has promised to go with us.

Elisabeth Elliot

The purposes of God are his concealed promises; the promises—his revealed purposes!

Philip Henry

God's promises are like the stars; the darker the night the brighter they shine.

David Nicholas

Faith in the promises works obedience to the precepts.

George Swinnock

God is the God of promise. He keeps His word, even when that seems impossible; even when the circumstances seem to point to the opposite.

Colin Urquhart

You never pray with greater power than when you plead the promises of God.

William J.C. White

Property, *see* Possessions; Wealth

Prophets and Prophecy

See also Jesus Christ, Prophet

But Moses said to him, "Are you jealous for my sake? Would that all the LORD's people were prophets, and that the LORD would put his spirit on them!"

Numbers 11:29 NRSV

Ever since your ancestors left Egypt, I have been sending my servants the prophets to speak for me. But you have ignored me and become even more stubborn and sinful than your ancestors ever were!

Jeremiah 7:25–26 CEV

Jesus said to them, "Prophets are not without honor except in their own country and in their own house."

Matthew 13:57 NRSV

And God hath set some in the church, first apostles, secondarily prophets. . . .

1 Corinthians 12:28 KJV

The prophets whom we should look for are not the plants forced in the hot-house of sectarian religious experience, but those great men and women who, usually swimming against the current of the age, have spoken unwelcome but forceful truths to the Church.

A.T. & R.P.C. Hanson

Do thou speak, O Lord God, the Inspirer and Enlightener of all the prophets; for thou alone without them canst perfectly instruct me, but they without thee will profit nothing.

Thomas à Kempis

Prophecy is not given to make men prophets, but as a witness to God when it is fulfilled.

Sir Isaac Newton

Prophets are the beating hearts of the Old Testament.

Walter Rauschenbusch

An interest in prophecy which is merely speculative and sensational comes perilously close to being sinful.

William Graham Scroggie

I would not give much for prophetic intelligence if it does not begin, continue, and end with the person, work, and glory of Christ.

H.H. Snell

Scholars can interpret the past; it takes prophets to interpret the present.

Aiden Wilson (A.W.) Tozer

A prophet is one who knows his times and what God is trying to say to the people of his times.

Aiden Wilson (A.W.) Tozer

We are not diplomats but prophets, and our message is not a compromise but an ultimatum.

Aiden Wilson (A.W.) Tozer

Prophetic movements are not exempt from sin. Even as feminism announces judgment on patriarchy and calls for repentance and change, it needs ever to be aware of its own potential for idolatry.

Phyllis Trible

Prosperity, *see* Health and Wholeness; Wealth

Protection

See also Guidance

Withhold not thou thy tender mercies from me, O Lord: let thy lovingkindness and thy truth continually preserve me.

Psalm 40:11 KJV

He will cover you with his wings; you will be safe in his care; his faithfulness will protect and defend you.

Psalm 91:4 GNB

He guards the course of the just and protects the way of his faithful ones.

Proverbs 2:8 NIV

Holy Father, protect them in your name that you have given me, so that they may be one, as we are one. While I was with them, I protected them in your name that you have given me. I guarded them and not one of them was lost. . . . I am not asking you to take them out of the world, but I ask you to protect them from the evil one.

John 17:11–12, 15 NRSV

My dearest Lord, / Be Thou a bright flame before me, / Be Thou a guiding star above me, / Be Thou a smooth path behind me. / Be Thou a kindly shepherd behind me, / Today and evermore.

St. Columba

In the morning prayer is the key that opens to us the treasures of God's mercies and blessings; in the evening, it is the key that shuts us up under his protection and safeguard.

Jacques Ellul

This is a wise, sane Christian faith: that a man commit himself, his life, and his hopes to God; that God undertakes the special protection of that man; that therefore that man ought not to be afraid of anything.

George MacDonald

Providence

See also God, Goodness of

While the earth remaineth, seedtime and harvest, and cold and heat, and summer and winter, and day and night shall not cease.

Genesis 8:22 KJV

Abraham named that shrine "The Lord will provide"; and to this day the saying is: "In the mountain of the Lord it was provided."

Genesis 22:14 REB

The lot is fallen unto me in a fair ground: yea, I have a goodly heritage.

Psalm 16:7 BCP

Are not two sparrows sold for a penny? Yet not one of them will fall to the ground apart from your Father. And even the hairs of your head are all counted. So do not be afraid; you are of more value than many sparrows.

Matthew 10:29–31 NRSV

But my God shall supply all your need according to his riches in glory by Christ Jesus.

Philippians 4:19 KJV

Trust the past to the mercy of God, the present to his love, and the future to his Providence.

St. Augustine of Hippo

God moves in a mysterious way his wonders to perform; / He plants his footsteps in the sea, and rides upon the storm.

William Cowper

We sleep in peace in the arms of God, when we yield ourselves up to his Providence.

François de la Mothe Fénelon

Providence is the care God takes of all existing things.

St. John of Damascus

God wishes each of us to work as hard as we can, holding nothing back but giving ourselves to the utmost, and when we can do no more, then is the moment when the hand of Divine Providence is stretched out to us and takes over.

Don Orione

You will never need more than God can supply.

James Innell (J.I.) Packer

In all created things discern the Providence and wisdom of God, and in all things give Him thanks.

St. Teresa of Avila

Divine care supplies everybody with the means necessary for salvation, so long as he on his part does not put up obstacles.

St. Thomas Aquinas

A firm faith in the universal providence of God is the solution to all earthly problems. It is almost equally true that a clear and full apprehension of the universal providence of God is the solution to most theological problems.

Benjamin Breckinridge Warfield

Providence has at all times been my only dependence, for all other resources seem to have failed us.

George Washington

God is to be trusted when his providences seem to run contrary to his promises.

Thomas Watson

I firmly believe in Divine Providence. Without it, I think I should go crazy. Without God the world would be a maze without a clue.

(Thomas) Woodrow Wilson

Punishment

See also Last Judgment

If you do not keep your promise, I warn you that you will be sinning against the Lord. Make no mistake about it; you will be punished for your sin.

Numbers 32:23 GNB

He will show how angry and furious he can be with every selfish person who rejects the truth and wants to do evil. All who are wicked will be punished with trouble and suffering. It doesn't matter if they are Jews or Gentiles.

Romans 2:8–9 CEV

These [who do not obey the gospel of our Lord Jesus] will suffer the punishment of eternal destruction, separated from the presence of the Lord and from the glory of his might.

2 Thessalonians 1:9 NRSV

Each man's sin is the instrument of his punishment, and his iniquity is turned into his torment.

St. Augustine of Hippo

I am not judged by the light I have, but by the light I have refused to accept.

Oswald Chambers

He whose throne is built on justice and righteousness will see that righteousness prevails. That is why sin must, and will, be punished.

John C. Chapman

God aims at satisfying justice in the eternal damnation of sinners.

Jonathan Edwards

We are not punished for our sins, but by them.

Elbert Green Hubbard

No man is condemned for anything he has done; he is condemned for continuing to do wrong. He is condemned for not coming out of the darkness, for not coming to the light.

George MacDonald

God will be glorified in the punishment of sin as well as in the reward of obedience.

Thomas V. Moore

Purity

See also Holiness

Who shall ascend into the hill of the Lord? or who shall stand in his holy place? He that hath clean hands, and a pure heart; who hath not lifted up his soul unto vanity, nor sworn deceitfully.

Psalm 24:3–4 KJV

Purge me with hyssop, and I shall be clean: wash me, and I shall be whiter than snow.

Psalm 51:7 KJV

Your eyes are too pure to look on evil; you cannot countenance wrongdoing.

Habakkuk 1:13 REB

Blessed are the pure in heart, for they will see God.

Matthew 5:8 NRSV

Do not ordain anyone hastily, and do not participate in the sins of others; keep yourself pure.

1 Timothy 5:22 NRSV

Unto the pure all things are pure: but unto them that are defiled and unbelieving is nothing pure; but even their mind and conscience is defiled.

Titus 1:15 KJV

Only a passionate love of purity can save a man from impurity.

William Barclay

The insight that relates us to God arises from purity of heart, not from clearness of intellect.

Oswald Chambers

Spiritual truth is discernable only to a pure heart, not to a keen intellect. It is not a question of profundity of intellect, but of purity of heart.

Oswald Chambers

The pure soul is a beautiful rose, and the Three Divine Persons descend from Heaven to inhale its fragrance.

The Curé d'Ars

He who would be serene and pure needs but one thing—detachment.

Meister Eckhart

Vigilance and prayer are the safeguards of chastity.

St. Jean Baptist de la Salle

There cannot be perfect transformation without perfect pureness.

St. John of the Cross

Chastity enables a soul to breathe pure air in the foulest places.

Joseph Joubert

Still to the lowly soul / He doth Himself impart, / And for His cradle and His throne / Chooseth the pure in heart.

John Keble

Simplicity reaches out after God; purity discovers and enjoys him.

Thomas à Kempis

If there is joy in the world, surely the man of pure heart possesses it.

Thomas à Kempis

My strength is as the strength of ten, / Because my heart is pure.

Alfred, Lord Tennyson

Purposes, *see* Goals

Quiet and Stillness

See also Rest; Silence

The Lord is my shepherd; I shall not want. He maketh me to lie down in green pastures: he leadeth me beside the still waters.

Psalm 23:1–2 KJV

Be still before the Lord and wait patiently for him; do not fret when men succeed in their ways, when they carry out their wicked schemes.

Psalm 37:7 NIV

Be still, and know that I am God.

Psalm 46:10 KJV

Then they cried to the LORD in their trouble, and he brought them out from their distress; he made the storm be still, and the waves of the sea were hushed. Then they were glad because they had quiet, and he brought them to their desired haven.

Psalm 107:28–30 NRSV

For thus saith the Lord God, the Holy One of Israel; In returning and rest shall ye be saved; in quietness and in confidence shall be your strength.

Isaiah 30:15 KJV

It is good to wait quietly for the salvation of the Lord.

Lamentations 3:26 NIV

In such a time, therefore, it is prudent to stay quiet, for it is an evil time.

Amos 5:13 REB

Make a point of living quietly, attending to your own business and earning your living, just as we told you to.

1 Thessalonians 4:11 NJB

If we have not quiet in our minds, outward comfort will do no more for us than a golden slipper on a gouty foot.

John Bunyan

O God, make us children of quietness, and heirs of peace.

St. Clement I of Rome

Speak, Lord, in the stillness, / While I wait on Thee; / Hushed my heart to listen / In expectancy.

E. May Crawford

The very best and utmost attainment in this life is to remain still and let God act and speak in thee.

Meister Eckhart

Nothing in all creation is so like God as stillness.

Meister Eckhart

Christ is the still point of the turning world.

Thomas Stearns (T.S.) Eliot

A little with quiet is the only diet.

George Herbert

"Rest in the Lord; wait patiently for Him." In Hebrew, "Be silent to God and let Him mold thee." Keep still, and He will mold thee to the right shape.

Martin Luther

All the troubles of life come upon us because we refuse to sit quietly for a while each day in our room.

Blaise Pascal

The quiet of quiet places is made quieter by natural sounds. In a wood on a still day the quiet is increased by the whisper of the trees.

Mark Rutherford

Be still, my soul: the Lord is on thy side; / Bear patiently the cross of grief or pain; / Leave to thy God to order and provide; / In ev'ry change he faithful will remain. / Be still, my soul: thy best, thy heav'nly friend / Through thorny ways leads to a joyful end.

Katharina von Schlegel

I cannot be the man I should be without times of quietness. Stillness is an essential part of growing deeper.

Charles R. Swindoll

God is a tranquil Being, and abides in a tranquil eternity. So must thy spirit become a tranquil and clear little pool, wherein the serene light of God can be mirrored.

Gerhard Tersteegen

Drop thy still dews of quietness / Till all our strivings cease; / Take from our souls the strain and stress, / And let our ordered lives confess / The beauty of thy peace.

John Greenleaf Whittier

Race and Racism

See also Nations and Nationhood; Prejudice

So God created man in his own image, in the image of God created he him; male and female created he them.

Genesis 1:27 KJV

Then Peter addressed them, "I now really understand," he said, "that God has no favorites, but that anybody of any nationality who fears him and does what is right is acceptable to him."

Acts 10:34–35 NJB

From one person God made all nations who live on earth, and he decided when and where every nation would be.

Acts 17:26 CEV

There is neither Jew nor Greek, slave nor free, male nor female, for you are all one in Christ Jesus.

Galatians 3:28 NIV

After this I looked, and there was a great multitude that no one could count, from every nation, from all tribes and peoples and languages, standing before the throne and before the Lamb.

Revelation 7:9 NRSV

Race prejudice is as thorough a denial of the Christian God as atheism, and a far more common form of apostasy.

Harry Emerson Fosdick

Human blood is all one color.

Thomas Fuller

Jesus throws down the dividing prejudices of nationality and teaches universal love, without distinction of race, merit, or rank. A man's neighbor is everyone that needs help.

John Cunningham Geikie

Skin color does not matter to God, for he is looking upon the heart. . . . When men are standing at the foot of the cross, there are no racial barriers.

William Franklin (Billy) Graham

We must recognize that the motives and forces behind racism are the Antichrist, denying that man is made in the divine image.

Ernest Urban Trevor Huddleston

A doctrine of black supremacy is as evil as a doctrine of white supremacy.

Martin Luther King Jr.

After all, there is but one race—humanity.

George Moore

The lifting up of every voice, the celebration of diversity, the affirmation of plurality, help us to see glimpses of the amazing grace of God in all cultures and all peoples.

Kwok Pui-Lan

We can't enrich the common good of our country by driving out those we don't care for.

Oscar Romero

War springs from the love and loyalty being offered to God being applied to some God-substitute, one of the most dangerous being nationalism.

Robert Runcie

In the gates of eternity the black hand and the white hand hold each other with an equal clasp.

Harriet Beecher Stowe

Reading

See also Education; Study

Now there was an Ethiopian eunuch, a court official of the Candace, queen of the Ethiopians, in charge of her entire treasury. He had come to Jerusalem to worship and was returning home; seated in his chariot, he was reading the prophet Isaiah.

Acts 8:27–28 NRSV

Devote yourself to the public reading of Scripture, to preaching and to teaching.

1 Timothy 4:13 NIV

Blessed is he that readeth, and they that hear the words of this prophecy, and keep those things which are written therein: for the time is at hand.

Revelation 1:3 KJV

A real book is not one that we read, but one that reads us.

W.H. Auden

Read to contradict and confute, not to believe and take for granted, not to find talk and discourse—but to weigh and consider.

Francis Bacon

They do most by Books, who could do much without them, and he that chiefly owes himself unto himself, is the substantial Man.

Sir Thomas Browne

The reading of all good books is like a conversation with the finest men of past centuries.

René Descartes

It is impossible to mentally or socially enslave a Bible-reading people.

Horace Greeley

At that day of judgment we shall not be asked what we have read but what we have done.

Thomas à Kempis

If thou wilt receive profit, read with humility, simplicity, and faith; and seek not at any time the fame of being learned.

Thomas à Kempis

The book to read is not the one which thinks for you, but the one that makes you think. No other book in the world equals the Bible for that.

James McCosh

A good book is the precious life-blood of a master spirit, embalmed and treasured up on purpose to a life beyond life.

John Milton

I read my Bible to know what people ought to do, and my newspaper to know what they are doing.

John Henry Newman

Reading is good prayer. . . . [I]n reading, when the heart feels delight, devotion is increased, and that is worth many prayers.

Ancrene Riwle

Books are good enough in their own way, but they are a mighty bloodless substitute for life.

Robert Louis Stevenson

We find the Bible difficult because we try to read it as we would read any other book, and it is not the same as any other book.

Aiden Wilson (A.W.) Tozer

The things you read will fashion you by slowly conditioning your mind.

Aiden Wilson (A.W.) Tozer

Be careful what books you read; for as water tastes of the soil it runs through, so does the soul of the authors that a man reads.

John Trapp

Leave not off reading the Bible till you find your hearts warmed. . . . Let it not only inform you but inflame you.

Thomas Watson

Reason

See also Mind; Thoughts and Thinking

Come now, and let us reason together, saith the Lord: though your sins be as scarlet, they shall be as white as snow; though they be red like crimson, they shall be as wool.

Isaiah 1:18 KJV

Always be prepared to give an answer to everyone who asks you to give the reason for the hope that you have.

1 Peter 3:15 NIV

The Almighty does nothing without reason though the frail mind of man cannot explain the reason.

St. Augustine of Hippo

God does not expect us to submit our faith to him without reason, but the very limits of our reason make faith a necessity.

St. Augustine of Hippo

No man can understand spiritual mysteries by carnal reason.

Thomas Benton Brooks

Reason is itself a matter of faith. It is an act of faith to assert that our thoughts have any relation to reality at all.

Gilbert Keith (G.K.) Chesterton

Reason can never show itself more reasonable than in ceasing to reason about things which are above reason.

John Flavel

Natural reason is a good tree which God has planted in us; the fruits which spring from it cannot but be good.

St. Francis de Sales

Reason is a God-given faculty, and is to be valued enormously, but you must put it in its right place. And the right place is certainly not when it says, like a blind man in a sunlit garden, "Anything I can't see doesn't exist."

Michael Green

Reason can ascertain the profound difficulties of our condition; it cannot remove them.

John Henry Newman

The heart has its reasons of which reason knows nothing.

Blaise Pascal

Reason's last step is the recognition that there are an infinite number of things which are beyond it. It is merely feeble if it does not go as far as to realize that.

Blaise Pascal

Where reason cannot wade, there faith may swim.

Thomas Watson

Rebellion

See also Disobedience

For rebellion is no less a sin than divination, and stubbornness is like iniquity and idolatry.

1 Samuel 15:23 NRSV

Why do the heathen so furiously rage together, and why do the people imagine a vain thing? The kings of the earth stand up, and the rulers take counsel together, against the Lord, and against his Anointed.

Psalm 2:1–2 BCP

He ruleth by his power for ever; his eyes behold the nations: let not the rebellious exalt themselves.

Psalm 66:7 KJV

This is the Lord's message for his rebellious people: "You follow your own plans instead of mine; you make treaties without asking me, and you keep on sinning."

Isaiah 30:1 CEV

Watch over your heart that you may not give way, in the very least to bitterness, spite, complaints, or voluntary rebellion.

Jean Pierre de Caussade

There is endless room for rebellion against ourselves.

George MacDonald

Reconciliation

See also Peace, between People and Nations; Salvation

When you are offering your gift at the altar, if you remember that your brother or sister has something against you, leave your gift there before the altar and go; first be reconciled to your brother or sister, and then come and offer your gift.

Matthew 5:23–24 NRSV

It is all God's work; he reconciled us to himself through Christ and he gave us the ministry of reconciliation. I mean, God was in Christ reconciling the world to himself, not holding anyone's faults against them, but entrusting to us the message of reconciliation. So we are ambassadors for Christ; it is as though God were urging you through us, and in the name of Christ we appeal to you to be reconciled to God.

2 Corinthians 5:18–20 NJB

Through the Son, then, God decided to bring the whole universe back to himself. God made peace through his Son's blood on the cross and so brought back to himself all things, both on earth and in heaven.

Colossians 1:20 GNB

Never once is God said to be reconciled to man; it is always man who is reconciled to God.

William Barclay

It takes two sides to make a lasting peace, but it only takes one to make the first step.

Edward M. Kennedy

To reconcile man with man and not with God is to reconcile no one at all.

Thomas Merton

Reconciliation sounds a large theological term, but it simply means coming to ourselves and arising and going to our Father.

John Wood Oman

A love of reconciliation is not weakness or cowardice. It demands courage, nobility, generosity, sometimes heroism, and overcoming of oneself rather than of one's adversary. At times it may even seem like dishonor, but it never offends against true justice or denies the rights of the poor. In reality, it is the patient, wise art of peace, of loving, of living with one's fellows, after the example of Christ, with a strength of heart and mind modeled on his.

Paul VI

Some people think reconciliation is a soft option, that it means papering over the cracks. But the biblical meaning means looking facts in the face and it can be very costly: it cost God the death of his own Son.

Desmond Tutu

Redemption

See also Salvation

For I know that my Redeemer lives, and that at the last he will stand upon the earth.

Job 19:25 NRSV

For even the Son of Man came not to be ministered unto, but to minister, and to give his life a ransom for many.

Mark 10:45 KJV

All have sinned and fall short of the glory of God and are justified freely by his grace through the redemption that came by Christ Jesus.

Romans 3:23–24 NIV

When the fullness of time had come, God sent his Son, born of a woman, born under the law, in order to redeem those who were under the law, so that we might receive adoption as children.

Galatians 4:4–5 NRSV

For no one is redeemed except through unmerited mercy, and no one is condemned except through merited judgment.

St. Augustine of Hippo

The great Christian invitation is to be asked by Christ to share in his redemptive work— to enter into Jerusalem with him.

Fr. Peter Ball

When Jesus Christ shed his blood on the cross, it was not the blood of a martyr, or the blood of one man for another; it was the life of God poured out to redeem the world.

Oswald Chambers

Redemption means that Jesus Christ can put into any man the disposition that ruled his own life.

Oswald Chambers

An understanding of redemption is not necessary to salvation any more than an understanding of life is necessary before we can be born into it.

Oswald Chambers

The strangest truth of the Gospel is that redemption comes through suffering.

Milo L. Chapman

Redemption does not only look back to Calvary. It looks forward to the freedom in which the redeemed stand. Precisely because they have been redeemed at such a cost, believers must be God's men.

Leon Lamb Morris

The believer is not redeemed by obedience to the law but he is redeemed unto it.

John Murray

People will never take evil seriously nor even see much need to tap the resources of God until they join in with the costly redemptive purposes of love.

John Bertram (J.B.) Phillips

Justification and sanctification are two aspects or the two sides of the one coin of divine redemption.

W. Stanford Reid

Unless our civilization is redeemed spiritually, it cannot endure materially.

(Thomas) Woodrow Wilson

Regeneration, *see* Holy Spirit and Regeneration; New Birth

Rejection

My God, my God, why have you forsaken me? Why are you so far from . . . heeding my groans?

Psalm 22:1 REB

He was despised and rejected by others; a man of suffering and acquainted with infirmity; and as one from whom others hide their faces he was despised, and we held him of no account.

Isaiah 53:3 NRSV

He came into his own world, but his own nation did not welcome him.

John 1:11 CEV

Come to him, the living Stone—rejected by men but chosen by God and precious to him.

1 Peter 2:4 NIV

To accept Christ is to know the meaning of the words "as he is, so are we in this world." We accept his friends as our friends, his enemies as our enemies, his ways as our ways, his rejection as our rejection, his cross as our cross, his life as our life, and his future as our future.

Aiden Wilson (A.W.) Tozer

Have you not learned great lessons from those who reject you, and brace themselves against you? Or who treat you with contempt, or dispute the passage with you?

Walt Whitman

Rejection is the sand in the oyster, the irritant that ultimately produces the pearl.

Burke Wilkinson

Relatives, *see* Families

Relaxation, *see* Rest

Religions and Religion

See also Christianity; Gospel

Men of Athens! I see that in every way you are very religious. For as I walked around and looked carefully at your objects of worship, I even found an altar with this inscription: To AN UNKNOWN GOD.

Acts 17:22–23 NIV

Pure religion and undefiled before God and the Father is this, To visit the fatherless and widows in their affliction, and to keep himself unspotted from the world.

James 1:27 KJV

Religion is not proficiency in the fine art of spiritual knowledge, but just the love of God and our neighbor.

Fr. Andrew

For true religion is that by which the soul is united to God so that it binds itself again by reconciliation to Him from Whom it had broken off, as it were, by sin.

St. Augustine of Hippo

A religion that is small enough for our understanding is not great enough for our need.

Lord Arthur James Balfour

He who begins by loving Christianity better than truth will proceed by loving his own sect or church better than Christianity and end in loving himself better than all.

Samuel Taylor Coleridge

Man will wrangle for religion; write for it; fight for it; die for it; anything but live for it.

Charles Caleb Colton

Religion is like the vaccine that stops you from getting the real thing.

William Franklin (Billy) Graham

All other religions are oblique: the founder stands aside and introduces another speaker. . . . Christianity alone is direct speech.

Søren Kierkegaard

Organized Christianity has probably done more to retard the ideals that were its founder's than any other agency in the world.

Richard Le Gallienne

Do not call yourselves Lutherans, call yourselves Christians. Has Luther been crucified for the world?

Martin Luther

Anything that makes religion a second object makes it no object. He who offers to God a second place offers him no place.

John Ruskin

The heart of religion is not an opinion about God, but a personal relationship with him.

William Edwyn Robert Sangster

Humanism is not wrong in its cry for sociological healing, but humanism is not producing it.

Francis August Schaeffer

In the midst of finitude to be at one with the Infinite and in every moment to be eternal is the immortality of religion.

Friedrich Schleiermacher

The sum total of religion is to feel that, in its highest unity, all that moves us in feeling is one; to feel that anything singular and particular is only possible by means of this unity; to feel, that is to say, that our being and living is a being and living in and through God.

Friedrich Schleiermacher

Religion that is merely ritual and ceremonial can never satisfy. Neither can we be satisfied by a religion that is merely humanitarian or serviceable to mankind. Man's craving is for the spiritual.

Samuel Moor Shoemaker

Christianity is not a religion, it is a relationship.

Dr. Thieme

You can find more carnal, unregenerate, self-centered characters who have religion and are sensitive toward it than you can bury in the Grand Canyon.

Aiden Wilson (A.W.) Tozer

Communism is a religion and only as we see it as a religion, though a secular religion, will we understand its power.

(David) Elton Trueblood

Some people have just enough religion to make them feel uncomfortable.

John Wesley

Remembrance

See also Past

Then shall he bring it to the priest, and the priest shall take his handful of it, even a memorial thereof, and burn it on the altar, according to the offerings made by fire unto the Lord: it is a sin offering.

Leviticus 5:12 KJV

Remember the whole way by which the Lord your God has led you these forty years in the wilderness to humble and test you, and to discover whether or not it was in your heart to keep his commandments.

Deuteronomy 8:2 REB

Remember the marvels he has done, his wonders, the judgments he has spoken.

Psalm 105:5 NJB

The righteous shall be in everlasting remembrance.

Psalm 112:6 KJV

Let us now praise famous men, and our fathers in their generations.

Ecclesiasticus 44:1 RSV

Thou hast remembered me, O God, and hast not forsaken those who love you.

Bel and the Dragon 38 RSV

Then he took bread, and when he had given thanks, he broke it and gave it to them, saying, "This is my body given for you; do this in remembrance of me."

Luke 22:19 NJB

The Comforter, which is the Holy Ghost, whom the Father will send in my name, he shall teach you all things, and bring all things to your remembrance, whatsoever I have said unto you.

John 14:26 KJV

Memory tempers prosperity, mitigates adversity, controls youth, and delights old age.

Anon.

They shall grow not old, as we that are left grow old: / Age shall not weary them, nor the years condemn. / At the going down of the sun and in the morning. / We will remember them.

Laurence Binyon

Most of our human emotions are closely related to our memory. Remorse is a biting memory, guilt is an accusing memory, gratitude is a joyful memory, and all such emotions are deeply influenced by the way we have integrated past events into our way of being in the world.

Henri J.M. Nouwen

When remembrance of God lives in the heart and there maintains the fear of him, then all goes well; but when this remembrance grows weak or is kept only in the head, then all goes astray.

Theophan the Recluse

Renewal

See also Longing for God; Prayer; Revival

Turn thou us unto thee, O Lord, and we shall be turned; renew our days as of old.

Lamentations 5:21 KJV

Do not conform any longer to the pattern of this world, but be transformed by the renewing of your mind. Then you will be able to test and approve what God's will is—his good, pleasing and perfect will.

Romans 12:2 NIV

Though this outer human nature of ours may be falling into decay, at the same time our inner human nature is renewed day by day.

2 Corinthians 4:16 NJB

Do not lie to one another, seeing that you have stripped off the old self with its practices and have clothed yourselves with the new self, which is being renewed in knowledge according to the image of its creator.

Colossians 3:9–10 NRSV

The difference between worldliness and godliness is a renewed mind.

Erwin W. Lutzer

By the reading of Scripture I am so renewed that all nature seems renewed around me and with me.

Thomas Merton

Charismatic Renewal fostered loyalty to the Church, recourse to the Sacraments, love of the Scriptures, a spirit of confidence and

hope, growth in prayer—especially spontaneous prayer of praise and thanksgiving—and an awareness of God's presence, in particular of the Holy Spirit.

Leon Joseph Suenens

A humble, lowly, contrite heart, / Believing, true, and clean, / Which neither life nor death can part / From Him that dwells within; / Thy nature, gracious Lord, impart; / Come quickly from above; / Write Thy new Name upon my heart, / Thy new best Name of love.

Charles Wesley

Repentance

See also Confession

I have heard of thee by the hearing of the ear: but now mine eye seeth thee. Wherefore I abhor myself, and repent in dust and ashes.

Job 42:5–6 KJV

The time is fulfilled, and the kingdom of God is at hand: repent ye, and believe the gospel.

Mark 1:15 KJV

I tell you, there will be more joy in heaven over one sinner who repents than over ninety-nine respectable people who do not need to repent.

Luke 15:7 GNB

Now you must repent and turn to God, so that your sins may be wiped out, and so that the Lord may send the time of comfort.

Acts 3:19–20 NJB

Who errs and mends, to God himself commends.

Miguel de Cervantes

To him who still remains in this world no repentance is too late. The approach to God's mercy is open, and the access is easy to those who seek and apprehend the truth.

St. Cyprian

No man ever enters heaven until he is first convinced that he deserves hell.

John Everrett

Amendment is repentence.

Thomas Fuller

Repentance if it be true strikes at the root and washes the heart from wickedness.

Matthew Henry

When thou attackest the roots of sin, fix thy thoughts upon the God whom thou desirest rather than upon the sin which thou abhorrest.

Walter Hilton

For right as by the courtesy of God He forgets our sins when we repent, right so will He that we forget our sin, and all our heaviness, and all our doubtful dreads.

Julian of Norwich

To do so no more is the truest repentance.

Martin Luther

Repentance is the golden key that opens the palace of eternity.

John Milton

Man is born with his face turned away from God. When he truly repents, he is turned right round toward God; he leaves his old life.

Dwight Lyman (D.L.) Moody

Repentance is an ongoing process. One must be forever repentant. It is not enough to once feel sorrow over sin. True repen-

tance affects the whole man and alters the entire life style.

Richard Owen Roberts

Repentance is a thorough change of a man's natural heart on the subject of sin.

John Charles Ryle

The world, as we live in it, is like a shop window into which some mischievous person has got overnight, and shifted all the price-labels so that the cheap things have the high price-labels on them and the really precious things are priced low. We let ourselves be taken in. Repentance means getting those price-labels back in the right place.

William Temple

How inconsistent it is to expect pardon of sins to be granted to a repentance which they have not fulfilled. This is to hold out your hand for merchandise, but not produce the price. For repentance is the price at which the Lord has determined to award pardon.

Quintus Tertullian

To move across from one sort of person to another is the essence of repentance: the liar becomes truthful, the thief, honest.

Aiden Wilson (A.W.) Tozer

God puts away many in anger for their supposed goodness, but not any at all for their confessed badness.

John Trapp

Repentance must be something more than mere remorse for sins; it comprehends a change of nature befitting heaven.

Lewis Wallace

One of the first things for which we have to pray is a true insight into our condition.

Olive Wyon

It can take less than a minute to commit a sin. It takes not as long to obtain God's forgiveness. Penitence and amendment should take a lifetime.

Hurbert van Zeller

Resentment, *see* Anger; Bitterness

Respect

See also Dignity; Reverence

Rise in the presence of the aged, show respect for the elderly and revere your God. I am the Lord.

Leviticus 19:32 NIV

Them that honor me I will honor, and they that despise me shall be lightly esteemed.

1 Samuel 2:30 KJV

The fear of the Lord is the beginning of wisdom.

Psalm 111:10 KJV

A good name is rather to be chosen than great riches, and loving favor rather than silver and gold.

Proverbs 22:1 KJV

Pay to all what is due them—taxes to whom taxes are due, revenue to whom revenue is due, respect to whom respect is due, honor to whom honor is due.

Romans 13:7 NRSV

Respect everyone, love other believers, honor God, and respect the Emperor.

1 Peter 2:17 GNB

Religionism is the result of a lack of respect for the followers of another religious faith. But, then, it is also a lack of respect for God.

Tissa Balasuriya

Friendship unites affection with respect. There is no need to bow down before a friend. We can look him in the eye. We neither look up to him nor down on him.

Jürgen Moltmann

This is the final test of a gentleman: his respect for those who can be of no possible service to him.

William Lyon Phelps

Responsibility

See also Duty

Am I my brother's keeper?

Genesis 4:9 KJV

Pilate saw that there was nothing he could do and that the people were starting to riot. So he took some water and washed his hands in front of them and said, "I won't have anything to do with killing this man. You are the ones doing it!"

Matthew 27:24 CEV

Where someone has been given much, much will be expected of him; and the more he has had entrusted to him the more will be demanded of him.

Luke 12:48 REB

We do not live to ourselves, and we do not die to ourselves. If we live, we live to the Lord, and if we die, we die to the Lord; so then, whether we live or whether we die, we are the Lord's.

Romans 14:7–8 NRSV

Work out your own salvation with fear and trembling. For it is God which worketh in you both to will and to do of his good pleasure.

Philippians 2:12–13 KJV

It is almost as presumptuous to think you can do nothing as to think you can do everything.

Phillips Brooks

Expect great things from God. Attempt great things for God.

William Carey

The price of greatness is responsibility.

Sir Winston Churchill

A wrong decision can make me very miserable. But I have trust in God. If you have this trust you don't have to worry, as you don't have sole responsibility.

Alfred Thompson, Lord Denning

To let oneself be bound by a duty from the moment you see it approaching is part of the integrity that alone justifies responsibility.

Dag Hammarskjöld

The whole secret of abundant living can be summed up in this sentence: "Not your responsibility but your response to God's ability."

Carl F.H. Henry

What difference does it make to you what someone else becomes, or says, or does? You do not need to answer for others, only for yourself.

Thomas à Kempis

Half the world is starving; the other half is on a diet. We are not privileged because we deserve to be. Privilege accepted should mean responsibility accepted.

Madeleine L'Engle

The world takes its notions of God from the people who say that they belong to God's family. They read us a great deal more than they read the Bible. They see us; they only hear about Jesus Christ.

Alexander Maclaren

Responsibility brings accountability.

Ken Robins

Man must cease attributing his problems to his environment, and learn again to exercise his will—his personal responsibility in the realm of faith and morals.

Albert Schweitzer

The most important thought I ever had was that of my individual responsibility to God.

Daniel Webster

Rest

See also Quiet and Stillness; Silence

One thing have I desired of the Lord, that will I seek after; that I may dwell in the house of the Lord all the days of my life, to behold the beauty of the Lord, and to enquire in his temple.

Psalm 27:4 KJV

And I said, O that I had wings like a dove: for then would I flee away, and be at rest.

Psalm 55:6 BCP

Look to the Lord and be strong; at all times seek his presence.

Psalm 105:4 REB

For thus said the Lord GOD, the Holy One of Israel: In returning and rest you shall be saved; in quietness and in trust shall be your strength.

Isaiah 30:15 NRSV

Come unto me, all ye that labor and are heavy laden, and I will give you rest. Take my yoke upon you, and learn of me; for I am meek and lowly in heart; and ye shall find rest unto your souls.

Matthew 11:28–30 KJV

After sending the crowds away he went up into the hills by himself to pray. When evening came, he was there alone.

Matthew 14:23 NJB

So many people were coming and going that Jesus and the apostles did not even have a chance to eat. Then Jesus said, "Let's go to a place where we can be alone and get some rest." They left in a boat for a place where they could be alone.

Mark 6:31–32 CEV

The promise to enter the place of rest is still good, and we must take care that none of you miss out. . . . Only people who have faith will enter the place of rest. . . . God has promised us a Sabbath when we will rest, even though it has not yet come. On that day God's people will rest from their work, just as God rested from his work. We should do our best to enter that place of rest, so that none of us will disobey and miss going there, as they did.

Hebrews 4:1, 11 CEV

You have made us for yourself, and our hearts are restless till they find their rest in you.

St. Augustine of Hippo

Jesus knows we must come apart and rest awhile, or else we may just plain come apart.

Vance Havner

Recreation is not the highest kind of enjoyment; but in its time and place it is quite as proper as prayer.

St. Irenaeus

No soul can have rest until it finds created things are empty. When the soul gives up all for love, so that it can have Him that is all, then it finds true rest.

Julian of Norwich

There is nothing so insupportable to man as complete repose, without passion, occupation, amusement, care. Then it is that he feels his nothingness, his isolation, his insufficiency, his dependence, his impotence, his emptiness.

Blaise Pascal

Jesus, I am resting, resting / In the joy of what Thou art; / I am finding out the greatness / Of Thy loving heart, / Thou hast bid me gaze upon Thee, / And Thy beauty fills my soul, / For by Thy transforming power / Thou hast made me whole.

Jean Sophia Pigott

Life lived amidst tension and busyness needs leisure. Leisure that re-creates and renews. Leisure should be a time to think new thoughts, not ponder old ills.

Neil C. Strait

He enjoys true leisure who has time to improve his soul's estate.

Henry David Thoreau

Resurrection

See also Easter; Jesus Christ, Resurrection of

And many of them that sleep in the dust of the earth shall awake, some to everlasting life, and some to shame and everlasting contempt.

Daniel 12:2 KJV

Martha said to him, "I know that he will rise again in the resurrection on the last day."

Jesus said to her, "I am the resurrection and the life. Those who believe in me, even though they die, will live."

John 11:24–25 NRSV

So also is the resurrection of the dead. It is sown in corruption; it is raised in incorruption: It is sown in dishonor; it is raised in glory: it is sown in weakness; it is raised in power: It is sown a natural body; it is raised a spiritual body. There is a natural body and there is a spiritual body.

1 Corinthians 15:42–44 KJV

He will change our weak mortal bodies and make them like his own glorious body, using that power by which he is able to bring all things under his rule.

Philippians 3:21 GNB

Our Lord has written the promise of the resurrection not in books alone, but in every leaf in springtime.

Martin Luther

The edges of God are tragedy; the depths of God are joy, beauty, resurrection, life. Resurrection answers crucifixion; life answers death.

Marjorie Hewitt Suchocki

Fellowship with Christ is participation in the divine life which finds its fullest expression in triumph over death. Life is a larger word than resurrection; but resurrection is, so to speak, the crucial quality of life.

William Temple

Retaliation, *see* Revenge

Retreat, *see* Rest

Revelation

See also Bible; Jesus Christ; Prophets and Prophecy; Word of God

All things are delivered unto me of my Father: and no man knoweth the Son, but the Father; neither knoweth any man the Father, save the Son, and he to whomsoever the Son will reveal him.

Matthew 11:27 KJV

Simon Peter answered, "You are the Christ, the Son of the living God." Jesus replied, "Blessed are you, Simon son of Jonah, for this was not revealed to you by man, but by my Father in heaven."

Matthew 16:16–17 NIV

For what can be known about God is perfectly plain to them, since God has made it plain to them: ever since the creation of the world, the invisible existence of God and his everlasting power have been clearly seen by the mind's understanding of created things. And so these people have no excuse.

Romans 1:19–20 NJB

As it is written, "What no eye has seen, nor ear heard, nor the human heart conceived, what God has prepared for those who love him"—these things God has revealed to us through the Spirit.

1 Corinthians 2:9–10 NRSV

The first and most important thing we know about God is that we know nothing about him except what he himself makes known.

Heinrich Emil Brunner

Man cannot cover what God would reveal.

Thomas Campbell

Revelation consists of the initiative of God, who personally came to meet man, in order to open with him a dialogue of salvation. It was God who began the talk, and it is God who carries it forward.

John Paul II

The core of Christian revelation is that Jesus Christ is the sole legitimate Lord of all human lives.

Hendrik Kraemer

We do not believe that God has added, or ever will add, anything to his revelation in his Son. But we can now see many things in that revelation which could not be seen by those who first received it. Each generation of Christians, and each people to which the Christian gospel is preached, makes its own contribution to the understanding of the riches of Jesus Christ.

C.B. Moss

As prayer is the voice of man to God, so revelation is the voice of God to man.

John Henry Newman

In revelation, God is the agent as well as the object. It is not just that men speak about God, or for God; God speaks for Himself, and talks to us in person.

James Innell (J.I.) Packer

Apart from special, saving revelation—the revelation that centers upon the Lord Jesus Christ—we do not and cannot know God.

James Innell (J.I.) Packer

We affirm, then, that unless all existence is a medium of revelation, no particular revelation is possible.

William Temple

Every revelation of God is a demand, and the way to knowledge of God is by obedience.

William Temple

Human salvation demands the divine disclosure of truths surpassing reason.

St. Thomas Aquinas

Revenge

Thou shalt not avenge, nor bear any grudge against the children of thy people, but thou shalt love thy neighbor as thyself: I am the Lord.

Leviticus 19:18 KJV

Don't take it on yourself to repay a wrong. Trust the Lord and he will make it right.

Proverbs 20:22 GNB

Beloved, never avenge yourselves, but leave room for the wrath of God; for it is written, "Vengeance is mine, I will repay, says the Lord." No, "if your enemies are hungry, feed them; if they are thirsty, give them something to drink; for by doing this you will heap burning coals on their heads." Do not be overcome by evil, but overcome evil with good.

Romans 12:19–21 NRSV

Revenge is the most worthless weapon in the world.

David Augsburger

O Lord, deliver me from this lust of always vindicating myself.

St. Augustine of Hippo

A man that studieth revenge keeps his own wounds green.

Francis Bacon

By taking revenge, a man is but even with his enemy; but in passing over it, he is superior.

Francis Bacon

The noblest vengeance is to forgive.

Henry George Bohn

Revenge, at first though sweet, / Bitter ere long back on itself recoils.

John Milton

There is no passion of the human heart that promises so much and pays so little as revenge.

Henry Wheeler Shaw

The only people with whom you should try to get even are those who have helped you.

John E. Southard

Reverence

See also Fear; Respect

The friendship of the LORD is for those who fear him, and he makes his covenant known to them.

Psalm 25:14 NRSV

Let us purify ourselves from everything that makes body or soul unclean, and let us be completely holy by living in awe of God.

2 Corinthians 7:1 GNB

We have been given possession of an unshakeable kingdom. Let us therefore be grateful and use our gratitude to worship God in the way that pleases him, in reverence and fear.

Hebrews 11:28 NJB

I fear God, yet I am not afraid of him.

Sir Thomas Browne

We must fear God through love, not love Him through fear.

Bishop Jean Pierre Camus

Wonder is the basis of worship.

Thomas Carlyle

The remarkable thing about fearing God is that when you fear God, you fear nothing else, whereas if you do not fear God, you fear everything else.

Oswald Chambers

O how I fear Thee, Living God, / With deepest, tenderest fears, / And worship Thee with trembling hope, / And penitential tears!

Frederick William Faber

We must rejoice in God, but still with a holy trembling.

Matthew Henry

When we cannot, by searching, find the bottom, we must sit down at the brink and adore the depth.

Matthew Henry

Fear the Lord, then, and you will do everything well.

Hermas

Reverence is the attitude which can be designated as the mother of all moral life, for in it man first takes a position toward the world which opens his spiritual eyes and enables him to grasp values.

Dietrich von Hildebrand

We pay God honor and reverence, not for his sake, because he is of himself full of glory to which no creature can add anything, but for our own sake.

St. Thomas Aquinas

More spiritual progress can be made in one short moment of speechless silence in the awesome presence of God than in years of mere study.

Aiden Wilson (A.W.) Tozer

Revival

See also God, Greatness of; Renewal

Will you not revive us again, so that your people may rejoice in you?

Psalm 85:6 NRSV

Oh, that you would rend the heavens and come down, that the mountains would tremble before you! As when fire sets twigs ablaze and causes water to boil, come down to make your name known to your enemies and cause the nations to quake before you!

Isaiah 64:1–2 NIV

O LORD, I have heard of your renown, and I stand in awe, O LORD, of your work. In our own time revive it; in our own time make it known; in wrath may you remember mercy.

Habakkuk 3:2 NRSV

Prayer is the backbone of a revival. . . . Instead of substituting new ideas such as religious films or social entertainments, why not really try the God-given method for revivals: "Pray without ceasing"?

John W. Basham

Revival is the exchange of the form of godliness for its living power.

John Bonar

The experience of revival is nothing more than a new beginning of obedience to God.

Charles Grandison Finney

A revival may be expected whenever Christians are found willing to make the sacrifices necessary to carry it on. They must be willing to sacrifice their feelings, their business, their time, to help forward the work.

Charles Grandison Finney

Every revival that ever came in the history of the world, or in the history of the Church, laid great emphasis on the holiness of God.

William Franklin (Billy) Graham

Revival is a sovereign act of God upon the Church whereby he intervenes to lift the situation completely out of human hands and works in extraordinary power.

Geoffrey R. King

The best way to revive a church is to build a fire in the pulpit.

Dwight Lyman (D.L.) Moody

Waiting for general revival is no excuse for not enjoying personal revival.

Stephen Olford

Revival is the inrush of the Spirit into a body that threatens to become a corpse.

D.M. Panton

Evangelism affects the other fellow; revival affects me.

Leonard Ravenhill

There is a sense in which revival is like a prairie fire ignited by a bolt of lightning from the heavens. Without organization, advertising, or even sometimes human leadership, revivals have altered the hearts of men, the social attitudes of millions, and the destinies of nations.

Richard Owen Roberts

God is more willing to give revival than we are to receive it.

Erlo Stegan

They tell me a revival is only temporary; so is a bath, but it does you good.

William Ashley (Billy) Sunday

Revival is . . . God revealing himself to man in awful holiness, and irresistible power. . . . If we find a revival that is not spoken against, we had better look again to ensure that it is a revival.

Arthur Wallis

Brokenness is not revival; it is a vital and indispensable step toward it.

Arthur Wallis

The greatest hindrance to revival is pride amongst the Lord's people.

Arthur Skevington Wood

Reward

You who fear the Lord, trust in him, and your reward will not be lost.

Ecclesiasticus 2:8 NRSV

Blessed are ye, when men shall revile you, and persecute you, and shall say all manner of evil against you falsely, for my sake. Rejoice, and be exceeding glad: for great is your reward in heaven.

Matthew 5:11–12 KJV

Then the king will say to those on his right, "Come, you who are blessed by my Father; take your inheritance, the kingdom prepared for you since the creation of the world. For I was hungry and you gave me something to eat, I was thirsty and you gave me something to drink, I was a stranger and you invited me in, I needed clothes and you clothed me, I was sick and you looked after me, I was in prison and you came to visit me."

Matthew 25:34–36 NIV

Christ is the only foundation. Whatever we build on that foundation will be tested by fire on the day of judgment. Then everyone will find out if we have used gold, silver, and precious stones, or wood, hay and straw. We will be rewarded if our building is left standing.

1 Corinthians 3:11–14 CEV

The "wages" of every noble work do yet lie in heaven or else nowhere.

Thomas Carlyle

The reward of a thing well done is to have done it.

Ralph Waldo Emerson

Today, let us rise and go to our work. Tomorrow, we shall rise and go to our reward.

Richard Buckminster Fuller

I have had many things in my hands and have lost them all. But whatever I have been able to place in God's hands I still possess.

Martin Luther

Faith in God will always be crowned.

William S. Plummer

An inheritance is not only kept for us, but we are kept for it.

Richard Sibbes

Before the judgment seat of Christ my service will not be judged by how much I have done but by how much of me there is in it.

Aiden Wilson (A.W.) Tozer

Riches, *see* Possessions; Wealth

Right and Wrong

If you are doing right, surely you ought to hold your head high! But if you are not doing right, Sin is crouching at the door hungry to get you.

Genesis 4:7 NJB

I do not understand what I do. For what I want to do I do not do, but what I hate I do. And if I do what I do not want to do, I agree that the law is good. As it is, it is no longer I myself who do it, but it is sin living in me. I know that nothing good lives in me, that is, in my sinful nature. For I have the desire to do what is good, but I cannot carry it out. For what I do is not the good I want to do; no, the evil I do not want to do—this I keep on doing. Now if I do what I do not want to do, it is no longer I who do it, but it is sin living in me who does it.

Romans 7:15–20 NIV

If you endure when you are beaten for doing wrong, what credit is that? But if you endure when you do right and suffer for it, you have God's approval.

1 Peter 2:20 NRSV

Whoever is evil must go on doing evil, and whoever is filthy must go on being filthy; whoever is good must go on doing good, and whoever is holy must go on being holy.

Revelation 22:11 GNB

Better, though difficult, the right way to go / Than wrong, tho' easy, where the end is woe.

John Bunyan

And fierce though the fiends may fight, and long though the angels hide / I know that truth and right have the universe on their side.

Washington Gladden

Right is right, even if everyone is against it; and wrong is wrong, even if everyone is for it.

William Penn

If your morals make you dreary, depend upon it, they are wrong.

Robert Louis Stevenson

Ethical behavior is concerned above all with human values, not with legalism.

A.M. Sullivan

If you would convince a man that he does wrong, do right. Men will believe what they see. Let them see.

Henry David Thoreau

Ideas of what is right and wrong vary from age to age and from place to place, but the significant thing is that there is a distinction between right and wrong. The inner compulsion to do right and the shame we feel when we are aware of having done wrong are an experience of God.

Leslie J. Tizard

To be right with God has often meant to be in trouble with men.

Aiden Wilson (A.W.) Tozer

Righteousness

See also Holiness; Justification; Purity

Abram believed the Lord, and he credited it to him as righteousness.

Genesis 15:6 NIV

The work of righteousness shall be peace; and the effect of righteousness quietness and assurance for ever.

Isaiah 32:17 KJV

Let justice flow like a stream, and righteousness like a river that never goes dry.

Amos 5:24 GNB

Blessed are those who hunger and thirst for righteousness, for they will be filled.

Matthew 5:6 NRSV

Christ came to reveal what righteousness really is, for nothing will do except righteousness, and no other conception of righteousness will do except Christ's conception of it—his method and secret.

Matthew Arnold

Unclean in the sight of God is everyone who is unrighteous: clean therefore is everyone who is righteous; if not in the sight of men, yet in the sight of God, who judges without error.

St. Augustine of Hippo

There is no way to kill a man's righteousness but by his own consent.

John Bunyan

Any talk about God that fails to take seriously the righteousness of God as revealed in the liberation of the weak and downtrodden is not Christian language.

James Cone

If there be ground for you to trust in your own righteousness, then all that Christ did to purchase salvation, and all that God did to prepare the way for it, is in vain.

Jonathan Edwards

Righteousness delivers from the sting of death, but not from the stroke of it.

Matthew Henry

Whereas obedience is righteousness in relation to God, love is righteousness in relation to others.

A. Plummer

The righteousness of Jesus is the righteousness of a Godward relationship of trust, dependence, receptivity.

(Arthur) Michael Ramsey

Risk

See also Courage

The Three Warriors sneaked through the Philistine camp and got some water from the well near Bethlehem's gate. They took it back to David, but he refused to drink it . . . and said, "Drinking this water would be like drinking the blood of these men who risked their lives to get it for me." The Three Warriors did these brave deeds.

1 Chronicles 11:18–19 CEV

Cast thy bread upon the waters: for thou shalt find it after many days.

Ecclesiastes 11:1 KJV

Our beloved Barnabas and Paul, who have risked their lives for the sake of our Lord Jesus Christ.

Acts 15:26 NRSV

Welcome him [Epaphroditus] in the Lord with great joy, and honor men like him, because he almost died for the work of Christ, risking his life to make up for the help you could not give me.

Philippians 2:29–30 NIV

Every advance in spiritual life has its corresponding dangers; every step that we rise nearer to God increases the depths of the gulf into which we may fall.

Robert Hugh Benson

If only I could persuade timid souls I meet to listen to that inner voice of the Spirit, which challenges us to attempt great things for God and expect great things from God. Oh, if only I could inspire them to heed that inner urging that tells them, "Go for it!" I cannot say what a person should do with life, but I can say what a person should not do with it. No one should devote one's life to safety, to a course of action that offers no challenge and no fun.

Tony Campolo

Love releases us for taking one more risk than we might dare; glory breaks through dark and danger, shows the Lord transfigured there. God who planted our affections, help your gifts to grow more free, fan in us the fires of loving, daring, dancing Trinity.

Michael Hare Duke

The way to be safe is never to be secure.

Thomas Fuller

I believe you won't find anywhere absolute criteria that will give you the certainty of not being wrong, and this risk of being wrong has to be taken because you can't be a person without taking the risk of being wrong.

Giulio Girardi

There is never an act of faith without risk.

Eric James

The Christian is not shut up in a tragedy from which there is no issue. The solution, in the spiritual order, the saints have taught him is a love stronger than hell. In the temporal order, also, I hold, there is a solution; it can only be found by going ahead, by accepting the risks of our creative freedom. . . .

Jacques Maritain

Do not be one of those who, rather than risk failure, never attempt anything.

Thomas Merton

If you want to help other people you have got to make up your mind to write things that some men will condemn.

Thomas Merton

Love is the greatest of all risks . . . the giving of myself. But dare I take this risk, diving into the swirling waters of loving fidelity?

Jean Vanier

Ritual, *see* Tradition; Worship

Rulers

See also Government and Politics; Leadership

Do not speak evil of God, and do not curse a leader of your people.

Exodus 22:28 GNB

First of all, then, I urge that supplications, prayers, intercessions, and thanksgivings be made for everyone, for kings and all who are in high positions, so that we may lead a quiet and peaceable life in all godliness and dignity.

1 Timothy 2:1–2 NRSV

Remind the people to be subject to rulers and authorities, to be obedient, to be ready to do whatever is good.

Titus 3:1 NIV

The church belongs to God, therefore it ought not to be assigned to Caesar. The temple of God cannot be Caesar's by right. No one can deny that I say this with respectful feeling for the emperor. For what is more respectful than to call the emperor the son of the church? . . . For the emperor is within the church, not above it.

St. Ambrose

No one can rule except one who can be ruled.

Anon.

Those who rule must above all be able to rule themselves.

St. Catherine of Siena

When a man assumes a public trust, he should consider himself as public property.

Thomas Jefferson

Rulers who prefer popular opinion to trust have as much power as robbers in the desert.

St. Justin Martyr

Bad officials are elected by good citizens who do not vote.

George Jean Nathan

Sabbath

Remember that the Sabbath Day belongs to me. You have six days when you can do your work, but the seventh day of each week belongs to me, your God. No one is to work on that day—not you, your children, your slaves, your animals, or the foreigners who live in your towns. In six days I made the sky, the earth, the oceans, and everything in them, but on the seventh day I rested. That's why I made the Sabbath a special day that belongs to me.

Exodus 20:8–11 CEV

If you refrain from trampling the sabbath, from pursuing your own interests on my holy day; if you call the sabbath a delight and the holy day of the LORD honorable; if you honor it, not going your own ways, serving your own interests, or pursuing your own affairs; then you shall take delight in the LORD, and I will make you ride upon the heights of the earth; I will feed you with the heritage of your ancestor Jacob, for the mouth of the LORD has spoken.

Isaiah 58:13–14 NRSV

The sabbath was made for man, and not man for the sabbath: Therefore the Son of man is Lord also of the sabbath.

Mark 2:27–28 KJV

God ended all the world's array, / And rested on the seventh day: / His holy voice proclaimed it blest, / And named it for the sabbath rest.

The Venerable Bede

Where sabbaths are neglected all religion sensibly goes to decay.

Matthew Henry

You show me a nation that has given up the sabbath and I will show you a nation that has got the seed of decay.

Dwight Lyman (D.L.) Moody

Man was made to worship every day, but work is eliminated on the sabbath to show its proper perspective in God's divine plan.

Clyde Narramore

A weekly sabbath walls in our wild nature.

Christopher Nesse

Common sense, reason, conscience, will combine, I think, to say that if we cannot spare God one day in a week we cannot be living as those ought to live who must die one day.

John Charles Ryle

Sacraments, *see* Baptism; Eucharist

Sacrifice

See also Jesus Christ, Death of; Self-Denial

Does the Lord delight in burnt offerings and sacrifices as much as in obeying the voice of the Lord? To obey is better than sacrifice, and to heed is better than the fat of rams.

1 Samuel 15:22 NIV

Sacrifice gives you no pleasure, burnt offering you do not desire. Sacrifice to God is a broken spirit, a broken, contrite heart you never scorn.

Psalm 51:16–17 NJB

I, the Lord, hate and despise your religious celebrations and your times of worship. I won't accept your offerings or animal sacrifices—not even your very best. No more of your noisy songs! I won't listen when you play your harps. But let justice and fairness flow like a river that never runs dry.

Amos 5:21–24 CEV

Go ye and learn what that meaneth, I will have mercy, and not sacrifice: for I am not come to call the righteous, but sinners to repentance.

Matthew 9:13 KJV

I appeal to you therefore, brothers and sisters, by the mercies of God, to present your bodies as a living sacrifice, holy and acceptable to God, which is your spiritual worship.

Romans 12:1 NRSV

Every Jewish priest performs his services every day and offers the same sacrifices many times; but these sacrifices can never take away sins. Christ, however, offered one sacrifice for sins, an offering that is effective for ever, and then he sat down at the right side of God.

Hebrews 10:11–12 GNB

To sacrifice something is to make it holy by giving it away for love.

Frederick Buechner

He is no fool who gives what he cannot keep to gain what he cannot lose.

Jim Elliot

Come, let us offer Christ the great, universal sacrifice of our love, and pour out before him our richest hymns and prayers. For he offered his cross to God as a sacrifice in order to make us all rich.

St. Ephrem

Without sacrifice there is no resurrection. Nothing grows and blooms save by giving.

All you try to save in yourself wastes and perishes.

André Gide

Was anything real ever gained without sacrifice of some kind?

Sir Arthur Helps

We cannot be sure we have something worth living for unless we are ready to die for it.

Eric Hoffer

Ministry that costs nothing, accomplishes nothing.

John Henry Jowett

All along the Christian course, there must be set up altars to God on which you sacrifice yourself, or you will never advance a step.

Alexander Maclaren

The sign of our professed love for the gospel is the measure of sacrifice we are prepared to make in order to help its progress.

Ralph P. Martin

God will be our compensation for every sacrifice we have made.

Frederick Brotherton (F.B.) Meyer

If Jesus Christ be God and died for me, then no sacrifice can be too great for me to make for him.

Charles Thomas (C.T.) Studd

The principle of sacrifice is that we choose to do or to suffer what apart from our love we should not choose to do or to suffer.

William Temple

Sacrifice releses power. The greater the sacrifice, the greater the power released.

John Richard Wimber

The only life that counts is the life that costs.

Frederick P. Wood

Sadness

See also Grief; Happiness; Tears

Why am I so sad? Why am I so troubled? I will put my hope in God, and once again I will praise him, my savior and my God.

Psalm 42:5 GNB

Choose sorrow over laughter because a sad face may hide a happy heart.

Ecclesiastes 7:3 CEV

There is no greater sorrow than to recall a time of happiness when in misery.

Dante Alighieri

You cannot prevent the birds of sorrow from flying over your head, but you can prevent them from building nests in your hair.

Anon.

There is only one sadness, the sadness of not being a saint.

Leon Bloy

Sorrow makes us all children again, destroys all differences in intellect. The wisest knows nothing.

Ralph Waldo Emerson

If one man should suffer all the sorrows of all the saints in the world, yet they are not worth one hour's glory in heaven.

St. John Chrysostom

In sorrow and suffering, go straight to God with confidence, and you will be strengthened, enlightened, and instructed.

St. John of the Cross

You learn your theology most where your sorrows take you.

Martin Luther

Earth has no sorrow that Heaven cannot heal.

Thomas V. Moore

The miserable have no other medicine / But only hope.

William Shakespeare

There is a sweet joy that comes to us through sorrow.

Charles Haddon Spurgeon

One son God hath without sin, but none without sorrow.

John Trapp

Saints

See also Fellowship

Precious in the sight of the Lord is the death of his saints.

Psalm 16:3 KJV

To the church of God that is in Corinth, to those who are sanctified in Christ Jesus, called to be saints, together with all those who in every place call on the name of our Lord Jesus Christ.

1 Corinthians 1:2 NRSV

Fornication and impurity of any kind, or greed, must not even be mentioned among you, as is proper among saints.

Ephesians 5:3 NRSV

A saint is a creature of vast possibilities, knit into shape by the ruling personality of God.

Oswald Chambers

A saint is never consciously a saint; a saint is consciously dependent on God.

Oswald Chambers

The saints are God's jewels, highly esteemed by and dear to him; they are a royal diadem in his hand.

Matthew Henry

The way of the world is to praise dead saints and to persecute living ones.

Nathaniel Howe

God creates out of nothing. Wonderful, you say. Yes, to be sure, but He does what is still more wonderful: he makes saints out of sinners.

Søren Kierkegaard

It certainly takes grace to make a man into a saint. Anyone who doubts this does not know what a saint is—nor what a man is.

Blaise Pascal

All personality has a radiation. The radiations of those in whom God dwells are mighty beyond measurement.

W.E. Sangster

The saints in each generation are joined to those who have gone before, and filled like them with light to become a golden chain in which each saint is a separate link, united to the next by faith, works, and love. So in the one God they form a single chain which cannot quickly be broken.

Simeon the New Theologian

The saint is saint, not because he is "good" but because he is transparent for something that is more than he himself is.

Paul Tillich

What is a saint? A particular individual completely redeemed from self-occupation; who,

because of this, is able to embody and radiate a measure of eternal life.

Evelyn Underhill

A saint is a human creature devoured and transformed by love.

Evelyn Underhill

Salvation

See also Heaven; Jesus Christ, Savior

The Lord is my light and my salvation; whom should I fear? The Lord is the stronghold of my life; of whom then should I go in dread?

Psalm 27:1 REB

With joy shall ye draw water out of the wells of salvation.

Isaiah 12:3 KJV

Lord, now lettest thou thy servant depart in peace, according to thy word; for mine eyes have seen thy salvation, which thou hast prepared before the face of all people, to be a light to lighten the Gentiles, and to be the glory of thy people Israel.

Luke 2:29–32 BCP

For whosoever shall call upon the name of the Lord shall be saved.

Romans 10:13 KJV

God our Savior . . . desires everyone to be saved and to come to the knowledge of the truth.

1 Timothy 2:3–4 NRSV

How shall we escape, if we neglect so great salvation?

Hebrews 2:3 KJV

Our salvation, thank God, depends much

more on His love of us than on our love of Him.

Fr. Andrew

There is no salvation outside the Church.

St. Augustine of Hippo

The essential fact of Christianity is that God thought all men worth the sacrifice of his Son.

William Barclay

Salvation means the incoming into human nature of the great characteristics that belong to God.

Oswald Chambers

A person may go to heaven without health, without riches, without honors, without learning, without friends; but he can never go there without Christ.

John Dyer

Man needs, above all else, salvation. He needs to turn round and see that God is standing there with a rope ready to throw to him if only he will catch it and attach it to himself.

Norman Goodacre

All our salvation consists in the manifestation of the nature, life, and Spirit of Jesus in our inward new man.

William Law

Looking at the wound of sin will never save anyone. What you must do is to look at the remedy.

Dwight Lyman (D.L.) Moody

Salvation is worth working for. It is worth a man's going round the world on his hands and knees, climbing its mountains, crossing its valleys, swimming its rivers, going through all manner of hardship in order to attain it. But we do not get in that way. It is to him who believes.

Dwight Lyman (D.L.) Moody

The way to be saved is not to delay, but to come and take.

Dwight Lyman (D.L.) Moody

The terms for "salvation" in many languages are derived from roots like *salvus, saos, whole, heil,* which all designate health, the opposite of disintegration and disruption. Salvation is healing in the ultimate sense; it is final, cosmic, and individual healing.

Paul Tillich

Sanctification, *see* Holiness; Holy Spirit and Sanctification

Sanctity, *see* Holiness

Satan, *see* Devil

Savior, *see* Jesus Christ, Savior; Salvation

Scripture, *see* Bible; Word of God

Search for God, *see* Seeking God

Second Coming, *see* Jesus Christ, Second Coming of

Seeking God

See also Longing for God

But if from thence thou shalt seek the Lord thy God, thou shalt find him, if thou seek him with all thy heart and with all thy soul.

Deuteronomy 4:29 KJV

Seek ye the Lord while he may be found, call ye upon him while he is near.

Isaiah 55:6 KJV

When you search for me, you will find me; if you seek me with all your heart. I will let you find me, says the LORD.

Jeremiah 29:13–14 NRSV

Ask, and you will receive; seek, and you will find; knock, and the door will be opened to you. For everyone who asks will receive, and anyone who seeks will find, and the door will be opened to those who knock.

Matthew 7:7–8 GNB

Draw nigh to God, and he will draw nigh to you. Cleanse your hands, ye sinners; and purify your hearts, ye double minded.

James 4:8 KJV

All heaven is waiting to help those who will discover the will of God and do it.

J. Robert Ashcroft

Thou hast made us for Thyself, and the heart of man is restless until it finds rest in Thee.

St. Augustine of Hippo

He alone is God who can never be sought in vain; not even when he cannot be found.

St. Bernard of Clairvaux

If we seek God for our own good and profit, we are not seeking God.

Meister Eckhart

Amiable agnostics will talk cheerfully about man's search for God. For me, they might as well talk about the mouse's search for a cat. . . . God closed in on me.

Clive Staples (C.S.) Lewis

Two men please God—who serves him with all his heart because he knows him, who seeks him with all his heart because he knows him not.

Nikita Ivanovich Panin

If you find God, you find life: if you miss God you miss the whole point of living.

Kenneth Pillar

We do not seek God—God seeks us.

Frederick William Robertson

To have found God is not an end in itself but a beginning.

Franz Rosenzweig

Those who seek God in isolation from their fellow-men . . . are apt to find, not God, but a devil whose countenance bears an embarrassing resemblance to their own.

Richard Henry Tawney

Religion is the first thing and the last thing, and until a man has found God, and been found by God, he begins at no beginning and works to no end.

Herbert George (H.G.) Wells

It is only as God seeks us that we can be found of him. God is seeker rather than sought.

Arthur Skevington Wood

Self-Control

See also Temperance

Like a city breached, without walls, is one who lacks self-control.

Proverbs 25:28 NRSV

The fruit of the Spirit is . . . self-control.

Galatians 5:22–23 NIV

The end of all things is upon us; therefore to help you to pray you must lead self-controlled and sober lives.

1 Peter 4:7 REB

Self-control is the ability to keep cool while someone is making it hot for you.

Anon.

The man who cannot control himself becomes absurd when he wants to rule over others.

Isaac Arama

One of the first things that happens when a man is really filled with the Spirit is not that he speaks with tongues, but that he learns to hold the one tongue he already has.

J. Sidlow Baxter

We are no more responsible for the evil thoughts that pass through our minds than a scarecrow for the birds which fly over the seedplot he has to guard. The sole responsibility in each case is to prevent them from settling.

John Churton Collins

Moderation is the silent string running through the pearl chain of all virtues.

Joseph Hall

Those who wish to transform the world must be able to transform themselves.

Konrad Heiden

If you would learn self-mastery, begin by yielding yourself to the One Great Master.

Johann Friedrich Lobstein

Our response to temptation is an accurate barometer of our love for God.

Erwin W. Lutzer

Man's greatest danger is the combination of his increased control over the elements and his lack of control over himself.

Albert Schweitzer

Self-discipline never means giving up anything, for giving up is a loss. Our Lord did not ask us to give up the things of earth, but to exchange them for better things.

Fulton John Sheen

He that commands others is not so much as free, if he doth not govern himself. The greatest performance in the life of man is the government of his spirit.

Benjamin Whichcote

The best way to break a bad habit is to drop it.

H.S. Yoder

Self-Denial

See also Unselfishness

If any man will come after me, let him deny himself, and take up his cross daily, and follow me. . . . For whosoever will lose his life for my sake, the same shall save it.

Luke 9:23–24 KJV

Jesus must become more important, while I become less important.

John 3:30 CEV

I tell you the truth, unless a kernel of wheat falls to the ground and dies, it remains only a single seed. But if it dies, it produces many seeds.

John 12:24 NIV

If others have this right of support from you, shouldn't we have it all the more? But we did not use this right. On the contrary, we put up with anything rather than hinder the gospel of Christ.

1 Corinthians 9:12 NIV

If there is no element of asceticism in our lives, if we give free rein to the desires of the flesh . . . we shall find it hard to train for the service of Christ.

Dietrich Bonhoeffer

All men who have had spiritual power to prevail with God and man have been men who learned to sternly deny themselves and keep their bodies under.

Samuel Brengle

The more a man denies himself, the more shall he obtain from God.

Horace Bushnell

All great virtues bear the imprint of self-denial.

William Ellery Channing

There is no other way to live this Christian life than by a continual death to self.

François de la Mothe Fénelon

That you may have pleasure in everything, seek your own pleasure in nothing. That you may know everything, seek to know nothing. That you may possess all things, seek to possess nothing. That you may be everything, seek to be nothing.

St. John of the Cross

The one true way of dying to self is most simple and plain . . . if you ask what is the one true, simple, plain, and immediate and unerring way? It is the way of patience, meekness, humility, and resignation.

William Law

You will be dead so long as you refuse to die.

George MacDonald

They that deny themselves for Christ shall enjoy themselves in Christ.

John Mason

There was a day when I died to George Müller; his opinions and preferences, tastes and will; died to the world, its approval or censure; died to the approval or blame even of my brethren or friends; and since then I have striven only to show myself approved unto God.

George Müller

What does it mean for me to be "crucified"? I think the answer is best summed up in the words the crowd used of Jesus: "Away with him!"

Watchman Nee

One secret act of self-denial, one sacrifice of inclination to duty, is worth all the mere good thoughts, warm feelings, passionate prayers in which idle people indulge themselves.

John Henry Newman

Surrender of self applies as much to the daily affairs of life as it does to the affairs of the soul. They cannot be separated. We are all of a piece.

Br. Roger (Schutz)

There is a great difference between denying yourself things and denying yourself.

Adrian Rogers

He best can part with life without a sigh whose daily living is to daily die.

Charles Haddon Spurgeon

Prepare yourselves, my younger brethren, to become weaker and weaker; prepare yourselves for sinking lower and lower in self-esteem; prepare yourselves for self-annihilation—and pray God to expedite the process.

Charles Haddon Spurgeon

It is never too late to give up your prejudices.

Henry David Thoreau

The cross that Jesus tells us to carry is the one that we willingly take up ourselves—the cross of self-denial in order that we might live for the glory of the Father.

Colin Urquhart

Self-Discipline, *see* Self-Control

Self-Examination

LORD, let me know my end and what is the measure of my days; let me know how fleeting my life is.

Psalm 39:4 NRSV

I have reflected on my ways, and I turn my steps to your instructions.

Psalm 119:59 NJB

For I know that nothing good dwells within me, that is, in my flesh. I can will what is right, but I cannot do it.

Romans 7:18 NRSV

Let a man examine himself, and so let him eat of that bread, and drink of that cup. For he that eateth and drinketh unworthily, eateth and drinketh damnation to himself, not discerning the Lord's body. For this cause many are weak and sickly among you, and many sleep. For if we would judge ourselves, we should not be judged.

1 Corinthians 11:28–31 KJV

Examine yourselves to see whether you are living in the faith. Test yourselves. Do you not realize that Jesus Christ is in you?—unless, indeed, you fail to meet the test!

2 Corinthians 13:5 NRSV

Incline us, oh God!, to think humbly of ourselves, to be severe only in the examination of our own conduct, to consider our fellow-creatures with kindness, and to judge of all they say and do with that charity which we would desire from them ourselves.

Jane Austen

A man has many skins in himself, covering the depths of his heart. Man knows so many things; he does not know himself. Why, thirty or forty skins or hides, just like an ox's or a bear's, so thick and hard, cover the soul. Go into your own ground and learn to know yourself there.

Meister Eckhart

Determine a plan of action in the morning, and then evaluate yourself at night. How have you behaved today? What were your words, your deeds, your thoughts?

Thomas à Kempis

A humble knowledge of thyself is a surer way to God than a deep search after learning.

Thomas à Kempis

For every one look within, take ten looks at Christ.

Robert Murray M'Cheyne

The man who does not like self-examination may be pretty certain that things need examining.

Charles Haddon Spurgeon

Beware of no man more than yourself; we carry our worst enemies within us.

Charles Haddon Spurgeon

It is a great grace of God to practice self-examination; but too much is as bad as too little.

St. Teresa of Avila

Do not think of the faults of others but of what is good in them and faulty in yourself.

St. Teresa of Avila

It is good to find out our sins, lest they find us out.

Thomas Watson

Every man must be allowed to judge himself; but he must not be allowed to bury the evidence.

Morris West

Self-Pity

We wish the Lord had killed us in Egypt. When we lived there, we could at least sit down and eat all the bread and meat we wanted. But you have brought us out here into this desert, where we are going to starve.

Exodus 16:3 CEV

He himself [Elijah] went a day's journey into the wilderness, and came and sat down under a juniper tree: and he requested for himself that he might die; and said, It is enough; now, O Lord, take away my life; for I am not better than my fathers.

1 Kings 19:4 KJV

Why so downcast, why all these sighs? Hope in God! I will praise him still, my Savior, my God.

Psalm 43:5 NJB

If you have the whine in you, kick it out ruthlessly.

Oswald Chambers

As Christians we should never feel sorry for ourselves. The moment we do so, we lose our energy, we lose the will to fight and the will to live, and are paralyzed.

David Martyn Lloyd-Jones

Self-pity . . . cuddle and nurse it as an infant and you'll have on your hands in a brief period of time a beast, a monster, a raging, coarse brute that will spread the poison of bitterness and paranoia throughout your system.

Charles R. Swindoll

What poison is to food, self-pity is to life.

Oliver G. Wilson

Self-Righteousness, *see* Pride

Selfishness

See also Love, for Self; Unselfishness

They are like greedy dogs that never get enough. These leaders have no understanding. They each do as they please and seek their own advantage.

Isaiah 56:11 GNB

For those who are self-seeking and reject the truth and follow evil, there will be wrath and anger.

Romans 2:8 NIV

We should think about others and not about ourselves.

1 Corinthians 10:24 CEV

Living in our selfishness means stopping at human limits and preventing our transformation into divine love.

Carlo Corretto

Since I am determined to join myself to God, I find that I am also bound to be the enemy of his enemies. And since I find nothing that is more his enemy than the self that is in me, I am constrained to hate this part of me more than any other.

Catherine of Genoa

For most men the world is centered in self, which is misery: to have one's world centered in God is peace.

Donald Hankey

No indulgence of passion destroys the spiritual nature so much as respectable selfishness.

George MacDonald

I have more trouble with D.L. Moody than with any man I ever met.

Dwight Lyman (D.L.) Moody

Nine-tenths of our unhappiness is selfishness, and is an insult cast in the face of God.

G.H. Morrison

Self-centeredness of any kind is always a movement away from God and consequently a very serious form of disorder.

Philip Pare

The man who lives by himself and for himself is apt to be corrupted by the company he keeps.

Charles Henry Parkhurst

Christ regarded the self-loving, self-regarding, self-seeking spirit as the direct antithesis of real living. His two fundamental rules for life were that "love-energy," instead of being turned in on itself, should go out first to God and then to other people.

John Bertram (J.B.) Phillips

When a man is wrapped up in himself, he makes a pretty small package.

John Ruskin

If I really love God, my innate and persistent selfishness will have received its death-blow.

Alexander Smellie

Self-centeredness completely vitiates communication—with either God or man.

Hubert van Zeller

Serenity, *see* Peace, of Mind

Sermons

See also Preaching

My message and my preaching were not with wise and persuasive words, but with a demonstration of the Spirit's power.

1 Corinthians 2:4 NIV

Every man is a priest, even involuntarily; his conduct is an unspoken sermon, which he is for ever preaching to others.

Henri-Frédéric Amiel

One act of obedience is better than a hundred sermons.

Dietrich Bonhoeffer

Great sermons lead the people to praise the preacher. Good preaching leads the people to praise the Savior.

Charles Grandison Finney

It requires great listening as well as great preaching to make a great sermon.

John Andrew Holmes

Aim at pricking the heart not stroking the skin.

St. Jerome

He that has but one word of God before him, and out of that word cannot make a sermon, can never be a preacher.

Martin Luther

A sermon is not made with an eye upon the sermon, but with both eyes upon the people and all the heart upon God.

John Owen

A sermon is a proclamation of the generous love of God in Christ, or it is not a Christian sermon.

Norman Pittenger

A crowd is not an achievement, only an opportunity.

William Edwyn Robert Sangster

The sermons most needed today are sermons in shoes.

Charles Haddon Spurgeon

Effective sermons are the offspring of study, of discipline, of prayer, and especially of the unction of the Holy Ghost.

James Henley Thornwell

Once in seven years I burn all my sermons for it is a shame if I cannot write better sermons now than I did seven years ago.

John Wesley

It is a poor sermon that gives no offense; that neither makes the hearer displeased with himself nor with the preacher.

George Whitefield

Some clergy prepare their sermons; others prepare themselves.

Samuel Wilberforce

Good sermons happen when the twofold listening, to tradition and to the present, really becomes a listening to and for God, so that something emerges almost begging to be put into words.

Rowan Williams

It takes a lifetime to prepare a sermon because it takes a lifetime to prepare a man of God.

Arthur Skevington Wood

Seven Last Words

See also Cross; Jesus Christ, Death of; Jesus Christ, Prayers of

About the ninth hour Jesus cried with a loud voice, saying, Eli, Eli, lama sabachthani? that is to say, My God, my God, why hast thou forsaken me?

Matthew 27:46 KJV

Then Jesus said, "Father, forgive them; for they do not know what they are doing."

Luke 23:34 NRSV

He answered him, "In truth I tell you, today you will be with me in paradise."

Luke 23:43 NJB

Then Jesus uttered a loud cry and said, "Father, into your hands I commit my spirit"; and with these words he died.

Luke 23:46 REB

When Jesus saw his mother and his favorite disciple with her, he said to his mother, "This man is now your son." Then he said to the disciple, "She is now your mother." From then on, that disciple took her into his own home.

John 19:26–27 CEV

After this, Jesus knowing that all things were now accomplished, that the scripture might be fulfilled, saith, I thirst.

John 19:28 KJV

Jesus drank the wine and said, "It is finished!" Then he bowed his head and gave up his spirit.

John 19:30 GNB

Sex and Sexuality

So God created humankind in his image, in the image of God he created them; male and female he created them.

Genesis 1:27–28 NRSV

That's why a man will leave his own father and mother. He marries a woman, and the two of them become like one person. Although the man and his wife were both naked, they were not ashamed.

Genesis 2:24–25 CEV

The husband must give to his wife what she has a right to expect, and so too the wife to her husband. The wife does not have authority over her own body, but the husband does; and in the same way, the husband does not have authority over his own body, but the wife does. You must not deprive each other except by mutual consent for a limited time, to leave yourselves free for prayer, and to come together again afterwards; otherwise Satan may take advantage of any lack of self-control to put you to the test.

1 Corinthians 7:3–5 NJB

But among you there must not be even a hint of sexual immorality, or of any kind of impurity, or of greed, because these are improper for God's holy people.

Ephesians 5:3 NIV

It is God's will that you should be sanctified: that you should avoid sexual immorality.

1 Thessalonians 4:3 NIV

Nuptial love maketh mankind; friendly love perfecteth it; but wanton love corrupteth and embaseth it.

Francis Bacon

Whenever Christ was confronted by people in sexual disarray, he took good care to safeguard sexuality by reminding them that they had to avoid sin; that is to say to use their sexuality in a fully human way.

Jack Dominian

The love of a man and a woman gains immeasurably in power when placed under divine restraint.

Elisabeth Elliot

Only in a marriage—a marriage where love is—can sex develop into the delightfully positive force God meant it to be. Here is where the excitement of sex really is. When a man and a woman make a lifelong commitment to love and cherish each other, they are giving themselves the time they will need to dismantle the barriers of restraint, shyness, defensiveness, and selfishness that exist between all human beings. It cannot be done in a night or with a rush of passion. It takes time to know and be known.

Colleen Townsend Evans

Most of the so-called sexual incompatibility in marriage springs from the delusion that sex is an activity when it is primarily a relationship; if the relationship is faulty, the activity cannot long be self-sustaining or truly satisfactory.

Sydney J. Harris

We use for passions the stuff that has been given to us for happiness.

Joseph Joubert

God never intended that man could find the true meaning of his sexuality in any other relationship than that of the total self-giving involved in marriage.

Al Martin

Love can wait to give; it is lust that can't wait to get.

Josh McDowell

Sexuality throws no light upon love, but only through love can we learn to understand sexuality.

Eugen Rosenstock-Huessy

For aught that I could ever read, / Could ever hear by tale or history, / The course of true love never did run smooth.

William Shakespeare

The expression "free love" is a contradiction in terms. If it's free, it's not love; if it's love, it's not free.

David Watson

Shame

See also Guilt

He said, "I heard the sound of you in the garden, and I was afraid, because I was naked; and I hid myself."

Genesis 3:10 NRSV

Whosoever therefore shall be ashamed of me and my words in this adulterous and sinful generation; of him also shall the Son of man be ashamed, when he cometh in the glory of his Father with the holy angels.

Mark 8:38 KJV

I see no reason to be ashamed of the gospel, it is God's power for the salvation of everyone who has faith.

Romans 1:16 NJB

I am not ashamed, because I know whom I have believed, and am convinced that he is able to guard what I have entrusted to him for that day.

2 Timothy 1:12 NIV

I am a Christian; we do nothing to be ashamed of.

Blandina

I reckon him a Christian indeed that is neither ashamed of the gospel nor a shame to it.

Matthew Henry

To be discontented with the divine discontent, and to be ashamed with the noble shame, is the very germ and first upgrowth of all virtue.

Charles Kingsley

It is only when we have lost all love of ourselves for our own sakes, that our past sins cease to give us the anguish of shame.

Thomas Merton

A man should never be ashamed to own he has been in the wrong, which is but saying, in other words, that he is wiser to-day than he was yesterday.

Alexander Pope

I never wonder to see men wicked, but I often wonder to see them not ashamed.

Jonathan Swift

Man is the only animal that blushes. Or needs to.

Mark Twain

Be ashamed of nothing but sin: not of fetching of wood, or drawing water, if time permit; not of cleaning your own shoes or your neighbor's.

John Wesley

Shepherd, *see* Church, Leaders of; Pastoral Care

Signs and Wonders, *see* Jesus Christ, Miracles of; Miracles

Silence

See also Quiet and Stillness; Rest

Even fools may be thought wise and intelligent if they stay quiet and keep their mouths shut.

Proverbs 17:28 GNB

He was oppressed, and he was afflicted, yet he did not open his mouth; like a lamb that is led to the slaughter, and like a sheep that before its shearers is silent, so he did not open his mouth.

Isaiah 53:7 NRSV

But the Lord is in his holy temple: let all the earth keep silence before him.

Habakkuk 2:20 KJV

The chief priests accused him of many things. So again Pilate asked him, "Aren't you going to answer? See how many things they are accusing you of." But Jesus still made no reply, and Pilate was amazed.

Mark 15:3–5 NIV

It is in silence that God is known, and through mysteries that He declares Himself.

Robert Hugh Benson

We are silent at the beginning of the day because God should have the first word, and we are silent before going to sleep because the last word also belongs to God.

Dietrich Bonhoeffer

Mere silence is not wisdom, for wisdom consists in knowing when and how to speak and when and where to keep silent.

Bishop Jean Pierre Camus

True silence is the key to the immense and flaming heart of God. It is the beginning of a divine courtship that will end only in the immense, creative, fruitful, loving silence of final union with the Beloved.

Catherine de Hueck Doherty

In silence a man can most readily preserve his integrity.

Meister Eckhart

How can you expect God to speak in that gentle and inward voice which melts the soul, when you are making so much noise with your rapid reflections? Be silent, and God will speak again.

François de la Mothe Fénelon

One reason we can hardly bear to remain silent is that it makes us feel so helpless. We are so accustomed to relying upon words to manage and control others. If we are silent, who will take control? God will take control; but we will never let him take control until we trust him. Silence is intimately related to trust.

Richard J. Foster

Outward silence is indispensable for the cultivation and improvement of inner silence.

Jeanne Guyon

Our safest eloquence concerning him is our silence, when we confess without confession that his glory is inexplicable, his greatness above our capacity and reach.

Richard Hooker

Be silent about great things; let them grow inside you. Never discuss them: discussion is so limiting and distracting. It makes things grow smaller. You think you swallow things when they ought to swallow you. Before all greatness, be silent—in art, in music, in religion.

Baron Friedrich von Hügel

The Father uttered one Word; that Word is his Son, and he utters him for ever in everlasting silence; and in silence the soul has to hear it.

St. John of the Cross

Better to remain silent and be thought a fool than to speak and to remove all doubt.

Abraham Lincoln

God is the friend of silence. Trees, flowers, grass grow in silence. See the stars, moon, and sun, how they move in silence.

Mother Teresa

Silence is not much preached today, so it is for prayer to preach it. If we do not listen we do not come to the truth. If we do not pray we do not even get as far as listening. The four things do together: silence, listening, prayer, truth.

Hubert van Zeller

Simplicity

See also Single-Mindedness

The entrance of thy words giveth light; it giveth understanding unto the simple.

Psalm 119:130 KJV

For it is written: "I will destroy the wisdom of the wise; the intelligence of the intelligent I will frustrate." Where is the wise man? Where is the scholar? Where is the philosopher of this age? Has not God made foolish the wisdom of the world? For since in the wisdom of God the world through its wisdom did not know him, God was pleased through the foolishness of what was preached to save those who believe.

1 Corinthians 1:19–21 NIV

I fear, lest by any means, as the serpent beguiled Eve through his subtlety, so your minds should be corrupted from the simplicity that is in Christ.

2 Corinthians 11:3 KJV

Be simple; take our Lord's hand and walk through things.

Fr. Andrew

Simplicity is the ordinary attendant of sincerity.

Richard Baxter

One can acquire "simplicity" but "simpleness" is innate. Education and culture may bring "simplicity"—indeed, it ought to be one of their essential aims—but simpleness is a gift.

Dietrich Bonhoeffer

The inward reality of holy obedience to the divine Center is so central to everything about simplicity.

Richard J. Foster

Hold fast to simplicity of heart and innocence. Yes, be as infants who do not know the wickedness that destroys the life of men.

Hermas

The more we know of God the more unreservedly we will trust him; the greater our progress in theology, the simpler and more childlike will be our faith.

John Gresham Machen

Make it clear. Make it simple. Emphasize the essentials. Forget about impressing. Leave some things unsaid. Let the thing be simplified.

Charles R. Swindoll

Simplicity is found in the unfettered joy of a brother who forsakes an obsession with his own progress or backslidings in order to fix his gaze on the light of Christ.

The Taizé Rule

Our life is frittered away by detail. . . . Simplicity, simplicity, simplicity!

Henry David Thoreau

Hair-splitting can be left to theologians and

legalists; simplicity is the aim in the life of prayer.

Hubert van Zeller

Sin

See also Confession; Forgiveness; Jesus Christ, Death of; Repentance

Avoidance of

I treasure your word in my heart, so that I may not sin against you.

Psalm 119:11 NRSV

In the same way, you must think of yourselves as dead to the power of sin. But Christ Jesus has given life to you, and you live for God. Don't let sin rule your body. After all, your body is bound to die, so don't obey its desires or let any part of it become a slave of evil. Give yourselves to God, as people who have been raised from death to life. Make every part of your body a slave that pleases God. Don't let sin keep ruling your lives. You are ruled by God's kindness and not by the Law.

Romans 6:11–14 CEV

Encourage one another daily, as long as it is called Today, so that none of you may be hardened by sin's deceitfulness.

Hebrews 3:13 NIV

If hell were on one side and sin on the other, I would rather leap into hell than willingly sin against my God.

St. Anselm of Canterbury

Kill sin before it kills you.

Richard Baxter

Naught but the name of Jesus can restrain the impulse of anger, repress the swelling of

pride, cure the wound of envy, bridge the onslaught of luxury, extinguish the flame of carnal desire, can temper avarice, and put to flight impure and ignoble thoughts.

St. Bernard of Clairvaux

From envy, hatred, and malice, and all uncharitableness, Good Lord, deliver us.

Book of Common Prayer

It is the great moment of our lives when we decide that sin must die right out, not be curbed or suppressed or countenanced, but crucified.

Oswald Chambers

Sin is to be overcome, not so much by direct opposition to it as by cultivating opposite principles. Would you kill the weeds in your garden, plant it with good seed; if the ground be well occupied there will be less need of the hoe.

Abraham Fuller

When thou attackest the roots of sin, fix thy thought more upon the God whom thou desirest than upon the sin which thou abhorrest.

Walter Hilton

It would be better to eschew sin than to flee death.

Thomas à Kempis

To mourn a mischief that is past and gone / Is the next way to draw new mischief on.

William Shakespeare

Essence and Effects of

But if ye will not do so, behold, ye have sinned against the Lord: and be sure your sin will find you out.

Numbers 32:23 KJV

Your iniquities have been barriers between you and your God, and your sins have hidden his face from you so that he does not hear.

Isaiah 59:2 NRSV

O thou that art waxen old in wickedness, now thy sins which thou hast committed aforetime are come to light.

History of Susanna 52 KJV

For the wages of sin is death; but the gift of God is eternal life through Jesus Christ our Lord.

Romans 6:23 KJV

One leak will sink a ship, and one sin will destroy a sinner.

John Bunyan

Sin is the dare of God's justice, the rape of his mercy, the jeer of his patience, the slight of his power, and the contempt of his love.

John Bunyan

The greatest fault is to be conscious of none.

Thomas Carlyle

Sin is a power in our life: let us fairly understand that it can only be met by another power.

Henry Drummond

The root of sin is indolence of heart.

Alan Ecclestone

Sins are like circles in the water when a stone is thrown into it; one produces another. When anger was in Cain's heart, murder was not far off.

Philip Henry

As long as we be meddling with any part of sin, we shall never see clearly the blissful countenance of our Lord.

Julian of Norwich

Would to God we had behaved ourselves well in this world, even for one day.

Thomas à Kempis

Almost all our faults are more pardonable than the methods we think up to hide them.

François, Duc de La Rochefoucauld

Sin is essentially a departure from God.

Martin Luther

Sin is always loving badly, or not loving at all.

Michel Quoist

Little foxes ruin the vineyards; and little sins do mischief to the tender heart. These little sins burrow in the soul, and make it so full of that which is hateful to Christ, that He will hold no comfortable fellowship and communion with us.

Charles Haddon Spurgeon

No sin is small. No grain of sand is small in the mechanism of a watch.

Jeremy Taylor

Whatever we do that creates deadness is a sin.

John V. Taylor

For the religious man to do wrong is to defy his King; for the Christian, it is to wound his Friend.

William Temple

Sincerity

See also Integrity

Fear the Lord, and serve him in sincerity and truth: and put away the gods which your fathers served on the other side of the flood, and in Egypt; and serve ye the Lord.

Joshua 24:14 KJV

Love must be sincere.

Romans 12:9 NIV

Let us celebrate the festival, not with the old yeast, the yeast of malice and evil, but with the unleavened bread of sincerity and truth.

1 Corinthians 5:8 NRSV

It is often said it is no matter what a man believes if he is only sincere. But let a man sincerely believe that seed planted without plowing is as good as with; that January is as favorable for seed-sowing as April; and that cockle seed will produce as good a harvest as wheat, and is it so?

Henry Ward Beecher

Be what thou seemest.

Horatius Bonar

Jesus Christ makes us real, not merely sincere.

Oswald Chambers

The kindling power of our words must not come from outward show but from within, not from oratory but straight from the heart.

St. Francis de Sales

The devil is sincere, but he is sincerely wrong.

William Franklin (Billy) Graham

If you take heed what you are within, you shall not reckon what men say of you. Man looks on the visage and God on the heart. Man considers the deeds and God praises the thoughts.

Thomas à Kempis

The conduct of our lives is the only proof of the sincerity of our hearts.

Robert Dick Wilson

Sinful Nature

I have sinned and done wrong since the day I was born.

Psalm 51:5 CEV

For all have sinned and fall short of the glory of God.

Romans 3:23 NIV

What the Law could not do because of the weakness of human nature, God did, sending his own Son in the same human nature as any sinner to be a sacrifice for sin, and condemning sin in that human nature. This was so that the Law's requirements might be fully satisfied in us as we direct our lives not by our natural inclinations but by the Spirit. Those who are living by their natural inclinations have their minds on the things human nature desires; those who live in the Spirit have their minds on spiritual things. And human nature has nothing to look forward to but death, while the Spirit looks forward to life and peace, because the outlook of disordered human nature is opposed to God, since it does not submit to God's Law, and indeed it cannot, and those who live by their natural inclinations can never be pleasing to God. You, however, live not by your natural inclinations, but by the Spirit, since the Spirit of God has made a home in you.

Romans 8:3–9 NJB

For what our human nature wants is opposed to what the Spirit wants, and what the Spirit wants is opposed to what our human nature wants. These two are enemies, and this means that you cannot do what you want to do.

Galatians 5:17 GNB

The goodness of God knows how to use our disordered wishes and actions, often lovingly turning them to our advantage whilst always preserving the beauty of His order.

St. Bernard of Clairvaux

There is no crime of which one cannot imagine oneself to be the author.

Johann Wolfgang von Goethe

If you cannot mold yourself as you would wish, how can you expect other people to be entirely to your liking?

Thomas à Kempis

Humanity does not pass through phases as a train passes through a station: being alive, it has the privilege of always moving yet never leaving anything behind. Whatever we have been, in some sort we are still.

Clive Staples (C.S.) Lewis

Original sin is in us, like the beard. We are shaved today and look clean, and have a smooth chin; tomorrow our beard has grown again, nor does it cease growing while we remain on earth. In like manner original sin cannot be extirpated from us; it springs up in us as long as we live.

Martin Luther

I more fear what is within me than what comes from without.

Martin Luther

If there is a God, since there is a God, the human race is implicated in some terrible aboriginal calamity. It is out of joint with the purposes of its Creator.

John Henry Newman

We are born unrighteous; for each one tends to himself, and the bent toward self is the beginning of all disorder.

Blaise Pascal

Our old nature is no more extinct than the devil; but God's will is that the dominion of both should be broken.

John R.W. Stott

Worst of all my foes, I fear the enemy within.

John Wesley

Singing

Sing a new song to the Lord! Sing to the Lord, all the world! Sing to the Lord, and praise him! Proclaim every day the good news that he has saved us.

Psalm 96:1–2 GNB

Like one who takes away a garment on a cold day, or like vinegar poured on soda, is one who sings songs to a heavy heart.

Proverbs 25:20 NIV

Let the word of Christ dwell in you richly in all wisdom; teaching and admonishing one another in psalms and hymns and spiritual songs, singing with grace in your hearts to the Lord.

Colossians 3:16 KJV

Are any among you suffering? They should pray. Are any cheerful? They should sing songs of praise.

James 5:13 NRSV

What though my joys and comforts die? / The Lord my Savior liveth; / What though the darkness gather round? / Songs in the night he giveth; / No storm can shake my inmost calm, / While to that refuge clinging; / Since Christ is Lord of heaven and earth, / How can I keep from singing?

Robert Lowry

Still in the enormous silence of the desert we sing like birds.

Sara Maitland

When your heart is full of Christ, you want to sing.

Charles Haddon Spurgeon

O for a thousand tongues to sing my great Redeemer's praise.

Charles Wesley

Single-Mindedness

One thing I have desired of the Lord, that will I seek after; that I may dwell in the house of the Lord all the days of my life, to behold the beauty of the Lord, and to enquire in his temple.

Psalm 27:4 KJV

They will be my people, and I will be their God. I will give them singleness of heart and action, so that they will always fear me for their own good and the good of their children after them.

Jeremiah 32:38–39 NIV

The light of the body is the eye: if therefore thine eye be single, thy whole body shall be full of light.

Matthew 6:22 KJV

The main thing is to keep the main thing the main thing!

Anon.

He that loves God seeks neither gain nor reward but only to lose all, even himself.

St. John of the Cross

There are many activities I must cut out simply because I desire to excel in my pursuit after God and holiness.

Wendell W. Price

The body has two eyes, but the soul must have but one.

William Secker

Love has a clear eye; but it can see only one thing—it is blind to every interest but that of its Lord; it sees things in the light of his glory and weighs actions in the scales of his honor; it counts royalty but drudgery if it cannot reign for Christ, but it delights in servitude as much as in honor, if it can thereby advance the Master's kingdom; its end sweetens all its means; its object lightens its toil and removes its weariness.

Charles Haddon Spurgeon

A man's heart has only enough life in it to pursue one object fully.

Charles Haddon Spurgeon

Singleness

The disciples said, "If that's how it is between a man and a woman, it's better not to get married." Jesus told them, "Only those people who have been given the gift of staying single can accept this teaching. Some people are unable to marry because of birth defects or because of what someone has done to their bodies. Others stay single in order to serve God better. Anyone who can accept this teaching should do so."

Matthew 19:10–12 CEV

I wish that all were as I myself am. But each has a particular gift from God, one having one kind and another a different kind.

1 Corinthians 7:7 NRSV

I want you to be free from anxious care. An unmarried man is concerned with the Lord's business; his aim is to please the Lord.

1 Corinthians 7:32 REB

The essence of chastity is not the suppression of lust, but the total orientation of one's life toward a goal.

Dietrich Bonhoeffer

Chastity is the most unpopular of the Christian virtues. There is no getting away from it: the Christian rule is "Either marriage, with complete faithfulness to your partner, or else total abstinence."

Clive Staples (C.S.) Lewis

Chastity is a requisite of Christian singleness. Furthermore, chastity is possible. There will always be somebody to suggest that such thinking is legalistic, unreasonable, and unlikely to succeed. My reply can only be: "When it's bigger than I am, so is God."

Rosalie de Rosset

Sinners, *see* Unbelievers

Sisters, *see* Families

Skill, *see* Ability

Slavery, *see* Bondage; Freedom

Sleep

It is in vain that you rise up early and go late to rest, eating the bread of anxious toil; for he gives sleep to his beloved.

Psalm 127:2 NRSV

Love not sleep, lest thou come to poverty; open thine eyes, and thou shalt be satisfied with bread.

Proverbs 20:13 KJV

You belong to the light and live in the day. We don't live in the night or belong to the dark. Others may sleep, but we should stay awake and be alert. People sleep during the night, and some even get drunk. But we belong to the day. So we must stay sober.

1 Thessalonians 5:5–8 CEV

A sleeping pill will never take the place of a clear conscience.

Eddie Cantor

Sleep recreates. The Bible indicates that sleep is not meant only for the recuperation of a man's body, but that there is a tremendous furtherance of spiritual and moral life during sleep.

Oswald Chambers

Sleep with clean hands, either kept clean all day by integrity, or washed clean at night by repentance.

John Donne

Don't count sheep if you can't sleep. Talk to the shepherd.

Paul Frost

Sleep is, in fine, so like death I dare not trust it without my prayers.

Thomas Fuller

Those whose spirits are stirred by the breath of the Holy Spirit go forward even in sleep.

Brother Lawrence

Sloth, *see* Laziness

Society

You are the salt of the earth; but if salt has lost its taste, how can its saltiness be restored? It is no longer good for anything, but is thrown out and trampled under foot. You are the light of the world. A city built on a hill cannot be hid.

Matthew 5:13–14 NRSV

Therefore, as opportunity offers, let us work for the good of all, especially members of the household of the faith.

Galatians 6:10 REB

The test of every civilization is the point below which the weakest and most unfortunate are not allowed to fall.

Herbert Henry Asquith

If a man be gracious and courteous to strangers, it shows he is a citizen of the world.

Francis Bacon

Religion is the main determining element in the formation of a culture or civilization.

Hilaire Belloc

No man is an island, entire of itself; every man is a piece of the Continent, a part of the main.

John Donne

No true civilization can be expected permanently to continue which is not based on the great principles of Christianity.

Tryon Edwards

The true test of civilization is, not the census, nor the size of cities, nor the crops, but the kind of man that the country turns out.

Ralph Waldo Emerson

To seek the society of others and to shun it are two blameworthy extremes in the devotion of those who live in the world.

St. Francis de Sales

The true civilization is where every man gives to every other every right that he claims for himself.

Robert Green Ingersoll

Civil society was renovated in every part by the teachings of Christianity. In the strength of that renewal the human race was lifted up to better things. Nay, it was brought back from death to life.

Leo XIII

The worth of a state, in the long run, is the worth of the individuals composing it.

John Stuart Mill

God is the judge of all social systems.

Oscar Romero

Civilization is always in danger when those who have never learned to obey are given the right to command.

Fulton John Sheen

Death is what takes place within us when we look upon others not as gift, blessing or stimulus but as threat, danger, competition. It is the death that comes to all who try to live by bread alone. . . . [I]t is that purposeless, empty existence devoid of genuine human relationships and filled with anxiety, silence and loneliness.

Dorothy Soelle

A society is conceivable in which no person is left totally alone, with no one to think of him and stay with him. Watching and praying are possible.

Dorothy Soelle

We have the gospel of Jesus Christ which transforms society, not just glues all the bits together.

Elaine Storkey

There is no structural organization of society which can bring about the coming of the Kingdom of God on earth, since all systems can be perverted by the selfishness of man.

William Temple

All that is best in the civilization of today is the fruit of Christ's appearance among men.

Daniel Webster

Whatever makes men good Christians makes them good citizens.

Daniel Webster

Solitude

See also Loneliness

When you pray, go into a room alone and close the door. Pray to your Father in private. He knows what is done in private, and he will reward you.

Matthew 6:6 CEV

After he had dismissed them, he went up on a mountainside by himself to pray. When evening came, he was there alone.

Matthew 14:23 NIV

In the morning, rising up a great while before day, he went out, and departed into a solitary place, and there prayed.

Mark 1:35 KJV

The soul that is growing in holiness is the least lonely when it is most alone.

Fr. Andrew

Enter into the inner chamber of your mind. Shut out all things save God and whatever may aid you in seeking God; and having barred the door of your chamber, seek him.

St. Anselm of Canterbury

The more any man loves Christ, the more he delights to be with Christ alone. Lovers love to be alone.

Thomas Benton Brooks

It is known to many that we need solitude to find ourselves. Perhaps it is not so well known that we need solitude to find our fellows. Even the Savior is described as reaching mankind through the wilderness.

Henry Havelock Ellis

It is easy in the world to live after the world's opinion; it is easy in solitude to live after your own; but the great man is he who in the midst of the crowd keeps with perfect sweetness the independence of solitude.

Ralph Waldo Emerson

Solitude is essentially the discovery and acceptance of our uniqueness.

Lawrence Freeman

Solitude is bearable only with God.

André Gide

Solitude is a wonderful thing when one is at peace with oneself and when there is a definite task to be accomplished.

Johann Wolfgang von Goethe

It is a fine thing to be out on the hills alone. A man can hardly be a beast or a fool alone on a great mountain.

Francis Robert Kilvert

This great misfortune—to be incapable of solitude.

Jean de La Bruyère

Take time to be holy, the world rushes on; / Spend much time in secret with Jesus alone. / By looking to Jesus like Him thou shalt be; / Thy friends, in thy conduct, His likeness shall see.

William Dunn Longstaff

Every man must do two things alone; he must do his own believing, and his own dying.

Martin Luther

Great eagles fly alone; great lions hunt alone; great souls walk alone—alone with God.

Leonard Ravenhill

Settle yourself in solitude and you will come upon Him in yourself.

Teresa of Avila

I never found the companion that was so companionable as solitude.

Henry David Thoreau

Language has created the word loneliness to express the pain of being alone, and the word solitude to express the glory of being alone.

Paul Tillich

To go up alone into the mountain and come back as an ambassador to the world, has ever been the method of humanity's best friends.

Evelyn Underhill

Practice the art of "aloneness" and you will discover the treasure of tranquility. Develop the art of solitude and you will unearth the gift of serenity.

William Arthur Ward

Solitude permits the mind to feel.

William Wordsworth

Son of God, *see* Jesus Christ

Sons and Daughters, *see* Children; Parents and Parenthood

Sorrow, *see* Sadness

Soul and Spirit

See also Longing for God; Seeking God

He restores my soul. He leads me in right paths for his name's sake.

Psalm 23:3 NRSV

Fear not them which kill the body, but are not able to kill the soul: but rather fear him which is able to destroy both soul and body in hell.

Matthew 10:28 KJV

Take my yoke upon you and learn from me, for I am gentle and humble in heart, and you will find rest for your souls.

Matthew 11:29 NIV

Mary said, "My soul magnifies the Lord, and my spirit rejoices in God my Savior."

Luke 1:46–47 NRSV

May the God of peace himself sanctify you entirely; and may your spirit and soul and body be kept sound and blameless at the coming of our Lord Jesus Christ.

1 Thessalonians 5:23 NRSV

For what human being knows what is truly human except the human spirit that is within? So also no one comprehends what is truly God's except the Spirit of God.

1 Corinthians 2:11 NRSV

The word of God is alive and active. It cuts more keenly than any two-edged sword, piercing so deeply that it divides soul and spirit, joints and marrow; it discriminates among the purposes and thoughts of the heart.

Hebrews 4:12 REB

Despise the flesh, for it passes away; be solicitous for your soul which will never die.

St. Basil the Great

The human soul is God's treasury, out of which he coins unspeakable riches. Thoughts and feelings, desires and yearnings, faith and hope—these are the most precious things which God finds in us.

Henry Ward Beecher

If sin and worldly preoccupation have not weighed the soul down, if dangerous passion has not sullied it, then, lifted up by the natural goodness of its purity, it will rise to the heights on the lightest breath of meditation and, leaving the lowly things, the things of earth, it will travel upward to the heavenly and the invisible.

John Cassian

If you put grapes into the wine-press there will come out a delicious juice; our souls, in the winepress of the Cross, give out juice which nourishes and strengthens.

The Curé d'Ars

I do believe every soul has a tendency towards God.

Dorothy Day

Since, O my soul, thou art capable of God, woe to thee if thou contentest thyself with anything less than God.

St. Francis de Sales

We take excellent care of our bodies which we have for only a lifetime; yet we let our souls shrivel which we will have for eternity.

William Franklin (Billy) Graham

The soul, like the body, lives by what it feeds on.

Josiah Gilbert Holland

The real value of an object is that which one who knows its worth will give for it. He who made the soul, knew its worth and gave His life for it.

Arthur Jackson

God never deserts the soul, but abides there in bliss for ever.

Julian of Norwich

For as to the spiritual direction of my soul, I think that God Himself has taken it in hand from the start and still looks after it.

Simone Weil

Sovereignty of God, *see* God, Sovereignty of

Speech

See also Gossip

Be brief; say much in few words; be as one who knows and can still hold his tongue.

Ecclesiasticus 32:8 NRSV

No foul word should ever cross your lips; let your words be for the improvement of others, as occasion offers, and do good to your listeners.

Ephesians 4:29 NJB

Be pleasant and hold their interest when you speak the message. Choose your words carefully and be ready to give answers to anyone who asks questions.

Colossians 4:6 CEV

We all stumble in many ways. If anyone is never at fault in what he says, he is a perfect man, able to keep his whole body in check. When we put bits into the mouths of horses to make them obey us, we can turn the whole animal. Or take ships as an example.

Although they are so large and are driven by strong winds, they are steered by a very small rudder wherever the pilot wants to go. Likewise the tongue is a small part of the body, but it makes great boasts. Consider what a great forest is set on fire by a small spark. The tongue also is a fire, a world of evil among the parts of the body. It corrupts the whole person, sets the whole course of his life on fire, and is itself set on fire by hell. All kinds of animals, birds, reptiles and creatures of the sea are being tamed and have been tamed by man, but no man can tame the tongue. It is a restless evil, full of deadly poison.

James 3:2–8 NIV

It is easier to look wise than to talk wisely.

St. Ambrose

Speaking without thinking is shooting without aiming.

Sir William Gurney Benham

Speak when you are angry and you will make the best speech you will ever regret.

Ambrose Bierce

When you have nothing to say, say nothing.

Charles Caleb Colton

Our words are a faithful index of the state of our souls.

St. Francis de Sales

Take my voice, and let me sing / Always, only for my King; / Take my lips, and let them be / Filled with messages from Thee.

Frances Ridley Havergal

Good words are worth much, and cost little.

George Herbert

Good words quench more than a bucket of water.

George Herbert

Talking and eloquence are not the same: to speak, and to speak well, are two things.

Ben Jonson

Cold words freeze people, and hot words scorch them, and bitter words make them bitter, and wrathful words make them wrathful. Kind words also produce their image on men's souls; and a beautiful image it is. They smooth, and quiet, and comfort the hearer.

Blaise Pascal

Be humble and gentle in your conversation; and of few words, I charge you; but always pertinent when you speak.

William Penn

An evil-speaker differs from an evil-doer only in the lack of opportunity.

Marcus Fabius Quintillian

Men of few words are the best men.

William Shakespeare

Whatever moves the heart wags the tongue.

Charles Thomas (C.T.) Studd

They converse as those would who know that God hears.

Quintus Tertullian

Little keys can open big locks. Simple words can express great thoughts.

William Arthur Ward

With courage and with love, we must expand our religious images, open up our metaphors, and make sure our God-language is representative of all.

Miriam Therese Winter

Spiritual Blindness

See also Unbelief

They do not know, nor do they comprehend; for their eyes are shut, so that they cannot see, and their minds as well, so that they cannot understand.

Isaiah 44:18 NRSV

Let them alone: they be blind leaders of the blind. And if the blind lead the blind, both shall fall into the ditch.

Matthew 15:14 KJV

To you is granted to understand the secrets of the kingdom of God; for the rest it remains in parables, so that they may look but not perceive, listen but not understand.

Luke 8:10 NJB

Even if our gospel is veiled, it is veiled to those who are perishing. The god of this age has blinded the minds of unbelievers, so that they cannot see the light of the gospel of the glory of Christ.

2 Corinthians 4:3–4 NIV

There is no greater darkness than ignorance of God.

John Calvin

There's none so blind as those who will not see.

Matthew Henry

He who hates not in himself his self-love and that instinct which leads him to make himself a God, is indeed blind.

Blaise Pascal

Spiritual Gifts

See also Gifts

They were all filled with the Holy Ghost, and began to speak with other tongues, as the Spirit gave them utterance.

Acts 2:4 KJV

I long to see you so that I may impart to you some spiritual gift to make you strong.

Romans 1:11 NIV

There are different kinds of spiritual gifts, but they all come from the same Spirit. There are different ways to serve the same Lord, and we can each do different things. Yet the same God works in all of us and helps us in everything we do. The Spirit has given each of us a special way of serving others. Some of us can speak with wisdom, while others can speak with knowledge, but these gifts come from the same Spirit. To others the Spirit has given great faith or the power to heal the sick or the power to work mighty miracles. Some of us are prophets, and some of us recognize when God's Spirit is present. Others can speak different kinds of languages, and still others can tell what these languages mean. But it is the Spirit who does all this and decides which gifts to give to each of us.

1 Corinthians 12:4–11 CEV

Pursue love and strive for the spiritual gifts, and especially that you may prophesy.

1 Corinthians 14:1 NRSV

It was he who "gave gifts to people"; he appointed some to be apostles, others to be prophets, others to be evangelists, others to be pastors and teachers. He did this to prepare all God's people for the work of Christian service, in order to build up the body of Christ.

Ephesians 4:11–12 GNB

As every man hath received the gift, even so minister the same one to another, as good stewards of the manifold grace of God.

1 Peter 4:10 KJV

It is easy to want things from the Lord and yet not want the Lord himself; as though the gift could ever be preferable to the Giver.

St. Augustine of Hippo

Each one has a place in the community of Christ, and ought to fill it, but he ought not to be everywhere and want to take part in everything. . . . Take note of what God gives you, then you will also know the task he sets you.

Heinrich Emil Brunner

Spiritual gifts are not toys with which to play; they are tools of the Spirit with which to do the Lord's work effectively.

G. Raymond Carlson

Spiritual gifts are no proof of spirituality.

Samuel Chadwick

The Holy Spirit is composer and conductor. He gives each member of the worshiping congregation sounds—which He weaves together in heavenly harmony.

Fr. John Harper

To consider the charismata as intended merely to adorn and benefit the person endowed would be just as absurd as to say, "I light the fire to warm not the room but the stove."

Abraham Kuyper

The gifts of the Spirit have nothing to do with personal ambition or career orientation. They are not given to build individual reputations, to warrant superior positions in the local church, or to demonstrate spiritual advancement. They are not trophies, but tools—tools for touching and blessing others.

John Richard Wimber

Spiritual Growth

See also Fruitfulness; Harvest; Maturity

So we shall all come together to that oneness in our faith and in our knowledge of the Son of God; we shall become mature people, reaching to the very height of Christ's full stature. Then we shall no longer be children carried by the waves and blown about by every shifting wind of the teaching of deceitful men, who lead others into error by the tricks they invent. Instead, by speaking the truth in a spirit of love, we must grow up in every way to Christ, who is the head.

Ephesians 4:13–15 GNB

People who live on milk are like babies who don't really know what is right. Solid food is for mature people who have been trained to know right from wrong. We must try to become mature and start thinking about more than just the basic things we were taught about Christ. . . . Let's grow up.

Hebrews 5:13–6:1, 3 CEV

You must make every effort to support your faith with goodness, and goodness with knowledge, and knowledge with self-control, and self-control with endurance, and endurance with godliness, and godliness with mutual affection, and mutual affection with love.

2 Peter 1:5–7 NRSV

Grow in grace, and in the knowledge of our Lord and Savior Jesus Christ.

2 Peter 3:18 KJV

Measure your growth in grace by your sensitiveness to sin.

Oswald Chambers

Faith does not grow by being pulled up by the roots time and again to see how it is getting on. Faith grows when we look steadily toward God for the supply of all our needs and concentrate on him. There is little point in becoming engrossed with our faith as if that were the thing we believed in!

J.C.P. Cockerton

It is only when men begin to worship that they begin to grow.

Calvin Coolidge

There is only one way of getting rid of one's faults and that is to acquire the habits contradictory to them.

Ernest Dimnet

Growth in the Christian life depends on obedience in times of crisis.

James Dobson

The strongest principle of growth lies in human choice.

George Eliot

What lies behind us and what lies before us are tiny matters compared to what lies within us.

Ralph Waldo Emerson

Little things come daily, hourly within our reach, and they are not less calculated to set forward our growth in holiness than are the greater occasions, which occur but rarely. Moreover, fidelity in trifles, and an earnest seeking to please God in little matters, is a test of real devotion and love. Let our aim be to please our dear Lord perfectly in little things, and to attain a spirit of childlike simplicity and dependence.

Jean-Nicolas Grou

Spiritual growth consists most in the growth of the root, which is out of sight.

Matthew Henry

They who would grow in grace must be inquisitive.

Matthew Henry

The work of God is held back not by bad men and women, but by good ones who have stopped growing.

M.P. Horban

Happy is he who makes daily progress and who considers not what he did yesterday but what advance he can make today.

St. Jerome

We get no deeper into Christ than we allow him to get into us.

John Henry Jowett

Growing spiritually can be like a roller coaster ride. Take comfort in the knowledge that the way down is only preparation for the way up.

Rebbe Nachman

Growth is the only evidence of life.

John Henry Newman

Progress in the spiritual life comes from climbing a ladder of which the rungs are made alternately of belief and doubt.

Edward Patey

I am learning to see, I do not know why it is, but everything penetrates more deeply within me, and no longer stops at the place, where until now, it always used to finish.

Rainer Maria Rilke

All God's giants have been weak men who did great things for God because they reckoned on God being with them.

James Hudson Taylor

Interior growth is only possible when we commit ourselves with and to others.

Jean Vanier

Growth begins when we start to accept our own weakness.

Jean Vanier

To grow is to emerge gradually from a land where our vision is limited, where we are seeking and governed by egotistical pleasure, by our sympathies and antipathies, to a land of unlimited horizons and universal love, where we will be open to every person and desire their happiness.

Jean Vanier

When we stop growing we stop living and start existing.

Warren W. Wiersbe

Spiritual Healing, *see* Healing

Spiritual Hunger, *see* Longing for God; Seeking God

Spiritual Journey, *see* Pilgrimage; Seeking God

Spiritual Renewal, *see* Renewal

Spiritual Search, *see* Seeking God

Spiritual Warfare

See also Conflict; Demons; Devil

For though we live in the world, we do not wage war as the world does. The weapons we fight with are not the weapons of the world. On the contrary, they have divine power to demolish strongholds. We demolish arguments and every pretension that sets itself up against the knowledge of God, and we take captive every thought to make it obedient to Christ.

2 Corinthians 10:3–5 NIV

Put on the whole armor of God, so that you may be able to stand against the wiles of the devil. For our struggle is not against enemies of blood and flesh, but against the rulers, against the authorities, against the cosmic powers of this present darkness, against the spiritual forces of evil in the heavenly places.

Ephesians 6:11–12 NRSV

Fight the good fight of faith, lay hold on eternal life.

1 Timothy 6:12 KJV

I have fought a good fight, I have finished my course, I have kept the faith.

2 Timothy 4:7 KJV

You were rubbed with oil like an athlete, Christ's athlete, as though in preparation for an earthly wrestling-match, and you agreed to take on your opponent.

St. Ambrose

While some weep, as they do now, I'll fight; while little children go hungry, I'll fight; while men go to prison, in and out, in and out, as they do now, I'll fight; while there is a drunkard left, whilst there is a poor, lost girl upon the streets, while there remains one dark soul without the light of God—I'll fight! I'll fight to the very end!

William Booth

Anyone who witnesses to the grace of God revealed in Christ is undertaking a direct assault against Satan's dominion.

Thomas Cosmades

You are but a poor soldier of Christ if you think you can overcome without fighting, and suppose you can have the crown without the conflict.

St. John Chrysostom

Prayer is that mightiest of all weapons that created natures can wield.

Martin Luther

There can never be peace in the bosom of a believer. There is peace with God, but constant war with sin.

Robert Murray M'Cheyne

Fight the good fight with all thy might; / Christ is thy strength, and Christ thy right; / Lay hold on life, and it shall be / Thy joy and crown eternally.

John Samuel Bewley Monsell

When Christians evangelize, they are not engaging in some harmless and pleasant pastime. They are engaging in a fearful struggle, the issues of which are eternal.

Leon Lamb Morris

No soldiers of Christ are ever lost, missing, or left dead on the battlefield.

John Charles Ryle

The spiritual battle, the loss of victory, is always in the thought-world.

Francis August Schaeffer

There may be persons who can always glide along like a tramcar on rails without a solitary jerk, but I find that I have a vile nature to contend with, and spiritual life is a struggle with me. I have to fight from day to day with inbred corruption, coldness, deadness, barrenness, and if it were not for my Lord Jesus Christ my heart would be as dry as the heart of the damned.

Charles Haddon Spurgeon

The Christian life is not a playground; it is a battleground.

Warren W. Wiersbe

Spirituality

See also Longing for God; Maturity; Seeking God

Those who live as their human nature tells them to, have their minds controlled by what human nature wants. Those who live as the Spirit tells them to, have their minds controlled by what the Spirit wants. To be controlled by human nature results in death; to be controlled by the Spirit results in life and peace. And so people become enemies of God when they are controlled by their human nature; for they do not obey God's law, and in fact they cannot obey it. Those who obey their human nature cannot please God. But you do not live as your human nature tells you to; instead, you live as the Spirit tells you to—if, in fact, God's Spirit lives in you.

Romans 8:5–9 GNB

We have not received the spirit of the world but the Spirit who is from God, that we may understand what God has freely given us. This is what we speak, not in words taught us by human wisdom but in words taught by the Spirit, expressing spiritual truths in spiritual words. The man without the Spirit does not accept the things that come from the Spirit of God, for they are foolishness to him, and he cannot understand them, because they are spiritually discerned. The spiritual man makes judgments about all things, but he himself is not subject to any man's judgment.

1 Corinthians 2:12–15 NIV

You are only as spiritual as you are scriptural.

Myron Augsburger

Spirituality is the basis and foundation of human life. . . . It must underlie everything. To put it briefly, man is a spiritual being, and the proper work of his mind is to interpret the world according to his higher nature, and to conquer the material aspects of the world so as to bring them into subjection to the spirit.

Robert Seymour Bridges

What we call crises, God ignores; and what God reveals as the great critical moments of a man's life, we look on as humdrum commonplaces. When we become spiritual, we discern that God was in the humdrum commonplace and we never knew it.

Oswald Chambers

To live according to the Spirit is to think, speak, and act according to the virtues that are in the Spirit and not according to the senses and sentiments which are in the flesh.

St. Francis de Sales

True spirituality seeks for bitterness rather than sweetness in God, inclines to suffering rather than to consolation.

St. John of the Cross

You will never be an inwardly religious and devout man unless you pass over in silence the shortcomings of your fellow men, and diligently examine your own weaknesses.

Thomas à Kempis

There is no good in trying to be more spiritual than God. God never means man to be a purely spiritual creature. . . . He likes matter. He created it.

Clive Staples (C.S.) Lewis

Spiritual life depends on the purposes we cherish.

Charles Haddon Spurgeon

Spirituality really means "Holy Spirit at work," a profound action of the Holy Spirit in his Church, renewing that Church from the inside.

Leon Joseph Suenens

True spirituality manifests itself in:

1. The desire to be holy rather than happy
2. The desire to see the honor of God advanced through his life
3. The desire to carry his cross
4. The desire to see everything from God's viewpoint
5. The desire to die right rather than live wrong
6. The desire to see others advance at his expense
7. The desire to make eternity-judgments instead of time-judgments.

Aiden Wilson (A.W.) Tozer

A spiritual life is simply a life in which all that we do comes from the center, where we are anchored in God: a life soaked through and through by a sense of his reality and claim, and self-given to the great movement of his will.

Evelyn Underhill

Stewardship

See also Responsibility

The kingdom is also like what happened when a man went away and put his three servants in charge of all he owned. The man knew what each servant could do. So he handed five thousand coins to the first servant, two thousand to the second, and one thousand to the third. Then he left the country.

Matthew 25:14–15 CEV

Think of us in this way, as servants of Christ and stewards of God's mysteries. Moreover, it is required of stewards that they be found trustworthy.

1 Corinthians 4:1–2 NRSV

As every man hath received the gift, even so minister the same one to another, as good stewards of the manifold grace of God.

1 Peter 4:10 KJV

If you do not give the tenth part to God, He will take the nine parts.

St. Ambrose

Surplus wealth is a sacred trust which its possessor is bound to administer in his lifetime for the good of the community.

Andrew Carnegie

Stewardship is what a man does after he says, "I believe."

W.H. Greever

Someday all that we will have is what we have given to God.

M.P. Horban

The two things which, of all others, most want to be under a strict rule, and which are the greatest blessings to ourselves and to others, when they are rightly used, are our time and our money.

William Law

Stewardship is the acceptance from God of personal responsibility for all of life and life's affairs.

Roswell C. Long

God will not merely judge us on the basis of what we gave but also on the basis of what we did with what we kept for ourselves.

Erwin W. Lutzer

There is no portion of our time that is our time, and the rest God's; there is no portion of our money that is our money, and the rest God's money. It is all his; he made it all, gives it all, and he has simply trusted it to us for his service. A servant has two purses, the master's and his own, but we have only one.

Adolphe Theodore Monod

The use of our possessions shows us up for what we actually are.

Charles Caldwell Ryrie

When a man becomes a Christian, he becomes industrious, trustworthy, and prosperous. Now, if that man, when he gets all he can and saves all he can, does not give all he can, I have more hope for Judas Iscariot than for that man!

John Wesley

Stillness, *see* Quiet and Stillness; Rest; Silence

Strength, *see* Power

Stress

See also Anxiety; Rest

"In my distress I called to the Lord, and he answered me. From the depths of the grave I called for help, and you listened to my cry."

Jonah 2:1–2 NIV

I came to bring fire to the earth, and how I wish it were already kindled! I have a baptism with which to be baptized, and what stress I am under until it is completed!

Luke 12:49–50 NRSV

In his anguish he prayed more earnestly, and his sweat became like great drops of blood falling down on the ground.

Luke 22:44 NRSV

So in the hardships we underwent in Asia, we want you to be quite certain, brothers, that we were under extraordinary pressure, beyond our powers of endurance, so that we gave up all hope even of surviving.

2 Corinthians 1:8 NJB

God did not say, "You shall not be tempest-tossed, you shall not be work-weary, you shall not be discomforted." But he said "you shall not be overcome."

Julian of Norwich

When you're laughing, your attention is focused. You can't do anything else. Everything else, whether it's depression or stress, stops.

Robert Leone

It is not the outward storms and stresses of life that defeat and disrupt personality, but its inner conflicts and miseries. If a man is happy and stable at heart, he can normally cope, even with zest, with difficulties that lie outside his personality.

John Bertram (J.B.) Phillips

Drop thy still dews of quietness, / Till all our strivings cease; / Take from our souls the strain and stress, / And let our ordered lives confess / The beauty of thy peace.

John Greenleaf Whittier

Stubbornness

To day if ye will hear his voice, Harden not your heart, as in the provocation, and as in the day of temptation in the wilderness.

Psalm 95:7–8 KJV

And when he had looked round about on them with anger, being grieved for the hardness of their hearts, he saith unto the man, Stretch forth thine hand. And he stretched it out: and his hand was restored whole as the other.

Mark 3:5 KJV

By your hard and impenitent heart you are storing up wrath for yourself on the day of wrath, when God's righteous judgment will be revealed.

Romans 2:5 NRSV

Hardening of the heart ages people more quickly than hardening of the arteries.

Anon.

To those whom God finds impenitent sinners he will be found to be an implacable Judge.

Matthew Henry

Keep thy heart in a soft and tractable state lest thou lose the impress of His hands on thy life.

St. Irenaeus

All sin hardens the heart, stupefies the conscience, and shuts out the light of truth.

William S. Plummer

The eye may be watery and the heart flinty. An apricot may be soft without, but it has a hard stone within.

Thomas Watson

Study

See also Knowledge

Furthermore, my child, you must realize that writing books involves endless hard work, and that much study wearies the body.

Ecclesiastes 12:12 NJB

You diligently study the Scriptures because you think that by them you possess eternal life. These are the Scriptures that testify about me, yet you refuse to come to me to have life.

John 5:39–40 NIV

Study to shew thyself approved unto God, a

workman that needeth not to be ashamed, rightly dividing the word of truth.

2 Timothy 2:15 KJV

The study of God's Word for the purpose of discovering God's Will is the secret discipline which has formed the greatest characters.

James W. Alexander

Reading maketh a full man; conference a ready man: and writing an exact man.

Francis Bacon

We learn more by five minutes' obedience than by ten years' study.

Oswald Chambers

He will make the best divine that studies on his knees.

John Flavel

How easy is pen-and-paper piety! I will not say it costs nothing; but it is far cheaper to work one's head than one's heart to goodness. I can write a hundred meditations sooner than subdue the least sin in my soul.

Thomas Fuller

He who would fully and feelingly understand the words of Christ, must study to make his whole life conformable to that of Christ.

Thomas à Kempis

I study my Bible as I gather apples. First, I shake the whole tree that the ripest might fall. Then I shake each limb, and when I have shaken each limb, I shake each branch and every twig. Then I look under every leaf.

Martin Luther

To pray well is the better half of study.

Martin Luther

I never saw a useful Christian who was not a student of the Bible.

Dwight Lyman (D.L.) Moody

Disregard the study of God and you sentence yourself to stumble and blunder through life, blindfolded, as it were, with no sense of direction and no understanding of what surrounds you.

James Innell (J.I.) Packer

Wisely and slow; they stumble that run fast.

William Shakespeare

An honest man with an open Bible and a pad and pencil is sure to find out what is wrong with him very quickly.

Aiden Wilson (A.W.) Tozer

Submission

Every person must submit to the authorities in power, for all authority comes from God, and the existing authorities are instituted by him.

Romans 13:1 REB

Obey your leaders and submit to their authority. They keep watch over you as men who must give an account. Obey them so that their work will be a joy, not a burden, for that would be of no advantage to you.

Hebrews 13:17 NIV

Submit yourselves therefore to God. Resist the devil, and he will flee from you.

James 4:7 NRSV

In submission we are free to value other people. Their dreams and plans become important to us. We have entered into a new, wonderful, glorious freedom, the freedom to give up our own rights for the good of others.

Richard J. Foster

A few conquer by fighting, but more battles are won by submitting.

Elbert Green Hubbard

Carry the cross patiently and with perfect submission and in the end it shall carry you.

Thomas à Kempis

Success

See also Failure

May he grant you your heart's desire and crown all your plans with success!

Psalm 20:4 NJB

Without counsel, plans go wrong, but with many advisers they succeed.

Proverbs 15:22 NRSV

If the ax is dull and its edge unsharpened, more strength is needed but skill will bring success.

Ecclesiastes 10:10 NIV

Success comes to those who are neither afraid to fail nor discouraged by failures.

Anon.

The figure of the Crucified invalidates all thought which takes success for its standard.

Dietrich Bonhoeffer

The dangers to our spiritual welfare from success are far greater than the dangers from failure.

Arthur C. Custance

The religious man is the only successful man.

Frederick William Faber

Fame is sometimes like unto a kind of mushroom, which Pliny recounts to be the greatest miracle in nature, because growing and having no root.

Thomas Fuller

Success consists of getting up just one more time than you fall.

Oliver Goldsmith

Let us work as if success depended on ourselves alone, but with the heartfelt conviction that we are doing nothing and God everything.

St. Ignatius of Loyola

A great many people go through life in bondage to success. They are in mortal dread of failure. I do not have to succeed. I have only to be true to the highest I know—success or failure are in the hands of God.

E. Stanley Jones

Better to love God and die unknown than to love the world and be a hero; better to be content with poverty than to die a slave to wealth; better to have taken some risks and lost than to have done nothing and succeeded at it; better to have lost some battles than to have retreated from the war; better to have failed when serving God than to have succeeded when serving the devil. What a tragedy to climb the ladder of success, only to discover that the ladder was leaning against the wrong wall.

Erwin W. Lutzer

The person who succeeds is not the one who holds back, fearing failure, nor the one who never fails . . . but rather the one who moves on in spite of failure.

Charles R. Swindoll

God has not called me to be successful; he has called me to be faithful.

Mother Teresa

Four steps to achievement. Plan purposefully. Prepare prayerfully. Proceed positively. Pursue persistently.

William Arthur Ward

Suffering

See also Healing; Jesus Christ, Death of; Trials

And now my soul is poured out within me; days of affliction have taken hold of me. The night racks my bones, and the pain that gnaws me takes no rest.

Job 30:16–17 NRSV

Yea, though I walk through the valley of the shadow of death, I will fear no evil: for thou art with me; thy rod and thy staff they comfort me.

Psalm 23:4 KJV

Turn thee unto me, and have mercy upon me; for I am desolate and afflicted.

Psalm 25:16 KJV

My heart is in anguish within me, the terrors of death have fallen upon me. Fear and trembling come upon me, and horror overwhelms me.

Psalm 55:4–5 NRSV

Didn't you know that the Messiah would have to suffer before he was given his glory?

Luke 24:26 CEV

I consider that the sufferings of this present time are not worth comparing with the glory about to be revealed to us.

Romans 8:18 NRSV

Stand up to him [the devil], firm in your faith, and remember that your fellow-Christians in this world are going through the same kinds of suffering.

1 Peter 5:9 REB

The diamond cannot be polished without friction, nor the man perfected without trials.

Anon.

If suffering went out of life, courage, tenderness, pity, faith, patience, and love in its divinity would go out of life, too.

Fr. Andrew

Never judge God by suffering, but judge suffering by the Cross.

Fr. Andrew

A Christian is someone who shares the sufferings of God in the world.

Dietrich Bonhoeffer

If we had no winter, the spring would not be so pleasant; if we did not sometimes taste of adversity, prosperity would not be so welcome.

Anne Bradstreet

When one is in very great pain and fear it is extremely difficult to pray coherently, and I could only raise my mind in anguish to God and ask for strength to hold on.

Dr. Sheila Cassidy

Out of suffering have emerged the strongest souls; the most massive characters are seared with scars.

Edwin Hubbel (E.H.) Chapin

We often learn more of God under the rod that strikes us, than under the staff that comforts us.

Stephen Charnock

One sees great things from the valley; only small things from the peak.

Gilbert Keith (G.K.) Chesterton

Jesus did not come to explain away suffering or remove it. He came to fill it with His Presence.

Paul Louis Charles Claudel

Pain can either make us better or bitter.

Tim Hansel

To live by the law of Christ and accept him in our hearts is to turn a giant floodlight of hope into our valleys of trouble.

Charles R. Hembree

God will not look you over for medals, degrees, or diplomas, but for scars.

Elbert Green Hubbard

We could never learn to be brave and patient, if there were only joy in the world.

Helen Adams Keller

He who knoweth how to suffer will enjoy much peace. Such a one is a conqueror of himself and lord of the world, a friend of Christ, and an heir of Heaven.

Thomas à Kempis

No man is fit to comprehend heavenly things who hath not resigned himself to suffer adversities for Christ.

Thomas à Kempis

It is cruel and false to brand every sufferer as a sinner: much suffering and sickness is due to the sin either of other persons or of society in general.

Lambeth Conference Report 1958

Adversity is the diamond dust Heaven polishes its jewels with.

Robert Leighton

When pain is to be borne, a little courage helps more than much knowledge, a little

human sympathy more than much courage, and the least tincture of the love of God more than all.

Clive Staples (C.S.) Lewis

God whispers to us in our pleasures, speaks in our conscience, but shouts in our pains; it is his megaphone to rouse a deaf world.

Clive Staples (C.S.) Lewis

It is a glorious thing to be indifferent to suffering but only to one's own suffering.

Robert Lund

Our suffering is not worthy the name of suffering. When I consider my crosses, tribulations, and temptations, I shame myself almost to death; thinking what are they in comparison to the sufferings of my blessed Savior Christ Jesus.

Martin Luther

Afflictions are but the shadow of God's wings.

George MacDonald

Every painful event contains in itself a seed of growth and liberation.

Anthony de Mello

Jesus refuses to swallow the drugged drink normally provided as an act of compassion to those about to be crucified; he has to be aware of his suffering. His supreme sacrifice, to be valid, must be conscious.

Malcolm Muggeridge

The first thing that Jesus promises is suffering: "I tell you . . . You will be weeping and wailing . . . And you will be sorrowful." But he calls these pains birth pains. And so, what seems a hindrance becomes a way; what seems an obstacle becomes a door; and what seems a misfit becomes a cornerstone. Jesus changes our history from a random series of sad incidents and accidents into a constant opportunity for a change of heart.

Henri J.M. Nouwen

Suffering passes; having suffered never passes.

Charles Peguy

No pain, no palm; no thorn, no throne.

William Penn

The greatness of our God must be tested by the desire we have of suffering for his sake.

St. Philip Neri

There has never yet been a man in our history who led a life of ease whose name is worth remembering.

Theodore Roosevelt

There is no gain without pain.

Robert Harold Schuller

Suffering makes one more sensitive to the pain in the world. It can teach us to put forth a greater love for everything that exists.

Dorothee Soelle

As sure as ever God puts his children in the furnace he will be in the furnace with them.

Charles Haddon Spurgeon

Tell me how much you know of the sufferings of your fellow men and I will tell you how much you have loved them.

Helmut Thielicke

Calvary is God's great proof that suffering in the will of God always leads to glory.

Warren W. Wiersbe

Sundays, *see* Sabbath

Superstition

See also Deceit

You have abandoned your people, the house of Jacob. They are full of superstitions from the East; they practice divination like the Philistines and clasp hands with pagans.

Isaiah 2:6 NIV

Paul stood in the midst of Mars' hill, and said, Ye men of Athens, I perceive that in all things ye are too superstitious.

Acts 17:22 KJV

Superstition is a religion of feeble minds.

Edmund Burke

Superstition is godless religion, devout impiety.

Joseph Hall

The devil divides the world between atheism and superstition.

George Herbert

Superstition is the cruelest thing in the world. Faith is to live in the sun. Superstition is to sit in darkness.

Katherine T. Hinkson

Sympathy

See also Compassion; Pity

Then there came to him all his brothers and sisters and all who had known him before, and they ate bread with him in his house; they showed him sympathy and comforted him for all the evil that the Lord had brought upon him.

Job 42:11 NRSV

Reproach hath broken my heart; and I am full of heaviness: and I looked for some to take pity, but there was none; and for comforters, but I found none.

Psalm 69:20 KJV

Rejoice with those who rejoice, weep with those who weep. Live in harmony with one another; do not be haughty, but associate with the lowly; do not claim to be wiser than you are.

Romans 12:15 NRSV

Jesus understands every weakness of ours, because he was tempted in every way that we are. But he did not sin!

Hebrews 4:15 CEV

Remember those who are in prison, as though you were in prison with them; those who are being tortured, as though you yourselves were being tortured.

Hebrews 13:3 NRSV

Finally: you should all agree among yourselves and be sympathetic; love the brothers, have compassion and be self-effacing.

1 Peter 3:8 NJB

Sympathy is your pain in my heart.

Anon.

The highest privilege there is, is the privilege of being allowed to share another's pain.

Fr. Andrew

Sympathy is derived from two Greek words, *syn* which means together with, and *paschein* which means to experience or to suffer. Sympathy means experiencing things together with the other person, literally going through what he is going through.

William Barclay

It is sympathy with human life that inspires

genial activities and keeps men within suitable restraint.

Henry Ward Beecher

The truest help we can render an afflicted man is not to take his burden from him, but to call out his best strength that he may be able to bear the burden.

Phillips Brooks

Pity may represent no more than the impersonal concern which prompts the mailing of a check, but true sympathy is the personal concern which demands the giving of one's soul.

Martin Luther King Jr.

Sympathy is no substitute for action.

David Livingstone

To help a brother up the mountain while you yourself are only just able to keep your foothold, to struggle through the mist together—that surely is better than to stand at the summit and beckon.

Forbes Robinson

O the joy of that vast elemental sympathy which only the human soul is capable of generating and emitting in steady and limitless floods.

Walt Whitman

Talent, *see* Ability

Teachers and Teaching

See also Jesus Christ, Teaching of

Never forget these commands that I am giving you today. Teach them to your children. Repeat them when you are at home and when you are away, when you are resting and when you are working.

Deuteronomy 6:6–7 GNB

The Holy Spirit will come and help you, because the Father will send the Spirit to take my place. The Spirit will teach you everything and will remind you of what I said while I was with you.

John 14:26 CEV

And those whom God has appointed in the Church are, first apostles, secondly prophets, thirdly teachers. . . .

1 Corinthians 12:28 NJB

If anyone teaches false doctrines and does not agree to the sound instruction of our Lord Jesus Christ and to godly teaching, he is conceited and understands nothing.

1 Timothy 6:3–4 NIV

As for you, teach what is consistent with sound doctrine.

Titus 2:1 NRSV

Not many of you should presume to be teachers, my brothers, because you know that we who teach will be judged more strictly.

James 3:1 NIV

A teacher affects eternity; he can never tell where his influence stops.

Henry Brooks Adams

Teaching a Christian how he ought to live does not call so much for words as for daily example.

St. Basil the Great

All television is educational television. The only question is, what is it teaching?

Nicholas Johnson

No teacher should strive to make men think as he thinks, but to lead them to the living Truth, to the Master himself, of whom alone they can learn anything.

George MacDonald

Christian action in the world will not be sustained or carried out in an intelligent and effective manner unless it is supported by doctrinal convictions that have achieved some degree of clarity.

John Macquarrie

The fundamental qualification for teaching is learning.

Andrew McNab

Teach your son to love and fear God whilst he is still young, that the fear of God may grow up with him; and the same God will be a husband to you, and a father to him—a husband and father which cannot be taken from you.

Sir Walter Raleigh

Teaching is a partnership with God. You are not molding iron nor chiseling marble; you are working with the Creator of the universe in shaping human character and determining destiny.

Ruth Vaughn

Tears

See also Bereavement; Grief; Sadness

They that sow in tears shall reap in joy. He that goeth forth and weepeth, bearing precious seed, shall doubtless come again with rejoicing, bringing his sheaves with him.

Psalm 126:5–6 KJV

In the days of his flesh, Jesus offered up prayers and supplications, with loud cries and tears, to the one who was able to save him from death, and he was heard because of his reverent submission.

Hebrews 5:7 NRSV

The Lamb in the center of the throne will be their shepherd. He will lead them to streams of life-giving water, and God will wipe all tears from their eyes.

Revelation 7:17 CEV

People can cry much easier than they can change.

James Arthur Baldwin

Tears shed for self are tears of weakness, but tears shed for others are a sign of strength.

William Franklin (Billy) Graham

God has a bottle and a book for his people's tears. What was sown as a tear will come up as a pearl.

Matthew Henry

The tears of saints more sweet by far than all the songs of sinners are.

Robert Herrick

Tears: the best gift of God to suffering man.

John Keble

There are times when God asks nothing of his children except silence, patience, and tears.

Charles Seymour Robinson

Winners of souls must first be weepers for souls.

Charles Haddon Spurgeon

A teardrop on earth summons the King of heaven.

Charles R. Swindoll

We should be thankful for our tears; they prepare us for a clearer vision of God.

William Arthur Ward

Temperance

See also Self-Control

Those who sleep sleep at night, and those who are drunk get drunk at night. But since we belong to the day, let us be sober.

1 Thessalonians 5:7–8 NRSV

Deacons must be respectable, not double-tongued, moderate in the amount of wine they drink. . . . Similarly, women must be respectable, not gossips, but sober and wholly reliable.

1 Timothy 3:8, 11 NJB

Add to your faith . . . knowledge; And to knowledge temperance: and to temperance patience. . . .

2 Peter 1:5–6 KJV

Temperance is to the body what religion is to the soul—the foundation of health, strength, and peace.

Tryon Edwards

Temperance is the control of all the functions of our bodies. The man who refuses liquor, goes in for apple pie, and develops a paunch, is no ethical leader for me.

John Erskine

If we give more to the flesh than we ought, we nourish our enemy; if we give not to her necessity what we ought, we destroy a citizen.

St. Gregory I

One great piece of mischief has been done by the modern restriction of the word temperance to the question of drink. It helps people to forget that you can be just as intemperate about lots of other things. A man who makes his gold or his motor bicycle the center of his life, or a woman who devotes all her thoughts to clothes or bridge or her dog, is being just as intemperate as someone who gets drunk every evening. Of course, it does not show on the outside so easily; bridge-mania or golf-mania do not make you fall down in the middle of the road. But God is not deceived by externals.

Clive Staples (C.S.) Lewis

Temperance, that virtue without pride, and fortune without envy, that gives vigor of frame and tranquility of mind; the best guardian of youth and support of old age, the precept of reason as well as religion, the physician of the soul as well as the body, the tutelar goddess of health and universal medicine of life.

William Temple

Temptation

See also Self-Control; Trials

If you carry burning coals, you burn your clothes; if you step on hot coals, you burn your feet.

Proverbs 6:27–28 CEV

Lead us not into temptation, but deliver us from evil. . . .

Matthew 6:13 KJV

Watch and pray so that you will not fall into temptation. The spirit is willing, but the body is weak.

Matthew 26:41 NIV

Jesus, full of the Holy Spirit, returned from the Jordan and was led by the Spirit in the wilderness, where for forty days he was tempted by the devil. He ate nothing at all during those days, and when they were over, he was famished.

Luke 4:1–2 NRSV

Wherefore let him that thinketh he standeth take heed lest he fall. There hath no temptation taken you but such as is common to man: but God is faithful, who will not suffer you to be tempted above that ye are able; but will with the temptation also make a way to escape, that ye may be able to bear it.

1 Corinthians 10:12–13 KJV

He who with his whole heart draws near unto God must of necessity be proved by temptation and trial.

Albert the Great

The devil tempts that he may ruin; God tests that he may crown.

St. Ambrose

The devil's snare does not catch you unless you are first caught by the devil's bait.

St. Ambrose

God tested Abraham. Temptation is not meant to make us fail; it is meant to confront us with a situation out of which we emerge stronger than we were. Temptation is not the penalty of manhood; it is the glory of manhood.

William Barclay

O let me feel Thee near me: / The world is ever near; / I see the sights that dazzle, / The tempting sounds I hear; / My foes are ever near me, / Around me and within; / But, Jesus, draw Thou nearer, / And shield my soul from sin.

John Ernest Bode

Temptations, when we first meet them, are as the lion that roared upon Samson; but if we overcome them, the next time we see them we shall find a nest of honey within them.

John Bunyan

The devil only tempts those souls that wish to abandon sin and those that are in a state of grace. The others belong to him: he has no need to tempt them.

The Curé d'Ars

Every moment of resistance to temptation is a victory.

Frederick William Faber

To realize God's presence is the one sovereign remedy against temptation.

François de la Mothe Fénelon

Temptation has its source not in the outer lure but in the inner lust.

D. Edmund Hiebert

Temptations discover what we are.

Thomas à Kempis

Temptation is not a sin; it is a call to battle.

Erwin W. Lutzer

Each temptation leaves us better or worse; neutrality is impossible.

Erwin W. Lutzer

Nothing is so conducive to real humility as temptation. It teaches us how weak we are.

Donald MacDonald

Christ will not keep us if we carelessly and wantonly put ourselves into the way of temptation.

Frederick Brotherton (F.B.) Meyer

Ten Commandments

See also Law

Then God spoke all these words: I am the LORD your God, who brought you out of the land of Egypt, out of the house of slavery; you shall have no other gods before me. You shall not make for yourself an idol, whether in the form of anything that is in heaven above, or that is on the earth beneath, or that is in the water under the earth. You shall not bow down to them or worship them; for I the LORD your God am a jealous God, punishing children for the iniquity of parents, to the third and the fourth generation of those who reject me, but showing steadfast love to the thousandth generation of those who love me and keep my commandments. You shall not make wrongful use of the name of the LORD your God, for the LORD will not acquit anyone who misuses his name. Remember the sabbath day, and keep it holy. Six days you shall labor and do all your work. But the seventh day is a sabbath to the LORD your God; you shall not do any work—you, your son or your daughter, your male or female slave, your livestock, or the alien resident in your towns. For in six days the LORD made heaven and earth, the sea, and all that is in them, but rested the seventh day; therefore the LORD blessed the sabbath day and consecrated it. Honor your father and your mother, so that your days may be long in the land that the LORD your God is giving you. You shall not murder. You shall not commit adultery. You shall not steal. You shall not bear false witness against your neighbor. You shall not covet your neighbor's house; you shall not covet your neighbor's wife, or male or female slave, or ox, or donkey, or anything that belongs to your neighbor.

Exodus 20:1–17 NRSV

His Light gives wisdom and knowledge, and

his Love gives power and strength, to run the ways of his commandments with delight.

John Bellers

If God had wanted us to have a permissive society he would have given Ten Suggestions instead of Ten Commandments.

M.M. Hershman

The Ten Commandments completed by the evangelical precepts of justice and charity, constitute the framework of individual and collective survival.

John XXIII

The Ten Commandments, when written on tablets of stone and given to man, did not then first begin to belong to him; they had their existence in man and lay as a seed hidden in the form and maker of his soul.

William Law

The commands of God are all designed to make us more happy than we can possibly be without them.

Thomas Wilson

Thankfulness and Thanksgiving

See also Prayer, Thanksgiving

Offer to God a sacrifice of thanksgiving and pay your vows to the Most High.

Psalm 50:14 NRSV

One of them [ten lepers], when he saw that he was healed, turned back, and with a loud voice glorified God, And fell down on his face at his feet, giving him thanks: and he was a Samaritan.

Luke 17:15–16 KJV

Let us thank God for his priceless gift!

2 Corinthians 9:15 GNB

I do not cease to give thanks for you as I remember you in my prayers.

Ephesians 1:16 NRSV

Nor should there be obscenity, foolish talk or coarse joking, which are out of place, but rather thanksgiving.

Ephesians 5:4 NIV

Speak to one another in psalms, hymns, and songs; sing and make music from your heart to the Lord; and in the name of our Lord Jesus Christ give thanks every day for everything to our God and Father.

Ephesians 5:19–20 REB

With thankful hearts offer up your prayers and requests to God.

Philippians 4:6 CEV

Be joyful always; pray continuously; give thanks in all circumstances, for this is God's will for you in Christ Jesus.

1 Thessalonians 5:16–18 NIV

No duty is more urgent than that of returning thanks.

St. Ambrose

A true Christian is a man who never for a moment forgets what God has done for him in Christ and whose whole comportment and whose activity have their root in the sentiment of gratitude.

John Baillie

Pride slays thanksgiving, but a humble mind is the soil out of which thanks naturally grows. A proud man is seldom a grateful man, for he never thinks he gets as much as he gives.

Henry Ward Beecher

In ordinary life we hardly realize that we receive a great deal more than we give, and that it is only with gratitude that life becomes rich. It is very easy to overestimate the importance of our own achievements in comparison with what we owe others.

Dietrich Bonhoeffer

Thanksgiving is good but thanks-living is better.

Matthew Henry

Thou has given so much to me. . . . Give me one thing more—a grateful heart.

George Herbert

Gratitude is born in hearts that take time to count up past mercies.

Charles Edward Jefferson

Life without thankfulness is devoid of love and passion. Hope without thankfulness is lacking in fine perception. Faith without thankfulness lacks strength and fortitude. Every virtue divorced from thankfulness is maimed and limps along the spiritual road.

John Henry Jowett

Thankfulness is a soil in which pride does not easily grow.

Michael Ramsay

Gratitude to God makes even a temporal blessing a taste of heaven.

William Romaine

If the Church is in Christ, its initial act is always the act of thanksgiving, of returning the world to God.

Alexander Schmemann

From David learn to give thanks for everything. Every furrow in the book of Psalms is sown with the seeds of thanksgiving.

Jeremy Taylor

The best way to show my gratitude to God is to accept everything, even my problems, with joy.

Mother Teresa

And then be thankful; O admire his ways, / Who fills the world's unempty'd granaries! / A thankless feeder is a thief, his feast / A very robbery, and himself no guest.

Henry Vaughan

The Christian is suspended between blessings received and blessings hoped for, so he should always give thanks.

Marvin Richardson (M.R.) Vincent

Gratitude is not only the memory but the homage of the heart—rendered to God for his goodness.

Nathaniel Parker Willis

Theology

See also God; Knowledge; Study

In the beginning was the Word, and the Word was with God, and the Word was God.

John 1:1 NIV

I have not the slightest interest in a theology which doesn't evangelize.

James Denney

Love is the abridgment of all theology.

St. Francis de Sales

Theology does not produce pastoral activity—rather it reflects upon it. . . . This is a theology which does not stop with reflecting on the world, but rather tries to be part of the process through which the world is transformed.

Gustavo Gutiérrez

Nothing dies harder than a theological difference.

Ronald Arbuthnott Knox

No one can understand God or His Word who has not received such understanding directly from the Holy Spirit. But no one can receive it from the Holy Spirit without experiencing, proving and feeling it. In such experiences the Holy Spirit instructs us as in His own school, outside of which naught is learned save empty words and idle fables. . . . Only experience makes a theologian. Experience is necessary to the understanding of the Word. It is not merely to be repeated and known, but also to be lived and felt.

Martin Luther

Your theology is what you are when the talking stops and the action starts.

Colin Morris

The word God is a theology in itself, indivisibly one, inexhaustibly various.

John Henry Newman

Live to explain thy doctrine by thy life.

Matthew Prior

What Jesus showed us is how to do theology with people daily involved in the joys and sorrows of this life.

Choan-Seng Song

My entire theology can be condensed into four words, "Jesus died for me."

Charles Haddon Spurgeon

The publican stood afar off and beat his breast and said, "God be merciful to me, a sinner." I tell you that man had the finest theology of any man in all England.

Charles Haddon Spurgeon

If your theology doesn't change your behavior, it will never change your destiny.

Charles Haddon Spurgeon

A doctrine has practical value only as far as it is prominent in our thoughts and makes a difference in our lives.

Aiden Wilson (A.W.) Tozer

You can be as straight as a gun-barrel theologically—and as empty as one spiritually.

Aiden Wilson (A.W.) Tozer

Thirst, *see* Hunger and Thirst

Thoughts and Thinking

See also Mind

Search me, O God, and know my heart: try me, and know my thoughts: And see if there be any wicked way in me, and lead me in the way everlasting.

Psalm 139:23–24 KJV

For my thoughts are not your thoughts, nor are your ways my ways, says the LORD. For as the heavens are higher than the earth, so are my ways higher than your ways and my thoughts than your thoughts.

Isaiah 55:8–9 NRSV

What do you think about the Messiah?

Matthew 22:42 GNB

We demolish arguments and every pretension that sets itself up against the knowledge of God, and we take captive every thought to make it obedient to Christ.

2 Corinthians 10:5 NIV

Finally, my friends, keep your minds on whatever is true, pure, right, holy, friendly, and proper. Don't ever stop thinking about what is truly worthwhile and worthy of praise.

Philippians 4:8 CEV

You should not wait till you are cleansed from wandering thoughts before you pray.

Abraham of Nathpar

Thought is a kind of sight of the mind.

St. Augustine of Hippo

When evil thoughts come into your heart, dash them at once on the rock of Christ.

St. Benedict

Think through me, thoughts of God, / And let my thoughts be / Lost like the sand-pools on the shore / Of the eternal sea.

Amy Wilson Carmichael

A man is what he thinks about all day long.

Ralph Waldo Emerson

Even in good thoughts there is a fickleness and inconstancy which may well be called vanity. It concerns us to keep a strict guard upon our thoughts, because God takes particular notice of them. Thoughts are words to God, and vain thoughts are provocations.

Matthew Henry

Certain thoughts are prayers. There are moments when whatever the attitude of the body, the soul is on its knees.

Victor Hugo

A great many people think they are thinking when they are merely rearranging their prejudices.

Sir William Jones

It is the very energy of thought / Which keeps thee from thy God.

John Henry Newman

You can't think rationally on an empty stomach, and a whole lot of people can't do it on a full one either.

Lord Reith

As soon as man does not take his existence for granted, but beholds it as something unfathomably mysterious, thought begins.

Albert Schweitzer

What we think about when we are free to think about what we will—that is what we are or will soon become.

Aiden Wilson (A.W.) Tozer

May the mind of Christ my Savior / Live in me from day to day, / By His love and power controlling / All I do and say.

Kate B. Wilkinson

Time

As thy days, so shall thy strength be.

Deuteronomy 33:25 KJV

For if thou altogether holdest thy peace at this time, then shall there enlargement and deliverance arise to the Jews from another place; but thou and thy father's house shall be destroyed: and who knoweth whether thou art come to the kingdom for such a time as this?

Esther 4:14 KJV

Teach us to count our days that we may gain a wise heart.

Psalm 90:12 NRSV

This is the day which the Lord hath made; we will rejoice and be glad in it.

Psalm 118:24 KJV

For everything there is a season, and a time for every matter under heaven: a time to be born, and a time to die; a time to plant, and a time to pluck up what is planted; a time to kill, and a time to heal; a time to break down, and a time to build up; a time to weep, and a time to laugh; a time to mourn, and a time to dance; a time to throw away stones, and a time to gather stones together; a time to embrace, and a time to refrain from embracing; a time to seek, and a time to lose; a time to keep, and a time to throw away; a time to tear, and a time to sew; a time to keep silence, and a time to speak; a time to love, and a time to hate; a time for war, and a time for peace.

Ecclesiastes 3:1–8 NRSV

I returned, and saw under the sun, that the race is not to the swift, nor the battle to the strong, neither yet bread to the wise, nor yet riches to men of understanding, nor yet favor to men of skill; but time and chance happeneth to them all.

Ecclesiastes 9:11 KJV

For who has despised the day of small things?

Zechariah 4:10 KJV

Jesus told them, "The right time for me has not yet come; for you any time is right."

John 7:6 NIV

For he saith, I have heard thee in a time accepted, and in the day of salvation have I succored thee: behold, now is the accepted time; behold, now is the day of salvation.

2 Corinthians 6:2 KJV

These are evil times, so make every minute count.

Ephesians 5:16 CEV

Beloved, be not ignorant of this one thing, that one day is with the Lord as a thousand years, and a thousand years as one day.

2 Peter 3:8 KJV

Time is a three-fold present: the present as we experience it, the past as a present memory, and the future as a present expectation.

St. Augustine of Hippo

Time lost is time when we have not lived a full human life, time unenriched by experience, creative endeavor, enjoyment and suffering.

Dietrich Bonhoeffer

Time is not yours to dispose of as you please; it is a glorious talent that men must be accountable for as well as any other talent.

Thomas Benton Brooks

Time is not a commodity that can be stored for future use. It must be invested hour by hour, or else it is gone for ever.

Thomas Alva Edison

Do not squander time, for it is the stuff of which life is made.

Benjamin Franklin

To sensible men, every day is a day of reckoning.

John (William) Gardner

One always has time enough if one will apply it.

Johann Wolfgang von Goethe

A Christian is not his own master, since all his time belongs to God.

St. Ignatius of Antioch

God does nothing in time which he did not design to do from eternity.

William Jay

The great rule of moral conduct is, next to God, to respect time.

Johann Kaspar Lavater

What is Time? The shadow on the dial, the striking of the clock, the running of the sand, day and night, summer and winter, months, years, centuries—these are but arbitrary and outward signs, the measure of Time, not Time itself. Time is the Life of the soul.

Henry Wadsworth Longfellow

Only eternal values can give meaning to temporal ones. Time must be the servant of eternity.

Erwin W. Lutzer

What we weave in time we wear in eternity.

John Charles Ryle

Time is the deposit each one has in the bank of God and no one knows the balance.

Ralph Washington Sockman

Time shall be no more when judgment comes, and when time is no more change is impossible.

Charles Haddon Spurgeon

I would the precious time redeem, / And longer live for this alone, / To spend, and to be spent, for them / Who have not yet my Savior known; / Fully on these my mission prove, / And only breathe, to breathe Thy love.

Charles Wesley

Procrastination is the thief of time.

Edward Young

Tiredness

See also Rest

Have you not known? Have you not heard? The LORD is the everlasting God, the Creator of the ends of the earth. He does not faint or grow weary; his understanding is unsearchable. He gives power to the faint, and strengthens the powerless. Even youths will faint and be weary, and the young will fall exhausted; but those who wait for the LORD shall renew their strength, they shall mount up with wings like eagles, they shall run and not be weary, they shall walk and not faint.

Isaiah 40:28–31 NRSV

Come to me, all you who are weary and burdened, and I will give you rest.

Matthew 11:28 NIV

Now Jacob's well was there. Jesus, therefore, being wearied with his journey, sat thus on the well.

John 4:6 KJV

Don't get tired of helping others. You will be rewarded when the time is right, if you don't give up.

Galatians 6:9 CEV

It is the same with people who travel: if they tire themselves out on the very first day by rushing along, they will end up wasting many days as a result of sickness. But if they start out walking at a gentle pace until they have got accustomed to walking, in the end they will not get tired, even though they walk great distances.

Evagrius of Pontus

Weariness maketh way for wandering.

Thomas Manton

It is good to be tired and wearied by the vain

search after the true good, that we may stretch out our arms to the Redeemer.

Blaise Pascal

Don't let Satan make you overwork and then put you out of action for a long period.

Charles Simeon

Tithing, *see* Giving; Stewardship

Tolerance

See also Judging Others; Respect

Your eyes are too pure to look on evil; you cannot tolerate wrong. Why then do you tolerate the treacherous?

Habakkuk 1:13 NIV

Despiseth thou the riches of his goodness and forbearance and longsuffering; not knowing that the goodness of God leadeth thee to repentance?

Romans 2:4 KJV

The person who will eat anything is not to despise the one who doesn't; while the one who eats only vegetables is not to pass judgment on the one who will eat anything; for God has accepted that person.

Romans 14:3 GNB

Tolerance implies a respect for another person, not because he is wrong or even because he is right, but because he is human.

John Cogley

It is only imperfection that complains of what is imperfect. The more perfect we are, the more gentle and quiet we become toward the defects of others.

François de la Mothe Fénelon

Men boast of their tolerance, who should be ashamed of their indifference.

William H. Houghton

If we cannot end our differences, at least we can make the world safe for diversity.

John Fitzgerald Kennedy

The modern theory that you should always treat the religious convictions of other people with profound respect finds no support in the Gospels. Mutual tolerance of religious views is the product not of faith, but of doubt.

Sir Arnold Lunn

O God, help us not to despise or oppose what we do not understand.

William Penn

Tongues, *see* Spiritual Gifts

Tradition

See also Worship

You [Pharisees] have made God's word ineffective by means of your tradition.

Matthew 15:6 NJB

The Pharisees, and all the Jews, do not eat unless they thoroughly wash their hands, thus observing the tradition of the elders; and they do not eat anything from the market unless they wash it; and there are also many other traditions that they observe.

Mark 7:3–4 NRSV

Beware lest any man spoil you through philosophy and vain deceit, after the tradition of men, after the rudiments of the world, and not after Christ.

Colossians 2:8 KJV

Therefore, brethren, stand fast, and hold the traditions which ye have been taught, whether by word, or our epistle.

2 Thessalonians 2:15 KJV

Scripture has been God's way of fixing tradition, and rendering it trustworthy at any distance of time.

Henry Alford

There is a difference between apostolic tradition and ecclesiastical tradition, the former being the foundation of the latter.

Oscar Cullmann

Tradition is the living faith of the dead: traditionalism is the dead faith of the living.

Jaroslav Pelikan

Tradition will be our guide to the interpretation of the Bible through the appeal to the total life and experience of the Church from the ancient Fathers onwards.

(Arthur) Michael Ramsey

The Spirit who interprets the Scriptures is none other than the Risen Lord himself; the tradition of the Church is actually shaped and guided by the Spirit of the Risen Christ.

Alan Richardson

Every church should be engaged in continuous self-reformation, scrutinizing its traditions in the light of Scripture and where necessary modifying them.

John R.W. Stott

Christian work is constantly crippled by clinging to blessings and traditions of the past. God is not the God of yesterday. He is the God of today. Heaven forbid that we should go on playing religious games in one corner when the cloud and fire of God's presence have moved to another.

David Watson

Transformation, *see* Change

Travel, *see* Journeys

Trials

See also Suffering; Temptation; Trouble

My brothers and sisters, whenever you face trials of any kind, consider it nothing but joy, because you know that the testing of your faith produces endurance.

James 1:2–3 NRSV

Happy are those who remain faithful under trials, because when they succeed in passing such a test, they will receive as their reward the life which God has promised to those who love him.

James 1:12 GNB

Dear friends, do not be surprised at the painful trial you are suffering, as though something strange were happening to you.

1 Peter 4:12 NIV

The gem cannot be polished without friction, nor man perfected without trials.

Anon.

Trials enable people to rise above Religion to God.

Fr. Andrew

Prosperity is the blessing of the Old Testament; adversity is the blessing of the New.

Francis Bacon

It is trial that proves one thing weak and another strong. A house built on the sand is in fair weather just as good as if builded on a rock. A cobweb is as good as the mightiest cable when there is no strain upon it.

Henry Ward Beecher

The brightest crowns that are worn in heaven have been tried, and smelted, and polished, and glorified, through the furnace of tribulation.

Edwin Hubbel (E.H.) Chapin

In this life we will encounter hurts and trials that we will not be able to change; we are just going to have to allow them to change us.

Ron Lee Davis

Every wise workman takes his tools away from the work from time to time that they may be ground and sharpened; so does the only-wise Jehovah take his ministers oftentimes away into darkness and loneliness and trouble, that he may sharpen and prepare them for hard work in his service.

Robert Murray M'Cheyne

If we are intended for great ends, we are called to great hazards.

John Henry Newman

Problems are the cutting-edge that distinguishes between success and failure. Problems . . . create our courage and our wisdom. It is only because of problems that we grow mentally and spiritually.

M. Scott Peck

There is a strange perversity in men concerning their trials in life, and only grace can cure it.

William S. Plummer

As sure as ever God puts his children in the furnace, he will be in the furnace with them.

Charles Haddon Spurgeon

In shunning a trial we are seeking to avoid a blessing.

Charles Haddon Spurgeon

Whilst I continue on this side of eternity, I never expect to be free from trials, only to change them. For it is necessary to heal the pride of my heart that such should come.

George Whitefield

Trinity, *see* God, Trinity

Trouble

See also Suffering

Human beings are born to trouble just as sparks fly upward.

Job 5:7 NRSV

This poor man called, and the Lord heard him; he saved him out of all his troubles.

Psalm 34:6 NIV

This small and temporary trouble we suffer will bring us a tremendous and eternal glory, much greater than the trouble.

2 Corinthians 4:17 GNB

He is not drowning His sheep when He washeth them, nor killing them when He is shearing them. But by this He showeth that they are His own; and the newborn sheep do most visibly bear His name or mark, when it is almost worn out and scarce discernible on them that have the longest fleece.

Richard Baxter

Troubles are often the tools by which God fashions us for better things.

Henry Ward Beecher

The Lord does not measure out our afflictions according to our faults, but according to our strength, and looks not what we have deserved, but what we are able to bear.

George Downame

Difficulties are not a passing condition that we must allow to blow over like a storm so that we can set to work when calm returns. They are the normal condition.

Charles de Foucauld

Let us belong to God even in the thick of the disturbance stirred up round about us by the diversity of human affairs. True virtue is not always nourished in external calm any more than good fish are always found in stagnant waters.

St. Francis de Sales

Tribulation: God's fastest road to patience, character, hope, confidence, and genuine love.

Bill Gothard

There is no man in the world without some troubles or affliction, though he be a king or a pope.

Thomas à Kempis

Only in the hot furnace of affliction do we as Christians let go of the dross to which, in our foolishness, we ardently cling.

David Kingdon

Adversity is the diamond dust Heaven polishes its jewels with.

Robert Leighton

Jesus promised his disciples three things— that they would be completely fearless, absurdly happy, and in constant trouble.

F.R. Maltby

God will never permit any troubles to come upon us unless he has a specific plan by which great blessing can come out of the difficulty.

Peter Marshall

Trouble is the structural steel that goes into character-building.

Douglas Meador

When I am in the cellar of affliction, I look for the Lord's choicest wines.

Samuel Rutherford

Grace grows best in the winter.

Samuel Rutherford

The Lord gets his best soldiers out of the highlands of affliction.

Charles Haddon Spurgeon

I am never afraid for my brethren who have many troubles, but I often tremble for those whose career is prosperous.

Charles Haddon Spurgeon

Nothing influences the quality of our life more than how we respond to trouble.

Erwin G. Tieman

He that rides to be crowned will not think much of a rainy day.

John Trapp

There is more evil in a drop of sin than in a sea of affliction.

Thomas Weston

Trust

See also Belief; Confidence; Faith

As for God, his way is perfect; the word of the Lord is tried: he is a buckler to all them that trust in him. For who is God, save the Lord? and who is a rock, save our God? God is my strength and power: and he maketh my way perfect. He maketh my feet like hinds' feet: and setteth me upon my high places.

2 Samuel 22:31–34 KJV

Though he slay me, yet will I trust in him.

Job 13:15 KJV

I will lay me down in peace, and take my rest: for it is thou, Lord, only, that makest me dwell in safety.

Psalm 4:9 BCP

Trust in the Lord, and do good; so shalt thou dwell in the land, and verily thou shalt be fed. Delight thyself also in the Lord; and he shall give thee the desires of thine heart. Commit thy way unto the Lord; trust also in him; and he shall bring it to pass.

Psalm 37:3–5 KJV

O put not your trust in princes, nor in any child of man: for there is no help in them.

Psalm 146:2 BCP

Trust in the LORD with all your heart, and do not rely on your own insight.

Proverbs 3:5 NRSV

May the God of hope fill you with all joy and peace as you trust in him, so that you may overflow with hope by the power of the Holy Spirit.

Romans 15:13 NIV

Trusting means drawing on the inexhaustible resources of God.

Anon.

He who trusts in himself is lost. He who trusts in God can do all things.

St. Alphonsus Liguori

Trust the past to God's mercy, the present to God's love, and the future to God's providence.

St. Augustine of Hippo

O Lord, in thee have I trusted: let me never be confounded.

Book of Common Prayer

It is not our trust that keeps us, but the God in whom we trust who keeps us.

Oswald Chambers

Trust involves letting go and knowing God will catch you.

James Dobson

Put thou thy trust in God, / In duty's path go on; / Walk in His strength with faith and hope, / So shall thy work be done.

Paul Gerhardt, tr. John Wesley

Trust God where you cannot trace him. Do not try to penetrate the cloud he brings over you; rather look to the bow that is on it. The mystery is God's; the promise is yours.

John R. Macduff

Let God do with me what he will, anything he will; whatever it be, it will be either heaven itself of some beginning of it.

William Mountford

What is more elevating and transporting, than the generosity of heart which risks everything on God's word?

John Henry Newman

Trust is one of the fundamental aspects of life for every human existence . . . only trust allows the soul room to breathe.

Wolfhart Pannenberg

The more we depend on God, the more dependable we find he is.

Sir Cliff Richard

God knows what he's about. If he has you sidelined, out of the action for a while, he knows what he's doing. You just stay faithful

. . . stay flexible . . . stay available . . . stay humble, like David with his sheep (even after he had been anointed king!).

Charles R. Swindoll

Trust is a treasured item and relationship. Once it is tarnished, it is hard to restore it to its original glow.

William Arthur Ward

Truth

See also Falsehood

The LORD is the true God; he is the living God and the everlasting King.

Jeremiah 10:10 NRSV

Great is truth, and strongest of all!

1 Esdras 4:41 RSV

If you stand by my teaching, you are truly my disciples; you will know the truth, and the truth will set you free.

John 8:31–32 REB

Jesus saith unto him, I am the way, the truth, and the life: no man cometh unto the Father, but by me.

John 14:6 KJV

Jesus answered, "You are right in saying I am a king. In fact, for this reason I was born, and for this I came into the world, to testify to the truth. Everyone on the side of truth listens to me." "What is truth?" Pilate asked.

John 18:37–38 NIV

Speaking the truth in love.

Ephesians 4:15 KJV

Truth is not only violated by falsehood; it may be equally outraged by silence.

Henri-Frédéric Amiel

Truth which is merely told is quick to be forgotten; truth which is discovered lasts a lifetime.

William Barclay

I thirst for truth, but shall not reach it until I reach the source.

Robert Browning

Truth is the highest thing that man may keep.

Geoffrey Chaucer

Truth and love are wings that cannot be separated, for truth cannot fly without love, nor can love soar aloft without truth.

Ephraem the Syrian

Don't be so arrogant as to suppose that the truth is no bigger than your understanding of it.

Michael Green

Christianity is not true because it works. It works because it is true.

Os Guinness

For each truth revealed by grace, and received with inward delight and joy, is a secret murmur of God in the ear of a pure soul.

Walter Hilton

A Church which abandons the truth abandons itself.

Hans Küng

Superstition, idolatry, and hypocrisy have ample wages, but truth goes a-begging.

Martin Luther

It is obvious that to be in earnest in seeking the truth is an indispensable requisite for finding it.

John Henry Newman

No truth can really exist external to Christianity.

John Henry Newman

Truth often suffers most by the heat of its defenders than from the arguments of its opposers.

William Penn

Truth is given, not to be contemplated, but to be done. Life is an action, not a thought.

Frederick William Robertson

I think the most important quality in a person concerned with religion is absolute devotion to truth.

Albert Schweitzer

Let us rejoice in the truth wherever we find its lamp burning.

Albert Schweitzer

We are more likely to catch glimpses of truth when we allow what we think and believe to be tested.

Choan-Seng Song

No generation can claim to have plumbed to the depths the unfathomable riches of Christ. The Holy Spirit has promised to lead us step by step into the fullness of truth.

Leon Joseph Suenens

Every truth without exception—and whoever may utter it—is from the Holy Ghost.

St. Thomas Aquinas

What God's Son has told me, take for true I do; / Truth himself speaks truly or there's nothing true.

St. Thomas Aquinas

Nothing can ever destroy truth.

Leslie Weatherhead

Any human being can penetrate to the kingdom of truth, if only he longs for truth and perpetually concentrates all his attention upon its attainment.

Simone Weil

Tyranny,   *see*   Injustice;   Oppression; Persecution

Unbelief

See also Agnosticism and Atheism; Belief; Doubt

Jesus answered, "What an unbelieving and perverse generation! How long shall I be with you?"

Matthew 17:17 REB

Jesus said unto him, If thou canst believe, all things are possible to him that believeth. And straightway the father of the child cried out, and said with tears, Lord, I believe; help thou mine unbelief.

Mark 9:23–24 KJV

Thomas said, "First I must see the nail scars in his hands and touch them with my finger. I must put my hand where the spear went into his side. I won't believe unless I do this" . . . [Jesus] said to Thomas, "Put your finger here and look at my hands! Put your hand into my side. Stop doubting and have faith!"

John 20:25, 27 CEV

In all unbelief there are these two things: a good opinion of one's self and a bad opinion of God.

Horatius Bonar

All unbelief is the belief of a lie.

Horatius Bonar

Our own unbelief is the only impediment which prevents God from satisfying us largely and bountifully with all good things.

John Calvin

One result of the unbelief of our day is the tragedy of trying to live a maximum life on a minimum faith.

Rufus Matthew Jones

Every man will have to decide for himself whether or not he can afford the terrible luxury of unbelief.

Aiden Wilson (A.W.) Tozer

It is unbelief that prevents our minds from soaring into the celestial city, and walking by faith with God across the golden streets.

Aiden Wilson (A.W.) Tozer

Unbelievers

See also Unbelief

No one who has faith in God's Son will be condemned. But everyone who doesn't have faith in him has already been condemned for not having faith in God's only Son. The light has come into the world, and people who do evil things are judged guilty because they love the dark more than the light.

John 3:18–19 CEV

The god of this world has blinded the minds of the unbelievers, to keep them from seeing the light of the gospel of the glory of Christ, who is the image of God.

2 Corinthians 4:4 NRSV

Do not team up with unbelievers. What partnership can righteousness have with wicked-ness? Can light associate with darkness?

2 Corinthians 6:14 REB

No man is an unbeliever, but because he will be so; and every man is not an unbeliever, because the grace of God conquers some, changes their wills, and binds them to Christ.

Stephen Charnock

What greater rebellion, impiety, or insult to God can there be than not to believe his promises?

Martin Luther

Evil people have a kind of enamorment with their own will. When there is conflict between their conscience and their will, it is the conscience which has to go. They are extraordinarily willful people and extraordinarily controlling people.

M. Scott Peck

The seeming peace a sinner has is not from the knowledge of his happiness but the ignorance of his danger.

Thomas Watson

Understanding

See also Knowledge; Wisdom

Be ye not as the horse, or as the mule, which have no understanding: whose mouth must be held in with bit and bridle.

Psalm 32:9 KJV

Wisdom is the principal thing; therefore get wisdom: and with all thy getting get understanding.

Proverbs 4:7 KJV

When anyone hears the word of the kingdom without understanding, the Evil One comes and carries off what was sown in his heart: this is the seed sown on the edge of the path. . . . And the seed sown in rich soil is someone who hears the word and understands it; this is the one who yields a harvest and produces now a hundredfold, now sixty, now thirty.

Matthew 13:19, 23 NJB

When Philip ran up he heard him reading from the prophet Isaish and asked, "Do you understand what you are reading?"

Acts 8:30 REB

The peace of God, which surpasses all understanding, will guard your hearts and your minds in Christ Jesus.

Philippians 4:7 NRSV

Understanding is the reward of faith. Therefore seek not to understand that you may believe, but believe that you may understand.

St. Augustine of Hippo

Don't try to reach God with your understanding; that is impossible. Reach him in love; that is possible.

Carlo Carretto

He that will believe only what he can fully comprehend must have a very long head or a very short creed.

Charles Caleb Colton

What we do not understand we do not possess.

Johann Wolfgang von Goethe

Understanding can wait. Obedience cannot.

Geoffrey Grogan

It's taken me all my life to understand that it is not necessary to understand everything.

René-Jules Gustave

When men understand what each other mean, they see, for the most part, that controversy is either superfluous or hopeless.

John Henry Newman

What is most necessary for understanding divine things is prayer.

Origen of Alexandria

To be surprised, to wonder, is to begin to understand.

José Ortega y Gasset

All, everything that I understand, I understand only because I love.

Count Leo Tolstoy

Union with God

See also Fellowship

If we have been united with him like this in his death, we will certainly also be united with him in his resurrection.

Romans 6:5 NIV

I have been crucified with Christ; and it is no longer I who live, but it is Christ who lives in me.

Galatians 2:19–20 NRSV

You have made us for yourself and our hearts are restless until they find their rest in you.

St. Augustine of Hippo

A Christian has a union with Jesus Christ more noble, more intimate, and more perfect than the members of a human body have with their head.

St. John Eudes

Ecstasy is naught but the going forth of a soul from itself and its being caught up in God, and this is what happens to the soul that is obedient, namely, that it goes forth from itself and from its own desires, and thus lightened becomes immersed in God.

St. John of the Cross

The soul that is united with God is feared by the devil as though it were God himself.

St. John of the Cross

When I am with God / My fear is gone / In the great quiet of God. / My troubles are as pebbles on the road, / My joys are like the everlasting hills.

Walter Rauschenbusch

Making my will one with the will of God, this is the union which I myself desire and should like to see in everyone; and not just a few of those raptures, however delightful, which go by the name of union.

St. Teresa of Avila

If you genuinely desire union with the unspeakable love of God, then you must be prepared to have your "religious" world shattered.

Rowan Williams

Unity, *see* Church, Unity

Unselfishness

See also Selfishness

The soul who blesses will prosper, whoever satisfies others will also be satisfied.

Proverbs 11:25 NJB

We who are strong ought to put up with the failings of the weak, and not to please ourselves. Each of us must please our neighbor for the good purpose of building up the neighbor. For Christ did not please himself.

Romans 15:1–3 NRSV

Hereby perceive we the love of God, because he laid down his life for us: and we ought to lay down our lives for the brethren.

1 John 3:16 KJV

The most satisfactory thing in life is to have been able to give a large part of oneself to others.

Pierre Teilhard de Chardin

There is no great valor nor no sterner fight than that for self-effacement, self-oblivion.

Meister Eckhart

The secret of being loved is in being lovely; and the secret of being lovely is in being unselfish.

Josiah Gilbert Holland

All greatness grows by self-abasement and not by exalting itself.

Nestorius

Once you say the yes of faith to Jesus and accept his blueprint for the fullness of life, the whole world can no longer revolve around you, your needs, your gratifications; you'll have to revolve around the world, seeking to bandage its wounds, loving dead men into life, finding the lost, wanting the unwanted, and leaving far behind all the selfish, parasitical concerns which drain our time and energies.

Sir John Powell

The least-used words by an unselfish person are, I, me, my, and mine.

Charles R. Swindoll

Lord, grant that I may seek to comfort rather than be comforted; to love rather than be loved.

Mother Teresa

When you empty yourself, God Almighty rushes in!

Aiden Wilson (A.W.) Tozer

It is not my business to think about myself. My business is to think about God. It is for God to think about me.

Simone Weil

The princes among us are those who forget themselves and serve mankind.

(Thomas) Woodrow Wilson

Usury, *see* Debt

Vanity

See also Conceit

You have made my days a few handbreadths and my lifetime is as nothing in your sight. Surely everyone stands as a mere breath.

Psalm 39:5 NRSV

Turn away mine eyes from beholding vanity; and quicken thou me in thy way.

Psalm 119:37 KJV

All is vanity. All go unto one place; all are of the dust and all turn to dust again.

Ecclesiastes 3:19–20 KJV

Vainglory blossoms but never bears.

Anon.

We know nothing vainer than the minds of men.

John Calvin

Whatsoever we have over-loved, idolized, and leaned upon, God has from time to time broken it, and made us to see the vanity of it; so that we find the readiest course to be rid of our comforts is to set our hearts inordinately upon them.

John Flavel

Nothing is more foolish than a security built upon the world and its promises, for they are all vanity and a lie.

Matthew Henry

At all times, but especially now, it is pertinent to say, "Vanity of vanities, all is vanity."

St. John Chrysostom

Do not concern yourself with anxiety for the show of a great name.

Thomas à Kempis

Most of us would be far enough from vanity if we heard all the things that are said of us.

Joseph Rickaby

Vain thoughts defile the heart as well as vile thoughts.

William Secker

Victory

See also Spiritual Warfare; War and Warfare

Do not fear, for I am with you, do not be afraid, for I am your God; I will strengthen you, I will help you, I will uphold you with my victorious right hand.

Isaiah 41:10 NRSV

But thanks be to God, which giveth us the victory through our Lord Jesus Christ.

1 Corinthians 15:57 KJV

There [on the cross] he disarmed the cosmic powers and authorities and made a public spectacle of them, leading them as captives in his triumphal procession.

Colossians 2:15 REB

Everyone born of God overcomes the world. This is the victory that has overcome the world, even our faith.

1 John 5:4 NIV

True triumphs are God's triumphs over us. His defeats of us are our real victories.

Henry Alford

God is never defeated. Though He may be opposed, attacked, resisted, still the ultimate outcome can never be in doubt.

Br. Andrew

If Christ is with us, who is against us? You can fight with confidence where you are sure of victory. With Christ and for Christ victory is certain.

St. Bernard of Clairvaux

Let us be as watchful after the victory as before the battle.

Andrew Alexander Bonar

The first step on the way to victory is to recognize the enemy.

Corrie ten Boom

Victory begins with the name of Jesus on our lips. But it is not consummated until the nature of Jesus is in our heart.

Francis Frangipane

There is no more dangerous moment in our lives than that which follows a great victory.

Stephen Olford

God wants us to be victors, not victims; to grow, not grovel; to soar, not sink; to overcome, not to be overwhelmed.

William Arthur Ward

Violence

See also Oppression

The earth also was corrupt before God, and the earth was filled with violence.

Genesis 6:11 KJV

The LORD tests the righteous and the wicked, and his soul hates the lover of violence.

Psalm 11:5 NRSV

The overseer must be above reproach . . . not violent but gentle.

1 Timothy 3:2–3 NIV

Violence is always an offense, an insult to man, both to the one who perpetrates it and to the one who suffers it.

John Paul II

Violence is a lie, for it goes against the truth of our faith, the truth of our humanity. Violence destroys what it claims to defend: the dignity, the life, the freedom of human beings. Violence is a crime against humanity for it destroys the very fabric of society.

John Paul II

Violence ends by defeating itself. It creates bitterness in the survivors and brutality in the destroyers.

Martin Luther King Jr.

Much violence is based on the illusion that life is a property to be defended and not a gift to be shared.

Henri J.M. Nouwen

We have never preached violence, except the violence of love, which left Christ nailed to a cross, the violence we must each do to ourselves to overcome our selfishness and such cruel inequalities among us.

Oscar Romero

He who achieves power by violence does not truly become lord or master.

St. Thomas Aquinas

A good portion of the evils that afflict mankind is due to the erroneous belief that life can be made secure by violence.

Count Leo Tolstoy

Violence obliterates anybody who feels its touch.

Simone Weil

Virginity, *see* Singleness

Virtues and Vices

When self-indulgence is at work the results are obvious: sexual vice, impurity, and sensuality, the worship of false gods and sorcery; antagonisms and rivalry, jealousy, bad temper and quarrels, disagreements, factions and malice, drunkenness, orgies and all such things.

Galatians 5:19–21 NJB

Clothe yourselves with compassion, kindness, humility, gentleness and patience. Bear with each other and forgive whatever grievances you may have against one another. . . . And over all these virtues put on love, which binds them all together in perfect unity.

Colossians 3:12–14 NIV

. . . [A]dd to your faith virtue; and to virtue knowledge; And to knowledge temperance; and to temperance patience; and to patience godliness; And to godliness brotherly kindness; and to brotherly kindness charity. For if

these things be in you, and abound, they make you that ye shall neither be barren nor unfruitful in the knowledge of our Lord Jesus Christ.

2 Peter 1:5–8 KJV

Virtue is nothing but well-directed love.

St. Augustine of Hippo

We make a ladder of our vices, if we trample those same vices underfoot.

St. Augustine of Hippo

Prosperity doth best discover vice, but adversity doth best discover virtue.

Francis Bacon

This is the definition of vice: the wrong use, in violation of the Lord's command, of what has been given us by God for a good purpose.

St. Basil the Great

The inherent vice of capitalism is the unequal sharing of blessings, the inherent vice of socialism is the equal sharing of miseries.

Sir Winston Churchill

We are more apt to catch the vices of others than their virtues, as disease is far more contagious than health.

Charles Caleb Colton

There is a capacity of virtue in us, and there is a capacity of vice to make your blood creep.

Ralph Waldo Emerson

Do not think that you have acquired virtue, unless you have struggled for it to the point of shedding your blood.

Evagrius of Pontus

Cheerfulness is among the most laudable virtues. It gains you the good will and friendship of others. It blesses those who practice it and those upon whom it is bestowed.

B.C. Forbes

Passions are vices or virtues in their highest powers.

Johann Wolfgang von Goethe

But oftentimes if we brace ourselves with strong energy against the incitements of evil habits, we turn even those very evil habits to the account of virtue.

St. Gregory I

If every year we root out one vice, we should soon become perfect.

Thomas à Kempis

Make a virtue of necessity.

Brother Lawrence

The strength of a man's virtue should not be measured by his special exertions, but by his habitual acts.

Blaise Pascal

Teach thy necessity to reason thus: / There is no virtue like necessity.

William Shakespeare

Charity is the form, mover, mother, and root of all the virtues.

St. Thomas Aquinas

What man call social virtues, good fellowship, is commonly but the virtue of pigs in a litter, which lie close together to keep each other warm. It brings men together in crowds and mobs in bar-rooms and elsewhere, but it does not deserve the name of virtue.

Henry David Thoreau

Visions

See also Dreams

The boy Samuel was ministering to the LORD under Eli. The word of the LORD was rare in those days; visions were not widespread.

1 Samuel 3:1 NRSV

Where there is no vision, the people perish.

Proverbs 29:18 KJV

For the vision is yet for an appointed time, but at the end it shall speak, and not lie: though it tarry, wait for it; because it will surely come, it will not tarry.

Habakkuk 2:3 KJV

Some of the women . . . could not find his body. They came back saying they had seen a vision of angels who told them that he is alive.

Luke 24:22–23 GNB

A vision without a task is a dream; a task without a vision is drudgery; a vision and a task is the hope of the world.

Anon.

I was created to see God, and I have not yet accomplished that for which I was made.

St. Anselm of Canterbury

A man with the vision of God is not devoted simply to a cause or a particular issue but to God himself.

Oswald Chambers

Only he who can see the invisible can do the impossible.

Frank Gaines

This truly is the vision of God: never to be satisfied in the desire to see him. But one must always, by looking at what he can see, rekindle his desire to see more.

St. Gregory of Nyssa

The vision must be followed by the venture. It is not enough to stare up the steps—we must step up the stairs.

Vance Havner

A blind man's world is bounded by the limits of his touch; an ignorant man's world by the limits of his knowledge; a great man's world by the limits of his vision.

E. Paul Hovey

There is nothing as powerful as an idea whose time has now come.

Victor Hugo

Vision is of God. A vision comes in advance of any task well done.

Katherine Logan

The Christians who have turned the world upside down have been men and women with a vision in their hearts and the Bible in their hands.

T.B. Maston

Vision is the art of seeing things invisible.

Jonathan Swift

Vision encompasses vast vistas outside the realm of the predictable, the safe, the expected.

Charles R. Swindoll

Vocation

Then I heard the voice of the LORD saying, "Whom shall I send, and who will go for us?" And I said, "Here am I; send me!" And he said, "Go and say to this people: 'Keep listening, but do not comprehend; keep looking, but do not understand.' Make the mind of this people dull, and stop their ears, and shut their eyes, so that they may not look with their eyes, and listen with their ears, and comprehend with their minds, and turn and be healed."

Isaiah 6:8–10 NRSV

Consider your own call, brothers and sisters: not many of you were wise by human standards, not many were powerful, not many were of noble birth.

1 Corinthians 1:26 NRSV

May the God of our Lord Jesus Christ, the Father of glory, give you a spirit of wisdom and perception of what is revealed, to bring you to full knowledge of him. May he enlighten the eyes of your mind so that you can see what hope his call holds for you, how rich is the glory of the heritage he offers among his holy people, and how extraordinarily great is the power that he has exercised for us believers.

Ephesians 1:17–19 NJB

Do not despise your situation. In it you must act, suffer, and conquer. From every point on earth, we are equally near to heaven and the infinite.

Henri-Frédéric Amiel

No man can do properly what he is called upon to do in this life unless he can learn to forget his ego and act as an instrument of God.

W.H. Auden

When Christ calls a man, he bids him come and die.

Dietrich Bonhoeffer

When I have learned to do the Father's will,

I shall have fully realized my vocation on earth.

Carlo Carretto

A good vocation is simply a firm and constant will in which the called person has to serve God in the way and in the places to which Almighty God has called him.

St. Francis de Sales

God has created me to do him some definite service; he has committed some work to me which he has not committed to another. I have my mission—I never may know it in this life, but I shall be told it in the next.

John Henry Newman

The vocation of every man and woman is to serve other people.

Count Leo Tolstoy

A "religious vocation" if it is real must be an attraction to a life, not a work. The truest vocation would be best described as a supernatural attraction to the Cross.

Fr. William of Glasshampton

Voice of God, *see* God, Voice of

Vows, *see* Promises

Vulnerability

See also Weakness

The sacrifices of God are a broken spirit; a broken and contrite heart, O God, you will not despise.

Psalm 51:17 NIV

A bruised reed shall he not break, and smoking flax shall he not quench.

Matthew 12:20 KJV

Vulnerability . . . is the willingness and ability to be seen as well as to see, to be touched as well as to touch. Vulnerability is the giving up of control.

Carter Heyward

To love all is to be vulnerable. Love anything, and your heart will certainly be wrung and possibly broken. If you want to make sure of keeping it intact, you must give your heart to no one. . . . Wrap it carefully round with hobbies and little luxuries; avoid all entanglements; lock it safe in a casket or coffin of your selfishness. But in that casket—safe, dark, motionless, airless—it will change. It will not be broken; it will become unbreakable, impenetrable, irredeemable. . . . The only place outside Heaven where you can be perfectly safe from all the dangers of love is—Hell.

Clive Staples (C.S.) Lewis

But what am I? / An infant crying in the night: / An infant crying for the light: / And with no language but a cry.

Alfred, Lord Tennyson

Jesus reveals a God who comes in search of us, a God who makes room for our freedom even when it costs the Son's life, a God who is vulnerable.

Philip Yancey

Vulnerability means that we let go of protective mechanisms that close us to the possibility of being deeply influenced by the other.

Katehrine Zappone

Waiting

See also Patience

I wait for the LORD, my soul waits, and in his word I hope; my soul waits for the LORD more than those who watch for the morning.

Psalm 130:5–6 NRSV

They that wait upon the Lord shall renew their strength; they shall mount up with wings as eagles; they shall run, and not be weary; and they shall walk and not faint.

Isaiah 40:31 KJV

If we hope for what we do not yet have, we wait for it patiently.

Romans 8:25 NIV

There is no place for faith if we expect God to fulfill immediately what he promises.

John Calvin

We must wait for God, long, meekly, in the wind and wet, in the thunder and lightning, in the cold and the dark. Wait, and he will come. He never comes to those who do not wait.

Frederick William Faber

Simply wait upon him. So doing, we shall be directed, supplied, protected, corrected, and rewarded.

Vance Havner

Adequate time for daily waiting on God . . . is the only way I can escape the tyranny of the urgent.

Charles Hummel

They also serve who only stand and wait.

John Milton

In the rush and noise of life, as you have intervals, step within yourselves and be still. Wait upon God and feel his good presence; this will carry you through your day's business.

William Penn

He went to the Garden of Gethsemane to wait upon the outcome. Waiting can be the most intense and poignant of all human experiences—the experience which, above all others, strips us of our needs, our values, and ourselves.

W.H. Vanstone

Waiting patiently in expectation is the foundation of spiritual life.

Simone Weil

War and Warfare

See also Oppression; Spiritual Warfare

Armies may surround me, but I won't be afraid; war may break out, but I will trust you.

Psalm 27:3 CEV

And he shall judge among the nations, and shall rebuke many people: and they shall beat their swords into plowshares, and their spears into pruninghooks: nation shall not lift up sword against nation, neither shall they learn war any more.

Isaiah 2:4 KJV

And ye shall hear of wars and rumors of wars: see that ye be not troubled: for all these things must come to pass, but the end is not yet. For nation shall rise against nation, and kingdom against kingdom: and there shall be famines, and pestilences, and earthquakes, in diverse places.

Matthew 24:6–7 KJV

War has thus become the ultimate anti-Christ, the obscene god of death, condemning all life to capital punishment.

Daniel Berrigan

War can only be a desperate remedy in a desperate situation, used in order to spare humanity a still greater evil when all essentially reasonable and peaceful means have proved ineffective.

René Coste

As peace is of all goodness, so war is an emblem, a hieroglyphic, of all misery.

John Donne

Mankind must put an end to war, or war will put an end to mankind.

John Fitzgerald Kennedy

Truth is the first casualty in any war.

John Nevin Sayre

We (Christians at war) are called to the hardest of all tasks; to fight without hatred, to resist without bitterness, and in the end, if God grant it so, to triumph without vindictiveness.

William Temple

Sin, Satan, and war have all one name; evil is the best of them. The best of sin is deformity, of Satan enmity, of war misery.

John Trapp

To be prepared for war is one of the most effectual means of preserving peace.

George Washington

Weakness

See also Failure; Power; Vulnerability

Strengthen ye the weak hands, and confirm the feeble knees.

Isaiah 35:3 KJV

The spirit indeed is willing, but the flesh is weak.

Mark 14:38 NRSV

To the weak I became weak, so that I might by all means save some.

1 Corinthians 9:22 NRSV

He replied, "My kindness is all you need. My power is strongest when you are weak." So if Christ keeps giving me his power, I will gladly brag about how weak I am. Yes, I am glad to be weak or insulted or mistreated or to have troubles and sufferings, if it is for Christ. Because when I am weak, I am strong.

2 Corinthians 12:9–10 CEV

God lets himself be pushed out of the world on to the cross. He is weak and powerless in the world, and that is precisely the way, the only way, in which he is with us and helps us. Matthew makes it quite clear that Christ helps us, not by virtue of his omnipotence, but by virtue of his weakness and suffering.

Dietrich Bonhoeffer

One with God is a majority.

William Carey

Weak things united become strong.

Thomas Fuller

The acknowledgment of our weakness is the first step toward repairing our loss.

Thomas à Kempis

The martyrs shook the powers of darkness with the irresistible power of weakness.

John Milton

We should keep up in our hearts a constant sense of our own weakness, not with a design to discourage the mind and depress the spirits, but with a view to drive us out of ourselves in search of the Divine assistance.

Hannah More

We have no power from God unless we live in the persuasion that we have none of our own.

John Owen

I have a great need for Christ; I have a great Christ for my need.

Charles Haddon Spurgeon

All God's giants have been weak men who did great things for God because they reckoned on his being with them.

James Hudson Taylor

The greatest saints have always shown the perfect combination of nearness to our Lord on the one hand, and a deep sense of their own unworthiness and weakness on the other.

Abbé Henri de Tourville

Wealth

See also Possessions; Poverty

You may say to yourself, "My power and the strength of my hands have produced this wealth for me." But remember the Lord your God, for it is he who gives you the ability to produce wealth, and so confirms his covenant, which he swore to your fore-fathers, as it is today.

Deuteronomy 8:17–18 NIV

And he said, This will I do: I will pull down my barns, and build greater; and there will I bestow all my fruits and goods. And I will say to my soul, Soul, thou hast much goods laid up for many years; take thine ease, eat, drink, and be merry. But God said unto him, Thou fool, this night thy soul shall be required of thee: then whose shall those things be, which thou hast provided? So is he that layeth up

treasure for himself, and is not rich toward God.

Luke 12:18–21 KJV

When Jesus heard this, he said to him, "There is still one more thing you need to do. Sell all you have and give the money to the poor, and you will have riches in heaven; then come and follow me." But when the man heard this, he became very sad, because he was very rich. Jesus saw that he was sad and said, "How hard it is for rich people to enter the Kingdom of God! It is much harder for a rich person to enter the Kingdom of God than for a camel to go through the eye of a needle."

Luke 18:22–25 GNB

Charge them that are rich in this world, that they be not highminded, nor trust in uncertain riches, but in the living God, who giveth us richly all things to enjoy.

1 Timothy 6:17 KJV

If any person, because of his state of life, cannot do without wealth and position, let him at least keep his heart empty of love of them.

St. Angela Merici

In this world it is not what we take up, but what we give up that makes us rich.

Henry Ward Beecher

For every one hundred men who can stand adversity, there is only one who can withstand prosperity.

Thomas Carlyle

Great wealth and content seldom live together.

Thomas Fuller

Riches are gotten with pain, kept with care, and lost with grief.

Thomas Fuller

The real measure of our wealth is how much we'd be worth if we lost all our money.

John Henry Jowett

It ill disposes the servant to seek to be rich and great and honored in this world where his Lord was poor and mean and despised.

George Müller

The use of riches is better than their possession.

Fernando de Rojas

Many a man's gold has lost him his God.

George Swinnock

Gain all you can, save all you can, give all you can.

John Wesley

To lay up treasure on earth is as plainly forbidden by our Master as adultery and murder.

John Wesley

Weariness, *see* Rest; Tiredness

Weeping, *see* Tears

Whitsun, *see* Pentecost

Wholeness, *see* Health and Wholeness

Wilderness, *see* Desert

Will, *see* Free Will; God, Will of

Wisdom

See also Foolishness; God, Wisdom of

But where shall wisdom be found? and where is the place of understanding? Man knoweth not the price thereof; neither is it found in the land of the living.

Job 28:12–13 KJV

The fear of the Lord is the beginning of wisdom.

Psalm 111:10 KJV

Happy is he who has found wisdom, he who has acquired understanding, for wisdom is more profitable than silver, and the gain she brings is better than gold! She is more precious than red coral, and none of your jewels can compare with her. In her right hand is long life, in her left are riches and honor. Her ways are pleasant ways and her paths all lead to prosperity. She is a tree of life to those who grasp her, and those who hold fast to her are safe.

Proverbs 3:13–18 REB

Doth not wisdom cry? and understanding put forth her voice? She standeth in the top of high places, by the way in the places of the paths. She crieth at the gates, at the entry of the city, at the coming in at the doors. Unto you, O men, I call; and my voice is to the sons of man. O ye simple, understand wisdom: and, ye fools, be ye of an understanding heart.

Proverbs 8:1–5 KJV

Learn where there is wisdom, where there is strength, where there is understanding, so that you may at the same time discern where there is length of days, and life, where there is light for the eyes, and peace.

Baruch 3:14 RSV

God was wise and decided not to let the people of this world use their wisdom to learn about him. Instead, God chose to save only those who believe the foolish message we preach.

1 Corinthians 1:21 CEV

The wisdom from above is first pure, then peaceable, gentle, willing to yield, full of mercy and good fruits, without a trace of partiality or hypocrisy.

James 3:17 NRSV

The first key to wisdom is assiduous and frequent questioning. For by doubting we come in inquiry and by inquiry we arrive at truth.

Peter Abelard

Wisdom is the foundation, and justice the work without which a foundation cannot stand.

St. Ambrose

If you are wise you will show yourself rather as a reservoir than a canal. For a canal spreads abroad the water it receives, but a reservoir waits until it is filled before overflowing, and this shares without loss to itself its superabundance of water.

St. Bernard of Clairvaux

There is a deep wisdom inaccessible to the wise and prudent, but disclosed to babes.

Christopher Bryant

Mere silence is not wisdom, for wisdom consists in knowing when and how to speak and when and where to keep silent.

Bishop Jean Pierre Camus

Wisdom is the ability to use knowledge so as to meet successfully the emergencies of life. Men may acquire knowledge, but wisdom is a gift direct from God.

Bob Jones

Common sense suits itself to the ways of the world. Wisdom tries to conform to the ways of heaven.

Joseph Joubert

We must not trust every word of others or feeling within ourselves, but cautiously and patiently try the matter, whether it be of God.

Thomas à Kempis

To have a low opinion of our own merits, and to think highly of others, is an evidence of wisdom. All men are frail, but thou should'st reckon none as frail as thyself.

Thomas à Kempis

A wise man will always be a Christian, because the perfection of wisdom is to know where lies tranquility of mind, and how to attain it, which Christianity teaches.

Walter Savage Landor

Accumulated knowledge does not make a wise man. Knowledgeable people are found everywhere, but we are cruelly short of wise people.

Michel Quoist

Wisdom is nine-tenths a matter of being wise in time.

Theodore Roosevelt

The doorstep to the temple of wisdom is a knowledge of our own ignorance.

Charles Haddon Spurgeon

Wisdom is the right use of knowledge. To know is not to be wise. . . . There is no fool so great as a knowing fool. But to know how to use knowledge is to have wisdom.

Charles Haddon Spurgeon

Witness

See also Church, Mission and Ministry of; Evangelism; Holy Spirit, Witness of

I heard the voice of the Lord, saying, Whom

shall I send, and who will go for us? Then said I, Here am I; send me.

Isaiah 6:8 KJV

When the Advocate comes, whom I will send to you from the Father, the Spirit of truth who comes from the Father, he will testify on my behalf. You also are to testify because you have been with me from the beginning.

John 15:26–27 NRSV

You will receive power when the Holy Spirit comes on you; and you will be my witnesses in Jerusalem, and in all Judea and Samaria, and to the ends of the earth.

Acts 1:8 NIV

The real mark of a saint is that he makes it easier for others to believe in God.

Anon.

Witnessing is not something we do; it is something we are.

Anon.

Be patterns, be examples in all countries, places, islands, nations, wherever you come, that your carriage and life may preach among all sorts of people, and to them; then you will come to walk cheerfully over the world, answering that of God in every one.

George Fox

Witnessing is removing the various barriers of our self-love to allow Christ, living within us, to show himself to our neighbors.

Paul Frost

The way from God to a human heart is through a human heart.

Samuel Dickey (S.D.) Gordon

Be to the world a sign that whilst we as Christians do not have all the answers, we do know and care about the questions.

William Franklin (Billy) Graham

We are the Bibles the world is reading; we are the creeds the world is needing; we are the sermons the world is heeding.

William Franklin (Billy) Graham

The Christian's task is to make the Lord Jesus visible, intelligible, and desirable.

Len Jones

A witness in a court of law has to give evidence; a Christian witness has to be evidence. It is the difference between law and grace!

Geoffrey R. King

If he has faith, the believer cannot be restrained. He betrays himself. He breaks out. He confesses and teaches this gospel to the people at the risk of life itself.

Martin Luther

The Spirit of Christ is the spirit of missions, and the nearer we get to him, the more intensely missionary we must become.

Henry Martyn

The world is far more ready to receive the Gospel than Christians are to hand it out.

George W. Peters

The Gospel is nothing but a frozen asset unless it is communicated.

John Bertram (J.B.) Phillips

It would be illusory, useless, and even blasphemous to claim to bear witness to God without engaging in practical activity to repair creation.

Jon Sobrino

To be a witness does not consist of engaging in propaganda or in stirring people up. It means to live in such a way that one's life would not make sense if God did not exist.

Emmanuel Suhard

The only New Testament precedents for spreading the Gospel are godly living, praying, and bold speaking.

Geoffrey Thomas

Our task as laymen is to live our personal communion with Christ with such intensity as to make it contagious.

Paul Tournier

Wives, *see* Husbands and Wives

Women and Womanhood

See also Adam and Eve; Husbands and Wives; Mothers and Motherhood

To the woman he said, "I will greatly increase your pangs in childbearing; in pain you shall bring forth children, yet your desire shall be for your husband, and he shall rule over you."

Genesis 3:16 NRSV

Charm is deceptive and beauty fleeting; but the woman who fears the Lord is honored.

Proverbs 31:30 REB

A man of quality is never threatened by a woman of equality.

Jill Briscoe

It takes some extra examination to find the numerous women who worked side by side with Paul and the other "well-knowns." Possibly we are slow to notice their names because our own culture has trained us to see women more in strictly family roles than in ministry roles.

Winnie Christensen

Much of what we as women do is in a supportive role, but imagine what would happen to a building if its support pillars were removed.

Judy Hubbekk

Our families can survive with less of what we do. They just can't get by with less of what we give them out of who we are. Maybe we can't "do it all." But we can still give our families our hearts. We can turn our houses into homes, our families into, well, families. And one of the ways we can do it is by cherishing, not relegating, our special place as women, wives, and mothers in our homes.

Karen Scalf Linamen

No one can make you feel inferior without your consent.

Eleanor Roosevelt

The full personhood of women is one of the touchstones for testing our faithfulness to the vision of redemption in Christ. By this norm much of mainstream tradition must be judged as deficient.

Rosemary Radford Ruether

Perhaps it is no wonder that the women were first at the Cradle and last at the Cross. They had never known a man like this Man— there never has been such another. A prophet and teacher who never nagged at them, never flattered or coaxed or patronized; who rebuked without querulousness and praised without condescension; who took their questions and arguments seriously; who never mapped out their sphere for them.

Dorothy Leigh Sayers

It was to a virgin woman that the birth of the Son of God was announced. It was to a fallen woman that his resurrection was announced.

Fulton John Sheen

Christianity brings liberation through the Gospel in faith and action. But the Christian Church has not been a sufficiently liberating institution for women, in the sense of not opening up to them the full range of possibilities.

Pauline Webb

The ability to find joy in the world of sorrow and hope at the edge of despair is woman's witness to courage and her gift of new life to all.

Miriam Therese Winter

Wonders, *see* Miracles

Word of God

See also Bible; Jesus Christ

One does not live by bread alone, but by every word that comes from the mouth of the LORD.

Deuteronomy 8:3 NRSV

Thy word is a lamp unto my feet, and a light unto my path.

Psalm 119:105 KJV

For as the rain and the snow come down from heaven and do not return there until they have watered the earth, making it bring forth and sprout, giving seed to the sower and bread to the eater, so shall my word be that goes out from my mouth; it shall not return to me empty, but it shall accomplish that which I purpose, and succeed in the thing for which I sent it.

Isaiah 55:10–11 NRSV

Before the world was created, the Word already existed; he was with God, and he was the same as God. From the very beginning the Word was with God. Through him God made all things; not one thing in all creation was made without him. The Word was the source of life, and this life brought light to mankind.

John 1:1–4 GNB

Let the Word of Christ, in all its richness, find a home with you. Teach each other, and advise each other, in all wisdom.

Colossians 3:16 NJB

For the word of God is quick, and powerful, and sharper than any two-edged sword, piercing even to the dividing asunder of soul and spirit, and of the joints and marrow, and is a discerner of the thoughts and intents of the heart.

Hebrews 4:12 KJV

The Word of God is not a sounding but a piercing word, not pronounceable by the tongue but efficacious in the mind, not sensible to the ear but fascinating to the affection.

St. Bernard of Clairvaux

Wherever we see the Word of God purely preached and heard, there a church of God exists, even if it swarms with many faults.

John Calvin

Our primary task is to create the space for the word of God once again to cut into our daily life experience, in order to redeem and liberate it.

Thomas Cullinan

Men turn this way and that in their search for new sources of comfort and inspiration, but the enduring truths are to be found in the Word of God.

Elizabeth, the Queen Mother

The Word of God is not just for domestic consumption; it is also for export.

William Freel

The words of God which you receive by your ear, hold fast in your heart. For the Word of God is the food of the soul.

St. Gregory I

He who hath heard the Word of God can bear his silences.

St. Ignatius of Loyola

We need never tremble for the Word of God, though we may tremble at it and the demands which it makes upon our faith and courage.

William Robertson Smith

Work

The LORD God took the man and put him the garden of Eden to till it and keep it.

Genesis 2:15 NRSV

You have six days when you can do your work, but the seventh day of each week belongs to me, your God. No one is to work on that day—not you, your children, your slaves, your animals, or the foreigners who live in your towns.

Exodus 20:9–10 CEV

Whatsoever thy hand findeth to do, do it with thy might; for there is no work, nor device, nor knowledge, nor wisdom, in the grave, whither thou goest.

Ecclesiastes 9:10 KJV

The laborer deserves his wages.

Luke 10:7 NJB

Let him that stole steal no more: but rather let him labor, working with his hands the thing which is good, that he may have to give to him that needeth.

Ephesians 4:28 KJV

Whatever your task, put yourselves into it, as done for the Lord and not for your masters.

Colossians 3:23 NRSV

A dictionary is the only place where you will find success before work.

Anon.

He who labors as he prays lifts up his heart to God with his hands.

St. Bernard of Clairvaux

If people knew how hard I have to work to gain my mastery, it would not seem wonderful at all.

Michelangelo Buonarroti

O Lord, I do not pray for tasks equal to my strength: I ask for strength equal to my tasks.

Phillips Brooks

Hard work is a thrill and a joy when you are in the will of God.

Robert A. Cook

I never did anything worth doing by accident, nor did any of my inventions come by accident; they came by work.

Thomas Alva Edison

Great works do not always lie in our way, but every moment we may do little ones excellently, that is, with great love.

St. Francis de Sales

Work is not a curse, it is a blessing from God who calls man to rule the earth and transform it, so that the divine work of creation may continue with man's intelligence and effort.

John Paul II

A dairy maid can milk cows to the glory of God.

Martin Luther

To have too much to do is for most men safer than to have too little.

Henry Edward Manning

Work without a love relationship spells burnout.

Lloyd John Ogilvie

It is a sublime mystery that Christ should begin to work before he began to teach; a humble workman before being the Teacher of all nations.

Pius XII

You will become a saint by complying exactly with your daily duties.

Mary Joseph Rossello

Work is the natural exercise and function of man. . . . Work is not primarily a thing one does to live, but the thing one lives to do. It is, or should be, the full expression of the worker's faculties, the thing in which he finds spiritual, mental, and bodily satisfaction, and the medium in which he offers himself to God.

Dorothy Leigh Sayers

Thou, O God, does sell us all good things at the price of labor.

Leonardo da Vinci

He who turns up his nose at his work quarrels with his bread and butter.

Charles Haddon Spurgeon

World, *see* Creation; Environment

Worldliness

See also Covetousness

I passed your word on to them, and the world hated them, because they belong to the world no more than I belong to the world. I am not asking you to remove them from the world, but to protect them from the Evil One. They do not belong to the world any more than I belong to the world.

John 17:14–16 NJB

As a matter of fact, my friends, I could not talk to you as I talk to people who have the Spirit; I had to talk to you as though you belonged to this world, as children in the Christian faith. I had to feed you milk, not solid food, because you were not ready for it. And even now you are not ready for it, because you still live as the people of this world live. When there is jealousy among you and you quarrel with one another, doesn't this prove that you belong to this world, living by its standards? When one of you says, "I follow Paul," and another, "I follow Apollos"— aren't you acting like worldly people?

1 Corinthians 3:1–4 GNB

Godly grief produces a repentance that leads to salvation and brings no regret, but worldly grief produces death.

2 Corinthians 7:10 NRSV

For the grace of God that bringeth salvation hath appeared to all men, Teaching us that, denying ungodliness and worldly lusts, we should live soberly, righteously, and godly, in this present world.

Titus 2:11–12 KJV

Do not love the world or anything in the world. If anyone loves the world, the love of the Father is not in him. For everything in the world—the cravings of sinful man, the lust of his eyes and the boasting of what he has and does—comes not from the Father but from the world. The world and its desires pass away, but the man who does the will of God lives forever.

1 John 2:15–17 NIV

All the ways of this world are as fickle and unstable as a sudden storm at sea.

The Venerable Bede

Our labor here is brief, but the reward is eternal. Do not be disturbed by the clamor of the world, which passes like a shadow. Do not let the false delights of a deceptive world deceive you.

St. Clare of Assisi

We must look upon all things of this world as none of ours, and not desire them. This world and that to come are two enemies. We cannot therefore be friends to both; but we must resolve which we would forsake and which we would enjoy.

St. Clement I of Rome

Just as the cloud of unknowing lies above you, between you and your God, so you must fashion a cloud of forgetting beneath you, between you and every created thing.

The Cloud of Unknowing

We ought to love what Christ loved on earth, and to set no store by those things which he regarded as of no account.

The Curé d'Ars

Perfection does not consist in not seeing the world, but in not having a taste or relish for it.

St. Francis de Sales

I beg of you for the love and reverence of God our Lord to remember the past, and reflect not lightly but seriously that the earth is only earth.

St. Ignatius of Loyola

Have no intercourse with the people in the world. Little by little you will get a taste for their habits, get so drawn into conversation

with them that you will no longer be able out of politeness to refrain from applauding their discourse, however pernicious it may be, and it will lead you away into unfaithfulness.

St. Jean Baptist de la Salle

During eight-and-twenty years of prayer, I spent more than eighteen in that strife and contention which arose out of my attempts to reconcile God and the world.

St. Teresa of Avila

Worry, *see* Anxiety

Worship

See also Praise; Prayer; Reverence

Thou shalt have no other gods before me. Thou shalt not make unto thee any graven image, or any likeness of any thing that is in heaven above, or that is in the earth beneath, or that is in the water under the earth.

Exodus 20:3–4 KJV

O come, let us sing unto the Lord; let us heartily rejoice in the strength of our salvation. Let us come before his presence with thanksgiving; and shew ourselves glad in him with psalms. For the Lord is a great God; and a great King above all gods. In his hand are all the corners of the earth; and the strength of the hills is his also. The sea is his, and he made it; and his hands prepared the dry land. O come, let us worship and fall down, and kneel before the Lord our Maker. For he is the Lord our God; and we are the people of his pasture, and the sheep of his hand.

Psalm 95:1–7 BCP

These people draw near with their mouths and honor me with their lips, while their hearts are far from me, and their worship of me is a human commandment learned by rote.

Isaiah 29:13 NRSV

Bless the Lord, all you works of the Lord; sing praise to him and highly exalt him forever.

Prayer of Azariah 35 NRSV

They went into the house, and when they saw the child with his mother Mary, they knelt down and worshiped him. They brought out their gifts of gold, frankincense, and myrrh, and presented them to him.

Matthew 2:11 GNB

Worship the Lord your God, and serve only him.

Matthew 4:10 NRSV

The hour cometh, and now is, when the true worshippers shall worship the Father in spirit and in truth: for the Father seeketh such to worship him. God is a Spirit: and they that worship him must worship him in spirit and in truth.

John 4:23–24 KJV

I urge you, brothers, in view of God's mercy, to offer your bodies as living sacrifices, holy and pleasing to God—this is your spiritual act of worship.

Romans 12:1 NIV

Now unto the King eternal, immortal, invisible, the only wise God, be honor and glory for ever and ever. Amen.

1 Timothy 1:17 KJV

When all Thy mercies, O my God, / My rising soul surveys, / Transported with the view, I'm lost / In wonder, love, and praise.

Joseph Addison

Without the worship of the heart liturgical prayer becomes a matter of formal routine.

St. Aelred

There is only one perfect act of worship ever offered and that was the life of Jesus Christ himself. From his conception to his ascension, he ever offers that life to the Father as the perfect act of worship in Heaven, and when we worship all we do is to join him.

Fr. Peter Ball

Wonder is the basis of worship.

Thomas Carlyle

To worship God is to realize the purpose for which God created us.

Herbert M. Carson

It is only when men begin to worship that they begin to grow.

Calvin Coolidge

Glory to Christ. Come, let us offer him the great, universal sacrifice of our love, and pour out before him our richest hymns and prayers. For he offered his cross to God as a sacrifice in order to make us all rich.

St. Ephrem

The divine priority is worship first and service second.

Richard J. Foster

If worship does not change us, it has not been worship. To stand before the Holy One of eternity is to change. Worship begins in holy expectancy; it ends in holy obedience.

Richard J. Foster

A little lifting of the heart suffices; a little remembrance of God, one act of inward worship are prayers which, however short, are nevertheless acceptable to God.

Br. Lawrence

It is a law of man's nature, written into his very essence, and just as much a part of him as the desire to build houses and cultivate the land and marry and have children and read books and sing songs, that he should want to stand together with other men in order to acknowledge their common dependence on God, the Father and Creator.

Thomas Merton

Liturgy can only really live, worship can only truly express joy, sorrow, hope, faith, and love if it is firmly rooted in the actual lives and experience of the people who are worshiping.

Ianthe Pratt

Worship is the celebration of life in its totality. Worship is the sacramental appropriation of all of life in celebration. Worship is the festival of creation.

William Stringfellow

To worship is to quicken the conscience by the holiness of God, to feed the mind with the truth of God, to purge the imagination by the beauty of God, to open the heart to the love of God, and to devote the will to the purpose of God.

William Temple

Worship, then, is not a part of the Christian life; it is the Christian life.

Gerald Vann

The worship of God is not a rule of safety— it is an adventure of the spirit.

Alfred North Whitehead

Wrong, *see* Right and Wrong

Youth

Remember not the sins of my youth, nor my transgressions: according to thy mercy remember thou me for thy goodness' sake, O Lord.

Psalm 25:7 KJV

Remember now thy Creator in the days of thy youth, while the evil days come not, nor the years draw nigh, when thou shalt say, I have no pleasure in them.

Ecclesiastes 12:1 KJV

Let no one despise your youth, but set the believers an example in speech and conduct, in love, in faith, in purity.

1 Timothy 4:12 NRSV

Flee the evil desires of youth, and pursue righteousness, faith, love and peace, along with those who call on the Lord out of a pure heart.

2 Timothy 2:22 NIV

Every adult Christian generation owes its young people a divine demonstration of the reality of what it believes and preaches.

Anon.

People sometimes say to youth, "The world is at your feet!" But this is not true unless heaven is in your heart.

P. Ainsworth

Young people do the impossible before they find out it's impossible—that's why God uses them so often.

Loren Cunningham

Young people will respond if the challenge is tough enough and hard enough. Youth wants a master and a controller. Young people were built for God, and without God as the center of their lives they become frustrated and confused, desperately grasping for and searching for security.

William Franklin (Billy) Graham

You yourself know how slippery is the path of youth—a path on which I myself have fallen, and which you are now traveling not without fear.

St. Jerome

One other thing stirs me when I look back at my youthful days, the fact that so many people gave me something or were something to me without knowing it.

Albert Schweitzer

Some call them Generation X. Others call them baby busters. I call them our future.

John Richard Wimber

Zeal

See also Fanaticism

His disciples recalled the words of scripture: "Zeal for your house will consume me."

John 2:17 REB

Do not lag in zeal, be ardent in spirit, serve the Lord.

Romans 12:11 NRSV

Titus not only welcomed our appeal, but he is coming to you with much enthusiasm and on his own initiative.

2 Corinthians 8:17 NIV

I know your eagerness to help, and I have been boasting about it to the Macedonians . . . and your enthusiasm has stirred most of them to action.

2 Corinthians 9:2 NIV

Just as there is an evil bitter zeal which cuts us off from God, and leads to hell, so there is a good zeal which shields us from vice and leads to God and eternal life.

St. Benedict

Zeal without knowledge is always less useful and effective than regulated zeal, and very often it is highly dangerous.

St. Bernard of Clairvaux

I want my religion like my tea—hot!

William Booth

Zeal is like fire; in the chimney it is one of the best servants; but out of the chimney it is one of the worst masters.

Thomas Benton Brooks

Attempt great things for God; expect great things from God.

William Carey

Men ablaze are invincible. Hell trembles when men kindle.

Samuel Chadwick

Nothing great was ever achieved without enthusiasm.

Ralph Waldo Emerson

Zeal without knowledge is fire without light.

Thomas Fuller

Zeal is fit only for wise men, but is found mostly in fools.

Thomas Fuller

Be not afraid of enthusiasm; you need it; you can do nothing effectively without it.

François Pierre Guillaume Guizot

It is still one of the tragedies of human history that the "children of darkness" are frequently more determined and zealous than the "children of light."

Martin Luther King Jr.

Earnestness is enthusiasm tempered by reason.

Blaise Pascal

In the case of virtues, it is very easy to pass from defect to excess, from being just to being rashly zealous. It is said that good wine easily turns to vinegar, and that health in the highest degree is a sign of approaching illness.

Vincent de Paul

If by excessive zeal we die before reaching the average age of man, worn out in the Master's service, then glory be to God, we shall have so much less of earth and so much more of heaven.

Charles Haddon Spurgeon

Enthusiasm, like fire, must not only burn, but must be controlled.

Augustus Hopkins Strong

All true zeal for God is a zeal for love, mercy, and goodness.

Robert Ellis Thompson

Apathy can only be overcome by enthusiasm, and enthusiasm can only be aroused by two things; first an ideal which takes the imagination by storm, and second, a definite intelligible plan for carrying that ideal into practice.

Arnold Joseph Toynbee

Get on fire for God and men will come and see you burn.

John Wesley

INDEX OF BIBLICAL SOURCES

INDEX OF AUTHORS

Erskine, John
Temperance
Estienne, Henri
Compassion
God, Grace and Mercy of
Ethelwold
Hunger and Thirst
Eusebius of Caesarea
Christianity
Eusebius of Vercelli, St.
Pastoral Care
Evagrius of Pontus
Angels
God, Infiniteness of
Prayer, Encouragements to
Tiredness
Virtues and Vices
Evans, Colleen Townsend
Sex and Sexuality
Evans, Louis H.
Prayer, Encouragements to
Evdokimov, Paul
Love, for God
Evely, Louis
God, Presence of
Everrett, John
Repentance
Faber, Frederick William
Discouragement
Fathers and Fatherhood
God, Grace and Mercy of
God, Greatness of
God, Voice of
God, Will of
Immortality
Kindness
Motives
Perfection
Reverence
Success
Temptation
Waiting
Farrell, Joseph
Knowledge
Farrer, Austin
Eucharist
Jesus Christ, Resurrection of
Holy Spirit, Indwelling of
Faulkner, William
Immortality
Felix, Marcus M.
God, Greatness of
Fénelon, François de la Mothe
Corruption
Cross

Death
Discipline
Discouragement
Faithfulness
Freedom
Kingdom of God
Perfection
Prayer, Attitudes in
Prayer, Definitions of
Prayer, Encouragements to
Providence
Self-denial
Silence
Temptation
Tolerance
Fernando, Benjamin E.
Persecution
Fey, Imogene
Birth
ffrench-Beytagh, Gonville
Atonement
Prayer, Adoration
Field, Henry Martyn
Fellowship
Figgis, J.N.
Peace, of Mind
Finney, Charles Grandison
Devil
Grace
Revival
Sermons
Holy Spirit, Power of
Flavel, John
Bible, Purpose of
Opportunity
Perfection
Reason
Study
Vanity
Fletcher, Joseph
Law
Fletcher, Lionel
Evangelism
Flint, Annie Johnson
God, Grace and Mercy of
Florovsky, Georges V.
God, Creator
Forbes, B.C.
Virtues and Vices
Ford, Henry
Education
Ford, Leighton Frederick Sandys
God, Anger of
Jesus Christ, Example of

BRIEF NOTES ON AUTHORS

Abelard, Peter 1079–1142
French philosopher and theologian

Acton, Lord John 1834–1902
English historian and philosopher

Adams, Henry Brooks 1838–1918
American historian and author

Addison, Joseph 1672–1719
English essayist

Aelred, St. 1109–1167
Abbot of Rievaulx

Albert the Great c. 1200–1280
Dominican scholar

Alcuin of York c. 740–804
English theologian and scholar

Alexander, Cecil Francis 1818–1895
British hymnwriter

Alford, Henry 1810–1871
Dean of Canterbury and hymn writer

Alighieri, Dante 1265–1321
Italian poet and philosopher

Alphonsus Liguori, St. 1696–1787
Founder of the Redemptorists and moral
theologian

Alstyne, Frances Jane van 1820–1915
American hymn writer

Ambrose, St. c. 339–397
Bishop of Milan

Amiel, Henri-Frédéric 1821–1881
Swiss philosopher and poet

Andrew, Br. b. 1928
Founder of Open Doors

Andrewes, Lancelot 1555–1626
Bishop of Winchester

Angela Merici, St. 1474–1540
Founder of the Ursulines

Anselm of Canterbury, St. 1033–1109
Italian-born Archbishop of Canterbury

Antony of Egypt, St. c. 251–356
Hermit

Antony of Padua, St. c. 1188–1231
Franciscan friar

Aphrahat
The first Syriac Father (early 4th century)

Appleton, George
Anglican archbishop in Jerusalem
and religious writer

Armstrong, John 1709–1779
English poet and essayist

Arnold, Matthew 1822–1888
English poet and literary critic

Asquith, Herbert Henry 1852–1928
British statesman

Athanasius of Alexandria, St. c. 293–373
Bishop of Alexandria

Auden, W.H. 1907–1973
British poet

Augsburger, David b. 1938
American pastoral theologian

Augustine of Hippo, St. 354–430
Bishop of Hippo

Austen, Jane 1775–1817
English novelist

Bacon, Francis 1561–1626
English philosopher
and statesman

Baker, Augustine 1575–1641
Benedictine writer

Balasuriya, Tissa
Sri Lankan theologian

Baldwin, James Arthur 1924–1987
American novelist and essayist

Baldwin, Stanley 1867–1947
British statesman

Balfour, Lord Arthur James 1848–1930
British philosopher and statesman

Barclay, William 1907–1978
Scottish biblical scholar

Barnardo, Dr. Thomas John 1845–1905
Philanthropist and pioneer
in social work

Barnes, Albert 1798–1870
Presbyterian minister

Barnhouse, Donald Grey   1895–1960
Presbyterian minister and radio preacher

Barrie, Sir James Matthew (J.M.)   1860–1937
Scottish dramatist and novelist

Barrow, Isaac   1630–1677
Mathematician and Anglican divine

Barth, Karl   1886–1968
Swiss theologian

Barton, Bruce Fairchild   1886–1967
Advertising executive, author,
and U.S. Representative

Basil the Great, St.   c. 329–379
Cappadocian Father

Baughen, Michael   b. 1930
Bishop of Chester

Baxter, Richard   1615–1691
English Puritan minister

Beaverbrook, Lord   1879–1964
British politician and publisher

Bede, The Venerable   c. 673–735
Father of English church history

Beecher, Henry Ward   1813–1887
American congregational minister

Beethoven, Ludwig van   1770–1827
German composer

Belloc, Joseph Hilaire Pierre   1870–1953
Roman Catholic historical writer and
critic

Benedict, St.   c. 480–c. 550
Father of Western Monasticism

Benét, Stephen Vincent   1898–1943
American poet and novelist

Benham, Sir William Gurney   1859–1944
English compiler

Benson, Edward White   1829–1896
Archbishop of Canterbury

Benson, Robert Hugh   1871–1914
Roman Catholic apologist

Berdyaev, Nikolai Aleksandrovich 1874–1948
Russian philosopher and writer

Bernanos, Georges   1888–1948
French novelist

Bernard of Clairvaux, St.   1090–1153
Cistercian abbot and theologian

Bethune, Mary McLeod   1875–1955
American educator and college president

Bierce, Ambrose   1842–1914
American author

Bingemer, Maria Clare
English novelist

Binyon, Laurence   1869–1943
British poet

Blackstone, Sir William   1723–1780
British jurist and legal scholar

Blake, William   1757–1827
English poet and artist

Blanchard, John   b. 1932
British author, evangelist, and Bible teacher

Blandina, St.   d. 177
Early Christian martyr

Bliss, Philipp Paul   1833–1876
American hymn writer

Bloom, Anthony   b. 1914
Russian Orthodox archbishop

Bode, John Ernest   1816–1874
English priest and hymn writer

Boethius, Anicius Manlius   c. 480–524
Torquatus Severinus
Roman philosoper and statesman

Boff, Leonardo
Brazilian liberation theologian

Böhme, Jacob   1575–1624
German mystical theologian and writer

Boice, James Montgomery   1939–2000
American pastor and theologian

Bonar, Andrew Alexander   1810–1892
Scottish minister

Bonar, Horatius   1808–1889
Scottish minister and hymn writer

Bonaventure, St.   c. 1217–1274
Franciscan theologian

Bonhoeffer, Dietrich   1906–1945
German pastor and theologian

Boom, Betsie ten   1885–1944
Dutch evangelist

Boom, Corrie ten   1892–1983
Dutch evangelist and author

Booth, Catherine Bramwell   1829–1890
Co-founder of the Salvation Army

Booth, Evangeline Cory   1865–1950
Salvation Army general

Booth, William   1829–1912
Founder of the Salvation Army

Boreham, Francis William (F.W.)   1871–1956
English preacher and writer

Borman, Frank   b. 1928
American astronaut

Bossuet, Jacques Bénigne   1627–1704
Roman Catholic bishop

Bounds, Edward M.   1835–1913
Methodist minister and devotional writer

Bradley, Omar Nelson   1893–1981
American general

Bradstreet, Anne   1612–1672
English-born poet

Brainard, Mary Gardiner   fl. 1860
American poet

Bray, Billy   b. 1794
Evangelist and preacher

Breeman, Peter G. van
Dutch Jesuit

Brengle, Samuel Logan   1860–1936
Salvationist holiness writer

Bridges, Robert Seymour   1844–1930
British poet

Bridget of Sweden, St.   1303–1373
Visionary and founder of the Brigittines

Briscoe, Jill   b. 1935
English-born Bible teacher and writer

Briscoe, Stuart   b. 1930
Pastor and Bible expositor

Bronte, Charlotte   1816–1855
English novelist

Brooks, Phillips   1835–1893
American preacher

Brooks, Thomas Benton   1608–1680
Nonconformist writer

Broun, Heywood Campbell   1888–1939
American journalist

Brown, Henry G.   1800–1859
American abolitionist

Browne, Sir Thomas   1605–1682
Natural historian and moralist

Browning, Elizabeth Barrett   1806–1861
English poet

Browning, Robert   1812–1889
English poet

Bruce, F.F.   1910–1990
Scottish biblical scholar

Brueggemann, Walter
North American biblical scholar

Brunner, Heinrich Emil   1889–1966
Swiss theologian

Bryan, William Jennings   1860–1925
Populist, editor and congressman

Bucer, Martin   1491–1551
German Protestant reformer

Buck, Pearl S.   1892–1973
American novelist

Buechner, Frederick   b. 1926
American spiritual writer

Bulgakov, Sergei Nikolaevich   1871–1944
Russian theologian and philosopher

Bunyan, John   1628–1688
English nonconformist author

Buonarroti, Michelangelo   1475–1564
Sculptor, painter, and architect

Burke, Edmund   1728–1797
English statesman and philosopher

Burkitt, Francis Crawford   1864–1935
New Testament scholar

Bush, Barbara   b. 1925
American First Lady, wife of President
George H.W. Bush

Bushnell, Horace   1802–1876
American Congregational theologian

Butler, Nicholas Murray   1862–1947
American educator

Butler, Samuel   1612–1680
English poet and satirist

Caedmon   d. 680
Earliest English Christian poet

Caird, John   1820–1898
Scottish philosopher and theologian

Calvin, John   1509–1564
French Protestant reformer

Câmara, Dom Helder Passoa   b. 1909
Brazilian theologian and archbishop

Campolo, Tony   b. 1935
American sociologist

Camus, Bishop Jean Pierre   1582–1652
French bishop

Cardenal, Ernesto
Nicaraguan priest, poet, and political
activist

Carey, William   1761–1834
Missionary and educator in India

Carlyle, Thomas   1795–1881
Scottish historian and moralist

Carmichael, Amy Wilson   1867–1951
Irish missionary to India

Carnegie, Andrew   1835–1919
Scottish philanthropist

Carrel, Alexis   1873–1944
French surgeon

Carretto, Carlo   b. 1910
Italian spiritual writer

Carson, Herbert M.   b. 1922
British pastor

Carter, (James Earl) Jimmy   b. 1924
American president

Cassian, John   360–435
Monk

Cassidy, Dr. Sheila   b. 1937
British doctor and writer

Catherine of Genoa   1447–1510
Mystic

Catherine of Siena, St.   1347–1380
Mystic and patron saint of Italy

Caussade, Jean Pierre de   1675–1751
French mystic

Cecil, Richard   1748–1810

Cervantes, Miguel de   1547–1616
Spanish author

Chadwick, Samuel   1832–1917
English evangelist

Chambers, Oswald   1874–1917
Scottish evangelist and devotional
writer

Channing, William Ellery   1780–1842
American Unitarian minister

Chapman, John Jay   1862–1933
American poet, playwright, and
essayist

Chapman, John Wilbur   1859–1918
American pastor and evangelist

Chardin, Pierre Teilhard de   1881–1955
Jesuit writer and paleontologist

Charnock, Stephen   1628–1680
English Puritan theologian and pastor

Chaucer, Geoffrey   c. 1342–1400
English poet

Chekhov, Anton Pavlovich   1860–1904
Russian dramatist

Chesterfield, Philip Dormer   1694–1773
Stanhope, Lord
English writer and statesman

Chesterton, Gilbert Keith (G.K.)   1874–1936
English writer and Christian apologist

Christensen, Winnie
American Bible teacher

Churchill, Sir Winston   1874–1965
British prime minister

Ciardi, John   1916–1986
American poet, teacher, and critic

Clare of Assisi, St.   1193–1253
Founder of the Poor Clares

Claudel, Paul Louis Charles   1868–1955
French Catholic poet and diplomat

Claudian   365–408
Roman poet

Cleave, Derek   b. 1941
Bible teacher and evangelist

Clement I of Rome, St.   c. 30–100
Early Church Father

Clement of Alexandria, St.   c. 150–c. 215
Early Christian scholar

Climaecus, John   c. 570–c. 649
Ascetic and spiritual writer

Coggan, (Frederick) Donald   1909–2000
Archbishop of Canterbury

Coleridge, Samuel Taylor   1772–1834
English poet and theologian

Collins, John Churton   1848–1908
English critic

Colson, Charles W.   b. 1931
Founder of Prison Fellowship Ministries

Colton, Charles Caleb   1780–1832
English writer

Columba, St.   c. 521–597
Abbot of Iona and missionary

Conant, James Bryant   1893–1978
American chemist, diplomat, and educator

Conder, Josiah   1789–1855
English hymn writer

Condorcet, Marquis de   1743–1794
French philosopher and political leader

Cone, James
African American theologian

Conklin, Edwin G.   1863–1952
American biologist

Cooke, Alistair   b. 1908
International correspondent

Coolidge, Calvin   1872–1933
American president

Cotter, Jim
English Anglican priest and liturgical
writer

Countryman, William
North American Episcopal theologian

Cowper, William   1731–1800
English poet and hymn writer

Cox, Harvey   b. 1929
American Baptist theologian and
educator

Cranmer, Thomas   1489–1556
Archbishop of Canterbury

Crashaw, Richard   c. 1613–1649
English mystical poet

Crawford, E. May   1868–1927
English hymn writer

Cromwell, Oliver   1599–1658
English revolutionary soldier and statesman

Crossman, Samuel   1624–1683
English hymn writer

Cullinan, Thomas   b. 1932
English monk

Cullmann, Oscar   1902–1972
German New Testament scholar and
theologian

Cunningham, Loren
Founder of Youth With A Mission

Curé d'Ars, The   1786–1859
French priest and spiritual guide

Cyprian, St.   c. 200–258
Bishop of Carthage

Davies, J.G.   1565–1618
English poet

Day, Dorothy   1897–1950
American journalist and reformer

De Vries, Peter   1910–1993
American novelist and
short-story writer

Denck, Hans   c. 1495–1527
Anabaptist leader

Denney, James   1856–1917
Scottish theologian

Denning, Alfred Thompson, Lord   b. 1899
British judge

Dickens, Charles   1812–1870
English novelist

Dickinson, Emily   1830–1886
American poet

Dillard, Annie
North American author

Dionysios the Areopagite, St.   c. 500
Syriac mystical writer

Dobson, James   b. 1936
Founder and President of Focus on
the Family

Dodd, Charles Harold (C.H.)   1884–1973
Welsh New Testament scholar and
congregational minister

Dominian, Jack   b. 1929
English psychiatrist and author

Donne, John   1572–1631
English poet and Dean of St. Paul's

Dostoevsky, Fyodor   1821–1881
Russian novelist

Drake, Francis   ?1540–1596
English admiral

Drummond, Henry   1851–1897
Scottish writer and evangelist

Dryden, John   1651–1701
English poet and dramatist

Duhamel, Georges   1884–1966
French writer

Duns Scotus, John   c. 1265–1308
Scottish Franciscan philosopher and
theologian

Dwight, Timothy   1752–1817
American educator and Congregational
minister

Dyke, Henry van   1852–1933
American pastor and educator

Ecclestone, Alan   1904–1992
English spiritual writer

Eckhart, Meister   c. 1260–1327
German mystic

Edison, Thomas Alva   1847–1931
American inventor

Edman, Victor Raymond   1900–1967
Missionary and educator

Edwards, Jonathan   1703–1758
American theologian

Ehrlich, Paul   1854–1915
German bacteriologist

Eliot, George   1819–1880
English novelist

Eliot, Thomas Stearns (T.S.)   1888–1965
Poet, dramatist, and critic

Elizabeth of Hungary   1207–1231
Wife of Louis II, king of Thuringia

Elizabeth, the Queen Mother   b. 1900
Consort of King George VI

Elizabeth of the Trinity   1880–1906
French Carmelite nun

Elliot, Elisabeth   b. 1927
Missionary, writer, and radio show host

Elliot, Jim   1927–1956
Missionary to South America

Ellis, Henry Havelock   1859–1939
English psychologist

Emerson, Ralph Waldo   1803–1882
American essayist and poet

Emmons, Nathanael   1745–1840
American Congregational minister

Ephrem, St.   c. 306–373
Syriac biblical scholar and hymn writer

Erasmus, Desiderius   c. 1466–1536
Dutch humanist and first editor of
the Greek New Testament

Erskine, John   1509–1589
American novelist and educator

Estienne, Henri   1528–1598
Printer

Ethelwold   c. 908–984
Bishop of Winchester

Eusebius of Caesarea   c. 265–c. 339
Father of Church history

Eusebius of Vercelli, St.   d. 371
Bishop of Vercelli

Evagrius of Pontus   346–399
Spiritual writer and preacher

Evdokimov, Paul
Russian Orthodox lay theologian

Faber, Frederick William   1814–1863
English devotional writer and hymn writer

Farrer, Austin   1904–1968
English preacher and theologian

Faulkner, William   1897–1962
American writer

Fénelon, François de la Mothe   1651–1715
French mystic and archbishop of
Cambrai

Fernando, Benjamin E.   b. 1918
Sri Lankan layman

Figgis, J.N.   1866–1919
Anglican historian and theologian

Finney, Charles Grandison   1792–1875
American revivalist

Flavel, John   c. 1630–1691
English Presbyterian minister

Fletcher, Joseph   1905–1991
American ethicist

Florovsky, Georges V.   1893–1979
Russian theologian

Ford, Henry   1863–1947
Founder of the Ford Motor Company

Ford, Leighton Frederick Sandys   b. 1931
International evangelist

Forsyth, Peter Taylor   1848–1921
Scottish Congregational theologian

Fosdick, Harry Emerson   1878–1969
American Baptist minister and preacher

Foster, Richard J.   b. 1942
American spiritual writer

Foucauld, Charles de   1858–1916
French explorer and hermit

Fox, George   1624–1691
Founder of the Society of Friends

Fox, Matthew   b. 1940
American priest and theologian

France, Anatole   1844–1924
French novelist

Francis de Sales, St.   1567–1622
French Roman Catholic bishop and
spiritual writer

Francis of Assisi, St.   1182–1226
Founder of the Franciscans

Francis of Paola   c. 1416–1507
Italian Franciscan reformer

Francis Xavier, St.   1506–1552
Jesuit teacher and missionary in India

Franklin, Benjamin   1706–1790
American statesman and philosopher

Freeman, Lawrence
English Benedictine

Froude, James Anthony   1818–1894
English historian

Fry, Elizabeth   1780–1845
English Quaker prison reformer

Fuller, Richard Buckminster   1895–1983
American architect, inventor, and
philosopher

Fuller, Thomas   1608–1661
English clergyman

Furlong, Monica   b. 1930
English essayist and spiritual writer

Gardner, John (William)   b. 1912
American educator and social
activist

Garrison, William Lloyd   1805–1879
American emancipationist

Gerhardt, Paul   1607–1676
German poet and hymn writer

Gibbons, James   1834–1921
American Roman Catholic cardinal

Gide, André   1869–1951
French author

Giles (of Assisi), Br.   d. 1262
Italian companion of Francis

Gill, Arthur Eric Rowton   1882–1940
British sculptor, letterist, and wood
engraver

Glegg, A. Lindsay   1882–1975
British evangelist

Glover, Terrot Reaveley (T.R.)   1869–1943
English Baptist scholar

Goethe, Johann Wolfgang von   1749–1832
German poet and dramatist

Goldsmith, Oliver   1730–1774
Anglo-Irish novelist and dramatist

Goodier, Alban   1869–1939
Jesuit writer

Goodwin, Thomas   1600–1680
English theologian

Gordon, Adoniram Judson (A.J.)   1836–1895
Fundamentalist and Baptist pastor

Gordon, Samuel Dickey (S.D.)   1859–1936
American devotional writer

Gore, Charles   1853–1932
Anglican bishop and theologian

Graham, Ruth Bell   b. 1920
American devotional writer (wife of
Billy Graham)

Graham, William Franklin (Billy)   b. 1918
American evangelist

Gray, Thomas   1716–1771
English poet

Greeley, Horace   1811–1872
American journalist and political leader

Green, Michael   b. 1930
English biblical scholar and evangelist

Gregory I, St.   c. 540–604
Pope, Church Father, administrator, teacher

Gregory of Nazianzus   c. 330–c. 390
Church Father from Cappadocia
(in modern Turkey)

Gregory of Nyssa, St.   c. 335–c. 394
Bishop of Nyssa

Grenfell, Sir Wilfred Thomason   1865–1940
Missionary to Labrador

Griffiths, Bede
English Benedictine monk who lived in an
ashram in India

Grogan, Geoffrey   b. 1925
British theologian and Bible-college
lecturer

Grou, Jean-Nicolas   1731–1803
French spiritual writer

Guinness, Os   b. 1941
Sociologist

Guizot, François   1787–1874
Pierre Guillaume
French statesman and historian

Gunstone, John
American pastoral historian and
devotional writer

Gurnall, William   1617–1679
English minister and writer

Gutiérrez, Gustavo   b. 1928
Peruvian theologian

Guyon, Madame Jeanne Marie   1648–1717
de la Mothe
French Quietist author

Hadwijch of Brabant   (early 13th century)
Belgian mystic

Haggai, John Edmund
Founder of the Institute for Advanced
Leadership Training

Haldane, Richard Burdon   1856–1928
British philosopher and statesman

Hall, Joseph   1574–1656
Bishop of Norwich

Hallesby, O.   1879–1961
Norwegian evangelical theologian

Halverson, Richard Christian   b. 1916
Presbyterian minister and
chaplain of the U.S. Senate

Hammarskjöld, Dag   1905–1961
Swedish secretary general of
the United Nations

Hammerstein, Oscar   1895–1960
American songwriter

Hankey, Donald   1874–1917
English soldier and essayist

Hardy, Thomas   1840–1928
English novelist

Harkness, Georgia
North American Methodist theologian and
social activist

Havergal, Frances Ridley   1836–1879
English hymn writer

Havner, Vance   b. 1901
Devotional writer

Hawthorne, Nathaniel   1804–1864
American novelist

Haydn, Franz Joseph   1732–1809
Austrian composer

Hazlitt, William   1778–1830
English essayist

Hecker, Isaac Thomas   1819–1888
Founder of the Paulists

Helps, Sir Arthur   1813–1875
English author

Henry, Carl F.H.   b. 1913
American Baptist theologian and
evangelical leader

Henry, Matthew   1662–1714
Nonconformist minister and Bible
commentator

Herbert, George   1593–1633
English poet and hymn writer

Hermas   2nd century
Early Christian writer

Herrick, Robert   1591–1674
English poet

Hesburgh, Theodore Martin   b. 1917
American clergyman

Heyward, Carter
North American feminist theologian

Heywood, John   c. 1494–1578
English dramatist and epigrammatist

Hildebert of Lavardin   1056–1133
Archbishop of Tours, poet, and
canonist

Hildegard of Bingen, St.   1098–1179
German mystic

Hill, Rowland   1744–1833
English evangelist

Hilton, Walter   c. 1343–1396
English mystic

Hinkson, Katherine T.   1861–1931

Hodge, Archibald Alexander   1823–1886
(A.A.)
American theologian

Hodge, Charles   1797–1878
American Presbyterian theologian

Hoffer, Eric   1902–1983
American philosopher

Holland, Josiah Gilbert   1819–1881
American novelist and poet

Holmes, John Haynes   1879–1964
American Unitarian minister and
social reformer

Holmes, Oliver Wendell   1809–1894
American novelist and poet

Hooker, Richard   1554–1600
Anglican divine

Hooker, Thomas   1586–1647
Puritan minister and father of
American democracy

Hoover, Herbert   1874–1964
American president

Hoover, J. Edgar   1895–1972
American criminologist and director
of the F.B.I.

Hopkins, Gerard Manley   1844–1889
English Roman Catholic poet

Hopkins, Mark   1802–1887
American educator and theologian

Horn, Robert   b. 1933
British writer and student leader

Howe, John   1630–1705
English Puritan minister and writer

Howe, Julia Ward   1819–1910
American writer and activist in the
women's suffrage movement

Hubbard, Elbert Green   1859–1915
American essayist

Huddleston, Ernest Urban Trevor   b. 1913
Anti-apartheid campaigner and archbishop

Hügel, Baron Friedrich von   1852–1925
Roman Catholic scholar

Hugo, Victor   1802–1885
French novelist

Hulse, Erroll   b. 1931
South African–born pastor and writer

Hume, David   1711–1776
Scottish philosopher and historian

Hume, George Basil   1923–1999
Cardinal Archbishop of Westminster

Hus, Jan   1373–1415
Bohemian reformer

Huvelin, Abbé Henri   1838–1910
Priest and spiritual director

Ibsen, Henrik   1828–1906
Norwegian dramatist

Ignatius of Antioch, St.   d. c. 110
Bishop of Antioch and martyr

Ignatius of Loyola, St.   c. 1491–1556
Founder of the Jesuits

Inge, William Ralph   1860–1954
Dean of St. Paul's

Ingersoll, Robert Green   1833–1899
American lawyer

Irenaeus, St.   c. 130–c. 200
Bishop of Lyons

Israel, Martin
Lecturer in pathology, priest,
and spiritual director

Jackman, David   b. 1942
British preacher

Jackson, Helen Maria Fiske Hunt   1830–1885
American novelist and poet

James, William   1842–1910
American philosopher

Jay, John   1745–1829
American diplomat and statesman

Jean Baptiste de la Salle, St.   1651–1719
French cleric and educator

Jefferson, Charles Edward   1860–1937
Congregational minister

Jefferson, Thomas   1743–1826
American president

Jerome, St.   c. 347–c. 419
Biblical scholar

Jewel, John   1522–1571
Bishop of Salisbury

John of Avila   1500–1569
Spanish reformer, preacher, and mystic

John Bosco, St.   1815–1888
Founder of the Salesians

John Chrysostom, St.   c. 347–407
Patriarch of Constantinople

John Climacus, St.   c. 570–c. 649
Ascetic and spiritual writer

John of the Cross, St.   1542–1591
Spanish mystic

John of Damascus, St.   c. 675–749
Greek Orthodox monk and scholar

John Eudes, St.   1601–1680
French missioner

John of Kronstadt   1829–1908
Russian priest

John Paul I   1912–1978
Pope

John Paul II   b. 1920
Pope

John XXIII   1881–1963
Pope

Johnson, Lyndon B.   1908–1973
American president

Johnson, Samuel   1709–1784
Author and lexicographer

Jones, Bob   1883–1968
American evangelist and educator

Jonson, Ben   1572–1637
Poet, dramatist, and critic

Joubert, Joseph   1754–1824
French novelist

Jowett, John Henry   1864–1923
English Congregational minister

Julian of Norwich   c. 1342–c. 1416
English mystic

Justin Martyr, St.   c. 100–165
Christian apologist

Kaiser, Henry J.   1882–1967
American industrialist

Keble, John   1792–1866
English theologian, poet, and Leader of
the Oxford Movement

Keller, Helen Adams   1880–1968
American author and lecturer

Kelsey, Morton T.
North American theologian
and spiritual writer

Kempis, Thomas à   c. 1380–1471
German spiritual writer

Kennedy, Edward M.   b. 1932
U.S. senator

Kennedy, G.A. Studdart   1883–1929
Anglican priest and Chaplain
to the British Forces

Kennedy, John Fitzgerald   1917–1963
American president

Kettering, Charles Franklin   1876–1958
American engineer and inventor

Kevan, Ernest F.   1903–1965
English pastor and writer

Kierkegaard, Søren   1813–1855
Danish philosopher

Kilvert, Francis Robert   1846–1879
English clergyman and diarist

King, Martin Luther, Jr.   1929–1968
American civil rights leader

Kingdon, David   b. 1934
English theologian and writer

Kingsley, Charles   1819–1875
Anglican social reformer and writer

Knox, John   c. 1513–1572
Scottish reformer

Knox, Ronald Arbuthnott   1888–1957
Roman Catholic scholar

Kraemer, Hendrik   1888–1965
Dutch theologian

Kroll, Una
English doctor and Anglican deacon

Küng, Hans   b. 1928
Swiss Roman Catholic theologian

Kuyper, Abraham   1837–1920
Dutch Reformed theologian and
political leader

L'Engle, Madeleine   b. 1918
American novelist and spiritual writer

La Bruyère, Jean de   1645–1696
French educator and writer

La Rochefoucauld, François,   1613–1680
Duc de
French classical writer

Lamb, Charles   1775–1834
English essayist

Landers, Ann   b. 1918
American journalist

Landor, Walter Savage   1775–1864
English poet and essayist

Langland, William   c. 1330–c. 1400
English poet

Latimer, Hugh   c. 1485–1555
English Protestant martyr and Bishop
of Worcester

Lavater, Johann Kaspar   1741–1801
Swiss theologian and writer

Law, Henry   1797–1844
Anglican dean and evangelical writer

Law, William   1686–1761
Anglican spiritual writer

Lawrence, Br.   c. 1605–1691
Carmelite mystic

Le Gallienne, Richard   1866–1947
British journalist

Leech, Kenneth
English priest and spiritual writer

Leighton, Robert   1611–1684
Archbishop of Glasgow

Leo XIII   1810–1903
Pope

Leopold, Aldo   1887–1948
American conservationist

Lewis, Clive Staples (C.S.)   1898–1963
Irish-born spiritual writer and
literary critic

Lewis, Peter   b. 1945
Pastor

Lincoln, Abraham   1809–1865
American president

Little, Paul E.   1928–1975
American student evangelist

Livingstone, David   1813–1873
Scottish missionary and explorer

Llewelyn, Robert
English spiritual writer

Lloyd-Jones, David Martyn   1900–1981
Welsh Bible expositor, minister,
and author

Locke, John   1632–1704
English philosopher

Longfellow, Henry Wadsworth   1807–1882
American poet

Lowell, James Russell   1819–1891
American poet

Luce, Clare Boothe   1903–1987
American playwright, legislator,
and diplomat

Lull, Raymond   c. 1232–1316
Spanish spiritual writer and missionary

Lum, Ada   b. 1926
American Bible-study trainer and
student leader

Lunn, Sir Arnold   1888–1974
Indian–born Roman Catholic apologist

Luther, Martin   1483–1546
Leader of the Reformation in
Germany

Lyte, Henry Francis   1793–1847
Scottish hymn writer

M'Cheyne, Robert Murray   1813–1843
Scottish minister

MacArthur, Douglas   1880–1964
American general

MacDonald, George   1824–1905
Scottish minister and writer

Machen, John Gresham   1881–1937
American Presbyterian theologian

Maclaren, Alexander   1826–1910
British Baptist pastor

MacLeod, Lord George Fielden   1895–1991
Presbyterian minister and founder of
the Iona Community

Macquarrie, John   b. 1919
Scottish theologian

Maeterlinck, Maurice   1862–1949
Belgian poet and essayist

Main, John   1926–1982
English monk and spiritual guide

Manning, Henry Edward   1808–1892
Cardinal Archbishop of Westminster

Manton, Thomas   1620–1677
English minister

Maritain, Jacques   1882–1973
French Roman Catholic philosopher

Markham, Edwin   1852–1940
American poet

Marquis, Donald Robert (Don)   1878–1937
American author

Marshall, Catherine Wood   1914–1983
American spiritual writer

Marshall, Peter   1902–1949
Presbyterian minister and chaplain
of the U.S. Senate

Martin, Al
American pastor and writer

Martin, Ralph P. b. 1925
American biblical scholar

Martyn, Henry 1781–1812
Anglican missionary to India

Matheson, George 1842–1906
Scottish minister and hymn writer

Maurice, John Frederick Denison 1805–1872
Anglican theologian

Maximus the Confessor, St. c. 580–662
Byzantine theologian and ascetic writer

May, Rollo 1909–1994
American psychoanalyst

McCosh, James 1811–1894
Scottish philosopher

Mechtilde of Magdeburg c. 1220–c. 1280
German nun and mystic

Mello, Anthony de
Indian Jesuit

Melville, Herman 1819–1891
American novelist

Menninger, Karl (Augustus) 1893–1990
American psychiatrist

Mercier, Désiré Joseph 1851–1926
Belgian philosopher and priest

Merton, Thomas 1915–1968
American Trappist monk, author, and poet

Meyer, Frederick Brotherton (F.B.) 1847–1929
English evangelical writer

Mill, John Stuart 1806–1873
English philosopher and economist

Miller, Calvin b. 1936
American Baptist pastor, scholar, and writer

Miller, Henry 1891–1980
American writer

Milne, Bruce J. b. 1940
Baptist pastor

Milton, John 1608–1674
English poet

Mitchell, Fred 1897–1953
Methodist preacher and mission leader

Moltmann, Jürgen b. 1926
German Reformed theologian

Monica, St. c. 331–387
Mother of St. Augustine of Hippo

Monod, Adolphe Theodore 1802–1856
Protestant preacher in France

Montgomery, James 1771–1854
Scottish poet and hymn writer

Moody, Dwight Lyman (D.L.) 1837–1899
American evangelist

Moore, George 1853–1933
Irish novelist, poet, and playwright

Moore, Thomas V. 1779–1852
Irish poet

Moran, Gabriel
Roman Catholic theologian

More, Hannah 1745–1833
English writer and philanthropist

More, Sir Thomas 1478–1535
English statesman and writer

Morgan, George Campbell 1863–1945
English Congregational minister

Morris, Colin b. 1929
Methodist writer

Morris, Leon Lamb b. 1914
Australian biblical scholar

Moses 4th century
Desert Father

Mote, Edward 1797–1874
English hymn writer

Motyer, J. Alec b. 1924
Irish theologian and preacher

Moule, Charles F.D. b. 1908
English biblical scholar

Muggeridge, Malcolm 1903–1990
English journalist

Müller, George 1805–1898
Pastor and philanthropist

Murray, Andrew 1828–1917
South African minister

Murray, John 1898–1975
Presbyterian theologian

Neander, Joachim 1650–1680
German hymn writer and teacher

Nee, Watchman 1903–1972
Leader of the "Little Flock"

Neill, Bishop Stephen Charles 1900–1984
English biblical scholar and missiologist

Nestorius d. c. 451
Archbishop of Constantinople, deposed on grounds of unorthodoxy

Newbigin, James Edward Lesslie b. 1909
Missionary bishop and theologian

Newman, John Henry 1801–1890
English cardinal and theologian

Newton, John 1725–1807
Anglican clergyman and hymn writer

Newton, Sir Isaac   1642–1727
Mathematician and natural philosopher

Nicholas Cabasilas, St.   b. 1322
Byzantine mystic

Niebuhr, (Karl Paul) Reinhold   1892–1971
American theologian

Nightingale, Florence   1820–1910
Reformer of hospital nursing

Niles, Daniel Thambirajah (D.T.)   1908–1970
Sri Lankan minister and
ecumenical leader

Nouwen, Henri J.M.   1932–1997
Dutch spiritual writer and pastor

O'Connell, Daniel   1775–1847
Irish statesman

O'Connor, Mary Flannery   1925–1964
American novelist and short-story writer

Olford, Stephen   b. 1918
American Baptist preacher

Oman, John Wood   1860–1939
Scottish Presbyterian theologian

Origen of Alexandria   c. 185–c. 254
Theologian and biblical scholar

Ortega y Gasset, José   1883–1955
Spanish writer and philosopher

Ortiz, Juan Carlos
Argentinian pastor

Ortlund, Anne
American writer and speaker

Owen, John   1616–1683
English theologian

Packer, James Innell (J.I.)   b. 1926
Evangelical theologian

Page, Kirby   1890–1957
Minister and social reformer

Paine, Thomas   1737–1809
English-American political theorist

Palamas, Gregory   1296–1359
Greek mystical theologian

Palau, Luis   b. 1934
Argentinian evangelist

Pannenberg, Wolfhart
German Lutheran theologian

Parker, Joseph   1830–1902
English Congregational minister

Parkhurst, Charles Henry   1842–1933
American Presbyterian preacher

Pascal, Blaise   1623–1662
French mathematician, scientist, and
religious writer

Pasteur, Louis   1822–1895
French chemist and biologist

Paton, Alan Stewart   1903–1988
South African writer and social reformer

Patrick, St.   c. 389–c. 461
Apostle of the Irish

Paul VI   1897–1978
Pope

Paulinus, St.   c. 353–431
Bishop of Nola

Peale, Norman Vincent   1898–1993
Reformed Church of America minister

Peck, M. Scott   b. 1936
American psychiatrist and writer

Peguy, Charles   1873–1914
French Roman Catholic writer

Penn, William   1644–1718
Quaker leader and founder of
Pennsylvania

Peter Damian, St.   1007–1072
Roman Catholic reformer

Peterson, Eugene H.   b. 1932
American devotional and pastoral writer

Philip Neri, St.   1515–1595
Apostle of Rome

Phillips, John Bertram (J.B.)   1906–1982
English Bible translator

Pierson, Arthur Tappan (A.T.)   1837–1911
American Presbyterian minister
and writer

Pink, Aiden Wilson (A.W.)   1886–1952
English preacher and writer

Pippert, Rebecca Manley   b. 1948
American writer and speaker

Pittenger, Norman   b. 1905
American–born theologian

Pius XI   1857–1939
Pope

Pius XII   1876–1958
Pope

Polycarp, St.   c. 70–c. 155
Bishop of Smyrna

Pope, Alexander   1688–1744
English poet

Porette, Margaret   d. 1310
Spiritual writer and martyr

Powell, Vavasor   1617–1670
Welsh Puritan minister

Price, Eugenia   b. 1916
American author

Primavesi, Anne
Irish theologian and writer on
ecological issues

Prior, Matthew   1664–1721
English poet

Pui-Lan, Kwok
Chinese biblical scholar

Pusey, Edward Bouverie   1800–1882
Anglican theologian

Quincey, Thomas de   1785–1859
English writer

Quoist, Michel   b. 1921
French spiritual writer

Rad, Gerard von
German biblical scholar

Rahner, Karl   1904–1984
Roman Catholic theologian

Raleigh, Sir Walter   1554–1618
English poet and literary scholar

Ramsey, (Arthur) Michael   1904–1988
Archbishop of Canterbury

Rauschenbusch, Walter   1861–1918
American pastor and social activist

Redpath, Alan   1907–1989
Evangelist and Bible teacher

Reed, Thomas Brackett   1839–1902
American representative

Rees, Paul Stromberg   1900–1991
American evangelical pastor and leader

Reith, Lord   1889–1971
British statesman and broadcaster

Retz, Cardinal de   1613–1679
Archbishop of Paris

Rice, John R.   1896–1980
American author, educator, radio preacher,
and revivalist

Richard of Chichester, St.   c. 1198–1253
Bishop of Chichester and church
reformer

Richard of St. Victor   d. 1173
British-born mystic and theologian
in France

Richard, Sir Cliff   b. 1940
English pop singer

Richardson, Alan   1905–1975
English biblical theologian

Richter, Johann Paul Friedrich   1763–1825
German novelist

Rilke, Rainer Maria   1875–1926
Austro-German poet and novelist

Rinkart, Martin   1586–1649
German pastor, poet, and hymn writer

Robert Bellarmine, St.   1542–1621
Roman Catholic cardinal and apologist

Robertson, Frederick William   1816–1853
English preacher

Robinson, Bishop John Arthur   1919–1983
Thomas
Anglican bishop and theologian

Robinson, Donald William Bradley   b. 1922
Australian bishop and New Testament
scholar

Robinson, Forbes   1867–1904
English university chaplain

Robinson, John   c. 1575–1625
Pastor to the Pilgrim Fathers

Roger (Schutz), Br.   b. 1915
Cofounder of the ecumenical
community of Taizé, France

Rolle of Hampole, Richard   c. 1295–1349
English hermit and mystic

Romaine, William   1714–1795
Anglican clergyman

Romero, Oscar
El Salvadorian Roman Catholic
archbishop and martyr

Roosevelt, Eleanor   1884–1962
American stateswoman and writer;
wife of Franklin D. Roosevelt

Roosevelt, Franklin D.   1882–1945
American president

Roosevelt, Theodore   1858–1919
American president

Rossetti, Christina Georgina   1830–1894
English poet and hymn writer

Royden, Agnes Maud   1876–1956
English preacher and campaigner for
women's rights

Ruether, Rosemary Radford   b. 1936
American feminist theologian

Runcie, Robert   1921–2000
Archbishop of Canterbury

Ruskin, John   1819–1900
British art critic and social reformer

Russell, Letty M.
North American theologian

Rutherford, Mark   1831–1913
Religious author (pseudonym of
William Hale White)

Rutherford, Samuel   1600–1661
Scottish theologian

Ruysbroeck, Jan van   1293–1381
Flemish mystic

Ryle, John Charles   1816–1900
Bishop of Liverpool

Ryrie, Charles Caldwell   b. 1925
American pastor, administrator, and scholar

Saltmarsh, John   d. 1647
English preacher and writer

Sanders, J. Oswald   1902–1992
Missionary statesman and Bible teacher

Sangster, William Edwyn Robert   1900–1960
Methodist minister

Sankey, Ira David   1840–1908
American hymn singer and organist,
accompanied D.L. Moody

Santer, Mark   b. 1936
Bishop of Birmingham

Sarnoff, David   1891–1971
Russian-born American broadcaster

Saunders, Cicely
Pioneer of the English hospice movement

Sayers, Dorothy Leigh   1893–1957
English novelist and Christian apologist

Schaeffer, Francis August   1912–1984
American spiritual writer

Schiller, (Johann) Friedrich von   1759–1805
German poet, dramatist, and historian

Schlegel, Katharina von   b. 1697
German hymn writer

Schleiermacher, Friedrich   1768–1834
German theologian

Schmemann, Alexander   1921–1983
Eastern Orthodox liturgical theologian

Schreiner, Olive   1855–1920
South African writer and campaigner for
women's rights

Schuller, Robert Harold   b. 1926
Minister of the Reformed Church in
America and host of "Hour of Power"

Schweitzer, Albert   1875–1965
German theologian, medical missionary,
and musician

Scroggie, William Graham   1877–1959
Baptist minister and writer

Scudder, Vida   1861–1954
Indian-born social activist

Secker, Thomas   1693–1768
Archbishop of Canterbury

Segundo, Juan Luis   b. 1932
Uruguayan Jesuit liberation theologian

Seton, Elizabeth Ann Bayley   1774–1821
American founder of
The Sisters of Charity

Shaftesbury, Anthony Ashley   1801–1885
Cooper, Seventh Earl of
Evangelical social and industrial reformer

Shakespeare, William   1564–1616
English dramatist and poet

Shaw, Luci   b. 1928
American poet

Sheen, Fulton John   1895–1979
American Roman Catholic bishop and
broadcaster

Shoemaker, Samuel Moor   1893–1963
American Episcopal priest and writer

Sibbes, Richard   1577–1635
Puritan theologian and preacher

Sider, Ronald J.   b. 1939
American evangelical theologian and
social activist

Silesius, Angelus   1624–1677
Mystical poet

Simeon the New Theologian, St.   949–1022
Byzantine mystic and spiritual writer

Simeon, Charles   1759–1836
Anglican evangelical leader and cofounder
of the Church Missionary Society

Singh, Sadhu Sundar   1889–c. 1929
Indian evangelist

Skinner, Thomas   1942–1994
American evangelist, lecturer, and writer

Slessor, Mary   1848–1915
North American Presbyterian missionary

Smith, Hannah Whitall   1832–1911
American Quaker and cofounder of the
Women's Christian Movement

Smith, Logan Pearsall   1865–1946
American critic and essayist

Smith, William Robertson   1846–1894
Scottish Old Testament scholar

Sobrino, Jon
El Salvadorian liberation theologian

Soelle, Dorothee
German theologian

Solzhenitsyn, Alexander   b. 1918
Russian novelist

Song, Choan-Seng
Taiwanese theologian

Soper, Donald
British Methodist preacher

Southey, Robert   1774–1843
English poet

Spalding, John Lancaster   1840–1916
American Catholic theologian

Spencer, Herbert   1820–1903
Philosophical and scientific thinker

Spenser, Edmund   1552–1599
English poet

Sproul, Robert Charles (R.C.)   b. 1939
Presbyterian pastor and theologian

Spurgeon, Charles Haddon   1834–1892
English Baptist preacher

Stanley, Arthur Penrhyn   1815–1881
Dean of Westminster

Stein, Edith   1861–1921
Jewish-Christian nun and martyr

Stevenson, Robert Louis   1850–1894
Scottish writer

Stewart, James   1896–1990
Scottish pastor and scholar

Stibbs, Alan M.   1901–1971
British preacher and theologian

Still, William   1911–1987
Scottish pastor

Stone, Samuel John   1839–1900
English priest, poet, and hymn writer

Storkey, Elaine   b. 1943
Anglican evangelical theologian, writer,
and broadcaster

Stott, John R.W.   b. 1921
Anglican evangelical leader and author

Stowe, Harriet Beecher   1811–1896
American novelist

Strong, Augustus Hopkins   1836–1921
American Baptist theologian and
educator

Studd, Charles Thomas (C.T.)   1862–1931
Missionary to China, India, and Africa

Studdert-Kennedy, Geoffrey   1883–1929
Anketell
Anglican priest and Chaplain
to the British Forces

Suenens, Leon Joseph   b. 1904
Roman Catholic cardinal

Sunday, William Ashley (Billy)   1862–1935
American evangelist

Suso, Heinrich   c. 1295–1366
German spiritual writer

Swann, Donald   1923–1994
English humorist, composer, and
song writer

Swedenborg, Emanuel   1688–1772
Swedish scientist and religious thinker

Swift, Jonathan   1667–1745
English satirist

Swindoll, Charles R.   b. 1934
American pastor and author

Tabb, John Bannister   1845–1909
American poet

Tada, Joni Eareckson
American writer and speaker

Talmage, Thomas De Witt   1832–1902
American pastor and preacher

Tauler, Johann   c. 1300–1361
German mystic

Tawney, Richard Henry
English economic historian

Taylor, Edward   c. 1645–1729
American poet

Taylor, James Hudson   1832–1905
Founder of the China Inland Mission

Taylor, Jeremy   1613–1667
Anglican bishop and theologian

Taylor, John V.
English Anglican bishop

Temple, William   1881–1944
Archbishop of Canterbury

Tennyson, Alfred, Lord   1809–1892
English poet

Teresa of Avila, St.   1515–1582
Spanish Carmelite mystic and reformer

Teresa, Mother   1910–1997
Missionary to India

Tersteegen, Gerhard   1697–1769
German pietist hymn writer

Tertullian, Quintus   c. 160–c. 220
African Christian apologist

Theophan the Recluse   1815–1900
Russian monk and spiritual writer

Thérèse of Lisieux, St.   1873–1897
French Carmelite nun

Thielicke, Helmut
German Lutheran theologian
and preacher

Thomas Aquinas, St.   1225–1274
Italian theologian and philosopher

Thomas, Geoffrey   b. 1938
Welsh pastor and preacher

Thoreau, Henry David　　　　1817–1862
American essayist and poet

Thornwell, James Henley　　　1812–1862
Southern Presbyterian minister and
educator

Thurman, Howard　　　　　　b. 1900
American minister, theologian, and
educator

Tikhon of Zadonsk　　　　　1724–1783
1st Russian bishop and spiritual writer

Tillich, Paul　　　　　　　1886–1965
German-born American theologian
and philosopher

Tillotson, John　　　　　　1630–1694
Archbishop of Canterbury

Todi, Jacopone da　　　　c. 1230–1306
Franciscan poet

Tolstoy, Count Leo　　　　1828–1910
Russian novelist and social reformer

Torrey, Reuben Archer (R.A.)　1856–1928
Presbyterian evangelist, educator, and
writer

Tournier, Paul　　　　　　1898–1986
Swiss physician

Tourville, Abbé Henri de　　1842–1903
French spiritual writer

Toynbee, Arnold Joseph　　1889–1975
British historian

Tozer, Aiden Wilson (A.W.)　1897–1963
American pastor and author

Traherne, Thomas　　　　c. 1636–1674
English metaphysical poet

Trench, Richard Chenevix　　1807–1886
Archbishop of Dublin

Trible, Phyllis　　　　　　b. 1932
North American theologian

Trueblood, (David) Elton　　1900–1994
Quaker philosopher and theologian

Tugwell, Simon　　　　　　b. 1943
English Dominican writer

Tutu, Desmond　　　　　　b. 1931
South African archbishop, ecumenist,
and social reformer

Twain, Mark　　　　　　　1835–1910
American author

Tyndale, William　　　　c. 1495–1536
English biblical translator and martyr

Tyrrell, George　　　　　　1861–1909
Roman Catholic modernist

Ullathorne, William Bernard　1806–1889
Roman Catholic Bishop of Birmingham

Underhill, Evelyn　　　　　1875–1941
English mystical writer

Urquhart, Colin　　　　　　b. 1940
Bible teacher and devotional writer

Vanier, Jean　　　　　　　b. 1928
French-Canadian founder of L'Arche
communities

Vann, Gerald　　　　　　　1906–1963
English Dominican writer

Vanstone, W.H.
American spiritual writer

Vaughan, Henry　　　　　　1622–1695
English poet

Vénard, Theophane　　　　1829–1861
French missionary and martyr

Verwer, George　　　　　　b. 1938
Founder and international director of
interdenominational mission

Viannes, Jean　　　　　　1786–1859
French priest

Vincent de Paul, St.　　　　1580–1660
French Roman Catholic priest
and philanthropist

Vinci, Leonardo da　　　　1452–1519
Italian artist and scientist

Visser't Hooft, Willem Adolf　1900–1985
Dutch ecumenical leader

Waddell, Helen
Irish Presbyterian scholar

Waite, Terry　　　　　　　b. 1939
Anglican churchman and former
hostage

Wallace, Lewis　　　　　　1827–1905
American military leader and writer

Wallis, Jim
American writer and cofounder of the
Sojourners Community

Walton, Izaak　　　　　　1593–1683
English author

Wand, John William Charles　1885–1977
(J.W.C.)
English bishop and church historian

Warfield, Benjamin Breckinridge　1851–1921
American Presbyterian theologian

Washington, Booker T.　　　1859–1915
American educator and author

Washington, George　　　　1732–1799
American president

Watson, David　　　　　　1933–1984
English evangelical preacher
and writer

Watson, Thomas   c. 1557–1592
English poet

Watts, Alan W.   1915–1973
American spiritual writer

Watts, Isaac   1674–1748
English hymn writer and theologian

Waugh, Evelyn   1903–1966
English author

Weatherhead, Leslie
British Methodist minister

Webb, Pauline   b. 1927
English Methodist writer

Webster, Daniel   1782–1852
American statesman and orator

Weil, Simone   1909–1943
French philosopher and mystic

Wells, Herbert George (H.G.)   1866–1946
English novelist

Wesley, Charles   1707–1788
Methodist hymn writer

Wesley, John   1703–1791
Founder of Methodism

Wesley, Susanna   1669–1742
Mother of John and Charles Wesley

West, Morris
Roman Catholic novelist

Wharton, Edith Newbold   1862–1937
American novelist

Whately, Richard   1787–1863
Anglican Archbishop of Dublin

Whichcote, Benjamin   1609–1683
Cambridge Platonist

White, John   b. 1924
Psychiatrist and author

Whitefield, George   1714–1770
English Methodist evangelist

Whitehead, Alfred North   1861–1947
English philosopher

Whitman, Walt   1819–1892
American poet and essayist

Whittier, John Greenleaf   1807–1892
American Quaker poet and hymn writer

Whyte, Alexander   1836–1921
Scottish minister

Wiersbe, Warren W.   b. 1929
Author, broadcaster, and pastor

Wilberforce, Samuel   1805–1873
Anglican bishop

Wilberforce, William   1759–1833
English abolitionist and philanthropist

Willard, Dallas   b. 1935
American philosopher

Williams, H. A.
English theologian

Williams, Rowan
Archbishop of Wales, theologian, and
social activist

Willis, Love Maria   1824–1908
North American writer and editor

Wilson, Geoffrey B.   b. 1929
English pastor and writer

Wilson, Robert Dick   1856–1930
Presbyterian minister and Old Testament
scholar

Wilson, (Thomas) Woodrow   1856–1924
American president

Wimber, John Richard   1934–1997
Founder of the Vineyard Movement

Winter, Miriam Therese
North American Medical Mission sister
and liturgist

Wirt, Sherwood Eliot   b. 1911
American journalist and author

Witherspoon, John   1723–1794
Presbyterian minister

Woolman, John   1720–1772
American Quaker preacher

Wordsworth, William   1770–1850
English poet

Wren, Brian   b. 1936
English theologian and hymn writer

Wren, Christopher   1632–1723
English architect

Wright, Tom
English biblical scholar

Wyon, Olive   1881–1966
English Methodist spiritual writer
and translator

Yancey, Philip   b. 1949
American author and editor

Young, Edward   1683–1765
English poet

Zappone, Katherine
North American-born feminist
theologian

Zeller, Hubert van   b. 1905
English monk and spiritual writer

Zwingli, Ulrich   1484–1531
Swiss reformer

Black Sea

ISTANBUL
(Constantinople)
Sea of Marmara
Dardanelles Straits

Caspian Sea

Smyrna

Anatolia

·Antalya

·Aleppo
Cyprus   SYRIA

Tigris River

·Urmia   ·Teheran

·n e a n

Beirut
·Damascus

Euphrates River

MESOPOTAMIA   PERSIA

PALESTINE
·Jaffa
·Jerusalem

·Baghdad

·Alexandria
·Cairo

·Basra

EGYPT

·Asyut

Persian
Gulf

Straits of
Harmuz

·Medina

Nubia
·Wadi Halfa

Muscat·

Red Sea

·Mecca

Nile River

Fourth Cataract

·Khartoum
AN
Bahar al
Abiad·
·Sennar

Yemen

El Obeid ·

Ottoman Territories